JEWISH SPIRITUALITY
From the Bible through the Middle Ages

World Spirituality

An Encyclopedic History of the Religious Quest

1. Asian Archaic Spirituality
2. European Archaic Spirituality
3. African and Oceanic Spirituality
4. South and Meso-American Native Spirituality
5. North American Indian Spirituality
6. Early Hindu and Jain Spirituality
7. Post-Classical Hindu and Sikh Spirituality
8. Buddhist Spirituality: Indian, Siri Lankan, Southeast Asian
9. Buddhist Spirituality: Chinese, Tibetan, Japanese, Korean
10. Taoist Spirituality
11. Confucian Spirituality
12. Ancient Near Eastern Spirituality: Zoroastrian, Sumerian, Assyro-Babylonian, Hittite
13. Jewish Spirituality: From the Bible to the Middle Ages
14. Jewish Spirituality: From the Sixteenth-Century Revival to the Present
15. Classical Mediterranean Spirituality: Egyptian, Greek, Roman
16. Christian Spirituality: Origins to the Twelfth Century
17. Christian Spirituality: High Middle Ages and Reformation
18. Christian Spirituality: Post-Reformation and Modern
19. Islamic Spirituality: Foundations
20. Islamic Spirituality: Manifestations
21. Modern Esoteric Movements
22. Spirituality and the Secular Quest
23. Encounter of Spiritualities: Past to Present
24. Encounter of Spiritualities: Present to Future
25. Dictionary of World Spirituality

Board of Editors and Advisors

Ewert Cousins, *General Editor*

Volume 13 of
World Spirituality:
An Encyclopedic History
of the Religious Quest

JEWISH SPIRITUALITY

FROM THE BIBLE through the MIDDLE AGES

Edited by
Arthur Green

CROSSROAD • NEW YORK

1987
The Crossroad Publishing Company
370 Lexington Avenue, New York, NY 10017

World Spirituality, Volume 13
Diane Apostolos-Cappadona, Art Editor

Printed in the United States of America

Library of Congress Cataloging in Publication Data

Main entry under title:
Jewish spirituality.
(Vol. 13 of World spirituality)
Bibliography: v. 1. p.
Includes index.
Contents: v. 1. From the Bible through the Middle Ages.
1. Spiritual life—Judaism—Addresses, essays, lectures.
2. Spiritual life—Biblical teaching—Addresses, essays, lectures.
3. Rabbinical literature—History and criticism—Addresses, essays, lectures.
4. Judaism—History—Addresses, essays, lectures.
I. Green, Arthur, 1941– . II. Series: World spirituality ; v. 13–
BM723.J487 1985   296.7   85-11287
ISBN 0-8245-0762-2 (v. 1)

Acknowledgments

Grateful acknowledgment is made to the following individuals and publisher
for permission to reprint copyrighted material: David Goldstein for the poems by
Isaac Ibn Gi'at and Judah Halevi from *Hebrew Poems from Spain* (Schocken Books, 1966);
Daniel Matt for "The Secret of Sabbath" from his *Zohar* (Paulist Press, 1983);
Stephen Mitchell for the passage from *Into the Whirlwind* (Doubleday & Co., 1979);
and the Jewish Publication Society of America for selections from *The Holy Scriptures*.

למרנן ורבנן

To the generation of
Jewish scholars, rabbis, and teachers
    who fled the Nazi inferno
    and devoted their lives
    to establishing new centers of Jewish learning
    in America, Israel, and elsewhere,
    this collection is gratefully dedicated.

Contents

Part Two: Emergence
The Rabbinic Age

Part Three: Reflections
The Medieval Age

Preface to the Series

THE PRESENT VOLUME is part of a series entitled World Spirituality: An Encyclopedic History of the Religious Quest, which seeks to present the spiritual wisdom of the human race in its historical unfolding. Although each of the volumes can be read on its own terms, taken together they provide a comprehensive picture of the spiritual strivings of the human community as a whole—from prehistoric times, through the great religions, to the meeting of traditions at the present.

Drawing upon the highest level of scholarship around the world, the series gathers together and presents in a single collection the richness of the spiritual heritage of the human race. It is designed to reflect the autonomy of each tradition in its historical development, but at the same time to present the entire story of the human spiritual quest. The first five volumes deal with the spiritualities of archaic peoples in Asia, Europe, Africa, Oceania, and North and South America. Most of these have ceased to exist as living traditions, although some perdure among tribal peoples throughout the world. However, the archaic level of spirituality survives within the later traditions as a foundational stratum, preserved in ritual and myth. Individual volumes or combinations of volumes are devoted to the major traditions: Hindu, Buddhist, Taoist, Confucian, Jewish, Christian, and Islamic. Included within the series are the Jain, Sikh, and Zoroastrian traditions. In order to complete the story, the series includes traditions that have not survived but have exercised important influence on living traditions—such as Egyptian, Sumerian, classical Greek and Roman. A volume is devoted to modern esoteric movements and another to modern secular movements.

Having presented the history of the various traditions, the series devotes two volumes to the meeting of spiritualities. The first surveys the meeting of spiritualities from the past to the present, exploring common themes that

A longer version of this preface may be found in Christian Spirituality: Origins to the Twelfth Century, *the first published volume in the series.*

can provide the basis for a positive encounter, for example, symbols, rituals, techniques. Finally, the series closes with a dictionary of world spirituality.

Each volume is edited by a specialist or a team of specialists who have gathered a number of contributors to write articles in their fields of specialization. As in this volume, the articles are not brief entries but substantial studies of an area of spirituality within a given tradition. An effort has been made to choose editors and contributors who have a cultural and religious grounding within the tradition studied and at the same time possess the scholarly objectivity to present the material to a larger forum of readers. For several years some five hundred scholars around the world have been working on the project.

In the planning of the project, no attempt was made to arrive at a common definition of spirituality that would be accepted by all in precisely the same way. The term "spirituality," or an equivalent, is not found in a number of the traditions. Yet from the outset, there was a consensus among the editors about what was in general intended by the term. It was left to each tradition to clarify its own understanding of this meaning and to the editors to express this in the introduction to their volumes. As a working hypothesis, the following description was used to launch the project:

> The series focuses on that inner dimension of the person called by certain traditions "the spirit." This spiritual core is the deepest center of the person. It is here that the person is open to the transcendent dimension; it is here that the person experiences ultimate reality. The series explores the discovery of this core, the dynamics of its development, and its journey to the ultimate goal. It deals with prayer, spiritual direction, the various maps of the spiritual journey, and the methods of advancement in the spiritual ascent.

By presenting the ancient spiritual wisdom in an academic perspective, the series can fulfill a number of needs. It can provide readers with a spiritual inventory of the richness of their own traditions, informing them at the same time of the richness of other traditions. It can give structure and order, meaning and direction to the vast amount of information with which we are often overwhelmed in the computer age. By drawing the material into the focus of world spirituality, it can provide a perspective for understanding one's place in the larger process. For it may well be that the meeting of spiritual paths—the assimilation not only of one's own spiritual heritage but of that of the human community as a whole—is the distinctive spiritual journey of our time.

EWERT COUSINS

Introduction

Hear, O Lord, when I cry aloud;
have mercy on me, answer me.
In Your behalf my heart says:
"Seek My face!"
O Lord, I seek Your face.
Do not hide Your face from me;
do not thrust aside Your servant in anger;
You have ever been my help.
Do not forsake me, do not abandon me,
O God, my deliverer.

Psalm 27:8–9

SEEKING THE FACE OF GOD, striving to live in His presence and to fashion the life of holiness appropriate to God's presence—these have ever been the core of that religious civilization known to the world as Judaism, the collective religious expression of the people Israel. Such a statement of supreme value—aside from questions of how precisely it is to be defined and how it is achieved—could win the assent of biblical priest and prophet, of Pharisee and Essene sectarian, of Hellenistic contemplative and law-centered rabbi, of philosopher, Kabbalist, *ḥasid*, and even of moderns who seek to walk in their footsteps.

Life in the presence of God—or the cultivation of a life in the ordinary world bearing the holiness once associated with sacred space and time, with Temple and with holy days—is perhaps as close as one can come to a definition of "spirituality" that is native to the Jewish tradition and indeed faithful to its Semitic roots. Within this definition there is room for an array of varied types, each of which gives different weight to one aspect or another of the spiritual life. For some the evocation of God's presence includes an "ascent" to a higher realm and implies knowledge other than that vouchsafed to most mortals. Others content themselves with "preparing the table of the Lord" or, alternatively, seek to discover "the tabernacle within the heart" and allow the *shekhinah* (Presence) to find a dwelling there. The ultimate vision may be one of a highly anthropomorphic Deity seated on His throne, an utterly abstract sense of mystical absorption within the presence, the imminent arrival of messiah, or simply that of a life lived in the fulfillment of God's will. What all these have in common is a commitment to the life of holiness, a faith in the power of Israel's ancient code to embody that holiness, and a knowledge that such a life fulfills God's intent in creation and in the election, however understood, of His "kingdom of priests," the people Israel. This consensus has lasted until modern times when we find, as we shall see, Jews in search of the spiritual life who can no longer accept its premises as classically outlined by Judaism.

The definition of Jewish spirituality offered here has rather little to do, it will be noticed, with the term "spirituality" itself, for which there *is* a precise Hebrew equivalent, *ruḥaniyyut*. The reader sensitive to the nuances of Hebrew speech will recognize this word as a latecomer to the ancient Hebrew tongue. It is an artifice of the medieval translators that was created first to express philosophical and scientific concepts that were Hellenic in origin. It was taken over only later by Kabbalists and pietists to describe a religious ideal that by then indeed was a thorough amalgam of the spiritual legacies of Israel and Greece. Spirituality in the Western sense, inevitably opposed in some degree to "corporeality" or "worldliness" (all apologies to the contrary notwithstanding), is unknown to the religious world view of ancient Israel; it is rather a late element, though an important one, among those factors that make up the religious legacy of medieval and later Jewry.

Defining spirituality as the cultivation and appreciation of the "inward" religious life, we find both assent and demurral in the sources of Judaism. Surely the Psalmist was a master, indeed perhaps the original Western master, of inwardness, and the early rabbis knew well to speak of "the service within the heart" and the values of silence and solitude. There are latter-day Hasidic treatises focused almost entirely on the cultivation of *ruḥaniyyut* and *penimiyyut* ("inwardness"). At the same time, concern is aroused lest the inner be praised at the expense of the outer. The rabbi, the spiritual descendant of both priest and prophet in this matter, will perforce rise to defend the externals. If inwardness implies a depreciation of the outer and dismisses religious behavior (in the moral as well as the ritual realm) as mere ceremony or trappings, the rabbi will find this a notion hard to tolerate. Religion, as far as the rabbi is concerned, is the living word of God, ever evolving through interpretation, a word that concerns itself with proper behavior in every domain of life at least as much as it does with matters of the heart.

Aware of these reservations, and wary generally of applying to a particular tradition terms and categories that are alien to it ("mysticism" too is a category that does not exist within classical Jewish sources), we nevertheless permit ourselves to speak of Jewish spirituality, defining it as we have: Israel's striving for life in the presence of God. This should allow talmudist, halakhist, and commentator to take their deserved place within the collective "spiritual" enterprise alongside the more obvious prophet, philosopher, and mystic.

This view is also meant to dispel the ancient and widely held notion that there are in fact two Judaisms, one of the flesh or the law and the other of the spirit, or one of the mind and the other of the heart. This idea has a surprisingly long history and has been held by Christian detractors of Judaism who reflect the biases of the New Testament, but also by many Jews themselves. The Kabbalists supported a version of this idea, claiming that their teaching was the "soul" of Judaism and that without it rabbinic practice was but a lifeless body. Students of Judaism in the early twentieth century, themselves rebels against the stultifying world of the Eastern European *shtetl* ("small town"), also put forth a version of this idea (one thinks here of Buber, Berdyczewski, and Horodezky), by which they hoped to save and renew the heart of Judaism while casting off its outer shackles. From the historian's point of view, there is no single secret doctrine that serves to quicken Judaism, to save it from becoming a life-threatening morass of detail. Jews throughout the ages, including the early rabbis themselves, have struggled with this issue of providing meaning and spiritual content to the tradition. Some have done so in highly systematic fashion, creating such grand edifices as Jewish Aristotelianism and classical Kabbalah. Others, including the Hasidic preacher, have chosen to do so in a more spontaneous and sporadic manner. The very notion of a divine or primordial Torah, a thought that has accompanied rabbinic Judaism since its earliest days, seems, as Gershom Scholem has pointed out, to call forth a sense that there is some deeper esoteric meaning to the text at hand, some secret that is more than any ordinary human reading of Torah can provide. All of the systems of meaning that have emerged within the classical Jewish context have made use of this idea and have found within it the theological license for that exegetical creativity which is in fact the tradition's very lifeblood. "Turn it over, turn it over, for all is in it" has allowed sages and seekers of the most varied sorts to see their own thought, influenced as it may be by spiritual currents far from those of ancient Israel, as the true meaning of their own religious legacy. There are not *two* Torahs, a revealed and a hidden, but rather both *one* and *many*, as many as the ongoing creativity of the Jewish people can provide.

A history of Judaism from the viewpoint of the phenomenology of religion has yet to be written. The ways in which classic patterns of myth, symbol, and archetype survive the great transformations wrought by biblical religion and reappear, *mutatis mutandis,* in rabbinic and later Judaism are yet to be fully traced. The unique element of diaspora, spreading the Jews throughout the Western world at an early and crucial stage in their religion's development, also needs here to be taken into account. The traditions that grew out of that monotheistic and iconoclastic revolution in ancient Canaan, overlaid with memories of the Babylonian exile and its Persian aftermath as well as with evidence of the early contacts of Israel with Greece and Rome, were carried throughout the known world by bands of faithful wanderers. Yet who would dare say that Judaism, even of the most pious and traditionalist sort, remained unaffected by the cultural patterns of those in whose midst particular groups of Jews happened to settle? It is not at all clear that a Jew in Spain in the twelfth century and one in Poland or Bohemia some five hundred years later, even if performing the very same ritual actions, were in fact doing the same thing. Distinctive religious subcultures emerged within the history of Jewry. Even in latter-day terms, if one thinks of Lithuania, Italy, and Yemen, highly diverse images of Judaism come to mind. These, it should be added, were not simply mirror images of the respective non-Jewish cultures amid which they were created: Jewish communities themselves, separated by distances of both time and space, created cultural and religious life patterns that differed greatly both from one another and from those of the host cultures in whose shadow they flourished.

Nor were differences in religious types attributable only to variations in historical or geographical circumstance. The same Amsterdam of the seventeenth century was home to rationalists and messianic Kabbalists, both of them probably nurtured by the same combination of Marrano past and expanding future. Warsaw at the turn of the twentieth century housed *hasidim* of various stripes alongside socialists, Zionists, Yiddishists, and Hebraists in every imaginable combination—all of them products of, some of them rebels against, the same cultural milieu. Any account of the spiritual life of Jewry undoubtedly is in need of the word "varieties" somewhere in its title. Indeed it may be that a major lesson the Jewish experience has to offer the historian of religion is just that: even within this "smallest of all the nations" there lies a vast array of different religious types, spiritual activities, and attempts at self-understanding. No single characterization or typology of "Jewish spirituality" could possibly comprehend them all. How much more true must this be for religious empires far more vast than the relatively circumscribed realm of Jewry!

What then is it that coinhabitants of this religious and cultural phenomenon known as Judaism have in common? First, it must be said that they all are Jews, and this is no mere tautology. Judaism is the religious path of a distinct national group, one that has defined itself in ethnic as well as religious terms throughout the ages. The shared legacy of national symbols, including language, land (held dear, as history has shown, despite long absence), and common history, including but not limited to a history of persecution, is quite inseparable from Jewish religious identity. Yet the historian of religion must probe further, asking what it is within this legacy of the past that makes for the vital and ongoing thread of Judaism as a religious enterprise. In this search, one is first tempted to go the route of essentialism: somewhere at the core there must be an essence of Judaism that all its many bearers hold in common. This was, in fact, the path taken by most presentations of Judaism for the Western reader, including both attempts at "objective" religious history and works of advocacy by Jewish theologians, in the nineteenth and early twentieth centuries. Of course this essence was usually articulated in theological terms—and then often in terms not unsurprisingly accommodating either to the writer's particular religious stance within the Jewish community or to the properly liberal and Western values that an author might have thought his readers would find most comfortable. Thus, ethical monotheism, the struggle against idolatry, and a vague commitment to "the rule of law"—though not to particular laws—were emphasized by liberal Jewish writers, whereas *halakhah* in its specific sense, but also expanded to "the halakhic mind," was brought to the fore by traditionalists.

Aside from the obviously self-serving quality of some of these presentations (and our selection from them admittedly borders on caricature), the attempts at arriving at such an essence have been largely discredited in Jewish scholarly circles because of recent developments in historical research. Essentialism always wound up positing a "mainstream" in the history of Jewry; those who diverged from whatever the particular set of norms was said to be were then characterized as minor groups of dissenters, who cut themselves off from the ongoing stream of Jewish history. But the work of mid-twentieth-century Jewish scholarship has almost entirely discredited the notion of *any* theological mainstream. Erwin R. Goodenough, researching the archaeological remains of Jewry throughout the eastern Mediterranean world, gave the lie to the widely held view that a rabbinic mainstream, puritanical, iconoclastic, and uncompromisingly anti-syncretistic, dominated Palestinian and Babylonian Jewry in the first centuries of the common era. Harry A. Wolfson has shown how thoroughly Jewish philosophers from Philo to Spinoza were part and parcel of the Western philosophical tradition, at times having more intellectually in common with their Christian and Muslim counterparts than they did with Jews who stood outside philosophy. Above all, Gershom Scholem and his studies of medieval Jewish mysticism and seventeenth-century Sabbatian messianism have had a revolutionary impact on the field of Jewish studies as a whole. Scholem has forced us to realize that notions of mainstream were posited largely out of ignorance and were sustained by the selective suppression of evidence. This process reflects the cultural biases to which historians, perhaps only slightly less than theologians, were themselves subject.

The elusive quality of any essentials that might still be said to underlie, even in an unspoken way, most or all Jewish theologies is heightened by the nonfundamentalist relationship that traditional Jewry has always had with its sacred Scripture. Although the veracity and theoretical authority of the Bible were taken for granted from the Hellenistic era down to modern times, unanimity about the meaning of any but the most bland of biblical phrases was utterly lacking. There is no postbiblical Jewish theology in any age that could claim to base itself on a *peshat,* that is, an obvious and straightforward reading of the biblical text. The contest between interpreters is not about which have Scripture on their side, but rather about which display the greater ingenuity in marshaling scriptural support for their views. When in medieval times certain dogmatic formulations achieved a status that was nearly canonical (belief in divine omnipotence, or in creation *ex nihilo*), Kabbalists and others played freely with these, reinterpreting their meaning to suit their own ideas.

What then, if not theological essentials, will serve as the binding substance for the variety of Jewish spiritual expressions? It seems safe to begin with the *text* itself. All Judaisms since approximately the first century c.e. have had in common a defined body of sacred Scripture. Though exegetical license has indeed reigned free, it is not fair to assume that the text has made no claims on those who are faithful to it. These claims, the ones least bendable by interpretation, exist first in the realm of religious deed and, second— but by no means insignificantly—in that of religious language, imagery, and style.

The relative unanimity of premodern Jews in matters of religious action, codified as *halakhah* or the "path" is well known. The commandments of the Torah as defined and elaborated by the early rabbis were accepted as binding by all Jews except the Karaite minority at least from the early Middle Ages down to the seventeenth century. There were, to be sure, ongoing debates concerning both details of the law and the seemingly large matter of what exactly it was that constituted the 613 commandments of the Torah itself. But these were dwarfed by the overwhelming unanimity in most matters of praxis, including both those matters "between man and God" and those "between man and man," or the ritual-devotional and the moral-ethical spheres. It is worthy of note that neither premodern Hebrew nor Yiddish has a term that may be properly used to translate "orthodox"; *shomer miz-wot* ("observer of the commandments") or, in the more casual Yiddish vernacular, *shoimer shabes* ("Sabbath keeper") is as close as one could come. It was this unanimity of life pattern that allowed for Moses Mendelsohn's claim in the eighteenth century that Judaism was in fact a matter of "revealed legislation." This, of course, allowed for the wide berth of intellectual freedom that he as an enlightener sought. This view of Judaism, though thoroughly discredited by the nineteenth-century "essentialists," was based in the reality of long experience with one aspect of the tradition, the relative unanimity of deed and form.

Deeds, of course, are an aspect of symbolic speech, especially so when they take the regularized and repeated form of ritual. Alongside this type of speech-act, then, contemporary scholarship suggests that Judaism (like any religious tradition) has a unique pattern of verbal tropes and rubrics that constitute a unifying style of expression, one that transcends even great chasms in theological meaning. Any theology of Judaism, for example, must claim to believe in one God; monotheism is embodied in the essential trope of *shema' yisra'el* ("Hear, O Israel, the Lord our God, the Lord is one" [Deut 6:4, recited in the daily liturgy]). A theology that denies the truth of the *shema'* or openly proclaims belief in a multiplicity of heavenly powers can hardly claim a place within Judaism. But the range of meaning given to the *shema'* remains quite open; the One may be a unity of ten powers, as for the Kabbalist, or the *shema'* may attest to the absolute oneness of God and world, as for the *HaBaD hasid*. The fact that both of these views stand in utter contradiction to the theology of Hebrew Scripture constitutes no real problem in the history of Judaism, but stands rather as a monument to the exegetical success and freedom of these latter-day thinkers.

Another such basic trope is the belief in Torah as revealed at Mount Sinai. Again, a Judaism without some sort of Sinaitic revelation is inconceivable, but the range of beliefs about exactly what was given at Sinai, or what it means to speak of revelation, or the degrees of difference between inspiration and revelation is tremendous, especially if one takes into account the great variety of modern Jewish positions on this matter. Realistically speaking, the traditional claim that "whoever says 'This verse' or 'This word is not from heaven' is one who 'despises the word of the Lord'" comes down to mean that those who can find no place for *some* concept of *Torah mi-Sinai* have rejected an essential rubric of Jewish discourse and thus have placed themselves outside the theological consensus of Israel.

Do we then propose naught but a new essentialism, one of tropes and rubrics rather than of dogmas and ideas? It should not be difficult to compile a list of essential religious vocabulary of which the would-be Jewish theologian could make rather free use. Of course (Heaven be praised! we should perhaps add), the matter is not so simple. Having used rather obvious and easily labeled examples, we speak of a literary and theological *style*, one carried in part by the mention of certain key terms but hardly reducible to them. The ways in which these terms are used, the frequency with which they appear, how they are juxtaposed with one another, and a whole host of other more-or-less intangible elements collectively constitute the religious language of Judaism. The well-trained eye of a text scholar or ear of a native speaker learns to detect unusual patterns, changes in meaning, and shifts of emphasis even in the seemingly most standard bit of rabbinic discourse. Especially interesting here are two late genres of premodern Jewish theological literature. Scholem's studies of the seventeenth- and eighteenth-century documents in which Sabbatian heresy was masked behind the language of traditional piety are instructive in illuminating the outermost limits of Jewish religious language and the ways in which even an exaggeratedly pietistic Jewish style can be distorted to produce radically new meanings. Similarly, the literature of Hasidism, though hardly heretical in the same way, offers the careful reader a chance to explore the traditional language and style of Judaism pushed to the extreme, as the masters use it to legitimize the particular religious values for which they stand.

The Judaism that all held in common was, we are claiming, a shared religious *language*, rooted in a body of sacred Scripture and anchored to daily life by a prescribed pattern of deeds. Like any language in currency over a wide geographical area and through the course of many centuries, it evolved, changed, grew, and developed its own varied "dialects." A multiplicity of religious types found within it sufficient breadth and depth to express their differences of vision and understanding; even those labeled "sinners" or "heretics" in times of controversy continued to make use, often the most creative use, of this religious language. Only in modern times has the language itself suffered a serious challenge, as the weakening of its own faith claims has combined with the tremendous assimilatory pressures on Jewry to diminish greatly the hold it has maintained over the Jewish people. But the challenge to tradition, the various attempts to buttress it, and the large and highly variegated movements of modern or postmodern Jews seeking to return to its fold are themselves all a part of the ongoing history of Jewish spirituality.

* * * * *

The volume here presented to the reader is the first of a two-volume collection of essays by leading scholars of our time on aspects of the spiritual life as manifest in the history of Judaism. No unified history has here been attempted, nor has uniformity of approach or style been imposed upon the authors. At the same time, this collection is not a random one, such as might appear in a *Festschrift* or a periodical collection. Each essay in these volumes was *commissioned* by the editor, who felt that its inclusion was essential to presenting a well-rounded picture of the Jewish spiritual enterprise in its historical development.

The ordering of these individual essays in historical sequence is revealing of the editor's historical and evolutionary bias, one shared with most of the contributors to this effort and with the community of Judaic scholars as a whole. An alternative, a topical arrangment using the now conventional rubrics of the history of religious ("Sacred Time," "Sacred Space," "Sacred Person," etc.) was considered and rejected as leading to too static a portrayal. Developed originally for the description of archaic and largely preliterate societies, these seemingly timeless categories take on a certain awkwardness when applied to those relatively recent and Western societies about whose historic evolution so much is known.

The history of Judaism has been written and rewritten many times over in the course of the past century and a half, or since the time when Jewry's love of its past combined with the West's emerging sense of critical history to make the study of Jewish history a passionate, almost religious, pursuit among a well-defined community of scholars. Insofar as this history has focused on Judaism, as distinct from the history of the Jewish people, it has largely been a history of religious ideas and religious or religiosocial institutions. The particular language and style of devotional life, a subtle matter in any case, has often eluded the historians. The psychological states to be achieved in the attempt at communion with God and the techniques employed to attain them have generally been among the closely guarded secrets of most esoteric traditions; Jewish esotericism has been particularly stringent in its proscriptions against the revealing of such secrets, and these too have been little noticed by historians until very recent times. Although the essays of this collection by no means concentrate exclusively on these matters, the prominence they are given here is in no way accidental. The history offered is not comprehensive, but has opted for in-depth treatment of selected themes rather than for the model of survey or encyclopedia. Important individuals (Yehudah Halevi, Nahman of Bratslav) are notable in their absence from this collection, and certain historical phenomena (medieval philosophy, Sabbatianism) have not been given their due. But from a thematic point of view, the reader who takes the time to be fully immersed in the essays of this collection will have as full an understanding as is available of the range of spiritual life as it has manifested itself in Judaism.

This first volume deals with the classical ages of the Jewish spiritual tradition. The volume opens with the religion of the biblical period, an age to which the name "Jewish" may not quite yet be properly applied but which nonetheless stands as the basis on which all of later Judaism is erected. The rebellion of Israel's prophets against the religious world view of Near Eastern paganism, combined with their own deep roots in that very religious language they so fiercely rejected, places ancient Israel at the crossroads of religious history in the West. The exclusive and ultimately universal claims made for its God set Israel over against all the surrounding cultures, while the borrowings in cultic form, institutions, and metaphor provide for an often unseen continuity of humanity's most ancient sacred forms into the Judaism that was to emerge in the postbiblical era.

The saga of biblical Israel makes it clear for all time that no separation is possible between the study of Israel as a nation and an appreciation of its peculiar spiritual legacy. The forging of the tribes, probably of varied origins, into a nation, the centralization of the cult in Jerusalem, and the prophetic denunciation and finally the destruction of that center are all crucial events in the sociopolitical history of that people. They are also, as we well know, formative happenings in the spiritual life of Israel, a life that often revolved around the priest and his sanctuary, the prophet and his message, and the king and his throne. It is in the tensions between these three, never resolved before the destruction, that the spiritual uniqueness of ancient Israel is most clearly reflected.

Biblical religion presents itself as one that readily sees the hand of God in the events of human life, including both those happenings that we call "natural"—for example, birth, death, the passing of the seasons—and those that we ascribe to the realm of "history"—the exodus from Egypt, the conquest of Canaan, and so forth. It is not, on the face of things, a literary tradition, one in which texts, readers, and interpreters play a central role. But appearances are in this case deceiving. Both prophet and psalmist work within emerging literary patterns, and it has already been quipped that "R," the so-called "Redactor" of the various strands of Pentateuchal traditions, is in fact "Rabbenu," our master, the proto-rabbi of all later Judaism.

The opening essay in this section, David Sperling's "Israel's Religion in the Ancient Near East," deals with the issues of Israel's continuity and break with its Near Eastern past, evaluating in the light of current knowledge various scholarly theories that have emerged concerning the genesis of Israelite religion. Jon D. Levenson and Michael Fishbane then respectively address Temple-centered piety and prophetic experience as aspects of spiritual life in the biblical period. Joel Rosenberg and James Kugel address themselves to literary aspects of Israelite religiosity, the former discussing issues of the emerging canon and tradition in biblical writings, the latter treating the specific genre of Psalms and their place in the life of worship as it developed in Israel. All of these essays have in common a focus on the question of how the biblical world laid the groundwork for the growth of Judaism as it came to be defined in the postbiblical world.

The final essay in the biblical section, Martha Himmelfarb's treatment of The Book of the Watchers, provides a first step in our transition from the biblical age to the religious world that was to emerge in the aftermath of its destruction. Her essay, along with that of Jacob Neusner, which serves as the introduction to the second section of this volume, and David Winston's treatment of Philo of Alexandria, refer to what is called the Hellenistic Age in Jewish history, or the period between the decline of biblical forms of religious life and the emergence of those we term "rabbinic" (an age referred to in Christian scholarship as the "Intertestamental" period). Himmelfarb shows how prophecy, eclipsed after the early Second Temple period, reemerges in the form of apocalypse. This again shows continuity and change in both experience and literary form. Some might want to follow her essay directly by reading that of Joseph Dan, "The Religious Experience of the *Merkavah*," in which similar phenomena of a somewhat later period are treated. Both authors write with an eye to a question of religious experience and literary convention. Winston offers us a view of the contemplative ideal as taught in the highly sophisticated writings of the Alexandrian Jewish philosopher, a mere few hundred miles distant but culturally worlds apart from his contemporaries in Erez Israel.

The rabbinic period is, of course, the great age of institutionalization in the history of Judaism. The authority of law, the virtue of constant Torah-study, and the rabbi as embodiment of the Jewish ideal all belong to this age, as Neusner so rightly reminds us. At the same time, it is a great mistake to depict this period as one of spiritual aridity, as was so often done by the rabbis' detractors. Dan's essay calls to our attention the fact that mystical practices flourished in circles not far removed from those in which fine points of law were elaborated. Robert Goldenberg's essay goes to the heart of the matter, dealing with law and spirit in talmudic religion and showing that dichotomies alien to the world view of the rabbis may not be helpful in achieving a serious understanding of their religion. Steven D. Fraade, in dealing with the question of asceticism, offers an exemplary treatment which shows how much the rabbis were the products of the religious struggles that had dominated the centuries that preceded them as well as of the broader late Hellenistic world in which they lived. The picture that emerges from these studies, taken as a whole, is of an age when ideals of wisdom and sober piety achieved a long-sought victory over the passionate and sometimes destructive upheavals of the turn of the era. It was also the age, of course, when the rule of law and attention to proper performance of the commandments became the defining marks of Jewry for many centuries to come.

The medieval age in Jewish history, termed here the age of "Reflection," is the period in which Jewish tradition, now received as a wholly formed body of lore and praxis from ages past, became itself the object of study and investigation. A new spirit of inquiry, born of Jewry's contact with Greco-Islamic philosophy, sought to find meaning in this legacy, as well as to reinterpret it in the light of its own ways of thought. First philosophers and later Kabbalists were active in the rereading of rabbinic sources, which they saw as proof texts for their own distinctive—and clearly nonrabbinic, in the historical sense—ways of thinking. The canons of such reinterpretation were much discussed in both philosophic and mystical circles, as is shown in our lead essay by Frank Talmage, "The Inner Meaning of Sacred Texts in Medieval Judaism."

A particular branch of this reinterpretive activity of medieval Jewry was that discipline known as *ta'amey ha-mizwot*, investigation of "the meanings of the commandments." This too, though initiated by philosophers, was most fully developed in the kabbalistic schools, as shown to us by Daniel C. Matt in "The Mystic and the *Mizwot*," which opens with a historical survey of prekabbalistic efforts to understand the commandments.

Studies of Jewish philosophy and mysticism in the Middle Ages have often concentrated on the world of *sefaradim*, the Jews of Spain and the Mediterranean regions, where a great deal of this intellectual activity was concentrated. The religious life of Jewish communities peripheral to this central area, whether in ashkenazic northern Europe or to the east in Iran or Yemen, is often left aside. Ivan G. Marcus helps us to rectify some part of this imbalance with his treatment of the devotional ideals of Jewish pietists in the Rhineland during the thirteenth century, where a religious life quite different from that of the nearly contemporary Spanish Kabbalists was being developed.

Our volume and our all-too-brief consideration of the medieval period closes with an essay by Moshe Idel on the term *hitbodedut* and its history in the medieval and postmedieval periods. Literally meaning "self-isolation," the term was first used by Jews to describe Muslim Sufi mystics who wandered off to be alone with God. As the term was brought into Judaism and was used in prescriptive as well as descriptive contexts, it underwent a shift in meaning. Rather than simply "being alone" with God, *hitbodedut* also came to refer to mental *concentration* on divine matters, or an "isolation" of the mind from things of this world to focus only on God. In the course of tracing this philological shift, Idel surveys some of the most fascinating and little-known texts of the later Middle Ages and shows, again in paradigmatic fashion, how a new term used to describe a phenomenon of the past becomes, for later generations, the statement of a major religious value.

For the editor as historian, there remains only a final disclaimer. The presentation of Jewish spirituality in historical form is not intended to serve as a barrier between the materials presented and the present-day reader who is a would-be practitioner. The knowledge that a particular technique, first manifest in thirteenth-century Spain, was the probable result of Sufi influence, or that the use of certain prayer directions was abandoned by the Hasidim some two hundred years ago should not make either of these into "dead letters" in the potential spiritual repertoire of contemporary Jewry. The entirety of the creative past is part of the legacy of the present; none of its embers is extinguished entirely. But historical presentation is also paradigmatic: as Jewish spiritual life in ages past was subject to growth, the development of new forms, new systems of meaning, cautious but definite borrowings from its surrounding cultures, and surprising renewal and affirmation in the face of changed circumstances and even cataclysm—so may it, indeed must it, grow yet again in times to come.

ARTHUR GREEN

Part One
FOUNDATIONS
The Biblical Age

O Lord, You have examined me and know me.
When I sit down or stand up You know it;
  You discern my thoughts from afar.
You observe my walking and reclining,
  and are familiar with all my ways.
There is not a word on my tongue
  but that You, O Lord, know it well.
You hedge me before and behind;
  You lay Your hand upon me.
It is beyond my knowledge;
  it is a mystery; I cannot fathom it.
Where can I escape from Your spirit?
Where can I flee from Your presence?
If I ascend to heaven, You are there;
  if I descend to Sheol, You are there too.
If I take wing with the dawn
  to come to rest on the western horizon,
  even there Your hand will be guiding me,
  Your right hand will be holding me fast.
If I say, "Surely darkness will conceal me,
  night will provide me with cover,"
  darkness is not dark for You;
  night is as light as day;
  darkness and light are the same.

                              Psalm 139:1–12

Raise a shout to the Lord, all the earth,
  break into joyous songs of praise!
Sing praise to the Lord with the lyre,
  with the lyre and melodious song.
With trumpets and the blast of the horn
  raise a shout before the Lord, the king.
Let the sea and all within it thunder,
  the world and its inhabitants;
  let the rivers clap their hands,
  the mountains sing joyously together
  at the presence of the Lord,
  for He is coming to rule the earth;
  He will rule the world justly,
  and its people with equity.

                              Psalm 98:4–9

Where were you when I planned the earth?
  Tell me, if you are so wise.
Do you know who took its dimensions,
  measuring its length with a cord?
What were its pillars built on?
  Who laid down its cornerstone,
while the morning stars burst out singing
  and the angels shouted for joy!

Were you there when I stopped the waters,
  as they issued gushing from the womb?
when I wrapped the ocean in clouds
  and swaddled the sea in shadows?
when I closed it in with barriers
  and set its boundaries, saying,
"Here you may come, but no farther;
  here shall your proud waves break."

Have you ever commanded morning
  or guided dawn to its place—
to hold the corners of the sky
  and shake off the last few stars?
All things are touched with color;
  the whole world is changed.

Have you walked through the depths of the ocean
  or dived to the floor of the sea?
Have you stood at the gates of doom
  or looked through the gates of death?
Have you seen to the edge of the universe?
  Speak up, if you have such knowledge.
                    Job 38:4–18

1. The Lisbon Bible Carpet,
Manuscript illumination, OR 2628, Vol. II

2. Last passages from the *Manual of Discipline*

3. Mosaic from Herod's Palace, Masada

4. The Temple of Jerusalem, Dura-Europos Synagogue
[copy of the wall painting by Herbert Gute]

1

Israel's Religion in the Ancient Near East

DAVID SPERLING

The Religious Teachings of the Hebrew Bible

THE BIBLE, which serves as the spiritual underpinning for all of later Judaism, itself reflects Near Eastern culture and its long history. The writers of the Bible were greatly influenced by their predecessors and by the surrounding culture at the same time that they rejected much of what had been transmitted to them. Before we begin our discussion of the Bible and its relationship to its cultural and religious antecedents, it is important to clarify certain terms that will be used in this chapter.

We may begin with the terms "Jewish" and "Israelite." Although the Bible as a book was compiled by members of the postexilic Jewish community, most of its contents had been composed during the preexilic period properly called "Israelite" (ca. 1225–586 B.C.E.). In fundamental matters the teachings of the Israelite authors differed from the beliefs and practices of their Jewish descendants. It will be useful to examine these differences before turning to the major concerns of our study: revolution and continuity.

The Israelite writers of the bulk of the Bible agreed that Yahweh (usually translated "Lord") was to be worshiped by all Israelites to the exclusion of all other divinities (e.g., Exod 20:3; 22:19). Yahweh was known also as El, Elohim, (El) Shaddai, (El) Elyon, and Adonai. In addition He was known by numerous epithets, some of which referred to His attributes, some to His relations with His people or their ancestors, and some which we now know to have been originally the names of other gods.

5

These same Israelite writers differed with regard to the idea of Yahweh as sole god. Some apparently took the existence of other gods for granted (Gen 1:26; 6:2; Exod 12:12; 15:11; Ps 82). Deuteronomy 4:18 credited Yahweh with the institution of astral worship for the benefit of the Gentiles. In contrast, Deutero-Isaiah was a thoroughgoing monotheist who insisted that Yahweh was the sole god in existence, who alone must be worshiped by all peoples.

According to the older sources of the Bible, authority was usually not vested in books or sets of writings. Prophets and judges (male and female) and priests (male) were the living sources of Yahweh's word (Deut 17:8–13). The earlier biblical authors generally understood the worship of Yahweh to be permissible only in the land of Israel. All other land was unclean (Deut 28:64; 1 Sam 26:19; Amos 7:17; Ps 137:4). Exile from Israel's land was tantamount to exile from the divine presence, which could be approached only by someone in a cultically pure state.

Most of the biblical writers taught that the righteous would be rewarded and the wicked punished in what the rabbis would later call "this world." The righteous were promised longevity, fecundity, prosperity, respect, and tenure in the promised land (Pss 127, 128). The wicked were warned that they would die rootless and fruitless at a relatively young age despised by all. Wickedness would be punished within the ideal extent of an individual's life, three to four generations (Exod 20:5; Ps 128:6; Job 42:16).

Classical Judaism began to emerge during the Babylonian exile. Although many varieties of Judaism were in competition for centuries, they agreed in differing with the older Israelite religion on the issues of Yahweh's uniqueness, on the source of religious authority, and on the proper place of Yahweh's worship. No form of classical Judaism attributed divinity to any god but Yahweh. The phrase *YHWH 'ehad* (Deut 6:4), was transformed into a monotheistic credo, "The Lord is One." Adherents of ancient polytheism as well as those who favored the newer Persian dualism had to disguise or modify their beliefs. Originally autonomous divinities such as the god of death and the god of the sea were demoted to the status of angelic delegates of Yahweh, who would assign them their proper functions.

The exilic period witnessed the selective collection of earlier Israelite writings into the beginnings of a canon. This Jewish literary activity proved compatible with the Persian imperial policy of encouraging minorities within its borders to govern themselves by their own laws. The literature of the Torah now became law, binding on every Jew. The very presence of the written word which was both holy and binding gradually undermined the authority of priests and prophets. The scribe's ability to read and interpret texts moved him into a position of leadership at the expense of those who claimed priestly lineage or direct divine communication.

The rise of a Jewish diaspora coupled with a zealous monotheism made it both possible and imperative to worship Yahweh all over the world. If Yahweh was indeed the sole god in existence, then it was necessary to bring all the peoples of the earth to His service. If Deutero-Isaiah was to be proved right, then the land outside Israel's borders had to become less unclean.

Finally, many Jews abandoned those biblical teachings which limited reward and punishment to this world. In ever larger numbers they became receptive to foreign notions of life beyond the grave. In sum, the religious teachings of the Hebrew Bible were preserved by communities which no longer accepted them fully. Instead the earlier doctrines were understood and interpreted in the light of the later ones. Thus began the process of *midrash*.

But now we must examine those earlier biblical teachings on their own in order to understand the spiritual life of ancient Israel. Where a modern employs the term "spirituality," an ancient Israelite employs *yir'at YHWH* ("fear of Yahweh") or *'avodat YHWH* ("service of Yahweh"). Analogously, an ancient Babylonian said *palāḥ ilī* ("fear of the gods") just as he said *palāḥ šarri* ("fear of the king"; see Prov 24:21). The same individual referred to divine service as *dullu* ("work") and employed the identical term to describe labor in the fields. "Fear" and "service" of divinity in ancient Babylonia, Egypt, and Israel included such diverse activities as keeping the gods closely informed of military developments, feeding them high quality food, keeping their temples in good repair, feeding the ancestral ghosts, abstaining from certain foods, not touching a woman in her menses, and keeping honest weights and measures. We may think of *yir'āh* and *'avodāh* as categories summarizing the realities of ancient Israel's spirituality. This brings us to the question of what those realities were and how we can study them.

Although convention refers to the period under discussion as biblical, the fact is that the religious life of Israel was much more diverse than the canon indicates. We do not know if the individual works that make up the present Bible were at all influential in their own time. We do not know the size of the following that individual writers had. The basic question remains unanswered: How accurately does the Bible reflect the spiritual life of ancient Israel?

Modern scholarly descriptions of ancient Israel are mostly based on critical readings of the Bible and employ such tools as text criticism, form criticism, tradition history, redaction criticism, and canon criticism. Unfortunately, the best biblical criticism can tell us only about the texts studied.

The world outside those texts remains unknown. Ideally, students of ancient Israel should have adequate means of confirming or contradicting statements made by biblical authors, but this is seldom the case. Archaeology has been a useful corrective to overreliance on the Bible; the archaeological record of a period is far less subject to change than its constantly developing literary traditions. Nonetheless, the limitations of geographical study of the holy land are severe when it comes to settling important matters of detail. For one thing, very few original Hebrew texts outside the canon survived the Israelite period. In addition the many nonliterary remains, though very informative about material culture, generally provide only indirect background for the Bible. The biblical writers, it will be recalled, often made evaluative statements that do not admit of empirical verification. Just as often they told stories of individuals who spoke with God in dreams and visions. A further difficulty is the infrequency with which the identification of a major excavation site or the function of a particular building is absolutely certain. As a result of these difficulties much modern comparative study is necessarily dependent on parallels and analogies drawn between Israel and less recalcitrant sites such as Egypt, Mesopotamia, parts of northern Syria, and Turkey. Finally, even where linguistic and cultural parallels between the Bible and extrabiblical sources have been demonstrated, the channels of transmission have been difficult to trace.

Israel and Other Ancient Cultures

In spite of these limitations it is now clear that the Israelites continued in many ways to transmit the culture that had preceded them. From a linguistic point of view, the Amarna letters demonstrate that Israelite Hebrew represented no radical break with the earlier Canaanite dialects. Neither is Hebrew far removed from the Canaanite dialects of Moabite, Phoenician, and Ammonite spoken by Israel's contemporaries. Even the archaizing Ugaritic texts of northern Syria, whose language is somewhat more removed, have remarkable affinities with the poetic diction and style of Israelite Hebrew.

Similar continuities between Canaanite and Israelite culture are found in the area of the cult. The Hebrew terms zevah ("slain offering"), shelāmim ("tribute offering"), neder ("votive offering"), kohen ("priest"), minhāh ("gift-offering"), qādesh ("[illicit] cultic functionary") and kālil ("holocaust") are found in virtually identical form in Ugaritic and Phoenician. The Solomonic temple itself was built with Phoenician labor on Phoenician models.

The artisan Hiram, who cast the two freestanding pillars Yakin and Boaz, was the son of an Israelite mother and a Phoenician father.

Other religious continuities are demonstrable from the Ugaritic texts of northern Syria, none later than 1200 B.C.E. From these texts it is apparent that El, the head of the Ugaritic pantheon, had both his name and his reputation for generosity and good counsel usurped by Yahweh. Baal suffered a similar fate. From them Yahweh appropriated his epithet "rider of the clouds" and much of his storm god imagery.

The obvious explanation for the continuities between Israelite and Canaanite culture is that Israel did not originate simply as a unified ethnic group which had invaded the promised land. Rather, as a careful reading of the Bible demonstrates, Israel was made up of diverse elements, many of which were autochthonous or had already been assimilated to Canaanite culture.

Various biblical traditions explicitly mention the absorption of diverse peoples into Israel. We may cite the "mixed multitude" (Exod 13:38) and "riffraff" (Num 11:4), the descendants of Rahab the harlot (Josh 6:25), and the Gibeonites (Josh 9:15). But because the Bible often encapsulates complex social and political developments in stories about individuals, these too can contain important historical information. On this reading, Jacob's marriages to Aramean women (Gen 29:23–28; Hos 12:13), Judah's marriage to a Canaanite woman (Gen 38:2), Joseph's marriage to an Egyptian (Gen 41:45), and Moses' marriage to a Midianite (Exod 2:21) reflect ancient Israel's heterogeneity. A slightly more veiled detail is provided by the land grant to Caleb the Kenizzite (Josh 14:14; cf. Gen 15:19) and by the transformation of the Canaanite cities Hepher and Tirzah into Mannasite clans (Josh 12:17, 24; Num 27:1, 36:11). At the same time, however, as these details are visible in the biblical texts, these same writings present an ideological viewpoint of "Israel," a self-conscious entity distinct from its surroundings, which assumes the existence of that self-consciousness from earliest times. All members of the group "Israel" are traced to a remote ancestor with the proper (Canaanite) name Israel, and ultimately to Abraham. But the claim of common kinship runs counter to the details of the narratives and the genealogies. Therefore the claim should be understood as an ideological expression of a socio-political reality that was based not originally on kinship or simple blood-relationship but, as we shall see, on religious and political union.

The writers' ideological self-consciousness is also apparent in the repeated biblical denial of the Canaanite heritage. This is especially true of the Pentateuch, according to which the priesthood, the sacrificial cult (contrast

Amos 5:25), the tabernacle, the festivals, most of the covenant traditions to serve Yahweh exclusively, and the laws governing most of life's activities originated outside of the promised land. Yet we have seen how great was Israel's debt to its country's past. By claiming that Israel's most important institutions originated in the desert (Deut 32:10), the biblical writers disowned both Canaan and Egypt (Lev 18:2). In reality, however, Israel's origins must be sought in both of these locations.

The Amarna letters of the fourteenth century B.C.E. provide useful background information on the origins of Israel and enable us to evaluate the biblical material in historical perspective. Some of these documents illustrate the burdens of taxation and compulsory corvée labor, which weighed heavily on the populations of Syria-Palestine. Local rulers, theoretically subject to Pharaoh, often feared uprising by lower classes, notably the ḫāpiru, whose name may or may not be related to "Hebrew." Itinerant workers known as ḫupšu, some of whom had been slaves (cf. ḥofsh in Exod 21:2, 6), were another source of disturbance feared by rulers. In their desperation for food, the ḫupšu moved from city to city and often joined outlaw bands. Corvée workers, who made up the massu, were another source of discontent. Like their counterparts, the mas of Solomon's time, the men who made up the compulsory labor forces could be shifted from one region to another. Their movement among work areas was supervised by local rulers, who were, in theory, responsible to Pharaoh.

The social structure of ancient Ugarit, which is documented as late as the end of the thirteenth century B.C.E., supplements the picture. Ugarit was a feudal society in which all land was technically assigned by the king. Scholars have noted that the antimonarchic statements made in the eighth chapter of 1 Samuel reflect the realities of royal exactions such as those attested at Ugarit in the late second millennium. It was well known in Canaan that the mishpaṭ ha-melekh ("the king's custom") weighed heavily on the people. The internal restiveness of the area was aggravated by the local rulers, who jockeyed for power among themselves and did not shrink from encouraging revolts in territories subject to their rivals. Egyptian internal policy generally benefited from the internal disharmony and squabbling, because they minimized the possibility of revolt.

In the thirteenth and twelfth centuries matters worsened when the turmoil of the western Mediterranean brought new peoples into the area. Among them were elements who carried with them traditions of escape from Egyptian servitude. Though these traditions have been reworked, embellished, and exaggerated, it is unlikely that the servitude was simply invented. The god Yahweh was given credit for the liberation. Many natives of the country were attracted to the ranks of the invaders, whose own numbers must have been small. The new coalition of invaders and natives made up "Israel," a name which is a proper Canaanite word and which appears as the name of a people for the first time in history in a stele dating from the fifth regnal year of Pharaoh Merneptah (ca. 1225 B.C.E.).

Political union between the invaders from Egypt and native Canaanites was aided by their hostility to a common enemy—the feudal axis of Egypt and the Canaanite city-states. Biblical sources blend internal and external traditions that associate Canaanite and Egyptian oppressors. The genealogies of Genesis 9 and 10 make Ham the father of Canaan and Canaan the brother of Kush, Egypt, and Put. Similarly, the writer of Leviticus 18 compares the "way of Egypt" with the "way of Canaan."

A like association of Canaan and Egypt is demonstrated in the Amarna letters. As soon as Egypt had carved out its empire in Syria-Palestine, most inhabitants of Canaan had the Pharaoh as their master. Reports about corvée labor were sent to Egypt (El Amarna 365). We may be certain that even if a local ruler did not bother to tell the workers that they were toiling for Pharaoh, that information would be supplied by others. In a letter to the Egyptian court from the loyalist Rib-Addi there is a quotation from the rhetoric of the revolutionary Abdi-Ashirta: "We shall drive the governors (i.e., the city-state rulers) out of the lands so that all the land will be come ḫāpiru-land and so justice will be done in all the lands. (Our) sons and daughters will be undisturbed forever. If then the King (of Egypt) ventures forth with all the lands in opposition to him, then what can be done to us?" Rib-Addi continues, "To this end they have sworn an oath among themselves (El Amarna 74)."

It is clear that native Canaanites could be instigated to rebel against local rulers who were in league with Egypt. Expulsion of the kinglets was tantamount to expulsion of the Pharaoh, which would bring justice and freedom to the land. M. Astour has pointed out Canaan's "intense and consistent anti-royalism."[1] The Amarna letters inform us of popular revolts in several areas. In some of these cases the city rulers were slain by their rebellious subjects.

The invasion of what we may conveniently call the "Moses group" was able to feed on the native opposition to combined Egyptian-Canaanite rule. Whereas the fourteenth century rebellions had been sporadically successful, the entry of the outsiders coupled with the general political turmoil of the thirteenth century had more permanent consequences. Both natives and invaders opposed Egyptian authority. The invaders, by escaping from Egypt, had shown that Egyptian authority could be thrown off. In consequence, the traditions of the exodus came to overshadow those of the natives who had joined the invaders to become Israel.

Local traditions did not disappear entirely. It is virtually certain that the Israelite tribal name Issachar, which means "hireling," has no ethnic referent. Indeed, Gen 49:15 specifically says that Issachar "inclined his shoulder to the corvée basket." In other cases stories of escape from servitude or rebellion against political subjugation were subordinated to the "all-Israel" traditions of exodus and conquest. Among these we may count the tales of the Rahabites, the Gibeonites, and the Kenites.

In some cases stories of native subjugation were relocated to Egypt. Exodus 1:11 reads: "Over them they appointed *mas*-overseers in order to humble them with their *sevel.*" The words in italics are technical terms. We have already noted that *mas* in the Amarna letters refers to corvée work. The *sevel*, another institution of forced labor, was native to Syria. M. Held has shown that both male and female minors were recruited for the *sevel.*[2] The attribution to the Pharaoh of *mas* and *sevel*, both west Semitic rather than Egyptian institutions, should be viewed as original native traditions of Canaanites who became part of Israel. The members of the new group, though ethnically and geographically diverse, found common ground in opposition to Egyptian servitude in Canaan as well as in Egypt.

The diversity of the new group accounts for the different biblical traditions of the length of Egyptian servitude as well as for the differences in its institutional nature. The long figure of 430 years (Exod 12:40–41) fits remarkably well with the chronology of the eighteenth to twentieth Egyptian dynasties (ca. 1560–1080), which witnessed the rise and fall of Egyptian imperialism in Asia Minor, and thus represents the sentiments of Israel's Canaanite elements. In contrast, Num 26:59 informs us that Jochebed, the mother of Aaron, Moses, and Miriam, was born to Levi in Egypt. Inasmuch as her children were associated with the exodus, the tradition in Numbers reckons an enslavement lasting one and a half generations, a figure more plausibly associated with a runaway slave group.

A similar explanation accounts for discrepancies in the descriptions of Israel's status in Egypt. One set of traditions (Lev 26:13; Deut 15:15; 24:18) speaks of Israel as "slave" (Hebrew *'eved*), whereas another refers to corvée (Exod 1:11). Both would fit native Canaanite conditions. In contrast the texts that speak of Israel as *ger* ("sojourner") would be more appropriate to describe subjugation in a foreign land (Exod 22:20; 23:9; Lev 19:34; Deut 10:19; 23:8).

In sum, the extant sources show how various traditions were subordinated to the motifs of exodus from Egypt and inheritance of the land. In theory, all Israel had invaded Canaan; in reality, many, if not most, Israelites could trace their origins locally.

The Spiritual Life of Israel

What was new about the spiritual life of the new entity Israel? For one thing, the worship of the god Yahweh. Though alleged by some scholars to be attested in pre-Israelite sources, it has been found for certain only in Israel. The nature of Israelite worship of Yahweh has been hotly debated. The classical theory is associated with Julius Wellhausen (1844–1918), the great German Bible scholar who employed a literary-critical study of the Bible as the basis for a reconstruction of Israelite religious history. Wellhausen's theory traced the evolution of Israelite religion from animism through totemism and polytheism to monolatry and finally to monotheism. According to Wellhausen, most of the earlier biblical material reflected the polytheistic stage in which Yahweh was viewed as a national god. Yahweh had delivered his people and continued to protect them, much as Chemosh had done for the Moabites. The Moabites did not insist that Chemosh was the sole god in existence nor that he alone should be worshiped. The Bible, said Wellhausen, tells us in no uncertain terms that Israelites worshiped many gods in addition to Yahweh. Because Yahweh, like Chemosh, was a national god, every Israelite owed Him allegiance. Before the rise of classical prophecy, however, no one understood the rejection of all other gods to be a corollary of that allegiance. The extant books of the Bible, to be sure, describe Israelite worship of other gods at all periods as "sin," but that point of view is an anachronism, a postprophetic retrojection. According to Wellhausen, Israel did not begin to break with polytheism until the rise of the classical prophets of the eighth century B.C.E. In their confrontations with the religions of Canaan, Hosea and Amos had stressed the moral and ethical demands of Yahweh at the expense of the Israelite sacrificial cult. According to these prophets and their successors, Yahweh demanded absolute justice and uncompromising righteousness rather than bulls and fatted calves. Such demands made sense only if Yahweh was powerful enough to enforce them. To the prophets, the political upheavals of the eighth century were a clear demonstration of that necessary power. Yahweh had moved all the nations of the earth about for His moral purposes. He had not merely brought Israel out of Egypt but had relocated the Philistines and the Arameans as well (Amos 9:7). In prophetic theory, argued Wellhausen, the increasingly ethical Yahweh became increasingly powerful, supplanting His divine rivals at home and abroad. These prophetic teachings had little effect on the popular religion for centuries. Only during the Babylonian exile did the guilt-ridden Jewish masses come to accept Yahweh as the sole God. The Pentateuch, in its final form a product of the postexilic

Jewish church, recast ethical monotheism in legalistic terms. For Well-hausen, the pentateuchal notion of "covenant" was a prime example of legalistic recasting.[3]

According to the authors of the Pentateuch, Yahweh and Israel had been joined in a covenant that placed demands on the people. Adherence to the prescriptions of that covenant would bring prosperity to Israel and would assure its tenure in the promised land. Disobedience would bring exile and destruction. Wellhausen was certain that this legalistic formulation of Israel's relation to God had not originated at an early period of religious "naturalness." It was more suited to the thinking of the postexilic Jewish community, in which "the creator of heaven and earth becomes the manager of a petty scheme of salvation; the living God descends from his throne to make way for the law."[4]

Wellhausen viewed covenant as a monotheistic metaphor suitable to the Jewish church. He traced the covenant notions to the marriage imagery employed by the classical prophets. Hosea had been the first to depict Israel as the bride of Yahweh. Jeremiah and Ezekiel further developed this same image, which became generally accepted by the masses of Israelites as they moved closer to monotheism. The authors of the Pentateuch accepted the metaphor of Israel and Yahweh as bride and groom, but, in keeping with the legalism characteristic of postexilic Judaism, chose to emphasize the contractual aspects of marriage. As Yahweh's bride, Israel was legally bound by the detailed stipulations of her marriage contract.

For all its ingenuity the Wellhausenian scheme is seriously flawed. First, Wellhausen's history of Israelite religion was derived from his source criticism of the Pentateuch. Few scholars today find this procedure accept-able. As we have already mentioned, the knowledge of a book's develop-mental history does not necessarily tell us about the world outside that book. Second, if one challenges the dating of the sources, which is being done quite vigorously at present (1984), then one must rewrite the religious history accordingly.

Wellhausen was certainly wrong about the earliest stages of Israelite religion. Our present knowledge of the ancient Near East demonstrates that Israel and its neighbors had long passed the primitive phases of animism and totemism before the appearance of their earliest written sources. Egyptians, Mesopotamians, Hurrians, Hittites, and Canaanites all worshiped high gods with distinctive personalities and rich mythologies.

Wellhausen erred as well in seeing a necessary connection between ethics and monotheism. The Akkadian incantation series Shurpu enumerates as sins cheating on weights and measures, marking boundaries falsely, having intercourse with the wife of a neighbor, omitting the name of a god from an incense offering, and eating the tabooed food of a city. The approximately contemporary prophecies of Amos condemn cheating on weights and measures, trampling the heads of the poor, and giving wine to Nazirites. The much earlier Egyptian guidebook for the dead, *Going Forth by Day*, instructed its readers to proclaim their innocence of blaspheming god, doing violence to a poor man, depriving cattle of fodder, having homosexual relations with boys, and passing the time of sacrifice. If Wellhausen were correct, one would have to explain why the teachings of Amos led to monotheism while the similar Egyptian and Mesopotamian writings did not have a like effect.

We must also take issue with the alleged connection between ethics and power. Yahweh did not have to await the emergence of ethical prophecy in the eighth century in order to extend His power beyond the borders of His people's territory. The great gods of the ancient Near East were not geographically limited. To be sure, many gods had favorite habitations. Sippar, for example, was the home of Shamash, the sun god. Yet worshipers did not doubt that he might be in the heavens, under the earth, at the bottom of the sea, or in all simultaneously if he so chose. A major difference between humans and immanent numina on the one hand and high divinities on the other was the freedom of the great gods from the constraints of time and space. Heightened ethical consciousness was not required to convince Babylonians, Hittites, or Egyptians that their gods had power outside of their immediate places of worship. Had they believed otherwise they scarcely would have attempted foreign conquests.

Wellhausen's view of legalism is likewise in need of correction. It was not only postexilic Judaism that stressed a connection between law and divinity. In Egypt justice was embodied in the figure of the goddess Maʿat. In Mesopotamia law was often incarnated in the gods Kittu (justice) and Misharu (equity). At other times Justice and Equity were spoken of as independent powers to which the gods were subject. Shamash the sun god was lauded as "Judge of gods and humans" and "Lord of law." Kings Hammurapi and Lipit-Ishtar compiled law codes because the gods had summoned them to promote law and justice.

Though the above criticisms of Wellhausen are cogent, none goes to the heart of the matter. Neither the marriage metaphor nor the covenant metaphor alleged by Wellhausen and by some contemporary writers to be monotheistic is in fact more than monolatrous. Indeed, the closest parallels to Hosea's marriage imagery come from the sacred marriage texts found in the polytheistic cultures of the Near East. Quite possibly Hosea resorted to the image of marriage with Yahweh in the belief that "the devil shouldn't have the best tunes," as he was addressing himself to Israelite aherents of the fertility worship associated with Baal. Hosea claimed that Israel the bride owed her husband marital fidelity. The unavailability of other lovers was not the issue. Indeed, the use of the marriage metaphor points to a belief that Israel must be faithful to Yahweh despite the presence of other gods.

The objection to interpreting the covenant between divinity and humanity as a monotheistic image is even stronger. Such a notion is found in polytheistic religions and is particularly appropriate to them. The model of religious covenant was borrowed from treaty terminology, where it was necessary to demand loyalty in the face of competition. Human kings drew up covenants because they knew that they had rivals. Covenants between Israel and Yahweh were necessary because other gods could be served. It is noteworthy that those unquestionably late texts such as Ezra and Chronicles, which are consistently monotheistic, do not employ living covenant terminology. As H. L. Ginsberg has pointed out, Hosea had already abandoned the older political covenant notion for the marriage metaphor.[5]

Despite the criticisms of the classical position outlined here, its view that monolatry ("the worship of one god where other gods may be supposed to exist") preceded monotheism is correct. But before that position is defended, it will be useful to compare the Wellhausenian classical view with its opposite, the hypothesis of Yehezkel Kaufmann.

In his magnum opus, *Toledot Ha-Emunah Ha-Yisre'elit* (abridged in English as *The Religion of Israel*), Kaufmann agreed with most modern Bible scholars that the tales of the Hebrew patriarchs reflected a polytheistic milieu. Moses, however, had fomented a religious revolution that eradicated all traces of the older gods. Moses had brought Israel to acknowledge Yahweh as the sole god in existence. All other gods became, for Israel, no-gods. Biblical references to other gods are vestigial, or literary conceits not to be taken seriously by students of the religion of Israel. In other words, monotheism came to Israel very early and was never thereafter seriously threatened. So fundamental had been the influence of Moses that there was very little difference between prophetic and popular religion. True, imported foreign worship was sometimes to be found in the royal courts. The wives of Solomon had private chapels for their own use. Jezebel had brought Baal and Asherah along with their prophets into Samaria. For Kaufmann, however, these aberrations were not reflective of the actual religion of Israel.

Other scholars, notably W. F. Albright, had maintained the early appearance of monotheism in Israel, but none had gone so far as Kaufmann in denying the presence of polytheism in the religion of the masses. Because they contained abundant and repeated denunciations of Israel's worship of other gods, the prophetic and historical books stood in the way of Kaufmann's thesis. Ingeniously, Kaufmann explained that the prophets had denounced the worship not of other gods but of "stick and stone" fetishes. By the eighth century B.C.E., according to Kaufmann, Israel had become so removed from paganism that she had forgotten its true nature and had assumed that the Gentiles worshiped the plastic representations of their gods. In other words, the Israelites mistook the gods of the Gentiles for fetishes. Occasionally some Israelites turned to these fetishes in a low-level superstitious manner. The Hebrew prophets denounced these practices vigorously because their zeal for monotheistic Yahwism would not tolerate even minor lapses into superstition. Furthermore, the prophets and the writers of the historical books had to explain Israel's political defeats and its subjugation by foreigners. It was natural for them to condemn this vestigial fetishism and to see in it a rebellion against Yahweh grave enough to warrant His harshest punishments, including exile.

Having advanced the claim that the Bible's explicit statements about Israelite worship of other gods are not authentic polytheism, Kaufmann set out to redefine the true nature of the Mosaic revolution. Moses had not simply reduced the number of the gods to one, but had taught his people to reject the universal pagan belief in a realm beyond the gods. In a scholarly *tour de force*, Kaufmann surveyed many pagan religions of East and West to show that all of them shared the concept of a "primordial" or "meta-divine" realm inhabited by autonomous powers to which the gods themselves were subject. For Kaufmann, this notion of a primordial realm was the real difference between paganism and Israelite monotheism. In accepting Yahweh as the sole god in existence, Israel had asserted His independence of any other power. The neighbors of Israel placed great emphasis on magic, incantation, and divination, each of which assumed the ability of humans to circumvent the gods by going beyond them to the primordial realm. In contrast to the pagans, Israel rejected the belief in a meta-divine realm, as evidenced by the Israelite cult, which was free of magic, incantation, and divination. So fundamental were their conceptual differences with regard to the nature of divinity that Israelites could not understand pagans. Israelites could not truly worship foreign gods because they did not know how to do so.[6]

Each element of this remarkable thesis must be examined critically. For one thing, it is difficult to find unequivocal monotheistic statements in the Pentateuch, which contains the bulk of the traditions about the Mosaic period. Instead, what are found are demands that Israelites worship Yahweh to the exclusion of all other gods. The most famous passage in this connection is at the beginning of the Decalogue: "You shall have no other gods beside Me . . . You shall not prostrate yourself before them nor shall you serve them. For I, Yahweh your God, am a jealous God, requiting the iniquity of ancestors upon descendants to the third and fourth generations of My enemies" (Exod 20:3–5=Deut 5:7–10).

The commandment does not assert the sole divine existence of Yahweh at all. Unlike clear monotheistic statements (Isa 43:10–13; 44:6–8; 45:5–7, 14, 18, 21–22, 46:9), the passage in the Decalogue does not deny the existence of all other gods. Kaufmann argues that biblical monolatry is simply a corollary of biblical monotheism, that one can understand the prohibition against the worship of all other gods as an outgrowth of the belief that only Yahweh is God. This is surely to put the cart before the horse. As the contemporary American Bible scholar M. Tsevat observes: "It would have been easy for Israel to recognize Yahweh as its only God once it was convinced that there were no other gods in existence. It was another thing altogether to be faithful to Him in the face of a plethora of gods from among whom they might choose their deity."[7]

When we turn to Kaufmann's argument based on the alleged absence of magic from the Israelite cult, we find a good deal of imprecision and exaggeration. Scholars have frequently noted that the Pentateuch and Hammurapi's code alike prescribe the death penalty for magicians. In Israel and in the larger world of the ancient Near East, the words for "magic" and "magician" were social terms of abuse applied to people, often foreigners or women, who were believed to practice rituals designed to harm the larger society. The prohibitions against magic in the Bible and in Hammurapi's code as well as the many Akkadian rituals against the effects of sorcery share similar concerns about the well-being of society, not about the existence of a primordial realm.

Whether an Israelite ritual was "magical" (*keshāfim*) or "divine service" (*'avodāh*) depended on its performers, on the group with which is was associated, and on the writer responsible for its extant description. The Pentateuch, for example, speaks admiringly of the ability of Moses and Aaron to create live crocodiles out of staves (Exod 7:9–10) and to turn the waters of the Nile into blood (Exod 7:20). The same biblical writer disparages the identical feats of the Egyptians. In other biblical traditions, Yahweh is credited with the instruction to sculpt a bronze serpent with the power to heal snakebite (Num 21:8–9), with the formulation of a ritual to topple the walls of a city (Josh 6:2–5), and with the command to employ a divine staff to get water from a stone (Num 20:7–11). Very similar rituals were associated with the Babylonian gods Ea and Marduk. To say that the Bible prohibits magic is to make no statements about primordial realms. The ancient Hebrews shared with their contemporaries the belief that certain rituals were approved by the gods and that others were disapproved.

The question of prayer versus incantation is more complicated. Form criticism and philology demonstrate that the ancients distinguished between these two ways of approaching the gods. Prayer was usually petitionary. In prayer, the gods were invoked with great respect, and much attention was paid to their attributes and epithets. The suppliant attempted to persuade the gods to respond favorably, since they might just as easily turn a deaf ear. In contrast, in incantation the names of the gods might be omitted or dropped casually, in the expectation that their mere mention would automatically compel the execution of the suppliant's will. Incantations were often in rhyme or doggerel and had to be recited in a particular way for a specified number of times. Wishes and hopes were not expressed as such but were phrased in the indicative mood, as if to say that the very statement of the words would bring about the desired result.

Kaufmann drew on the formal differences between prayer and incantation in order to argue that the Israelites disbelieved in the meta-divine realm in which incantation was effective. According to Kaufmann it was only on the soil of Israelite religion that incantation grew into prayer. Had he been correct it would be difficult to explain why polytheists bothered to pray. In fact, prayer and incantation had always coexisted. In most cases the differences between the two approaches were stylistic rather than substantive. Mesopotamian worshipers, for example, considered prayer and incantation complementary, as in Akkadian texts prescribing prayers to be offered by incantation priests so that their incantations might be successful. Other ritual texts from Mesopotamia instruct priests to recite incantations designed to make sure that the prayers of worshipers would be answered. Social factors also played a part. In Mesopotamia, at least, incantation was the province of specially trained priests, and prayer the duty of the individual worshiper. Kaufmann's assumption that incantation was not found in Israel is questionable. We cannot always tell whether a text served a cult as prayer or incantation. The Akkadian "Lifting of the Hand" series, compiled early in the second millennium B.C.E., consists in the main of texts that employ the verbal forms and petitionary tone usually associated with prayer. Yet each member of the series is marked with the Sumerian subscript EN "incantation" and followed by instructions about the number of times the text is to be recited and by details about its accompanying ritual. The closest biblical analog to the "Lifting of the Hand," the Psalms, is not as well supplied with rubrics; we do not understand many of the rubrics we have. In consequence, it is difficult for a modern student to tell which Psalms were intended for prayer and which for incantation. What is certain is that in later centuries the Psalms were put to incantational use. It is noteworthy that pious Jews who lived in the period of late antiquity, who were surely more consistent monotheists than their Israelite ancestors, did not object to

the use of incantations. Indeed, some of the most prominent rabbis cited in
the Talmuds were credited with the authorship of effective incantations.
Believing Christians likewise often had recourse to incantations. In other
words, there is no necessary link between incantation and the supposed
meta-divine realm of polytheism.

In a similar vein, Kaufmann differentiated sharply between prophecy and
divination. In paganism the diviner initiated divine–human communication. Kaufmann saw this as a limitation of the gods' power. In contrast, the
Israelite prophet was called by Yahweh. On this analysis, apostolic prophecy
was intimately bound up with the belief in a single God, completely
transcendent, who chose as messengers whomever he wished.

Here too the facts are otherwise. Were Kaufmann correct, we should not
expect to find apostolic prophecy in pagan cultures or divination in Israel.
Yet the biblical writers do not regard prophecy as uniquely Israelite, but
refer to the prophets of Baal and Asherah by the term *nevi'im* (1 Kgs 18:19).
The biblical designation *hozeh* ("seer," 2 Kgs 17:13) finds its pagan parallel in
the *hazayin* who were sent by the god Baalshamayin to King Zakur of
Hamath in the eighth century. The Mari letters of the eighteenth century
B.C.E., whose testimony is apparently corroborated by the much older
archives discovered in Ebla in Syria, speak of various male and female
mantics who speak, uninvited, in the name of a god who sent them. In none
of these instances are these prophets or their listeners monotheists. There
is, in fact, no inherent reason why many gods cannot have many apostolic
prophets. Conversely, as H. M. Orlinsky has remarked, there is no theoretical reason why a monotheist could not employ divinatory means to learn
of Yahweh's will.[8]

Prophecy and divination differed in form but not in substance. The
ancients believed that the powers that be had provided valuable information
about the past, present, and future in the heavens, in the entrails of animals,
in the motions of birds and beasts, in the movements of liquids, in voices
and sounds of unknown origin, in chance utterances, and in the actions of
certain people. The prophet, who was subject to seizure by the hand of God
(1 Kgs 18:46), depended on ravens for food (1 Kgs 17:6), walked about naked
and barefoot for three years (Isa 20:2–3), remained on his left side 390 days
and on his right for 40 days (Ezek 4:4–6), and gave names to his children
on the order of Pillage-Speed-Hurry-Plunder, was himself a "sign and
wonder" (Isa 8:18) through whom divinity provided oracle and message.

The evidence available at present suggests that prophecy was more highly
regarded than divination in the Syria-Palestine area, whereas in Mesopotamia the arts of the diviner were considered more reliable. Both prophecy
and divination were found in Israel (1 Sam 28:1ff.). Biblical objections to

divination were as selective as biblical objections to magic. The '*ov* and *yid'oni* were condemned by biblical writers (Deut 18:11; 2 Kgs 21:8), though certainly not by the people (Isa 8:19; 29:4). The *urim* (Num 27:21), the *efod* (1 Sam 23:9; 30:7), and the *goral* (Lev 16:8; Josh 15:1), in contrast, were considered perfectly legitimate. It will also be recalled that monotheistic Judaism of late antiquity recognized the legitimacy of many kinds of divination and did not regard them as inconsistent with the unity of God.

Kaufmann's boldness in asserting the differences between Israel and its neighbors is especially striking in his statements about myth. He claims that Israelites told no myths about Yahweh and assumed naively that pagans told no myths about their gods. If, argues Kaufmann, the Israelites did not realize that pagans told no myths about their gods, then the Israelites must have believed that the pagan gods were mere fetishes. The most apt rejoinder to Kaufmann is Albright's remark: "The ignorance presupposed by Kaufmann's view is simply incredible."[9] Comparative studies of Near Eastern mythology demonstrate that Israel told its myths about Yahweh and was aware that its neighbors told myths about other gods.

There are two final criticisms to be made of Kaufmann. He himself conceded that there had been some periods of true idolatry in Israel, confined in the main to court circles. How would these have been possible in an Israel with no understanding of paganism? How would the "limpers" of Elijah's day have expected Baal to answer his prophets if Baal were no more than a fetish? How would Ezekiel have known that El lived in the heart of the seas (Ezek 28:2)? Why would the Baal worshipers of Hosea's day think that Baal was the donor of corn and oil (Hos 2:10)? The plain sense of the biblical texts is that those Israelites who worshiped gods other than Yahweh, or "beside" Yahweh, believed in their power. The classical prophets were aware of these beliefs but condemned them.

Finally, Kaufmann's method is paradoxical. He denies the explicit statements of the biblical texts but relies on the Bible almost exclusively for evidence to support his arguments. Still, Kaufmann has performed the valuable task of forcing scholarship to focus on the basic problem of monotheism's development: How could monotheistic Judaism have developed out of Israelite religion unless there was something in its structure fundamentally different from other ancient religion, or unless some revolutionary historical development had taken place?

Covenant

In fact, Israelite religion from earliest times was different from the religion of its surroundings. The difference, however, was not in ethics, as Wellhausen had it. Still less is Israelite uniqueness to be found in the alleged absences of magic, incantation, or myth from its cult, or in its assumed naïveté about the religions of its neighbors. The crucial difference between Israel and its neighbors was the emphasis of the Hebrews on the role of Yahweh as liberator, as redeemer from slavery, as donor of land and political sovereignty to a newly formed people. Because the exodus tradition was so pervasive in Israel, it made for a concentration on the role of Yahweh in history rather than in nature. Israel was not unique in crediting its God with historical concerns. But historical concerns had a far greater influence on the cult of Yahweh than similar concerns had on the cults of Israel's neighbors. The three great agricultural festivals, for example, had their "natural" character subordinated to the themes of exodus and settlement. The offering of the first fruits celebrated Israel's transformation from a "wandering Aramean" (Deut 26:5) into a people with its own land. The Sabbath, whatever its origin, became a reminder of Egyptian servitude (Deut 5:15). The dedication of the firstborn of animals and humans (Exod 13:11–16) was related to the punishment of the Egyptians. The covenant of circumcision was related to the promise of the land (Gen 17:7–14).

As we have noted, the traditions of freedom from oppression by Egypt and its Canaanite vassals appealed to those Canaanites who affiliated with the invaders to become "Israel," who subsumed their own struggles under the rubric of "exodus." In consequence, the new polity celebrated Yahweh's saving acts in the cult and drew its religious metaphors primarily from what we would now call "politics" or "government." Early Israel was viewed as the kingdom of Yahweh (Judg 9:23; 1 Sam 8:7) to whom the people were allied by *berit* or "covenant."

George Mendenhall was the first biblical scholar to realize the significance of ancient Near Eastern treaties for the understanding of biblical covenant.[10] One particularly important treaty that has been adduced was concluded between the Hittite king of the fourteenth century Mursilis II and his vassal Duppi-Teshub of Amurru. It reads in part:

> When your father died, in accordance with your father's word I did not drop you. Since your father mentioned to me your name, I sought after you. To be sure, you were sick and ailing, but though you were ailing, I, the Sun, put you in the place of your father and took your brothers, sisters and the Amurru land in oath for you.

This introduction is followed by stipulations that require loyalty to Mursilis and his descendants. In return, Mursilis promises his protection. Duppi-Teshub, the vassal (literally, "servant"), is instructed to present his tribute and to maintain his undivided devotion to Mursilis:

> Do not turn to anyone else. Your fathers presented tribute to Egypt; you shall not do that. . . . With my friend you shall be friend and with my enemy you shall be enemy.

Various divinities are called on to witness the treaty. In order to discourage disloyalty, curses are invoked on the "vassal," his possessions, and his country. The gods are also called upon to bless him if he obeys his obligations and fulfills them.

Because of its similarities to the biblical covenants between Yahweh and Israel, much attention has been given this treaty and others like it. Some scholars have questioned the extent of the formal similarities while others have held that the later Assyrian treaties are closer to the biblical forms, but it is now certain that the political covenant is the inspiration of the biblical divine–human *berit*. No longer can *berit* be viewed as a prophetic metaphor of marriage adapted to the unromantic needs of Jewish legalism.

If the reconstruction of early Israelite history presented above is correct, then it is natural that early Israel would have conceived of its bond with Yahweh in terms of deliverance and continuing political protection akin to the wording of the Hittite treaties. Just as King Mursilis II was entitled to the sole allegiance of Duppi-Teshub in return for putting him on his throne when he was sick and ailing, so was Yahweh entitled to the sole allegiance of the people whom he had freed.

Why sole allegiance? We have noted above that political covenants were drawn up in the face of competition. Duppi-Teshub was explicitly reminded that his ancestors had served the Egyptians. He, in contrast, was to turn to no king apart from Mursilis. When worshipers of Yahweh adopted the covenant notion as a religious metaphor, they themselves could have only been polytheistic. A covenant to serve Yahweh alone would have been necessary only in a society in which the existence of other gods was taken for granted. As the gnostics of a much later date were to ask: How could Yahweh be both a jealous God and the sole God? If there were no other gods, of whom could He be jealous?

What enabled polytheistic Israelites to make the transition to the monolatry that is implicit in the covenant metaphor? The question actually has several facets. First, we must examine religious analogues within and without Israel. Second, we must attend to the political and social circumstances that made the metaphor of covenant and its attendant monolatry more significant in Israel than elsewhere.

Monolatry was not entirely unknown in the ancient Near East. At fourteenth century Amarna in Egypt (ancient Akhetaton), the royal family of Akh-en-aton gave their sole adoration to the Aton, whereas the rest of

Egypt gave its sole adoration to the Pharaoh. Similarly A. van Selms has identified what he terms "temporary henotheism" in Mesopotamian sources.[11] In the Atra-hasis epic, for example, the people are advised to forsake temporarily the worship of all gods and goddesses with the exception of Namtara. According to van Selms a similar tendency to temporary henotheism motivated the removal of foreign gods in the Bible (see Gen 35; Josh 24; Judg 10; 1 Sam 7 and 1 Kgs 15).

The prayer literature of the Near East was also helpful in smoothing the path to monolatry. In Egypt, it was not unusual to flatter a deity as the "sole god." Mesopotamia in particular provides evidence of a tendency of worshipers to engage in a kind of verbal monolatry. Each high god might be approached in turn as if he were the only god who mattered. There were different ways in which Mesopotamian worshipers expressed verbal monolatry. Suppliants might speak of all the gods worshiping the divinity to whom the immediate prayer was directed, while noting that none of these gods was comparable in power. Alternatively, they might transfer to the god they were worshiping those qualities primarily associated with other gods. Thus, the moon god might be told that his sparkle was like the fire-god's and his heat like the sun-god's. In some cases the worshiper described all the other gods as mere attributes of the one to whom he was praying or, similarly, as the limbs of the god to whom he was praying.[12]

The prayers do not exhibit a serious tendency to deplete the ranks of the gods. There was no suggestion in them that the cult of Shamash, for example, should be discontinued because Ishtar rivaled his brightness. In effect, what the worshiper said was, "You, the god I now approach, are as good as any divinity at its best." The very same worshiper who insisted on the sole importance of Ishtar when addressing her would make the same kind of statement about Ea when addressing him. Yet despite the difference in substance between the flattery of verbal monolatry and the actuality of cultic monolatry, it is clear that the availability of monolatrous language played an important part in the ability to worship a single god.

Some scholars have claimed that the idea of a divine–human covenant is uniquely Israelite. Were this accurate, it would be more difficult to retrace the steps that made covenant so important in Israel. We should not expect the notion of divine–human covenant to be unique. In the ancient Near East gods could be kings, queens, judges, counselors, fathers, mothers, secretaries, canal inspectors, warriors, physicians, midwives, torches, and heralds, to name just a few. Why might a god not be a suzerain or an ally?

The biblical writers did not believe that a covenant with a god was unique. Exod 23:32 contains the warning, "You shall not make a covenant with them [Hivites, Canaanites, and Hittites], nor with their gods." Obviously, the writer of this early passage knew that one could covenant with other gods. To do so was not impossible, but it was sinful.

Extrabiblical sources point in the same direction. The word *salāmu* is used regularly in Akkadian to describe covenanting and political alliance. The same word is very well attested in Akkadian prayer literature to describe the reconciliation of a god with a worshiper. That the two senses of *salāmu* could simultaneously be suggested to a Mesopotamian is demonstrated by a twelfth-century "prophecy" attributed to Marduk: "That prince shall rule all the lands. For I alone, all you gods, have a covenant with him. He shall destroy Elam." Similarly, a Phoenician inscription from Arslan Tash reads in part: "Eternal covenants were made with us. Asshur made them with us as did every divinity and great one, the council of all our holy beings."[13]

The notion of covenant did not play its central role in Israelite religion because of any alleged uniqueness. What made the metaphor so much more important in Israel than elsewhere was its relevance to the historical circumstances that brought Israel into being. We have already mentioned that Israel was a composite group. The union of its diverse elements came about by means of covenant, as may be seen in several instructive biblical accounts.

The ninth chapter of Joshua tells of a treaty between Joshua and the Gibeonites. Like most of our biblical sources, it is written from the viewpoint of all Israel on one side of the covenant and the Gibeonites on the other. Nevertheless, covenant is said to have brought Gibeon into Israel. In all likelihood, a similar treaty united the diverse ethnic elements who inhabited Shechem in the premonarchic period, whose god was called El-Berith or Baal-Berith (Judg 8:33; 9:4; 46), names that express religiously the relation or union of the god's worshipers.

The twenty-fourth chapter of Joshua is especially important for the information it provides about fusion through covenant in early Israel. Shechem, the setting of the story, is unconnected with the conquest traditions of the rest of Joshua and Judges. Joshua has summoned all the leaders of Israel to stand before God. In their presence, Joshua relates the story of Israel's ancestors "who lived beyond the river . . . and served other gods." After a summary of the events that led to the exodus and the settlement, Joshua turns to the people and admonishes them to serve Yahweh exclusively. They have, he says, the options of serving the gods of Egypt, the gods beyond the river, or the local Amorite gods, if they do not wish to serve Yahweh. The people choose to serve Yahweh. At that point, Joshua warns them that their service must be exclusive. Yahweh is a jealous God who will not forgive the worship of other divinities. Accepting the responsibility for their choice, the people agree to bear their own witness to it. Once the people have agreed to abandon the worship of all "foreign gods," Joshua makes a covenant on behalf of all of them and writes its stipulations in a book of divine instructions (*sefer torat 'elohim*). Finally, Joshua erects a memorial stone under the oak in Yahweh's sanctuary.

Though the story has undergone an "all-Israel" adaptation, its basic narrative must be taken seriously. It appears to be independent both of the rest of Joshua and the Pentateuch. For example, in contradiction to chapter 6, 24:11 refers to warfare with the inhabitants of Jericho. The presence of a tree in Yahweh's sanctuary is in violation of Deut 6:21. The statement that Israel's ancestors served other gods "beyond the river" is unique. Most striking is the lack of reference to any earlier covenant at Sinai or Horeb, to a theophany, or to a gift of the law.

Many scholars have remarked on the similarity of the covenant ceremony in Joshua 24 to the treaty tradition of the ancient Near East that has been referred to above. The long historical introduction is reminiscent of second-millennium treaty style, in which the great king demands undivided loyalty in return for past saving acts. Yahweh, like Mursilis II, the Hittite king, was aware of rivalry—that presented by the local gods, the gods beyond the river, and the gods of Egypt—a significant indication of the diversity of "all the tribes of Israel" whom Joshua had summoned to Shechem.

If we must decide between the reliability of the Joshua covenant story and the traditions that describe the covenant as pre-settlement, then the decision must be in favor of Joshua. It is much more likely that a new polity which arose in Canaan would have had access to ancient traditions of treaty making than to suppose that these came out of the desert. Furthermore, the very fact that this covenant ceremony was not, like so much else, transferred to the desert is a sign of its antiquity and reliability. Even in its present form, the covenant tradition of the chapter reveals that Israel, a new group allied with Yahweh, came into existence in Canaan. The theological construct of covenant with Yahweh was a means of expressing the mundane fact of political union. Through covenant to Yahweh and to each other, diverse groups became Israel, which then began to describe itself as a kinship group unrelated to Canaan. It was only natural after that to find common blood ancestors. In the course of time as Israel coalesced, opposition grew to the continuing inclusion of new members. Covenants with them were forbidden (Exod 23:32), and early traditions were reworked to distinguish sharply between Israel and Canaan.

The formation of Israel was a victory for the sole worship of Yahweh. For the time being, the needs of the new polity could be met by the worship of one God to the exclusion of all others. But the practices associated with polytheism began quickly to reassert themselves. There is no reason to be skeptical about such statements as Judg 2:11ff.: "The Israelites did that which was evil in the sight of Yahweh and served the Baals. They abandoned Yahweh the God of their ancestors, who had brought them out of Egypt, and served other gods from among the gods of the surrounding nations. They prostrated themselves before them and so angered Yahweh. . . . They served Baal and the Astartes."

It is easy to see why this happened. At the time of Israel's formation, the exclusive worship of Yahweh unified various groups who sought independence and autonomy. Yahwism served as a kind of political banner for those whose concerns were primarily with warfare. The early text Exod 23:24–25 is illuminating: "You shall serve Yahweh your God and He will bless your bread and water; and I will take sickness away from your midst. None shall lose her young or be barren within your land. I will give you the full number of your days." It will be noticed that there is no mention here of the fertility of soil or beast (contrast Deut 11:14–15). Instead, the promises reflect the needs of landless warriors who require food and a healthy population to keep on fighting. Yahweh the conqueror God did not immediately become a fertility deity with the ability to provide farmers with sun, wind, and rain at the proper time. But, as we have seen, among the members of Israel were many people who had long practiced the Baal cults well-attested in the second millennium B.C.E. and now documented at Ebla in the third. These former Canaanites knew the effectiveness of time-honored myth and ritual. Indeed, the denial of the powers of the old fertility gods must have seemed tantamount to the denial of what is now called "nature." The second chapter of Hosea presents the Baalist view succinctly in order to combat it. Hosea compares Israel to a foolish adulteress who has falsely credited her lovers with the provision of luxurious gifts which had, in reality, come from her husband. In the same fashion had Israel thanked Baal, instead of Yahweh, for rich harvests and the ensuing prosperity of the country: "For she did not know that it was I who provided her with the new grain, the wine, and the oil, I who lavished silver on her and gold which they used for Baal" (Hos. 2:10).

Hosea, fully cognizant of the claims made for Baal's powers, retorted that Yahweh would soon show that He was a god of fertility. For Hosea, the older political metaphor of covenant was no longer effective. Instead, he pictured Israel as Yahweh's bride, an indication of his awareness that the Baal cults celebrated the powers of sexuality and fecundity.

The exchange between Hosea and his contemporaries reveals the tension inherent in Israelite monolatry. Monolatry is inherently polytheistic in that it does not deny the powers of the divinities whose worship it chooses to ignore. To serve a god in the ancient world was both to acknowledge and to relate to a source of power. To ignore a god was to abdicate a certain amount of both understanding and control. The average polytheist was always delighted to discover a new divinity, for that provided him with a greater understanding of his surroundings and with the potential to manipulate them to his advantage. Monolaters had two kinds of choices. They might propitiate the many gods whose existences they had never denied and run the risk of angering Yahweh. It is clear that most Israelites were willing to take that risk. A minority, however, began to elevate Yahweh to a position where his exclusive worship made sense. Gradually, Yahweh became the most powerful of the gods (Exod 15:11; Ps 89:7), who, in true mythic fashion, could defeat all His divine foes (Isa 27:1; Ps 74:13–14; Job 26:12–13). The next step was the declaration that Yahweh alone was powerful and all other gods powerless and temporary (Jer 10:1–16). Finally came the uncompromising monotheism of Deutero-Isaiah.

The tension within monolatry accounts for the unique course taken by Israelite religion. The early demand for the exclusive worship of Yahweh, as expressed in the metaphor of covenant, was too rooted historically in the rise of Israel for it to be eradicated entirely. Especially in times of war, crisis, and national disaster the call to serve Yahweh alone was a potential force to rally the people. At the same time, an inherent difficulty in monolatry, the requirement to ignore the service of powerful gods, forced its advocates to assume a more radical stance and ultimately to become monotheists.

Monotheism's evolution was slow owing to several factors. First, the world view of the ancients was not unitary. Before the teachings of Epicurus and Lucretius became influential in the Near East, no one spoke of "nature" or "universe" or "cosmos." Polytheism was the religious expression of fundamental disunity, and it accounted very well for the infinitude of phenomena.

Polytheism had several other appealing features. First, it was dramatic. The mythic descriptions of the loves and wars of the ancient Near Eastern gods, many of which were reenacted in the cult, continue to charm the modern reader. Second, polytheism makes "moral" sense. Human suffering and toil were more understandable in a world in which the gods were perceived as in conflict than in one in which everything was supposed to reflect the will of a god both omnipotent and just. True, paganism did not fail to confront the problem of theodicy. Nonetheless, the books of Job and Ecclesiastes were not produced by pagan societies. Finally, paganism affirmed all of the life force. In Israel, women were generally excluded from positions of power and Hebrew religious imagery tended to depict Yahweh as male. As increasing numbers of Israelites began to take monolatry and then monotheism seriously, Yahweh absorbed most of the attributes and functions of the older gods, especially El and Baal. It was more difficult, though it will be seen not impossible, for Yahweh to arrogate to Himself the qualities of Near Eastern goddesses.

Some contemporary authors have attempted to find female divine imagery related to Yahweh in the Bible, but their efforts are not convincing. Generally the masculinity of Yahweh is taken for granted by the biblical writers. The absence of that female imagery accounts for the widespread popular worship of goddesses which is condemned by the biblical authors. The mother of King Asa, for example, had constructed an image of the ancient goddess Asherah. An image of the same divinity stood in the Jerusalem temple in Josiah's time (2 Kgs 21:7). The goddess Astarte was popular in her Canaanite form and as the Arameo-Mesopotamian Queen of Heaven (Jer 7:18; 44:17ff.).[14]

Extrabiblical sources support the impression that goddess worship was popular. The fifth-century B.C.E. archives left by the Jewish garrison at Elephantine in Egypt refer to a divinity named Anatyahu, presumably an androgynous blend of Yahweh with the ancient Canaanite goddess Anat. The recent discoveries at Khirbet el Qom and Kuntillet Ajrud in the holy land have unearthed inscriptions of the ninth to eighth centuries referring to "Yahweh of Samaria and his Asherah" and to "Yahweh of Teman and his Asherah." It is not certain whether Asherah retains its proper name status in these phrases or whether it has become a common noun in the sense of "consort." In either case, these new discoveries provide important information about the spiritual life of ancient Israel. It is even possible that the marriage metaphor discussed above, originated by Hosea and amplified by Jeremiah and Ezekiel, served in part as a rejoinder to this popular conception.

Our essay has attempted to show that Israel was very much a part of the world of its time. Yet certain historical circumstances conspired to implant in Israel the seeds of uniqueness in matters spiritual. Perhaps "historical" is the key word, because that made for differences in the celebrations of Israelite cult. The varied strands of Israelite religion, popular and prophetic, shared common beliefs about the importance of the role of Yahweh in what we would call history. By linking its beliefs, practices, and religious metaphors to memories of formative historical events, some accurate and some no doubt imagined, Israelite faith gradually became Judaism.

Notes

1. M. Astour, "The Amarna Age Forerunners of Biblical Anti-Royalism," in *For Max Weinreich on His Seventieth Birthday* (The Hague: Mouton, 1974) 13.

2. M. Held, "The Root Zbl/Sbl in Akkadian, Ugaritic and Biblical Hebrew," in *Essays in Memory of B. A. Speiser*, ed. W. W. Hallo, American Oriental Series 53 (New Haven, CT: American Oriental Society, 1968) 94.

3. J. Wellhausen, *Prolegomena*, 417–19.

4. Ibid., 509.

5. H. L. Ginsberg, "Hosea, Book of," in *Encyclopaedia Judaica* (Jerusalem: Encyclopaedia Judaica; New York: Macmillan, 1971) 1011.

6. Y. Kaufmann, *The Religion of Israel*, 21–121.

7. M. Tsevat, *The Meaning of the Book of Job and Other Biblical Studies* (New York: Ktav, 1981) 132.

8. H. M. Orlinsky, "The Seer-Priest," in *Judges*, ed. B. Mazar. (Givatayim, Israel: Jewish History Publications; New Brunswick, NJ: Rutgers University Press, 1971) 344.

9. W. F. Albright, *Yahweh and the Gods of Canaan*, 207.

10. G. Mendenhall, "Covenant Forms in Israelite Tradition," 25–53.

11. A. van Selms, "Temporary Henotheism," in *Symbolae Biblicae et Mesopotamicae F. M. T. de Liagre Böhl Dedicatae* (Leiden: Brill, 1973) 341–48.

12. S. D. Sperling, "A šu-il-la to Ištar," *Die Welt des Orients* 12 (1981) 14.

13. S. D. Sperling, "An Arslan Tash Incantation: Interpretations and Implications," *Hebrew Union College Annual* 53 (1982) 9–10.

14. See M. Held, "Studies in Biblical Lexicography in the Light of Akkadian," in *Harry M. Orlinsky Volume*, ed. J. Aviram et al., Eretz-Israel 16 (Jerusalem: Magnes Press, 1982) *254.

Bibliography

There is a large body of critical literature on the history and religion of ancient Israel. Such reference works as the Anchor Bible series (Garden City, NY: Doubleday), the *Interpreter's Dictionary of the Bible* (Nashville: Abingdon), and so forth are readily available in libraries. The standard historical works on the period are those by Bright, Noth, and de Vaux. All of these will, in varying degrees, deal with religion as well as with national history.

On the specific question of Israel's religion and its relationship to Near Eastern antecedents, see Albright (*Yahweh and the Gods of Canaan*), Cross. Other important works on Israelite religion, in addition to those discussed in the text of this essay, include Fohrer, Levine.

Albright, William Foxwell. *From the Stone Age to Christianity: Monotheism and the Historical Process*. Garden City, NY: Doubleday, 1957.

———. *Yahweh and the Gods of Canaan*. Garden City, NY: Doubleday, 1968.

Bright, John. *A History of Israel*. Rev. ed. Philadelphia: Westminster, 1981.

Cross, F. M. *Canaanite Myth and Hebrew Epic*. Cambridge, MA: Harvard University Press, 1973.

Emerton, J. A. "New Light on Israelite Religion: The Implications of the Inscriptions from Kuntillet 'Ajrud." *Zeitschrift für die alttestamentliche Wissenschaft* 94 (1982) 1–20.

Fohrer, G. *History of Israelite Religion*. Translated by D. E. Green. New York: Abingdon, 1972.

Freedman, David Noel, and D. F. Graf, eds. *Palestine in Transition*. Sheffield: Almond Press, 1983.

Gaster, T. H. *Myth, Legend, and Custom in the Old Testament.* New York: Harper & Row, 1969.

Geus, C. H. J. de. *The Tribes of Israel: An Investigation into Some of the Presuppositions of Martin Noth's Amphictyony Hypothesis.* Studia Semitica Neerlandica 18. Assen: Van Gorcum, 1976.

Glock, A. "Early Israel as the Kingdom of Yahweh," *Concordia Theological Monthly* 41 (1970) 558–605.

Gottwald. N. K. *The Tribes of Yahweh: A Sociology of the Religion of Liberated Israel 1250-1050 B.C.E.* Maryknoll, NY: Orbis Books, 1979.

Hallo, W. "New Moons and Sabbaths: A Case-Study in the Contrastive Approach." *Hebrew Union College Annual* 48 (1978) 1–18.

———. "Cult Statue and Divine Image: A Preliminary Study." In *Scripture in Context II*, 1–17. Edited by W. Hallo, J. Moyer, and L. G. Perdue. Winona Lake, IN: Eisenbrauns, 1983.

Hillers, Delbert. *Covenant: The History of a Biblical Idea.* Baltimore, MD: Johns Hopkins University Press, 1969.

Kaufmann, Yehezkel. *The Religion of Israel.* Translated by and abridged by M. Greenberg. Chicago: University of Chicago Press, 1960. [Hebrew original, 1938-1956.]

Levine, Baruch A. *In the Presence of the Lord: A Study of Cult and Some Cultic Terms in Ancient Israel.* Studies in Judaism in Late Antiquity 5. Leiden: Brill, 1974.

McCarthy, Dennis. *Treaty and Covenant.* Analecta Biblica 21a. Rome: Pontifical Biblical Institute, 1978.

Mendenhall, George. "Covenant Forms in Israelite Tradition," in *The Biblical Archaeologist Reader 3*, 25–53. Garden City, NY: Doubleday, 1970. [First published in *Biblical Archaeologist* 17 (1954) 52–76.]

———. "The Hebrew Conquest of Palestine." In *The Biblical Archaeologist Reader 3*, 100–120. Garden City, NY: Doubleday, 1970. [First published in *Biblical Archaeologist* 25 (1962) 66–87.]

———. *The Tenth Generation: The Origins of the Biblical Tradition.* Baltimore, MD, and London: Johns Hopkins University Press, 1973.

Milgrom, J. "Religious Conversion and the Revolt Model for the Formation of Israel." *Journal of Biblical Literature* 101 (1982) 169–176.

Noth, Martin. *The History of Israel.* Edinburgh: T. & T. Clark, 1960.

Pettinato, G. *The Archives of Ebla.* Garden City, NY: Doubleday, 1981.

Van Seters, J. *Abraham in History and Tradition.* New Haven, CT: Yale University Press, 1975.

Vaux, Roland de. *Ancient Israel: Its Life and Institutions.* Translated by John McHugh. New York: McGraw-Hill, 1965.

Weippert, M. *The Settlement of the Israelite Tribes in Palestine: A Critical Survey of Recent Scholarly Debate.* Studies in Biblical Theology 2/21. Naperville, IL: Allenson, 1971.

Wellhausen, Julius. *Prolegomena to the History of Israel with Reprint of the Article Israel from the "Encyclopaedia Britannica."* Translated by J. Sutherland Black and Allan Menzies. Edinburgh: A. & C. Black, 1885.

2

The Jerusalem Temple in Devotional and Visionary Experience

Jon D. Levenson

Temple and Tent

A CENTRAL PARADOX of Jewish spirituality lies in the fact that so much of it centers upon an institution that was destroyed almost two millennia ago, the Jerusalem Temple. The enduring centrality of the Temple in Jewish consciousness and the tenacity of its hold upon it are attested by the tendency of modern students of Jewish history to periodicize distant antiquity in terms of the First Temple period (ca. 960–587 B.C.E.) and the Second Temple period (ca. 515 B.C.E.–70 C.E.). In fact, the existence or absence of the Temple is a point of great relevance even to the observance of Jewish law. To cite only one example from among many, the Mishnah, a law code promulgated about 200 C.E., stipulates that the prohibition of the slaughter of an animal and its young on the same day (Lev 22:28) applies both "in the presence of the Temple and in the absence of the Temple" (*m. Hul.* 5:1). But other commandments, especially many found in the last of the six "orders" of the Mishnah, which deals with matters of ritual purity, apply only when the Temple is standing.

The paradox is compounded when one considers that the Pentateuch has been, in principle, the foundational document of Judaism since some point in that Second Temple period. For the Pentateuch neither names Jerusalem nor refers directly to the sacred building(s) that were erected there. Instead it treats at length the construction of the *'ohel mo'ed*, the Tent of Assembly or Tent of Meeting, which served as a portable temple during the period between the revelation at Sinai (e.g., Exod 25–30; 35–40) and the entrance into Canaan, or perhaps even the construction of Solomon's Temple, the First Temple (1 Kgs 8:4). Modern critical scholarship has tended to doubt the historicity of that portable temple and to regard it as a retrojection of a later institution, usually the Second Temple, which the text thus anchors in primordial events. This tendency has been mitigated in our century by research into tribal palladia and other tentlike structures which, even in modern times, have accompanied some nomadic Arabian tribes in their movements. Descriptions of analogous shrines appear in Phoenician sources contemporaneous with much biblical literature.[1] Thus, the possibility that the traditions about the Tent of Meeting contain a nucleus of historical fact has gained ground, especially in the more conservative American circles. On the other hand, the notion that the Tent as described in Exodus could have been carried about in the wilderness for some forty years is still implausible.[2]

If, as seems likely, the Tent of Meeting and the Temple, in whatever of its phases, are not simply to be identified, we are led to wonder what statement is being made by the emphasis of some ancient Israelite traditions upon the portable shrine.[3] Is it as judgment upon the Temple, a statement that the Jerusalem shrine does not conform to the ancient archetype? If so, then the very portability of the Tent may have served as a critique of the tendency to regard Jerusalem and its Temple as immutable cosmic realities, a tendency which we shall examine and which became more developed in postbiblical literature. Similarly, the availability of God in His portable home probably did serve as a source of consolation to an Israel in exile (sixth century B.C.E.) far from their Temple, which lay in ruins. To them the most meaningful image of God was not that of a king enthroned in his massive stone palace; it was that of a delicate tabernacling presence, on the move with His people. In rabbinic literature, this presence acquires a name, the *shekhinah* (from the root *shakhan*, "to set up tent," "to dwell"), and there it is often said to envelop those who involve themselves in Torah (e.g., *m. Abot* 3:3). This conjunction of the tabernacling presence and Torah is, in a sense, natural, in light of the emphasis in the Pentateuch itself upon God's mobility and availability to all Israel, attributes that He shares with the Book. Finally, we should note that, if the Pentateuchal concern with the tent-shrine is indeed a judgment on the Jerusalem Temple, it is probably also a judgment upon the latter's character as a royal shrine, built, patronized, and abused by the House of David. The placement of the ideal arrangement in the days of Aaron and Moses, when a king had not yet reigned in Israel, may have played a role in a political polemic now lost to us.

If, to some segments of ancient Israel in some situations, the Tent of Meeting served as a vehicle for critique of the Jerusalem Temple, the fact remains that the dominant impression one receives from the Hebrew Bible is one of an easy harmony between the two. In fact, one scholar has recently gone so far as to argue for the historical accuracy of the statement of 1 Kgs 8:4 (=2 Chr 5:5) and several texts in Chronicles that the Tent was moved into the Temple.[4] In support of this, he points to texts such as Ps 26:8:

> O LORD, I love Your temple abode,
> the dwelling-place (*meqom mishkan*) of Your glory.[5]

Here, the psalmist puts "temple" and "tent" (*mishkan*) into synonymous parallelism. Essentially the same use of language can be found in Ps 27:4–5, in which the poet longs "to live in the house (*beyt*) of the LORD," which he also describes as "His pavilion" (*sukkoh*) and "His tent" (*'oholo*). Finally, Psalm 74, whose occasion is the destruction of one of the Jerusalem Temples (v. 2), most likely the First in 587 B.C.E., puts "sanctuary" (*miqdash*) and "tent" (*mishkan*) into parallelism and laments the torching of all of "God's [of El's] tabernacles" (*mo'adey-'El,* vv. 7–8). This kind of evidence, of which there exists much more, suggests that we may, with all due caution, include the Tent of Meeting in our discussion of the spiritual experience of the Jerusalem Temple when it stood. In a sense, the rabbis institutionalized such a homologization, when, centuries later, they matched passages from the Torah about the construction of the Tent of Meeting with prophetic lections (*haftarot*) describing the erection or reconstruction of the Temple in Jerusalem. For example, the *haftarah* for the portion *Tezawweh* (Exod 27:20–30:10) is Ezek 43:10–27, and that for *Wayaqhel* (Exod 35:1–38:20) is 1 Kgs 7:40–50. Judaism tends to continue those streams in biblical tradition which homologized the Tent and the Temple.

The Presentness and Practice of Salvation

It is often said that Israel established her identity through the recitation of her *Heilsgeschichte,* the sacred story which, with many embellishments and digressions, dominates the Pentateuch or the Hexateuch (Genesis–Joshua). The most compressed résumé of the story occurs in 1 Sam 12:8: "When Jacob came to Egypt,[6] . . . your fathers cried out to the LORD, and the LORD sent Moses and Aaron, who brought your fathers out of Egypt and settled them in this place." This résumé is extraordinary only in its implication that Moses and Aaron came into the land with the people; the Pentateuch dates their deaths before the entrance into the land (Num 20:27–29; Deut 34:4–7).[7] The absence of mention of the revelation at Sinai/Horeb is not extraordinary. It is paralleled in the Pentateuch (e.g., Deut 26:5b–9). In fact, it is this omission which has generated the controversial hypothesis that the settlement tradition and the Sinai tradition were originally separate and distinct, having been combined only at a certain point within historical memory.[8] Whether the hypothesis is historically valid or not, it remains true that the present shape of the Pentateuch presents us with two different perspectives concerning the point at which the relationship between Israel and its God (YHWH)[9] was consummated, the *telos*, so to speak, of the foundational drama. The settlement tradition holds that the story is consummated only outside the Pentateuch, with the allocation of the land, at long last, to the tribes (Josh 21:41–43). Until "everything was fulfilled" (v. 43), the hand of God was restless, discontented with the status quo, and upsetting eventually each obstacle to the fulfillment of the promise, whether it arises from Pharaoh, from Canaanite land tenure, or from the faithlessness and lawlessness of the Israelites themselves. The other perspective finds the climax at the point at which God graciously signals the acceptability of the complex and elaborate system of worship mandated and executed at Sinai:

> Moses and Aaron then went inside the Tent of Meeting. When they came out, they blessed the people; and the Presence of the LORD appeared to all the people. Fire came forth from before the LORD and consumed the burnt offering and the fat parts on the altar. And all the people saw, and shouted, and fell on their faces. (Lev 9:23–24)

At last, the basis has been laid for insuring the eternal availability of that elusive "presence" (*kavod*, usually rendered "glory"), which all the people saw. The visitation of God to Israel, the vision of God in Israel, need no longer be episodic or arbitrary. An enduring means of access of YHWH to Israel and of Israel to YHWH has been inaugurated, service without end, "an eternal ordinance for all generations" (Lev 10:9 and often). From now on, all that remains is the issue of whether or not Israel is observing the commandments, moral, ritual, and both, which entitle her to be graced by the electrifying divine presence manifest in the Tent and to remain in the presence of the fire that burned on Mount Sinai, wherever she may go. Whereas in the first perspective, the land symbolizes and manifests spiritual fulfillment, in this second one it is the Tent of Meeting that performs this climactic function. The relationship of YHWH and Israel is consummated in her unending repetition of His sacred rites. In both perspectives, the assumption, perhaps a naïve one, is that only Israel's sin can rupture the beatified life.

The two climactic movements define two poles not only of the Torah but of biblical spirituality in general, and perhaps of the Jewish world view itself. The first, the settlement tradition, evokes images of instability, of political change, of an alternation of divine presence and absence, of the quest for new fulfillments. For even the land soon proves to be something very different from paradise, and each new consummation—the defeat of the Philistines, the establishment of the House of David, the erection of the Jerusalem Temple, the centralization of the liturgy there—yields to a successor, in a dynamic whose logical fulfillment came in the vision of a definitive end to all history in apocalyptic literature (Dan 2:44–45). In this perspective, the status quo is forever on the verge of obsolescence, and its radical critique is an indispensable component of the spiritual life. The second perspective, the Sinai tradition, at least as it appears in Priestly materials (P), evokes images of stasis, regularity, repetition, constancy, and intimacy. It places salvation in the present and not only in the future and offers the means for a partial immanentization of the God who is still transcendent. Those means are essentially the liturgy centered upon the Tent of Meeting. They are beyond critique, although the people obligated by them is not. Salvation, the beatific vision, which is the definitive teleological end of life, cannot be surpassed.

Within this second perspective, the emphasis lies on absorption into the divine order of things, that is, participation in the rhythm of the divine life itself, which is the nearest approximation to *unio mystica* that Hebraic thought can tolerate. Thus, the Sabbath, which in Deuteronomic tradition (D) is a humanitarian ordinance and a commemoration of the liberation from Egypt (Deut 5:12–15), appears in P as a sign of the eternal covenant and a commemoration of the act of creation (Exod 31:12–17). In P, in other words, observance of the Sabbath is an example of *imitatio Dei*. Through it, Israel replicates the rhythm of the primordial act, participating endlessly in an institution which, until Sinai, had been observed by God alone (Gen 2:1–3). The dietary laws speak to the same point. In D, they seem to be a consequence of the election and consecration of Israel (Deut 14:1–21). P, which also assumes election and consecration, suggests a connection between Israel's "separation" (*hivdaltem*) of clean from unclean beasts and God's "separation" (*hivdaltiy*) of Israel from the nations, and it presents divine holiness as the rationale for Israel's mandated holiness (Lev 20:25–26).[10] Once again, sacred rites are grounded in *imitatio Dei;* mortal persons are offered some access into the divine life. Furthermore, it seems likely that the emphasis upon the verb "to separate" (*hivdil*) here is intended to suggest the primordial acts of separation that punctuate the act of creation in P (Gen 1:4, 6, 7, 14, 18). If so, then the implication is that the separation of Israel from the nations is a continuation of creation and that Israel's own separation of fit from unfit foods is a perpetuation of the very process that brought order out of chaos. Israel draws near to God, in part, by perpetuating the primordial within the world of historical change, and the sacred amidst profanity. And at the center of Israel, quite literally, lies what is most sacred, the Tent of Meeting (Num 2). Israel lies at the intersection of God and the world, but she faces God.

The dichotomy between these two perspectives must not be sharply drawn. Although D is closer in spirit to the first, and P, to the second, the perspectives are ideal types that are not coterminous with literary sources or historical periods. Nor should we fall into the common mistake of identifying one perspective as indigenous and essential, and the other as foreign and peripheral. Both are well attested in the Hebrew Bible, and both have antecedents and parallels elsewhere in the ancient Near East. More important, the final shape of the Hebrew Bible and of the Torah in particular includes both perspectives. In that sense, the Book is bipolar: the whole is larger than the sum of its parts, and the tension between perspectives yields a spiritual dynamic that neither perspective alone could have produced.

The Presence and the Omnipresence of God

All the developed theology of temples in Israel points to the presence of God as the core of spiritual meaning:

> For there I will meet with you, and there I will speak to you, and there I will meet with the Israelites, and it shall be sanctified by My Presence. I will sanctify the Tent of Meeting and the altar, and I will consecrate Aaron and his sons to serve me as priests. I will abide among the Israelites, and I will be their God. And they shall know that I the LORD am their God, who brought them out from the land of Egypt that I might abide among them, I the LORD their God. (Exod 29:42b–46)

This passage offers a rich network of interconnected associations. The Tent is the vehicle for communication with God; in it oracles are received. God's visible "Presence" (kavod) renders the Tent and its sacrificial apparatus sacred. But the sanctity does not preclude immediate human contact; it only restricts it to the chosen priesthood (kohanim), Aaron and his male descendants. The Tent is a visible relationship between God and Israel, a relationship whose other great testimony is the exodus. Here, we see the effect of the nearer climax of the sacred history that appears in P: the goal of the exodus is not so much the promised land as it is the intimacy with YHWH made available to Israel in the Tabernacle. He rescued her so that He might set up Tent in her midst (leshokniy betokham, v. 46). The endless rendezvous in the portable temple is the teleological consummation of the history of redemption.

Another aspect of the sanctified and sanctifying presence of God in His Temple is the idea of blessing. We have already examined the passage in

which Moses and Aaron blessed the people after they came out of the Tent
and before the presence, or glory, of YHWH appeared to all (Lev 9:23–24).
In fact, blessing was a part of the regular liturgy of the Jerusalem Temple:

> A song of ascents.
> Now bless the LORD,
>   all you servants of the LORD
>   who stand nightly
>   in the house of the LORD.
> Lift your hands toward the sanctuary
>   and bless the LORD.
> May the LORD,
>   maker of heaven and earth,
>   bless you from Zion.
>   (Ps 134)

The setting of this poem was probably the changing of the guard in the
Jerusalem Temple, which sat atop Mount Zion. The night shift, who seem
to be going on or off duty (v. 1), are summoned to bless YHWH before
doing so. Verse 3 may be the response from the other shift; if so, they return
YHWH's blessing to those who have just blessed him (cf. Ruth 2:4). At all
events, two points are noteworthy in the psalm. First, the direction of blessing is twofold: God is blessed and blesses; persons both give and receive a
benediction. The image is one of nearness, mutuality, reciprocity, communication. Second, the psalmist's assertion of God's sovereignty over the
entire cosmos, "heaven and earth," is in no tension with his allegiance to
Zion as the source of YHWH's blessing (v. 3). Zion is not another spot in
the world. It is the capital of the world, the place from which the divine
beatification of humanity proceeds. In this, Psalm 134 is typical of Hebraic
thought, which usually does not view the presence of God as finite in
quantity: His presence in one place does not imply a corresponding absence
of God elsewhere. Thus can the God enthroned on Zion bestow a blessing
to those outside. This is not an easy conception for modern persons to
grasp. Perhaps it will prove useful to envision the Temple as the center of
a wheel, equidistant from each point on the rim, which is the world. The
sanctifying and beatifying presence of God shoots out along the spokes. The
points on the rim then discharge sanctity and blessing back toward the
center. The rim and the center are not identical. But so long as the process
of sanctification and beatification continues, neither is bereft of God. Zion
is the conduit through which the plenitude of divine blessings surges into
the world. In fact, the Temple is sometimes seen as the earthly antitype to
a heavenly archetype:

The LORD is in His holy palace;
   the LORD—His throne is in heaven;
His eyes behold, His gaze searches mankind.
(Ps 11:4)

The "holy palace" (*heykhal qodsho*) is both the Temple (e.g., Ps 79:1) and the supernal archetype which it manifests.[11] YHWH's presence in His Temple does not diminish His presence in the heavens. On the contrary, the two "places" are the same. The relationship of the Temple to the world is not one of simple spatiality. The Temple is the objective correlative of the paradoxical doctrine of God's simultaneous otherness and omnipresence.

Refuge for the Just
in the House of YHWH

Nowhere is it written that sins and sanctity can cohabitate. In some passages, the conditionality of God's presence in the Temple is underscored:

> Then the word of the LORD came to Solomon, "With regard to this House you are building—if you follow My laws and observe My rules and faithfully keep My commandments, I will fulfill for you the promise that I gave to your father David: I will abide among the children of Israel, and I will never forsake My people Israel." (1 Kgs 6:11–13)

Here, the dynastic covenant with David, which elsewhere is unconditional (2 Sam 7:14–16; Ps 89:20–38), has been rendered contingent upon the king's obedience.[12] The same note of conditionality governs YHWH's presence in the Temple. Once again, covenant and presence imply each other. Faithful observance of the commandments (*mizwot*), which are the stipulations of the covenant, evokes the presence of God. God graciously deigns to place His presence in the Temple until human disobedience renders the place unfit for Him. In prophetic preaching, the moral side of sanctity becomes a precious homiletical resource:

> When they [the Judean kings] placed their threshold next to My threshold and their doorposts next to My doorposts with only a wall between Me and them, they would defile My holy name by the abominations that they committed, and I consumed them in My anger. Therefore, let them put their apostasy and the memorials[13] of their kings far from Me, and I will dwell among them forever. (Ezek 43:8–9)

The last passage cited and probably the one before it as well are responses to the catastrophe of 587 B.C.E., when Solomon's Temple, the First (Jerusalem) Temple, fell to the Babylonians. They reflect the solemn note of conditionality that dominates Jeremiah, Deuteronomy, and the literature edited under the latter's influence, the block from Joshua through 2 Kings: Israel's breach of covenant, her violation or neglect of *mizwot*, can fell the House of YHWH. As we shall see, other literature from the Hebrew Bible affirms the unshakability and inviolability of the Temple and its mountain and city, leaving ambiguous the issue of whether this is pure grace or a conditional gift that may yet be withdrawn if the recipient proves undeserving. Between these two positions—the one resting the very existence of the Temple on Israel's desserts, the other ostensibly ignoring the issue of desserts —lies a third position. This one, most evident in the book of Psalms, sees in the Temple a source of boundless security, but one available only to those whose deeds prove worthy. The effect, then, is to highlight the unshakability and inviolability of the person of innocence and rectitude:

> A psalm of David.
> LORD, who may sojourn in Your tent,
>   who may dwell on Your holy mountain?
> He who lives without blame,
>   who does what is right,
>   and in his heart acknowledges the truth;
>   whose tongue is not given to evil;
>   who has never done harm to his fellow,
>   or borne reproach for [his acts toward] his neighbor;
>   for whom a contemptible man is abhorrent,
>   but who honors those who fear the LORD;
>   who stands by his oath even to his hurt;
>   who has never lent money at interest,
>   or accepted a bribe against the innocent.
> The man who acts thus shall never be shaken.
>
> (Ps 15)

In this poem, we hear the requirements for admission to the Temple. The assumption of most scholars has been that the original setting for this kind of literature was an "entrance liturgy," in which priests set forth the terms for admission to inquiring worshipers. Egyptian parallels, however, suggest an alternative hypothesis, that the requirements were inscribed on the doorposts or lintels of the Temple.[14] This recalls the injunction in Deuteronomy that the stipulations of the covenant be inscribed "on the doorposts of your house and on your gates" (Deut 6:9; 11:20), and it suggests a very practical background to Jeremiah's stress on the moral requirements for admission to the Temple, especially the Decalogue (Jer 7:9), which he is said to have proclaimed to "all you of Judah who enter these gates . . ." (v. 2; cf. 22:2). But who is applying for admission? Much of the literature suggests, as does Psalm 15, that it is ordinary people who seek to offer prayer or sacrifice in the House of YHWH. Elsewhere, however, we hear of the worshiper's desire not merely to visit the sacred shrine but to spend his whole life there, as in the close of the famous Twenty-Third Psalm:

> You spread a table for me in full view of my enemies;
>   You anoint my head with oil;
>   my drink is abundant.
> Only goodness and steadfast love shall pursue me
>   all the days of my life,
>   and I shall dwell in the house of the LORD
>   for many long years.
>
> (Ps 23:5–6)

The familiar words suggest an image perhaps unfamiliar to those who now make devotional use of the poem: In the Temple, the poet has found refuge from his pursuing enemies. There, his life is complete, lacking neither food nor drink. The passage recalls Adonijah's grasping the horns of the altar until his father, Solomon, swore not to put him to the sword (1 Kgs 1:50–53). The sacred shrine is a place of asylum for those falsely accused and for those who crime was unintentional (cf. Exod 21:14).[15] Apparently, its function in Israelite law was like that of the "cities of refuge," to which one guilty of homicide without malice aforethought could escape the vendetta of his victim's blood-avenger (Num 35:9–34). There he was entitled to remain in asylum until the death of the high priest (vv. 25–28), at which point, presumably, the right of vengeance expired, probably because of an amnesty proclaimed by the new high priest upon his accession (before the exile, it was the king who issued the amnesty).[16] The resultant interval could be decades. We should not be surprised, therefore, by the length of time which some psalmists seek to spend in the Temple:

> One thing I ask of the LORD,
>   only that do I seek:
>   to live in the house of the LORD
>   all the days of my life,
>   to gaze upon the beauty of the LORD,
>   to frequent His temple.
> He will shelter me in His pavilion
>   on an evil day,
>   grant me the protection of His tent,
>   raise me high upon a rock.
> Now is my head high
>   over my enemies roundabout;
>   I sacrifice in His tent with shouts of joy,
>   singing and chanting a hymn of the LORD.
>
> (Ps 27:4–6)

As in the Twenty-Third Psalm, so here again we read of the author's longing for a lifetime of asylum in the Temple in place of the enmity which seems to have driven him there. If, as we suggest, this request for a lifetime in the Temple was not originally an example of devotional hyperbole (which it became later), but had a precise, legal reference, how did the refugee spend his time those many years? Psalm 84 suggests an answer:

> How lovely is Your dwelling-place,
>   O Lord of hosts.
> I long, I yearn for the courts of the Lord;
>   my body and soul shout for joy to the living God.
> Even the sparrow has found a home,
>   and the swallow a nest for herself
>   in which to set her young,
>   near Your altar, O Lord of hosts,
>   my king and my God.
> Happy are those who dwell in Your house;
>   they forever praise You. (Selah)
> Happy is the man who finds refuge in You.
> Better one day in Your courts than a thousand [anywhere else];
>   I would rather stand at the threshold of God's house
>   than dwell in the tents of the wicked,
> For the Lord God is sun and shield;
>   the Lord bestows grace and glory;
>   He does not withhold His bounty from those who live without blame.
>   (Ps 84:2–6a, 11–12)

The two beatitudes of vv. 5 and 6 suggest that the refugees may have been employed as Temple singers, a position that in the postexilic era was redefined as a prerogative of the lesser clerical caste, the Levites (1 Chr 16:4). Verse 11 recalls another Temple chore, that of the doorkeepers, which also eventually became Levitical (1 Chr 9:19). Ps 27:6, which we have already examined, indicates that the refugee may also have been engaged in the sacred slaughter of animals, and many psalms indicate that he did, indeed, partake of the offerings:

> I bless You all my life;
>   I lift up my hands, invoking Your name.
> I am sated as with suet and fat,[17]
>   I sing praises with joyful lips
>   when I call You to mind upon my bed,
>   when I think of You in my watches of the night,
>   for You are my help,
>   and in the shadow of Your wings
>   I shout for joy.

> My soul is attached to You;
>   Your right hand supports me.
> May those who seek to destroy my life
>   enter the depths of the earth.
>
>   (Ps 63:5–10)

Elsewhere, the "as" of v. 6 disappears, and we hear of people who "feast on the rich fare of Your house" (Ps 36:9). These passages betray no awareness of the Priestly insistence that a layperson may not eat of the sacred donations (Lev 22:10–16).

We have argued that the Jerusalem Temple (and other Israelite shrines) served as places of asylum in a very practical, legal sense. Whether the institution of asylum was the original context for all the "entrance liturgies" is impossible to ascertain. Passages like Ezekiel 18, however, with its criteria for determining who is righteous and worthy of life and who is not, argue for a less limited context of these lists of criteria. In any event, the preservation of the "entrance liturgies" after the disappearance of the legal institution in question and their eventual inclusion in the Psalter demonstrates that their meaning was not thought to have been exhausted by any practical context. Instead, they became part of a manual of devotion. The refugee of those poems that do clearly speak of asylum became Everyman. The situation of an innocent person slandered and hunted by bloodthirsty enemies and seeking shelter and sustenance from his bountiful lord became a paradigm of the human condition. The recitation to this day of those psalms by people who have never suspected their original setting is stunning evidence for the phenomenal durability of the spiritual legacy of the Jerusalem Temple.

The apogee of the spiritual experience of the visitor to the Temple was a vision of God. In fact, "to see the face of YHWH"[18] is an idiom that indicates a visit to the Temple (e.g., Deut 16:16). Psalm 11 asserts a reciprocity of vision: YHWH, enthroned in His Temple, conducts a visual inspection of humanity, and those found worthy are granted a vision of his "face":

> The Lord is in His holy palace;
>   the Lord—His throne is in heaven;
>   His eyes behold (yeḥezu), His gaze searches mankind.
> The Lord seeks out the righteous man,
>   but loathes the wicked one who loves injustice.
> He will rain down upon the wicked blazing coals and sulfur;
>   a scorching wind shall be their lot.

> For the LORD is righteous;
>   He loves righteous deeds;
>   the upright shall behold (*yeḥezu*) His face.
>
>   (Ps 11:4–7)

We shall see that the vision of God in His Temple or a vision of the Temple itself were occasionally powerful components of the revelation granted to prophets. But this was probably merely a specialization of the spiritual experience of the Temple available to any whose deeds merited it. The folk etymology of the Land of Moriah at which Abraham was to sacrifice Isaac underscores the association with visionary experience: "And Abraham named that site Adonai-Yireh, whence the present saying, 'On the mount of the LORD there is vision.'" (Gen 22:14)[19] The last clause can just as well be translated, "on the mount of the LORD He is seen." One senses that the author has a particular mountain in mind. Postexilic tradition may well be correct in identifying it with the Temple Mount in Jerusalem, where YHWH "had appeared to [Solomon's] father David" (2 Chr 3:1). If so, then one function of the story of the binding of Isaac in its present form was to connect the ongoing vision of God in the Temple with the visionary experience of the patriarchs. Abraham's experience has been assimilated to David's (2 Sam 24:15–25); both now serve as a foundation myth for the Jerusalem Temple. If, as seems equally possible, in Genesis 22 Moriah has not yet become a name for any part of Jerusalem but refers to another sacred spot, the connection between theophany and sacrifice remains valid and important. Particularly noteworthy is the association of vision, sacrifice, and oracle, which appear together not only in Genesis 22 and 2 Samuel 24 but also, for example, in the story of the Gentile seer Balaam (Num 23:1–5) and in the annunciation of Samson's birth (Judges 13). The last passage indicates that a divine being might be imagined to have been glimpsed in the flames leaping up to the sky from the altar on which the sacrificial offering was burning (vv. 19–23; cf. Exod 3:2).

The importance of icons of the deity in Near Eastern temples suggests another candidate for the object beheld in the epiphanic moment. To be sure, images of the deity, in fact *all* images, became strictly prohibited in ancient Israel. The prohibition came into the Decalogue itself (Exod 20:4),[20] and Aaron's and Jeroboam's casting of golden calves (Exod 32 and 1 Kgs 12:28–32) came to serve as archetypes of sin. The question is the date at which the cultus became aniconic and the extent of acceptance of the anti-iconic theology in ancient Israelite society. From the Torah itself one might not suspect that the heyday of iconoclasm in Israel began in the days of Hezekiah, king of Judah late in the eighth century B.C.E., and was resumed with a ferocious passion almost a century later, in the reign of Josiah. It was Hezekiah who "broke into pieces the bronze serpent which Moses had made" (2 Kgs 18:4), the very sight of which had been thought to produce healing in the viewer (Num 21:6–9). Josiah, acting on the basis of a new-found "book of the Torah," which most scholars think was some form of Deuteronomy, carried out a far-reaching purge, which included the destruction of iconography on the grounds of the Jerusalem Temple (2 Kgs 22–23). The history of Israel that comes to us in the books from Joshua through 2 Kings was edited in Deuteronomistic circles who presupposed the normativeness and antiquity of the aniconic cultus. But traces of the other perspectives remain. There is, for example, the golden "ephod" that the YHWHistic hero Gideon made; to a Deuteronomistic editor of the book of Judges, it was only "a snare to Gideon and his household" (Judg 8:27). But there is no reason to think that it represented any deity except YHWH. Similarly, the mother of an Ephraimite name Micah dedicated silver to YHWH, out of which a smith at her request apparently made two images, one sculptured and one molten. These Micah set up in his temple (Judg 17:1–6). The precise nature of all these images must remain a matter of speculation. Nonetheless, the application of bovine imagery to YHWH may provide a clue. Not only is YHWH described as being endowed with something "like the horns of a wild ox" (Num 24:8), but one of his epithets is 'avir ya'aqov, a term often rendered as "Mighty One of Jacob," but better rendered "Bull of Jacob" (Gen 49:24; Ps 132: 2, 4).[21] The bovine imagery and epithets are a carryover from the Canaanite god 'El, with whom YHWH was identified even in "orthodox" theology (e.g., Gen 33:20; Isa 43:12). Was there ever a bull image or similar icon in the Jerusalem Temple? In answer, one must first note that the radical iconoclasm of Deuteronomic tradition, which prohibited *all* plastic art (Deut 4:15–18), never seems to have taken root in the Jerusalem Temple. There, in contrast, one encountered a dazzling display of art, including olive-wood cherubim, reliefs of trees and flowers, bronze columns, topped with capitals and festooned with chainwork, a bronze tank called the "Sea," supported by twelve oxen (!), and much else (1 Kgs 7). The blunt truth is that, if we judged from the descriptions of Solomon's Temple and the Tent of Meeting (Exod 25–30; 35–40) alone, we should never guess the depth of anti-iconic feeling in ancient Israel. Whether the gallery of visual delights that was the Jerusalem Temple included at some points in its checkered history an icon of YHWH, bovine or other, is impossible to say with certainty. Deuteronomic tradition insists that the Ark of the Covenant contained only the Decalogue (Deut 10:1–5). Some modern scholars have conjectured that at one point it contained an icon instead.[22] If so, it is likely that the "face" which was seen in the Temple or the "beauty of the LORD" which one psalmist longed to behold there for his entire life (Ps 27:4) were more than metaphorical. In that case, what is most remarkable is that this language of vision remained central to the religious vocabulary even after its literal referent had vanished. In this, the language of vision resembles the Jerusalem Temple itself.

A Locus for the Vision of God

We have seen that central to the idea of the Temple as a place of asylum is the assertion that the person qualified for admittance to it is inviolable. He "shall never be shaken" (Ps 15:5), and he holds his "head high/over [his] enemies roundabout" (Ps 27:6). The same inviolability is predicated not only of the right-doing person sheltered within, but of the Temple itself, the mount upon which it rests, and the holy city in which it is found. That is to say, the protection that the Temple affords one Israeliate against the enmity of another is available also to the larger community when it is under attack by its enemies:

> A song. A psalm of the Korahites.
> The LORD is great and much acclaimed
>   in the city of our God,
>   His holy mountain —
>   fair-crested, joy of all the earth,
>   Mount Zion, summit of Zaphon,
>   city of the great king.
> Through its citadels, God has made Himself known as a haven.
> See, the kings joined forces;
>   they advanced together.
> At the mere sight of it they were stunned,
>   they were terrified, they panicked;
>   they were seized there with a trembling,
>   like a woman in the throes of labor,
>   as the fleet of Tarshish was wrecked
>   in an easterly gale.
> The likes of what we heard we have now witnessed
>   in the city of the LORD of hosts,
>   in the city of our God —
>   may God preserve it forever!
> Selah.
>
> In Your temple, God,
>   we meditate upon Your faithful care.
> The praise of You, God, like Your name,
>   reaches to the ends of the earth;
>   Your right hand is filled with beneficence.

Let Mount Zion rejoice!
  Let the towns of Judah exult,
  because of Your judgments.

Walk around Zion,
  circle it;
  count its towers,
  take note of its ramparts;
  go through its citadels,
  that you may recount it to a future age.
For God—He is our God forever;
  He will lead us evermore.

                    (Ps 48)

In this poem, recited today by traditional Jews on Monday mornings, the Temple is the objective correlative of the omnipotence and trustworthiness of God. The very sight of it throws an alliance of hostile kings into a panic (vv. 4–8). Zion, the Temple Mount, is the visible form, the "incarnation," so to speak, of the sacred story of YHWH's commitment to rescue those loyal to Him (v. 9): it is in the Temple that the psalmist and his circle "form an image" (*dimminu*, v. 10)[23] of God's care for His worshipers. Here the dichotomy is not between the innocent within and the wicked outside the Temple, or between the homicide without malice aforethought and his victim's avenger. Rather, the critical distinction is between the Temple (and Zion and Jerusalem) as the state shrine of the entire kingdom of Judah, on the one hand, and those outside Judah, on the other, those who are, presumably, vulnerable to military defeat, as Judah, ruled by "the great king" (v. 3), is not. Whether "the great king" is YHWH or His Davidic viceroy and son is impossible to ascertain and ultimately irrelevant, given the indefectible commitment of YHWH to the House of David in Judean royal theology (e.g., Pss 89:20–28; 110:1–5). In fact, the inviolability of the Temple/Zion/Jerusalem served, in part, as the ideology associated with Davidic imperialism. The utility of this mythos for propaganda and psychological warfare must not be overlooked:

Why do nations assemble,
  and peoples plot vain things;
  kings of the earth take their stand,
  and regents intrigue together
  against the LORD and against His anointed?
"Let us break the cords of their yoke,
  shake off their ropes from us!"
He who is enthroned in heaven laughs;
  the LORD mocks at them.

> Then He speaks to them in anger,
>   terrifying them in His rage,
> "But I have installed My king
>   on Zion, My holy mountain!"
> Let me tell of the decree:
>   the LORD said to me,
> "You are My son,
>   I have fathered you this day.
> Ask it of Me,
>   and I will make the nations your domain;
>   your estate, the limits of the earth.
> You can smash them with an iron mace,
>   shatter them like potter's ware."
>
> So now, O kings, be prudent;
>   accept discipline, you rulers of the earth!
> Serve the LORD in awe;
>   tremble with fright,
>   pay homage in good faith,
>   lest He be angered, and your way be doomed
>   in the mere flash of His anger.
> Happy are all who take refuge in Him.
>
> (Ps 2)

In this poem, as in Psalm 48, we hear of a conspiracy of kings and of the ease with which it is overcome. But here the kings are already in vassalage to YHWH and to His anointed regent (*mashiah*, v. 2); v. 3 is the manifesto of their revolution, the declaration of their independence. With three points, however, they have failed to reckon. First, ultimate sovereignty is not an earthly prerogative; it resides in the skies, where YHWH, the king of kings, is enthroned. No challenge to His kingship can succeed (v. 4). Second, the human king against whom they are in rebellion has been installed by the ultimate king on Mount Zion, which is sacred space (v. 6). Presumably, an attack upon him there would be equivalent to an invasion of the Temple precincts by a blood-avenger in pursuit of his prey — in short, an outrageous sacrilege. Third, the rebellious vassals do not recognize the closeness and the durability of YHWH's relationship to the anointed king enthroned upon Zion. The latter rectifies this by reading the protocol by which he became God's son and thus the vice-regent of the universal dominion (vv. 7–9). The action of Psalm 2, therefore, takes place upon a split set. The nexus between heavenly and earthly sovereignty is Davidic kingship, which is an extension of YHWH's reign into the murky world of human politics. In other words, the authority of the House of David is in this world, but not of it. The link between the two worlds, the world of divine power and the world of power politics, is Mount Zion, the capital of the universe, from which the House of David exercises its divine commission to rule. The divine origin of that commission ensures the immunity and invulnerability of the Temple Mount to the challenges of ordinary political life. It is on Zion that the higher world is available. Zion is the *axis mundorum*.

The Judean royal theology, with its bold assertions about the indefectibility and absoluteness of God's commitments to David and Zion, must not be taken for the totality of biblical thought on these issues. There is, for example, a tension between this theology and the stern morality of much prophetic literature:

> Hear this, you rulers of the House of Jacob,
> You chiefs of the House of Israel,
> Who detest justice
> And make crooked all that is straight,
> Who build Zion with crime,
> Jerusalem with iniquity!
> Her rulers judge for gifts,
> Her priests give rulings for a fee,
> And her prophets divine for pay;
> Yet they rely upon the LORD, saying,
> "The LORD is in our midst;
> No calamity shall overtake us."
> Assuredly, because of you
> Zion shall be plowed as a field,
> And Jerusalem shall become a heap of ruins,
> And the Temple Mount
> A shrine in the woods.
> (Mic 3:9–12; cf. Jer 7:1–15)

Here, the divine commitment to Temple/Zion/Jerusalem is emphatically contingent upon the justice of the Judean ruling class. Jerusalem ceases to benefit from God's special protection when its prosperity results from corruption and victimization of the innocent; to build Jerusalem in this way is to invite God to level it. To be sure, no biblical source guarantees the Davidic king and the inhabitants of Jerusalem immunity from punishment for sins they commit. In fact, even the texts that promise David an everlasting dynasty warn that the reigning dynasty can be chastised, even though the throne is inalienable from his family (2 Sam 7:14–15; Ps 89:31–38). The Davidic covenant does not provide exemption from the Sinaitic. And, in fact, Israelite kings, like kings throughout the ancient Near East, were expected to promote and enforce social justice (e.g., Pss 72 and 101). On the other hand, the very indefectibility of the grant to David does imply that one punishment for breach of the Sinaitic covenant is not a possibility, the deposition and exile of the king (Deut 28:36). When, in 597 B.C.E., a Davidic king was dragged into exile and, in 587 B.C.E., the Temple atop Mount Zion was torched and the sacred city destroyed (2 Kgs 24:8–25:17), the Sinaitic covenantal tradition must have seemed vindicated and the spiritual experience articulated in the royal theology, discredited:

> The breath of our life, the LORD's anointed,
> Was captured in their traps—
> He in whose shade we had thought
> To live among the nations.
> (Lam 4:20)

Yet Judaism as it developed in the exile and in the period of the Second Temple was not a religion of pure conditionality untouched by vision and grace. Instead, the impregnable Temple of yesteryear and Zion, the seat of a glorious empire, were increasingly projected onto an eschatological future. God would redeem Zion, David, and all Israel from their present state of degradation and subjugation (e.g., Zech 9:9–10). Or, to change the metaphor from the temporal to the spatial, the glories of the past could still be glimpsed, but only in the form of their heavenly archetypes now that the earthly antitypes were ruined or diminished: apocalyptic seers and initiated mystics could still attain to a vision of the messiah and even of the throne of God in the supernal realm, which has not yet come to the mundane world (e.g., Dan 7; *1 Enoch* 14). Despite all these transformations, something of the Judean royal theology lives even today in the Jewish messianic hope and its Christian counterpart, the expectation of the Second Coming and the kingdom, and in the place that Zion and Jerusalem play in the Jewish religious imagination.

The effect of the inclusion of these two spiritual postures in one set of scriptures is to create a spiritual dialectic which, like any dialectic, is more than the sum of its parts. The one perspective, represented by the royal theology, speaks of the mysterious and all-encompassing grace of God, which provides absolute security in the here-and-now. The second perspective, represented by the Sinaitic covenantal perspective, also includes a note of grace, for example, in its assertion of the perdurable openness of God to repentance (e.g., Deut 4:29–31) and its occasional emphasis upon the eternal, unconditional covenant with the patriarchs (e.g., Lev 26:39–42). But the predominant note in the Sinaitic traditions is the note of ultimate conditionality, the life-and-death choice which it is fully in Israel's power to make (e.g., Deut 30:19–20). Together these two positions prescribe a religion in which, to use the Christian terminology, neither "grace" nor "works" is asserted at the expense of the other. The emphasis on grace in the royal and Temple theologies threatens to depreciate the deed, to render ethics dispensable, in short, to make Israel merely a passive bystander in her own spiritual life. The emphasis on works, on *mizwot,* on the traditions of the Sinai covenant, threatens to make God merely a mechanism for the dispensation of rewards and punishments and to make the *mizwot* themselves into magical practices through which Israel can manipulate her God, who thus becomes the passive partner in the relationship. By refusing to dichotomize spiritual experience into grace and works, by affirming both simultaneously, the religion prescribed by the Jewish Bible maintains the two-sidedness of the relationship of God and Israel. It preserves both activity and passivity as proper postures for both partners, and it affirms the ultimate importance both of this world and of the higher or future world. To some, the juxtaposition of the two theologies will seem to have resulted in an unacceptable *contradiction.* To others, it will seem to have resulted in a contradiction that is indeed to be accepted, a *paradox,* one that lies at the heart of Jewish spirituality throughout the ages.

Temple and Creation

In postbiblical Jewish literature, both Hellenistic and rabbinic, we find the notion that the Jerusalem Temple (or the Tent of Meeting) was a cosmic institution, either the center of the world, from which the world was created, or itself a microcosm, a miniature world. For example, the first-century historian Josephus describes the veil over its door as an *eikon,* an image, of the world.[24] In our century this notion that the Temple was conceived as cosmic has received some confirmation from archaeologists studying the iconography of the Temple and its Near Eastern sources and parallels. For example, the metal "Sea" (*yam*) in its courtyard (1 Kgs 7:23–26) suggests "the Mesopotamian *apsû,* employed both as the name of the subterranean fresh-water ocean ... and as the name of a basin of holy water erected in the Temple."[25] As the god of the subterranean freshwater ocean, *apsû* played an important role in some Mesopotamian cosmogonies, just as the Sea (*yam*) did in some Israelite creation stories (e.g., Ps 74:12–17; Isa 51:9–11).[26] This suggests that the metal Sea in the Temple courtyard served as a continual testimony to the act of creation. Similarly, the name of the foundation of the altar of the Temple envisioned in Ezek 43:13–17, "Bosom of the earth" (*ḥeq ha'arez*), might suggest the sort of cosmic understanding that will become common in Hellenistic and rabbinic speculation, and the name *har'el* there (v. 15) may signify either "the mountain of God" (Hebrew) or "a cosmic locality opposite of heaven" (Akaddian *arallû*). The last example of many that might be cited is the platform (*kiyor*), upon which Solomon stands as he dedicates his Temple in 2 Chr 6:13. It has been connected with Akkadian *kiūru*, which may indicate the earth or a sacred place.[28] In sum, the likelihood is that the Temple appurtenances were conceived as symbolic of the cosmos and reminiscent of the great cosmogonic acts of YHWH. If so, then the association of Zion/Jerusalem with "heaven and earth" (e.g., Ps 134:3; Isa 65:17–18), the merism through which biblical Hebrew denotes the world (e.g., Gen 1:1), is not coincidence.[29]

There is also literary evidence to support this connection of creation and Temple in ancient Israelite culture. Since rabbinic times, scholars have noticed verbal parallels between the account of the completion of the world in Gen 2:1–4 and the account of the completion of the Tent of Meeting in Exodus 39–40.[30] World building and Temple building seem to be homologous activities. In fact, some of the same language can be found in the description of "the establishment of the sanctuary in the land and the distribution of the land among the tribes"[31] in Joshua 18–19. Therefore, we should not be surprised to find other thematic parallels between these three moments. One is the theme of "rest." God "rested" (*wayyanah*) on the seventh day (Exod 20:11), the crown of creation; Zion is his "resting-place" (*menuhatiy*, Ps 132:4); and the land of Israel is the place in which he provides "rest" for his people (*menuhah*, Deut 12:9). According to 1 Chr 22:9, it is because Solomon, unlike David, was "a man at rest" ('*ish menuhah*) that he was permitted to build the Temple. The Temple is the place at which that primordial moment of repose remains eternally available. Yet the Sabbath, another memorial to creation (e.g., Exod 20:11), makes available the same experience. The Sabbath is a kind of democratization of the Temple experience, and the land of Israel is an extended Temple, a whole land of holiness, which, like temples, must be zealously guarded against pollution (e.g., Lev 18:24–30). The sanctity of the Sabbath, the sanctity of the Temple, and the sanctity of the land are homologous. They are not ultimately distinguishable. Each testifies to God's triumph, to His invincibility—whether in cosmogony, when He overcame the primordial watery chaos (Gen 1:2), or in history, when He overcame all the enemies of His people, settled them in the land, gave them respite, and allowed His sacred palace to be built at last. Ultimately, the cosmogonic and the historical myths are not to be distinguished: their end point is the same, YHWH and Israel at rest in His sacred precincts. It was for this reason that the definitive triumph of YHWH over Pharaoh, a historical enemy, could be celebrated with a hymn about victory at the waters, a hymn that ends with the appropriate image of YHWH enthroned on his mountain in the Temple which His own hands built and acclaimed king by the people He acquired through manumission

(Exod 15:1–8).[32] It is here that we see the convergence of the two perspectives outlined above, the settlement tradition and the (Priestly) Sinai tradition. It is true that the consummation of the foundational story comes at the assumption of the promised land in one case and at the inauguration of the tent-shrine in the other. In the settlement tradition, the fulfillment lies ahead for a longer time. In the (Priestly) Sinai tradition, it is a present reality from Sinai on. But once the homology of land and Temple is recognized, it becomes clear that, although the story comes to rest later in one case than the other, the rest to which it comes is the same.

This conception of the Temple as a world, a microcosm, recalls the recent statement by a distinguished historian of religion that "*ritual represents the creation of a controlled environment. . . . [It is] a means of performing the way things ought to be in conscious tension to the way things are in such a way that this ritualized perfection is recollected in the ordinary, uncontrolled, course of things.*"[33] The Temple is the world as it ought to be. It is a world in which God's reign is unthreatened, and his justice is manifest, in which life is peaceful, and every Israelite is without blemish. It is no wonder that prophets could call the mountain of God "Eden" or compare Zion glorified to that paradisaical garden (Ezek 28:13–14; Isa 51:3).[34] In this theology, the Temple was a piece of primal perfection available within the broken world of ordinary experience—heaven on earth.

The House of YHWH
and the Renewal of the World

The contiguity of a heavenly entity, the Jerusalem Temple, and mundane reality, with all its corruption and defilement, accounts for one of the most powerful spiritual dynamics in the Hebrew Bible. We see it in its sharpest form in the experience of the prophet Isaiah:

> In the year that King Uzziah died, I beheld my LORD seated on a high and lofty throne; and the skirts of His robe filled the Temple. Seraphs stood in attendance on Him. Each of them had six wings: with two he covered his face, with two he covered his legs, and with two he would fly.
>
> > And one would call to the other,
> > "Holy, holy, holy!
> > The LORD of Hosts!
> > His presence fills all the earth!"
>
> The doorposts would shake at the sound of the one who called, and the House kept filling with smoke. I cried,

> "Woe is me; I am lost!
> For I am a man of unclean lips
> And I live among a people
> of unclean lips;
> Yet my own eyes have beheld
> The King LORD of Hosts."

Then one of the seraphs flew over to me with a live coal, which he had taken from the altar with a pair of tongs. He touched it to my lips and declared,

> "Now that this has touched your lips,
> Your guilt shall depart
> And your sin be purged away."

Then I heard the voice of my LORD saying, "Whom shall I send? Who will go for us?" And I said, "Here am I; send me." And He said, "Go, say to that people. . . ." (Isa 6:1–9)

Here Isaiah is privileged to see the difference between the earthly antitype and the heavenly archetype disappear: iconography becomes the reality it symbolizes. To the prophet, the Temple as it fills with smoke (probably from burning incense) suggests the world as it is filled with the "presence" (*kavod*) of God, no longer restricted to the sacred precincts (vv. 3–4; cf. Exod 40:34; 1 Kgs 8:11). Not only does the earthly Temple become one with the heavenly one, but the world becomes one with the Temple —or almost. For the vision of God in His majesty and holiness and the seraphic announcement of the universal scope of His presence induce in Isaiah an acute awareness of his own defilement. He is a man "of unclean lips" from a people "of unclean lips," a status that is incompatible with a vision of God. The vision would have doomed him, had not a seraph cauterized his lips and thus purified him of whatever blasphemy or slander he had uttered (Isa 6:5–7). Only then does Isaiah become fit to bear the verdict of the divine council out into the profane world (vv. 8–9).

The affinity of Isaiah's throne-vision with the spirituality of the Temple as it appears in the Psalms is patent. As we have noted, the apogee of a visit to the Temple was a vision of God, but entrance was granted only to those qualified for it. Sins of the tongue are prominent among the disqualifications (e.g., Ps 15:3; 24:4). In Isaiah's case, the dissonance between the holiness of YHWH enthroned in his Temple and the unholiness of the outside world impelled his prophetic career. The people of Zion have become unfit receptacles for that overpowering holiness whose invasion of the ordinary world was announced by the seraphim. They must be reformed:

> Sinners in Zion are frightened,
> The godless are seized with trembling:
> "Who of us can dwell with the devouring fire:
> Who of us can dwell with the never-dying blaze?"
> He who walks in righteousness,
> Speaks uprightly,
> Spurns profit from fraudulent dealings,
> Waves away a bribe instead of grasping it,
> Stops his ears against listening to infamy,
> Shuts his eyes against looking at evil—
> Such a one shall dwell in lofty security,
> With inaccessible cliffs for his stronghold,
> With his food supplied
> And his drink assured.
>
> (Isa 33:14–16)

In this oracle, the "entrance liturgy" serves as the basis for prophetic indictment, as the entire nation is exhorted to act as if it seeks admission to the Temple. Moreover—and here we see the connection with the seraphic hymn of 6:3—the holy God is not satisfied with remaining within His palace, but is, instead, determined to make the world His palace: He is a "devouring flame," scorching sinners not only in Zion/Jerusalem but also in Israel and throughout the world. Isaiah's message is, in large measure, founded upon the ethical imperative that follows from the experience of the Temple. For him, YHWH is, first and foremost, the "Holy One of Israel," and the deadliest sin is arrogance, which he interprets as the idolatrous act of self-enthronement:

> Yea, man is bowed,
> And mortal brought low;
> Brought low in the pride of the haughty.
> And the LORD of Hosts is exalted by judgment,
> The Holy God proved holy by retribution.
> (Isa 5:15–16; cf. 2:10–17).

"Just as Isaiah's own life is exposed to the eyes of the Holy One, so he sees his people in their world *sub specie sanctitatis Dei*."[35]

The invasion of the world by the Temple is the theme of an oracle of uncertain authorship, two variations of which appear in Isaiah and in Micah:

> In the days to come,
> The Mount of the Lord's House
> Shall stand firm above the mountains
> And tower above the hills;
> And all the nations

Shall gaze on it with joy.
And the many peoples shall go and say:
"Come,
Let us go up to the Mount of the Lord,
To the House of the God of Jacob;
That He may instruct us in His ways,
And that we may walk in His paths."
For instruction shall come forth from Zion,
The word of the Lord from Jerusalem.
Thus He will judge among the nations
And arbitrate for the many peoples,
And they shall beat their swords into plowpoints[36]
And their spears into pruning hooks:
Nation shall not take up
Sword against nation;
They shall never again know war.
                    (Isa 2:2–4; cf. Mich. 4:1–5)

Here we see numerous reflections of the Temple mythos which we have been delineating. The language of the eschatological establishment of the Temple (*nakon*, "stand firm," v. 2) recalls both YHWH's founding of a temple after His battle with Pharaoh at the Sea (*konenu*, Exod 15:17) and the language of creation, in which YHWH sets the earth upon its foundation (e.g., *yekoneneha*, Ps 24:1–2). The Temple is about to be refounded, and the world, renewed. The exaltation of the Temple Mount (*nissa"* Isa 2:2) recalls Isaiah's vision of YHWH seated on a high and lofty (*ram wenissa'*) throne" (6:1). Apparently, the famous oracle of 2:2–4 is a description of the world as it is to be after YHWH's final and irreversible enthronement, when He assumes direct rule by His universal dominion. Like so much of biblical literature, it is a historicization of the enthronement experience, this time (as often) in the future tense. The theme of peace (v. 4) is, as we have seen, also an integral element in the Temple mythos. In this oracle, it is extended beyond the vicinity of Zion, or, to be more precise, Zion so dominates the world that all war becomes as futile as an attack upon the inviolable and impregnable Temple Mount itself. The affirmation that God "puts a stop to wars throughout the earth" (Ps 46:10) seems to have had a place in the Temple theology (cf. vv. 9–12). Finally, the prediction of "instruction" (*torah*, Isa 2:3) proceeding from Zion recalls the career of Isaiah himself, who bore his message from the Temple out into the world. The prediction is another reflex of the idea, common throughout the ancient Near East, of the temple as a place for oracles. But, in this vision, alongside the outward motion of the oracle as it leaves Zion/Jerusalem lies the inward motion of the nations as they march toward the Temple in quest of sacred knowledge. The image of the Gentiles converging on Zion, now resplendent and triumphant after a period of humiliation and desolation, became an important element in later Jewish eschatology (e.g., Isa 60–62). It was an essential constituent of the vision of YHWH's ultimate victory, which was complete and manifest only when He had assumed His throne in the palace upon His sacred mountain. "A new heaven and a new earth" were inextricably associated with a new Jerusalem, (re-)created "as a joy/and her people as a delight" (Isa 65:17–18). Visions of that (re)new(ed) temple and the proleptic experience of it were important in Jewish utopias (e.g., Ezek 40–48).

Temple and Synagogue

The groundwork for Jewry's survival of the destruction of the Second Temple by the Romans in 70 c.e. was laid after the Babylonians had razed the First in 597 b.c.e. The unavailability of the Temple to all Jews for another two generations and for Diaspora Jews ever after aided mightily in the emergence of ideas and institutions that stood in succession to the national shrine, principally the synagogue. Until the emergence of liberal Judaism in the nineteenth century, however, the succession of the Jerusalem Temple by the synagogue was not regarded as final. Rather, the synagogue was seen as a temporary measure, although, sadly, a long-lived one, until the reconstruction of the Temple. In fact, the traditional liturgy continues to pray for the return of the Temple and the reinstitution of its sacrificial system, and even synagogues of liberal groups, although they often assume the name "temple," tend to continue to face Jerusalem. In short, prayer and sacred study replaced sacrifice, but sacrifice remained a central concern of prayer and sacred study. This curious arrangement, in which one institution replaces another without altogether displacing it, is adumbrated in the Hebrew Bible, in the longest biblical meditation upon the use of the Temple, Solomon's dedication speech in 1 Kgs 8:12–53. The speech shows an acute consciousness of the possibility of national defeat in war and a consequent exile (vv. 33–34, 46–53), but it never once mentions the most frequent and obvious function of the Temple, to serve as a place for sacrifice! Instead it stresses prayer (*tefillah*) and supplication (*tehinnah*) unremittingly.[37] The Temple, in fact, has become the place toward which Israel in exile directs their prayers (v. 48); from there they are referred to God's heavenly abode, the supernal Temple. The survival of the Temple as a spiritual focus long after the physical entity had been destroyed is one of the most remarkable aspects of Judaism. It is not that the Temple was spiritualized after its destruction. Instead, the spiritual role of the Temple after its destruction was a continuation of the role the Temple had long played in the devotional and visionary experience of Israel in the biblical period.

Notes

1. See F. M. Cross, "The Priestly Tabernacle," in *The Biblical Archaeologist Reader,* ed. G. Ernest Wright and David Noel Freedman (Garden City, NY: Doubleday, 1961) 217–19 (first published in *Biblical Archaeologist* 10 [1974] 45–78).

2. See Menaham Haran, "The Priestly Image of the Tabernacle," *Hebrew Union College Annual* 35 (1965) 191–226.

3. It has been argued that the elaborate description of the Tent is not intended as the norm for any single shrine, but only for Israelite shrines in general, that is, that centralization is not presumed or mandated. The classic argument appears in Yehezkel Kaufmann, *The Religion of Israel,* trans. and abridged by Moshe Greenberg (Chicago: University of Chicago Press, 1960; New York: Schocken Books, 1972) 175–200. The argument has not met with much success.

For a view of the Tent tradition as conservative but also a judgment on the high Temple theology, see Virgil W. Rabe, "Israelite Opposition to the Temple," *Catholic Biblical Quarterly* 29 (1967) 228–33.

4. Richard E. Friedman, "The Tabernacle in the Temple," *Biblical Archaeologist* 43 (1980) 241–48; idem, *The Exile and Biblical Narrative,* Harvard Semitic Monographs 22 (Chico, CA: Scholars Press, 1981) 44–61.

5. The biblical translations in this study have been taken from the new Jewish Publication Society of America Bible (Philadelphia)(JPS): *The Torah* (1962), *The Prophets* (1978), and *The Writings* (1982). Permission to quote is gratefully acknowledged. Since the enumeration of verses differs in most other English Bibles, note that the references here are to the Hebrew text and not the English.

6. The Septuagint reads here "the Egyptians oppressed them."

7. See G. W. Ahlström, "Another Moses Tradition," *Journal of Near Eastern Studies* 39 (1980) 65–69. But if one reads the last two verbs in the singular, with the Septuagint, then the contradiction disappears.

8. As argued in Gerhard von Rad, "The Form-Critical Problem of the Hexateuch," in *The Problems of the Hexateuch and Other Studies,* trans. E. W. Truemann Dicken (New York: McGraw-Hill, 1966) 1–78 [German original, 1938]. On the scholarly debate, see Brevard S. Childs, *Introduction to the Old Testament as Scripture* (Philadelphia: Fortress, 1979) 124–27.

9. "YHWH" is the tetragrammaton, the four-letter proper name of the God of Israel, the pronunciation of which Jewish law now prohibits. Therefore, in this study, it appears as in Hebrew Bibles, without its vowels, even when I quote scholars who did not observe this prohibition. In prayer and public readings, Jews pronounce the tetragrammaton as 'Adonay, ("my Lord"); otherwise, they usually read it as Ha-shem ("the Name"). Biblical translations conventionally render it as "Lord."

10. Source critics generally refer to Leviticus 17–26 as "H," that is, the Holiness Code. Nonetheless, it is agreed that H is a stream within the Priestly tradition (P).

11. See G. W. Ahlström, "Heaven on Earth—at Hazor and Arad," in *Religious Syncretism in Antiquity,* ed. Birger A. Pearson (Missoula, MT: Scholars Press, 1975) 67–83; and Mircea Eliade, *The Myth of the Eternal Return or, Cosmos and History,* trans.

Willard R. Trask, Bollingen Series 46 (Princeton, NJ: Princeton University Press, 1971) 6–11.

12. On this issue, see Jon D. Levenson, "Who Inserted the Book of the Torah?" *Harvard Theological Review* 68 (1975) 203–33, esp. 223–27; idem, "From Temple to Synagogue: 1 Kings 8," in *Traditions in Transformation,* ed. Baruch Halpern and J. D. Levenson (Winona Lake, IN: Eisenbrauns, 1981) 145–47; and Friedman, *The Exile,* 1–43.

13. Here we translate "memorials" in place of the JPS "corpses" for Hebrew *pigrey.* See the rationale in Walther Zimmerli, *Ezekiel 2,* trans. James D. Martin, Hermeneia (Philadelphia: Fortress, 1983) 417.

14. Moshe Weinfeld, "Instructions for Temple Visitors in the Bible and in Ancient Egypt," in *Egyptological Studies,* ed. Sarah Israelit-Groll, Scripta Hierosolymitana 28 (Jerusalem: Magnes Press, 1982) 224–50.

15. See L. Delekat, *Asylie und Schutzorakel am Zionheiligtum* (Leiden: Brill, 1967).

16. See Weinfeld, "'Justice and Righteousness' in Ancient Israel against the Background of 'Social Reforms' in the Ancient Near East," in *Mesopotamien und seine Nachbarn,* ed. Hans-Jörg Nissen and Johannes Renger (Berlin: Reimer, 1982) part 2, 491–519, esp. 493–99. But see also the plausible alternative explanation of Moshe Greenberg, "The Biblical Concept of Asylum," *JBL* 78 (1959) 125–32.

17. "Suet and fat," the alternative translation in the JPS version, is preferable to the euphemistic reading that appears in their text, "a rich feast."

18. The idiom should read *yir'eh* ("he shall see") rather than *yera'eh* ("he shall be seen"). Where the latter appears, it is most likely a deliberate change of vocalization to obviate the anthropomorphism. See Wolf Wilhelm Grafin Baudissin, "'Gott schauen' in der alttestamentlichen Religion," *Archiv für Religionswissenschaft* 18 (1915) 181–82.

19. "There is vision" (*yera'eh*) is similar in sound (and identical in spelling) to *yir'eh* ("will see"), which appears in the name Abraham gives the site. Both terms are also puns on the name of the land, the mysterious *ha-moriyah* (v. 2).

20. But the secondary character of verse 4 is suggested by the fact that verses 3 and 4 can be read in continuity smoothly. See Walther Zimmerli, "Das Zweite Gebot," in *Festschrift Alfred Bertholet* (Tübingen: Mohr-Siebeck, 1950) 550–63; and William L. Moran, "The Conclusion of the Decalogue (EX 20, 17=DT 5, 21)," *Catholic Biblical Quarterly* 29 (1967) 553–54. On the nature and origin of the aniconic theology, see Sigmund Mowinckel, "Wann wurde der YHWHkultus in Jerusalem offiziell bildlos?" *Acta orientalia* 8 (1930) 257–79; and Tryggve Mettinger, "The Veto on Images and the Aniconic God in Ancient Israel," in *Religious Symbols and Their Functions,* ed. Harold Biezais, Scripta Instituti Donneriana Aboensis 10 (Stockholm: Almqvist & Wiksell, 1978) 15–29. Mettinger traces the prohibition on iconography back to Hosea (late eighth century B.C.E.) (p. 24). On the calves of Aaron and Jeroboam, see Cross, *Canaanite Myth and Hebrew Epic* (Cambridge, MA: Harvard University Press, 1973) 73 n. 117. Cross argues that "the young bulls were no doubt conceived as pedestals for the same God [i.e., YHWH] in the two national shrines," but he concedes that the god "also is immanent in the animal so that the two may be confused." The pedestal theory does not fit well with the fact that the Ugaritic god 'El, with whom YHWH was identified (see below), is called *Twr* ("bull").

21. See Cross, *Canaanite Myth,* 4, n. 6, in which it is noted that the word "originally meant 'bull,' or 'stallion.'" The discovery of a bronze figurine of a bull on a site from early in the Iron Age (i.e., the era of the "judges") that is probably Israelite commends the translation "bull" over "stallion." See Amichai Mazar, "The 'Bull Site'—An Iron Age I Open Cult Place," *BASOR* 247 (1982) 27–42.

22. See Mowinckel, "Wann wurde," 275–79.

23. The word translated as "meditate" in the JPS version may be a denominative piel from *demut* ("image"). Cf. the evolution of the English word "imagine."

24. Josephus, *The Jewish War*, trans. H. St. J. Thackeray, Loeb Classical Library (London: Heinemann; New York: G. P. Putnam's Sons, 1928) vol. 3, 265 (=Book 5, section 5, paragraph 4).

25. W. F. Albright, *Archaeology and the Religion of Israel* (Baltimore, MD: Johns Hopkins University Press, 1956; London: Oxford University Press) 148.

26. See Cross, *Canaanite Myth*, 112–44.

27. *The Assyrian Dictionary* (Chicago: Chicago Oriental Institute, 1968) vol. 1, part 2, 226–27.

28. See Albright, *Archaeology*, 153–54. *The Assyrian Dictionary* lists two words of the form *kiūru*, one, "a metal cauldron," of foreign origin, and another, "earth," "(sacred) place," of Sumerian origin (vol. 8 [1971], 476). It is possible that under the influence of the homology of world and Temple, the two meanings collapsed into one, at least among those whose native language was not Akkadian.

29. See Ahlström, "Heaven and Earth."

30. Particularly noteworthy are these correspondences: Gen 2:1–2 with Exod 39:32 and 40:33b–34; Gen 1:31 with Exod 39:43; Gen 2:3 with Exod 39:43 and 40:9. See M. Weinfeld, *Shabbat, Miqdash, Wehamlakat H'*; *Bet Miqra* (5737/1977) 188–93; idem, "Sabbath, Temple, and the Enthronement of the Lord," in *Mélanges bibliques et orientaux en L'honneur de M. Henri Cazelles*, ed. A. Caquot and M. Delcor; Alter Orient und Altes Testament 212 (Neukirchen-Vluyn: Neukirchener Verlag, 1981) 501–12; Joseph Blenkinsopp, *Prophecy and Canon*, University of Notre Dame Center for the Study of Judaism and Christianity in Antiquity 3 (Notre Dame, IN, and London: University of Notre Dame Press, 1977) 59–69; Arthur Green, "Sabbath as Temple: Some Thoughts on Space and Time in Judaism," in *God and Study: Essays and Studies in Honor of Alfred Jospe*, ed. Raphael Jospe and Samuel Z. Fishman (Washington, DC: B'nai B'rith Hillel Foundations, 5741/1980) 287–305; and Levenson, "The Temple and the World," *Journal of Religion* 64 (1984) 275–98.

31. Blenkinsopp, *Prophecy*, 61.

32. Is the mountain of YHWH's sanctuary and the goal of the exodus in Exod 15:17 Mount Sinai, the land of Israel, some unknown shrine in the land, or the Jerusalem Temple itself? In light of the mythical concept of the Temple which we are exploring, the question is misleading. The mountain of Exod 15:17 could have been and probably was all of these, at various times. Cross's argument for Gilgal is correct, but needlessly specific and exclusive (*Canaanite Myth*, 141–43).

33. Jonathan Z. Smith, *Imagining Religion: From Babylon to Jonestown*, Chicago Studies in the History of Judaism (Chicago and London: University of Chicago Press, 1982) 63 (italics in original).

34. See Levenson, *Theology of the Program of Restoration of Ezekiel 40–48*, Harvard Semitic Monographs 10 (Missoula, MT: Scholars Press, 1976) 25–36.

35. Th. C. Vriezen, "Essentials of the Theology of Isaiah," in *Israel's Prophetic Heritage: Essays in Honor of James Muilenburg*, ed. Bernhard W. Anderson and Walter Harrelson (New York: Harper & Row, 1962) 146.

36. "Plowpoints" has been substituted for the JPS "plowshares," which, although traditional, is less accurate. Israelite plows were wooden; this term refers to the iron point on the tip, as the note in the JPS version indicates.

37. See Levenson, "From Temple," 164.

Bibliography

The most recent major study of the problems concerning temples in Israel is Haran. Also useful are Clements, Cross. On the mountain traditions and their affinities, see Clifford. For the specific Jewish issues, including the postbiblical periods, Patai is valuable and accessible. Finally, the present author has developed some of the themes of this study in greater detail in *Sinai and Zion,* especially chapter 2.

Clements, R. E. *God and Temple.* Oxford: Blackwell, 1965.

Clifford, Richard J. *The Cosmic Mountain in Canaan and the Old Testament.* Harvard Semitic Monographs 4. Cambridge, MA: Harvard University Press, 1972.

Cross, F. M., ed. *Symposia Celebrating the Seventy-Fifth Anniversary of the Founding of the American Schools of Oriental Research (1900-1975).* Cambridge, MA: American Schools of Oriental Research, 1979.

Haran, Menahem. *Temples and Temple-Service in Ancient Israel.* Oxford: Clarendon Press, 1977.

Levenson, Jon D. *Sinai and Zion: An Entry into the Jewish Bible.* Minneapolis, MN: Winston-Seabury, 1985.

Patai, Raphael. *Man and Temple.* New York: Ktav, 1967.

3

Biblical Prophecy as a Religious Phenomenon

Michael Fishbane

THE MODERN CRITICAL STUDY of biblical prophecy has produced a voluminous literature. It has been concerned, on the one hand, with the textual and linguistic analysis of the received discourses and oracles of the prophets or their tradents. It has striven to isolate the authentic words, the *ipsissima verba*, of the prophets and their subsequent reformulation or readaptation in later times. On the other hand, contemporary biblical scholarship has attempted to locate the phenomena of biblical prophecy within the context of the larger contemporary ancient Near Eastern environment in which it occurred. It has also examined prophecy within the framework of one or another modern methodology of the social sciences or the history of religions. Accordingly, there are valuable studies that trace (or relate) the origins of Israelite prophecy to comparable phenomena in ancient West Asia (like the mantic-ecstatic type of prophet known from twelfth-century Byblos or ninth- to eighth-century Aram)[1] or in Mesopotamia proper (like the messenger type known from eighteenth-century Mari);[2] and there are inquiries into the social role of the prophet or the prophet's dominant psychological characteristics.[3] Moreover, summarizing or synthetic reviews of this material are also readily available.[4] Given this state of affairs, and the relative absence of inquiries into the peculiarly religious and spiritual aspects of the prophet, both within the larger context of ancient Israelite religion and as a uniquely focused expression of its dynamics and structures, I have decided to redress this imbalance through the following essay.[5] Such a perspective may, moreover, be further justified by the present forum, which locates the phenomenon of ancient Israelite prophecy as a foundational element of biblical religion and as a generative feature of later trajectories of Jewish spirituality.

Naturally, any summarizing inquiry into the phenomena of biblical prophecy will have to make certain choices and acknowledge a certain selectivity of focus and emphasis, for biblical prophecy was not one thing in one place or at one time. Indeed, it is a series of phenomena spanning a full millennium—roughly from 1200 to 200 B.C.E.—with a broad variety of subtypes even within its major divisions. No investigation can ignore the complex historical diversity of biblical prophecy without collapsing it into distorting uniformities or without harmonizing or streamlining the range of theologies and ideologies in biblical religion to which the prophets (among others) gave verbal expression. Nevertheless, the large literary corpus preserving traits of ancient Israelite prophecy in biblical literature does in fact project distinctly uniform spiritual physiognomies of the prophet over several centuries, so that certain recurrent phenomenological features may be responsibly isolated. On this basis, the peculiarly classical type of the prophet in ancient Israel emerges as a recognizable type who can be differentiated from other contemporary types, like the Israelite sage or priest, or from such subsequent rabbinic types as the disciple of the wise or the mystic (to name just two). It may be noted that the decision to focus the present discussion on the classical phase of biblical prophecy, which flourished between the eighth and the fifth centuries B.C.E., is based on the determination that it is precisely here that the uniquely Israelite prophetic type comes to expression—as against the professional mantic types that preceded it (and even coexisted with it) or the apocalyptic types that followed centuries later. Accordingly, these two latter phenomena, which frame the classical period of Israelite prophecy, shall be touched upon only briefly for purposes of contrast in the present chapter.

Prophecy as an Overwhelming Event in the Life of the Prophet

Even now the awesome visions of the divine majesty which are reported in Isaiah 6 and in Ezekiel 1 can jolt the reader—no matter how jaded such a reader may be to these texts, whether because of personal familiarity through habitual recitation or because of some secular cynicism about the reality of transcendental religious experiences. For even this modern reader is overcome by the august formulations of language that are found here; by the eerie otherness but explosive immediacy of the divine presence which dramatically unfolds in these visions; and by the symbolic mixing of sound and sight or of anthropomorphic and theriomorphic images which radiate through the texts as the literary vapors of shattering religious experiences. Now if this is so, how much more must these events have struck holy dread into the lives of the two prophets, Isaiah and Ezekiel, in whose name the visions are reported as having occurred at the onset or renewal of their prophetic careers?[6] Indeed, as reported, these theophanies of "the King Lord of Hosts" royally enthroned in the heavenly realms and attended by a retinue of mysterious divine beings, fill both men with the terrifying awareness that they have been fatefully chosen for a life of divine service. Isaiah shudders and recoils with a sense of profound disease and inadequacy (6:5), saying "Woe is me, for I am undone; for I am a man of impure lips" (a reaction that recalls the shocked response of Moses and his remonstrance at being "heavy of mouth" and "uncircumcised of lips" when contronted by the Lord in the wilderness, and Jeremiah's cry "Woe, Lord YHWH! Surely I cannot prophesy, for I am but a novice," when confronted with his prophetic destiny);[7] and Ezekiel falls to his face in abject terror, until he is subsequently commanded to rise up to his new life and task (1:28–2:7). Moreover, the suddenness and transforming character of these experiences suggests that they were not the climax of spiritual or contemplative exercises, or the inheritance of some spiritual lineage. Amos, the first of the classical prophets whose words have been preserved, expresses this fact clearly, as he seeks to differentiate himself from earlier prophetic types: "I am neither a prophet nor the son of a prophet," he confesses, "but a herdsman and pruner of sycamore trees; and YHWH took me from behind the flock, and YHWH said to me: 'Go, prophesy to My people, Israel'" (7:14–15).

With this we come to the core of the prophetic commission, of the experience that reoriented the chosen individual to a life of divine service. For not only do the commissioning or recommissioning theophanies erupt unexpectedly, and not only are they divinely initiated; but they also give their recipients an apostolic task, the task to be a human messenger of a divine word.[8] For such reasons alone it would be valid to conclude that the throne visions of Isaiah and Ezekiel are far removed from the contemplative ecstasies of later Jewish mystics, who beheld, at the culmination of private spiritual quests and group séances, the glory of the Lord enthroned in the supernal realms.[9] To be sure, what these visionaries of the cosmic palaces shared with their prophetic forebears was the fundamental religious awareness of the transcendent Otherness of divinity. But for these mystics the goal was the ecstatic contemplation of the supernal realm of divinity (and in some instances the envisioning of esoteric secrets); for them the vision did not serve primarily as the *prelude* to a supernatural divine communication for the nation as a whole, as it did for the classical prophets. To put this point in further perspective, it will be instructive briefly to turn from the afterlife of "Ezekielian visions" in the early rabbinic period to throne visions in pre-Ezekielian strata. We may, thereby, also get a brief glance at some features of the preclassical Israelite prophecy that were rejected by Amos in the passage quoted earlier.

A striking and instructive antecedent of prophetic throne imagery may be found in 1 Kings 22.[10] Indeed, within the framework of this historical narrative, we are treated to a visionary report of a remarkable and dramatic episode that occurred in the heavenly realm. The onset of this vision lies in the course of a divinatory consultation requested by King Jehoshaphat of Ahab's prophetic entourage, after Ahab had asked the Judean king to join him in a coalition against Aram. With remarkable unanimity of divine inspiration, the full complement of these Israelite prophets, four hundred strong, counseled their royal lord to proceed with his military plans against Aram. Struck skeptical by this remarkable concord, Jehoshaphat quizzically besought the independent opinion of one Micaiah ben Imlah, a prophet known to depart from the self-serving instincts of royally sponsored court prophecy. Subsequently, after an initial hesitation, Micaiah revealed to the king his vision of the Lord YHWH enthroned in heaven with the heavenly host roundabout, and of the divine decision to send a "false spirit" to deceive Ahab through his prophets—therewith bringing ruin upon him and all Israel. Although many moderns agree that this passage has been modified in part by later prophetic (and Deuteronomistic) values, certain constitutive elements of the older, preclassical strand of biblical prophecy nevertheless remain. For one thing, the prophetic entourage constituted a guild under court sponsorship, and the oracular prognostications of its members were in response to a mantic situation initiated by another human regarding private or institutional interests.[11] Even Micaiah, who is recognizably marginal to this collective phenomenon and whose nonconformity to current political interests is reminiscent of the adversarial role played by the later prophets, reveals the content of his vision only under royal duress. He is not under any divine compulsion to speak as a messenger responsible only to his Lord God.

Micaiah's experience of the divine throne is thus decisively different from that of Isaiah and Ezekiel. Indeed, as suggested earlier, these classical, non-institutional prophets are "sent" to the people not to confirm or disconfirm a royal question concerning the military success or failure of a contemplated venture. Their principal task is rather to proclaim to the entire nation God's unsolicited message of rebuke, exhortation, warning, or doom. Hence, as divine emissaries, neither Isaiah nor Ezekiel (nor all their congeners) initiates his speech to Israel. Their prophetic discourse is rather God's self-initiated *davar:* his event-filled and event-begetting word. Thus, Isaiah is told precisely what to say to the wayward nation (6:9); Ezekiel ingests divine

words (of woe), thereby concretizing the nonhuman character of the proclamations he is forced to speak (2:8–3:11); and Jeremiah is "sent" by God to
Israel and the nations, with divine words put into his mouth (1:4–10). The
degree to which Jeremiah's life was in fact radically transformed by this
consuming prophetic destiny is strikingly evident from Jeremiah 20:7–10,
among many passages, where the prophet wails in despairing torment over
a divine message that he can neither bear to speak nor, at the same time,
withhold.[12]

> You have enticed me, YHWH, and I've been had:
> You have overwhelmed me and prevailed;
> I am mocked all day long,
> Everyone reviles me
> Whenever I speak or shout, I say: "violence and plunder"—
> The word of YHWH is become my daily shame
> and reproach
> And whenever I would think: "I won't mention Him,
> Nor speak in His name ever again"—
> Then His word burned me up like a consuming
> fire locked in my bones;
> I have tried to contain it but to no avail.
>
> (Jer 20:7–9)

The tremendous power of the divine claim over this and other Israelite
prophets results in a striking state of self-surrender: the singular self shud-
deringly succumbs to the force of a divine presence that finds thereby both
a "mouth" and a means of earthly expression. Amos, a pivotal figure in the
history of biblical prophecy, signals the whole movement from earlier prophetic phenomena to the classical expressions just described. For he knows,
profoundly, that he is not a guild prophet in solidarity with institutional
concerns, but a solitary one, a person jerked out of normal consciousness
to prophesy to the people of Israel (Amos 7:14–15). As he reports, "[If] a lion
roars who does not fear? [Now] my Lord YHWH has spoken, who can but
prophesy?" (3:8). Palpably, the fateful pathos of God's charge upon Amos is
still felt despite the elevated rhetoric of the received discourse. In it he
singularly reveals that this mighty divine charge upon him—which exceeds
all natural terror—manifests itself in his life as an unearthly compulsion to
speak God's bidding. In turn, this compulsion and the content of the divine
message set the prophet apart. "Because of your hand upon me [viz., your
inspiring, compelling presence] I sat solitary," Jeremiah elsewhere cried
(15:17). Indeed, to be a prophet in Israel was to undergo a rupture in social
solidarity and a transformation of one's religious consciousness. It was to be
God's servant and spokesman, serving and speaking as God alone would will

it. In the end, therefore, any revolt against one's prophetic destiny, against the divine *davar* infused in one's mouth, was futile. Such is at once the lesson taught by Jeremiah's pathetic protests against God and his prophetic destiny in the passage quoted above; it is similarly the root of the parody about Balaam, the pagan prophet, and his talking ass, which obeys God even when his master is obtuse; and, in the end, the issue of the ineluctable fatefulness of one's prophetic task is the core theme of the book of Jonah as well. For all other thematics aside, this little prophetic book is distinctively a confession of just this truth, grudgingly realized.

Prophecy and the Biblical Break with Near Eastern Myth

Up to this point, we have explored selected elements of the classical prophetic commission scenes and seen that they are marked by a rupture in self-consciousness which transforms the chosen person into a special emissary of the divine spirit and word. However, in order fully to appreciate this phenomenon in the context of biblical religion, it is necessary briefly to consider two other, more fundamental ruptures. The first of these may be called Israel's break with ancient Near Eastern mythical consciousness. By this characterization I mean Israel's decisive rejection of a monistic perspective which imagined the world as a great chain of being that emerged in primordial time from the recombinant matings of divine forces, and which received its recognizable differentiations as a result of a decisive theomachy and the organizational skill of a victorious god. In such a world view, most clearly presented in the Babylonian epic of creation called *Enumah elish*, there may be a complex hierarchy of powers and forces within the primal divine ground (a hierarchy typified mythologically by the political inter-relationships and dependencies of a pantheon of divine beings). But all being—which is to say, all of the vastness of conceivable existence—is nonetheless primordially, qualitatively, and indeed inherently, divine. In contrast, the normative religious vision brought to expression in the Hebrew Bible knows none of this. For it, not polytheistic monism but theistic dualism is the essential feature of its world view. Because of this difference, the teachers of ancient Israel do not, in their accounts of origins, portray a world of divine forces that emerge successively from a primordial *plenum*, but rather describe a world created from primordial stuff by an autonomous god who is qualitatively distinct from his creations (cf. Gen 1:1–2:4a). The upshot of this world view is of decisive comparative significance. For on its terms there is envisaged a creator God who is utterly Other than the world and its creatures, with the result that the world of divine

creation is divested of inherent divinity. What remains, therefore, is not a
world "full of gods" but a world that has the *possibility* of sacralization
through the attribution of sanctity to selected and chosen spheres of it by
the transcendent creator, and through the faithful human performance of
the commandments revealed by this same God to a chosen, sanctified
nation.[13]

Before proceeding further, the second of the two ruptures just mentioned
must be noted. It concerns the explicit and fateful portrayal in Genesis 3
of a primordial break in human religious consciousness. Indeed, for the
ancient writer of Genesis 3—a narrative description which bears all the
signs of being the product of considerable theological reflection—the enduring spiritual pathos of the "myth of Eden" is that it portrays sin as a
human revolt against the autonomous creator God, which in its first expression destroyed an archaic and aboriginal sense of a harmonious divine order.
In the dramatic, mythic terms of Genesis 3, humankind, because of self-
centered desire, disobeyed the primordial divine interdict safeguarding the
hierarchical boundaries of the divine creation and was forthwith evicted
from paradisaical harmony into the broken, barren world we know from
common human experience.[14] But the transformative revolt did not stop
there. As the successive episodes of the primeval cycle of Genesis make clear
(chaps. 4–11), the biblical narrator was concerned with emphasizing that
humankind's continuing acts of disobedience and desire, with their illusory
presumptions of human autonomy, drove an ever deeper wedge between
itself and the punishing, uniquely autonomous Lord of creation.

This said, we must properly note that this Lord is not only a punishing
god. For one of the most characteristic and recurring religious motifs of the
Hebrew Bible is that its Lord God, by revelations imparted through chosen
leaders, continuously attempts to reconcile His sinful creatures to His will.
Thus, the primordial rupture of harmonious existence in Genesis 3 results,
after twenty generations, in the selection of Abram and his seed for divine
grace and revelation. But the axial expression of this basic divine concern
is, of course, the covenant made with Israel at Sinai (Exod 19–20). Indeed,
as the different Pentateuchal theologies make clear, the deepest hope in the
transformation of the spiritual and natural sterility that humankind first
experienced after the sin in Eden lay in devoted fulfillment of the divine
commandments. In axiomlike fashion the covenantal texts found in the
books of Leviticus and Deuteronomy hammer this point insistently, stressing that rain and children and peace are the everlasting boons of obedience,
whereas drought and barrenness and strife are the dooms that may be
expected for rejection of the divine will (see especially Lev 26 and Deut 28).
Spiritually considered, obedience to God's convenantal will is the historical

anodyne for the broken religious consciousness caused (and reinforced) by sin: for obedience, from a biblical point of view, requires the rejection of the illusions of creaturely autonomy and subservience to the dictates of the divine teachings.

With these considerations in mind, we may now return to our consideration of the prophets. According to biblical tradition, Moses is portrayed as the archetypal biblical prophet, not solely through the depiction of his commission in Exodus 3–4 in language and imagery similar to the inauguration scenes of the classical prophets, but principally by means of the characterization of him found in Deuteronomy 18:15–18. In this essential document, it is reported that prophets like Moses will be continually established by God because of the people's fear of a continuous, unmediated relationship with divinity. Succinctly, then, and in a striking manner (for this passage is in fact an exegetical revision of Exod 20:6, where the people in fear of the awesome theophany at Sinai ask Moses to mediate the revelation to them), this text crystallizes a basic truth of classical biblical prophecy in its religious foundations. For at its core, the text implies, the voices of the prophets of Israel are to be regarded as the historical prolongation of Moses' voice, which first taught God's covenantal will to the people and the primacy of obedience to it. So viewed, the classical prophets of Israel are not so much the spokesmen of God as *the spokesmen of God in behalf of the covenant* which He established with His people. Their appointed destiny, therefore, is to speak for obedience to the stipulations of that covenant and thereby to reconcile the people to the God who revealed them. In addition, the prophets also speak against covenantal disobedience, and so against the sinful revolt against its divine giver and guarantor. It is significant that the dire consequences for covenantal malfeasance, as well as the rewards for faithfulness which the prophets announce, explicitly reecho the rewards and punishments announced in the Torah. In this way the prophets establish themselves as a chain of messengers empowered to reconcile a wayward people with God, and so to heal a breach whose origins preceded the Sinaitic law and originated, according to biblical theological myth, in the sinful revolt of the primordial human pair in Eden.

Prophecy as a Bridge Between God and Israel

As we have seen, biblical religion gives primary emphasis to obedience to the divine will, and may even be characterized as a pattern of holiness that demands active human service to supernatural stipulations. As we have suggested, the prophets may be properly viewed as the exemplary teachers of this demand. Brief contrast with other religious types will serve to highlight other aspects of this role.

In the Eastern religions, for example, one dominant pattern of the spiritual teacher is that of an exemplary master who provides a human model of salvific action. Just such a teacher was Gautama Buddha or Lao-tze. For while each of these masters claims to verbalize or enact the truths of (divine) reality, what each teaches is just that path of wisdom that has proved personally successful to him. Hence, that path of wisdom is not a universal revelation but a personal realization of the truth of reality. Accordingly, although a few spiritual virtuosos may in fact choose to emulate their teacher's way—the way he points to but does not prescribe—they do not and cannot imitate it, since every individual's path to illumination is necessarily unique. In contrast, the classical Hebrew prophet is the recipient (through Moses and the covenant) of supernatural divine stipulations that prescriptively instruct the entire nation of Israel in its path of obligation. Moreover, since the biblical God is not the essence of the eternal order of being, but rather an autonomous sovereign with a precise will and zealous regard for His exclusive preeminence in the hierarchy of being (i.e., His creations, which are subordinate to Him), the ideal religious quest in biblical Israel is devotion to the Lord of the covenant as expressed through faithful obedience to His will—not a quest for release from the round of rebirth, or sympathy with all sentient beings who share the pain of existence, and so forth. By the same token, the ancient Israelite prophet is not a perfected spiritual master who has transcended the illusions of common sense or the temptations of his ego. He is rather a person who is deeply aware of his own unperfected nature before the transcendent Otherness of his covenantal Lord, and one for whom a radical spiritual encounter has inspired an acute consciousness of the necessity to avoid sin and heed the stipulations of God's autonomous will.

But now, if the prophet's displacement of ego-centered subjectivity for a God-centered covenantal service may also be considered the overarching ideal of ancient Israelite covenantal piety, such that the prophets may be regarded as the exemplary models of this religious orientation, one must at the same time underscore the more fundamental displacement of subjectivity that marks prophetic consciousness. We can best begin by returning to our earlier characterization of the prophets as persons who believed themselves to be transmitters of divine words that obsessed and possessed them. A short detour through some related prophetic features will help to establish our point.

Certainly one of the remarkable features of biblical religion, which is of profound importance to the history of Judaism as well, is its emphasis on the fact that God establishes and maintains *verbal* contact with His creatures. Such contact is essentially twofold. On the one hand, there are the Sinaitic and post-Sinaitic revelations of national-foundational import reputedly given to Moses; on the other, there are the numerous revelations of divine intention and response vis-à-vis human behavior given through Moses' successors, the prophets of Israel. In this respect, at least, the God of the prophets is neither an intransitive nor otiose divine power, but a transcendent being who communicates His involvement in the actions of humankind through the speech of His chosen emissaries.

But once this claim that divinity communicates its will through mediaries attains widespread cognitive plausibility—and is furthermore institutionally reinforced by groups claiming to be the protectors and guardians of that will—intentional or disingenuous abuses of divine speech inevitably arise. Such manipulations of divine prescriptions and predictions pertain both to the foundational legal revelations—where a host of pseudepigraphic amendments introduced into the legal corpora and historical narratives serve to authorize subsequent legal needs or ideologies—and to the prophetic oracles. With respect to the latter material, a close investigation of our biblical sources reveals a wide diversity of latter-day revisions of ancient oracles that were presumed to have lapsed; of tendentious social and political claims advanced under the putative authority of earlier divine statements; and of assorted contradictory claims put forth by contending prophetic circles.[15]

During periods of crisis, the problem of discerning among contradictory divine communications and oracles was particularly acute and frequently led to much popular confusion and interinstitutional contestations (often intraprophetic) about the will of God for a given historic moment. Such contradictions and confusions are particularly evident in the prophecies found in the books of Jeremiah and Ezekiel—both antecedent to and concurrent with the final fall of the Judean state. In some cases these prophets blasted the claims of their prophetic rivals (see Jer 12:13–15; 23:9–40; Ezek 12:21; 14:10); in other instances these men were actually pilloried by other power groups (see Jer 7; 20:1–3). Given this state of affairs, new criteria were added to older ones for ascertaining the validity of specific prophetic claims. Sometimes these newer criteria were altogether unremarkable and obvious, as in the case of prophecies delivered in the name of non-Israelite gods or on behalf of their cultic praxes. Such prophecies were obviously invalid and could be forthrightly dismissed without further theological anxiety (Jer 23:13–14; cf. Deut 12:2–12; 18:20). Another apparently obvious criterion sought to rest the case of prophetic validity on the fulfillment or nonfulfillment of the oracular forecasts themselves (Jer 28; cf. Deut

18:21–22). But however obvious in principle, or in the long run, such a criterion was virtually useless in the interim—in the time that unfolds between the promise and its (announced) realization. For how could one ever be sure *in advance* that a particularly seductive oracle was not simply a self-serving announcement or even a divine test or deception to be resisted—like the oracles given by Ahab's prophets, discussed earlier (Ezek 14:9; cf. Deut 12:2–14)? Given such fateful ambiguities as these, it is of considerable interest to observe that Jeremiah's ultimate contention in behalf of prophetic veracity (with echoes in Ezekiel, too) turns on an entirely different axis and returns us to a consideration of the fundamental displacement of subjectivity that marks prophetic consciousness.

For Jeremiah, ultimately, true prophecy was not simply to be validated by objective linguistic elements (like references to YHWH as the source of the oracles, or to the national covenant, or even to such themes as doom or calls to repentance). Nor was it solely to be judged in terms of the fulfillment of the oracles forecast. Rather, for this prophet, the overriding criterion of a true prophecy lay in its subjective impact on the prophet himself. By his testimony, in fact, true prophecy is presented as having its onset in an inner explosion, a consuming compulsion, a rape of interiority (20:1–9; 23:29). It was thus categorically separate from the illusions of dreamwork, subjective fantasies, or even scholastic plagiarisms—a sampling of the pseudo-prophetic conditions which Jeremiah unyieldingly and repeatedly lambastes (23:26–32). Profoundly aware that he spoke God's words and not the concoctions of his own mind, Jeremiah (and his prophetic congeners) would have mockingly rebutted the modern suggestion that the prophets merely gave verbal release to some overbearing psychic pressure, thereby neutralizing psychologically the prophets' own claim that they transmitted divine words which erupt out of them. To be sure, there were already cynics in antiquity who gave scant heed to the histrionic pronouncements of these men—so frequently couched in fantastic or stylistically ornate imagery. Ezekiel, for one, laments that he knew such people, who were prone to dismiss his oracles as so many rhetorical tropes, thus disregarding the concrete divine truth of his message (21:5). But he has nothing but contempt for their illusions. He knows that he lies on his sides for 390 and 40 days apace, performs dramatic actions, forbears mourning his wife, and is struck with anxious fear after announcing horrid dooms not to relieve an inner psychic pressure but because God Himself speaks directly to him. Similarly, Isaiah runs naked for three years and Jeremiah convulses like a drunkard while pronouncing forecasts of national desolation not to relieve some vague emotional pressure but because God has displaced their natural subjectivity with His supernatural "I."

Accordingly, all modern predilections for emphasizing the so-called Promethean element in biblical prophecy—whereby a prophet reacts to or contends with a just-revealed horrific divine forecast—must be considered within this larger perspective.[16] It is thus true that Amos repeatedly responds to visions of Israel's destruction with the remonstration "Lord YHWH, please forgive/cease! For who will stand up for Jacob, since he is small?!" (Amos 7:2, 5). And we even find the remarkable depiction in the book of Ezekiel of the true prophet as one who will stand in the breach in behalf of the people as an intercessor against and container of divine wrath, as it were.

> And I (God) sought for a man among
> them who would build a hedge and stand
> in the breach before Me for the land, that
> I should not destroy it; but I found none.
> Therefore have I consumed them with the
> fire of My wrath. . . . (Ezek 22:30–31)

But it would be false to conclude from the few records of such remonstration that the Israelite prophet is a free-spirited protestor against divine judgments and not a person deeply under the sway of a divine power which he resists and seeks to contain. For is it not the case, as well, that these few protestations also break down under divine compulsion—as when Amos's protests strikingly subside when God forcefully determines to deliver a divine message of doom (7:8), or when Jeremiah is warned to cease his protests and told that they will not be successful (15:1)?[17] Indeed, when Jeremiah continues to protest he is forcefully stifled by God and allowed to return to his role as a divine "mouth" only if he repents of his misuse of selfhood.[18] On other occasions, as we have seen, Jeremiah could hardly get this far; the best he could achieve was merely a cry of protest against his divinely determined fate (20:7–12).

The Pathos of Prophecy

The remarkable notion that an utterly transcendent God should repeatedly choose to appoint human messengers to reveal His will leads to a deeper penetration into the religious phenomenon of biblical prophecy. It was earlier remarked that, as historical mediators, the classical prophets bring to sharp expression an active divine intention to reconcile sinful creatures to the covenantal stipulations—and so to the God who reveals His will thereby. Indeed, over and over again, in all historical periods and with a diversity of means, our scriptural sources give witness to a divine will that erupts through chosen human mediators in order to announce His response to human behavior: to denounce noncovenantal actions, to urge spiritual conversion and reconciliation with the God of Israel and His covenant, to warn against the consequences of disobedience, and to announce the advent of these consequences. Manifestly, the God of Israel does not leave His people alone. Indeed, the remarkable religious dimension of the mediating role of the prophets is not so much their attempts to inveigle a distant, omnipotent god to attend to the religious urges of his weak and needy creatures. This occasionally occurs in the prophetical sources, but is generally speaking more of a feature of the psalm literature. More common, indeed more decisively characteristic of biblical prophecy, is rather YHWH's attempt—through coaxing and warning—to inveigle a distant, wayward people to attend to the religious demands of His covenant. On reflection, this *divine quest for human acknowledgment and obedience* constitutes the profound pathos of biblical prophecy.[19] In a singular way the Israelite prophets are the bearers of a divine urgency to communicate the absolute dominion of YHWH over his people by announcing the lawful consequences of a covenant to which He—if not they—is absolutely committed.

These reflections serve to highlight the fundamental religious paradox and challenge of classical biblical prophecy. Succinctly put, the core of the paradox hinges on the fact that, whereas the biblical God is the transcendent Lord over His nation and claims absolute exclusiveness in this respect, the people always remain free to reject or at least to limit their allegiance to His will. It would appear that prolonged reflection on just this spiritual paradox lies at the root of the "Eden myth" of Genesis 3—discussed earlier as the expression of the fundamental cognitive rupture in divine–human harmony produced by sinful desire, and as the genesis of a negative dialectic (of human sin and divine punishment) which YHWH's covenant and the chain of prophets seek to reverse. Here, of course, some pause must be given to the resilient theological optimism which is a hallmark of biblical prophecy and which expresses itself in the (recurrent) possibilities of reconciliation between the sinner and God. And if confession and the recognition of guilt were in fact a precondition of atonement in the ancient Israelite cult, as some have maintained,[20] then the priests also shared an optimistic anthropology and theology of divine–human reconciliation comparable to that which highlights so much of biblical prophecy. However this be, such a possibility need not obscure the fact that most priests were particularly convinced of the singular power of divinely revealed ritual actions to effect divine reconciliation with the sinner. It may therefore be surmised that, in their focus upon the dynamics of the religious will and its capacity to turn against or toward God, with hardly a word said about priestly atonement (though often in mocking irony at popular notions of the independent or inherent efficacy of cultic reconciliation), the prophets must have aroused the ire of the priestly establishment. In retrospect, the prophets' emphasis on repentance as an independent and inherently valuable spiritual force anticipates the historical possibility, which for Jews was fateful—namely, of being reconciled with God even when and where the ancient cultic rituals of expiation no longer existed.

While rooted in an optimistic theology, however, the pathos whereby the divine Sovereign sends His prophets to preach liege submission to His covenant—through blandishments for faithfulness or threats of doom for disobedience—deserves separate comment. For although it is a well-worn truth that the prophets stress a relative hierarchy of religious values, giving striking and dramatic preference to moral over purely cultic considerations,[22] it may be less obvious that their obsession with the dispossessed and the need for a purification of cultic service (on many levels) are equally part and parcel of their fundamental obsession with Israel's exclusive obedience to YHWH. To phrase it differently and to cast a different light on covenantal observance, we may observe that though the will of the sovereign God of the prophets manifested itself in particular stipulations, of paramount importance was *the very fact of obedience* as expressed by the religious vassal through performance of the commandments given by his commanding Lord—not the commandments per se. Although these commandments do, of course, have inestimable worth in the prophets' minds, and their contents are unquestionably the agency for morality and justice, it is nevertheless precisely *through* the performance of the covenantal stipulations that the religious vassal demonstrates fealty to God. Consequently, all Israelites must, like the exemplary prophets, relinquish their wills to the supreme revealing will of God and perform His dictates.

For this reason as well there is in prophetic-covenantal religiosity no final peacefulness with God, no relaxed indifference to obligations and tasks. On the contrary, the prophets' teachings stress that allegiance to the covenant lies in an ongoing obedient service to God through His stipulations, in vigilant attentiveness to the obligations of a religious treaty. For, finally, God is Himself never indifferent to these stipulated actions, and for this reason He has sent a succession of messengers over many generations in order to warn, reproach, or encourage His vassals to faithfulness. The prophet Jeremiah reveals this reality with fearsome clarity:

> Then the word of YHWH came to me: Can I not deal with you, Israel— oracle of YHWH—as the potter deals with his clay? . . . At any moment I may threaten to uproot a nation or a kingdom, to pull it down and destroy

it. But if the nation which I have threatened turns back from its wicked ways, then I shall think better of the evil which I had in mind to bring on it. Or at any moment I may decide to build or to plant a nation or a kingdom. But if it does evil in my sight and does not obey me, I shall think better of the good I had in mind for it (Jer 18:5–10).

It has been argued that the prophet Jonah rejected this radical view of the divine–human relationship and the radical conditionality of divine orders—preferring the dependability of unalterable prophecies of doom (or salvation).[22] Perhaps he felt that such a conditionality gave humans a modicum of manipulative power over God, and so he protested for the sake of divine freedom. From this perspective, the divine response to Jonah's grievance, at the withering of his gourd, is designed to acknowledge the supremacy and mystery of divine grace and to indicate that even human repentance does not in itself coerce God. Nevertheless, the fact that God desires repentance is a theological point also underscored in this prophetic narrative, even as it is particularly emphasized in other prophetic and historiographical postexilic sources as well.[23] For repentance is the human action that may lead to covenantal reconciliation and to the subsidence of divine wrath, of the vented fury of an unacknowledged deity.

But there is a further aspect of the matter. If the prophets tremble at the reality of imminent divine wrath and desperately warn the people to heed their divinely initiated exhortations, the potential advent of destruction is nevertheless not that most feared of ancient religious realities. This wrath is not the mysterious or irrational eruption of a demonic power or divine vindictiveness into human life, but is rather the manifestation of a forewarned punishment by a just and rational divine sovereign. In short, the prophetic theodicy (with deep pentateuchal roots) maintains that the people of Israel were punished for sinful disregard of its covenantal obligations by an attentive divine judge. Indeed, if anything, the prophets are overly subscribed to this religious interpretation of reality and face the thankless challenge of converting the people's attention to it and to its implications. So considered, the prophets serve as *divinely inspired interpreters of reality from a covenantal perspective.* The historical terrors on Israel's horizon and the natural disasters present and future are thus all raised to supernatural religious significance as signs of a God whose justice is in accord with His powers—and are, therefore, denied as independent manifestations of political adventurism or ecological catastrophe. Belief in God's covenantal providence thus served to transform historical reality from a zone of random evil and meaninglessness to a sphere of order and justice.

The fundamental subordination of reality to the regulation of a divine justice whose principles are articulated in the covenant is thus the ultimate theodicy of classical Israelite prophecy. Characteristically, the classical prophets scanned the historical horizon and the phenomena of nature for the sure signs of divine involvement in Israelite history. For them, history and nature were the potential and recurrently actual arenas of theophany, and it was to the facts and nuances of such theophanies that the prophets were intensely sensitive. Notwithstanding—and this is crucial to their religious consciousness—the prophets did not believe that their acute consciousness of God's involvement in Israel's destiny was meant for them alone, whether as a personal religious experience or as a feature of some private soteriology. Such theophanies were rather considered to be events of divine communication *through them to the entire nation,* for the sake of their collective salvation. For ancient Israelite covenant theology, the terrors of history are the consequences of sinful human actions. The prophets, profoundly aware of this fact, warn or alert the people—at God's insistence —to the implications of sin, repentance, and obedience. By this means they give active voice to what we may characterize as a committed divine immanence. Human sin and earthly disaster, like human obedience and natural beneficence, are locked into a divinely sealed nexus—not as some karmic law of cause and effect, and not even as some natural law of order and balance. In the Bible, sin and punishment are singularly correlated as the distributive (or retributive) personal justice of a sovereign Lord. In this way, the prophets gave profound expression to their belief that the transcendent creator-god was immanently present to Israel's historical existence: warning, judging, forgiving, and punishing. Transcendence of the terrors of historical existence was thus to be achieved solely through an inner-worldly conformity to the stipulations of the covenant.

Through their searing words and, even more fundamentally, through the more august and didactic utterances of the Pentateuch, the deep abyss at the heart of Israel's rupture with mythic consciousness (whereby the qualitative interconnectedness of god–humanity–world was sundered) can be seen to have been bridged by the covenantal principle of divine justice. To the classical prophets, this theodicy was no abstract speculation but a personally shattering awareness rooted in revelation. To them God was overwhelmingly present; there was no escape. But this is only one side of the prophets' pathos. The other aspect is the people's resistance or indifference to their divinely revealed assertions and predictions. Indeed, the prophetic corpus is itself the profound witness to the fact that the people were not always convinced or impressed by the theology of God's covenantal immanence—or at least not in the puristic and dogmatic terms enunciated by the classical prophetic tradition. Thus, we return to the paradoxical divine concern for human acknowledgment, noted earlier, that stands at the root of the prophets' emissary role. And nowhere is this concern—nay, pathos—more poignantly felt than in the vehemently wrathful prophecies of Ezekiel, shortly before the final Judean catastrophe.[24] Repeatedly, at the crescendo of numerous destructive images, which are projected as the just divine consequences of Israel's disobedience, the prophet tells the people that all this will befall them "that they [thereby] know that I am the Lord."

Prophecy and Temporality

Aside from its essential characteristic as a divine enunciation delivered through a human medium, a secondary but no less vital characteristic of the prophetic oracle is that it gives religious significance to time. At first glance the oracle would seem to be fundamentally different in this respect from the covenantal revelation. The covenantal stipulations establish the positive and negative counters of divine beneficence and punishment, the indicia of divine providence and the religious valorization of historical existence; but the oracles are revelations that give meaning to time through its uniquely bipolar structure of divine promise and fulfillment. Repeatedly the two poles of the latter structure establish the framework of significance for the events that occur therein: by projecting a future end point they provide the standard whereby occurrences *within* history may be judged or assessed. Notwithstanding this formal difference, the bipolar structures of the covenantal revelation (reward and punishment) and prophetic oracles (promise and fulfillment) dovetail reciprocally. The covenantal revelation, by virtue of the projected blessings and curses for obedience and disobedience partakes of the bipolar structure of promise and fulfillment, while, correlatively, prophetic oracles predict doom for covenantal disobedience and envision eras of peace and restoration as the reward for obedience. From this perspective, prophetic oracles are linked to and profoundly valorize the same theodicy as the covenantal theology itself.

But what happens when the oracles of approaching dooms or blessings are not fulfilled as expected? Quite obviously, the theological crisis that may unfold at such moments will go significantly beyond the issue of true or false prophecies discussed earlier and encroaches on the basic covenantal theodicy, which maintains that God providentially rewards obedience and punishes evildoers. For this reason, a host of *theologoumena*, casuistic revisions, and new teachings abound in biblical sources that attempt to shore up the potential ruin of the covenantal world view. For its part, the prophetic corpus also responds to this theodicean concern. In terms of the present discussion, the particular solution that counteracts the apparent nonfulfillment of divine oracles through their reinterpretation is of decisive interest. To the discriminating eye, traces of this phenomenon can be detected in a host of pre- and postexilic texts. Amid this welter of (frequently camouflaged) creativity, where divine projects are adjusted to human perceptions and human projects are adjusted to authoritative divine timetables, the final chapters of the late book of Daniel are exemplary and deserve some comment. Herein, numerous older oracles, from the books of Isaiah and Jeremiah in particular, are reapplied and given their "current" historical application—centuries after they were first spoken. The result is that the parameters of significant time frames are extended from the relatively short scope of a few years or generations to the enormous scope of a half-millennium of world history. If, then, the religious presupposition of covenantal theology is that God's will, though transcendent, is not ultimately inscrutable, the corollary presupposition of prophetic oracles is that God's ways may be mysterious but are not ultimately inscrutable—for one thing, because God Himself reveals His plans to humankind; for another, because the apparent failure of certain oracles may actually be due to human errors of application; and finally, because the proper application of ancient oracles (which reorders retroactively the time hitherto believed to be outside God's caring justice) may be secondarily revealed to chosen adepts. This consideration returns us to Daniel, to the commission scenarios reviewed at the outset of this chapter and even to the veritable end of biblical prophecy itself.

Among the many oracles that are cited and reapplied in Daniel 9–12, certainly the most famous and central one is the old divine oracle forecasting seventy years of doom before a national restoration. This oracle was received by the prophet Jeremiah (25:9–12) and had already undergone several reapplications between the seventh and the second century, the time of Daniel. Among the striking features of the reapplication of this Jeremian oracle to the period of Seleucid hegemony over Judea and the desecration of the Temple by the pagan overlords and native collaborators, one must include the fact than an older divine word, which was originally addressed to a prophet and was intended to be comprehensible to all hearers, has been reduced to writing; that it is no longer assumed to mean literally what it appears to say; and, most fatefully, that it requires an angelic intermediary to decode its esoteric sense to a wise man for the sake of a small conventicle of the faithful. Indeed, it is on the basis of their secret knowledge of the true application of the old oracle that Daniel and his fellowship are able to endure their present persecution and martyrdom. They can withstand and even transcend the terrors of history *precisely because* the newly revealed divine timetable vindicates their suffering as part of a cosmic plan.[25]

Daniel is thus the enlightened bearer of the esoteric knowledge of the older prophets of Israel—but he is not himself a prophet. He is not addressed by God directly, but by an angelic intermediary; he does not speak God's oracular words, but reads and studies them; he is not sent to the people, but conveys his gnosis to a cabal of the faithful (self-designated "servants of the Lord"); and he does not warn the people to amend their ways in the hope of changing the course of history, but rather transmits knowledge of the fixed course of historical events which an enlightened person must steadfastly endure. From such contrasts it is evident that a long path has been charted from Amos, at the onset of classical Israelite prophecy, to Daniel, a latter-day inheritor. Indeed, as if to mark this remarkable transformation and the epigonic reliance on older divine words and religious models that marks the end of biblical prophecy, it is significant that the onset of Daniel's initiation into oracular mysteries (in Dan 10:4–19) is described in precisely *those terms* that were originally used to convey the commission of Ezekiel as a spokesman of God.[26] The shift from a prophet commissioned directly with a living oracular word to a sage commissioned indirectly by a divine messenger who instructs him in older divine words could not be more sharply nuanced. For the author of the book of Daniel, then, prophecy has become a religious phenomenon of the past and a subject for ongoing study and reuse by the faithful. Indeed, by the time of this author, but with clear signals centuries earlier, the religious phenomenon of classical prophecy had become part of the tradition of prophecy, and so had become the basis of a new religious consciousness—that of apocalyptic and comparable messianic pieties.[27]

Notes

1. See the discussion with bibliography in Robert Wilson, *Prophecy and Society in Ancient Israel* (Philadelphia: Fortress, 1950) 129–34.

2. Ibid., 98–115.

3. On the latter, see, for example, J. Lindblom, *Prophecy in Ancient Israel* (Philadelphia: Fortress, 1967) chap. 3.

4. See Wilson, *Prophecy and Society,* chaps. 4–5.

5. A valuable exception is that of A. J. Heschel, *The Prophets* (Philadelphia: Jewish Publication Society of America, 1962) esp. chaps. 1, 12, 14, 16, 24–25, 28. The present essay diverges from this work in many respects.

6. Whether Isaiah 6 is a commission or recommission scene has long exercised scholars, but this is not the place for an extended analysis. The interested reader is referred to such discussions as M. Kaplan, "Isaiah 6:1–11," *Journal of Biblical Literature* 45 (1926) 251–59; and J. Milgrom, "Did Isaiah Prophesy during the Reign of Uzziah?" *Vetus Testamentum* 14 (1964) 164–82.

7. See Exod 4:10; 6:12; Jer 1:7 and my discussion in *Text and Texture: Close Readings of Selected Biblical Texts* (New York: Schocken Books, 1979) 67–69.

8. The verb *shalaḥ* ("send") is the key word here, and it recurs in the commission scenes of Exod 3:10; Isa 6:7; Jer 1:7; and Ezek 2:3. See also J. Ross, "The Prophet as Yahweh's Messenger," in *Israel's Prophetic Heritage: Essays in Honor of James Muilenburg*, ed. Bernhard W. Anderson and Walter Harrelson (New York: Harper & Row, 1962) 98–107.

9. See the essay by J. Dan below, chapter 11.

10. For a review of the treatment of this passage in modern scholarship, see W. Roth, "The Story of the Prophet Micaiah (1 Kings 22) in Historical-Critical Interpretation 1876–1976," in *The Biblical Mosaic: Changing Perspectives*, ed. R. M. Polzin and E. Rothman (Philadelphia: Fortress, 1982; Chico, CA: Scholars Press) 105–37.

11. For other examples, see 1 Sam 9 and 1 Kgs 14:1–20.

12. For a full analysis, see my *Text and Texture*, chap. 7 ("Jeremiah 20:7–12: Loneliness and Anguish").

13. For a more extended discussion of these various matters, see my "Israel and the 'Mothers,'" in *The Other Side of God*, ed. Peter L. Berger (Garden City, NY: Doubleday, 1981) 28–47.

14. See my *Text and Texture*, 19–23.

15. I have treated the whole problem of the human amendment and/or reinterpretation of teachings and speeches attributed to God in my *Biblical Interpretation in Ancient Israel* (Oxford: Clarendon Press, 1984).

16. See S. Blank, "Men of God," *Journal of Biblical Literature* 72 (1953) 143; and the more forceful and advanced discussion by Y. Muffs in his "*Tefillatan shel Neviim*," in *Torah Nidreshet*, ed. A. Shapira (Tel Aviv: Am Oved, 1984) 39–87.

17. See Muffs, "*Tefillatan*," 60–64, 67–68.

18. Ibid., 64

19. My use here of the thematic of pathos is different from that explored by Heschel (*The Prophets*, chaps. 12, 15).

20. Notably, J. Milgrom, *Cult and Conscience: The Asham and the Priestly Doctrine of Repentance*, Studies in Judaism in Late Antiquity 18 (Leiden: Brill, 1976).

21. This well-known point has been trenchantly formulated by Y. Kaufmann as the "primacy of morality" over the cult. See his *The Religion of Israel*, trans. and abridged by M. Greenberg (Chicago: University of Chicago Press, 1960; New York: Schocken Books, 1972) 160.

22. See E. Bickerman, *Four Strange Books of the Bible* (New York: Schocken Books, 1967) 29–37.

23. This point has been generally overlooked. See the discussion of I. L. Seeligmann, "Die Auffassung von der Prophetic in der deuteronomischen und chronistischen Geschichtsschreibung (mit einem Exkurs über das Buch Jeremia)," in *Congress Volume: Göttingen, 1977*, Supplements to *Vetus Testamentum* 29 (Leiden: Brill, 1978) 254–84.

24. For a discussion of the content and concerns of the doom oracles of Ezekiel, see my "Sin and Judgment in the Prophecy of Ezekiel," *Interpretation* 38 (1984) 131–50.

25. See my *Biblical Interpretation in Ancient Israel*, 479–95.

26. See my "*Ha-'Ot ba-Miqra*," in *Shenaton: An Annual for the Biblical and Ancient Near Eastern Studies* 1 (1975) 224–25 n. 28.

27. See the discussion by M. Himmelfarb below, chapter 6.

4

Biblical Tradition: Literature and Spirit in Ancient Israel

JOEL ROSENBERG

"BIBLICAL TRADITION," a largely modern term with no real equivalent in the language of ancient Israel, is a name we can give to the sum total of the Hebrew Bible's lore, whether oral or written in origin, whether legal or narrative, whether authorial or the product of a "school"—thus, everything in and behind the text, but excluding commentary on it by later readers.[1] For convenience of discussion, we may consider biblical tradition to have become complete by the formation of a canon—a step which, for all practical purposes, was completed for Palestinian Jews by about the second century of the common era, and very likely some time before that. But we cannot assume the tradition-forming process to have come to an end at that point, nor can we ignore the fact that numerous prior efforts at canonization seem to be in evidence. Each complete literary unit (including whatever might be proved by modern critical method to have been original and Mosaic within Pentateuchal law) is a "canon" of a sort. The Pentateuchal sources, individually and in an edited synthesis, reflect earlier efforts to fix traditions for normative and communal use, each stage involving to some extent condensation, distillation, and selection. At each stage, exclusion of a much wider body of oral and written material seems to have occurred; yet the excluded substratum was not, as it were, frozen out, but continued alongside the definitive formulation as a living force, able to exert its claims at subsequent stages of traditionary development. The canonization process is thus not a unique and unrepeatable event in the history of a religious tradition, but rather a recurrent step in a dynamic process of expansion and contraction that is part of the ongoing discourse of a people and culture.[2] Biblical tradition is its result at one particular juncture.

The biblical textual evidence for earlier stages of canonization remains obscure to the modern observer, and much speculation surrounds the two main canonizing events: King Josiah's discovery and proclamation of a "scroll of instruction" (*sefer ha-torah*), as recorded in 2 Kings 22ff.; and Ezra the Scribe's New Year convocation of returned exiles in Jerusalem around 444 B.C.E., at which "scroll of the teaching of Moses" (*sefer torat Moshe*) was read aloud "with distinctness/with interpretation" (*meforash*), as recorded in Nehemiah 8. Whether the whole or some of our present Pentateuch was publicly instituted on either of those occasions, the exact details of the process continue to elude us, as does the canonic relation of the Pentateuch to the closely kindred narratives of Joshua through 2 Kings, or to the corpus of late books we know as Daniel, Ezra, Nehemiah, and 1 and 2 Chronicles, and, for that matter, to the whole corpus of biblical poetry, wisdom, and prophecy that makes up the rest of the Hebrew Bible. All that we can say is that there is a deep and resonant intertextual relation among the parts that constitute the whole and a kind of traditionary ecology, by which gaps were filled in, obscurities were glossed, and the major bodies of traditionary lore were brought into a kind of dialectical harmony—if harmony it can be called—which postbiblical generations of interpreters, among them the rabbinic and medieval Jewish exegetes, strove to make more explicit.

One thus cannot, properly speaking, understand biblical tradition in isolation from the ways it was appropriated and refashioned in the discourse of postbiblical interpreters, and though the makers and followers of the Jewish Scripture constitute only one among several biblically founded religious cultures of late antiquity, they were perhaps anchored the most firmly in the language and idioms of pre-Hellenistic Palestine (their own Hellenizations notwithstanding) and were, in a sense, canonical centrists. They preferred neither the Pentateuchally restricted canon of the Samaritans nor the more inclusive but conceptually less defined corpus (for "canon" it cannot be called)[3] of the Septuagint Greek translation, which emerged from Egypt from the third century B.C.E. onward and became the basis of the Christian Bibles. The Jewish Scripture is thus by no means identical with what Christianity calls "the Old Testament." It has a character of its own and represents a particular appropriation of religious lore that forms a single system with the various modes of discourse (mishnaic, talmudic, midrashic, exegetical, halakhic, liturgical, poetic, philosophic, and kabbalistic) that were born out of it.

To be sure, when we speak of biblical tradition, we refer to nothing in excess of the Masoretic Bible; at its most elemental, this tradition is exclusively a fabric of words.[4] But the process of tradition formation is not exclusively a literary one, at least in our familiar sense of the word "literary"; and, given the diversity of historical records and discursive systems embodied in the Hebrew Bible and the great disparity in the style, outlook, and concerns of its respective components, one cannot speak of biblical tradition as homogeneous and continuous. Yet a Jew of early post-Hadrianic Palestine saw in biblical tradition something of a systematic whole, a "world," if you will—a coherent and seemingly encyclopedic record of the Israelite past—one, indeed, that purports to be at once a manual of religious instruction, a national covenant, and, by virtue of Genesis 1–11 and Isaiah 2:2–4, among other texts, a history of humanity. What, then, did early postbiblical Jews see when they beheld biblical tradition? How conceptually distinct from their own discourse was it held to be? How does their vision of it stand in relation to what is currently known about the history of biblical literature? Above all, what is the character of this lore as a system of religious knowledge? How did it render the world more coherent for a literate Jew of late antiquity?

The Emergence of the "Postbiblical" Reader

We should remember above all that the term "postbiblical" is a relative one, our perception of which largely depends on our understanding of when the Hebrew Bible as we know it was perceived as a whole entity. As noted earlier, exact understanding of the process of canonization, and so of the concept "canon," has proved elusive. This is not the place to go into the complicated questions that have vexed the scholarship on the subject.[5] Certain practical conclusions of this research, however, can be stated here as a preparation for understanding the Hebrew Bible's intrinsic design—a design that was in some sense already complete before the literature was completed, and certainly long before there was a canon. What is especially striking about the canonization process is how blurred the line is between "biblical" and "postbiblical," how unobtrusive and self-effacing the activity of the canonizers seems to have been—as if the very authority of their action stemmed from its self-evidence and superfluity.

Relevant for present purposes, then, are the following reasonably certain facts. First, the Hebrew Bible was substantially complete by 165 B.C.E., when the book of Daniel (purporting to be prophecies from the time of the Babylonian exile) was written. Second, the only "canon" recognized at that time among all Jewish communities was the Torah (the Pentateuch, or five books of Moses), which had been so acknowledged at least since the mid-fifth century B.C.E. Third, other biblical books acquired nearly comparable sanctity or authority throughout the period of the Second Commonwealth without yet constituting a "canon"—if by that term we mean the result of an official *closure* of the authoritative Scripture.[6] Fourth, something of a tripartite division of authoritative Scripture was acknowledged by Ben Sira's grandson and translator (late second century B.C.E.), who refers to "the law and the prophets and the other books of our fathers" (Sirach, prologue). Fifth, a tradition of a fixed *number* of books is not attested until the first century C.E., namely of "22" (so Josephus, *Against Apion* 1.8.38–42) or "24" (so *4 Ezra* 14:18–48), though the latter source projects the origin of the number back into the days of Ezra and the so called Great Assembly. Sixth, it was not until Elias Levita's *Massoreth ha-Massoreth* (1538) that the present Masoretic order of the books was seen to have originated with Ezra. Seventh, as late as a certain rabbinical discussion at Jamnia (Yavneh) around 90 C.E., the canonical status of certain biblical books seems to have been debated, but it seems increasingly likely that this did not amount to a full-fledged "synod" that aimed at fixing the canon, as was widely maintained in scholarship until recently.[7] Nevertheless, the Pharisaic category of "books that defile the hands" (*m. Yadayim* 3:5; *m. Kelim* 15:6) presupposed some sort of firm definition of the sacred books. *B. Baba Batra* 14b–15a lists the Prophets and the Writings, though in a different order from the Masoretic; it likewise tries to sort out "the Twelve" chronologically and offers an interesting tradition regarding biblical authorship.[8]

In short, there seems to have been no universally recognized action *closing* the Hebrew canon during this time, despite the fact that it had been effectively closed for some time and was widely *perceived* as more or less complete. This curiously loose sense of canonicity, by which a classical era is determined while its continuing reverberations in and traditionary continuity with a present era are affirmed, is rooted in conceptions of Torah that developed in the early rabbinic era—though these conceptions are arguably a working out of processes of traditionary discourse begun within the Torah itself and sustained throughout the Hebrew Bible. The line between biblical and postbiblical was blurred, even as the distinction itself was affirmed, and something of this almost willful ambiguity inheres, as I shall argue later, in the image biblical literature projects of itself. Early rabbinic literature, at any rate, speaks far more of "Torah" than of "Scripture," and the emphasis is far more on continuity than on hieratic discontinuity. "Torah" in rabbinic parlance was more a process than a document: "engaging in Torah" meant teaching, interpreting, reciting, applying, and meditating on the words of Scripture, and, above all, transmitting one's deliberations to a successor generation.

What the Postbiblical Reader Saw

Metaphysical valorizations of Torah, and so of Scripture in general, abound in rabbinic literature:[9] "On three things the world stands: on Torah, on worship, and on acts of kindness" (*m. Abot* 1:1); "Were it not for Torah, heaven and earth could not be sustained" (*b. Pes.* 58a); "If two sit and exchange words of Torah, the Shekhinah (divine presence) dwells with them" (*m. Abot* 3:4); "The Torah says: I was the artist's tool for the Holy One, blessed be He (when the world was made)" (*Gen. Rab.* 1:1); "Turn it, and turn it, for everything is there" (*m. Abot* 5:27). Such encomia went hand-in-hand with exhortations to constant study, recitation, and contemplation of Torah (see *m. Abot* 1:5; 2:19; 4:12). Yet this labor of love was likewise seen as a form of *self*-knowledge: in what was very likely a gnostic turn of thought, rabbinic interpreters likened the commandments of Torah to the limbs and sinews of the human body (*Mak.* 23b), a notion that was to receive a much fuller expansion in kabbalistic and Hasidic literature centuries later. Lore about the alphabet letters and about the human speech apparatus and number system was projected onto the cosmogonic traditions of the Hebrew Bible, which yielded a distinctive linguistic mysticism and delight in cryptography that flourished through the Middle Ages in poetic, theosophic, and pietistic sources, and in the more exoteric legal and midrashic literature.[10]

The mythical and sacral dimensions inherent in this radical esteem of Torah would not have been possible without certain predisposing tendencies within the Hebrew Bible itself. Had the Bible been a legal corpus alone, or a national covenant alone, or a library of ancestral stories alone, or a book of wisdom sayings alone, or a manual of personal piety alone, it would not have mobilized the kind of total commitment to its study and enactment that was demanded by its rabbinic eulogizers. Only by understanding the way the Bible brings these multiple modes of discourse into a complementary relation, with a simultaneously individual and communal application, can we properly understand and evaluate its role as a book of religious knowledge. One could say that its otherwise very this-worldly precepts have been "spiritualized"—provided we do not mean by this any diminution of their concreteness or of their moral, ethical, and political import. Rather, they were made into a kind of traditionary gnosis, a manual of utopian restoration, suited to a people no longer territorially sovereign, whose reliving of Israelite realities was to occur, at least partly, in the realms of hope, dream, and memory. Part, if not most, of this program was capable of realization in the present, through the life of the family, the law court, the community, the houses of prayer and study; part of it was contingent on the sometime operation of the Temple and Aaronide priesthood; part of it was contingent on the anticipated return of the Davidic kingdom and of Israel's position of preeminence among the nations. But whatever the vicissitudes at play, Scripture's chief arena of enactment was the deeds, words, and thoughts of the individual believer, who internalized its stories and heroes, its cycles of time and seasons, its rituals, its sense of holiness and purity, its sensitivity to right and wrong, its rhythms of song and prayer—even its gaps, obscurities, and contradiction. "Not with our ancestors (alone) did YHWH make this covenant, but with us, the living, every one of us who is here today" (Deut 5:3). Already within Torah, its immortality is hinged on the activity of its heirs.

The Hebrew Bible, thus, did not present itself simply as a book to be read but as a text to be *reread*. This stress on repetition is rooted in the Torah's covenant function: the obligation to store in the Tabernacle a copy of the Sinai covenant and the supplements to it revealed in the wilderness encampments of Israel and the further obligation to renew this covenant regularly by public recitation of the laws and stories and by public pledge to its demands (see esp. Exod 34:27ff. and Deut 31:9–10, 16–30). These requirements reflect covenant idioms of ancient Near Eastern, not specifically Israelite, origin.[11] But in late monarchic, exilic, and postexilic Israel, this principle of repeated perusal and actualization of law was deepened and personalized, enriched by an accumulation of narrative, wisdom speculation, literary prophecy, and devotional material. Pentateuchal law cannot, properly speaking, be termed a civil code; it is not addressed exclusively to jurists and legal specialists. It is, rather, despite the often technical nature of its stipulations, first and foremost a component in a book of lay instruction. It was this function that helped to determine the nature and scope of the extra-pentateuchal biblical literature that was collected in the ensuing centuries.

As early as the Deuteronomist, and undoubtedly much earlier, personal rehearsal of the Mosaic teachings was a desired norm (Deut 6:6–7; 11:19–21; Josh 1:8). The exhortation to ceaseless study and meditation merged as a matter of course with wisdom and devotional texts that praised the scholar and sage, and projected a mythology of primordial Wisdom (*ḥokhmah*) and of a victorious fruition of the Torah's life-enhancing virtues (Ps 1:1–2; 19:8–11; Prov 3:18; 8:22ff. etc.). The Torah became ever more ancient, every more ubiquitous.

Despite the transcendence and holiness that rabbis ascribed to biblical tradition, their own operations on it were curiously atomistic and anti-contextual. Their deliberations were rarely concerned with units longer than a verse.[12] Each moment of biblical history was made to seem simultaneous with every other. ("There was no 'before' or 'after' in the Torah" was a commonly accepted principle.) Through a close and imaginative exegesis, attuned to word and even letter, biblical tradition took on concreteness and specificity of a distinctly Hellenistic sort, creating in the process certain strands of cultural and religious discourse that the makers of the Hebrew Bible might not have anticipated. Anonymous characters were identified with the known; time, place, and context of scenes were filled in; the presence of a superfluous "the" or "and" was read as indicating some extra stipulation not mentioned by the text; repeated commandments, or the presence of multiple clauses within a single one, were said to be so recorded, for example, "to compound the reward of the righteous in the world to come." Hermeneutic rules were devised that resembled those employed by the Hellenistic academies in the interpretation of Homer. Unusual words, archaisms, and grammatical forms were glossed. Observations on biblical language and rhetoric were made. Above all, new relations were discovered among the various texts of Scripture: narratives were illumined by quotations of psalm and prophecy; doublets were compared and contrasted; contradictions were spotted and resolved. The biblical text was turned in upon itself and made into an ever more organic and comprehensive entity.

The atomism of rabbinic exegesis had the paradoxical effect of reinforcing the unity of Scripture, though often at the expense of the dialectical tensions and polyphonic counterpoint that were the magic and art of biblical storytelling. At least one preoccupation of this exegesis, however, was wholly appropriate to the compositional technique of biblical literature: the verbal echo.[13] We shall return to the motivic use of words in its proper place, but here it may suffice to observe that the rabbis read the Hebrew Bible, so to speak, concordantially —alerted to verbal cross-reference and to the particular grammatical and syntactical musculature of each term. Words and verses had, in effect, independent careers in the postliterary oral tradition, which may reflect, in some cases, similarly independent careers in the preliterary.

The early postbiblical Jewish reader, then, defined the authoritative Scripture in several overlapping, at times incompatible, ways. Recognizing at least cultically the notion of "sacred writings" (*kitvey ha-qodesh*), under the category of "books that defile the hands," the reader nevertheless treated its exact definition and the identity of its definers with a certain delicacy. The sacred writings were known as such, in the reader's estimation, by common consensus more than by rabbinical decree. Rules concerning their reproduction, handling, and storage could be formulated and observed quite independently of understanding their intrinsic traditionary factors underlying their sacred status. To characterize the whole of Scripture, the reader rarely needed a word more precise than the very general and metonymic term "Torah." In the eyes of its interpreters, Torah was made to be commented upon—so destined, one could say, since creation. Its daily repetition, in prayer and study, was seen as its fulfillment, though an even riper realization might be held to lie in the future. It may seem odd that, among the early generations that viewed the emergence of a complete sacred Scripture, Torah could be both revered so transcendently and approached so familiarly. Yet this paradox lies at the heart of the tradition-forming process. Torah archaized and Torah contemporized are two aspects of the same interpretive activity.

What the Modern Reader Sees

Properly speaking, biblical tradition, as seen by its postbiblical Jewish transmitters, presented a double aspect: as a codification of collectively acknowledged history (in its function as a "Written Torah") and as an object of contemplation, a font of wisdom, a text to be deciphered and expounded (in its function as "Oral Torah"). The contradiction between these domains—one a perceived past, the other a theoretical and eternal present—was borne lightly. It was rarely, if ever, in question that the past could become thought—or, in modern parlance, "goods to think with." But the more analytical and technical the rabbinic interpretation, the more it presupposed a shared past, and a whole composite picture of that past was inevitably ready at hand in the minds of interpreters and readers. Despite the numerous ways the dialectical motions of the text were (often correctly) perceived, biblical tradition still held its chronological integrity: Noah still preceded Abraham, and Abraham preceded Jacob, who, in turn, preceded Moses, and all the former-born were not only seen as prior to the latter-born, but also were understood as present in the *memories* of the latter. Even if there was "no before and no after" in the Torah, where derivation of its atemporal wisdom was concerned, the whole venture of interpretation depended on the armature of historical time, on the inviolability of Scripture's purported chronology.

Quite a different set of assumptions governs the way a conscientious modern reader approaches the Hebrew Bible and biblical tradition. (We may here take "conscientious modern" to mean "willing to be guided by modern critical method and its findings," and therefore, "nonfundamentalist.") A nonfundamentalist reader, even one approaching the text out of religious motives, tries to understand the Bible as a record of human experience, therefore as a form of subjective expression, as a product of several eras and milieus, and as an evolving interpretation of Israelite and Jewish history. Turning to standard critical commentaries and histories, this reader will soon discover that the majority of biblical stories were put into written form long after the events they purportedly represented; that there were strata of authorship (if also much disagreement among modern observers about their exact boundaries);[14] that there was probably a long oral history underlying the written text (if also no way of understanding its contours short of sorting out all available bits of textual information on a given period, event, person, or theme, and somewhat arbitrarily deciding what is "early" and "late").[15] This reader will learn that the oldest nonlegal materials in the Bible are poetic—usually *fragments* of poems or songs, none older than Moses or Joshua, and most quite a bit younger. This reader will discover that psalms and prophetic oracles often preserve traditions differently from the narratives they refer to and therefore serve as a useful control for our understanding of the narrative material and vice-versa, and that the same can be said of archival and legal data.

Turning to archaeology, the modern reader will find essentially a new textual discipline.[16] The "text" here is an array of carbon-dated layers of excavation, all revealing aspects of the material history of ancient Canaan and environs, with little or nothing by way of explicit confirmation of the biblical record but with a rich fund of material for insight about how Canaanites and Israelites must have lived—their probable patterns of settlement and trade, their languages and dialects, their alphabets and their cultic and religious artifacts, their art and architecture, their epistles, records, and laws, and, even among the Canaanites of the north Syrian coast (at ancient Ugarit), their fiction and mythology.[17] However literary such remains might be, they are mute in one important respect—their material accidence, their apparent absence of cultural succession, and thus their inverse relation to biblical tradition (here considered in all of its Jewish, Christian, and perhaps Islamic variants), which precisely strove, successfully, to overcome the silent destiny of rocks and shards. In this sense, archaeology, however much it might uncover spiritual creations, cannot comprehend the Hebrew Bible's spiritual reality quite so well as the Bible's own intentional structure and unfolding. Biblical tradition is in a sense preinterpreted. The intentionality, the internal exegesis, the "argument," as it were, of that quiet order must be confronted.

So the conscientious modern reader comes perhaps to consult the realm of literary study as a means of unlocking the secrets of biblical thought. The past fifteen years have wrought something of a revolution in literary study of the Bible, both in quantity and in sophistication—though, indeed, the field has grown enough to become pedantic and technical as well as over-aestheticized and unwarrantedly abstract.[18] What literary study *has* shown effectively, however, is that we are confronting in the Hebrew Bible—whatever its claims as a document of revelation—various types of human discourse, each with its genres, rules, and conventions, each with its particular logic, cadence, coherence, and rhetorical purpose within the larger composition. All of these distinctions are useful, indeed essential, provided we remain aware that the literary forms are saying *something* and that this something is perhaps best understood at the widest level of textual organization—that of canon and completed text. Again, as with archaeology, we are drawn back to the intentionality and argument of biblical tradition. What is the tradition, with all its moments and movements, finally *saying*?

The critical disciplines mentioned here each occupy a different segment of the tradition-forming process: archaeology, the pretraditional archaic past, the realm perhaps of incipient biblical tradition; literary study, the purportedly posttraditional literary record, the realm of matured tradition; and tradition history, the largely inferred realm in between. For all that they can contribute to our understanding of biblical tradition, these modes of approach cannot view it in the way its makers expected it to be viewed, by an engaged and participating reader. This is both the strength and the weakness of critical method. Being attuned to the ways of human talk, it can spot coherence in biblical tradition that its religiously engaged readers are not always free to see; it can speak self-consciously of discourse and its properties; it can articulate the groundrules of tradition transmission and interpretation and can try to reconstruct the history of the tradition's elements. What it can do only in the most approximate way, however, is to follow the full subjective course of a line of thought within the tradition, enter the tradition's way of thinking, yield to its insistence that its interpreters make their own examined lives part of the text—asking its questions, living its contradictions. The present overview, rooted, I hope, in critical method, must leave those steps largely untraveled. We must content ourselves here with what I shall call a descriptive physiognomy.

A Descriptive Physiognomy of Biblical Tradition

What, then, is biblical tradition? What follows is a descriptive survey of some of its traits. We shall proceed in a discontinuous way, allowing the text's features to register each on its own terms. We can call this a "physiognomy," because it will at all times be rooted in specific features of the text, but it is traditionary, not specifically literary, processes that will be of special interest.

* * *

The Hebrew Bible, by the traditional count, consists of twenty-four books, though the division underlying this number is not identical to the way the books are arranged and labeled in today's printings of the Masoretic Text and its translations. Another enumeration is found in the writings of Josephus and of certain church fathers (among them, Origēn, Eusebius, Cyril of Jerusalem, Epiphanius, Jerome, and Augustine), for whom the books totaled twenty-two.[19] It is not clear how current this numbering was among Jewish readers, but the number's correspondence to the number of letters in the Hebrew alphabet suggests a Jewish basis for the custom, for alphabetology was a common motif not only in midrash but, indeed, in the acrostic psalms, proverbs, and lamentations.[20] Such an alphabetically defined Scripture expressed a sense of encyclopedic comprehensiveness and a preoccupation with language quite appropriate to readers of a body of texts so steeped in wordplay and verbal legerdemain.

* * *

The collection is, indeed, a monument to literacy itself, which essentially arose in its present form with the rise of the northwest Semitic alphabets (precisely in the centuries in which biblical literature itself arose), which permitted written communication of far greater ease and suppleness, and on a vaster social scale, than the cumbersome wedge and hieroglyphic syllabaries of the great Near Eastern empires had permitted. Although the present trend in scholarship has been to emphasize the role of oral processes in the formation of biblical tradition, it is clear that the spread of alphabet literacy has had something to do with the Hebrew Bible's implicit plea for traditionary literacy and that the relentless, almost addictive, punning and alliteration that we find among Israel's prophets, poets, and storytellers was more than a quirk, a stutter, or a decorative artifice. It was the currency of thought itself, the guarantor of intelligibility and form, binding events, assisting memory, providing surprise evaluations of character, of intention, of effect. Later rabbinic and mystical conceptions of the preexistence of language, of Torah, of sacred text, and of divine names, are not simply Hellenistic or medieval colorations; they represent, rather, efforts to make explicit a philosophy of language and signification already long present in Scripture itself.[21]

* * *

There is no basis for drawing a sharp line between the God lore and the human lore assembled in the twenty-two or twenty-four books. Person, family, tribe, league, state, settled world, cosmos, the temporal order, and, as it were, the divine perspective are presented in the Hebrew Bible as more or less an integrated system. So, at any rate, did they become in the de facto unity of the canon. Yet this unity was the fruit of centuries of traditionary evolution, so we cannot simply regard it as imposed from without. Because the components of biblical literature had, in some sense, demanded each other, had been called into being by the dialectic of an interpretive history, we cannot view the unity of the canon as imposed from without. It is this interpretive history, united in and, so to speak, flattened by the text, that formed a single and simultaneous reality in the spiritual universe of the Jewish believer. If the flatness of the text muted somewhat the dialectical tensions of biblical tradition, the notions of rabbinic and medieval Jewish interpretive history brought them alive again, even as the liturgical trajectory of daily Jewish prayer reharmonized and reintegrated them.[22] When one speaks of the "spiritual" reality of biblical tradition in Judaism, one is dealing at all times with the relations of texts and words that form the substance of tradition as such. Even when met in the rhythmic and meditative cadences of Jewish prayer, the biblical *traditum* carries the full weight of its interpretive history, including, in however attenuated a form, the weight of its particular moment in the pretextual, preliterary history of the Hebrew Bible. As such, there is no particular hierarchy to the traditionary information embodied in the Hebrew Bible. It is impossible to state a biblical theology without stating a biblical politics, a biblical order of time, a biblical portrait of the human body, a biblical typology of the household, a biblical morality, and a biblical anthropology.

* * *

Torah, Prophets, and Writings express, to be sure, something of a descending hierarchy of traditionary succession: from *the* prophet, par excellence, Moses; to prophets who arose ad hoc when there was none to lead or teach; to the singers, scribes, and sages who strove to lead and teach, more consistently and dependably, when there was none to prophesy.[23] The three segments of "TaNaKh" thus require and complete each other. Literally (and literarily) speaking, Torah, Prophets, and Writings constitute a linear sequence. But insofar as the history of the literary casting of the Pentateuchal tradition runs concurrently with the history of the remaining biblical literature, we can say that Torah, Prophets, and Writings evolved simultaneously.[24] Almost no book of the Hebrew Bible is devoid of the most archaic elements, the most fundamental and normative of ideas. Every book has an exegetical *raison d'être*, a role in the intertextual economy of the tradition.

* * *

The Pentateuch and Former Prophets form a single continuous story, bound in an insistently chronological succession of "generations": of the cosmos, of humanity, of national ancestors, of national leaders, and, lastly, of dynastic houses. Each generation of narrated history is told more realistically, though with no fewer symbolic and typological resonances. Starting with God alone in the universe, the narration depicts the gradual growth and complicating of the natural and social order, the ever greater detail and material encumbrance of the created world. Yet the progression is in another sense cyclic: from individual to household, to family, to tribe, to intertribal order; then, at the birth of national order, a return to a paradigmatic individual—to the king in his household as both the exceptional man and the "Everyman" of the kingdom. It is perhaps only in the protective shade of royal institutions that speculation about the fate of the individual could arise in ancient Israel. It seems no accident that the biblical lore that is most spoken, from the vantage point of the individual, is found chiefly in those books that appear under the rubric of royal authorship: the Psalms of David; the Song of Songs, Proverbs, and Ecclesiastes, all three ascribed to Solomon. This material exists in a certain complementary tension both with that of Genesis through 2 Kings and with the oracular discourse of the Latter Prophets. If the narrative history weighs its characters' motives and emotions by their terse words and conspicuous deeds, the royal books give free reign to the conversing subject—in exile and despair, in triumph and exultation, in love and passion, in the role of instructing parent, in the ruminations of old age. As divine subjectivity dominates the discourse of prophets,[25] human subjectivity dominates that of kings. Only the book of Job (rabbinically ascribed to the authorship of one who was at the same time Israel's most reluctant prophet and its most reluctant ruler: Moses) allows human and divine subjectivity to confront each other headlong.

* * *

Perhaps the most fundamental alternation of discourse in the Hebrew Bible is that between poetry and prose.[26] Torah, although it selectively integrates poetry into its total fabric, consists chiefly of a prose tradition. The Former and Latter Prophets form a complementary and interlocking prose and poetic tradition, respectively. The ratio of these two modes in the Writings is fairly even: Psalms, Proverbs, Song of Songs, Lamentations, Job, and Ecclesiastes being mostly poetic; Ruth, Esther, Daniel, Ezra, Nehemiah, and 1 and 2 Chronicles being mostly prose. The chiefly sacral, dynastic, and eschatological history represented in these latter books forms, in effect, a counter-tradition to the prose tradition of Genesis through 2 Kings. They represent the experience and hopes of exilic Israel; Genesis through 2 Kings, those of preexilic Israel. If we suspend judgment concerning the placing of Ruth, which, as one of the Five Megillot, appears amid poetic books, but which, as a historical book, sometimes appears between Judges and 1 Samuel, we can see that the Writings divides neatly into a prose half and a poetic half and therefore that the two prose traditions (Genesis–2 Kings; Esther–2 Chronicles) effectively sandwich the poetic tradition (the Latter Prophets; Psalms, Proverbs, etc.). The role of parenthetic interpolations in the prose tradition is exactly reversed: in the prose tradition, poetic oracles and *gnomoi* are interpolated; in the poetic tradition, prose narratives are interpolated or affixed as bracketings.

* * *

Considered in terms of its other alternations of discourse, the first prose tradition is a complex weave. Its narrative is riddled throughout with non-narrative material—poetic oracles, proverbs, etiological rubrics, law, genealogy, itinerary, traditions of sacred sites, namings of people and places. At times it seems as if the nonnarrative elements are the digression and the narrative the body. At other times, as with genealogies, it seems as if the narrative itself were the digression, sandwiched between the archival junctures it explains. If the Torah is a law book, then the narratives are commentaries on the laws: the Garden story on the law of procreation; the Cain and Abel story on the law of fugitives; the Noah story on the Noachian laws; the Abraham cycle on the law of circumcision; the Jacob cycle on the law of the thigh sinew; the Exodus cycle on the laws of Passover, the offering of firstfruits, and redemption of the firstborn; the Sinai narrative on the giving of the Ten Commandments and the covenant code, with its emphasis on treatment of slaves and former slaves, and on the civil code of the freeborn; the Tabernacle narratives on the laws of the sanctuary and the Aaronide priesthood, and on the so-called Holiness Code; the plague stories on the laws of disease and purification; stories of sin and rebellion on the laws of atonement; stories of early Israelite conquests on the laws of military organization and land inheritance; the story of Moses' last days on the Deuteronomic code.[27]

* * *

Though the representation of narrative time seems firmly subordinated to a genealogical and generational succession throughout Genesis–2 Kings, the actual progression from any one juncture to the next is anything but uniform: dream, oracle, flashback, redundancy, anticipatory information, resumptive repetition, simultaneity, tautological equivalance, and the like, all serve to jumble and complicate the narrative time, to steal away the artificial clarity gained by the chronological framework. Time proceeds unevenly and circuitously. The generations succeed each other, but the unresolved conflicts of the former ones resurface again and again in the lives of the latter ones. Contrary to common preconception (raised to the absurdity of theory by Thorleif Boman),[28] the biblical sense of time is not truly forward-moving, but cyclical, repetitive, laden with intertextual ironies.

The following passage will help to illustrate the literary complexities of the traditionary montage underlying a narrative:

> Israel took all of these cities. Israel dwelt in all the cities of the Amorite in Heshbon and in all its dependent regions. For Heshbon was the city of Sihon.
> (King of the Amorite he was: he fought with the first king of Moab, and took all his land from his hand up to Arnon.) Therefore do parablers say:

> > Come, Heshbon, be built,
> >   be established, O city of Sihon,
> > For a fire has gone out from Heshbon,
> >   a flame from the district of Sihon,
> > It has devoured the cities of Moab,
> >   the ba‘alim of the high places of Arnon.
> > Woe to thee, Moab,
> >   thou art lost, O people of Chemosh!
> > He has made his sons refugees,
> >   and his daughters captives
> >   —to the Amorite king
> > Sihon.
> > We have shot it to death
> >   —Heshbon as far as Dibon,
> > We have laid it to waste unto Nophah,
> >   as far as Medeba!
> > (Num. 21:25–30)

The three layers of quotation here—the story's narrator ("Israel took all of these cities . . ."); the archival annotator ("King of the Amorite he was . . ."); and quoted "parable" ("'Come, Heshbon, be built . . . !'")—together epitomize the irony of conquest and occupation. The king who is displaced is shown in parable as the erstwhile displacer. A prophecy of Sihon's victory has become his epitaph. The "parablers" speak on three levels: as riddlemakers (asking who can understand this image which is not yet realized fact); as oraclers (whose oracle is remembered years after it has been realized as historical fact); and as proverbists (coining the byword in the gossip of the nations, the image that has become fate in the discourse of later generations). The Israelite displacers must in their turn live with the volatility of a conquest that hinges on their own fluctuating worthiness before the one true Lord of the land, YHWH. All of these historical ironies are compressed into a few verses of prose and poetry.[29]

A similar ironizing can be viewed in the manner in which kingship is treated in the prose tradition. The outer lineaments of the narratives of national leadership in Judges, 1 and 2 Samuel, and 1 and 2 Kings conform to certain key themes in the poetic tradition's lore of kingship (especially in Psalms), which in its turn is rooted in a mythology of divine and earthly enthronement found among a great many cultures in the ancient Near East.[30] The king, like the divine protagonist of myth, is first a warrior, arising in a tense historical hour when chaos threatens the peace of the kingdom; enemies gather at the borders; they laugh and scoff; the councils are in an uproar. But, answering both to divine call and public clamor, the young warrior steps forth. At first he hesitates: he experiences a "dark night of the soul"; he is reassured, however, and comes to trust in YHWH. He is anointed in secret by a prophet and then proclaimed a *nagid* ("prince") to the people. He then sallies forth, in martial splendor and battle regalia, to meet the enemy, the cries of public approbation following him into the field. In some versions of the kingly tradition, he experiences setbacks in some of his initial engagements: he is hunted for his life; he despairs of refuge; he cries out for help; but he trusts in YHWH; and, rewarded for his trust, he rallies. Sooner or later, he routs the foe, amid claps of thunder and riotous shouting. He engages them, stuns them, breaks their bands, shatters their weapons, throws them into panic and disarray, and sends them scattering. The victorious king now returns amid the joyous cries, the beating of timbrels and the clanging of crescent bells, the huzzahs and ululations of the populace. He proceeds straightaway to the sanctuary, where he lays the spoils of victory and where he deposits the laws of his kingdom, as if promulgated anew. He purifies the sanctuary and reinaugurates its service. Proceeding to his throne, he is greeted by his bride, where, in sacred union, they assume rule over the kingdom: inaugurating the New Year, guaranteeing the turning of the times and seasons, fructifying the womb of earth, feeding the populace, encouraging procreation, and providing the conditions that make for generational continuity, for life and culture, as such.

* * *

The prose tradition, however, severely qualifies, almost satirizes, the psalmodic themes of sacral kingship that it incorporates. The people, in their weakness and venality, clamor for a king; they are warned by a prophet against the evils of monarchy; they persist in their vulnerability and sloth; pretenders to the throne arise and exact the cost of their dreams and fantasies on the lives of the populace; the people persist, and grudgingly the prophet allows a candidate to emerge; the disarray of the councils is the shame of the people; his emergence as king is contested; he is carried into battle by an especially crude and grotesque ecstatic rage; he routs the enemy only some of the time; his joyous return is marred by jealousies and antagonisms; the queen does not greet the king; or she greets him but their rapport is not good and they do not cohabit; or they cohabit, but the union is illicit; or she bears the king a son and the child dies; or she bears successfully, but the other children rebel; the succession is marred by rivalry; and the peace of the kingdom is continually threatened. The idealized kingship of the poetic tradition supplies the form but not the substance of the Hebrew Bible's monarchic history. Messianic prophecy and postexilic eschatology project an image of an idealized kingdom, but the daily reality of Israel never ceases to haunt this artificial perfection: the reality of master and slave, employer and worker, thief and wayfarer, debtor and widow, usurper and orphan. The utopian and the unredeemed are bound as one.

* * *

Units of biblical tradition have received further definition and qualification by their arrangement into symmetries.[31] Symmetries occur throughout the Bible. They comprise poetic couplets ("These are the generations of *heaven and earth* once they were created, / on the day that YHWH God made *earth and heaven*" [Gen 2:4]), legal maxims ("The *shedder* of *blood of a human*, / by a *human* his *blood* will be *shed*" [Gen 9:6]), episodes (see 2 Sam 11:19–25), stories (Gen 2–3; 6–9), story cycles (Gen 12–25; 25–36), and whole books (Job; Ruth; et al.). Symmetries are a principle for the arrangement of biblical books, as I shall suggest below. The symmetries are rarely perfect, rarely closed, static structures. Almost always some member of a symmetry rebels and spawns a new substructure, teaching something additional about the whole. If symmetries have a meaning, they can perhaps be said to express admirably well the Bible's sense of reciprocal justice. They show the protagonist reaping as he sows. They show the return of the repressed. They show the end in the beginning. But, considered simply as an expositional device, as a means of traditionary enjambment, symmetry serves other functions. It is a memory aid to storytellers. It is a mode of parenthetic interpolation. It, too, represents a structure of quotation: the innermost terms are "quoted" by the outermost. It was the great accomplishment of biblical tradition historians during the past few decades to have shown the Bible's patterns of traditionary infixing—a profound and radical means of traditionary revision whereby the addition of a word, a quotation, an etiological rubric,[32] a proverb, or even a genealogical datum,[33] influenced the meaning of the received tradition in fundamental ways.[34]

* * *

The Torah is a symmetry of sorts. Genesis is archaic history, ending with the last prepolitical, prehistoric, prenational generation. Exodus is a national epic of "exile," portraying a time when Israel's main existence was as slaves, wayfarers, and former slaves in lands surrounding Canaan. Leviticus, which is said to begin properly, at least in terms of source, at Exodus 25:1 and to end at Numbers 10:28, is part of a Sinai traditionary complex, prefaced by the Sinai pericope proper (Exod 19–24), and suffixed (at a point marked, for reasons unclear, by inverted letter *nuns*) by a resuming wilderness cycle that extends over the rest of Numbers and reaches into the narrative at the end of Deuteronomy. This wilderness material thus stands parallel to the exodus cycle of Exodus 1–18, continuing the national exilic epic. Deuteronomy, for its part, is parallel to Genesis: as Genesis ends with the last pre-exodus generation, Deuteronomy begins with the first post-exodus generation; as Genesis ends with the archaic poetry of Jacob's blessing of the tribes, Deuteronomy ends with the archaic poetry of Moses' departing words (Deut 32:1–43) and his blessing of the tribes (Deut 33). (2 Samuel, we note, similarly ends with the protagonist's poetic "last words.") The primeval history of Genesis 2–11 begins in the Garden of Eden and ends in the dispersal of the nations. The ancestral history of Genesis 12–50 begins with the entry into the promised land and ends in exile in Egypt. Deuteronomy begins and ends in the wilderness on the verge of Israel's reentry to the land. If Noth's revision of classical source criticism (1943) is correct, that is, if we have here an interlocking of two great narrative compositions—a "D-work" (Deuteronomy–2 Kings) and a "P-work" (Genesis–Numbers)—then both Genesis and Deuteronomy are prefatory. Deuteronomy is the archaic prehistory of settled Israel, just as Genesis is the archaic prehistory of confederate Israel.

* * *

It is essential that the Torah end in a conditional mood. Deuteronomy 27–30 presents a full tableau of the blessings and curses of civilized existence, sets them before Israel, and bids them choose. There is no Hexateuch, as von Rad has argued, no salvation history (*Heilsgeschichte*) in any permanent sense. Salvation and disaster, disaster and salvation, relentlessly succeed each other. Prior to the exile, at least, all is contingent on Israel's behavior.

* * *

The tradition's preoccupations are best seen in the disproportions of its narratives. The greatest narrative space is lavished on the generations of Moses and David, with Solomon, Saul, Samuel, Joshua, Joseph, Jacob, and Abraham as runners-up. Moses is the dominant figure of the most sacred corpus, but David is allotted more total narrative space, as well as being the attributive author and subject of most of Psalms. Moses and David are regarded as parallel figures in midrash—both having begun their careers as shepherds; both having shepherded Israel; each being the elect of prophets and kings, respectively (*Exod. Rab.* to Exod 3:1). In the literary montage of Genesis–2 Kings, each serves as founding figure of the two main institutional phases of ancient Israel's depicted history: Moses at the birth of the confederation, David at the birth of the dynastic monarchy. Genesis as pre-Mosaic and 1–2 Kings as post-Davidic history thus exhibit a certain parallelism. It is further suggested by the larger pattern of books: Solomon is both Israel's most worldly-wise king (as suggested both by 1 Kings 3–11 and Ecclesiastes) and her most "paradisic" figure (as suggested by Song of Songs). The story of the building of Solomon's Temple bears motifs in common with the creation story. The history of Israel's ancestors (Gen 11–50) and that of Solomon's successors (1 Kgs 12–2 Kgs 25) stand in a certain parallel, each coordinated by a formulaic temporal scheme: Genesis of "generations" (*toledot*), 1–2 Kings of reigns. The promises to the patriarchs in Genesis are shown to be realized in the days of Solomon (see 1 Kgs 3:8, 4:20–21) and to be whittled away in the reigns of his successors. It was noted earlier that Genesis, Deuteronomy, and 2 Samuel each end with a poetic supplement representing the "last words" of the respective protagonists. 2 Kings does not have a poetic supplement, unless the (preexilic) Latter Prophets be taken as such—for they span the same segment of time.

* * *

If Moses and David are in some respects parallel figures, they are in other respects opposites. Moses is a reluctant leader, David an ambitious one; Moses is humble, David self-promoting; Moses is clumsy of tongue (Exod 4:10), David a maker of songs and a genius of public relations; Moses is a prophet who challenged a king, David a king who subverted the institutions of the prophets; Moses' grave site is unknown, David's grave site is Mount Zion; Moses yielded to a successor from another tribe, David sired a dynasty; Moses wished for collective leadership (Num 11:29), David centralized it; Moses administered before a traveling sanctuary, David planned a permanent one. The chief institutional polarities of ancient Israel's pre-exilic history are present in these two polar figures.

* * *

Tradition historians have seen in the Mosaic and Davidic complexes two fundamentally different traditionary stocks, one be-speaking confederate values, the other monarchic.[35] One cannot, however, speak simply of promonarchic and antimonarchic tendencies, for the two traditionary stocks are inextricably bound up with each other. The Sinai complex, which includes the oldest confederate legal code (Exod 20–24), also incorporates enthronement motifs and serves as the setting for Tabernacle traditions that stem from monarchic and exilic times. The history of the monarchy, on the other hand, interpolates the confederate perspective in a variety of ways: by showing both the Davidic and the northern Israelite throne as fallible; by showing prophets occupying a pivotal role in the crises of the monarchy; by showing the ebbing power of the kings; and, in general, by embodying the Deuteronomistic (and so-called Elohistic) principles of conditional covenant and reciprocal justice.

* * *

Despite their integral—indeed, dialectical and symphonic—relation throughout Genesis–2 Kings, the two moods of the tradition (sometimes called "conditional" and "unconditional" covenants) reflect two main phases of Israel's institutional history: confederate and monarchic. (Noth has spoken of Israelite and Judean, "Rachelide" and "Leahide" traditions.) Prophetic critics of the monarchy harkened back to confederate days, eulogized the exodus and wilderness days, valorized the ethical aspects of Israel's covenant somewhat at the expense of the royal and cultic. Some tradition historians have spoken of a Mosaic and a Davidic covenant. The Abrahamic covenant, because of its strong association with the Hebronite milieu of the pre-Jerusalem Davidic court, has been seen as a part of the Davidic covenant tradition,[36] but the Abraham cycle (Gen 11:27–25:18) in fact carefully integrates the two senses of covenant: Genesis 15 speaking of a sojourn for Israel in Egypt, a four-generation cycle of iniquity and punishment (see Exod 20:5) for the land of Canaan, and an apparently moral *quid pro quo* underlying Israel's right to the land; Genesis 17, in turn, speaking of Israel as an "everlasting" kingdom with everlasting tenure of the promised land (17:7–8)—Abraham as a forebear of kings (17:6)—and projecting conditions of prosperity and security that most resemble those of the Solomonic era (despite the alleged "P" origin of Gen 17). The two covenant episodes are parallel in the Abraham cycle's symmetrical structure.

* * *

If the Abraham cycle concentrates on the parent–child relation and on succession of a favored heir, the Jacob cycle and its derivative Joseph story concentrate on the sibling relation and on the tribal and regional rivalries it bespeaks. The story of the rivalry of Jacob and Esau (Israel and Edom) frames the story of vying and conniving between Jacob and Laban (Israel and Aram/Syria), which, in turn, frames the story of the procreative rivalry among Jacob's wives and concubines. If the male rivalries of the cycle express Israel's relations with its Semitic neighbors to the northeast and east, the rivalry between Leah and Rachel expresses the relation of northern and southern, or confederate and Davidic, Israel; that between the wives and concubines, the rivalry of central and outying tribal territories or between reigning and subservient tribes. Rivalry likewise appears in a less elaborated form in the Abraham cycle: between Abraham's herdsmen and Lot's; between Sarah and Hagar; implicitly, between Isaac and Ishmael.

* * *

Abraham's journey recapitulates the entry to and the exodus from Egypt. The altars he builds at the beginning of the cycle correspond to certain centers of cultic life to the north and to the south of Jerusalem; the altar he builds at Mount Moriah near the end of the cycle was associated by the Chronicler and by later Jewish tradition with the Jerusalem Temple mount. Abraham, thus, can be said to cover periphery and center of the promised land. His border agreement with Lot (the ancestor of Moab and Ammon) anticipates later Israel's relation to its eastern neighbors; that with Abimelech, the "Philistine" king of Gerar (an anachronism, for the Philistines did not exist in the land in the days of Abraham), Israel's relation to the western coastal plain. Abraham's journey originates in Syria, crosses Canaan to Egypt, later to Philistia, and ends with him settled in the Hebron/Beersheba region and sending back to Syria for a kindred bride for Isaac (Gen 24). Most of Israel's later history, as well as most of its socioeconomic patterns (servitude and independence, seminomadism, sheepherding, cattle raising, farming, village life and city life), is prefigured in the patriarchal cycles of Genesis.

* * *

If Genesis and 1–2 Kings are parallel in certain formal respects, as noted earlier, Genesis and 1–2 Samuel have even more compelling similarities:

both are matchless narratives; both focus on the domestic life of their heroes; both are preoccupied with inheritance and succession; and both are dominated by Garden story and Cain-and-Abel motifs (temptation and sin; retribution; exile; sibling rivalry and fratricide; loss or exile of a son; note also the violating and dishonoring of a daughter). Both books manifest subtle causal patterns, extending across several story cycles, based on the notion of reciprocal justice. Abraham and Sarah's mistreatment and banishment of an Egyptian servant (Hagar) and Abraham's apparently later banishment of the children of a second servant, Keturah (Gen 25:6), entail the birth of offspring (Ishmael and Midian, respectively) whose descendants play an indispensable role in the descent of Joseph into Egypt (Gen 37:28, 36; 39:1), and so, eventually, of Israel into Egyptian servitude. Jacob's deception of his blind father finds an ironic parallel in Laban's later substitution of Leah for Rachel under cloak of darkness on Jacob's first wedding night. Similarly, David's careless remark that the "rich man" of Nathan's parable (2 Sam 12:1ff.) should pay for the theft of the poor man's ewe "four times over" leads to the fourfold devastation of David's own household for his theft of Bathsheba from Uriah the Hittite: the death of Bathsheba's first child by David; the rape of Tamar by her half-brother Amnon and Absalom's vengeful murder of Amnon; the death of Absalom by the hand of the man David had previously instructed to do away with Uriah; and the death of Adonijah by command of David's chosen successor Solomon. In every case, David, whether by the commands he utters or by the independent initiative of his courtiers, is the indirect agent of the violence done to each child. Abraham's near sacrifice of Isaac thus stands as a symbolic counterpart of David's effective slaughter of his own children.

* * *

In a sense, no human character in the Hebrew Bible is ever fully just, never fully justified by works or faith. Even Moses, the most pristine of YHWH's servants, is apparently fallible to one lapse of faith (see Num 20). All heroes die and are succeeded, by reason of nature and time; Moses, though still in his prime, is succeeded by divine decree. A lifetime is governed by cycles of waxing and waning. The Garden story and patriarchal cycles, especially, proceed through most stages of the human life-cycle: birth, weaning, instruction or commandment, leaving of the parental household, marriage, procreation, aging, and death. The period of a person's greatest public and political engagement is the era between the leaving of the parental household and the establishment of a new parental household—the period of travel, resettlement, political covenant, war and soldiering, marriage, sexual vigor, firstborn offspring. Procreation, however, marks the beginning of senescence, of retreat from political to biological realities. In the Garden story, this polarity between active and passive modes of life is symbolized by the alternating use of words for "man": 'adam ("human"), referring to the passive and biological phases, 'ish, ("man, male") to the intervening active and political phase.

* * *

In such a manner, the relation, noted initially, of the idealized lore of kingship to the jadedly realistic lore of confederate covenant can be seen more clearly. Counterposed to the mythological lore of kingship and its preoccupation with sacred enclaves and divine stewardship (as in the Babylonian poem "Adapa"; compare Utanapishtim in "Gilgamesh"; see also Ezek 28; Jonah 2; Ps 23; Song of Songs; and Gen 2:9–15, 3:22–24)[37] is the homespun fable of the disobedience at the Garden story's core. "Paradise" and "immortality," like monarchy, are shown to be part of the history of folly, even as their charms register their effect on the reader. This pattern conforms well to the jaded ruminations on human wealth and accomplishment voiced by the aged King Solomon ("Qohelet") in Ecclesiastes. If human immortality is shown to rest not in the bodily powers or accomplishments of the individual but in the cooperative labor of the generations—the "tree of life" thus being the family tree of humanity (Gen 5–11) and the cultural and spiritual "tree" of Torah (Prov 3:18)—then the fundamental argument of Israelite tradition is clearly the justification of generational succession, of the traditionary enterprise as such, and of the cultural and religious institutions that sustain it. The peaceful nexus of the generations, the bond of education and continuity, which seems so imperiled in the narratives and poetry of the Hebrew Bible, is presupposed in its genealogies and laws. Despite the Bible's preoccupation with Israel's reliance on paradigmatic heroes, it was the public background—the tribes, the people, the laity—on whom Israel's survival most depended. Confederate, monarchic, and postexilic Israel radically differ in patterns of leadership and social structure, but it is the people, with its elders and sages, who remain the implied protagonist throughout.

* * *

A chief paradox of biblical tradition rests in the fact that, whereas the monarchy symbolized the unity and sovereignty of Israel among the nations, the actual exercise of monarchic power entailed Israel's descent back to a condition resembling Egyptian servitude. Israel was, by one way of reckoning, the most autonomous when least governed but also the least, or (Judg 19–21) the most hazardously, self-governing. In the monarchic era Israel made a choice for a transtribal guarantor of peace and continuity; the people ceded certain rights in the process and incurred a large debt in resources and human labor, but gained a setting in which the collecting and systematizing of tradition, the life of culture and spirituality as such, could occur. The Deuteronomistic history (especially 1 Sam 8; 12; 2 Sam 5:1–3) clearly renders the choice for monarchy as a voluntary waiver of autonomy by Israel, under the warning, in the first case, of a prophet. The paradigmatic history of extraordinary persons (Gen 12–50; 1–2 Samuel) is thus still in some sense a corporate history. The institutional contradictions of Israel are in a sense the personal heritage of every Israelite. In this manner, political history is a domain of spiritual lore.

* * *

Since the people Israel are only significant as the historical creation of YHWH, it is perhaps the creator Himself who is the true hero and underlying subject of Scripture. His experimental undertaking of cosmos and history, His interchangeable names, His manifold postures of speaking and acting, His resistance to pictorial representation and definitive conceptualization, His repeated efforts to establish and renew a covenant with His creatures, His love affair with a nation, His pragmatic changes of plan, even compromise, to fit human actions and consequences, His restless juggling of personal and national fortunes in an effort to right the equilibrium of moral justice, His apparent pain and pathos over injustice, His feminine vulnerability, as it were, to the ravages of human history, His responsiveness to prayer and repentance, all are part of Scripture's lore of divinity. YHWH appears as King and as subverter of kings, as legislating and guerrilla divinity, as force of continuity and of surprise, as council-God and as divine warrior, as august commander and as grieving parent.

* * *

The lore of divinity was accumulated over many centuries and was reflected in many different social and religious outlooks, but the contradictory trends were seen in postbiblical commentary, especially in late medieval Kabbalism, as forming a single system bound by Scripture's apparent balance between divine hiddenness and revelation, love and justice, immanence and transcendence. The Kabbalistic conception of Scripture—including its otherwise very this-worldly narratives—as a web of divine names and potencies is grounded in the textual weave of action and utterance that postbiblical generations came to apprehend as a simultaneous structure. "The Holy One, blessed be He, Torah, and Israel—are one," a late but widespread precept, is, from the standpoint of biblical tradition history and Jewish spirituality alike, a reigning equation. Torah is body lore, time lore, household lore, tribal lore, confederate lore, national and royal lore, and lore of the divine alike. The implicit gnosis it already was, in the oldest phases of traditionary evolution, helped to shape the traditions and books that would accumulate in time around the verbal polarities of archaic poetry and daily life: YHWH and God; created and made; heaven and earth; light and darkness; land and water; human and man; acquisition and vanity; Jacob and Israel; blessing and curse; take and give; Rachel and Leah; thousand and ten thousand; and so on. Lexical variation, antonymic contrast, and verbal parallel, long understood as formative elements in biblical poetry, lie at the heart, as well, of biblical narrative and tradition formation. The rounded set, the pair, the couplet, and, later in rabbinic discourse, the triad, pentad, and heptad of traditionary garland are the means by which the generations communicated in ancient Israel. The artistry and mystery of Scripture rest in its weaving of inherited dichotomies into the full fabric of personal- and self-critique.

* * *

The affixing of a primordial history (Gen 1–11) to the otherwise very circumscribed locale of the remainder of Scripture is an interpretive act in harmony with the affixing of eschatological and sacral concerns to the end of the Writings. It sets the history of a nation in the context of humanity and cosmos. It makes the Israelite traditionary venture an experiment in literacy as such, in human continuity and reverence for God, which had its first fitful origins at least in the generation of Enosh: "Then was begun [the custom of] calling upon the name of YHWH" (Gen 4:26). This self-conscious presentation of Israel's religion in the light of world history may flow from the nation's situation at the juncture of three continents, from her position "at the heart of the seas" (see Ezek 28:2), crowning the Mediterranean basin at the gateway between East and West. That the people of this relentlessly invaded, trampled, and abused land should have ample cause to reflect on the ravages of history is not an especially remarkable situation. What is remarkable is the manner in which their ruminations captured the attention and inflamed the religious imaginations of surrounding peoples and nations. The life of the spirit in ancient Israel was inextricably bound up with the categories of daily life, political existence, and historical change. However utopian Israel's tradition eventually became, in however theologized, mythologized, or, in a narrower sense of the term, spiritualized a way her lore evolved, that very this-worldly core was never lost. The people Israel's sense of the holy grew from her vocation as a living, literate, and persevering culture in an intensely multicultural environment. Her awareness of past, present, and future was from the start conditioned by the interplay of voices and memories that makes up biblical tradition. The quotational and dialogic rhythms of her lore and learning attest to the seriousness with which she undertook the Hebrew Bible's mandate for survival and continuity. Her devotional life was appropriately familial and communal, and her evolving task collectively assumed: the gradual elaboration of the name and essence of the tradition's ultimate source, the Sovereign whose majesty the world has not yet fully come to know. The labor of the anonymous tradents of the earliest tradition and that of its latter-day interpreters are in this sense one and continuous.

NOTES

1. On the definition of "biblical tradition," see D. A. Knight, *Rediscovering the Traditions of Israel: The Development of the Traditio-Historical Research of the Old Testament* (Missoula, MT: Scholars Press, 1975) 26–36. See also P. R. Ackroyd, "The Old Testament in the Making," in *Cambridge History of the Bible* [*CHB*] (Cambridge: University Press, 1970) 1:67–113; B. W. Anderson, "Martin Noth's Traditio-Historical Approach in the Context of Twentieth-Century Biblical Research," trans. B. W. Anderson (Englewood Cliffs, NJ: Prentice-Hall, 1972) xiii–xxxii.

2. For a detailed description of an analogous process in postbiblical Judaism, see I. Twersky, "The *Shulhan Arukh*: Enduring Code of Jewish Law," *Judaism* 16 (1967) 141–59. On the question of an earlier canon, see, most recently, D. N. Freedman, "The Earliest Bible," *Michigan Quarterly Review* 22 (1983) 167–75.

3. On this matter, see A. C. Sundberg, *The Old Testament of the Early Church* (Cambridge, MA, and London: Harvard University Press, 1964); G. W. Anderson, "Canonical and Non-Canonical," in *CHB* 1:145–49; B. S. Childs, *Introduction to the Old Testament as Scripture* (Philadelphia: Fortress, 1979) 53.

4. On the Masoretic Text, see, among others, the extensive article and bibliography by A. Dotan, "Masorah," *Encyclopaedia Judaica* (Jerusalem: Encyclopaedia Judaica; New York: Macmillan, 1971–72) vol. 16, supplementary entries, cols. 1401–82, esp. 1418–19, 1479–82. See also S. Leiman, ed., *The Canon and Masorah of the Hebrew Bible* (New York: Ktav, 1974). On the distinction between text and canon, see Childs, *Introduction,* 94–96.

5. O. Eissfeldt presents a useful overview (*The Old Testament: An Introduction,* trans. P. R. Ackroyd [New York: Evanston, and San Francisco: Harper & Row, 1965] 560–71) as does G. W. Anderson ("Canonical and Non-Canonical," 113–59). S. Leiman includes extensive rabbinic sources (*The Canonization of Hebrew Scripture* [Hamden, CT: Archon Books, 1978]). Childs offers a recent critique of the major scholarship (*Introduction,* 46–83).

6. See Childs, *Introduction,* 57–60.

7. See Leiman, *Canonization,* 120–24; Childs, *Introduction,* 53.

8. "Our rabbis taught: the order of Prophets is Joshua and Judges, Samuel and Kings, Jeremiah and Ezekiel, Isaiah and the Twelve. . . . Hosea was the first of the four prophets who prophesied at that period, namely, Hosea, Isaiah, Amos, and Micah. . . . Since his prophecy is written along with those of Haggai, Zechariah, and Malachi, [the latter having been] at the end of Prophets, he is reckoned with them. . . . Since his book

is so small, it might be lost [if copied separately]. . . . The order of Writings is Ruth and the book of Psalms, and Job, and Proverbs, Song of Songs and Lamentations, Daniel and the scroll of Esther, Ezra (including Nehemiah) and Chronicles. . . . And who wrote which books? Moses wrote his own book [i.e., the Pentateuch] and the portion of Balaam, and Job; Joshua wrote his own book and [the last] eight verses of the Torah; Samuel wrote his own book and Judges, and Ruth; David wrote the book of Psalms, in which is found as well the work of Adam, Melchizedek, Abraham, Moses, Heman, Jeduthun, Asaph, and the three sons of Korah; Jeremiah wrote his own book and the book of Kings and Lamentations; Hezekiah and his circle wrote . . . Isaiah[!], Proverbs, Song of Songs, and Ecclesiastes; the people of the Great Assembly wrote Ezekiel and the Twelve, Daniel, and the scroll of Esther; Ezra wrote his own book, and the genealogies of Chronicles up to his own time. . . . Who finished it? Nehemiah b. Hachaliah." One finds in this discussion perhaps one of the earliest examples of biblical source criticism. The attributions themselves may contain useful clues for reconstructing biblical tradition history.

9. The following discussion is based in part on L. Ginzberg, *The Legends of the Jews*, 7 vols., trans. H. Szold and P. Radin (Philadelphia: Jewish Publication Society, 1910–37); S. Lieberman, *Hellenism in Jewish Palestine* (New York: Jewish Theological Seminary, 1950); I. Heinemann, *The Ways of Aggadah* [in Hebrew] (Jerusalem: Magnes Press, 1950); I. L. Seeligmann, "Voraussetzungen der Midraschexegese," in *Congress Volume: Copenhagen, 1953*, Supplements to *Vetus Testamentum* 1 (Leiden: Brill, 1953) 150–81; G. Vermes, *Scripture and Tradition in Judaism*, Studia Post-Biblica 4 (Leiden: Brill, 1961); W. S. Green, ed., *Approaches to Ancient Judaism* (Missoula, MT: Scholars Press, 1978).

10. On gnosis in rabbinic exegesis, see A. Altmann, "Gnostic Backgrounds of the Rabbinic Adam Legends," *Jewish Quarterly Review* 35 (1944–45) 371–91; G. Scholem, *Jewish Gnosticism, Merkabah Mysticism, and Talmudic Tradition*, 2nd ed. (New York: Jewish Theological Seminary, 1965). In his essay "Der Name Gottes und die Sprachtheorie der Kabbala" (*Judaica* 3 [Frankfurt-am-Main: Suhrkamp, 1973] 7–70), Scholem deals with the rabbinic and medieval career of linguistic mysticism.

11. See especially G. E. Mendenhall, "Ancient Oriental and Biblical Law," in *The Biblical Archaeologist Reader* 3 (Garden City, NY: Doubleday, 1970) 3–24 (first published in *Biblical Archaeologist* 17 [1954] 26–46); idem, "Covenant Forms in Israelite Tradition," in *The Biblical Archaeologist Reader* 3, 25–53 (first published in *Biblical Archaeologist* 17 [1954] 50–76); see also D. R. Hillers, *Covenant: The History of a Biblical Idea* (Baltimore, MD, and London: Johns Hopkins University Press, 1969) 25–45.

12. See J. Kugel, "Two Introductions to Midrash," *Prooftexts* 3 (1984) 131–55, esp. 145–47.

13. See J. Frankel, "Paronomasia in Aggadic Narratives," in *Studies in Hebrew Narrative Art*, ed. J. Heinemann, Scripta Hierosolymitana 27 (Jerusalem: Magnes Press, 1973); L. H. Silberman, "Toward a Rhetoric of Midrash: A Preliminary Account," in *The Biblical Mosaic: Changing Perspectives*, ed. R. M. Polzin and E. Rothman (Philadelphia: Fortress; Chico, CA: Scholars Press, 1982) 15–26. See n. 21 below.

14. Source-critical studies of the Bible have appeared at least since the eighteenth-century work of Jean Astruc and J. G. Eichhorn, among others, but the classical effort in this vein, on which most current research is based, is Julius Wellhausen's *Prolegomena to the History of Israel*, first published in German in 1878 (Eng. trans., New York: Meridian Books, 1957). See the full discussion by David Sperling above, chapter 1. For an updating of Wellhausen's Documentary Hypothesis, see Eissfeldt, *Introduction*, 158–241, esp. 194–212; C. R. North, "Pentateuchal Criticism," in *The Old*

Testament and Modern Study, ed. H. H. Rowley (London: Oxford University Press, 1961) 48–83; and the challenges to source criticism offered in the name of tradition history by I. Engnell, *A Rigid Scrutiny: Critical Essays on the Old Testament,* trans. and ed. J. T. Willis, with H. Ringgren (Nashville, TN: Vanderbilt University Press, 1969) 50–67; and in the name of Hebrew philology by B. Jacob, *Das erste Buch der Tora: Genesis* (Berlin: Schocken, 1936; the English abridgment [New York: Ktav 1974] is a greatly inadequate equivalent); and U. Cassuto, *The Documentary Hypothesis: Eight Lectures,* trans. I. Abrahams (Jerusalem: Magnes Press, 1961). As for source criticism outside the Pentateuch, see the essays by N. H. Snaith and O. Eissfeldt, among others, in the Rowley volume cited above.

15. The oral prehistory of the Hebrew Bible belongs to the domain of tradition history, the term for which (*Überlieferungsgeschichte*) was first coined by Hermann Gunkel in *Schöpfung und Chaos in Urzeit und Endzeit: Eine religionsgeschichtliche Untersuchung über Gen 1 und Ap Joh 12* (Göttingen: Vandenhoeck & Ruprecht, 1895) 3, 209, 256. (One should, however, compare Wellhausen's earlier, more "literary" use of the term "Geschichte der Tradition," *Prolegomena* [Eng. trans.], 169.) See Knight (*Rediscovering,* 72–83) on Gunkel's overall contribution to the field of tradition history. Since Gunkel, a series of seminal works in the field have appeared. One should note A. Alt's traditio-historical studies of Israelite settlement (1925), patriarchal religion (1929), Israelite monarchy (1930), and Israelite law (1935)—all four found in English in A. Alt, *Essays on Old Testament History and Religion,* trans. R. A. Wilson (Oxford: Blackwell, 1966; reprint, Garden City, NY: Doubleday, Anchor Books, 1968). G. von Rad's *The Problem of the Hexateuch and Other Essays,* trans. E. W. Trueman Dickman (Edinburgh and London: Oliver & Boyd, 1966) includes, as its title essay, one of the first attempts (published in German in 1938) to write the tradition history of a large narrative complex, which von Rad defined as the Hexateuch (Genesis through Joshua), a notion later challenged by Martin Noth (*Überlieferungsgeschichtliche Studien: Die sammelnden und bearbeitenden Geschichtswerke im Alten Testament* [Tübingen: Niemeyer, 1943]). Noth's *A History of Pentateuchal Traditions,* trans. B. W. Anderson (Englewood Cliffs, NJ: Prentice-Hall, 1972 [German original, 1948]) remains perhaps the single most ambitious work in the field, as well as being a major effort in the revision of Wellhausen's source criticism. For further discussion of biblical tradition history, see the sources cited in n. 1 above, and I. Engnell, *A Rigid Scrutiny: Critical Essays on the Old Testament,* trans. John T. Willis (Nashville, TN: Vanderbilt University Press, 1969) 3–11.

16. On archaeological research in relation to the Bible, see, among others, W. F. Albright, *From the Stone Age to Christianity: Monotheism and the Historical Process* (Baltimore, MD: Johns Hopkins, 1942); G. E. Wright, ed., *The Bible and the Ancient Near East* Garden City, NY: Doubleday, 1965); D. W. Thomas, ed., *Archaeology and Old Testament Study* (Oxford: Oxford University Press, 1967).

17. See, in general, J. B. Pritchard, ed., *Ancient Near Eastern Texts Relating to the Old Testament,* 3rd ed. (Princeton, NJ: Princeton University Press, 1969); and idem, ed., *The Ancient Near East in Pictures Relating to the Old Testament,* 2nd ed. (Princeton, NJ: Princeton University Press 1969).

18. Remarkably durable and creditable work in a less technical literary vein is represented by R. G. Moulton, *The Literary Study of the Bible* (Chicago: University of Chicago Press, 1895), and by the celebrated essay on Odysseus's scar and the sacrifice of Isaac by Erich Auerbach, *Mimesis: The Representation of Reality in Western Literature* (1953; reprint, Garden City, NY: Doubleday, Anchor Books, 1957) 1–20. More recently, M. Fishbane (*Text and Texture: Close Readings of Selected Biblical Texts* [New

York: Schocken Books, 1979]); R. M. Polzin (*Moses and the Deuteronomist: A Literary Study of the Deuteronomic History* [New York: Seabury, 1980]) and Robert Alter (*The Art of Biblical Narrative* [New York: Basic Books, 1981]), among others, have represented significant extensions of literary method. Some useful caveats on the method have been offered by James Kugel ("On the Bible and Literary Criticism," *Prooftexts* 1 [1981] 217–36) and A. J. Miles, Jr., ("Radical Editing: [Redactional History] and the Aesthetic of Willed Confusion," in *Traditions in Transformation: Turning Points in Biblical Faith,* ed. B. Halpern and J. D. Levenson [Winona Lake, IN: Eisenbrauns, 1981] 9–31). It should be noted that the form criticism of Gunkel and others has always been deeply immersed in literary study. Among tradition historians, von Rad in particular has been preoccupied with the literary phases of the tradition-forming process.

19. On the rootedness of this conception, see G. W. Anderson, "Canonical and Non-Canonical," 135–39.

20. On the possible antiquity of this numbering among both Alexandrian and Palestinian Jewry, see G. W. Anderson, "Canonical and Non-Canonical," 139.

21. On wordplay in the Bible, see M. Casanowicz, *Paronomasia in the Old Testament* (Baltimore, MD: Johns Hopkins, University Press, 1892); A. Guillaume, "Paronomasia in the Old Testament," *Journal of Semitic Studies* 9 (1964) 282–90; S. Gevirtz, "Of Patriarchs and Puns: Joseph at the Fountain, Jacob at the Ford," *Hebrew Union College Annual* 46 (1975) 33–53.

22. See my article "Some Notes on Traditional Prayer," *Response* 13 (1983) 15–22.

23. On the principle of prophetic legitimation (and, by implication, succession), see Deut 18:15–22; Jer 23:32. Jer 18:18 shows a complementary relation among priest, sage, and prophet. See P. R. Ackroyd, *Continuity: A Contribution to the Study of the Old Testament Religious Tradition* (Oxford: Blackwell, 1962) 18–19.

24. See M. Margolis, *The Hebrew Scriptures in the Making* (Philadelphia: Jewish Publication Society, 1922); Childs, *Introduction,* 53.

25. See A. J. Heschel, *The Prophets* (Philadelphia: Jewish Publication Society, 1962) 247–306.

26. See, however, the methodological cautions offered by J. L. Kugel (*The Idea of Biblical Poetry: Parallelism and Its History* [New Haven, CT, and London: Yale University Press, 1983] 59–95), who argues that the distinction between the two, if it can be drawn at all, may be more a matter of degree than of boundary and, in any case, that "poetic" is not the most interesting of formal traits. But since the distinction was an operative category in the Septuagint translation and, differently, in the Masoretic Text, I retain it where the shape of the canon as a whole is our concern, provided that we remember that Alexandrian and Palestinian Jews had undoubtedly dissimilar conceptions of poetic form and that, as Kugel shows, the devices of "heightened" style are not limited to poetic texts.

27. On the interplay of biblical law with other modes of biblical discourse, see E. L. Greenstein, "Biblical World and Biblical Law," in *Back to the Sources: A Guide to Reading the Classic Jewish Texts,* ed. B. W. Holtz (New York: Simon & Schuster, 1984).

28. T. Boman, *Hebrew Thought Compared with Greek* (London: SCM, 1960) 123–54; contra Boman, see J. Barr, *The Semantics of Biblical Language* (London: Oxford University Press, 1961).

29. See P. Hanson, "The Song of Heshbon and David's Nir," *Harvard Theological Review* 61 (1968) 297–320; and other sources cited by Elias Auerbach, *Moses* (Detroit, MI: Wayne State University Press, 1975) 165–66, 233 n. 135.

30. See, among others, H. Frankfort, *Kingship and the Gods: A Study of Ancient Near Eastern Religion and the Integration of Society and Nature* (Chicago: University of

Chicago Press, 1948); I. Engnell, *Studies in Divine Kingship in the Ancient Near East* (Oxford: Blackwell, 1967); B. Halpern, *The Constitution of the Monarchy in Israel* (Chico, CA: Scholars Press, 1981) 1–109. One should also compare the rich medieval Christian lore of kingship, as analyzed, for example, in E. Kantorowicz, *The King's Two Bodies: A Study in Medieval Political Theology* (Princeton, NJ: Princeton University Press, 1957). The two composite sketches offered in the discussion that follows are gleaned largely from Judges, 1 and 2 Samuel, 1 and 2 Kings, Psalms, and Song of Songs.

31. On symmetry, see, among others, Fishbane, *Text and Texture,* 40–62; J. P. Fokkelman, *Narrative Art in Genesis* (Assen: Van Gorcum, 1975); M. Dahood, "Chiasmus," in *Interpreter's Dictionary of the Bible: Supplementary Volume* (Nashville, TN: Abingdon, 1976) 144; J. W. Rosenberg, "The Garden Story Forward and Backward — the Non-Narrative Dimension of Gen. 2–3," *Prooftexts* 1 (1981) 1–27.

32. On etiology, see H. Gunkel, *The Legends of Genesis: The Biblical Saga and History,* trans. W. H. Carruth (1901; reprint, New York: Schocken Books, 1970) 13–36, esp. 25–34; B. O. Long, *The Problem of Etiological Narrative in the Old Testament,* Beihefte zur Zeitschrift für die alttestamentliche Wissenschaft 108 (Berlin: de Gruyter, 1968); J. F. Priest, "Etiology," *Interpreter's Dictionary of the Bible: Supplementary Volume,* 293–95.

33. See N. M. Sarna, "The Anticipatory Use of Information as a Literary Feature of the Genesis Narratives," in *The Creation of Sacred Literature: Composition and Redaction of the Biblical Text,* ed. R. Friedman (Berkeley, CA: University of California Press, 1982), 76–82.

34. See n. 21 above; also C. Westermann, *Genesis: Kapitel 1–11* (Neukirchen-Vluyn: Neukirchener Verlag, 1974) 256–68, esp. 264; and Knight, *Rediscovering,* 124–27.

35. For a useful overview of this problem, see W. Brueggemann, "Trajectories in Old Testament Literature and the Sociology of Ancient Israel," *Journal of Biblical Literature* 98 (1979) 161–85. See also F. M. Cross, *Canaanite Myth and Hebrew Epic* (Cambridge, MA: Harvard University Press, 1973) 219–73, concerning the conflicting ideologies as they affected kingship. Polzin (*Moses and the Deuteronomist,* 53–69) introduces a useful distinction between "dogmatic authoritarianism" and "critical tradtionalism," to account for the orchestrated interplay of conflicting ideologies in the finished text of Deuteronomy–Judges.

36. See R. E. Clements, *Abraham and David: Genesis 15 and Its Meaning for Israelite Tradition* (London: SCM, 1967); Hillers, *Covenant,* 98–119.

37. On the role of the Eden myth in the bible, see, among others, Fishbane, *Text and Texture,* 111–20; I. Engnell, "'Knowledge' and 'Life' in the Creation Story," in *Wisdom in Israel and in the Ancient Near East,* ed. M. Noth and D. W. Thomas, Supplements to *Vetus Testamentum* 3 (Leiden: Brill, 1955) 103–19. The paradisic enclave motif even finds satirical expression, according to J. S. Ackerman ("Satire and Symbolism in the Song of Jonah," in *Traditions in Transformation,* 213–46).

Bibliography

Underemphasized in the present article is the role of prophecy in the formation of Israelite tradition. Recommended in this area are Blenkinsopp, *A History of Prophecy* and *Prophecy and Canon;* Clements. Concerning the role of northern Israelite traditions in the formation of biblical tradition, see, among others, Jenks; Ackroyd, "Hosea and Jacob"; Good. On the role of Deuteronomy, see Nicholson, *Deuteronomy and Tradition;* Weinfeld; von Rad. Concerning the culture and traditions of exilic Israel, see Ackroyd, *Exile and Restoration;* Nicholson, *Preaching to the Exiles.* Miscellaneous works of use for understanding the development of biblical tradition are Noth; Knight; Smith; Gottwald.

Ackroyd, P. R. *Exile and Restoration.* Philadelphia: Westminster, 1968.
––––––. "Hosea and Jacob." *Vetus Testamentum* 13 (1963) 245–59.
Blenkinsopp, Joseph. *A History of Prophecy in Israel.* Philadelphia: Westminster, 1983.
––––––. *Prophecy and Canon.* Notre Dame, IN: University of Notre Dame Press, 1977.
Clements, R. E. *Prophecy and Tradition.* Atlanta, GA: John Knox, 1975.
Good, E. M. "Hosea and the Jacob Tradition." *Vetus Testamentum* 16 (1966) 137–51.
Gottwald, N. K. *The Old Testament: A Socio-Literary Introduction.* Philadelphia: Fortress, 1985.
Jenks, A. W. *The Elohist and North Israelite Tradition.* Missoula, MT: Scholars Press, 1977.
Knight, Douglas A., ed. *Tradition and Theology in the Old Testament.* Philadelphia: Fortress, 1977.
Nicholson, E. W. *Deuteronomy and Tradition.* Philadelphia: Fortress, 1967.
––––––. *Preaching to the Exiles.* New York: Schocken, 1970.
Smith, Morton. *Palestinian Parties and Politics That Shaped the Old Testament.* New York: Columbia University Press, 1971.
von Rad, G. *Studies in Deuteronomy.* Studies in Biblical Theology I/9. London: SCM, 1953.
Weinfeld, Moshe. *Deuteronomy and the Deuteronomic School.* Oxford: Clarendon, 1972.

5

Topics in the History of the Spirituality of the Psalms

JAMES L. KUGEL

N O BOOK OF THE BIBLE seems to summon up the concerns of spirituality in the biblical period more than the book of Psalms. Its prayers and songs of praise have long served as a model and focus of the spiritual concerns of later ages, and its words have been incorporated into, indeed have shaped, liturgies in Judaism and Christianity for two millennia. Little wonder, then, that the Psalter itself has served as the spiritual text *par excellence;* since late antiquity the mere recitation of individual psalms has been regarded as an act of piety; in certain circles the Psalter was viewed as the divinely ordained book of prayers and praises, while elsewhere it was seen as a book of divine revelation comparable to the Torah.[1] Because of it, Jews and Christians have exalted its traditional author, David, to the rank of prophet and divine spokesman.

Modern study of the Psalter, however, has not been kind to these traditional views. If past ages have delighted in poring over what they considered the "occasional, personal lyrics of King David,"[2] it has fallen to the present age to demonstrate that the Psalms are neither occasional, nor personal lyrics, nor David's. Indeed, it would not be unfair to say that research into the Psalms in this century has had a largely negative effect on the Psalter's reputation as the natural focus of Israelite spirituality, and much that was heretofore prized in this domain has undergone a somewhat reluctant reevaluation. A consideration of the Psalter's spirituality must, then, begin with the facts of this "de-spiritualization."

Authorship and Origins

Historically, it was the problem of the Psalter's reputed authorship that was the most obviously problematic element in the traditional picture, and the first in modern times to be openly disputed. Could David be the author of *all* the Psalms? Of course the name of David figures prominently in the Psalter: 73 of our 150 Psalms bear the superscription *le-dawid*, which from an early time was interpreted as implying Davidic authorship.[3] Moreover, David's long-standing reputation as a maker of music, as well as the Temple impresario (see, e.g., 1 Chr 6:16–18; 16:4–7; 25:1; 2 Chr 23:18), only strengthened this association. But the claim that David was the author of all the Psalms in the Bible, which apparently originated at the end of the biblical period,[4] seems to be contradicted *prima facie* by the mention of figures apart from David (Moses, Solomon, Asaph, the "sons of Korah," and others) in similar *le-X* superscriptions. Moreover, the editorial addition at Psalm 72:20 ("The prayers of David son of Jesse are concluded") must have once implied that *some* psalms are by another hand. Indeed, one can well imagine that the very idea of Davidic authorship wrinkled brows even as it was first being advanced; and, in characteristic fashion, rabbinic exegetes ingeniously turned the above-cited verse into a witness for the defense: "Rabbi Meir said: all the songs uttered in the book of Psalms were uttered by David, as it is written, 'The prayers of David son of Jesse are concluded (*kalu*)' Do not read it as *kalu*, but *kol ellu* [i.e., 'All these are the prayers of David son of Jesse']" (*b. Pes.* 117a). Why R. Meir chose so to argue need not detain us here; but it ought therefore not to be surprising that the issue remained a difficulty even after the close of the talmudic period[5] and, in more recent times, was disputed long before other elements in the Psalms were brought into question.[6]

Modern scholarship, heir to this tradition, began at the opposite pole, insisting that few, if any, of the Psalms go back to the time of David; indeed, at the turn of the century many eminent scholars held that a majority of the Psalms were written at least five centuries after David, that is, in the period following the Babylonian exile. This was the opinion of the biblical critic Julius Wellhausen; his contemporary B. Duhm went so far as to deny the existence of *any* preexilic psalms, holding Psalm 137 (whose apparent reference to the Babylonian exile had caused trouble for the claim of Davidic authorship centuries earlier) to be actually the oldest psalm in the Psalter.[7] Other scholars were still more extreme, limiting the whole phenomena of psalm composition in Israel to the period of Hellenistic domination, or even later, to the time of the Maccabees.

The question of dating has since taken a more moderate turn, and some parts of the Psalter are being justifiably assigned very ancient origins. Many more psalms are now accepted as preexilic. But in the meantime, the concept of the *Davidic* authorship remains thoroughly undermined (indeed, determining authorship on the basis of the psalm superscriptions has been quite justly rejected). Still more important, however, is the "opening" that the

Davidic authorship controversy provided. For once the Psalms, or at least a portion of them, were stripped of their Davidic connection, the traditional way of reading them (as the spontaneous, indeed, inspired, prayers and praises of a biblical hero) and the favored form of explicating them (i.e., connecting them to actual incidents in the life of David as related in the historical books, a phenomenon witnessed even in the psalm superscriptions themselves)[8] made little sense and was eventually abandoned. Who then composed these apparently anonymous documents? And, in the absence of biographical data from elsewhere in the Bible, what can be inferred from the text of each psalm itself about the purpose and circumstance of its composition?

To the possibility that some psalms were spontaneously jotted down by anonymous figures in response to unidentified dire straits or miraculous acts of salvation was eventually added another: that at least some psalms were not spontaneous, occasional, compositions at all, but were, on the contrary, prayers and praises composed by some people for recitation by others — that, in short, some psalms constituted a liturgy or ritual to be spoken by particular individuals at certain times. The effect of such an idea (which gained ground through the end of the nineteenth century) was, understandably, to jostle somewhat the traditional piety of the Psalter. For if the "I" of the Psalms is no longer anyone in particular, but a liturgical Everyman, a fiction, then the text's words inevitably start the slide from personal, sincere outpourings to compositions consciously crafted to fit a particular common, repeated, circumstance and couched in language sufficiently vague or general as to suit a variety of potential speakers and occasions — in short, a kind of "fill-in-the-blanks" psalmody.

This tendency can perhaps be made more vivid in the presence of a specific example. The Psalms frequently speak of "my enemies," "my foes," "those that hate me," and so forth.

> O LORD, how numerous are my foes!
>   How numerous those that rise against me!
>   (Ps 3:1)

> O LORD my God in whom I take refuge,
>   save me from all who pursue me, and deliver me,
>   lest like a lion they rend me,
>   tearing me to pieces with none to rescue.
>   (Ps 7:2–3)

> They close their hearts to pity;
>   with their mouths they speak arrogantly.

They track me down; now they surround me;
they set their eyes to cast me to the ground.
(Ps 17:10–11)

So long as the divinely inspired David was the putative author of such words, the identity of the enemies might be sought in details from David's own life: they were the allies of Saul, or court intriguers, or foreign nations bent on toppling the throne. Once the "I" of the speaker became diffuse, however, the identity of the enemies, and consequently the character of the compositions as a whole, became correspondingly shadowy. This issue has continued to puzzle even contemporary scholars. Were the words to be uttered by a, or *any*, Davidic king invoking divine help from enemies perhaps unknown even to him, indeed, from potential or actual *national* enemies?[9] Or was the intended speaker sometimes merely any ordinary Israelite trying to counteract the common practices of witchcraft and sorcery that he feared were being used against him?[10] Or was their identity still less precise, indeed left vague because of the "one-size-fits-all" mentality of these compositions? Such is the conclusion of one recent study, which observes:

> The enemies themselves are talked about in very typical stereotyped language. Clichés of all sorts are used throughout the psalms. The opponents are described in stark terms, usually with strong language and negative imagery. This stereotypical language should suggest caution in assuming that there is a single referent for the enemies or evildoers. Animal metaphors, war terminology, the language of the hunt can all be used to express the same reality. The adversaries seem to be characterized in the same way no matter what their actuality is for the one who sings or prays.[11]

The truth of these insights no doubt extends beyond the matter of the Psalmist's "enemies." For the same stereotypical language characterizes the Psalmist's description of the dire straits from which he has been (or would be) saved—"shame," "mocking," "lips of falsehood," "glozing lips," "false accusers," "the grave," "the pit," and so forth—or other details seemingly related to the speaker's particular circumstances.[12] The vague and sometimes highly metaphorical terms in which the speaker of the Psalms sometimes characterizes his own circumstances seem hardly the result of a desire *not* to be too specific, nor yet of a taste for literary embellishment even in the midst of distress; on the contrary, a needy suppliant ought to be as specific and direct about his circumstances as possible. Instead we should agree that the language of at least some psalms does seem to reflect the purpose named: to provide a text suitable for a broad variety of speakers, which, while containing descriptions and requests corresponding in general terms to the speaker's circumstances, was of a sufficiently broad character to be usable by almost all.[13] But whichever explanation one seeks among the foregoing, one point should be clear: they all lead away from the spontaneous and particular, and toward the stereotypical artifice.

Psalm Classifications

The critical concerns just described are representative of a major trend in modern Psalms criticism as a whole, the interest in discovering the basic literary forms and conventions of the Psalter. This interest is multifaceted and of diverse origins; but certainly one of its important starting points was the observation of resemblances between the Psalms and various hymns, prayers, and other compositions discovered among the writings of ancient Israel's neighbors, especially in Mesopotamia. (Important early studies were monographs by F. Stummer, C. G. Cumming, and G. Widengren, as well as briefer studies by B. Landsberger, J. Hempel, and others).[14] As is well known, this work has resulted in the discovering of striking resemblances between the basic themes and language of the Psalter and those of Babylonian hymnody: just as the God of Israel is praised as cosmic creator, benign manipulator of the natural environment, faithful and true, helper of the downtrodden, enemy of the unjust, etc., so were these same attributes hymned by the Babylonians in their praises of Marduk and other deities.[15] But, moreover, basic generic resemblances between Babylonian hymns and biblical psalms played a significant role in spurring scholars' interest in discerning basic *types* within the diverse material of the Psalter, and in classifying its material along the lines suggested by such comparisons with the hymnody of Israel's neighbors.

Another impetus to such a classification was the growing perception of formal resemblances between individual psalms and other compositions or passages found elsewhere within the Hebrew Bible. "It is not sufficient," wrote one critic at the beginning of this century, "to deal only with the biblical book of Psalms, where the great majority of psalms which originated in ancient Israel are to be found; rather we must ask ourselves whether there are other psalms that have been preserved outside the Psalter."[16] In the latter category certainly fall such psalmlike compositions as the Prayer of Hannah (1 Sam 2:1ff.) or the Song of the Sea (Exod 15:1ff.), works that are in every way comparable to others included within the Psalter. (Indeed, there are a few psalms or parts of psalms that appear both within the Psalter and outside of it, usually in the midst of narrative text, as for example Psalm 18, which is to be found in slightly different form in 2 Sam 22). This fundamental kinship of songs within and outside of the

Psalter was in fact recognized by early Jews and Christians and is attested in various ways, perhaps most strikingly in the early Christian practice of grouping together the "Psalms and Canticles," the latter category consisting of just such "Psalms outside the Psalter."[17] But the connections go beyond such obvious instances. For are not the communal laments within the Psalter to be connected with those of the book of Lamentations? And are not the Psalter's supplications to be viewed in common with the great prayers that mark the Deuteronomic history or the books of Daniel, Ezra-Nehemiah, or Chronicles? Where does "individual psalm of petition" leave off and "prayer" begin?[18] Indeed, do not Jeremiah's "confessions" bear a striking resemblance to petitions and laments within the Psalter?[19] Once the great variety of different genres within the Psalter is grasped, the difficulty in delineating the corpus of "psalmlike" compositions in the Bible is apparent.

   This difficulty has not been resolved, but it has been elucidated somewhat by the scholarly methodology known as form criticism, the approach pioneered by the German biblical critic Hermann Gunkel (1862–1932). In general, Gunkel sought to categorize different biblical texts by breaking them down to their smallest independent units and trying to discern in these the original purpose and life setting (*Sitz im Leben*) for which they might have been composed. In regard to the Psalms,[20] he was able to classify the contents of the Psalter (and some extra-Psalter material) into a few major types: hymns, laments of the community, laments of the individual, royal psalms, thanksgivings of the individual, and various minor categories, ("pilgrimage songs," "wisdom psalms," etc.).[21] For each category, he sought to define the recurrent, and hence characteristic, formal elements, as well as the circumstances in which the psalm might have been recited.

   Gunkel's work (which, incidentally, did much to undermine the then-ascendant approach to the Psalms championed by Julius Wellhausen and his followers)[22] inspired critics of various tendencies and orientations; primary among these was the Norwegian scholar Sigmund Mowinckel, who advanced what he liked to call the "cultic interpretation of the Psalms" even beyond what Gunkel had suggested. The Psalter, which had already been dislodged from the naïve, "personal religious poetry" reading of an earlier day, now became in Mowinckel's view almost exclusively the verbal accompaniment of cultic ritual; the exegete's task, as he saw it, was that of deducing from the words of each text what sort of cultic occasion it had been meant to accompany. Particularly suggestive, if controversial, was Mowinckel's theory that ancient Israel had had an annual divine enthronement festival, a mythic rite of renewal at the autumnal New Year, in which God's cosmic kingship was ritually reenacted by the celebrants. (Some later scholars, unconvinced by what they felt to be Mowinckel's sparse evidence, have offered variants on this theory.)[23]

The impact of the form-critical approach pursued by Gunkel, Mowinckel, and others is to be stressed: it remains the dominant element in Psalms research and has been of great influence with regard to contemporary perceptions of the Psalms overall. The Psalter, thanks to this line of inquiry, has been broken down into different classes of compositions, and its very compilation into a single book has been shown to be a somewhat arbitrary development that took place long after most of the psalms within it were composed.[24] It is thus an anthology of significantly different classes of writings, a collection whose several names[25] only serve to mask the diversity of its contents. It is, moreover, a collection whose contents might—but for the caprice of editors—have included songs and prayers presently found in other biblical books, and a collection (so form criticism was to show) whose fundamental forms and underlying functions are paralleled elsewhere in the literature of the ancient Near East. But recent form criticism has especially tended to concentrate on the connection between the Psalms and the cult, and this, probably more than any of the other factors mentioned, has affected current perceptions of the Psalms' spirituality. For—despite the work of some current writers on the subject—cult is still widely associated with all that is perfunctory and ritualistic in worship;[26] the Psalms, which to an earlier age had seemed quite the antipode of this perfunctoriness, have thus become subsumed by it. Were not these compositions as ritualistic a part of the ceremony as sacrifices themselves, an all-purpose set of liturgical formulas that were offered heavenward like so many fattened bulls?

The "Canaanite Connection"

A final factor affecting perceptions of the spirituality of the Psalms has been the connection drawn between them and the literature of Ugarit, the latter surviving in a collection of alphabetic cuneiform texts discovered earlier this century at Ras Shamra on the north Syrian coastline near Latakia. As mentioned above, clear resemblances had already been discerned between the Psalms and various compositions of ancient Israel's neighbors, principally in Mesopotamia and Egypt. But the linguistic and other parallels between the writings of the denizens of ancient Ugarit and the Bible are still more striking and have led some researchers to speak of a single "Canaanite" or "Syropalestinian literary tradition." For not only are Hebrew and Ugaritic themselves remarkably close (they are sometimes even described as "dialects" of a single language)[27] but much of the cultural background and religious vocabulary of the two civilizations is of a single fabric.

Unfortunately, a Ugaritic "Psalter" has not been found. Yet even within the mythological corpus, phrases, or even whole lines, have been found to bear striking resemblances to parts of the Psalter.[28] What is of perhaps still more far-reaching consequence for the Psalter than such spots of resemblance is the conclusion reached by some scholars that the diction of the Ugaritic texts bears the traces of a highly conventional literary idiom, one that functioned through a set of stock terms, "fixed pairs" of epithets and commonly associated terms. This language, they argued, also lies behind many of the common locutions of the Psalms and other biblical books; some even urged that the presence of these terms in the Hebrew Bible be read as a sign that the compositions in question had been created by a poet "on his feet," spontaneously weaving together standard literary motifs in the manner attributed to ancient Greek, or modern south Slavic, bards.[29] In the case of the Bible, the argument was somewhat hasty and has had to be tempered;[30] nevertheless, the existence of a standardized, and not specifically Israelite, literary idiom in the Psalms is now established.

Perhaps the most zealous pursuer of the "Canaanite connection" with regard to the Psalter in recent times has been the late Mitchell J. Dahood, whose three-volume commentary on Psalms has received wide exposure.[31] His retranslation of and commentary on the Psalms are in many respects radical—it has been described as a "Ugaritic" Psalter—and many of its suggested readings must be rejected. Despite such excesses, however, the comparative approach has proven itself in regard to the Psalter, and this has not been without consequence for the Psalter's spirituality. Ugaritologists have effectively argued for the appearance of Ugarit-style epithets, phrases, and even mythological motifs in the Psalter (an extreme example is that of Psalm 29, which as early as 1935 was argued by H. L. Ginsberg to be a "hymn to Baal" polemically readdressed to Israel's God).[32] Moreover, through hundreds of little proposed emendations and retranslations—to choose but one resonant example, Hebrew *nefesh*, traditionally translated as "soul," has, thanks in part to Ugaritic, had to be rerendered in places as "throat," "neck," or "appetite"—some of the most stirring bits of Psalter spirituality have been demoted into mundane pleas for the satisfaction of material wants, and where lofty yearnings for divine–human communion once prevailed, there now reign the somewhat less lofty requests for a good harvest, irrigation of parched pastureland, and similarly pedestrian, if nonetheless vital, matters. Even taking into account the fact that only some of these suggestions have found widespread acceptance, the cumulative effect has been significant.

In sum, the Psalter's spiritual side has been tarnished somewhat by our increased knowledge of the nature of its contents and the circumstances of its creation and original life setting. The Psalms no longer appear to us to be spontaneous or personal outpourings, but highly polished and stereo-typical, often ritual, acts. Their words were framed in what appears to be a deliberately vague and highly metaphorical manner so as to be adaptable to a variety of speakers and circumstances while seeming, nevertheless, to be specifically appropriate to each potential speaker. Moreover, comparison with other ancient Near Eastern texts has shown a communality of theme between the songs of Israel and those of surrounding, polytheistic cultures; apparently there is much that is not specifically Israelite about the words or even ideas of the Psalter. And when viewed in the light of such cognate texts, some, perhaps many, of the most exalted passages of Psalter spiritual-ity have had to be reunderstood in what would strike us as far less spiritual terms.

Such a de-spiritualization of the Psalter is, of course, paralleled elsewhere in the Bible: our story is but a representative chapter in the saga of modern biblical studies generally. Yet in presenting these findings as we have, the work of modern scholarship has been somewhat slighted. Although it is true that "spirituality" as it has traditionally been apprehended in the Psalter is now somewhat undermined—the result of the overthrowing of funda-mental misconceptions—our subject is not exhausted by exposing those misconceptions. The other, and more challenging, part of the task for modern critics has been the attempt to approach the Psalter anew, seeking to investigate the positive side of its spirituality with sympathetic historical imagination and taking full advantage of what is now known about the Psalms in their original setting. Various recent works have been suggestive in this regard,[33] and, though no single rubric would do justice to a multitude of studies of the Psalms from this standpoint, certainly many of them have concerned themselves with what might be called the phenomenology of the Psalms as speech-acts. Specifically, we might pose the problem in these terms: how are we to understand the significance of the Psalms texts in their most characteristic features, and is it possible to perceive behind the raw data of their classification something of the spiritual world in which they arose?

The Function of Praise

One interesting approach to the classification of the Psalms in recent times has been that advocated by the German scholar Claus Westermann, who has sought in the concepts of "praise" and "lament" (or, for the latter, "petition," "lament/petition," or "prayer," as others have urged) a fundamental polarity within the Psalter: "the literary categories of psalms of lament and psalms of praise are not only two distinct categories among others, but . . . they are literary forms which characterize the Psalter as a whole, related as they are as polar opposites."[34] All psalms, according to Westermann, may thus be categorized as belonging to these two fundamental modes, and then subclassified within them according to such variables as the intended speaker of the psalm, particular themes or formulas, and (in psalms of praise) the nature of the praising, whether "declarative" or "descriptive."[35] It is striking, however, that, even in this polar approach to taxonomy, praise itself does not dwell exclusively at one end of the polarity, for it has a role to play (as was certainly observed by earlier students of the Psalter) even within the biblical laments or petitions. These, Westermann argues, partake of a fundamental, stereotypical sequence in the Hebrew Bible, a sequence observable for example in biblical narratives: again and again, Israel (or some subdivision thereof) finds herself sorely pressed and cries out to her God, who "hearkens," "hears her cry," etc., and then saves the day for His grateful subjects. This sequence, prominent in the Pentateuch's long exodus narrative and various shorter recitations of it, also characterizes the salvation sequence presented in the book of Judges, according to Westermann. When it comes to the Psalms, this same sequence is represented by numerous petitions that begin with a narration of the Psalmist's distress, a narration that flows into (and/or out of) a request for relief. (Westermann writes: "Lamentation has no meaning in and of itself. That it functions as an appeal is evident in its structure. What the lament is concerned with is not a description of one's own sufferings or with self-pity, but with the removal of suffering itself.")[36] It is significant that, in this lament sequence, praise has no small part. It is, in the broadest sense, present even in the distress call itself, which often has recourse to what might be called a "jurisdictional appeal," an assertion that God is powerful, or merciful, or attentive to the needy, etc., and therefore is thoroughly capable, or likely, or obligated, to intervene in this particular circumstance. Moreover, praise is the essential element of this sequence's conclusion: Israel, saved from annihilation at the crossing of the Red Sea, sings a song of praise, as do Deborah, Hannah, David, and other individual figures; so the Psalmist, in seeking God's intervention in his behalf, invokes God's praise in the course of his petition or at its end, as a vow or foretaste of things to come.

Westermann's stress on the crucial function of praise throughout the Psalms challenges us to try to grasp its reality in a cultic setting. On the most basic level, it is striking that the Psalter often conjoins the motifs of praising God and sacrificing animals: "To You I bring a thanks-offering and call on the name of the Lord" (Ps 116:17); "Let me offer up a willing sacrifice to You and greatly praise Your name, LORD" (Ps 54:8); "Let my prayer be as incense before You, the raising of my hands (=prayer) as the evening offering" (Ps 141:2). Such frequent juxtapositions may point to something basic about how the act of praise was apprehended. Apparently it was not the spontaneous overflowing of a grateful worshiper or the simple expression of religious awe: rather was praise sometimes presented as an offering in and of itself and, in this sense, parallel to cultic sacrifice. So it is that (especially postexilic) biblical texts connect praise- and prayer-like acts with the general term for divine service: praise and sacrifice are both referred to as 'abodah.[37] Similarly, the psalmist frequently *vows* to offer praise to God: his is a vow of future action comparable to sacrificial vows and sometimes joined with them:[38]

> And I will offer in his tent sacrifices with shouts of joy;
> I will sing and make melody to the LORD.
> (Ps 27:6)

> With a free-will offering I will sacrifice to You;
> I will greatly praise Your name, O LORD.
> (Ps 54:6)

Moreover, biblical narratives sometimes suggest that praise, petition, and sacrifice were related in practice. 1 Kings 8, which recounts the inauguration of Solomon's Temple, is an oft-cited example: Solomon's sacrificial offerings are preceded by a lengthy royal speech whose beginning and end touch on themes of divine praise familiar elsewhere in biblical songs.[39] Perhaps most striking of all, it is the cultic sanctuary, the place of offerings *par excellence,* which is the clearly named locus of much of the praising to be found in biblical songs:

> I bow down to Your holy Temple,
> and praise Your name for Your love and faithfulness.
> (Ps 138:2)

> And in His Temple all proclaim [His] glory.
> (Ps 29:9)

> Happy are they that stay in Your Temple,
> ever do they praise You.
> (Ps 84:5)

> Bless the LORD, O you servants of the LORD,
> that stand in the LORD's Temple at night.
> (Ps 134:1)

> Acclaim the LORD, all men on earth;
> worship the LORD in exultation;
> enter before Him [i.e., at the sanctuary] with rejoicing.
>   (Ps 100:1)

Despite such obvious connections between praise and sacrifice and the depiction of praise as a cultic act, there is one difficulty (of which scholars have long been aware) in piecing together the cultic role of praise in ancient Israel: psalms of praise (or petition, for that matter) are nowhere discussed in Israel's cultic legislation.[40] The Priestly Code, which is so painstaking in its prescriptions regarding the procedures for various sacrificial offerings, individual and communal, the incense and other appurtenances of the Temple worship, the festive calendar, and so forth, prescribes nothing about psalms or hymns to accompany this ritual. Moreover, the Psalm headings or superscriptions, which contain all manner of information (not only, as we have seen, apparent ascriptions of authorship but also what has been interpreted as reference to the manner of performance, muscial modes, instruments for accompaniment, even contrafacts), do not offer much support for this cultic connection; here too is a curious near-silence.

These twin omissions have been variously explained, as, for example, a proof that the practice of Temple psalmody postdated the composition of the Priestly Code (hence no reference to the practice is to be found in it) or as an indication, on the other hand, of a striking innovation on the part of Israel's priests, who sought to eliminate all overtones of magic and pagan rites from Israel's cult by stripping away speech and song from the sacrifices proper. More convincingly, it has been suggested that the explanation is to be sought in the nature of the documents themselves; that in the eyes of the priests (and hence in their code) there was no need to mention psalmody in connection with sacrificial rites because psalmody was not their province, as the biblical material itself abundantly testifies.[41] The Psalter, on the other hand, whatever the stages of its compilation, in its final forms was certainly not a manual for Temple worship, so the absence of specific cultic instructions appended to the texts (as they are in, for example, Mesopotamian hymnody) need not be surprising.

But the omission of reference to psalms in the Priestly Code may also reflect a difference in the way psalms were viewed in Israel generally. The very fact that psalmody was not a priestly concern may not be the result merely of a convenient division of labor, but of psalmody's different, perhaps inferior, status vis-à-vis sacrifices. Suggestive too is the fact that praise and petition seem to be more flexible than sacrifices: the latter (as both statute and narrative attest) were generally limited to a cultic setting, whereas prayers and hymns could be, and were, offered up from anywhere and in any circumstances.[42] (True, according to some texts prayers seem to be *directed* toward a sanctuary locale, but the place of the verbal act seems less rigidly fixed than that of the sacrificial offering.) The "verbal component" may thus have been left unregulated, and left to non-priests, precisely because it was felt to be of a secondary, a nonobligatory, or a spontaneously offered character. The last seems to be a most suggestive possibility: for however much the actual words spoken or sung were in fact cultic hand-me-downs, the operating fiction may well have been that the words spoken were somehow tailor-made to the worshiper's precise situation, analogous to spontaneous speech and therefore not legislated. Otherwise the presence of so many differently nuanced expressions of thanks and petitions for various sorts of help within the Psalter (or even its various subgroups) is difficult to explain. If some merely formulaic act of praise or petition were required, would it not have been prescribed in just the manner of, for example, the words spoken by the worshiper at the firstfruits offering (Deut 26:3ff.)?[43] Again, the fact that a cultic site was the frequent, but hardly exclusive, locus of prayer may indicate that these words too (containing, as we have seen, praise proper) were viewed as by nature more flexible and hence not subject to prescription, however much they were the regular reality of Temple worship.

Praise as an Act

If one is correct in this view of the relationship of praise and sacrifice—the former held to be by nature more flexible, and whose operating fiction at least stipulated an element of individuality and appropriateness to a particular set of circumstances—it might be asked further: In what sense were words of praise and physical offerings conjoined or compared in the first place? Were they both essentially a form of thanksgiving and/or an attempt to manipulate divine favor? Perhaps such questions can never be answered with certainty, but in seeking to do justice to the "cultic spirituality" of the Psalms one must approach their words of praise with particular, perhaps unwonted, seriousness. The solemn, high significance of the act of praising is to be stressed: to offer praise was more than mere lip service. That this is the case may already be divined through the great emphasis placed on the act of praising in the Psalms themselves, and especially the vows of praise seen above: were simply "mere words" involved, they would not likely be so stressed.[44] The formal parallelism encountered between praise and sacrifice argues the same case and might lead us to assess words of praise as an offering only slightly less concrete than actual bulls and lambs.

This assessment can only be strengthened by examining the similarities that have been found to exist between Israelite psalmody and various ancient Near Eastern inscriptions of thanks and dedication. The basic form, and many of the formulas, of Israelite thanksgiving and praise have been found in various inscriptions and led one of the first writers on the subject, H. L. Ginsberg, to conclude that for the ancient Israelite to praise God aloud was something akin to commissioning an inscription elsewhere: "The Israelite public acknowledgment . . . was primarily verbal, the non-Israelite at least very often epigraphic."[45] Ginsberg compared the Ben Hadad inscriptions to various psalms of thanksgiving on the basis of language and theme and cited a further parallel with two Egyptian inscriptions of thanksgiving. Emphasizing the public nature of praise in the Psalms (and the frequent mention of the "tumult," "great throng," etc. with which such praising was to take place—see Pss 22:23–26; 35:18; 107:32; 149:1; etc.), he pressed the comparison of public utterance with public inscription and further suggested that some prayers and psalms themselves may have been recorded in inscriptional form. This same theme was taken up by L. Delekat in regard to individual laments in the Psalter.[46] More recently, Jonas Greenfield has written extensively on the parallelistic, and indeed "poetic," features of certain inscriptions and in particular has argued the structural and lexical similarity of the Zakir inscription to the song of thanksgiving as form-critically delineated by Gunkel.[47] The connection between psalms and inscriptions has been further illuminated by P. D. Miller, Jr., specifically with regard to inscriptions from Khirbet el Qom and Khirbet Beit Lei.[48] What exactly the status of oral praise in surrounding societies was cannot, of course, be divined from such inscriptions, and we should be uncomfortable with any simpleminded equation of oral and epigraphic praise. Nevertheless, one is left with the fact that the same sort of events that moved princes and potentates to erect stelae—that this or that god had seen their suffering, abject position, etc., or had heard their prayers and answered them resoundingly—moved ancient Israelites to the solemn declarations and songs preserved in the Psalter. (They may also have been moved to write inscriptions, possibly even the same texts, but the evidence for this is still inferential.)[49] If the events described were comparable and the linguistic formulas sometimes strikingly similar, ought one not to consider the act of praising witnessed in the Psalms as something like a verbal monument making, a formal *prise de position*, rather than a simple expression of thanks?

Indeed, the Psalms in one place specifically connect the two acts, and one can perhaps learn something of their relationship:

> Let this be written down for a later generation, so that a people yet unborn may praise the LORD: how He looked down from His holy height, from heaven the LORD looked at the earth, to hear the prisoner's groan, to set free those who were doomed to die; that men might recount the name of the LORD in Zion, and His praise in Jerusalem. (Ps 102:18–22)

According to this text, it is the act of praising that appears to be central; the purpose of writing things down is to prolong that act to "a later generation."

But what was it all about? Certainly a deity was pleased to receive some formal expression of thanks for services rendered, to be paid in words as well as sacrifice. Yet to understand praise in such terms is, I believe, to distort fundamentally its character. Indeed, the distortion is precisely parallel to that introduced by conceiving of sacrificial offerings merely as a god's "food." In both cases the acts are to be apprehended in that highly charged, *realized,* environment which the cultic site constituted. (To call cultic actions "symbolic" is helpful to the extent that we understand the term as indicating a pointing beyond the merely material reading of events, but it is misleading in the implication that the "real" is somehow elsewhere. On the contrary, the real is summoned up and made present by these cultic acts.) That is to say: to understand the significance of the praise of God in Israel's psalms, we have not to consider the "content" of the praise itself (which is, to follow up on our comparison, analogous to mere animal carcasses), but to understand praise as meaningful primarily as an act. Then it will be clear that to praise God is, as stated, a kind of *prise de position,* a formal setting up of the worshiper as subject to God (one might almost say, in the royal sense, a subject of God, dependent, indebted), in every sense a devotee. Hence the significance of the vow of praise, which was akin to a vow of subservience, a transfer of personal glory and honor to Israel's God and a public identification of oneself as a devotee of that deity; hence also the significance of praising God "greatly," "loudly," "in a large company," and so forth. (Still more desirable is it that "people praise You"; in a later age, it was conceived that foreign kings and the wealth of nations might come to Zion in a sign of fealty. See thus Isa 60 where, it is noteworthy, dumb beasts in bringing up their treasures *ipso facto* "proclaim the praises of the Lord" [60:6].)

One final bit of comparative material may further dramatize the point. In a recent discussion of prayers and inscriptions, the Assyriologist W. W. Hallo described what he perceives to be a ranking in the acts of piety available to the Mesopotamian worshiper. At the top of the list comes what

Hallo calls the "optimal dedicatory, or votive, offering: the statue of a worshiper set up in the cella of the deity and inscribed with his prayer, which was conceived thereby as proffered perpetually by the statue of the worshiper to the statue of the deity, both statues serving as images or surrogates of their originals."[50] Next in line were the less costly votive stone carvings and replicas of bowls, maceheads, seals, and other objects taken from daily life. They might be inscribed with such standard formulas as "for the sake of the long life of the donor," or for the life of the king, the donor's family, etc.; or a specific prayer, whether as petition for success in a given venture or as thanks for favors previously asked and now granted, might be added to the basic dedicatory inscription. However, for the "masses," even such votive objects were too expensive; the common people had to content themselves with a simple written message without any accompanying "goods," neither a statue of the worshiper delivering, as it were, the message to the god nor yet a votive object (presumably valuable or useful to the deity's representation) to which the message was attached. No doubt such messages required some fee to a scribe to write them and possibly an accompanying sacrifice as well; nevertheless, they must have been considerably less expensive.

What is suggestive in all this is not only the parallel that Hallo himself sets forth, namely, that some of our psalms may in fact be entirely analogous to these written messages (a point that, as was just seen, has been raised by other writers in connection with the language of Phoenician and other northwest Semitic inscriptions). But beyond this, if this "hierarchy" is a true one, one ought perhaps to see the bottom two rungs as constituting a more generalized form of the first. That is: one has a message to deliver to the deity, either petition or thanks. The most straightforward method is, in essence, to write a "letter" and have it put in the deity's sanctuary, where, presumably, it may be "read" and registered. But things get lost in the mail or overlooked in an oriental bureaucracy. Attaching the message to some votive object useful to the deity in his house (=temple) is thus an understandable expedient: it is the "special delivery" or "personal" label stuck on the message's envelope, a guarantee that the message will get through and, what is more, a means of predisposing the recipient to the sender's cause. But what of the "highest" form? To represent the sender in statuary bearing the message is, as it were, to offer nothing less than oneself. In the concentrated eternity of the temple, the worshiper's best course is simply to *be there*, to be there in the same way that the deity is there (through representation) and so to enable oneself to stand perpetually before the deity, pressing one's message on the divine king just as a servant or courtier might. The point is a subtle one, but worth insisting on: the deity is not simply conceived to be *collecting praises,* nor, for that matter, simply storing up oxidized calves and sheep in the supernal realms; but by acting the part of the domestic servant or the humble courtier, the worshiper is, as it were, paying with himself, setting himself in a subservient relationship to the god. This is rather abstract, and so one can only suppose that, when a polemical psalmist sought to exalt praise over sacrifice, it could only proceed by a misrepresentation of both, a concretization of the act of praise no less than of sacrifice:

> I will praise the name of God with a song;
> I will magnify Him with thanksgiving.
> This will please the LORD more than an ox,
> or a bull with horns and hoofs.
>   (Ps 69:31–32)

The Changing Role of Psalms

To imagine psalms of praise and petition in their original setting is an important part of any attempt to define the Psalter's spirituality, but it is not all. There came a time (or, rather, times) in Israel's history when the givens of that setting changed, and the conventions and words of psalmody acquired willy-nilly a new significance and status. It is impossible to chronicle the very earliest of such shifts, because it was a purely mental moment, in which what one writer has called the "original unity of men's words and deeds within the cult" began to break down: "Man becomes independent vis-à-vis the cult, he 'comes of age.' The cultic word separates itself from the cultic act. . . ."[51] Thereafter, the specialized terms of the cultic world enter into discourse with those of the world outside; they color one another, and forever alter the perception of cultic texts. This is as much as to say that a "purely cultic" approach to the words of the Psalms will probably always slight the perceptions of the ancient Israelite worshiper as best we can conceive of them: the "spiritualization" of the most basic concepts connected with the cult begins even while the cultic setting remains undisturbed.[52]

But certainly there did come in Israel's history political events and cultural changes that in a more definable fashion altered the setting of the Psalms and concretely brought about, or hastened, the rise of *words alone* as an acceptable form of divine service. Perhaps the earliest known phenomenon with which one might connect this gradual shift is the disappearance of various cultic sites in Israel through conquest or consolidation, and especially the effect on such sites of the centralization of worship associated with the reigns of Hezekiah and Josiah. For cultic sites exhibit great staying power in the ancient Near East: even when events or ideologies conspire to upset the religious order, their specialness persists. It is therefore not difficult to imagine that praise and petition, those potentially most flexible and equipmentless cultic acts, could have continued in sites, perhaps only "unofficially," even after some of their other cultic functions had been interrupted or discontinued.[53] This in turn would represent an important milestone in the Psalms' journey toward autonomy. N. M. Sarna has suggested that psalmody, along with incense offerings and some meal offerings, became the cultic activity of some provincial shrines after animal sacrifices had been discontinued in them,[54] and this would certainly be an important step in the aforementioned journey. At the same time, Sarna argues, conquest and final centralization may have sent members of the "independent nonpriestly musical guilds," which once flourished in the provinces, to the Jerusalem sanctuary, where they were incorporated into the Temple cult and so further enhanced the repertoire, and importance, of psalmody there. Both steps would certainly have contributed to the significance of the verbal element of cultic ritual and perhaps thereby to the ability of the people of Israel to survive the destruction of the Jerusalem sanctuary by the Babylonians, and the subsequent years of exile.

That conquest and exile in themselves certainly constitute the next great step in the history of Israel's psalmody, as in all aspects of her cultural life. In the reconstituted province of Judah that followed the exile, Jews kept to their sacred traditions and texts, but both of these were doubtless invested with new feelings—were "read" differently—in accordance with the new world view of the people. And when they sought to augment these traditions and texts with their own creations, even apparent instances of conservatism (or archaizing) betray a changed outlook. In regard to the Psalms, this is as much as to say that some of the "spiritualizing" approach to the Psalter which so much of modern psalms scholarship has aimed at unraveling began in the postexilic (or even exilic) period.[55] To sharpen the analogy we might say: just as prophecies of old were reinterpreted in postexilic Israel to bear on present circumstances, and just as the person of the prophet survived (for a time) in various postexilic figures (including the Psalmist?)—but whose changed circumstances are reflected in what he has to say as well as in the form in which he says it—so was it both that old psalms were "reinterpreted" (perhaps unconsciously) to fit new conditions and that new psalmists set themselves to composing works which, though related to their antecedents, reflect a rather different point of view. It is obviously easier to discuss the composition of new texts (whose very words may echo changed conditions) than the reinterpretation or reuse of already existing psalms, where we must proceed largely through inference. Nonetheless, both phenomena can be documented to some extent.

In the former category one might place, first of all, the whole phenomenon of "wisdom psalms" within our Psalter, whose existence is certainly connected to the emergence of the sage (*hakham*) as a figure of crucial importance in the postexilic community.[56] Most of the "wisdom psalms"[57] can be dated on linguistic and other grounds to this period; they thus represent a late turn in the history of Israelite psalmography. They are characterized by various recognizable features of wisdom literature as a whole—sayings and exhortations that begin "Happy is he who . . . ," "Better is X than Y . . ." or numerical formulas; occasional alphabetical construction; mention of those favorite heroes and villains of wisdom writing, the "righteous" and the "wicked" (or their equivalents, the wise or discerning and the fool); mention of actual wisdom genres such as *mashal* or *hidah* (both, roughly, "pithy saying"); and still others. It is more difficult to find clues to their intended place in daily life. Mowinckel, whose pursuit of the "cultic connection" has been mentioned above, felt compelled by the evidence to exclude wisdom psalms from cultic practice; instead, their authors were "learned psalmographers" who created a liturgy fashioned for personal piety, suitable for instruction or for an individual's private devotions.[58] This development, Mowinckel argues, was utterly natural in a society for which Scripture, sacred texts, was coming to play a central role: "among the learned and inspired collectors of the holy traditions of the ancients, a cult-free psalmography also grew into being." He and others thus see an element of pastiche and imitation in these works.

The wisdom connection hardly rules out a cultic *Sitz-im-Leben*—after all, the connection between wisdom personnel and the Temple is seen even in preexilic times, and so in general the cultic side of Israelite wisdom—nor, given our ignorance of Second Temple piety and the origins of the "proto-synagogue" ought one to rule out some new, yet fully liturgical, role for these psalms.[59] But Mowinckel's appellation for them, a "learned psalmography," certainly rings true. Compositions such as Psalms 34, 49, 111, 112 and others[60] do seem to belong squarely in the world of scribes and sages. Although they draw on motifs known to us from other psalms, psalms whose place in the cult can be easily imagined, these works seem strangely occasion-less and timeless: "I shall bless the LORD in every time, let His praise be ever in my mouth" (Ps 34:1), "Let me bless You every day, and praise Your name ever more" (Ps 145:2).[61] They are psalms whose addressees sometimes shift midway through the text, addressees who in any case can be exceptionally vague ("all peoples," "inhabitants of the world"). Most of all they are psalms whose authors seem imbued with the concerns of scribes and scholars: this is true not only of the wisdom themes cited above but also of the very alphabet that sometimes shapes their construction, the scribe's own stock-in-trade. Moreover, they frequently reveal a consuming interest in the task of Scripture, namely, the recounting of the glorious deeds of Israel's God (Pss 78, 105, 106, 127, etc.); indeed, one senses that in later times these deeds had become *texts*, "interpreted [*derushim*] by [or "for"] all who delight in them" [or "in all their details"]. Now interpretation, sometimes inspired interpretation, is the province *par excellence* of the sage. In this sense the long alphabetical Psalm 119 certainly typifies the wisdom theme in the Psalter, with its renewed plea for "understanding" of the divine laws:

Teach me, O LORD, the way of Your statutes, and I will keep it to the end. Give me understanding, so that I may keep Your law and observe it with my whole heart. Lead me in the path of Your commandments, for I delight in it. Incline my heart to Your testimonies, and not to gain. . . . (Ps 119:33–36)

It is noteworthy that the traditions of "learned psalmography" continued on into a late period, as is witnessed, for example, by the pseudepigraphic *Psalms of Solomon*, eighteen psalms that were written in the middle decades of the first century B.C.E. Their late date indicates the durability of the concerns that shaped this "learned psalmography," but, moreover, their relation to earlier Psalms is informative about the pastiche-like nature of the whole undertaking. Mowinckel describes them in these terms:

The species of compositions are here in the main the old classical ones—no new types have developed—but . . . [they] are much more intermixed than in the biblical psalms and do not keep to the rules. It is very difficult to classify this late Jewish psalmody according to genres, and such attempts are apt to become mechanical. But we constantly come across the old primary forms.[62]

A Noncultic Psalmody?

We have dealt above with the falsity of the view that identifies the cultic with the mechanical and insincere, and which consequently would view cultic praise as "mere words."[63] In the existence of some wisdom psalms that seem particularly suited to recitation in a noncultic setting (certainly Psalm 119 is one such), however, what we may be witnessing is the fusion of the language and style of cultic praise with a (long-standing?) tradition of personal, spontaneous prayer.[64] The result was a formal, elegant psalmody meant for recitation, but outside of specifically cultic circumstances. *If so, one must wonder if the originally cultic psalms themselves did not, during the same period, find a use outside of the cultic setting for similar purposes of personal piety.* This is, of course, a question for which little evidence can be adduced, but several items are nonetheless to be mentioned.

The most intractable of these is the very issue of the "spiritualization" of cultic concepts mentioned earlier. The question (occasionally raised in recent studies[65]) is: To what extent, given such a "cultic spread," might texts of an originally clear cultic setting and function have begun to partake of the same spiritualization process and to assume a significance—perhaps also a use—outside of the narrowly cultic. (N. M. Sarna's hypothesis, described above, about the fate of provincial sanctuaries usefully subdivides the question further, by proposing a cultic use of psalms which was, however, independent of animal offerings and in which, therefore, older psalms took on new meanings—and a new importance—while still remaining in the sanctuary setting.)[66] That such instances of "spiritualization" of old texts took place seems entirely probable. The difficulty is that this could occur without in any way affecting the texts themselves: the locus of the shift was in the minds of the text's performers and hearers. Equally perplexing is the possibility that new texts were composed on old cultic models—the language and conventions for praising God or appealing for help having become, through the cult, "classic"—texts whose intended meanings were, however, no longer connected with the old, cult-specific ones.[67] The result in either case is that some of the fundamental concepts of Israel's psalms (God's "presence," "countenance," "protection," "wings," etc., or even "holiness," "love," and terms relating to the realia of sacrifices)[68] might have begun to be "spiritualized"—that is, decontextualized—from a very early time.[69]

Numerous biblical narratives put songs of praise or prayers into the mouths of their heroes, and in some instances the texts are apparently not tailor-made for the occasion. This seems to be the case, for example, with Jonah's Prayer (Jon 2:2–9), a cultic piece that has been imaginatively transferred from an original sanctuary setting to the narrative's "innards of the fish" on the basis of its water imagery in verses 4 and 6.[70] The date of this transfer belongs to the domain of redaction history, but it may bespeak the same process described above, the real-life transfer of sanctuary songs and prayers to noncultic settings. Similarly, the adoption of the Hallel psalms for private Passover ritual may conceivably go back into the centuries before the common era, although the evidence we have of it is late.[71] From the Qumran documents have come other hints. A Psalms scroll found in Cave 11 (11QPs^a) may, as some have suggested, owe its anomolous arrangement of the material to an apparently liturgical recitation. (Alongside such biblical material, hymns were composed in imitation of biblical style and incorporating frequent allusions to the Psalms and other biblical books; these too, apparently, served a liturgical function. Philo's Therapeutae similarly sing, in their communal worship, "a hymn composed as an address to God, either a new one of [their] own position, or an old one by poets of an earlier day. . . ." [*On the Contemplative Life* (*De vita contemplativa*) 10 §80].[72])

It is hard to rest too much weight on such scant materials, but one may at least ask: Do not the existence of "wisdom" and other psalms apparently composed for use outside of a cultic setting, the insertion of psalms into noncultic situations in biblical narrative, and the hypothesized use of psalms in noncultic liturgies at Qumran (and perhaps elsewhere) suggest a gradual "reinterpretation" of the cultic praise of God and, with it, the corpus of songs and prayers that had originally been composed for the sanctuary? Here, as in so many areas, the distinction between "original meaning" and "later (mis)interpretation" becomes blurred; but, moreover, it is important to stress that some of our pre-critical "misinterpretation" of the Psalms seems to have its beginnings well within the biblical period, indeed, may even go back to preexilic times and constitute the very premise on which part of the Psalter was written.

Davidic Authorship

The tradition that David wrote some, if not all, of our Psalms and that he instituted psalmody in Israelite worship is similarly very old.[73] Although there is no extant preexilic attribution of the Temple psalmody to him, it seems reasonable that the tradition was not invented by the Chronicler, where it appears so forcefully (see 1 Chr 6:16–18; 15:16; 16:4–7; 23:5; 25:1; 2 Chr 7:6; 8:14; 23:18; 29:20; 25; and 35:15. Cf. Ezra 3:10; Neh 12:24, 45–46.) It rests in part on the well-known narrative connection of David with music making,[74] which in itself may have originally been presented to stress David's extraordinary gifts or kingly virtues. Such a tradition might also have been important in preexilic times in legitimating the practice of psalmody (or some aspect thereof).[75] In the Chronicler's work the Davidic theme played an important part in the exaltation of the Levites, and thence it apparently passed to still later statements of David's authorship of the Psalms: Ecclus (Ben Sira) 47:11–14; Josephus, *Antiquities* 7.12.3 §§ 305–6 and *Against Apion* 1.8 §§ 38–46; and others. As noted, it is not clear what the Psalm superscriptions that contain the name of David were intended to communicate—*le-dawid* being an ambiguous formulation—and even those superscriptions that tell more ("A psalm of David, when Nathan the prophet came to him, after he had gone in to Bathsheba" in Psalm 51, or "A psalm of David, when he feigned madness before Abimelech so that he drove him out and he went away" in Psalm 34) cannot be read as unambiguous assertions of authorship.[76] However, the note at Psalm 72:20 ("the prayers of David son of Jesse are concluded") certainly is a statement of authorship — and one that must predate the final editing of the Psalter, since it contradicts Davidic attributions later on in the book. What is interesting overall, however, is not precisely when the claim of Davidic authorship originated, but what pushed it forward. And here a hypothesis suggests itself: the Davidic claim was strengthened and extended the more that the Psalms themselves were perceived as revealed Scripture, a circumstance that was to raise the troubling question of authorship for the Psalter just as it did for the Pentateuch. For a moment arrived in the life of every biblical text when the fact of its being "hallowed by tradition" was no longer sufficient for Jews to treat it as sacred; it had to be of special provenance, communicated by one of God's chosen servants known from Israel's history. This is the essence of the issue of authorship,[77] and in regard to the Psalter it explains why the Davidic attribution, originally advanced in far smaller dimensions (and for purposes that may have been apologetic but of an entirely different nature),[78] continued to gain steam. As noted above, the Septuagint Psalter has more Davidic attributions than the Masoretic Text, and this may represent a similar intensification of the claim to Davidic authorship, as does the occasional secondary Greek change from "to David" to "of David," apparently a less ambiguous statement of authorship.[79] The great expansion of the titles in the Syriac apocryphal psalms, in the targum and the Peshitta, testifies that the same process continued.[80]

And it is of more than casual interest to note that these late attributions are all Davidic (as are, indeed, the attributions found among those psalms that are generally agreed to represent the latest stratum in the Psalter). Where are Asaph, the Korahites, or Jeduthun? But it was David on whom this latest stage of the tradition was exclusively centered — not only, one suspects, because of the earlier factors cited, but because *David above all* the other singers cited was, by Scripture's own account, God's chosen one. In this connection, it is to be noted that the Qumran psalm scroll mentioned above (11QPs^a) contains a brief note attributing prodigious authorial powers to David: he is alleged to have written 3,600 psalms (*tehillim*, "praises") and an additional 450 "songs" of various classes. What this may indicate about the antiquity of the claim for Davidic authorship is less interesting here than the note's final observation: "All these [compositions] he spoke in prophecy (*bi-nevu'ah*) which was given to him from before the Most High." Here is the felicitous conjunction of a statement of authorship with what seems to have been the ultimate concern of such statements: that is, it was important to assert that David wrote psalms and that David was a prophet, so that his psalms would have a fit place within Israel's collection of divine writings.

Possessed of praises and prayers of such exalted pedigree, why did the inhabitants of Qumran, or indeed Jews elsewhere, continue to create their own psalmlike compositions? Was it not enough to praise God or entreat Him with the very words of His anointed? Apparently not. Although the psalms and songs of the Bible played a role in Jewish (and, later, Christian) liturgies,[81] compositions such as the Qumran *hodayot,* blessings, and hymns bear witness—as do rabbinic prayers and hymns—to a felt need for newly composed material.[82] No doubt some of this need arose from the ever-present demand for (and delight in) the new and the specially created, the latter in particular an ongoing concern throughout the history of prayer. Yet when one examines the texts of these "substitute psalms," one is struck by their continuity with elements of the canonical psalms: the same (apparently deliberately) vague references to the speaker's needs or plight or to God's saving interventions, indeed, frequently the wholesale adoption of phrases from the Psalter itself. The demand for new words fitted to specific circumstances does not shine through such texts. Instead, it appears that what was crucial in the demand for new liturgies was precisely the process we have been describing in regard to the question of authorship, namely, the gradual "Scripturalization" of the Psalms. For as the Psalms became Scripture, they did so with an interpretive strategy attached: they were not to be interpreted as a self-standing book of prayers or praises, any more than Proverbs was to be a self-standing collection of wise sayings. Both were adjuncts to the rest of Scripture, to be read in the light of other books, to be interpreted and studied, in at least some cases to be connected to incidents in the narrated lives of their alleged authors[83]—and, *hence,* not wholly sufficient for the congregation's (or individual's) needs in worship. No categorical statement will do here,[84] but there is an apparent tension between the Psalms-as-texts-for-teaching (i.e., from God to man) and the Psalms-as-texts-for-worship (i.e., from man to God); the more they are familiar in the former role, the less suitable, it seems, they appeared in the latter.

This development, the "Scripturalization" of the Psalms (if we are right in seeing it as a decisive force), did not spell an end to their spirituality—quite the contrary! David continued to loom before the readers of Scripture as the man of prayer *par excellence,* the human sinner who could return as a penitent and seek forgiveness, or in time of distress "pour forth my complaint" (Ps 142:3). But it meant that for a time the Psalms were not to serve as the prayers and praises of every heart, at least not primarily; new hands were put to work setting the praise of God in words.

Notes

1. For a survey of the background of Jewish ideas about the Psalter since late antiquity, see Uriel Simon, *Four Approaches to the Book of Psalms from R. Saadya Gaon to R. Abraham Ibn Ezra* [in Hebrew] (Ramat Gan: Bar Ilan University Press, 1982). Saadya Gaon's "Introduction to the Book of Psalms" is a particularly strong presentation of the Psalter as revelation.

2. The "Davidic" element in this formulation began to fall away (slowly!) even in the eighteenth century, but the "occasional personal lyrics" approach showed remarkable tenacity. As G. W. Anderson has observed, "the attribution of a psalm to, say, Nehemiah in the fifth century rather than to David in the tenth leaves its presumed devotional character unchallenged" ("'Sicut Cervus': Evidence in the Psalter of Private Devotion in Ancient Israel" *Vetus Testamentum* 30 [1980] 389). Representative of Psalms scholarship at the turn of the century is A. F. Kirkpatrick's *The Book of Psalms* (Cambridge: University Press, 1902), which opined: "The Psalter, then, is a collection of religious lyrics. Lyric poetry is defined as 'that which directly expresses the emotions of the poet'; and religious lyric poetry is the expression of those emotions and feelings as they are stirred by the thought of God and directed God-wards. This is the common characteristic of the Psalms in all their manifold variety" (p. x). Reacting to R. Smend's claim (below, n. 9) that the "I" of the Psalter is a collective, Kirkpatrick observed: "The theory doubtless contains elements of truth; but it has been pressed to absurd extremes, and it is connected with the mistaken view that the Psalter was designed as a whole to be the hymn book of the congregation, and the Psalms were written for that purpose" (p. lii).

3. Note the line appended at the end of Psalm 72, discussed below. The Septuagint apparently expanded on the number of Davidic superscriptions: whereas four of the Davidic attributions of the Masoretic Text are omitted, fourteen (or fifteen) other psalms bear David's name. On this phenomenon see now M. Pietersma, "David in the Greek Psalms," *Vetus Testamentum* 30 (1980) 213–26.

4. See in general A. Cooper, "The Life and Times of King David According to the Book of Psalms," in *The Poet and the Historian: Essays in Literary and Historical Biblical Criticism,* ed. R. E. Friedman, Harvard Semitic Studies 26 (Chico, CA: Scholars Press, 1983) 117-32. On the colophon of 11QPs[a], see below.

5. See thus Rabbi Saadya Gaon, "Introduction to the Book of Psalms" in his *Psalms with Translation and Commentary* [Arabic and Hebrew], ed. J. Qafiḥ (Jerusalem: American Academy for Jewish Research, 1966) 24.

6. Again, U. Simon, *Four Approaches.*

7. A brief survey of Psalms scholarship in this period is contained in N. M. Sarna, "Prolegomenon" to M. Buttenwieser, *The Psalms,* 2nd ed. (New York: Ktav, 1969) xiii–xxxiv; cf. H. H. Rowley, *Worship in Ancient Israel* (Philadelphia: Fortress, 1967) 176–212. More detailed are J. J. Stamm, "Ein Vierteljahrhundert Psalmenforschung," *Theologische Rundschau* 23 (1955) 1-68; D. J. A. Clines, "Psalm Research since 1955," *Tyndale Bulletin* 18 (1967) 103–26 and 20 (1969) 105–25; and E. Gerstenberger, "Psalms," in *Old Testament Form Criticism,* ed. J. H. Hayes (San Antonio, TX: Trinity University Press, 1974) 179–224.

8. See B. Childs, "Psalm Titles and Midrashic Exegesis," *Journal of Semitic Studies* 16 (1971) 137–50.

9. This position goes back to R. Smend's ground-breaking essay "Ueber das Ich der Psalmen," *Zeitschrift für die alttestamentliche Wissenschaft* 8 (1888) 49–147. In recent

times, the theme has been renewed by H. Birkeland, *The Evildoers in the Book of Psalms* (Oslo: Komisjon Hos Jacob Dybwad, 1955); see G. W. Anderson's critique "Enemies and Evildoers in the Psalms," *Bulletin of the John Rylands Library* 48 (1965–66) 18-29. On this topic see also in general J. H. Eaton, *Kingship and the Psalms* (London: SCM, 1976). I. Engnell's evolved view of the king's role in Temple ritual led him to consider individual laments as ritual enactments performed by the king. His views had some influence on A. Bentzen, *King and Messiah* (Oxford: Blackwell, 1970), and H. Ringgren. See also M. Bič, "Das erste Buch des Psalters . . . ," in *La Regalità Sacra,* Supplements to *Numen* 4 (Leiden: Brill, 1959) 316–32.

10. This view was adopted by S. Mowinckel, though later modified somewhat (*The Psalms in Israel's Worship* [Nashville: Abingdon, 1962] 2:10).

11. P. D. Miller, Jr., "Trouble and Woe: Interpreting the Biblical Laments," *Interpretation* 37 (1983) 34.

12. This is the case as well, I believe, with the speaker's frequent reference to himself in the Psalms as "poor," "destitute," etc. One of the by-products of the vacuum created by the discrediting of Davidic authorship has been the attempt to find historical and other allusions in the precise wording of individual psalms, and this has led to (among other things) the reading of such self-descriptions as indicating the class or social standing of these psalms' author(s) or intended speakers. But, on the contrary, such self-abasing language, familiar in exaggerated form in the Amarna letters, Mesopotamian royal hymnody, and royal correspondence, may be no more indicative of the real circumstances of the speaker(s) than the references to the "enemies," the "grave," the "Pit," and so forth. In the presence of such consistently charged and highly metaphorical language and of a reasonable hypothesis to justify it (viz., reuse by a variety of speakers), such conclusions seem unwarranted. See J. H. Tigay, "On Some Aspects of Prayer in the Bible," *AJS Review* 1 (1979) 363–78.

13. Further evidence of this same mentality is to be found in the use of the Psalms themselves to create new prayers, as in the Qumran *hodayot* (for example, "You have heard my cry in the bitterness of my soul [a phrase borrowed from Ps 40:2]; You have taken account of my pains, recognized my lamenting, and saved a downtrodden soul in the lions' den [from Nah 2:12], whose tongues are sharp as swords [Ps 64:4] . . . ," etc.; see J. Licht, *The Thanksgiving Scroll* [Hebrew; Jerusalem: Bialik Institute, 1957] 101) or for that matter in the recycling of phrases from the Psalms in rabbinic prayers and the rabbinic "centos" known as *pesuqei rissui, selihot,* and so forth (see I. M. Elbogen and J. Heinemann, *Prayer in Israel* [Hebrew; Tel Aviv: Devir, 1972] 66, 166). Indeed, the Psalter itself illustrates such "recycling."

14. F. Stummer, *Sumerisch-akkadische Parallelen zum Aufbau Alttestamentlicher Psalmen* (Paderborn: F. Schöningh, 1922); C. G. Cumming, *The Assyrian and Hebrew Hymns of Praise* (New York: Columbia University Press, 1934); G. Widengren, *The Accadian and Hebrew Psalms of Lamentation* (Stockholm: Thule, 1937); B. Landsberger in *Orientalische Literaturzeitung* 28 (1925) 479–83; J. Hempel in *Zeitschrift der deutschen Morgenländischen Gesellschaft* 79 (1925) 20–110.

15. See F. Cruesemann, *Studien zur Formgeschichte von Hymnus und Danklied in Israel* (Neukirchen-Vluyn: Neukirchener Verlag, 1969) 135–54.

16. From the first edition of H. Gunkel's article on the Psalter in the German encyclopedia *Die Religion in Geschichte und Gegenwart* (Tübingen: Mohr-Siebeck, 1909–13); see H. Gunkel, *The Psalms: A Form Critical Introduction,* trans. T. M. Horner (Philadelphia: Fortress, 1967) 1n.

17. See H. Schneider, "Die biblischen Oden im christlichen Altertum," *Biblica* 30

(1949) 28–65, 239–72, 433–52, 479–500; also F. Cabrol, "Cantiques," in *Dictionnaire d'archéologie chrétienne et de liturgie,* vol. 2 (Paris: Letouzey et Ané, 1910).

18. M. Greenberg's recent study (*Biblical Prose Prayer As a Window to the Popular Religion of Ancient Israel* [Berkeley: University of California Press, 1983]) maintains, as do some earlier studies, the fundamental distinctness of the Psalter's praises and petitions from those "simple" blessings and psalms embedded in narratives elsewhere in the Bible: the Psalms are the work of "professionals," "experts," for only such "can compose prayers of the highest technical and ideational level" (p. 46). Whatever the truth of this assertion (and it would obviously be impossible to claim that *any* of the prayers embedded in biblical narrative is not, in one sense, the work of an "expert," the same whose expertise created the surrounding narrative), I believe that the continuum traced by Greenberg (and others) from human-to-human petitions, confessions, and thanksgivings to human-to-divine formulations of the same motifs in narrative is to be extended naturally to the Psalms as well (see E. Gerstenberger, *Der Bittende Mensch,* Wissenschaftliche Monographien zum Alten und Neuen Testament 51 [Neukirchen-Vluyn: Neukirchener Verlag, 1980] 17–63; note also M. Greenberg, "The Patterns of Prayers of Petition in the Bible," in *Harry M. Orlinsky Volume,* ed. J. Aviram et al., Eretz-Israel 16 [Jerusalem: Israel Exploration Society, 1982], Hebrew section, pp. 47–55).

19. On this last question there is a substantial literature: see P. E. Bonnard (*Le Psautier selon Jérémie* [Paris: Cerf, 1960]) and H. Graf Reventlow (*Liturgie und Prophetisches Ich bei Jeremia* [Gütersloh: Mohn, 1963]) for the history of this question, as well as R. P. Carroll (*From Chaos to Covenant: Prophecy in the Book of Jeremiah* [New York: Crossroad, 1981] 107–35).

20. Gunkel was not the first to interest himself in breaking down the Psalms into different classes; indeed, his work was carried out in a climate of classification, and C. Westermann rightly describes Gunkel's *Einleitung* as standing at the "end" of a development process (C. Westermann, *Praise and Lament in the Psalms,* trans. Keith R. Crim and Richard N. Soulen [Atlanta: John Knox Press, 1981] 16).

21. This categorization met with broad approval, but subsequently many scholars have questioned the validity of some of the categories or have sought alternate explanations for the purpose and life settings of different types. See the works listed above, n. 7; also J. H. Eaton, "The Psalms and Israelite Worship," in *Tradition and Interpretation: Essays by Members of the Society for Old Testament Study,* ed. G. W. Anderson (Oxford: Clarendon Press, 1979) 238–73.

22. See on this, N. M. Sarna, "Prolegomenon," 20–21.

23. H. J. Kraus reacted against the mythic side of Mowinckel's approach, seeking to connect proclamations of the kingship of Israel's God not with the natural cycle but with historical/political kingship (his views have evolved; see most recently *Die Psalmen,* 5th ed. [Neukirchen-Vluyn: Neukirchener Verlag, 1978]; also *Worship in Israel: A Cultic History of the Old Testament,* trans. Geoffrey Buswell [Richmond, VA: John Knox Press, 1966]). A. Weiser posited that the essence of the autumnal New Year rite was the renewal of Israel's divine covenant (*The Psalms,* trans. H. Hartwell [Philadelphia: Westminster, 1962]).

24. It is clear that the present book of the Psalter came into existence in stages. The note at Ps 72:20 mentioned above seems to indicate that there must have once existed a collection entitled "the prayers of David son of Jesse." Other clearly discernible units are the fifteen Songs of Ascents (Psalms 120–34) and, perhaps, the Korahite and Asaph psalms. The "Elohist" characteristics of Psalms 42–83 bespeak another stage in the editing of our present collection: indeed, Psalm 53 is a doublet of Psalm 14, Ps 70:2–6=Ps 40:14–18; Ps 71:1–3=Ps 31:2–4 (cf. Ps 108, which is a doublet of Ps 57:8–12 and

60:7-14). Other groups that may have existed as independent collections include those psalms known as the Egyptian Hallel, Psalms 113-18 (as distinct from the Great Hallel, Psalms 120-36) and the Halleluyah Psalms, Psalms 146-50. See S. Mowinckel, *Psalms in Israel's Worship*, 2:193-201; and H. Gese, "Die Entstehung der Buechereinteilung des Psalters," in *Vom Sinai zum Zion* (Munich: Kaiser, 1974) 159-67; and now G. H. Wilson, *The Editing of the Hebrew Psalter* (Chico, CA: Scholars Press, 1985).

25. The book is known in Hebrew as (*sefer*) *tehillim* (or *tillim*), literally (book of) "praises," a form first attested in the colophon of a Psalms scroll (11QPs^a) found in Cave 11 at Qumran (see below) and witnessed thereafter in early rabbinic texts, transcriptions of the name by Eusebius, Jerome, et al. The name apparently attests to the centrality of *praise* in the late-biblical perception of psalmody (see sections "The 'Canaanite Connection'" and "The Function of Praise" of the present article). The Greek *psalmos* translates a Hebrew word frequently used in psalm superscriptions, *mizmor*; as a name for the book, "Psalms" may thus go back to an (unattested) alternate Hebrew name using *mizmor*. *Psalterion* (=our "Psalter") is first found in the fifth-century Codex Alexandrinus of the Greek Bible as a name for the book of Psalms; the word designates a stringed instrument.

26. H. H. Rowley, in his discussion of the "cultic connection" in the Psalms (in *Worship in Ancient Israel*) still felt compelled to write in 1967: "It may be observed in passing that, as Aubert observes, cultic religion is not necessarily devoid of piety" (p. 178). For the Protestant bias against Temple and cult in still more recent works of scholarship, see J. D. Levenson, "The Temple and the World," *Journal of Religion* 64 (1984) 275-98.

27. It might again be appropriate, in connection with this oft-debated topic, to recall O. Pritsak's definition of the difference between a mere dialect and a separate language: "A language is a dialect that has an Army."

28. See briefly my *The Idea of Biblical Poetry* (New Haven, CT: Yale University Press, 1981) 25-40, and works cited.

29. The model for this approach is set forth in A. Lord, *The Singer of Tales* (Cambridge, MA: Harvard University Press, 1960).

30. See on this most recently A. Berlin, "Parallel Word Pairs: A Linguistic Explanation," *Ugarit Forschung* 15 (1983) 7-16.

31. *Psalms I, II, and III*, Anchor Bible (Garden City, NY: Doubleday, 1965, 1968, 1970).

32. H. L. Ginsberg, "A Phoenician Hymn in the Psalter," in *Atti del XIX Congresso Internazionale degli Orientalisti* (Rome: G. Bardi, 1935) 472-76.

33. See B. Childs, *Introduction to the Old Testament as Scripture* (Philadelphia: Fortress, 1979) 510-11.

34. *Praise and Lament*, 11.

35. On this distinction see *Praise and Lament*, 22-23.

36. Westermann, *Praise and Lament*, 266.

37. See M. Greenberg, "On the Refinement of the Conception of Prayer in Hebrew Scriptures," *AJS Review* 1 (1979) 59.

38. Westermann, *Praise and Lament*, esp. 75-78.

39. See Greenberg, "On the Refinement," 60.

40. See the discussion in M. Greenberg, *Biblical Prose Prayer*, 4-5, 30, 42.

41. N. M. Sarna, "The Psalm Superscriptions and the Guilds," in *Studies in Jewish Religious and Intellectual History Presented to A. Altmann*, ed. S. Stein and R. Loewe (University, AL: University of Alabama Press, 1979) 281-300.

42. S. Talmon, "The Emergence of Institutionalized Prayer in Israel . . . ," in *Qumrân:*

Sa piété, sa théologie et son milieu, ed. M. Delcor (Paris and Gembloux: Duculot, 1978) 265–84.

43. See M. Greenberg's observation that the words of the confession required in the *asham* rituals (Lev 5:1–5; Num 5:7; cf. Lev 16:21) are not specified, but are apparently left up the individual (see J. Milgrom, *Cult and Conscience: The Asham and the Priestly Doctrine of Repentance,* Studies in Judaism in Late Antiquity 18 [Leiden: Brill, 1976] 108; Greenberg, *Biblical Prose Prayer,* 19–30). Note, however, that the locus of the asham confession is not clear (Milgrom says: "The biblical evidence is beyond doubt: it was recited anywhere but at the sanctuary" [p. 108]).

44. One theme from the Psalter that is relevant here is that of praise as a person's final bargaining chip in his plea for help: "What profit is there in my stillness (traditionally "my blood," but "my [going to the place of] stillness," may be better; cf. Pss 94:17; 115:17), in my going down to the Pit? Can dust praise You or tell of Your faithfulness?" (Ps 30:9). "I shall not die, but I shall live to recount the deeds of the Lord" (Ps 118:17), "Even to old age and gray hairs, O God, do not forsake me, that I may proclaim Your power to all the generations to come" (Ps 71:18, following the Septuagint). The psalmist's ability to offer up future praises is thus sometimes advanced as an argument (beyond others) for his life being spared.

45. H. L. Ginsberg, "Psalms and Inscriptions of Petition and Acknowledgement," in *Louis Ginzberg Jubilee Volume* (New York: American Academy for Jewish Research, 1945) 169.

46. L. Delekat, *Asylie und Schutzorakel am Zionheiligtum* (Leiden: Brill, 1967). W. W. Hallo has argued that an evolutionary process is observable elsewhere in the ancient Near East from monumental forms to hymns and other genres; see his "Individual Prayer in Sumerian," *Journal of the American Oriental Society* 88 (1968) 71–89; and idem, "The Cultic Setting of Sumerian Poetry," *Actes de la 17e rencontre assyriologique internationale* (Brussels: Comité belge de recherche en Mésopotamie, 1970) 116–34.

47. J. Greenfield, "The Zakir inscription as Danklied," in *Proceedings of the Fifth World Congress of Jewish Studies* (Jerusalem: World Union of Jewish Studies, 1969) 174–91; see also H.-J. Zobel, "Das Gebet um Abwendung der Not . . . ," *Vetus Testamentum* 21 (1971) 91–99; note also Greenfield's "Scripture and Inscription," in *Near Eastern Studies in Honor of W. F. Albright,* ed. H. Goedicke (Baltimore, MD: Johns Hopkins University Press, 1971) 253–68; and D. R. Hillers, "Ritual Procession of the Ark and Psalm 132," *Catholic Biblical Quarterly* 30 (1968) 48–55.

48. P. D. Miller, Jr., "Psalms and Inscriptions," in *Congress Volume: Vienna, 1980,* Supplements to *Vetus Testamentum* 32 (Leiden: Brill, 1981) 311–32.

49. Ibid.

50. W. W. Hallo, "Letters, Prayers, and Letter-Prayers," in *Proceedings of the Seventh World Congress of Jewish Studies* (Jerusalem: World Union of Jewish Studies, 1981) 25.

51. H.-J. Hermisson, *Sprache und Ritus im Altisraelitischen Kult: Zur "Spiritualisierung" der Kultbegriffe im Alten Testament* (Neukirchen-Vluyn: Neukirchener Verlag, 1965) 9.

52. This is the theme of the study cited in n. 51, a theme not always innocent, however, of the polemical elements mentioned above in n. 26.

53. See now M. Smith, "Jewish Religious Life in the Persian Period," in *Cambridge History of Judaism,* ed. W. D. Davies and L. Finkelstein (Cambridge: University Press, 1984) esp. 234–35 and notes.

54. Sarna, "Psalm Superscriptions and the Guilds."

55. It is hard to assess the common claim that, in the "cultless" exilic community, the Psalms took on a new meaning and individual prayer attained new importance; the evidence is somewhat slim. Valuable in this connection, however, is J. D. Levenson,

"From Temple to Synagogue: 1 Kings 8," in *Traditions in Transformation*, ed. B. Halpern and J. D. Levenson (Winona Lake, IN: Eisenbrauns, 1981) 143–66. On the reinterpretation of cultic psalms in preexilic or exilic times, see also S. Holm-Nielsen, "The Importance of Late Jewish Psalmody . . . ," *Studia Theologica* 14 (1960) 1–53; and J. Becker, *Israel deutet seine Psalmen* (Stuttgart: Katholisches Bibelwerk, 1966).

56. For a recent summary, see H. Gese, "Wisdom Literature in the Persian Period," in *Cambridge History of Judaism*, ed. Davies and Finkelstein, 189–218.

57. On this category, see R. E. Murphy, "A Consideration of the Classification, 'Wisdom Psalms,'" in *Congress Volume: Bonn, 1962*, Supplements to *Vetus Testamentum* 9 (Leiden: Brill, 1963) 156–67.

58. Mowinckel, *Psalms in Israel's Worship*, 2:109.

59. Above, n. 55.

60. For various lists of potential wisdom psalms, see Murphy, "Wisdom Psalms," though this article, in my view, presents too narrow an approach to the phenomenon. A better view is F. DeMeyer, "La Sagesse psalmique et le Ps. 94," *Bijdragen* 42 (1981) 22–45.

61. "Eternal praise" is a motif known—one might say, "borrowed"—from the vows of praise; here, however, it is the "non-occasion" of the psalms cited. Cf. Ps 89:1 and H. Zirker, *Die Kultische Vergegenwärtigung der Vergangenheit* (Bonn: Hanstein, 1964) 74–79.

62. Mowinckel, *Psalms in Israel's Worship*, 2:118.

63. See especially in this connection J. Milgrom, *Cult and Conscience*.

64. Thus Mowinckel, *Psalms in Israel's Worship*, 2:109; and see Greenberg (*Biblical Prose Prayer*) for the "long-standing tradition."

65. See, for example, W. Beyerlin, *Die Rettung der Bedrängten in den Feindpsalmen der Einzelnen auf Institutionelle Zusammenhänge untersucht* (Göttingen: Vandenhoeck & Ruprecht, 1970) 18; K. Seybold, *Das Gebet des Kranken im AT* (Stuttgart: Kohlhammer, 1973) 168.

66. Sarna, "Psalm Superscriptions and the Guilds," esp. 291–94.

67. See E. S. Gerstenberger's postulate that ceremonies whose original life setting was in the clan proper were later shifted from the local community to national cult centers (*Der Bittende Mensch* [Neukirchen-Vluyn: Neukirchener Verlag, 1980]).

68. These and others are discussed in Hermisson, *Sprache und Ritus*.

69. The adaptation of Mesopotamian laments, prayers, etc., from the specific circumstances of their composition to a more generalized currency (above, n. 45) has already been analogized to the case of biblical psalms (see J. Tigay, "Some Aspects," 363–79). And, indeed (in a much later period), the psalm superscriptions themselves, as well as the Mishnah, attest to the fact that certain psalms were set (in fact or in exegetical fancy) to liturgical functions or connected with events which, from our own understanding of their genre and original *Sitz im Leben*, were at one time quite foreign to them (see Tigay, "Some Aspects," 374 and n. 83). All this argues for the principle of adaptability and reuse.

70. It should be noted that some writers have hypothesized that Jonah's Prayer and other such insertions are in fact new creations, pastiches based on the Psalms and written in "anthological style" (A. Robert's term). For this thesis in regard to Jonah and a summary of the debate, see most recently J. S. Ackerman, "Satire and Symbolism in the Song of Jonah," in *Traditions in Transformation*, ed. Halpern and Levenson, 213–46; and in regard to Hannah's Prayer, R. Tournay, "Le Cantique d'Anne," in *Mélanges Dominique Barthélemy*, ed. P. Casetti et al. (Fribourg: Éditions Universitaires, 1981) 553–76. For reasons discussed below, this hypothesis might support the same point I

have advanced, but I am compelled to reject it. There seems, in any case, little in either composition to suggest that they were put together specifically for inclusion in the narrative. On the contrary, the poor fit is all too obvious.

71. See Mowinckel, *Psalms in Israel's Worship*, 2:107.

72. Trans. F. H. Colson, Loeb Classical Library (London: Heinemann, 1941) 162–63.

73. Above, n. 4.

74. As a youth, David was known for his skill in playing (1 Sam 16:18), and his abilities in combating Saul's divinely sent derangements (1 Sam 16:14, 23) may have suggested divine powers in him (1 Sam 18:10–12; cf. 19:9). David's bringing up the ark to Jerusalem was likewise associated with music (contrast 2 Sam 6:5ff. with 1 Chr 13:8; 15:29; see Cooper, "Life and Times," 127); moreover, the epithet *ne'im zemirot yisra'el* in 2 Sam 23:1 was certainly interpreted as referring to his abilities in song (see Cooper, "Life and Times," 129). He is also credited with the authorship of the lament in 2 Sam 1:19–27 and the song of 2 Sam 22:2–51. A verse in Amos (6:5) seems to connect him with the invention of musical instruments—and so, certainly, did later writers (see Neh 12:36; 1 Chr 23:5; 2 Chr 7:6; 29:26–27).

75. Sarna, "Psalms Superscriptions and the Guilds."

76. It is clear, as noted earlier, that whatever the original significance of the Davidic superscriptions, they were at a later time understood as attributions of authorship. Thus, the superscription of Psalm 18, *la-maneseah l-'ebed YHWH le-dawid*, is paralleled in the doublet versio of that psalm in 2 Sam 22 by the introductory sentence "And David spoke to [of?] the Lord the words of this song at the time the Lord delivered him from all his enemies and from Saul." Moreover, Sarna has pointed out that, in those cases where the nota auctoris has added to it some phrase connecting the psalm to an incident in the life of David, the psalm itself is wholly or at least in part written in the first person. See his entry "Tehillim" ("Psalms") in *Biblical Encyclopedia* [Hebrew; Jerusalem: Bialik Institute, 1982] 8:445.

77. I would thus be forced to disagree with some of the conclusions of a recent discussion, B. Mack, "Under the Shadow of Moses: Authorship and Authority in Hellenistic Judaism," in *Society of Biblical Literature 1982 Seminar Papers*, ed. K. H. Richards (Chico, CA: Scholars Press, 1982) 298–318.

78. Above, n. 75.

79. A. Pietersma, "David in the Greek Psalms," 217.

80. Childs, "Psalm Titles and Midrashic Exegesis," 143 n. 2; cf. J. A. Fitzmyer, "David, 'Being Therefore a Prophet . . . ,'" *Catholic Biblical Quarterly* 34 (1972) 332–39.

81. See my "Is There but One Song?" *Biblica* 63 (1982) 329–50.

82. For Qumran and early prayers, see Talmon, "The Emergence."

83. This was clearly the case with some of the Psalm superscriptions; see Childs, "Psalm Titles and Midrashic Exegesis."

84. Cf. *m. Ta'anit* 2:3.

Bibliography

At present there is no wholly adequate modern scholarly commentary on the Psalms in English. As noted, Dahood's *Psalms I, II, and III* has widely affected perceptions of spirituality in the Psalms. This commentary does contain many suggestive readings, but these often require investigation beyond the evidence adduced, and other readings appear unjustified. The history of Jewish exegesis of the Psalms and various questions touching on their spirituality are discussed in Simon. Miller touches on the idea of praise and its function but appeared too late for inclusion in the notes to the present article.

Dahood, Mitchell. *Psalms*. 3 vols. Anchor Bible 16, 17, 17A. Garden City, NY: Doubleday, 1965–70.
Miller, P. D., Jr. "'Enthroned on the Praises of Israel.'" *Interpretation* 39 (1985) 5–19.
Simon, U. *Four Approaches to the Book of Psalms*. Ramat Gan: Bar Ilan University, 1982 [in Hebrew].

6

From Prophecy to Apocalypse: The *Book of the Watchers* and Tours of Heaven

MARTHA HIMMELFARB

THE FIRST ASCENT TO HEAVEN in Jewish literature appears in a third-century B.C.E. apocalypse that has as its hero the biblical patriarch Enoch: "Behold, in the vision clouds invited me and a mist summoned me, and the course of the stars and the lightnings sped and hastened me, and the winds in the vision caused me to fly and lifted me upward, and bore me into heaven. . . . And I looked and saw therein a lofty throne. . . . And the Great Glory sat thereon, and His raiment shone more brightly than the sun. . . ." (*1 Enoch* 14:8, 18, 20)[1]

Traditions about Enoch

Not only has Enoch gazed upon God, according to the Book of Watchers (*1 Enoch* 1–36); he has also traveled to the ends of the earth in the company of angels to learn the secrets of creation. "And they brought me to the place of darkness, and to a mountain the point of whose summit reached to heaven. And I saw the places of the luminaries and the treasuries of the stars and of the thunder . . ." (*1 Enoch* 17:2–3).

The Hebrew Bible offers an account of the life of Enoch that is only four verses long. It appears in the genealogy of Genesis 5, which links Adam to Noah, Enoch's great-grandson. Despite the brevity of the notice, it sets Enoch apart from the other figures in the genealogy. The others live, become fathers, and die. Not so Enoch. After he becomes a father, we read of him that "he walked with God." This is not said of anyone else in Genesis 5. Nor does Enoch simply die. Rather "he was not, for God took him" (Gen 5:24).

The traditions about Enoch in the Book of the Watchers and other works from the period of the Second Temple are clearly related to this mysterious summary of Enoch's life and the end of his existence on earth. The Book of the Watchers is also closely related to another cryptic biblical passage, Gen 6:1-4, which describes the descent of the sons of God to marry the daughters of men. Some students view the narrative of the Book of the Watchers as an exegetical development of the biblical passages, while others believe that Genesis alludes to the same early traditions on which the Book of the Watchers draws.[2]

Enoch is the first biblical hero to whom revelatory journeys are attributed by the authors of the Second Temple period, but he is not the only one. Among the patriarchs, prophets, and scribes who are taken on guided tours of realms usually inaccessible to human beings are Abraham, Levi, Isaiah, Zephaniah, and Baruch.[3] The contents of the tours vary, but all are concerned with subjects that appear in the Book of Watchers, the throne of God and the angels of heaven, the secrets of nature, and the fate of souls after death.

Apocalypses

These tours constitute one major group of apocalyses. The apocalypse is one of the characteristic forms of Jewish and Christian literature of the Greco-Roman period. The prophets had spoken in their own names. With the decline of prophecy, for reasons not fully understood, the authors of the apocalypse began to put their messages into the mouths of famous figures of the past.[4] The other major group of apocalypses consists of those concerned primarily with the end of history. The characteristic medium of revelation in these apocalypses is the symbolic vision, usually deciphered for the seer by an angel. The famous vision of the four beasts from the sea in Daniel is typical of these visions.

> Daniel related the following: "In my vision at night, I saw the four winds of heaven stirring up the great sea. Four mighty beasts different from each other emerged from the sea. The first was like a lion but had eagles' wings. . . . I approached one of the attendants and asked him the true meaning of all this. He gave me this interpretation of the matter: 'These great beasts, four in number [mean] four kingdoms will arise out of the earth. . . .'" (Dan 7:2-4, 16-17).[5]

The deciphering of the symbolic visions of the eschatological apocalypses has formal similarities to the description of sights seen in the course of tours.[6] Angels play a central role as interpreters or guides in both varieties of apocalypse.

The imminent, cataclysmic end of the world is rarely a central theme of the tour apocalypses, although it is an important subject in many of the larger works of which the tours form part.[7] The discussion of apocalyptic literature, however, has been dominated by the interest in apocalyptic eschatology, the conception of the end characteristic not only of many apocalypses but also of other types of literature of the Second Temple period.[8]

The certainty that God is about to destroy the wicked and after terrible upheaval reward the righteous seems to have grown out of prophetic eschatology well before the emergence of the first apocalypse, in the period after the return from the Babylonian exile, which took place toward the end of the sixth century B.C.E.. In their own land again, the people of Israel found themselves without their own king, powerless provincials in the great Persian empire. The last Persian emperor was succeeded not by a Davidic king but by Alexander and his generals, the founders of the Hellenistic empires. The restoration of Israel's past glory by human means began to seem unattainable.

Before the exile, prophetic eschatology looked forward to a future that was a better version of the past, a time of freedom and security, peace and prosperity. It was God who would bring about the change, but the people of Israel were also to play a role. Through repentance they were to create the moral preconditions for this new age. But as the hoped-for restoration remained in the future and disappointment followed disappointment, the prophetic view with its insistence on the importance of human participation gave way to determinism. Repentance would assure the individual of reward rather than punishment in the new age, but it would not affect the course of events. Regardless of the people's behavior, God would soon intervene in this hopelessly evil world to create an entirely new order.

Perhaps the most important reason for the scholarly emphasis on apocalypses devoted to the prediction and description of the end of the world is that the only two apocalypses to achieve canonical status, Daniel in the Hebrew Bible and the Revelation of John in the New Testament, are concerned almost exclusively with this end. (The Apocrypha, those books accepted as canonical by Roman Catholics but not by Jews and Protestants, include a single apocalypse, *4 Ezra,* which is like Daniel and Revelation in its concentration on eschatology.) But canonical status, the judgment of later Jews and Christians, should not influence the historian of the period before such judgments were made.[9]

A more defensible reason for the emphasis on apocalypses concerned primarily with eschatology is that until recently Daniel in the mid-second century B.C.E. was believed to be the earliest apocalypse. But the publication of the Qumran Aramaic fragments of two Enochic works, the Book of the Watchers and the Book of the Heavenly Luminaries (*1 Enoch* 72–82), has dramatically changed the situation.[10]

1 Enoch

The Book of the Watchers and the Book of the Heavenly Luminaries are two of the five separate Enochic apocalypses that make up the compilation referred to as *1 Enoch*.[11] The dates assigned to the Qumran manuscripts on the relatively objective basis of paleography show the Book of the Watchers and the Book of the Heavenly Luminaries to be from the third century B.C.E., considerably earlier than they had previously been dated.[12] They are, thus, the oldest extant apocalypses.

The Book of the Heavenly Luminaries, the oldest apocalypse of all on the evidence of the Qumran manuscripts, is devoted almost exclusively to the courses of the sun and the moon and their relation to the calendar. We have seen that the concerns of the slightly later Book of the Watchers are more diverse, but the end of history is not prominent among them. Thus, it is no longer possible to treat apocalyptic eschatology as the defining features of apocalypses generally on the grounds that it is central to the earliest apocalypse.

We have seen that the emergence of apocalyptic eschatology and of the apocalypses that center on the end of history is a reaction to the conditions of the postexilic period. I shall argue here that both of Enoch's tours in the Book of the Watchers must also be understood against the background of the shock of the exile and the developments in Jewish thought to which that experience gave rise. The Book of the Watchers stands at the beginning of a long tradition of tours. Although each responds to a different set of circumstances, the conditions that shape the Book of the Watchers influence later works because of the place of the Book of the Watchers at the beginning of the tradition and its wide influence. Thus, the Book of the Watchers can serve as a way of approaching the tradition as a whole.

Like most of the books of the Hebrew Bible, the Book of the Watchers is not a book in the modern sense, that is, a unified composition by a single author.[13] Rather it combines several originally independent traditions. The person responsible for the work as we have it appears to have been both editor and author, expanding and developing themes in the sources on which he drew. The third-century B.C.E. date applies to the finished work; elements of it are certainly earlier.

The setting for Enoch's tours in the Book of the Watchers is the story of the fall of the watchers, the angels alluded to in Gen 6:1–4, who take women as wives. This violation of the order of the universe has dire results both in Genesis and in the Book of the Watchers. According to the more extended account in the Book of the Watchers, the offspring of the sinful unions of the watchers and their wives are powerful and dangerous giants who wreak havoc on earth. When the suffering they have caused humanity becomes known in heaven, God sends the flood to cleanse the earth and instructs His archangels to imprison the watchers until the final judgment.

Enoch enters the narrative in the professional capacity of scribe. (The Book of the Watchers opens with Enoch's prophecy of the final judgment, but this section [*1 Enoch* 1–5] stands apart from the story line.) In chapter 12, Enoch is commissioned by the watchers who remain in heaven to announce their sentence to the fallen watchers. Deeply affected, the fallen watchers implore Enoch to petition God for mercy in their behalf. This petition provides the occasion for Enoch's ascent to heaven. In a dream Enoch stands before the throne of God and presents the petition. God rejects it, telling Enoch to tell the watchers, "You should intercede for men, and not men for you" (*1 Enoch* 15:2). Enoch's journey to the ends of the earth follows. It makes up the rest of the Book of the Watchers.

Enoch's Ascent and Biblical Antecedents

Even before the discovery of the Qumran fragments fixed the date of the Book of the Watchers so close to late prophetic literature, Gershom Scholem had pointed out that Enoch's ascent to heaven stands in a line of visions that begins with Ezekiel 1, which was anticipated at some points by Isaiah 6, and culminates in the *hekhalot* texts.[14]

> And I looked and saw therein a lofty throne: its appearance was as crystal, and the wheels thereof as the shining sun, and there was the vision of cherubim. And from underneath the throne came streams of flaming fire so that I could not look thereon. And the Great Glory sat thereon, and His raiment shone more brightly than the sun and was whiter than any snow. None of the angels could enter and could behold His face by reason of the magnificence and glory, and no flesh could behold Him. The flaming fire was round about Him, and a great fire stood before Him, and none around could draw nigh Him: ten thousand times ten thousand (stood) before Him, yet he needed no counsellor. And the most holy ones who were nigh to Him did not leave by night nor depart from Him. And until then I had been prostrate on my face trembling: and the Lord called me with His own mouth . . . . (*1 Enoch* 14:18–24)

The similarities of *1 Enoch* 14 to Ezekiel 1 are many: the imagery of clouds and wind, of fire, crystal, and ice (see the passage quoted at the beginning of this essay), the seer's falling on his face in the presence of God, the divine throne with wheels, the fiery figure on the throne.[15] These elements appear again and again in later apocalypses that describe the visionary's experience as he approaches God's throne.

But *1 Enoch* 14 departs from the pattern of Ezekiel 1 in one particularly significant way. Ezekiel is the only one of all the classical prophets to record the experience of being physically transported by the spirit of God (Ezek 3:12; 8:3; 11:24; 40:1–2, but even Ezekiel does not ascend to heaven.[16] The throne of God comes to him while he is standing by the river Chebar (Ezek 1–3). Enoch's is the first ascent in Jewish literature. With the exception of the second journey in the Book of the Watchers, during which Enoch remains earthbound, all later apocalyptic tours, whatever their subject, involve ascent.

In Enoch's vision, God is seated on a throne surrounded by a host of angels. In Isaiah 6 the angels about the throne serve as the council with which God consults as He sits in judgment of His people. The picture of God enthroned in the midst of the divine council appears elsewhere in the Bible as well.[17] Prophets claim to have overheard or, like Isaiah, to have participated in the deliberations of the council.

The divine council in biblical literature derives ultimately from the council of the gods presided over by El, the Canaanite patriarch of the gods.[18] In the Ugaritic texts the members of the council are distinct figures whose personalities play a part in the Canaanite myths. Since the multiplicity of gods was unacceptable to biblical thought, the Bible transforms the members of the council into angels or sons of gods, divine beings without individuality who exist merely to serve as heavenly courtiers. The function of giving counsel is alluded to in Enoch's vision, although negatively (*1 Enoch* 14:22). The divine council is in the background of the scene there, but a somewhat different understanding of the role of the angels about the throne dominates this vision.

Isaiah's vision of the divine council takes place in the Jerusalem Temple. The association of the divine council with the Temple goes back to its Canaanite origins. The mountain on which El and the gods assemble in the Ugaritic texts is the heavenly model for earthly temples.[19] The idea of a heavenly archetype for the earthly temple appears explicitly in the Bible in the instructions for the building of the tabernacle in the wilderness (Exod 25:9, 40; 26:30; 27:8). Mount Zion, the Temple Mount, takes the place of the holy mountain of the Canaanite gods.[20] Here heaven and earth come together, as in Isaiah's vision, where the Jerusalem Temple appears to be at once the heavenly and the earthly seat of God.

The view of the Temple as God's dwelling place is central to Isaiah's message. With Jerusalem under seige by a vast Assyrian army in the early seventh century, Isaiah argued against surrender: despite the many sins that he so powerfully condemned, Jerusalem could never be conquered, because God dwelt there.[21] The power of the Temple was confirmed for Isaiah's contemporaries when Isaiah's advice was followed. Hezekiah, king of Judah, did not surrender, but the Assyrian army returned home without entering Jerusalem. Modern historians are not certain how to explain this turn of events, but for Isaiah's generation and the generations that followed it was clear that God had miraculously defeated the foes of His people for the sake of His Temple. Indeed, because of the example of Isaiah's time, Jeremiah's contemporaries shortly before the fall of Jerusalem and the destruction of the Temple were certain that those disasters could never take place.[22]

J. Maier suggests that it is the prophetic condemnation of the Temple in the period just before the destruction and the experience of the destruction itself that bring an end to the view of the unity of heavenly and earthly in the Temple.[23] The intensity of that condemnation can be seen in Ezekiel's claim from far-off Babylonia, surely false, that idolatry was taking place in the Temple itself.[24] Restoration is no longer possible. Only an entirely new beginning under God's supervision can succeed. Its human imperfections quickly make the rebuilt Temple a disappointment. Thus, the First Temple in its last days and the Second Temple almost from the start come to be seen as mere copies of the heavenly Temple, the true Temple.

The visions of the chariot throne of God in Ezekiel express this view.[25] The chariot throne is the heavenly counterpart of the cherubim without a rider that stand as a throne for the invisible God in the earthly Temple. The chariot throne carries the glory of God away from the Jerusalem Temple before it is given over to the Babylonians for destruction (chaps. 8–11) and returns it to the eschatological temple in the elaborate vision of the restored Jerusalem at the end of the book (chaps. 40–48; return of the glory, 43:1–4).

The Book of the Watchers

Ezekiel's visions set the stage for the developments in the Book of the Watchers.[26] Since God is no longer present in the Temple on earth, the seer must ascend to His presence. The site of Enoch's vision is the heavenly abode of God. The description speaks of an outer and an inner house. This corresponds to the structure of the earthly Temple with its main hall and Holy of Holies. Because Enoch ascends to heaven, the chariot throne is not needed as a means of transportation. It stands stationary in the heavenly house of God.

The principle of correspondence between heaven and earth means that the heavenly temple must have priests. As far back as Isaiah 6 the angels of the divine council called out, "Holy, holy, holy," an acclamation that later became part of Israel's liturgy on earth. The angels of Enoch's vision are not explicitly described as offering praise, but they are said to stand before God even by night, which may hint at such a role.[27] The intercession that is so prominent a function of the angels in the Book of the Watchers is, of course, the work of priests on earth.

The priestly character of the angels becomes more explicit in the apocalypses that follow the Book of the Watchers. Angels assume the priestly (or Levitical) function of offering praise in a wide range of later works. In *Apocalypse of Zephaniah* 8, the visionary sees "thousands of thousands and myriads of myriads of angels" giving praise.[28] The *Testament of Levi* describes angels offering sacrifices in heaven (3:5–6). From Qumran there is preserved the *Angelic Liturgy*, which reports the blessings recited by the seven archangels in the course of the heavenly service.[29] In the *hekhalot* texts, the praise offered by the hosts of heaven includes hymns characterized by the repetitive description of God's greatness in formulaic language. Some of the hymns have become part of the liturgy of the synagogue.[30]

A state of purity is required for entrance into the earthly Temple, and access to the holiest parts is forbidden to all but priests. Contact with the holy can have dire consequences. When Uzzah reaches out and touches the ark, he dies (2 Sam 6:6–7). So too the ascent to God's throne is not for everyone, and even those chosen human beings who enter the realm of the angels must fear that they are intruding. When Isaiah sees God enthroned before him, he cries out, "Woe is me . . . I am lost, for I am a man of unclean lips" (Isa 6:5). His use of the language of purity is significant. In *Apocalypse of Zephaniah* 8, the prophet dons a special garment when he joins the angels, just as the priest dresses in special clothes when he serves in the Temple. Ezekiel, Enoch, and the heroes of later apocalypses tremble and fall on their faces as they approach the throne. The dangers experienced by the visionaries in some of the apocalypses that follow the Book of the Watchers also appear to be related to the understanding of the heavens as a temple. The Book of the Watchers, then, begins the transformation of the deliberations of the divine council into the service of the heavenly temple. The transformation is made possible by associations that go back to Isaiah and the Canaanite background of the council. In both the divine council and the heavenly temple God appears as king. Prophetic literature offers the image of God as Israel's husband, but this image and the emotions it inspires do not influence the picture in *1 Enoch* 14. Here, as in the *hekhalot* texts, the experience is of awe and fear.[31] It is wholly appropriate that Enoch calls God the Great Glory.

Mystical Experience

But how far does the account of the Book of the Watchers reflect actual experience? The fact of pseudepigraphy, of attributing the work to a hero of the past, suggests at least a certain distance between the author and the experience described. Enoch's ascent cannot be taken simply as a testimony to the author's own experience. Whatever else it may be, it is an episode in a story about Enoch. But this is not necessarily an argument against the view that personal experience stands behind the description of Enoch's ascent. The *hekhalot* texts too are pseudepigraphic with their attributions to great rabbis of the tannaitic period, yet they are generally regarded as reflecting actual ascents, in part because some describe the procedure for achieving ascent.[32]

Even the striking parallels to Ezekiel that at first glance might seem to indicate that Enoch's ascent is a literary creation, with details borrowed from an already prestigious earlier work, can be read another way. All accounts of mystical experience stand at some remove from the experience they attempt to describe. The expression of the experience, like all expression, is governed by convention. The mystic seeking to describe an experience beyond words draws on language endowed with power and validity by great visionaries of the past. Thus, the *hekhalot* texts show significant similarities to each other and to Ezekiel. For Jews of the Second Temple period and later, Ezekiel is a most suitable source for the description of such experiences.

Indeed, the experience itself may well be shaped by convention. Mystical visions are not independent of the visionary's assumptions about the world. Christian mystics have visions of Christ; Jewish mystics do not. Even while their feet were planted firmly on the ground, members of the circles that produced the *hekhalot* texts knew in broad outline how the heavens were arranged, how the hosts of angels spent their time, what the throne of God looked like. Those who experienced ascent went up through seven heavens filled with angels who sing God's praises and keep out intruders to stand before the chariot throne. The ascent confirmed what the visionary already knew. Thus, another factor in the close relationship between Enoch's vision and Ezekiel's may be the expectations of the author of *1 Enoch* 14. The similarities in themselves, then, are not an argument against seeing *1 Enoch* 14 as the description of a genuine experience.

To put it differently, the author of *1 Enoch* 14 knows what the experience of the vision of God on His throne is supposed to be like, but it is impossible to say whether he had had such experiences.[33] This conclusion applies as well to many of the ascents and tours that follow the Book of the Watchers, although not to all. The nature of the content of some of the tours predisposes us to view them as literary creations rather than as descriptions of actual experiences. Ecstatic experiences that take the seer to God's throne seem somehow more authentic than tours of the heavens that contain a great deal of astronomical data or tours of hell that detail the punishments of sinners. Yet Ezekiel's vision in chapters 40–48 includes precise instructions for the eschatological temple, and it is hard to doubt that Ezekiel elsewhere records genuine experiences. Once we take seriously the gap between the raw experience and the interpretation contained in any attempt to offer an account of it, it becomes more difficult to rule out an experiential element in many of the tours. Still, there are tours of hell that can safely be judged to be literary excursions. Some consist almost entirely of borrowings, often word for word, from earlier works. Other cases are less clear-cut, but the existence of a well-defined genre makes purely literary activity seem more likely.

The Social Setting of the Tours

The question of the experience behind these visionary tours is inextricably linked to the question of the social setting of the works in which the tours appear. Any hope of a better understanding of the nature of the experience lies in a better understanding of that background. Pseudepigraphy sets up effective barriers between the reader and the author and his community. Not only are we ignorant of the names of our authors and of the communities to which they belonged; in most cases we do not even know where and when their works were written except in the most general way. Despite the paucity of hard evidence, cautious comparison of the apocalypses with works like the gnostic ascents and the *hekhalot* texts may yield some clues.

Enoch's second journey takes him not to heaven but to the ends of the earth. In the course of this journey the geography of the cosmos is revealed to him. This tour is composed of two sources, each a complete tour. Chapter 20–36 develop the themes of chapters 17–19, the earlier source.[34] In both sources the only sight related to the story of Enoch and the watchers is the place where the watchers are punished (chaps. 18–19, 21). The tours are more interested in the foundations of the earth, the oceans and rivers upon it, and the astronomical and meteorological phenomena above it (chaps. 17–18, 23, 33–36). Both tours include a visit to the mountain throne of God (chaps. 18, 24–25), and the second contains the places where souls are stored after death to await the day of judgment (chap. 22) and an elaborate description of Jerusalem and its environs (chaps. 26–32).

From the *Odyssey* on, Greek literature offers tours of realms usually closed to human beings, and it is not unlikely that these influenced the Book of the Watchers. But the immediate ancestor of the tour to the ends of the earth is Ezekiel's tour of the eschatological temple and the new Jerusalem in Ezekiel 40–48.[35] Like Ezekiel, Enoch is led by an angel. Especially in the second source the sights of the tour are the subject of dialogue between Enoch and his guide.

> And I came to the Garden of Righteousness, and saw beyond those trees . . . the tree of wisdom whereof they eat and know great wisdom. . . . Then I said: How beautiful is the tree, and how attractive is its look! Then Raphael, the holy angel who was with me, answered me and said: "This is the tree of wisdom, of which thy father old (in years) and thy aged mother, who were before thee, have eaten, and they learnt wisdom and their eyes were opened, and they knew that they were naked and they were driven out of the garden."
> (*1 Enoch* 32:3, 5–6)

The guide's explanations of the sights consistently begin with demonstrative pronouns or adjectives. These questions and explanations are a developed version of a form found in Ezekiel 40–48. There the prophet remains silent, but the angel gives instructions for the conduct of affairs in the new commonwealth and occasionally describes sights using demonstrative pronouns or adjectives. These demonstrative explanations are related to a form of exegesis that was widespread in the ancient Near East, a form applied to dreams, omens, and texts. The symbolic visions of the eschatological apocalypses are often deciphered in this way. The tours of Ezekiel, Enoch, and the other apocalyptic seers also reveal heavenly secrets. Thus, a similar form of explication is suitable.[36] The content of the tour to the ends of the earth will reward further study. Some argue for Babylonian influence on the cosmology of the tour, others for Greek.[37] The interest in Jerusalem and the surrounding area in the second tour provides a point of contact with the content of Ezekiel's tour.

But the central theme of the second tour is the wonders of nature, and this suggests a link to wisdom literature. One of the distinctive features of wisdom literature within the biblical canon is that it ignores history as an arena of revelation and turns instead to creation.[38] For the early, optimistic wisdom represented by Proverbs and some of the wisdom psalms, the self-evident message of the created world is the greatness of the creator: "The heavens proclaim the glory of God . . ." (Ps 19:2). Wisdom literature is

almost alone before the exile in its interest in creation; the only major treatment of creation outside of wisdom is the J account in Genesis 2.

With the exile, the P account of creation—so different in its emphases
from J—takes shape, and creation appears for the first time as an explicit
theme of prophetic literature in the work of the anonymous prophet we
call Second Isaiah.[39] This new interest in creation is a reaction to the exile.
Israel's recent past constituted a challenge to the belief that God manifests
His power in the course of history. Since history no longer speaks clearly
of God's greatness, Second Isaiah turns to the created world.

> Lift high your eyes and see:
> Who created these?
> He who sends out their host by count,
> Who calls them each by name:
> Because of His great might and vast power,
> Not one fails to appear.
> Why do you say, O Jacob,
> Why declare, O Israel,
> "My way is hid from the LORD,
> My cause is ignored by my God"?
> Do you not know?
> Have you not heard?
> The LORD is God from of old,
> Creator of the earth from end to end,
> He never grows faint or weary,
> His wisdom cannot be fathomed.
> (Isa 40:26–28)[40]

The prophet moves from God as creator of the stars to Israel's lament
about the course of recent history to a triumphant conclusion based on the
evidence of the cosmos. The prophet has not abandoned the belief that God
is Lord of history, but he looks beyond history for evidence. The speech
attributed to Israel and the prophet's exhortation in response to it make it
clear that many in the prophet's audience were not as sure as he that their
God never grows weary.

Second Isaiah appeals to creation in another way as well in his allusions
to the ancient Near Eastern myth of the defeat of the chaos monster by a
warrior god.[41] The Babylonian form of the myth describes the victory of
Marduk over Tiamat and the creation of the world from the monster's
corpse. (Genesis 1 can be read as a polemic against this myth.[42]) In its
Canaanite form the myth recounts Ba'al's defeat of the sea god Yam and
the subsequent establishment of Ba'al's temple. This version of the myth
was an important influence on the Bible's understanding of the exodus and
the battles against Israel's enemies in the land. The God of Israel is given

many of the characteristics of Ba'al, the storm god, and even the events of the exodus are shaped according to the pattern of the myth. Like Ba'al's triumphant march to his mountain after his defeat of Yam, the wandering in the wilderness is depicted as a triumphant march to a holy mountain.

F. M. Cross points out that in the earliest biblical literature, including the Song at the Sea and the Song of Deborah, a process of demythologizing is at work.[43] Ba'al's defeat of Yam has been drastically historicized. The only divine actors in the biblical texts are the God of Israel and his heavenly host. God's enemies are human; the forces of nature are at God's command.

It is not surprising that Second Isaiah, who wrote in Babylonia, uses the Babylonian form of the myth. If early biblical literature demythologizes, Second Isaiah remythologizes.[44]

> Awake, awake, clothe yourself with splendor,
> O arm of the LORD!
> Awake as in days of old,
> As in former ages!
> It was you that hacked Rahab in pieces,
> That pierced the Dragon.
> It was you that dried up the Sea,
> The waters of the great deep;
> That made the abysses of the Sea
> A road the redeemed might walk.
> So let the ransomed of the LORD return,
> And come with shouting to Zion,
> Crowned with joy everlasting.
> (Isa 51:9–11)

The creation of the cosmos, understood as combat between God and a sea monster, is a model for the exodus from Egypt. In earlier accounts of the exodus, the sea appears as the instrument of God's vengeance on his enemies. Here as in the myth the sea is the embodiment of the forces against which God is struggling. The exodus has become a battle between God and the sea. Finally, the coming redemption will be modeled on the exodus and thus also on creation. Creation and the exodus serve to guarantee what is no longer universally accepted, God's ability to effect redemption once again.

We have seen that one aspect of apocalyptic eschatology is the devaluation of the role of human actors in history. In apocalypses like Daniel the events of history are described through the symbols of myth. History is thus emptied of its particulars. It is understood instead as reflecting conflicts taking place in the divine sphere. In Daniel 7 the enemies of Israel become beasts from the sea in an allusion to the combat myth. In Daniel 10–12 the real conflict is between Michael, the angelic guardian of Israel, and the angelic guardians of the nations.

Second Isaiah's use of myth is not as extended as that of the apocalypses, but his depiction of the exodus and the coming redemption in the language of myth is a step toward the new eschatology.[45] Thus, his contemporaries' sense that history has failed or at least that its message is no longer clear leads to the prophet's use of myth and also to his appeal to the wonders of creation. As the use of myth anticipates an important aspect of later apocalyptic literature, so too does the interest in the wonders of creation.

The book of Job represents a more radical response to the disappointment of the exile. In Second Isaiah the old prophetic view of God as revealing himself in history is not set aside, but a new element is added to it. The cosmos, visible to all, undeniable, is now seen as evidence for God's control of history, which the course of history itself has brought into question. Cross suggests that without the prologue and epilogue, almost universally recognized as secondary, Job can be read as a denial of the meaningfulness of history as Israel has experienced it.[46] Job is certain that his suffering has a meaning, that God will explain it to him. But though Job is granted his confrontation with God, God offers no explanation. God's appearance in the whirlwind and the questions He asks of Job affirm God's power. He could be Lord of history if He so desired. But His response to Job suggests that He does not so desire. He is the great and potent creator, not the God who redeemed the people of Israel from Egypt to make a covenant with them and who will redeem them once again.

For the book of Job, God's awesome power as creator has as its correlate the human person's inability to comprehend God's ways. This is the point of the rhetorical questions of Job 38–39.

> Where were you when I laid the earth's foundations?
> Speak if you have understanding.
> Do you know who fixed its dimensions
> Or who measured it with a line?
> Onto what were its bases sunk?
> Who set its cornerstone
> When the morning stars sang together
> And all the divine beings shouted for joy?
> (Job 38:4–7)

In a departure from the view of earlier wisdom literature nature has become a repository of secrets. It is precisely human ignorance about those secrets that demonstrates God's greatness. Nature is understood to testify to God but not because God's ways are readily accessible to human beings.

The interest of the Book of the Watchers and of later apocalypses in the works of creation can also be understood as a response to the experience of the exile and its aftermath. Like early wisdom literature and Second Isaiah, the Book of the Watchers sees nature as pointing to the creator. After each sight that he sees during his tour (chaps. 20–36), Enoch praises God. The tour and the Book of the Watchers as a whole conclude with such praise.

> And from thence I went to the south to the ends of the earth, and saw there three open portals of the heaven: and thence there come dew, rain, and wind. . . . And as often as I saw I blessed always the LORD of Glory, and I continued to bless the LORD of Glory who has wrought great and glorious wonders, to show the greatness of His work to the angels and to spirits and to men, that they might praise His work and all His creation. . . . (*1 Enoch* 36:1, 4)

But the Book of the Watchers has moved away from the optimistic certainty of Second Isaiah and early wisdom literature and comes closer to the outlook of Job. Like Job, the Book of the Watchers understands nature as full of secrets. The very fact of a tour in which the geography of the earth and astronomical and meteorological phenomena are the subject of revelation to a seer by an angel reflects such a view. Unlike Job, the Book of the Watchers claims that God does make those secrets known, although only to particularly righteous heroes. The concluding verse of the first source of the tour to the ends of the earth shows both the agreement and the disagreement: "And I, Enoch, alone saw the vision, the ends of all things: and no man shall see as I have seen" (19:3). Enoch is the righteous one who moves among angels, carrying messages from the watchers to God and back, traveling to the ends of the earth in the company of the archangels. This is the man who is worthy of having nature's secrets revealed to him.

The completed Book of the Watchers came three centuries after Second Isaiah. The more pessimistic view of the ability of human beings to read nature in the later work is probably in part the result of the fact that the great hopes of Second Isaiah, who saw himself living at the beginning of a new era, were disappointed. For Second Isaiah redemption is at hand, Cyrus is the anointed one of the God of Israel. But when Cyrus fulfilled the prophet's expectations by permitting the return and the rebuilding of the temple, the new Jerusalem turned out to be small, divided, and decidedly unredeemed.

The view of the Book of the Watchers and of later apocalypses[47] that the revelation of secrets is properly limited to the chosen seer—and thus also to those who read his work—goes hand in hand with the emergence of groups within Israel who regard themselves as the true Israel while all others are lost. This development becomes visible in the aftermath of the Maccabean revolt, but the processes that led to the growth of sects can be traced back to the exile and the efforts at defining membership in the community of Israel at a time when the natural boundaries of a people living in its own land under its own king were no longer in force.

The sectarian world view encompasses not only the secrets of creation but all revelation. As the Aramaic fragments show, the Book of the Watchers was read at Qumran. Although it is too early to have been written there, it was obviously congenial to this most sectarian (in the strictly sociological sense) of all Jewish groups of the Second Temple period.[48] The community at Qumran set up clear boundaries between itself and the rest of the Jewish people. The Jerusalem temple was polluted; the community constituted the true temple. The words of the prophets could be interpreted only with the aid of the insight of the Teacher of Righteousness, the community's revered founder. In short, only within the community was true revelation to be found.

Like the ascent in *1 Enoch* 14, the tour to the ends of the earth has an important influence on many later apocalyptic tours. Demonstrative explanations are a central feature in many of them,[49] and the contents of the tour provide a starting point for later developments. For example, the fate of souls after death, touched upon only briefly in Enoch's tour, becomes the subject of an extremely popular tradition of tours of hell and paradise that continues to flourish well into the Middle Ages in a variety of languages.[50]

But the main interests of Enoch's second tour, the secrets of nature and the geography of the earth, are considerably less prominent in later tours. Part of the reason for this is obvious. In the years after the Book of the Watchers the interest is more and more in heaven. Enoch's tour is the last to take place on earth. The causes of this shift in cosmography remain to be investigated. There is no uniformity to the new picture. For some works like the Parables of Enoch (*1 Enoch* 37–71) and many of the tours of paradise and hell, heaven is a single plane; after the initial ascent the visionary travels horizontally, much as Enoch does in his earthbound tour. But for others the heavens are plural, usually seven in number, and the visionary ascends from heaven to heaven. The levels of heavens available in this conception can be used to order the sights seen. In *2 Enoch,* for example, meteorological phenomena appear in the first heaven, the fallen watchers in the seond, paradise and hell in the third, astronomical phenomena in the fourth, watchers who did not sin in the fifth, and the angelic host in the sixth and seventh.

The move from the earth to the heavens can account for the loss of interest in elements of earthly geography like Jerusalem and environs, but it does not account for interest in the secrets of nature. As *2 Enoch* indicates, the heavens can provide a home for secrets formerly placed on earth. Tours of paradise and hell are produced well into the Middle Ages, and the tradition of apocalyptic ascents to the throne of God continues into late antiquity and the early Middle Ages—if we are willing to take the *hekhalot* texts as continuing the tradition. There is no such ongoing tradition concerned with the secrets of creation. Of the apocalypses that come after the Book of the Watchers, only the Parables of Enoch and *2 Enoch,* both of which draw on the Book of the Watchers, and *3 Baruch,* which seems to be dependent on *2 Enoch,* are interested in these secrets.[51]

Perhaps the shift in interest away from the secrets of nature can be explained by the potential of apocalyptic eschatology to lead to the devaluation of the created world or at least to a loss of interest in it. For the many Jews in the centuries from the Maccabean revolt to the destruction of the Second Temple and beyond who eagerly awaited the end they thought imminent, the world in which they actually lived paled in comparison to the new world they expected so soon. This aspect of what scholars have called apocalyptic dualism, a radical distinction between the present world and the redeemed world, tends to undercut the appeal of Deutero-Isaiah and the Book of the Watchers to natural phenomena as evidence for God's greatness and power. It should be remembered that most of the apocalyptic tours themselves contain predictions of the coming end or else form part of larger works that make such predictions. It is significant that such eschatology is strikingly absent from two of the apocalypses mentioned above as maintaining an interest in creation, *1 Enoch* and *3 Baruch.*

We have seen that the two quite different journeys of the Book of the Watchers can both be read as responses to the experience of the exile. The ascent to heaven in *1 Enoch* 14 represents an attempt to reach the God who is no longer understood to dwell in the Jerusalem temple. The journey to the ends of the earth claims nature as a source of knowledge about God, at least for the select few, at a time when history does not speak clearly enough.

The decline of biblical prophecy and the rise of pseudepigraphic apocalypses are often taken as reflecting a feeling that God had become distant. Communication was no longer direct. It took place instead through symbolic visions, and even these visions were attributed to great figures of the past.

This view seems to me to be based primarily on one aspect of apocalyptic literature, the symbolic visions. The apocalyptic tours point in a different direction. It is true that the God of the Book of the Watchers is found not in Jerusalem, but on His heavenly throne. Yet Enoch is able to ascend to stand before that throne! In doing so he continues the tradition of the prophets who stand in the heavenly council. The fact that the heroes of apocalyptic tours are able to take their place with the angels in the heavenly liturgy means that closeness to God is available at least for the elect. Although the significance of the attribution of the ascents to heaven to heroes of the biblical past cannot be denied, it must be remembered that Qumran offers us a contemporary example of a whole community that understood itself to enjoy fellowship with angels. Thus, the message of the apocalyptic tours is more than the claim that great men in the past could stand before God's throne. Attention to the tours, then, leads toward a fuller and richer understanding of the times in which these works were written and the spiritual life of Israel in these centuries of transition.

Notes

1. Quotations from *1 Enoch* are taken from R. H. Charles, *The Book of Enoch* (Oxford: Clarendon Press, 1912). This translation with an abbreviated version of the notes appears also in *Apocrypha and Pseudepigrapha of the Old Testament*, ed. R. H. Charles. A new translation by Ephraim Isaac appears in *Old Testament Apocrypha*, ed. J. H. Charlesworth.

2. For the Book of the Watchers as exegetical, see George W. E. Nickelsburg, *Jewish Literature Between the Bible and the Mishnah*, 49–52. For a radical version of the other view, see J. T. Milik, *The Books of Enoch: Aramaic Fragments of Qumran Cave 4* (Oxford: Clarendon Press, 1976) 31.

3. Abraham: *Apocalypse of Abraham, Testament of Abraham*; Levi: *Testament of Levi* 2–7 (in the *Testaments of the Twelve Patriarchs*); Isaiah: *Ascension of Isaiah*; Zephaniah: *Apocalypse of Zephaniah*; Baruch: *3 Baruch*. Enoch is the hero of tours not only in the Book of the Watchers but also in the Book of the Heavenly Luminaries (*1 Enoch* 72–82), the Parables of Enoch (*1 Enoch* 37–71), and *2 Enoch*. With the exception of the *Ascension of Isaiah*, all of these works appear in Charlesworth, *Old Testament Apocrypha*. The *Ascension of Isaiah* in its present form is a Christian work, but in my view a Jewish version stands behind the Christian. The *Ascension of Isaiah* appears in Edgar Hennecke, *New Testament Apocrypha*, ed. Wilhelm Schneemelcher, Eng. trans. ed. by R. Mcl. Wilson (Philadelphia: Westminster, 1965) vol. 2. For a brief discussion of all works except the *Ascension of Isaiah* and the *Apocalypse of Zephaniah*, see Nickelsburg, *Jewish Literature*.

4. For a discussion of pseudepigraphy, see John J. Collins, *The Apocalyptic Vision of the Book of Daniel*, Harvard Semitic Monographs 16 (Missoula, MT: Scholars Press, 1977) 67–74.

5. All quotations of biblical texts are taken from the new Jewish Publication Society translation (JPS).

6. Martha Himmelfarb, *Tours of Hell*, 58–60.

7. The only work in which strong eschatological interests appear during the tour itself is the Parables of Enoch. The ascent of the *Apocalypse of Abraham* culminates in a symbolic vision of world history like those of the eschatological apocalypses, and the

ascent of the *Ascension of Isaiah* ends with a vision of Christ in descent to earth, an event with eschatological significance.

8. For a discussion of the distinction between apocalyptic eschatology and the apocalypse as a genre, see Michael E. Stone, "Lists of Revealed Things in Apocalyptic Literature," in *Magnalia Dei: The Might Acts of God*, 439–43.

9. Stone considers these three apocalypses atypical ("Lists," 443).

10. The fragments are published by Milik in *Books of Enoch*.

11. Before the Qumran discoveries, scholars had divided *1 Enoch* into five sections on the basis of obvious internal indications. The Parables of Enoch (*1 Enoch* 37–71) does not appear at Qumran, but the Qumran manuscripts include fragments of the other four sections of *1 Enoch*. With the Qumran discoveries the old debate about whether Hebrew or Aramaic was the original language of *1 Enoch* has been resolved in favor of Aramaic (except for the Parables of Enoch). What is preserved in Aramaic, it should be emphasized, is extremely fragmentary. The complete *1 Enoch* survives only in Ethiopic. Where the Aramaic can be compared to the Ethiopic, the correspondence is close but not exact. The Ethiopic was probably translated from the Greek version that survives in fragments, including a long stretch of the Book of the Watchers. As the only complete text, the Ethiopic remains indispensable.

12. For dates, see Milik, *Books of Enoch*, 7, 22–24. For some implications of the dates, see Michael E. Stone, "The Book of Enoch and Judaism in the Third Century B.C.E.," *Catholic Biblical Quarterly* 40 (1978) 479–92.

13. See Nickelsburg, *Jewish Literature*, 48–55, for an analysis of sources in the Book of the Watchers.

14. G. Scholem, *Major Trends in Jewish Mysticism*, 3rd ed. (New York: Schocken Books, 1954) 43–44.

15. On the relationship of *1 Enoch* 14 to Ezekiel 1, see Nickelsburg, *Jewish Literature*, 52–54; and especially Nickelsburg, "Enoch, Levi, and Peter: Recipients of Revelation in Upper Galilee," *Journal of Biblical Literature* 100 (1981) 580–82.

16. Nickelsburg emphasizes this point ("Enoch," 580).

17. For example, 1 Kings 22, Isaiah 40, Psalm 82. See the discussion in F. M. Cross, *Canaanite Myth and Hebrew Epic*, 186–90.

18. Cross, *Canaanite Myth*, 177–86.

19. Ibid., 179–80.

20. Johann Maier, *Vom Kultus zur Gnosis, Kairos:* Religionswissenschaftliche Studien 1 (Salzburg: Otto Müller, 1964) 97–101.

21. On this episode, see, for example, John Bright, *A History of Israel*, 3rd ed. (Philadelphia: Westminster, 1981) 293, 298–309.

22. It is against this view that Jeremiah warns: "Don't put your trust in illusions and say, 'The Temple of the LORD, the Temple of the LORD, the Temple of the LORD are these [buildings]'" (Jer 7:4).

23. Maier, *Gnosis*, 105–6.

24. On this claim, see Yehezkel Kaufmann, *The Religion of Israel*, trans. and abridged by M. Greenberg (New York: Schocken Books, 1972) 430–32.

25. Maier, *Gnosis*, 112–14.

26. Nickelsburg, "Enoch," 581–82.

27. Nickelsburg suggests that the verb "approach" (Charles: "draw nigh") in *1 Enoch* 14:23 has a technical, priestly meaning ("Enoch," 580–81 n. 19, 585).

28. Trans. O. S. Wintermute, in *Old Testament Pseudepigrapha*, ed. Charlesworth.

29. Geza Vermes, *The Dead Sea Scrolls in English*, 2nd ed. (Harmondsworth: Penguin Books, 1975) 210–13.

30. On the *hekhalot* hymns, see Scholem, *Major Trends,* 57–63; and idem, *Jewish Gnosticism, Merkabah Mysticism, and Talmudic Tradition,* 2nd ed. (New York: Jewish Theological Seminary, 1965) 20–29.

31. On the nature of hekhalot mysticism, see Scholem, *Major Trends,* 54–57.

32. Ibid., 49–51.

33. For similar conclusions about Jewish apocalypses generally on the quite different grounds of cross-cultural prallels, see Susan Niditch, "The Visionary," in *Ideal Figures in Ancient Judaism,* ed. George W. E. Nickelsburg and John J. Collins; Septuagint and Cognate Studies 12 (Chico, CA: Scholars Press, 1980) 155–63.

34. Nickelsburg, *Jewish Literature,* 54–55.

35. Himmelfarb, *Tours of Hell,* 50–60, 67.

36. Ibid., 56–60.

37. Charles refers to "Greek elements" in his commentary on chapters 17–19 (*Book of Enoch,* 38), and Nickelsburg shares this view (*Jewish Literature,* 54) Milik views both tours as influenced by Babylonian cosmology (*Books of Enoch,* 29–31, 37–38), although he admits Greek and Ugaritic elements (pp. 38–39).

38. See, for example, Gerhard von Rad, *Wisdom in Israel* (Nashville: Abingdon, 1972) 289–304.

39. The words of this prophet are found in chapters 40–55 of the book of Isaiah. The prophet was active in Babylonia ca. 540, just before the fall of Babylonia to Cyrus of Persia. See, for example, John McKenzie, *Second Isaiah,* Anchor Bible (Garden City, NY: Doubleday, 1968) lviii–lx.

40. On this passage, see McKenzie, *Second Isaiah,* 23–25.

41. On this myth and its relation to biblical literature, see Cross, *Canaanite Myth,* 112–44.

42. See E. A. Speiser (*Genesis,* Anchor Bible 3rd ed. [Garden City, NY: Doubleday, 1979] 9–11) for a discussion of the relationship between the Babylonian myth and genesis 1.

43. Cross, *Canaanite Myth,* 156–63.

44. Ibid., 105–11.

45. Ibid., 343–46.

46. Ibid.

47. Stone shows that one apocalypse, 4 Ezra, can be read as a polemic against the claim that such secrets are ever revealed to human beings ("Lists," 419–26).

48. For an introduction to the Qumran community, see Vermes, *The Dead Sea Scrolls: Qumran in Perspective* (Cleveland: Collins & World, 1977).

49. Himmelfarb, *Tours of Hell,* 61–66.

50. Ibid., 52.

51. Stone points to the presence of lists of the contents of revelation that include secrets of nature in several eschatological apocalypses that otherwise have little interest in such secrets ("Lists"). The significance of the lists will have to be considered in any discussion of the relationship between the eschatological apocalypses and the tour apocalypses.

52. For a survey of recent positions on the subject, see W. C. van Unnik, "Gnosis und Judentum," in *Gnosis: Festschrift für Hans Jonas,* ed. Barbara Aland (Göttingen: Vandenhoeck & Ruprecht, 1978) 65–86.

53. See, for example, "The Apocalypse of Paul," "Zostrianos," "Marsanes," and "Allogenes," in the *Nag Hammadi Library,* ed. James M. Robinson (San Francisco: Harper & Row, 1977).

Bibliography

The apocalypses discussed above appear in one or both of two collections. Charles is the classic English-language collection; the new collection, Charlesworth, contains many additional texts. An excellent introduction to most of the works included in these volumes is Nickelsburg. Two excellent but quite different introductory treatments of the early Second Temple period are Bickerman and Stone, *Scriptures.* Stone's book emphasizes apocalyptic literature. A good example of a standard scholarly view of the apocalypses with an almost exclusive emphasis on eschatology is Russell. Some of the most important recent developments in the study of the emergence of apocalyptic eschatology derive from the insights of Cross. A recent attempt to take a fresh look at the relationship between genre and content is *Apocalypse,* ed. Collins.

The significance of the new dates for the Book of the Watchers and the Book of the Heavenly Luminaries is discussed in Stone, "Enoch." VanderKam treats the development of the Enoch traditions. Stone, "Lists," is a seminal discussion of the place of secrets of nature in apocalyptic literature. Himmelfarb traces the development of the concern with punishment in the afterlife in apocalyptic literature. Gruenwald offers an overview of the relationship between the apocalypses and early Jewish mysticism.

Bickerman, Elias. *From Ezra to the Last of the Maccabees: Foundations of Post-Biblical Judaism.* New York: Schocken Books, 1962.

Charles, R. H., ed. *The Apocrypha and Pseudepigrapha of the Old Testament.* 2 vols. Oxford: Clarendon Press, 1913.

Charlesworth, J. H., ed. *Old Testament Apocrypha.* 2 vols. Garden City, NY: Doubleday, 1983–84.

——, ed. *The Old Testament Pseudepigrapha.* Vol. 1, Apocalyptic Literature and Testaments (Garden City, NY: Doubleday, 1983).

Collins, John J., ed. *Apocalypse: The Morphology of a Genre.* Semeia 14. Chico, CA: Scholars Press, 1979.

Cross, F. M. *Canaanite Myth and Hebrew Epic.* Cambridge, MA: Harvard University Press, 1973.

Gruenwald, Ithamar. *Apocalyptic and Merkavah Mysticism.* Leiden: Brill, 1980.

Himmelfarb, Martha. *Tours of Hell: An Apocalyptic Form in Jewish and Christian Literature.* Philadelphia: University of Pennsylvania Press, 1983.

Nickelsburg, George W. E. *Jewish Literature Between the Bible and the Mishnah.* Philadelphia: Fortress, 1981.

Russell, D. S. *The Method and Message of Jewish Apocalyptic.* Philadelphia: Westminster, 1964.

Stone, Michael E. "The Book of Enoch and Judaism in the Third Century B.C.E." *Catholic Biblical Quarterly* 40 (1978) 479–92.

——. "Lists of Revealed Things in Apocalyptic Literature." In *Magnalia Dei: The Mighty Acts of God: Essays on the Bible and Archaeology in Memory of G. Ernest Wright.* Ed. F. M. Cross, W. E. Lemke, and P. D. Miller. Garden City, NY: Doubleday, 1976.

——. *Scriptures, Sects and Visions.* Philadelphia: Fortress, 1980.

VanderKam, James C. *Enoch and the Growth of an Apocalyptic Tradition.* Catholic Biblical Quarterly Monograph Series 16. Washington, DC: Catholic Biblical Association, 1984.

Part Two

EMERGENCE
The Rabbinic Age

My God
A pure soul have You placed within me.
You created it, fashioned it, breathed it into me;
You guard it within me
And You will take it from me
And return it to me
In time to come.
So long as that soul is within me
I acknowledge You, LORD,
My God and God of my ancestors,
Master of all deeds,
LORD of all souls.

Berakhot 60b; *Daily Liturgy*

Were our mouths filled with song like the sea,
  Our tongues with joyous shout like its endless waves;
Were our lips broad with praise like the very skies,
  Our eyes shining with light like sun and moon;
Were our arms stretched forth like the wings of heaven's eagles,
  Our feet as light and swift as birds—
All these would barely suffice to thank You,
  LORD, our parents' God and ours,
Even for a thousandth part of Your goodness to .us:
        You redeemed us from Egypt,
          brought us forth from bondage;
        You fed us in hungry times,
          sustained us in plenty;
        You saved us from the sword,
          protected us from plague,
        Uplifting us from all our most persistent ills.
Thus far have Your mercies been our help,
  Your kindness never failing.
Do not abandon us, LORD God,
  ever.

Sabbath Liturgy

Rivers of Joy,
Rivers of Gladness
Rivers of Happiness,
Rivers of Desire,
Rivers of Love,
Rivers of Endearment
Flow forth from before the Throne of Glory
Rushing through the pathways of heaven.
The musical sound of His beings' harps,
The beating sound of His holy ones' drums,
The tympanous sound of His cherubim's song
Go forth in a mighty and holy shout,
As Israel proclaim
"Holy Holy is the LORD of hosts,
Earth is filled with His glory!"

Seder Rav Amram

5. Moses receiving the Torah at Sinai
from the beginning of the Tractate Avot
of the Rothschild Mahzor, Ms. 8892, f. 139a

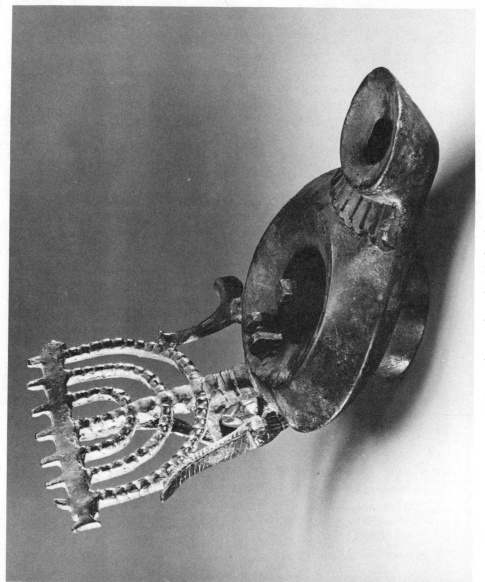

6. Bronze lamp, Alexandria (?), fourth century

7. Sacrifice of Isaac, Beth Alpha Synagogue

8. Zodiac Panel, Beth Alpha Synagogue

Varieties of Judaism
in the Formative Age

JACOB NEUSNER

THE FORM OF JUDAISM we know today as the world view and way
of life of the Judaic sector of the Jewish people reaches back to
the origins of ancient Israel. But its lines of structure flow more
immediately out of a brief period in the long history of Israel, the
Jewish people. Specifically, Judaism as we know it took shape before and
after the destruction of the Temple of Jerusalem in 70 C.E. By around 600
C.E., it was fully worked out.

Surveying the landscape of ancient Judaism from the perspective of the
Maccabean times, ca. 150 B.C.E., we search in vain for the rabbi as model and
authority, Torah as the principal and organizing symbol, study of Torah as
the capital religious deed, the life of religious discipline as the prime expression of what it means to be Israel, the Jewish people. These definitive
characteristics of Judaism as we now know it, and as the world has known
it from late antiquity, simply make no appearance. In particular, we find no
evidence whatever of the rabbi as the Torah incarnate and the human being
who shows what it means to be "like God," "in our image and likeness."
These twin notions define Judaism as it has flourished for nearly twenty
centuries, and, as I said, we find no evidence whatsoever that anyone held
them much before the first century, if then.

True, we may find in writers of books of wisdom, both canonical and
otherwise, values congenial to the system of Torah study that was later paramount. Stress on the holy way of life characteristic of all Israelites, familiar
in Judaism through nearly twenty centuries, may prove congruent to the
conception of the good life—life as a cultic act—expressed by priestly
writers. But the priests thought of themselves. Their caste in particular lived
by divinely ordained rules. The ideal of all Israel as a kingdom of priests and

171

a holy people for the priests was fully realized in their caste. Others attained holiness through finding a position in relationship to the consecrated caste.

Accordingly, the principal traits of Judaism, emphasis on study of Torah and practice of its religious precepts so as to define a holy way of life and give social expression to the distinctive ethos and ethic of Torah, the whole pointing toward the coming of the messiah—these scarcely coalesce. Writers of wisdom books represent one component, priests the second, and apocalyptic writers, the messianic constituent. In the Essene community at Qumran we find the three joined into a priestly commune, based on the study of Torah, preparing for a messianic war. But the Essenes scarcely prefigure Judaism as we have known it, for the Essenes stood for themselves only, not for all Israel. And the paramount trait of Judaism, once it had taken shape, lay in its insistence upon speaking for, and representing, all Israel, the entire Jewish people. Without the social aspiration, the components joined in the Judaism of which we speak—wisdom's stress on learning in ancient Scripture and traditions, the priesthood's focus upon living in accord with God's rules of sanctity and sanctification—never could have coalesced. Judaism, emerging from late antiquity, would unite the ethics of wisdom, the ethos of the priesthood, and the social focus of messianism, into the peoplehood of Israel. The catalyst, above all, would be the entry, into the mix, of the messianic hope.

The Rabbi

When people believed that by studying the Torah and keeping the commandments they would take a critical role in the coming of the messiah, Judaism as we have known it for nearly two millennia was born. When, further, Jews reached the conviction that the figure of the rabbi encompassed all three—the learning, the doing, the hope—Judaism had come to full and enduring expression. As I said, the rabbi as incarnate and avatar and model of the son of David embodied Judaism and gave to it his honorific, "rabbi," a mere commonplace title of respect when it first appeared. So Judaism became *rabbinic*. In due course, the entirety of Judaic existence, from remote past to yearned-for future, sustained a process of rabbinization: the rereading of everything in terms of the system of the rabbi.

When, again, we refer to the rabbi as avatar and incarnation of Torah, what do we mean? It is simple. The notion that humanity is made in God's image and likeness comes in the Torah. The rabbinical form of Judaism maintains that it is the task of every Jew to become "like God." So, for example, just as God is merciful and long-suffering, so must every Jew become merciful and long-suffering. Now when we ask: "Who among us now comes closest to the Torah's picture of God?" the answer is: "The one who knows Torah best." That of course is the rabbi. But the conception of the rabbi as "Torah incarnate" goes beyond the rather general allegation that the rabbi shows us the human face of God. The rabbi's deeds serve as sources of law. That is the definitive point in so law-centered a religious tradition as the rabbinical version of Judaism. If a rabbi were a model merely of pious virtue, the picture would be altogether too general. But if, as is the case, what a rabbi did on a given occasion serves as a model for the law, so that, on a later occasion, people will formulate for memorization a legal teaching in accord with the gesture of a respected sage, then the rabbi constitutes a living Torah. He is, as I said, the avatar and the incarnation of the Torah. So we should all be "like God," and when we are like the rabbi, we gain access to what it means to be "like God."

The rabbi remained human, anchored to this earth. True, he was the holy man. He was in the model of the son of David, so that the messiah would be a rabbi. The rabbi was a living Torah, a source of Torah teaching, including Torah law. This was through what he did, not only through what he said or could cite from his masters. But the rabbi remained at one with all other Jews. How so? He was first, human, always human, only human. His supernatural standing derived from the Torah he knew, not from any transformation effected because of what he knew. That is to say, Torah knowledge did not transform the one who knew it into a different sort of being from other Jews. The rabbi shared knowledge of revelation that God had given to Moses: that made him a holy man; it did not mean he was no longer a man. He was not God. He was like God.

The difference between the one and the other lies at the center of rabbinic Judaism. For the aspiration of the rabbi, as revealed in every line of rabbinic literature, was for all Israel, the community as a whole, to master the Torah and become, like rabbis, the people in the likeness and image of God. What made the rabbi different from other supernatural figures of antiquity was his aspiration *not* to be different from other Jews. What formed rabbinic Judaism was its insistence that all Israel be holy and be made holy. True, the rabbi was different from other Jews. But, as I just said, the rabbi's deepest aspiration was that other Jews be like him, so that he would not be different at all.

So when we speak of the rabbi as holy man, son of David, Torah incarnate, we do so in the context of the rabbi's own conviction, to begin with, that all Israel must become true to the Torah. The community must become the incarnation of the Torah's vision of Israel. What made the rabbi the norm—as he was for nearly two thousand years—was the rabbi's own aspiration to serve all Israel, his own insistence upon his this-worldly standing within Israel, his own unceasing demand that every Jew affirm his humanity, become like God, in the model of the Torah as the rabbi taught it. This, then, is the full vision for humanity offered by the rabbi to Israel.

Now, as I said, if in our imagination we stand in the time and place of the Maccabees and look out at the world of Judaism, we scarcely discern even an adumbration of the revolution in Israelite existence represented by the figure and fantasy of the rabbi. The world we should see knows an Israel governed by a king and centered on the Temple, a king who commanded the priesthood as high priest (much like the fantasy portrayed in Mishnah tractate *Sanhedrin*)—no rabbi here. If we leap forward to search for even incipient "rabbinism" in the portrayals of the life and teachings of Jesus, we find a picture of a community pretty much continuous with the one of the Maccabees. There is a Temple and a high priest in charge, alongside Jewish kings who ruled by the grace of a distant empire—still no rabbi. The constant point of reference remains Scripture, the revelation of God to Moses at Sinai and the interpretation and application of that revelation, that is, Torah, to the life of the people, on the one side, and to its destiny, on the other. Again, no rabbis here.

So into the first century the principal institutions of Israel remained priesthood and monarchy, Scripture and its way of life, holy Temple, land, and people. Various groups—Essenes, Pharisees—claimed to possess traditions in addition to Scripture. But in sources produced in the period (not merely those that refer to it but were produced much later on), we find no references to an additional, oral Torah, revealed to Moses at Sinai along with the written one, nor are there portraits of rabbis as holy men. In the Gospels, "rabbi" is an honorific, as I said, and not a title specific to a particular group, just as, for a long time, "rabbi" or "rabban" served as a title for holy men in Syriac Christianity as much as in rabbinic Judaism. The commanding concern of Israel focused, as it had for a long time, upon sanctification in the cult and salvation flowing from it, not on where things were heading and what events meant. These building blocks of political and social existence remained solid. The imaginative life of Israel encompassed long centuries past, essentially within a single vision, a cogent construction of reality, stable, enduring, properly classified.

If, now, we take the long step forward by yet another two hundred years, to the third century, the world has changed. Israel's life in the Land of Israel has come under the domination of not priests or kings but rabbis. No longer paramount in splendid isolation, Scripture shares the proscenium of Israel's mind and imagination. On the stage alongside it is the Mishnah, soon to be declared the other oral Torah of Sinai. There no longer is a Temple. People do not worship God any more by bringing animals, killing them, sprinkling the blood on the stones of an altar, and burning up the entrails on a fire, the smoke to please God's nose. So everything has changed. Yet all the critical constituents of the Israelite system of earlier days remained. What has happened is that they have undergone rearrangement, and, more important, everything has been reworked. In the rabbis' transvaluation of values, a priest no longer was what he had long been, and Torah too had come to stand for something else, something more. Accordingly, between the time of the composition of the Gospels, in the later first century, and the formation of the Mishnah, in the later second, Israel with all its heritage was turning in a direction never before taken, taking a path from which—we now know—there would be no returning.

The Types of Judaism

The task at hand is to sort out the main lines of movement in a confused age. Specifically, we ask about the diversity of the antecedent structures— the types of Judaism—and the symbols that embodied them. We want to know how these coalesced into Judaism as we have known it. Since we seek to describe and interpret modes of piety within late antique Israel, we ourselves imagine how things appeared to people whom we know only at a considerable distance. From what people said and did we attempt to figure out what they thought and how they felt. And this we do in such a way that what was complex we treat as simple; what was mixed, as pure.

In positing three ideal types of Israelite piety—priest, scribe, messiah—we suspend for the moment our disbelief that things can have ever been so simple. We recognize the opposite. The troops of a messianic army also observed Scripture's sacred calendar. Their goal was not only to enthrone the king-messiah, their general, but also to rebuild the Temple, to reestablish the priesthood, and to restore the sacrificial cult. The Essene community at Qumran, as we have already noted, joined together the themes and streams we treat as separate: priesthood, messiah, Torah study. By the earliest writers in Israelite Christianity, Jesus is often represented as king-messiah, but also as prophet and king, and, furthermore, as perfect priest and sacrifice, and always as sage, wise teacher, and rabbi (which accounts for the fact that the bulk of the ethical sayings attributed to him are commonplaces in the Judaism of the age). Accordingly, none of the symbolic systems at hand, with their associated modes of piety and faith and religious imagination, ever existed as we shall treat them, as pure and unalloyed, as ideal types awaiting description and interpretation.

The inquiry at hand centers on the symbols through which Jews expressed their feelings for God, their view of God's rule of the world, their own nation, and the lives they led. These symbols further embody and expose the way of life led by diverse groups of Jews, which allows us to grasp as a whole a sizable number of details about how things were done or not done. To seek a typology of the modes of piety, we look for the generative symbol of each of those modes: an altar for the priestly ideal; a scroll of Scripture for the ideal of wisdom; a coin marked "Israel's freedom: Year one" for the messianic modality. In each of these visual symbols we perceive the things we cannot touch, the hearts and minds we can only hope to evoke. Our supposition is that we enter into the imagination of someone else, long ago and far away, by our effort to appreciate and understand the way in which that other person framed the world, captured everything in some one thing: the sheep for the sacrifice, the memorized wise saying for the disciple, the stout heart for the soldiers of light.

Priest, sage, soldier—all of these figures stand for Israel, or part of the nation. When all would meld into one, that one would stand for some fresh and unprecedented Judaism. Jesus represented as perfect priest, rabbi, messiah, was one such protean figure. The talmudic rabbi as Torah incarnate, priest manqué, and model of the son of David, was another. In both cases we find a fresh reading of an old symbol and, more important, an unprecedented rereading of established symbols in fresh and striking ways. The history of piety in Israel is the story of the successive arrangements and revisions of available symbols. From ancient Israelite times onward, there would be no new classification beyond the three taxa. But no category would ever be left intact for long. When Jesus asked people what they thought he was, the enigmatic answer proves less interesting than the question. For the task he set before them was to reframe everything they knew in the encounter with the one they did not know: taxonomic. When, along these same lines, the rabbis of the later centuries of late antiquity rewrote in their own image and likeness the entire Scripture and history of Israel, dropping whole eras as though they had never been, ignoring vast bodies of old Jewish writing, inventing whole new books for the canon of Judaism, they did the same. They reworked the received in the light of what they proposed to give. No mode of piety could be left untouched, for all proved promising. But every mode of piety would be reworked in the light of the vast public events represented by the religious revolutionaries at hand, rabbi-clerks, rabbi-priests, rabbi-messiahs.

The issues of the symbols under discussion, Temple altar, sacred scroll, victory wreath for the head of the king-messiah, addressed Jewish society at large. We need not reduce them to their social dimensions to recognize that, at the foundations, we deal with the issues of the organization of society and the selection and interpretation of its history. Let us rapidly review the sectors of society addressed by the framers of these symbols.

The priest, as we know, viewed society as organized through lines of structure emanating from the Temple. His caste stood at the top of a social scale in which all things were properly organized, each with its correct name and proper place. The sanctity inhering in Israel, the people, came to its richest embodiment in him, the priest. Food set aside for his rations at God's command possessed that same sanctity; so too did the table at which he ate his food, when properly protected. To the priest the sacred society of Israel produced no history except for what happened in—and alas, on occasion, to—the Temple.

To the sage, the ongoing life of society demanded wise regulation. Relationships among people, guided by the laws and rules revealed of old and embodied in the Torah and best interpreted by the sage, were there to be governed. Accordingly, the task of Israel was to construct a way of life in accordance with the revealed rules of the Torah. The sage, master of the rules, stood at the head.

So far as prophecy's insistence that the fate of the nation depended upon the faith and moral condition of society, history testified to the context and inner condition of Israel, viewed whole. Both sage and priest saw Israel from the aspect of eternity. But the nation lived out its life in this world, among other people coveting the very same land, within the politics of empires. The messiah's kingship would resolve the issues of Israel's subordinated relationship to other nations and empires, establishing once for all time the correct context for priest and sage alike.

Implicit within the messianic framework was the perspective on a world out there of which priest and sage cared not at all—a society, nation, history. The priest saw the receding distances of the world beyond the Temple as less holy, then unholy, then unclean. All lands outside of the land of Israel were chronically unclean with corpse uncleanness. All peoples but Israel were inherently unclean as corpses were unclean. Accordingly, life abided within Israel, and, in Israel, within the Temple. Outside, in the far distance, were the vacant lands and dead peoples, all of them an undifferentiated wilderness. From such a perspective on the world, no doctrine of Israel among the nations and no interest in the history of Israel and in the meaning of its past and future were apt to emerge.

The sagacity of the sage, in general, pertained to the streets, marketplaces, and domestic establishments—the household units—of Israel. What the sage said was wise, therefore wise as much for Gentile as for Israel. Wisdom in the nature of things proved international, moving easily across boundaries of culture and language, from eastern to southern to western Asia. Its

focus, by definition, lay upon universal human experience, hence undifferentiated by nation, essentially unaffected by the large movements of history.
Wisdom spoke about fathers and sons, masters and disciples, families and
villages, not about nations, armies, and destiny.

So I suppose that, because of their diversity, the three principal motifs of
Israelite existence might readily cohere. Each focused upon a distinct and
particular aspect of the national life, so that none essentially intersected
with, or contradicted, any other. One could worship at the Temple, study
the Torah, and fight in the army of the messiah, and many did all three. Yet
we must see these modes of being, and their consequent motifs of piety, as
separate, each with its own potentiality of full realization wholly without
the others.

For the three modes of human existence expressed in the symbolic
systems of cult, Torah, and messiah do demand choices. If one thing is
important, then the others must be less important. History matters, or it
happens "out there" and does not matter. The proper conduct of the cult
determines the course of the seasons and the prosperity of the land, or it
is mere ritual. The messiah will save Israel, or he will ruin everything.
Accordingly, while we take for granted that people could live within the
vision of priest, sage, and messiah, we also recognize that it was vertiginous,
a blurred perception. Narratives of the war of 66–73 emphasize how priests
warned messianists not to endanger the Temple. Later sages, talmudic
rabbis, paid slight honor to the messianic struggle led by Bar Kokhba and,
after 70, claimed the right to tell priests what to do. It must follow that the
way in which the several symbols are arranged and rearranged settles everything. Symbol change is social change. A mere amalgam of all three, by
itself, hardly serves as a mirror for the mind of Israel. The way the three
are bonded reflects an underlying human and social reality.

That is how it should be, since the three symbols with their associated
myths, the world view they project, the way of life they define, stand for
different views of what really matters in life. In investigating the existential
foundations of the several symbolic systems available to ancient Jews, we
seek to penetrate to the bedrock of Israel's reality, the basis for the life of
the nation of Israel and each Israelite, the ground of being—even to the
existential core we share with them.

Time and Eternity

Let us unpack this notion of the two focuses of existence, public history and
private home, hearth, society, and village. We may call the one "time," in that
the focus of interest is in history, what happens day by day in the here and
now. The other we may call "eternity," in that the focus of interest is in the

ongoing patterns of life, birth, and death; planting and harvest; the regular movement of the sun, moon, and stars in heaven; and of the night and day, Sabbaths and festivals, and regular seasons on earth. The shared existential issue is this: How do we respond to the ups and downs of life? Every group that survives long enough experiences "history," those noteworthy events. The events of individual life, birth, maturing, marriage, death, do not make or add up to history, except for individuals. But the events of group life — formation of the group, developing social norms and patterns, depression or prosperity, war or peace—these do make history. When a small people coalesces and begins its course through history in the face of adversity, two things can happen.

Either the group disintegrates in the face of disaster and loses its hold on its individual members, or the group fuses and is strenthened by trial, is able to turn adversity into the occasion of renewal.

The triple focuses around which human and national existence were interpreted—priests', sages', messianists'—emerge, we must remember, from the national and social consciousness of ancient Israel. The heritage of the TaNaKH, the Hebrew Scriptures, was carried forward among all three approaches to Judaism. The Jewish people has known the mystery of how to endure through history, for it is one of the oldest peoples now alive on the face of the earth. Even in ancient Israel, adversity elicited self-conscious response. Things did not merely *happen* to the ancient Israelites. Events were shaped, reformed, and interpreted by them, made into the raw materials for a renewal of the life of the group. The reason is that the ancient Israelites regarded their history as important, as teaching significant lessons. History was not merely one thing after another; it had a purpose and was moving somewhere. The writers of Leviticus and Deuteronomy, of the historical books from Joshua through Kings, and of the prophetic literature, agreed that when Israel does God's will they enjoy times of peace, security, and prosperity, and that when they do not they are punished at the hands of mighty kingdoms, who are themselves raised up as instruments of God's wrath. This conception of the meaning of Israel's life produced a further question: How long? When do the great events of time come to their climax and conclusion? And in answer to that question, the hope for the messiah, the anointed of God who would redeem the people, set them on the right path forever, and thus end the vicissitudes of history, was born.

A Turning Point

Now, when we reach the first century C.E., we come to a turning point in the messianic hope. No one who knows the Gospels will be surprised to learn of the intense, vivid, prevailing expectation that the messiah was coming soon. And it is hardly astonishing that that should be the case. People who fix their attention on everyday events of world-shaking dimensions naturally will look forward to a better future.

What is surprising is the development of a second, quite different response to history. It is the response of people prepared once and for all to transcend everyday events, to take their leave of wars and rumors of wars, of politics and public life, and to attempt to construct a new reality above history, a way of viewing reality on the far side of the everyday life. At hand after 70 was not merely a craven or exhausted passivity in the face of world-shaking events. We witness the beginnings of the active construction of a new mode of being. The decision is to exercise freedom, autonomous of history, to reconstruct conceptions of the meaning and ultimate significance of what happens. It is a seeking of a world, not outside this one, but different from and better than the one formed by ordinary history. The second approach is a quest for eternity in the here and now, an effort to form a society capable of abiding amid change and storm. Indeed, it is a fresh reading of the meaning of history: the nations of the world make history and think that what they do matters; but Israel knows that it is God who makes history and that it is the reality formed in response to God's will which *is* history.

That reality, that conception of time and change, forms the focus and the vision of the priestly tradition, continuing later on in rabbinic Judaism. This sort of Judaism is essentially a metahistorical approach to life. It expresses an intense inwardness and lays its stress upon the ultimate meaning contained within small and humble affairs. Rabbinic Judaism in time to come would set itself up as the alternative to all the forms of messianic Judaism—whether leading to Christianity or to militaristic Zealotry and nationalism—that claimed to know the secret of history: the time of and the way to redemption.

This approach to the life of Israel, stressing continuity and pattern and promising change only at the end, represents the union of two trends, as I have stressed. The one was symbolized by the altar, the other by the scroll of the Torah: the priest and the sage. In actual fact, the union was effected by a *kind* of priest manqué and a *kind* of sage. The former was the Pharisee, the latter, the scribe; the former, a particular sect of people who pretended, at home, that they were priests in the Temple. The latter was the scribe, member not of a sect but of a profession. The scribes were a class of teachers of the Torah, petty officials and bureaucrats. The scribes knew and taught Torah. They took their interpretation of Torah very seriously, it goes without saying, and the act of study to them was of special importance. The Pharisees had developed, for their part, a peculiar perception of how to live and interpret life, which we may call an "as-if" perception. In very specific ways the Pharisees claimed to live as if they were priests, as if they had to obey at home the laws that applied to the Temple. When the Temple itself was destroyed, it turned out that the Pharisees had prepared for that tremendous change in the sacred economy. They continue to live as if—as if the Temple stood, as if there was a new Temple formed of the Jewish people. Joined to their mode of looking at life was the substance of the scribal ideal, the stress on learning of Torah and carrying out its teachings.

These, then, represent the alternatives to how great events were to be experienced and understood. One was the historical-messianic way, which stressed the importance of those events and concentrated upon their weight and meaning. The other was the metahistorical, priestly-rabbinic way, which laid emphasis upon the transcendence of events and the construction of an eternal, changeless mode of being, capable of riding out the waves of history.

The Destruction the Temple in 70 C.E.

Accordingly, once we have identified the principal strands of Judaic consciousness, we deal with two questions. First, what made one focus—the priestly and the sagacious, or the messianic trend—appear to people to be more compelling and consequential than another? The answer becomes obvious when we realize that each kind of piety addresses its own point of concern. The several of them speak about different things to different people. We may sort them out from one another if we return to an earlier observation. Priests and sages turn inward, toward the concrete everyday life of the community. Messianists and their prophetic and apocalyptic teachers turn outward, toward the affairs of states and nations. Priests see the world of life, in Israel, requiring no theory about the place of Israel among the nations. The nations, as we noticed, form an undifferentiated realm of death. Sages, all the more, speak of home and hearth, fathers and sons, husbands and wives, the village and enduring patterns of life within it. What place in this domestic scheme for the realities of history—wars and threats of war, the rise and fall of empires, encompassing the consciousness of a singular society amidst other societies?

Second, what drew the three focuses together and made them one? It was an event in which all were equally involved. This was important to those to whom great events of history appear momentous—but also beyond the (even feigned) act of ignoring history that was deliberately committed by priests and sages. Such an event proved paramount in the period at hand. The ultimate destruction of the Temple in 70 C.E. provided the catalyst that joined priest, sage, and, in time to come, messianist, thereby creating that amalgam that was the Judaism framed by the rabbis of the Mishnah and collections of Midrash and two Talmuds. The three definitive components were then bonded.

The principle that Judaism would constitute a way of life aimed at sanctification was contributed by the priestly trend. The notion that Judaism demanded a life of study of Torah and the application of Torah to the life of the community derived from the scribes. The conception that the community of Israel stood apart from the nations and lived out a destiny of its own was the gift of the prophetic, apocalyptic, messianic trend. Events then added up to history. The history of Israel was shaped by God's response to Israel's study of Torah and life of sanctification. When the whole came together, forming the perfect creation as the beginning, then would come the last and enduring Sabbath, counterpart of the Sabbath of creation: the messiah and his age.

So the single critical event of the age presented a crisis to the priestly caste, the sages' profession, and the political and messianic sectors of the nation alike. The decisive event, which cut across all classes and movements of history, the caesura of the life of the cult, the classroom, and the clerks of government alike, was the destruction of the Temple of Jerusalem in 70 C.E. What was important was not that the Temple was destroyed; that had happened not once but many times before. It was that the Temple was not then rebuilt. In 586 the Jerusalem Temple had fallen, but a scant three generations had to pass before it was rebuilt. From that time onward, whatever happened to the Temple building, the cult endured. So the entire history of Israel testified to the Temple's prominence in the world of Israel. If it should again be destroyed, then, following the established pattern, people had every reason to expect that it would be rebuilt. Accordingly, the fact of the destruction in 70, though it bore profound consequences, by itself merely raised a question. The calamity that, three generations later, Bar Kokhba's armies, intent on retaking the holy city and rebuilding the Temple, suffered total defeat, turned the question into a crisis, the earlier destruction into the decisive turning point. But in what direction? And, more important, with what meaning for the whole of the past of Israel? The answer, stated very briefly, is simple. In the aftermath of the cultic, political, military disaster of 70 and 135, everything would be reworked, the entire heritage revised and renewed.

Four Responses

It follows that the responses of diverse groups to the destruction of the Temple allow us to sort out the varieties of Judaic piety beforehand and to see how the renewed Judaism of the talmudic tradition related to what had gone before. Accordingly, we now examine four responses to the challenges of the destruction of Jerusalem, the end of the Temple, and the cessation of the cult of animal sacrifice. These responses had to deal with several crucial social and religious problems, all interrelated. First, how to achieve atonement without the cult? Second, how to explain the disaster of the destruction? Third, how to cope with the new age, to devise a way of life on an entirely new basis? Fourth, how to account for the new social forms consequent upon the collapse of the old social structure? As I said, it was in the process of answering these questions that rabbinic Judaism was born. Its success in responding to them guaranteed its future.

The four responses are of, first, the apocalyptic writers represented in the visions of Baruch and 2 Ezra; second, the Dead Sea community at Qumran; third, the Christian church; and finally, the Pharisaic sect. The apocalyptic visionaries were writers who tried to interpret the meaning of events. They expected the imminent end of time, a cosmic cataclysm in which God would destroy evil and establish righteousness. The Essene community at Qumran formed a kind of sectarian monastery, with its particular way of seeing the meaning of history. The Christian church needs no introduction. The Pharisaic sect does, however, and I shall take some trouble to explain who the Pharisees were and how we know about them.

The Apocalyptic Visionaries

We begin with the group most interested in the meaning of history, in the coming of the messiah and the end of time. They were the apocalyptic visionaries, who claimed to interpret the great events of the day and to know where they were leading. When the apocalyptic visionaries looked backward upon the ruins, they saw a tragic vision. So they emphasized future, supernatural redemption, which they believed was soon to come. The Essenes had met the issues of 70–135 long before, in a manner essentially similar to that of the Christians. Both groups abandoned the Temple and its cult and replaced them by means of the new community, on the one hand, and the service or pious rites of the new community, on the other. The Pharisees come somewhere between the first, and the second and the third groups. Like the apocalyptists, they saw the destruction as a calamity; but like the Dead Sea sect and the Christians, they sought the means, in both social forms and religious expression, of providing a new way to atonement and a new form of divine service, to constitute a new, interim Temple.

Two documents, the *Apocalypse of Ezra* and the *Vision of Baruch,* are representative of the apocalyptic state of mind. The compiler of the Ezra apocalypse (2 Ezra 3–14), who lived at the end of the first century C.E., looked forward to a day of judgment when the messiah would destroy Rome and God would govern the world. But he had to ask, How can the suffering of Israel be reconciled with divine justice? To Israel, God's will had been revealed. But God had not removed the inclination to do evil, so human beings could not carry out God's will: "For we and our fathers have passed our lives in ways that bring death. . . . But what is man, that thou are angry with him, or what is a corruptible race, that thou art so bitter against it? . . ." (2 Ezra 8:26 [2 Esdras 8:31, RSV]). Ezra was told that God's ways are inscrutable (4:10–11), but when he repeated the question "Why has Israel been given over to the Gentiles as a reproach," he was given the answer characteristic of this literature, that a new age was dawning that would shed light on such perplexities. Thus, he was told: ". . . if you are alive, you will see, and if you live long, you will often marvel, because the age is hastening swiftly to its end. For it will not be able to bring the things that have been promised to the righteous in their appointed time, because this age is full of sadness and infirmities . . ." (4:10–26).

An angel told him the signs of the coming redemption, saying: ". . . the sun shall suddenly shine forth at night and the moon during the day, blood shall drip from wood, and the stone shall utter its voice, and the peoples shall be troubled, and the stars shall fall . . ." (5:4–5). And he was admonished to wait patiently: "The righteous therefore can endure difficult circumstances, while hoping for easier ones, but those who have done wickedly have suffered the difficult circumstances, and will not see easier ones" (6:55–56). The writer thus regarded the catastrophe as the fruit of sin; more specifically, the result of the natural human incapacity to do the will of God. He prayed for forgiveness and found hope in the coming transformation of the age and the promise of a new day, when the human heart would be as able, as the mind even then was willing, to do the will of God.

The pseudepigraph in the name of Jeremiah's secretary, Baruch, likewise brought promise of coming redemption, but with little practical advice for the intervening period. The document exhibits three major themes. First, God acted righteously in bringing about the punishment of Israel: "Righteousness belongs to the Lord our God, but confusion of face to us and our fathers . . ." (Baruch 2:6). Second, the catastrophe came on account of Israel's sin: "Why is it, O Israel . . . that you are in the land of your enemies . . . ? You have forsaken the fountain of wisdom. If you had walked in the way of the Lord, you would be dwelling in peace forever" (3:10–12). Third, as surely as God had punished the people, so certainly would he bring the people home to their land and restore their fortunes. Thus Jerusalem speaks: "But I, how can I help you? For He who brought these calamities upon you will deliver you from the hand of your enemies. . . . For I sent you out with sorrow and weeping, but God will give you back to me with joy and gladness forever . . ." (4:17–18, 23). Finally, Baruch advised the people to wait patiently for redemption, saying:

> My children, endure with patience the wrath that has come upon you from God. Your enemy has overtaken you, but you will soon see their destruction and will tread upon their necks. . . . For just as you purposed to go astray from God, return with tenfold zeal to seek Him. For He who brought these calamities upon you will bring you everlasting joy with your salvation. Take courage, O Jerusalem, for He who named you will comfort you. (4:25, 28–30)

The saddest words written in these times come in *2 Baruch:*

> Blessed is he who was not born, or he who, having been born,
>   has died
> But as for us who live, woe unto us
> Because we see the affliction of Zion and what has befallen
>   Jerusalem . . . .
>
>   (10:6–7)
>
>
> You husbandmen, sow not again.
> And earth, why do you give your harvest fruits?
> Keep within yourself the sweets of your sustenance.
> And you, vine, why do you continue to give your wine?
> For an offering will not again be made therefrom in Zion.
> Nor will first-fruits again be offered.
> And do you, O heavens, withhold your dew,
> And open not the treasuries of rain.
> And do you, sun, withhold the light of your rays,
> And you, moon, extinguish the multitude of your light.
> For why should light rise again
> Where the light of Zion is darkened? . . .
>
>   (10:9–12)
>
>
> Would that you had ears, O earth,
> And that you had a heart, O dust,
> That you might go and announce in Sheol,
> And say to the dead,
> "Blessed are you more than we who live."
>
>   (11:6–7)

The issue before all groups is, What to do now, today? We have suffered disaster. What is its meaning and where are we heading? The answer of this sad poem is utter nihilism. Once we are told, "We have no answer but patience," the next step is going to be the end of patience. But there is no new beginning. The apocalyptic writers have nothing to say to those who wait but "wait some more." No wonder then they conclude that death is better than life. For those who live, however, such a message is curiously inappropriate. Before we proceed, let us consider how a rabbi of the period is portrayed as having responded to the nihilistic message of the disappointed messianists.

A leading rabbi after 70, Rabbi Joshua is described as meeting such people. It was reported that when the Temple was destroyed, "ascetics multiplied in Israel," who would neither eat flesh nor drink wine. Rabbi Joshua dealt with them thus:

> He said to them, "My children, On what account do you not eat flesh and drink wine?"
> They said to him, "Shall we eat meat, from which they used to offer a sacrifice on the altar, and now it is no more? And shall we drink wine, which was poured out on the altar, and now it is no more?"
> He said to them. "If so, we ought not to eat bread, for there are no meal offerings any more. Perhaps we ought not to drink water, for the water-offerings are not brought anymore."
> They were silent.
> He said to them, "My children, come and I shall teach you. Not to mourn at all is impossible, for the evil decree has already come upon us. But to mourn too much is also impossible, for one may not promulgate a decree for the community unless most of the community can endure it. . . . But thus have the sages taught: 'A man plasters his house, but leaves a little piece untouched. A man prepares all the needs of the meal, but leaves out some morsel. A woman prepares all her cosmetics, but leaves off some small item. . . . (b. Baba Batra 60B).[1]

The response of the visionaries is, thus, essentially negative. All they had to say is that God is just and Israel has sinned, but, in the end of time, there will be redemption. What to do in the meantime? Merely wait—not much of an answer.

The Essene Community

For the Essene community, the destruction of the Temple cult took place long before 70. By rejecting the Temple and its cult of sacrifice, the community had had to confront a world without Jerusalem even while the city was still standing. The founders of the Qumran community were Temple priests, who saw themselves as continuators of the true priestly line. For them the old Temple was destroyed in the times of the Maccabees when it fell into the hands of usurpers. Its cult was defiled not by the Romans but by the rise of a high priest from a family other than the true priestly family. They further rejected the calendar followed in Jerusalem. They therefore set out to create a new Temple to serve, until God, through the messiah in the line of Aaron, would establish the true Temple once again. The Essene community believed that the presence of God had left Jerusalem and had come to the Dead Sea. The community now constituted the new Temple, just as some elements in early Christianity saw the new Temple in the body of Christ, in the church, the Christian community. In some measure, this represents a "spiritualization" of the old Temple, for the Temple was the community, and the Temple worship was effected through the community's study and fulfillment of the Torah. But the community was just as much a reality, a presence, as was the Jerusalem Temple; the obedience to the law was no less material and concrete than the blood sacrifices. The Essenes, thus, represent a middle point between reverence for the old Temple and its cult and complete indifference in favor of the Christians' utter spiritualization of both, represented, for example, in the letter to the Hebrews. The conception that the community of the Essenes comes together to constitute God's people is expressed in the Community Rule:

[The Master shall teach the sai]nts to live [according to] the Book of the Community Rule, that they may seek God with a whole heart and soul, and do what is good and right before Him as He commanded by the hand of Moses and all His servants the Prophets; that they may love all that He has chosen and hate all that He has rejected; that they may abstain from all evil and hold fast to all good; that they may practise truth, righteousness, and justice upon earth and no longer stubbornly follow a sinful heart and lustful eyes committing all manner of evil. He shall admit into the Covenant of Grace all those who have freely devoted themselves to the observance of God's precepts, that they may be joined to the counsel of God and may live perfectly before Him in accordance with all that has been revealed concerning their appointed times, and that they may love all the sons of light, each according to his lot in God's design, and hate all the sons of darkness, each according to his guilt in God's vengeance.

All those who freely devote themselves to His truth shall bring all their knowledge, powers, and possessions into the Community of God, that they may purify their knowledge in the truth of God's precepts and order their powers according to His ways of perfection and all their possessions according to His righteous counsel. They shall not depart from any command of God concerning their times; they shall be neither early nor late for any of their appointed times, they shall stray neither to right nor to left of any of His true precepts. All those who embrace the Community Rule shall enter into the Covenant before God to obey all His commandments so that they may not abandon Him during the dominion of Satan because of fear or terror or affliction. (1QS 1:1-18)[2]

We see that, although the community states "spiritual" purposes, the community is a real, material, social entity, something concrete and this-worldly.

The purpose of the Essene community at Qumran was to fight a holy war, the final war in the history of the world, in which Rome (the Kittim in the following passage) would be ultimately destroyed and the people of God would be saved and achieve dominion. So the community saw itself as standing on the brink of a glorious eternity. These were Jews preparing to fight the last and greatest war between the children of light and the children of darkness. Here is how the vision is presented in the War Rule:

> For the M[aster, the Rule of] War on the unleashing of the attack of the sons of light against the band of Edom, Moab, and the sons of Ammon, and [against the army of the sons of the East and] the Philistines, and against the bands of the Kittim of Assyria and their allies the ungodly of the Covenant.
>
> The sons of Levi, Judah, and Benjamin, the exiles in the desert, shall battle against them in . . . all their bands when the exiled sons of light return from the Desert of the Peoples to camp in the Desert of Jerusalem; and after the battle they shall go up from there (to Jerusalem?).
>
> [The king] of the Kittim [shall enter] into Egypt, and in his time he shall set out in great wrath to wage war against the kings of the north, that his fury may destroy and cut off the horn of [the nations].
>
> This shall be a time of salvation for the people of God, an age of dominion for all the members of His company, and of everlasting destruction for all the company of Satan. The confusion of the sons of Japheth shall be [great] and Assyria shall fall unsuccoured. The dominion of the Kittim shall come to an end and iniquity shall be vanquished, leaving no remnant; [for the sons] of darkness there shall be no escape. [The seasons of righteous]ness shall shine over all the ends of the earth; they shall go on shining until all the seasons of darkness are consumed and, at the season appointed by God, His exalted greatness shall shine eternally to the peace, blessing, glory, joy, and long life of all the sons of light.[3]

The community then constitutes the new Israel, the children of light who will fight a holy war at the end of days and constitute, in its social being, the Temple.

If the old Temple is destroyed, then how will Israel make atonement? The Essene answer is that the life of the community in perfect obedience to the Law represents the true sacrifice offered in the new Temple. The community thus takes over the holiness and the functions of the Temple, and so are preserved the means of maintaining the holiness of Israel and making atonement for sin. The response of the Dead Sea sect, therefore, was in imagination to reconstruct the Temple and to reinterpret the nature and substance of sacrifice. The community constituted the reconstructed Temple. The life of Torah and obedience to its commandments formed the new sacrifice.

The Christian Church

For a long time the Christian was another kind of Jew. Moreover, the Christians, whether originally Jewish or otherwise, took over the antecedent holy books and much of the ritual life of Judaism. For our purposes their piety serves, therefore, as another form of Judaism, one that differed from the others primarily in regarding the world as redeemed through the word and cross of Jesus. But one must hasten to stress the complexity of the Christian evidences. Indeed, the response of the Christians to the destruction of the Temple cannot be simplified and regarded as essentially unitary.

Because of their faith in the crucified and risen Christ, Christians experienced the end of the old cult and the old Temple before it actually took place, much like the Essene sectarians. They had to work out the meaning of the sacrifice of Jesus on the cross, and whether the essays on that central problem were done before or after 70 is of no consequence. The issues of 70 confronted Essenes and Christians for reasons other than narrowly historical ones. For both groups the events of that month took place, to to speak, in modes other than military and political ones. But the effects were much the same. The Christians, therefore, resemble the Essenes in having had to face the end of the cult before it actually ended. But they were like the Pharisees in having to confront the actual destruction of the Temple, then and there.

Like the Essenes, the Christian Jews criticized the Jerusalem Temple and its cult. Both groups in common believed that the last days had begun. Both believed that God had come to dwell with them, as He had once dwelled in the Temple. The sacrifices of the Temple were replaced, therefore, by the sacrifices of a blameless life and by other spiritual deeds. but the Christians differ on one important point. To them, the final sacrifice had already taken place, the perfect priest had offered up the perfect sacrifice, his own body. So, for the Christians, Christ on the cross completed the old sanctity and inaugurated the new. This belief took shape in different ways. For Paul, in 1 Corinthians 3:16–17, the church is the new Temple, and Christ is the foundation of the "spiritual" building. Ephesians 2:18ff. has Christ as the cornerstone of the new building, the company of Christians constituting the Temple.

Perhaps the single most coherent statement of the Christian view of cult comes in Hebrews. Whether or not Hebrews is representative of many Christians or comes as early as 70 is not our concern. What is striking is that the letter explores the great issues of 70: the issues of cult, Temple, sacrifice, priesthood, atonement, and redemption. Its author takes for granted that the church is the Temple, that Jesus is the builder of the Temple, and that he is also the perfect priest and the final and most unblemished sacrifice. Material sacrifices might suffice for the ceremonial cleansing of an earthly sanctuary, but if sinners are to approach God in a heavenly sanctuary, a sacrifice different in kind and better in degree is required. It is Jesus who is that perfect sacrifice, who has entered the true, heavenly sanctuary and now represents his people before God: "By his death he has consecrated the new covenant together with the heavenly sanctuary itself." Therefore, no further sacrifice—his or others'—is needed.

The Christian response to the crisis of the day was both entirely appropriate and quite useless. It was appropriate for those who already shared the Christian belief that the messiah had come and that the Temple that had been destroyed in any case no longer mattered. But this was a message of little substance for those who did not stand within the Christians' circle of faith. To them, the crisis was real, the problem intense and immediate. So far as the Christians formed a small group within the Jewish people, their explanation and interpretation of the disaster was of limited appeal. What they offered was one messianism in place of another. It was the messianism built upon the paradox of the crucified messiah, the scandal of weakness in place of strength, suffering unto death in place of this-worldly victory. True, the messianism was to speak to millions of men and women through the ages. But to people who believed the messiah would be a general who would throw off the rule of pagans and lead the people to an age of peace and prosperity, the Christian messiah hanging on the cross proved to be an insufferable paradox. It was not that Christianity was irrelevant. It was that its answers could not be understood by people who were asking a different question.

The Pharisees

Regarding the Pharisees, first we want to know about their traits before the destruction of the Temple in 70. Then we shall ask about their message in the time of ultimate crisis. We know very little about the Pharisees before the time of Herod. During Maccabean days, according to Josephus, our sole reliable source, they appear as a political party, competing with the Sadducees, another party, for control of the court and government. Afterward, they all but fade out of Josephus's narrative. But the later rabbinical literature fills the gaps and tells a great many stories about Pharisaic masters from Shammai and Hillel, at the end of the first century B.C.E., to the destruction in 70 C.E. It also ascribes numerous sayings, particularly on matters of law, both to the master and to the Houses, or Schools, of

Shammai and of Hillel. These circles of disciples seem to have flourished in the first century, down to 70 and beyond.

The dominant trait of Pharisaism before 70 as depicted both in the later rabbinic traditions about the Pharisees and in the Gospels, was concern for certain matters of rite. In particular, Pharisees emphasized eating one's meals in a state of ritual purity as if one were a Temple priest and carefully giving the required tithes and offerings due to the priesthood. The Gospels' stories and sayings on Pharisaism also added fasting, Sabbath observance, affirming vows and oaths, and the like. But the main point was keeping the ritual purity laws outside of the Temple, as well as inside, where the priests had to observe ritual purity when they carried out the requirements of the cult. To be sure, the Gospels also include a fair amount of hostile polemic, some of it rather extreme, but these polemical matters are not our concern. All one may learn from the accusations—for instance, that the Pharisees were a brood of vipers, morally blind, sinners, and unfaithful—is one fact: Christian Jews and Pharisaic Jews were at odds.

The Pharisees believed that one must keep the purity laws outside of the Temple. Other Jews, following the plain sense of Leviticus, supposed that purity laws were to be kept only in the Temple, where the priests had to enter a state of ritual purity in order to carry out the requirements of the cult, such as animal sacrifice. Priests also had to eat their Temple food in a state of ritual purity, but lay people did not. To be sure, everyone who went to the Temple had to be ritually pure. But outside the Temple the laws of ritual purity were not widely observed, for it was not required that non-cultic activities be conducted in a state of Levitical cleanness.

But the Pharisees held, on the contrary, that even outside of the Temple, in one's own home, one had to follow the laws of ritual purity in the only circumstance in which they might apply, namely, at the table. They there-fore held that one must eat secular food, that is, ordinary, everyday meals, in a state of ritual purity as if one were a Temple priest. The Pharisees, thus, assumed for themselves—and therefore all Jews equally—the status and responsibilities of the Temple priests. The table in the home of every Jew was seen to be like the table of the Lord in the Jerusalem Temple. The commandment "You shall be a kingdom of priests and a holy people" was taken literally. The whole country was considered holy. The table of every Jew possessed the same order of sanctity as the table of the cult. But, at this time, only the Pharisees held such a viewpoint, and eating unconsecrated food as if one were a Temple priest at the Lord's table thus was one of the two significations that a Jew was a Pharisee, a sectarian.

The other was meticulous tithing. The agricultural rules required giving a portion of one's crops to the priests and Levites; planting seeds in such a way that several varieties were not mixed together; not making use of the fruit of trees before the fourth year after their planting; and various other taboos. The laws of tithing, and related agricultural taboos, may have been kept primarily by Pharisees. Of this we are not certain. Pharisees clearly regarded keeping the agricultural rules as a chief religious duty. But whether, to what degree, and how other Jews did so, is not clear. Both the agricultural laws and the purity rules in the end affected table fellowship—how and what one may eat—that is, they were "dietary laws."

The Dead Sea sect, the Christian Jews, and the Pharisees all stressed the eating of ritual meals. But whereas the Qumranians and the Christians tended to oppose sacrifice as such and to prefer to achieve forgiveness of sin through ritual baths and communion meals, the Pharisees before 70 continued to revere the Temple and its cult; and afterward they drew up the laws that would govern the Temple when it would be restored. While awaiting restoration, they held that "as long as the Temple stood, the altar atoned for Israel. But now a man's table atones for him."

This Pharisaic attitude would be highly appropriate to the time when the Temple no longer stood. The Pharisees had already entered that time, in a strange and paradoxical way, by pretending to be Temple priests. But the pretense contained within itself the germ of a great revolution. For the real issue is the matter of the sacred. Every Jew believed in holiness, in a God who set apart a place, the Temple, for the sacred. Every Jew knew that there was a certain hocus-pocus, a set of rites, that prepared one for the encounter with the sacred. What the Pharisees held before 70 was not merely the fantasy that they would act like priests. Their message before 70 was that the sacred is not limited to the Temple. The country is holy, the people is holy. The life of the people, not merely the cult of the Temple, is capable of sanctification. How do priests serve God? They purify themselves and offer sacrifices. How should the holy people serve God? They should purify themselves—sanctifying themselves by ethical and moral behavior. They should offer the sacrifice of a contrite heart, as the Psalmist had said, and they should serve God through loyalty and through love, as the prophets had demanded.

In other words, the Pharisaic message to the time of crisis was to recover in Scripture those elements that stressed the larger means of service to God than were available in the Temple. Their method—the way of living as if one were a priest—contained a message to all that the Jews had left in the aftermath of the messianic war of 70: the Temple that is left is the *people*. The surviving holy place is the home and the village. The cult is the life of the commmunity.

The Pharisees never opposed the Temple, though they were critical of the priesthood. While it stood, they seem to have accepted the efficacy of the cult for the atonement of sins, and in this regard, as in others, they were more loyal than other sects to what they took to be the literal meaning of Scripture. More radical groups moved far beyond that meaning, either by rejecting its continued validity, as in the Christian view, or by taking over the cult through their own commune, as in the Essene view.

Whereas the early Christians gathered for ritual meals and made them the climax of their group life, the Pharisees apparently did not. What expressed the Pharisees' sense of self-awareness as a group was not a similarly intense ritual meal. Eating was not a ritualized occasion, even though the Pharisees had liturgies to be said at the meal. No communion ceremony, no rites centered on meals, no specification of meals on holy occasions characterized Pharisaic table fellowship, which was a quite ordinary, everyday affair. The various fellowship rules had to be observed in a wholly routine circumstance—daily, at every meal, without accompanying rites apart from a benediction for the food. Unlike those of the Pharisees, the Christians' myths and rituals rendered table fellowship into a much heightened spiritual experience: Do these things in memory of me. The Pharisees told no stories about purity laws, except (in later times) to account for their historical development (for example, who had decreed which purity rule?). When they came to table, as far as we know, they told no stories about how Moses had done what they now did, and they did not "do these things in memory of Moses 'our rabbi.'"

In the Dead Sea commune, table fellowship was open upon much the same basis as among the Pharisees: appropriate undertakings to keep ritual purity and to consume properly grown and tithed foods. As we know it, the Essene meal was liturgically not much different from the ordinary Pharisaic gathering. The rites pertained to, and derived from, the eating of food and that alone.

Both Christians and Pharisees lived among ordinary folk, but the Essenes did not. In this respect the commonplace character of Pharisaic table fellowship is all the more striking. The sect ordinarily did not gather as a group at all, but kept their rites in the home. All meals required ritual purity. Pharisaic table fellowship took place in the same circumstances as did all nonritual table fellowship. Common folk ate everyday meals in an everyday way, among ordinary neighbors who were not members of the sect. They were engaged in workaday pursuits like everyone else. The setting for observance of the law was the field and the kitchen, the bed and the street. The occasion for observance was set every time a person picked up a nail, which might be unclean, or purchased a se'ah of wheat, which had to be tithed. There were no priests present to bless the Pharisees' deeds or sages to instruct them. Keeping the Pharisaic rule required neither an occasional exceptional rite at, but external to, the meal, as in the Christian sect, nor taking up residence in a monastic commune, as in the Qumranian sect. Instead, it imposed the perpetual ritualization of daily life, on the one side, and the constant inner awareness of the communal order of being, on the other.

Rabbinic Judaism

The response of the Pharisees to the destruction of the Temple is known to us only from later rabbinic materials, which underwent revisions over many centuries. What happened is that the Pharisees and other groups came together in Yavneh (Jamnia), a town near the Mediterranean coast, and there they developed over a period of years the main ideas of what we now know as rabbinic Judaism. "Yavneh," therefore, serves as a kind of symbol for response to crisis brought on by failed messianism, a symbol of rebuilding. There is another symbol, also a place-name, "Massada." Massada was a fortress near the Dead Sea, to which the surviving Zealots and messianists retreated for a last stand. As the end drew near, with the Roman fortifications pressing upward on the Jewish castle, the Zealots of Massada committed suicide. Massada stands for bravery, courage, and fortitude. But the end of zealous military courage was nihilistic, not much different from the message of the apocalyptists. Yavneh stands for something else. The people who came to Yavneh did not fight, to be sure; they made their peace with the reality of submission to Rome. If they were brave, it was not the courage of the battlefield. But, what is important, Yavneh did not end in suicide but in the renaissance, the utter revolution in the history of Judaism, accomplished by rabbinic Judaism. What is the great gesture of Yavneh, to match the grand, symbolic suicide of Massada?

A story contained in a fourth- or fifth-century compilation, about a leading rabbi, Yohanan ben Zakkai, and his disciple, Joshua ben Hananiah, tells us in a few words the grand gesture of Yavneh, the main outline of the later rabbinic view of the destruction:

> Once, as Rabbi Yohanan ben Zakkai was coming forth from Jerusalem, Rabbi Joshua followed after him and beheld the Temple in ruins.
> "Woe unto us," Rabbi Joshua cried, "that this, the place where the iniquities of Israel were atoned for, is laid waste!"
> "My son," Rabbi Yohanan said to him, "be not grieved. We have another atonement as effective as this. And what is it? It is acts of loving-kindness, as it is said, For I desire mercy and not sacrifice" [Hos 6:6]. (*Avot de-Rabbi Nathan,* chap. 6).

How shall we relate the arcane rules about ritual purity to the public calamity faced by the heirs of the Pharisees at Yavneh as portrayed four centuries later by fully realized rabbinic Judaism? What connection exists between the ritual purity of the "kingdom of priests" and the atonement of sins in the Temple?

To Yohanan ben Zakkai, portrayed in this story as a rabbi, preserving the Temple was not an end in itself. He taught that there was another means of reconciliation between God and Israel, so that the Temple and its cult were not decisive. What really counted in the life of the Jewish people? Torah and piety. For the Zealots and messianists of the day, the answer was power, politics, and the right to live under one's own rulers.

What was the will of God? It was doing deeds of loving-kindness: "I desire mercy, not sacrifice" (Hos 6:6) meant to Yohanan, "We have a means of atonement as effective as the Temple and it is doing deeds of loving-kindness." Just as willingly as people would contribute bricks and mortar for the rebuilding of a sanctuary, so they ought to contribute renunciation, self-sacrifice, and love, for the building of a sacred community. Earlier, Pharisaism had held that the Temple should be everywhere, especially in the home. Now, in the mind of fully developed Judaism, Yohanan taught that sacrifice greater than the Temple's must characterize the life of the community. If one were to make an offering to God in a time when the Temple was no more, it must be the gift of selfless compassion. The holy altar must be the streets and marketplaces of the world, as, formerly, the purity of the Temple had to be observed in the streets and marketplaces of Jerusalem. In a sense, therefore, by making the laws of ritual purity incumbent upon the ordinary Jew, the Pharisee already had effectively limited the importance of the Temple and its cult. The earlier history of the Pharisaic sect thus had laid the groundwork for Yohanan ben Zakkai's response to Joshua ben Hananiah. It was a natural conclusion for one nurtured in a movement based upon the priesthood of all Israel.

The imagery, then, is priestly, the substance of the message, that of the sage. The amalgam of the priests' form with the sages' substance constitutes the distinctive trait of rabbinic Judaism. At the same time, we must never forget that the purpose and the goal were the end of time: the coming of the messiah. Belief in the messiah served as the engine to pull the train down the tracks of the holy way of life and the study of Torah.

Here then is the amalgam. Heirs of the Pharisees, the rabbis of the second and later centuries determined to concentrate on what they believed was really important in politics, and that was the fulfillment of all the laws of the Torah, even ritual tithing, and the elevation of the life of the people, even at home and in the streets, to what the Torah had commanded: You shall be a kingdom of priests and a holy people. A kingdom was envisioned in which everyone was a priest, a people all of whom were holy—a community that would live as if it were always in the Temple sanctuary of Jerusalem. Therefore, in the eyes of the Pharisees, the purity laws, so complicated and inconvenient, were extended to the life of every Jew in the home. The Temple altar in Jerusalem would be replicated at the table of all Israel. To be sure, only a small minority of the Jewish people, to begin with, obeyed the law as taught by the Pharisaic party. Therefore, the group had to reconsider the importance of political life, through which the law might everywhere be effected.

The rabbis' entry into politics, in the nature of Israelite life and tradition, renewed the messianic quest. For when the issue was phrased in terms of one person's telling another what to do, addressed in the setting of the government of Israel in relationship to the powers and principalities of the world, claims concerning the messiah reappeared. In rabbinic Judaism, I believe these proved pressing in the fourth and fifth centuries, in the face of triumphant Christianity. It was appeal to the messiah in the future, who would come in response to the creation of an Israel in conformity to the Torah, an Israel fully sanctified by obedience to the Torah's laws of sanctification, that rabbinic piety would appeal—a fitting response to Christ's triumph after Constantine. Accordingly, within rabbinic Judaism the three elements were joined once more: the distinct traditions of priest, sage, and messianist. In the person of the rabbi, holy man, Torah incarnate, avatar and model of the son of David, rabbinic Judaism found its sole symbol. So the diverse varieties of Judaic piety present in Israel before 70 came to bonding in a new and wholly unprecedented way, with each party to the union imposing its logic upon the other constituents of the whole. The ancient categories remained. But they were so profoundly revised and transformed that nothing was preserved intact. Judaism, as we know it, the Judaism of Scripture and Mishnah, Midrash and Talmud, thereby effected the ultimate transvaluation of all the values, of all the kinds of Judaism that had come before, from remote Israelite times onward. Through the person and figure of the rabbi, the whole burden of Israel's heritage was taken up, renewed, handed on, from late antiquity to the present day.

Only when the union of time and eternity, of messianic hope and holy way of life, broke apart, with the modern shaking of the ancient iron consensus of the ages, did Judaism in its classic form unravel. Then its ancient strands were revealed to view once more one by one. Then history, the events of wars and nations, the life of the *citizen,* received Israel as the individual Jew once more. The remnant of believers in the ongoing holy way of life, leading toward a yet unrealized salvation in the messiah, went their solitary way. The result would be a renewed immediacy to the messianic expectation, just now, indeed, perceived and expressed most vividly by the generality of participants in the holy way of life themselves. With the rebirth of the near-term expectation that what we do here and now serves the messiah's cause, the Judaic world came to replicate, once more, the conditions in which, to begin with, the Temple earlier had been destroyed and rabbinic Judaism born. But with that observation, we leave ancient times and regain the hour at hand.

Notes

1. See also the treatment of this theme by Steven Fraade below, Chapter 10.
2. Translated by Geza Vermes (*The Dead Sea Scrolls in English* 2nd ed. [Harmondsworth: Penguin Books, 1975] 172).
3. Ibid., 124.

Bibliography

The writer of this essay is the author of numerous works in the history of Judaism in late antiquity. On an introductory level, his treatment of the Pharisees in *From Politics to Piety* (Englewood Cliffs, NJ: Prentice-Hall, 1972), his *Life of Yohanan ben Zakkai* (Leiden: Brill, 1962), and his discussion of Babylonian Jewry in *There We Sat Down* (Nashville: Abingdon, 1971) are all instructive. A thematic approach is taken in *Formative Judaism,* three series (Brown Judaic Studies; Chico, CA: Scholars Press, 1983). *Judaism: The Evidence of the Mishnah* (Chicago: University of Chicago Press, 1983) is a systematic presentation of the body of materials recorded in that central work.—ED.

8

Philo and the Contemplative Life

DAVID WINSTON

Philo of Alexandria (20 B.C.E.–50 C.E.) represents the high-water mark of that fascinating and multifaceted Jewish Hellenistic tradition which flourished in Alexandria, the hub of Greco-Roman civilization from its foundation by Alexander in 331 B.C.E. to its capture by the Arab conqueror Amr b. al-As in 642 C.E. The famous museum and library of this sparkling city were symbols of the highest achievements of the Greek world in literature and the arts, the sciences and philosophy. The most diverse cultural and religious streams poured into this metropolis, which made it virtually certain that the Jewish writings produced there would be susceptible to a syncretism of ideas of the widest possible range. This was particularly true of a polymath like Philo, who himself testifies to his voracious appetite for learning:

> We must not disown any learning made venerable through time, but attempt to read the writings of the sages and to attend to the maxims and narratives of those who treat of antiquities and ever fondly inquire about the men and deeds of old, for it is exceedingly pleasant to be ignorant of nothing. (*Sacr.* 79)[1]

Philo's voluminous Greek writings present a dazzling display of his Hellenic erudition. The only serious gaps in his knowledge belong to the Jewish side of his scholarship, where an inadequate mastery of Hebrew compelled him to rely almost completely on the Greek translation of the Bible.

Before we turn to the major theme of our essay, something must be said about the nature of the Philonic enterprise as a whole, since the webs of controversy in which his works have become entangled have barred the way to a proper understanding of his thought. Students of Philo remain sharply divided on how to construe the nature of his literary oeuvre. There can be little doubt that he is "a man between two worlds" and that his main concern was to effect reconciliation between Judaism and Hellenism. It is also clear that he cast the bulk of his work in the form of a running commentary on the Pentateuch, but it does not appear to be sufficiently clear whether he was a convinced Platonist who nevertheless considered it possible to translate the Bible into the language of that philosophy, or whether he was primarily an exegete of Scripture who, in his quest to render the latter palatable to a Hellenized Jewish readership, opted for the vocabulary and conceptuality of Platonic thought as offering the best vehicle for accomplishing that purpose. My own view is that Philo's primary education was Hellenic, as a result of which he was transformed into an ardent Platonist, but that at some stage in his career he decided to make a grand effort to obtain as detailed a knowledge of his Jewish heritage as he could manage, and that subsequently he resolved to concentrate all his energies on the task of harmonizing his ancestral faith with his philo-sophical world view. The present essay is hardly the place fully to sub-stantiate this view, and all I can do here is indicate very briefly the fundamental reasons that incline me to it.

First, it seems obvious to me that Philo's knowledge of Palestinian Jewish tradition is essentially that of an outsider, who is clearly dependent on translations and oral tuition and is not at home in any of the original sources. Second, it appears to me that the fervor with which he relays basic Platonic doctrine reveals a deep personal commitment and is not merely an external veneer used for the convenience of lending his Jewish beliefs intellectual respectability. Third, it seems to me highly improbable that he genuinely believed that the Platonist constructions that he put upon the Mosaic texts corresponded to their original intent any more than the Stoics genuinely believed that the philosophic interpretations that they read into the Homeric poems truly corresponded to that poet's original intentions. Like the Stoics and Middle Platonists, Philo was employing an accepted exegetical mode in order to bolster a particular set of philosophical convic-tions by reading them back into an older authority. Such eisegesis was common practice in his day and would hardly have raised any eyebrows even among his most sophisticated readers. Again, I have little doubt that the allegorical exegesis plied so skillfully by Philo was capable of resolving most of the inconsistencies between Platonism and Scripture and that it was only Philo's own Jewish sensibilities that ultimately stood in the way of his attempt to produce the fullest possible reconciliation between the two. Although the philosophical component in Philo's thought generally tends to predominate, there are certain aspects of Jewish religious tradition that seem to have become established in his mind as normative or indelibly characteristic of its fundamental approach to life; and he finds himself, in the final analysis, unwilling to read them away, although the virtually unlimited scope of his exegetical technique could readily have accommodated almost any interpretation that Philo was intent on presenting. This is not to say that in the course of interpreting any particular biblical passage, the inner dynamics of his exegetical mode would not generate certain details that were not entirely consistent with his views elsewhere. Minor inconsistencies of this kind had to be accepted and were clearly part of the price that had to be paid for playing this highly specialized game of philosophical allegorical exegesis of an authoritative text. Certainly it must have seemed a small price to pay in view of the larger gains involved in successfully maintaining the validity and authority of a religious tradition to which he owed so much and which was so very dear to his heart. Moreover, it is immediately evident to the reader of Philo that the latter is single-mindedly devoted to the task of reconciliation and that he has no pretensions either to make original contributions to the philosophical tradition that he has espoused or to provide his readers with a systematic presentation of that tradition as such. Furthermore, it is equally evident that Philo could hardly have been single-handedly responsible for the exuberantly rich exegesis exhibited in his scriptural commentaries. The enormous variety, the great subtlety, and the sheer quantity of his exegesis, in addition to his own many attestations of his predecessors, make it virtually certain that much of his commentary derived from a rich body of scholastic tradition. None of this, however, can detract from his own genius, which selected, modified, refined, amplified, and synthesized this great mass of material and placed it in the service of an elaborate religious-philosophical world view. Finally, it must be admitted that it is in the nature of so vast an enterprise of conceptual adaptation, that inner tensions must inevitably work their way ever so subtly to the surface at the more sensitive intersections of the disparate strands of thought which Philo was blending together, thus creating elements of stress that only an exposition employing systematic ambiguity could contain. The resulting ambivalences that characterize the Philonic construction are in fact an essential trait of any large-scale attempt to bridge divergent realms of thought indigenous to different peoples, each endowed with a creative genius distinctively its own. Indeed, it could be fairly said that had the Philonic commentary not engendered a considerable degree of ambiguity, that would have been a sure sign that it lacked the integrity and creativity essential for making its execution worthwhile in the first place.

What requires further explanation, however, is why Philo chose the genre of biblical exegesis for his philosophical interpretation of Judaism rather than a systematic exposition. It may well be, however, that he felt that the success of his enterprise was largely dependent on his ability to convince his readers through a detailed scriptural commentary that the mystical Platonism he championed was not a farfetched philosophical construct attached to the Bible by threads of gossamer, but could readily be deduced from every one of its verses.[2] Indeed, he was undoubtedly aware of the fact that for traditional Judaism, as Gershom Scholem has aptly remarked with regard to the rabbinic view, "It is not systematic exposition, but the commentary that is the legitimate form through which the truth can be developed."[3]

Antecedents of Philo's Logos Doctrine

The linchpin of Philo's religious thought is the doctrine of the Logos. Since without a clear understanding of this conception within its Greek and Jewish context we cannot fully appreciate Philo's special brand of spirituality, we turn our attention first to the antecedents of this central notion, which dominates almost everything he wrote. The Logos or Divine Mind is a polyonymous and polymorphic entity in whose description and praise Philo takes enormous delight. It is the Idea of Ideas, the first-begotten son of the uncreated father, the eldest and chief of the angels, the man or shadow of God, or even the second God, the pattern of all creation and archetype of human reason.[4] The Logos is God immanent, holding together and administering the entire chain of creation (*Mos.* 2.134; *Her.* 188). It is, thus, the primary vehicle for Philo's depiction of God as the supremely transcendent reality whose pervasive immanence controls and directs every aspect of cosmic activity. This notion of divine transcendence may go back in some measure to Speusippus, the successor of Plato as head of the Old Academy, but it is fairly explicit in the cosmology of the Middle Platonist Eudorus of Alexandria (fl. 25 B.C.E.) with his postulation of a supranoetic First Principle which he calls the Supreme God, above a pair of opposites: the Monad, representing Form, and the Unlimited Dyad, representing Matter. A similar notion of transcendence appears in Moderatus of Gades, a Neopythagorean philosopher of the first century C.E., the first of whose three Ones is supranoetic, above being and all essence.[5] The importance of transcendence for Philo is such that, given the broad semantic range of that term, a precisely nuanced description of it is essential. The conception of absolute transcendence must be seen as a product of the theological formula of creation *ex nihilo,* which introduces an unbridgeable gap between God and the cosmos rooted in the vacuous character of that formulation.[6] The transition between the utterly transcendent God and His creation is thereby shrouded in total mystery, which eliminates any possibility of glimpsing His essence through His creative act. Since ancient Greek philosophy was free of the *ex nihilo* formulation, it could yield only concepts of relative transcendence. Thus, the essential difference between the Platonist and Stoic concepts of deity involves two varieties of relative transcendence. The Stoic Logos is corporeal, albeit a corporeality of extraordinary subtlety, invisible to the naked eye, whereas the Platonic Nous is absolutely incorporeal. Within Platonism itself there existed yet a higher level of relative transcendence, the concept of a supranoetic entity entirely unknowable as it is in itself but made manifest through a process of self-modification or projection which can only be described in metaphorical terms. Still, inasmuch as there is no absolute discontinuity between the supranoetic One and its emanations or images, its transcendence remains relative rather than absolute (see Plotinus 5.1.7.1). Philo shares with the Stoics the notion of transcendent immanence, except that, unlike the Stoic Logos, whose transcendence scarcely conceals its essence, Philo's Logos yields only an image of the divine essence and itself mediates yet a further projection of that image in a cosmos that stands at a third remove from its source.

Philo's emphatic usage of the Logos has no direct parallel in Plato's *Timaeus,* which he otherwise follows so closely, and seems deliberately to replace the concept of a cosmic soul, which holds so central a place in that dialogue. The reason for this change was twofold. Under the influence of the "scientific" teachings of the Stoa, the Middle Platonists (such as Atticus and Albinus) merged Plato's Demiurge with his World Soul into the single concept of a Nous/Logos to designate the world-immanent activity of the divine. Following the Middle Platonist tradition, Philo made good use of the Stoic Logos, though like Plutarch and Atticus he made a sharp distinction between it and God.[7] But the special suitability of the Logos for Philo's exposition of God's creative aspect lies in the fact that it could readily be assimilated to the "word of God" in Scripture, which had been rendered in the Septuagint by the term *logos.*[8] Indeed, when the author of the Wisdom of Solomon states that God "made all things by his word (*logōgoi*), and through his wisdom (*sophiai*) framed man" (9:1–2), it is by no means clear that "word" and "wisdom" there refer to Logos/Sophia, and further analysis of the text is required before such an inference can be drawn. It was therefore a great convenience for the subtle exegete of Scripture that Philo was to employ the term Logos as the vehicle of God's creative activity. Moreover, since Jewish wisdom literature employed the term "Wisdom" synonymously with "word of God," it was only natural for Philo to use that term too as the equivalent of Logos. Dame Wisdom is the central figure in the Wisdom of Solomon, but she had already made her debut as a cosmic force in Proverbs (8:22–31; 1:20–2:6; 3:19) and Job 28:12–28; 15:7) under the guise of a charming female figure playing always before Yahweh, after having been created by Him at the beginning of His work (Prov 8:30). There was also an early Semitic reference (sixth century B.C.E.) to Wisdom who is dear to the gods and is "established in heaven, for the lord of holy ones has exalted her," in *The Words of Ahiqar* 95.[9] She appears again in Ben Sira (ca. 180 B.C.E.), where, as in Proverbs 8, she is described as having been created from the very beginning (1:4; 24:9) and as having been infused into all of God's works (1:9). She is further described as traversing the entire cosmos but finally, at the divine behest, making her home in Israel, in God's beloved city of Jerusalem (24:3–12). She is, moreover, identified with the Torah (24:23) and is thus paradoxically a cosmic figure which nevertheless maintains its focus in Zion and in the teachings of the Torah, which thus achieve a new universal significance.[10]

A further development of the Wisdom doctrine is found contemporaneously with Ben Sira in the scriptural commentary of Aristobulus (ca. 175–170 B.C.E.), who inaugurates an interpretative approach to Judaism that to some extent prefigures the thought of Philo. His goal was to demonstrate that the Torah represented the true philosophy and did not contradict philosophical reason. Indeed, Plato, Pythagoras, and Socrates, as well as Hesiod, Homer, and Linus, had drawn from the books of Moses, which, according to Aristobulus, had already been translated into Greek long before the Septuagint version (Eusebius *Praep. Evang.* 13.12). That the philosophy of Pythagoras was in certain points influenced by the Jews and Thracians had already been asserted by the Peripatetic Hermippus of Smyrna (ca. 200 B.C.E.) (Josephus, *Against Apion* 1.22 §§ 164–65), and even earlier Megasthenes (ca. 300 B.C.E.) had said that the teachings of Greek philosophy were already partially found among the Brahmans and Syrian Jewish philosophers (Clement *Stromateis* 1.72.5). Since Aristobulus is convinced that Moses was the teacher of the correct concept of deity, it is evident that the latter cannot have meant those passages that attribute to God anthropomorphic characteristics as they stand. To preserve "the appropriate conception of God" they must be interpreted allegorically. Thus, the "hand of God" means His power, and the "standing of God" refers to the existence and immutability of the world that He has created. Similarly, the descent of God on Sinai should not be understood locally, as God is omnipresent. The "voice of God" must also not be taken literally, but refers rather to "the construction of works," just as Moses has spoken of the whole creation of the world as words of God, for he constantly says of each work, "And God said and it was so." The resting of God on the seventh day does not mean the end of His work but only the "fixing of the order of things," and the work of the six days is to be understood as the establishment of the course of time and of gradations within the created world. Thus, it is not God but only His creation that is subject to the course of time (Eusebius *Praep. Evang.* 8.10). Similarly, according to the book of *Jubilees* (2:2, 30–33), the Sabbath had been celebrated in the heavenly world long before it was enjoined on Israel by Moses, inasmuch as it was regarded as an expression of the heavenly ordering of the world and of time. In a similar vein, too, Rabbi Berekiah commented in the name of Rabbi Judah b. Rabbi Simon: "'By the word of the Lord were the heavens made, and all the host of them by the breath of His mouth' (Ps 33:6): not by labor or toil but only by a word" (*Gen. Rab.* 3.2; cf. 12.2 and Cicero *De deorum natura* 1.52).

Although Aristobulus wishes the reader to understand the Torah "truly" (*physikōs*), that is, philosophically, "and not slip into the mythological mode" and chides those who cling to the letter for their lack of strength and insight and for providing a reading of the Torah in the light of which Moses fails to appear to be proclaiming great things, there is no evidence that the biblical text as a whole ever became for him an allegory in the Stoic and Philonic manner. Aristobulus further asserts that if anything unreasonable remains in the biblical text in spite of his interpretative skill, the cause is not to be imputed to Moses but to himself. This would seem to indicate that he is aware of using a relatively new exegetical method and that he could not rely on a well-established tradition. Aristobulus does not seem to know the terms *hyponoia* ("deeper sense"), *allēgoria* ("allegory"), or *tropikōs* ("figuratively"), using instead the terms *sēmainein* ("to signify," used also by Philo), *apaggellein* ("to interpret"), *diasaphein* ("to make clear).[11] The distance between Aristobulus and Philo is clearly manifest in the fact that Philo knows of firm canons of allegory, which shows his dependence on a school tradition, and by the complexity of these exegetical rules, which further indicates that that school tradition had already undergone considerable development.

In Pseudo-Aristeas we have an intermediary figure whose allegorical interpretation goes considerably further than Aristobulus's, since he allegorizes the dietary laws in a manner very similar to that of Philo. Like Aristobulus, Pseudo-Aristeas asserts that "nothing has been set down in Scripture heedlessly or in the spirit of myth, but rather," as he goes on to say, "in order that throughout our life and in our actions we may practice justice towards all men, being mindful of the sovereignty of God. All that is said of food, then, and of unclean creeping things and of animals is directed toward justice and just intercourse among men" (168–69). The dietary rules have as their purpose to promote holy contemplation and the perfecting of character, for the permitted animals are gentle and clean, whereas those which are forbidden are wild and carnivorous and with their strength oppress the rest and even do violence to men. All this is a symbol that those for whom the legislation was drawn up must practice righteousness and oppress no one. As for the "parting of the hoof" and the "cloven foot," which characterize the permitted animals, these are a symbol to discriminate in each of our actions with a view to what is right. An additional signification is that we are set apart from all human beings, for most of the rest of them defile themselves by their promiscuous unions, both homosexual and incestuous, but we have been kept apart from such things. Moreover, "parting the hoof and chewing the cud" signifies memory, and Moses thereby admonishes us to remember the great and marvelous things that God has done for us (144–55). This kind of allegorization may owe something to the influence of the Pythagoreans, since they too possessed dietary rules which they later justified philosophically (Iamblichus *De vita Pythagorica* 86; Aristotle *On the Pythagoreans*, frs. 5 and 7, Ross).[12]

The widespread use of allegorism in the Hellenistic age was due to its acceptance by the Stoic school of philosophy, which had inferred from its supposition that the Logos is the fundamental principle of everything that it must manifest itself in poetry too, though hidden there behind the veil of myth and legend. Zeno and Cleanthes initiated this new method, and Chrysippus perfected it. They enlisted the support of Homer and the other great poets in behalf of their own philosophy. An excellent example of cosmological allegory may be found in the commentary on the two Homeric poems by the Stoic philosopher Crates of Mallos (second century B.C.E.), who had been invited to the capital of Eumenes II, the founder of the library at Pergamum. In his allegorical interpretation of *Iliad* 18.483–608, which describes the making by Hephaestus of the shield of Achilles (a passage atheticized by Zenodotus), Crates claims that in depicting ten parts of the shield Homer meant the ten circles of the sky, which converts the Homeric account into a description of the genesis of the cosmos and its elements (Heraclitus Rhetor *Quaestiones Homericae* 43).[13] That Aristobulus knew the allegorical interpretation of Homer is clear from the way he applies allegory to a Homeric verse cited by him, though he does not appear to have applied allegory to the Torah in the same playful manner in which he applied it to Homer.[14]

In his interpretation of the Sabbath, Aristobulus introduces the notion of Logos/Sophia:

God created the world and, because life is troublesome for all, he gave us for rest the seventh day, which in reality (*physikōs*) could also be called the primal source of light, through which all things are comprehended. The latter could also metaphorically be transferred to Wisdom, for all light comes from her, just as some members of the Peripatetic school say that wisdom has the role of a beacon-fire, because those who follow her unremittingly will remain unruffled their whole life through. But one of our forefathers, Solomon, said more clearly and more beautifully that Wisdom existed before heaven and earth. (Eusebius *Praep. Evang.* 13.12)

The Pythagorean Philolaus had already associated the number seven with wisdom and light (Diels-Kranz, 44.A.12), and Philo later made a similar identification, asserting that "the reason why the man who guides himself in accordance with the seventh and perfect light is both blessed and holy is that the formation of things mortal ceases with the seventh day's advent" (*LA* 1.16–18; cf. *Deus* 12; *Spec.* 2.59; *Her.* 216). Aristobulus's luminous Wisdom is also further identified with the Logos, when he asserts that the seventh day is "a symbol of the seventh logos through which we have knowledge of human and divine things," and that the entire cosmos revolves through sevens" (cf. Philo, *Abr.* 28–29; *Her.* 225; *LA* 1.19). Thus, according to Aristobulus, preexistent Wisdom or Logos, which is identical with the primordial light (the archetypal sun or intelligible light of Philo) and is symbolized by the number seven, gives the true Sabbath rest to those who follow her.[15]

It is above all in the Wisdom of Solomon, however, that the figure of Wisdom comes into her own and offers the closest parallel to the centrality she possesses in Philo's writings. Sophia is described in this work as an effluence or effulgence of God's glory and His agent in creation (7:25–26; 8:4; 9:1–2), and it is implied that she contains the paradigmatic patterns of all things (9:8–9). A figure radiant and fairer than the sun, the author also refers to her as his bride or spouse and speaks of living with her and enjoying kinship with her (6:12; 7:29; 8:2–3, 16–17). Sophia anticipates those who desire her, and those who seek her will not weary. She has no fellowship with pining envy and must be wooed guilelessly (6:23; 7:13). Without her man is nothing, for all his words and thoughts are in God's hands (9:6; 7:16). She spans the entire range of scientific knowledge and is the source of both morality and prophecy (7:17–21, 27; 8:7). One must make one's soul a proper abode for Sophia, but the godless, inviting Death, make a pact with him (1:4, 16). Sophia is a direct bearer of revelation, functioning through the workings of the human mind, and supreme arbiter of all values (9:17; 10). The author's ebullient enthusiasm for Wisdom meets the readers at every turn and beckons them to share his experiences. His highly charged language seems to allude to a private mystical experience, which he believes is available also to others and is capable of opening up a path for them to some measure of union with the deity, at least under the aspect of Sophia. Although the more detailed description of the characteristics of the mystical experience which we shall find in Philo is lacking in Wisdom, the latter's words seem more intensely personal and less likely to be a matter of literary contrivance or a purely intellectual exercise.[16]

The question of whether Sophia or *Hokhmah* is conceived of in the texts cited above as an actual "hypostasis" or is merely to be regarded as a figure of speech has often been discussed. It is my view that, whereas in Proverbs and Job—as also in Ben Sira—Wisdom is not yet a hypostasis as that term was broadly defined by W. O. E. Oesterly and G. H. Box, (that is, "a quasi-personification of certain attributes proper to God, occupying an intermediate position between personalities and abstract beings")[17] since according to these texts she is clearly only the first creation of God, in Philo and in the Wisdom of Solomon, where Sophia is considered to be an eternal emanation of the deity, we undoubtedly have a conception of her as a divine hypostasis, coeternal with Him.[18] Since Philo's influence has been detected in the well-known statement of Rabbi Jose b. Halafta (second century C.E.) that the "Holy One is the place of His world but His world is not His place" (*Gen. Rab.* 68.9, Theodor-Albeck; 777), and also in the statement by Rabbi Hoshaya of Caesarea (third century C.E.) to the effect that the Torah served as God's paradigm in the creation of the world (*Gen. Rab.* 1.1),[19] it is worth pointing out that we also find in rabbinic literature that the divine "Word" is hypostatized after the manner of Philo's Logos. In *Song Rab.* 1.13, it is conceived of as a concrete, independent entity, encompassing all of the ten commandments (cf. *Mek.* on Exod 20:1):

> "Let Him kiss me with the kisses of His mouth." The Rabbis say: The commandment (*dibbur,* "utterance") itself went in turn to each of the Israelites and said to him, "Do you undertake to keep me?" . . . He would reply, "Yes, yes" and straightway the commandment kissed him on the mouth and taught him Torah.

It is but a short step from this to its conversion into a personal entity, a step that is taken in *Num. R.* 10.3 (= *Song Rab.* 6.3), where the *dibbur* speaks to God person to person:

> "His mouth is most sweet." R. Azariah and R. Aha in the name of R. Yohanan said: When the Israelites heard at Sinai the word "I," their souls left them, as it says, "If we hear the voice any more, then we shall die" (Deut 5:22). The Word then returned to the Holy Blessed One and said: "Sovereign of the Universe, Thou art full of life, and Thy law is full of life, and Thou hast sent

me to the dead, for they are all dead." Thereupon the Holy Blessed One sweetened the Word for them.

A similar hypostatization of the Holy Spirit is found in *Pesiqta Rabbati* 3.

The rabbis, however, never speak of the *dibbur* as God's son, as Philo does, nor do they employ the characteristic Stoic physical teachings concerning the pneumatic Logos which appear in Philo. Moreover, as is usual with them, they offer no systematic discussion concerning the *dibbur* and its relationship to God.[20] In short, it is not impossible that the rabbis had some oral knowledge of some of Philo's teachings and that they occasionally made use of them in their own biblical interpretations, but it is very unlikely that they ever studied his writings.

God and Logos

In Philo's hierarchical construction of reality the essence of God, though utterly concealed in its primary being, is nevertheless made manifest on two secondary levels, the intelligible universe constituting the Logos, which is God's image (*Som.* 1.239; *Conf.* 147–48), and the sensible universe, which is an image of that image (*Op.* 25). Thus, though the essence of God as it is in itself remains forever undisclosed, its effects, images, or shadows may be perceived. Philo further attempts to delineate the dynamics of the Logos's activity by defining and describing its two constitutive polar principles: Goodness or the Creative Power, and Sovereignty or the Regent Power.[21] It is not difficult to recognize in these two powers the *apeiron* and the *peras*, the Unlimited and the Limit of Plato's *Philebus* (23C–31A), which reappear in Plotinus's two moments in the emergence of *Nous*, where we find undefined or unlimited Intelligible Matter proceeding from the One and then turning back to its source for definition (2.4.5; 5.4.2; 6.7.17). Now, the various positive properties attributed to God by Philo may all be subsumed under either of these two polar forces, and they are therefore all expressions of the one Logos, which constitutes the manifestation of God as thinking-acting (*Sacr.* 65; *Mos.* 1.283; *Prov* 1.7). However, since God's essence as it is in itself is beyond any possibility of human experience or cognition, including the experience of mystic vision, the only attributes that may be applied to Him in His supreme state of concealment are those of the *via negativa* or of the *via eminentiae.*

Although at the summit the powers of the Logos may be grasped as constituting an indivisible unity, at lower levels there are those who cognize the Logos exclusively as the Creative Power, and those beneath them who cognize it as the Regent Power (*Fug.* 94–105; *Abr.* 124–25). Lower still are those who, sunk in the mire of sensible being, are unable to perceive the intelligible realities with any degree of continuity (*Gig.* 20). At each successively lower level of divine knowledge the image of God's essence is increasingly dimmed or veiled.

Students of Philo have generally inclined to the view that his Logos doctrine was introduced in order to bridge the gap between the absolutely transcendent and unknowable God and the world,[22] but this, it seems to me, is to put the cart before the horse. The fact is that the notion of a Logos or some rough equivalent of it was already one of the many components that constituted the Platonic account of reality. There were, thus, the supreme Form of the Good of *Republic* 6 (represented in the *Symposium* in its aspect of Beauty), the One of the first hypothesis of the *Parmenides,* the *Nous* Demiurge, the young gods, and the World Soul (in addition to the Receptacle) of the *Timaeus,* and the principles of the Unlimited and the Limit with a cosmic *Nous* above them of the *Philebus.* When this pluralistic schema of Plato was further elaborated and systematized by the Middle Platonists through their location of the Forms in the mind of God and their distinction between a first and second Intellect or God and was then finally transformed into the monistic system of Plotinus, it became essential to clarify as precisely as possible the relationship between the absolutely simple First Principle and its multiple consequents. Since Philo was committed to the monotheistic doctrine of the Bible, he was compelled to anticipate the central philosophical issue of Neoplatonism. It is therefore somewhat misleading to say that Philo and Plotinus resorted to a doctrine of intermediaries in order to bring the Unknowable God into a relationship with the world. It would be more accurate to say that the conversion of the multiple entities, which had been introduced by Plato in order to account for the structure of being, into aspects of a single reality required a shift of emphasis from a detailed description of the independent components of reality to a subtle analysis of the internal relationships of the various manifestations of the One.

The Philonic Logos is thus not literally a second entity by the side of God acting on His behalf, nor is it an empty abstraction, but rather a vivid and living hypostatization of an essential aspect of deity, the face of God turned toward creation. Whatever is effected by the Logos is effected by God Himself, though its referral to the Logos is a reminder that the effect does not constitute a disclosure of the divine essence as it is in itself. On the other hand, Philo's insistence on the impropriety of God's having any direct contact with the disordered primordial matter and the employment of His Powers instead for that purpose (Spec. 1.328; Fug. 71), signifies only that we may not impute to Him any interest in the material realm as a part of

His primary intentionality. Primordial matter and its ordering, as well as all evil, are indirect consequences of God's primary creative activity and must therefore not be ascribed directly to Him, even though as the only truly Existent, He alone is their ultimate source.[23]

In making the Logos the primary manifestation of the deity, Philo was naturally constrained not only to reject all anthropomorphic descriptions of God, but also to insist on His absolute rationality and on His insusceptibility to irrational emotions of any kind (*Deus* 52; *Abr.* 202). He could, however, as Emile Bréhier had correctly pointed out, ascribe to God what the Stoics designated as *eupatheiai* or rational emotions, the chief characteristics of the Stoic sage.[24] He thus describes God not only as beneficent but also as benevolent and kind (*Mut.* 129; *Op.* 81; *Abr.* 137), inasmuch as benevolence was classified by the Stoa (at least in its Roman phase) as a rational emotion.[25] By the same token, Philo could also speak of God's will and joy (*chara*), since these too were considered by the Stoics to be rational emotions (Stoicorium Veterum Fragmenta 3.432). He notes with apparent approval:

> It is said that even the Father and Creator of the universe continually rejoices in His life and plays and is joyful, finding pleasure in play which is in keeping with the divine in joyfulness. And He has no need of anything, but with joy He delights in Himself and in His powers and in the worlds made by Him. . . . Rightly, therefore, and properly does the wise man, believing his end to consist in likeness to God, strive, so far as possible, to unite the created with the uncreated and the mortal with the immortal, and not to be deficient or wanting in gladness and joyfulness in his likeness. (*QG* 4.188).

The wise man's joy, however, is not the equal of God's, since, because of the limited capacity of the finite creature, it is not characterized by the unbroken continuity that marks its divine archetype (*Abr.* 201–7).[26]

Turning from the rational emotions to those that are irrational, we find Philo in complete accord with the Stoics in rejecting anger as a feeling applicable to God and quite willing to stand Scripture on its head in order to avert such an attribution (*Deus* 70–73).[27] In ascribing pity (*eleos*) to God, however, Philo appears decisively to part company with the Stoics who had classified pity as a species of grief (*lypē*), which is one of the four primary passions.[28] It is of interest to note that although the Old Academy and the Middle Platonists generally adopted the Peripatetic ideal of *metriopatheia*, or moderation of one's passions, in lieu of the more rigorous Stoic goal of *apatheia/eupatheia*, which involved the complete conversion of one's passions into rational emotions,[29] Philo apparently was sufficiently attracted by the latter ideal to adopt it in preference to the former in spite of the difficulties and ensuing modifications that this choice entailed.[30] The ideal of *eupatheia* so intrigued him that he attributed it not only to the wise man but, after a fashion, even to the deity himself, although the Stoics may possibly have anticipated him in this. The one major deviation from Stoic theory in Philo's description of God is his insistence on attributing pity to the deity, and in so doing he was clearly acting under the influence of Jewish teaching.

The Allegory of Psychic Ascent

The fundamental goal of Philo's great biblical commentary was to uncover the hidden meaning of the Mosaic text, using the "method dear to men with their eyes opened" (*Plant.* 36). An unabashed Platonist, Philo considers himself one of those "who can contemplate the facts unbodied and naked, who live with the soul rather than with the body" (*Abr.* 236), and who "recognize that the letter is to the oracle as the shadow to the substance" (*Conf.* 190). In *On the Contemplative Life* he described the allegorical mode of biblical exposition practiced by the Therapeutae, "who have embraced the contemplation of nature and its constituent parts, and have lived in the soul alone, citizens of Heaven and the universe," as being made in accordance with Scripture's deeper meaning:

> For the whole of the Law seems to these people to resemble a living being [cf. Plato *Phaedrus* 264C] with the literal commandments for its body, and for its soul the invisible meaning stored away in its words. It is in the latter that the rational soul begins especially to contemplate the things akin to itself and, beholding the extraordinary beauties of the concepts through the polished glass of the words, unfolds and reveals the symbols, and brings forth the thoughts bared unto the light for those who are able by a slight jog to their memory to view the invisible through the visible. (*On the Contemplative Life* 78, 90)

Philo is sometimes ready to admit that the literal meaning of the Bible leaves him in a state of hopeless *aporia* (*Agr.* 131), and he is frequently quite prepared to reject the literal sense altogether.[31] Above all, however, he is concerned with "the hidden meaning which appeals to the few who study soul characteristics, rather than bodily forms" (*Abr.* 147), and much of his allegory is devoted to the psychic ascent to God. David M. Hay has noted that Philo mentions about sixty-three different interpretations of biblical passages as developed or shared by other allegorists, and he correctly concludes that "Philo was conscious of working alongside fellow allegorists, many of whom could be expected to approve of his efforts."[32]

We have already seen that it is Philo's view that God is characterized by a state of complete *apatheia,* so that when he proceeds to describe the *telos* or end of the human person as consisting in the "imitation of God" he clearly implies that the wise person must achieve a similar psychic state, in which all his *pathē* or irrational emotions are converted into *eupatheiai* or their rational equivalents. Thus, for example, the Peripatetic man of practical wisdom (the *sōphrōn,* characterized by self-mastery) would always feel the correct amount of fear or grief, whereas the Stoic wise man, who served as Philo's model, would never experience fear in the first place (since for him there is no correct amount of this emotion) but only a completely rational feeling of caution or wariness which constitutes its rational equivalent. Grief, on the other hand, which according to the Stoics has no rational equivalent, he would never be subject to in any form. He would experience at most a mental sting or minor soul contractions, which are morally neutral and betray not the slightest trace of irrationality. In his state of eupathy the sage, symbolized for Philo by Isaac, acts out of a fixity of disposition, no longer having to struggle to make rational decisions.[33]

From Philo's Platonist perspective the body is a corpse, "the dwelling place of endless calamities" (*Conf.* 177) and is symbolized in Scripture by Er:

> For this reason, in the matter of Er too, without evident cause, God knows him to be wicked and slays him (Gen 38:7). For he is not unaware that the body, our "leathery" bulk (Er means "leathery"), is wicked and a plotter against the soul, and is even a cadaver and always dead. For you must not imagine that each of us is anything but a corpse-bearer, the soul rousing and effortlessly bearing the body, which is of itself a corpse.[34]

The body is, moreover, the source both of *agnoia,* lack of knowledge, and *amathia,* fundamental ignorance:[35]

> But the chief cause of ignorance is the flesh and our affinity for it. Moses himself affirms this when he says "because they are flesh" the divine spirit cannot abide. Marriage, indeed, and the rearing of children, the provision of necessities, the ill repute that comes in the wake of poverty, business both private and public, and a host of other things wilt the flower of wisdom before it blooms. Nothing, however, so thwarts its growth as our fleshly nature. For this is the primary and main underlying foundation of ignorance and the diseased condition of an unknowing mind, on which each of the aforementioned qualities is constructed. For souls unfleshed and disembodied pass their days in the theatre of the universe and enjoy unhindered sights and sounds divine, possessed by an insatiate love for them. But those who bear the load of the flesh are unable, thus weighed down and oppressed, to gaze upward at the revolving heavens, but with necks wrenched downward are forcibly rooted to the ground like four-footed beasts. (*Gig.* 29–31)[36]

The soul may thus be seen as entombed in the body, on whose death it returns to its own proper life.[37] Alternatively, its sojourn in the body may be taken to be a period of exile:

> For the soul of the wise man when it comes from above from the ether and enters into a mortal and is sown in the field of the body, is truly a sojourner in a land not its own, for the earthy nature of the body is an alien to the pure mind and subjects it to slavery and brings upon it all kinds of suffering. (QG 3.10)

This theme of the soul's exile and its return to its homeland finds its analogue in Greek literature in the Neoplatonic allegorization of Odysseus's return to his dear fatherland, and traces of it may already be found in Plutarch (*Moralia* 745–46).[38]

Philo thus sees the psyche of ordinary mortals as the scene of constant warfare between its irrational and rational parts (*LA* 1.106), with the victory in this furious battle going to either of the two antagonists in turn, and symbolized in Scripture by the raising and lowering of Moses' arms in the battle between Israel and Amalek (*LA* 3.186). The gradual removal of the psyche from the sensible realm and its ascent to a life of perfection in God is represented for Philo by two triads of biblical figures, the first (Enosh, Enoch, Noah) symbolizing the initial stages of the striving for perfection, the second (Abraham, Isaac, and Jacob) its culmination (*Abr.* 7–59; *Praem.* 10–66). Of the three biographies of the patriarchs, however, only that of Abraham survives, although elements of those lost are scattered throughout Philo's allegorical commentary. We shall focus our attention, therefore, on the allegory of the life of Abraham.

The Abraham of Philo is a mystical philosopher who, after having mastered the encyclical studies (symbolized by Hagar), in which stage all he could produce was Ishmael or sophistry, has abandoned the realm of sense (symbolized by his parting with Lot) for the brighter regions of intelligible reality and, despite his initial flirtation with Chaldean (i.e., Stoic) pantheism, has attained to the highest vision of deity (the single vision as opposed to a triple vision), which results in his transformation into a perfect embodiment of natural law. Abraham thus represents the virtue-loving soul in search of the true God who arrives at a more purified understanding of the divine by studying himself as microcosm, and whose conversion from meteorologist to sage is attested in Scripture by the alteration of his name from Abram to Abraham.[39] The migration of Abraham to the realm of the intelligible is vividly described by Philo in his allegorical interpretation of Gen 12:1–3:

> "And the Lord said to Abraham, Go forth from your native land and from your kindred and from your father's house, to the land that I will show you. . . ." Intent on purifying man's soul, God initially assigns it as its starting point for full salvation its migration out of three regions, body, sense perception, and speech. "Lord" is a symbol of body, "kindred" of sense perception,

"father's house" of speech. . . . The words "Go forth from these" are not equivalent to "Disengage yourself from them in substance," since such a command would be a prescription of death. The words are equal instead to "Make yourself a stranger to them in your mental disposition; cleave to none of them and stand above them all; They are your subjects, never treat them as sovereigns; you are a king, be trained to rule, not to be ruled, throughout your life be getting to know yourself," as Moses teaches on many occasions, saying "Give heed to yourself" (Exod 24:12). . . . Go forth, then, from the earthly matter that envelops you. Escape, man, from the abominable prison, your body, and from the pleasures and lusts that act as its jailer. . . . Depart also from sense perception, your kin. For the moment you have made a loan of yourself to each of the senses and have become the alien property of those who have borrowed you, and the good thing that was your own you have lost. . . . Again, migrate also from speech, which Moses has called "your father's house," so that you may not be deceived by the beauties of words and expressions and be severed from the authentic beauty that lies in the matter disclosed. For it is absurd that shadow gain the advantage over objects, or a copy over originals. (*Mig.* 1–4, 7–12)

Returning now to Philo's two triads, we may briefly sketch the soul types they represent. The soul initially passes through three stages in its advance toward perfection: hope (Enosh) and repentance (Enoch), which lead to tranquillity (Noah). Abraham, Isaac, and Jacob represent the three components declared in the Platonist-Aristotelian tradition to be necessary to the attainment of perfect virtue: teaching, nature, and practice. This goes back at least to Protagoras (DK. 80.B.3), is alluded to by Plato at the beginning of the *Meno* (70A) and is formalized by Aristotle.[40]

But we must not fail to recognize that each of the three lays claim to the three qualities, but has received his name from that which greatly predominates in him; for teaching cannot be consummated without nature or practice, nor is nature capable of reaching its end without learning or practice, nor practice either unless there was the prior foundation of nature and teaching. (*Abr.* 52–53; cf. Quintilian *Institutiones Oratoriae* 27)

It is clear, however, from many passages, that the superior gift is that of the privileged few who are so naturally endowed that they achieve wisdom virtually without effort.[41] For the average person, on the other hand, it is necessary first to train within the sphere of everyday practical life before attempting loftier heights. The practicers, however, go continually up and down, and as mere *prokoptontes*, or men making progress, are liable to reverse course and slip back into their former habits (*LA* 1.89; *Gig.* 48).

If the man of progress is to attain wisdom, he must presently take flight from the sense-perceptible realm, leaving behind not only the passions but external goods too, though not through faintheartedness or inexperience of them, but rather under the guidance of right reason (*Deus* 150–53). In *Sacr.* 76–87, Philo presents a more elaborate description of the dialectical process of the mind's ascent. Citing the verse, "If you bring an offering of first-fruits" (Lev 2:14), he urges the reader to make such division as Holy Writ prescribes. "First the new": the mind must begin by rejecting the antique fables which have deceived the mortal race. Though not disowning the venerable learning of the past, having become God's apprentice, it must swiftly terminate human instruction as soon as the fresh shoots of self-taught wisdom blossom forth. "Then the roasted": the mind must now subject all things to the roast or test of reason. "Then the sliced": the process to be used is that of the division and classification of all things. "And last the pounded": the thoughts now presented to the mind must become the objects of constant reflection and practice. The mind thus perfected through the dialectical process is described by Philo as a "celestial and heavenly soul, which has left the region of the earth, has been drawn upwards, and dwells with divine natures" (*Deus* 151; cf. *Spec.* 1.207). Such a mind, as he says in connection with Moses, "has learned to gaze upward and frequent the heights, and as it ever haunts the upper atmosphere and closely examines the divine loveliness, it scoffs at earthly things, considering them to be mere child's play" (*Mos.* 1.190; cf. *Ebr.* 62). The same figure of speech was later used by Gregory of Nyssa, to whom human affairs are but the play of children building sand castles which are promptly washed away (*PG* 44, col. 628C).[42] Similarly, in Plato's allegory of the cave, the prisoner who is released and ascends the steep path to the real world above and is thus a figure of the soul's ascent to the intelligible region, is no longer willing to occupy himself with human affairs and would not voluntarily go down again to be among his former bondsmen who "fight one another for shadows" (*Republic* 7.514–21).

The locus classicus, however, for the upward flight of the soul is in Plato's *Theaetetus* 176A, a passage cited verbatim by Philo at *Fug.* 62–63:

The good is upward-mounting and should it ever come to us, through the bounty of its Father, it rightly hastens to reverse its path; but the evil thing remains here, far removed from the Divine Choir, making mortal life its prowling ground, and unable to die away and leave the human race. This sentiment was splendidly expressed by a man of distinction, one of those admired for their wisdom, when he said in his *Theaetetus:* "Evils cannot cease to exist, for there must ever be something opposed to the good; nor can they be established among the gods, but they haunt mortal nature and this region here. That is why we must attempt to take flight from 'here' to 'there' as swiftly as we can; flight means becoming like God as far as possible, and to become like God is to become just and intelligently devout."

Divine Worship

Sacrifice

Following the prophetic tradition in which he was reared, Philo locates the central significance of the sacrificial cult in the ethical sensitivity that should properly motivate it, a view which, as was often the case with the lofty spirituality of prophetic teachings, coincided with the Greek philosophical attitude toward ritual piety:

> Though wanting nothing, God bids us in the extravagance of His beneficence to our race to offer Him what is His own. For if we train ourselves to show Him gratitude and honor, we shall be clear of wrongdoing and purge away that which defiles our lives in word, thought, and deed. For it is absurd that one should not be permitted to enter the temples without having first bathed and cleansed his body, yet should attempt to pray and sacrifice with his mind still stained and sullied. . . . He who has deemed it right not only to refrain from any further evil but also to wash away the old may approach with joy, but let him who lacks these sentiments, since he is insusceptible of purification, keep far off. For he will never escape detection by Him who sees into the recesses of the mind and tarries amid its inmost shrines. (*Deus* 7–9)[43]

Heraclitus had already heaped ridicule on the primitive notion of purification which is here the object of Philo's critique: "They vainly purify themselves with blood when they are defiled with blood as though one who had stepped into mud were to wash with mud" (DK 22.B.5).[44] Plato scorned the vulgar understanding of sacrifice which saw in it an attempt to obtain favors from the gods, as equivalent to treating holiness as "an art of barter between gods and men" (*Euthyphro* 14E) and, using almost the same language as that employed by Philo, laid it down firmly that the gods cannot be bribed, for "from him that is defiled no good man, nor god can ever rightly receive gifts" (*Laws* 716E). At *QE* 2.101 Philo vividly represents the horns of the altar as "repelling the enemies of truth, goring every soul and showing up in their nakedness its unclean and unworthy deeds." Still, just as Plato recognized that the "faith in ritual catharsis was far too deeply rooted in the common mind for him to propose its complete elimination,"[45] so did Philo acknowledge the common man's need for ritual sacrifice. When the high priest, he notes, stands at the outer altar,

> the altar of common life, he will seem to pay much regard to skin and flesh and blood and all the bodily parts lest he should offend the thousands who, though they assign to the things of the body a value secondary to the things of the soul, yet do hold them to be good. But when he stands at the inner

altar, he will deal only with what is bloodless and is born of reason, which things are likened to the incense and the burnt spices. (*Ebr.* 87)[46]

Philo finds only an extrinsic significance in the sacrificial cult, one symbolically conveyed. God, who has no need of aught, "takes" in order to train us to piety and implant in us a zeal for holiness (*Her.* 123; cf. Dio Chrysostom, *Olymp.* 60). The true sacrifice, for Philo, is the worshiper's bringing of the self to God, that is, the fullness of moral nobility (*Spec.* 1.269–72). On occasion he even goes so far as to suggest that where the worshiper's heart is pure, no material sacrifices are necessary (*Mos.* 2.107; *Plant.* 108). He speaks, moreover, of two temples: the cosmos,[47] whose high priest is the Logos, and the rational soul, whose priest is the real Man (*Som.* 1.215). The theme of the "real Man" is very common in Philo and in Greek philosophy and refers to the inner voice of conscience, man at his rational best. Plato refers to the man "within us" who should dominate the entire person (*Republic* 589B), and Socrates facetiously refers to "that man who is continually refuting me, for he is a very near relative of mine and lives in the same house" (*Hip. Maj.* 304D).[48] The human mind, according to Philo, should become "an animate shrine of the Father" (cf. Plato *Timaeus* 37C), for no worthier house could be found for God in the realm of creation than a soul that is perfectly purified, and everyone should pray "that he may obtain the All-ruler as his occupant who shall exalt the paltry edifice of his mind high above the earth and join it to the ends of heaven" (*Sobr.* 62–64). The priest is thus identical with the sage, an assimilation that had already taken place in Stoic thought,[49] and the sacrifice is the allegorical designation of every act of philosophical reflection in which the mind, "filled with the breath of inspiration from heaven above is reduced to a single element" (inasmuch as the irrational part completely follows the rational) and is thus "fitly rendered in its entirety as a holy libation to Him who inspired it" (*Her.* 184).[50]

Prayer of Thanksgiving

Philo's preference for prayers of thanksgiving over those that are petitionary (*Spec.* 1.194–98) is rooted in his grading of the various human capacities to know God, according to which that which is based on love is higher than that which is based on fear (*Fug.* 97–98; *Deus* 64). This teaching of Philo is already adumbrated in Scripture, which speaks of the divine love for Israel which demands mutuality.[51] The same notion is expressed in the well-known statement of Rabbi Simeon b. Eleazar: "Greater is he who acts from love than he who acts from fear, because with the latter the merit remains effective for a thousand generations but with the former it remains effective for two thousand generations" (*b. Soṭa* 31a).

The obligation to render thanks to God for everything is all-pervasive in Philo's writings, and in one passage the various liturgical forms are all assimilated to this one category (Spec. 1.224). A similar tendency may be found in biblical literature. "In Hebrew Scripture," writes Moshe Greenberg, "the joyous singing of God's praises forms a class of hymns unto itself, with no petitional element. . . . A prime motive of praise, given repeatedly in the Psalms, is the sheer joy experienced in God's benefactions"[52] (Ps 92:2; 103:2; 71). This theme is lovingly elaborated by Philo. There is nothing that does not require our gratitude to God, since everything comes from Him (*Sac.* 97). Indeed, since all belongs to God, there is nothing else human beings can render to Him in return save thanks (*Det.* 56). And just as the psalmist imagines even the inanimate creation as breaking into song to God (65:12–14), Philo imagines that the world offers itself daily to God in ceaseless gratitude (*Her.* 200).

Petitionary Prayer

In spite of the fact that Philo often refers to petitionary prayer, a glance at its content will immediately reveal that he is no longer writing in the spirit of the biblical and early Jewish concept of such prayer, but rather in that of its Greek philosophical counterpart. The recurring pattern of these Philonic prayers rarely involves requests for external goods, their goal being instead the knowledge of God and spiritual perfection.[53] They are not so much entreaties as self-exhortations to seek the heights of spirituality, although they are couched in language that indicates that all spiritual achievement is in reality a gracious outflow of the divine. A fine example of the self-exhortatory type of petitionary prayer is Socrates' prayer at the conclusion of the *Phaedrus:*

> O beloved Pan and all ye other gods of this place, grant to me that I be made beautiful in my soul within, and that all external possessions be in harmony with my inner man. May I consider the wise man rich; and may I have such wealth as only the self-restrained man can bear or endure. Do we need anything more, Phaedrus? For me that prayer is enough. (279BC)[54]

For the Stoics, no less than for Philo, "the wise man will offer prayers and ask for good things from the gods" (Diogenes Laertius 7.124), but good things for the Stoics never refer to external goods, since these are assessed by them as morally indifferent. The kind of goods the Stoics should pray for is well illustrated by Marcus Aurelius: "One prays: 'How may I lie with that woman!' Thou: 'How may I not lust to lie with her!' Another: 'How may I be quit of that man!' Thou: 'How may I not wish to be quit of him!' Another: 'How may I not lose my little child!' Thou: 'How may I not dread to lose him!'" (9.40).

Contemplative Prayer

In delineating the contemplative or intellectual mode of prayer, which is for him the highest form it can assume, Philo is clearly going beyond the limits of his native Jewish tradition. In its journey to God, the mind abandons body and sense perception and becomes absorbed in a form of intellectual prayer which is wordless and unencumbered by petition:

> [For in this way only could that which is best in ourselves become inclined to serve the Best of all Existents] if reason sever and disperse that which seems to be closest to it, the uttered word, so that the thought within the mind may be left behind alone, bereft of body, bereft of sense-perception, bereft of the utterance of resonant speech. For thus left behind, it will live a life in accord with such solitude and will cleave in purity and without distraction to the Alone Existent. (*Fug.* 92)

The philosophical reason given by Philo for the inadequacy of speech is that it "attempts the impossible task of using shadows to point to substances," for "it is absurd that shadow gain the advantage over objects, or a copy over originals" (*Her.* 71; *Mig.* 12). This Philonic notion has its roots in Greek philosophical theory.

The inadequacy of language for the expression of truth had already received great emphasis in the Platonic *Seventh Letter*. At 341C there is a denial that the science of ultimate truth is expressible in words like other sciences. The reason is the inadequacy of names, definitions, sensible images, and human knowledge based on these, to express the nature of the Pure Form. The letter describes two ways of knowing the Forms, an imperfect way based on words and on the Forms' sensible images, and one that transcends these. Similarly, one of the ways in which *noēsis* in the *Republic* was claimed to be superior to *dianoia* was in dealing with the Forms themselves and making no use of their sensible images (510–11). The *Cratylus* too refers to the need for a faculty that will grasp Realities by themselves and independently of names, since only so can we be sure that our application of names is correct (438DE).[55] This conception is further amplified in Plutarch's *On the Sign of Socrates*, where we are told:

> Our recognition of one another's thought through the medium of the spoken word is like groping in the dark, whereas the thoughts of daemons are

luminous and shed their light on the daemonic man. Their thoughts have no need of verbs or nouns, which men use as symbols in their intercourse, and thereby behold mere counterfeits (*eidōla*, insubstantial forms or images) and likenesses of what is present in thought, but are unaware of the originals except for those persons who are illuminated, as I have said, by some special and daemonic radiance. (589C)

The concept of silent or contemplative prayer is alluded to in Plotinus 5.1.6.8: "We first invoke God Himself, not in resonant speech, but in that way of prayer which is always within our power, leaning in soul towards Him by aspiration, alone towards the Alone." Plotinus is referring here to the prayers of a sage capable of attaining the mystic vision, which is precisely what Philo has in mind in the passages cited above. We find this form of prayer again in Porphyry (*De abstinentia* 2.34) and Iamblichus (*De mysteriis* 8.3). Thus, the highest form of prayer for Philo is constituted by a mystical contemplation of God which ultimately preempts all its lower manifestations.

Study: Action versus Contemplation

From biblical times on, says Philo, it has been the practice for Jews "to pursue their ancestral philosophy every seventh day, dedicating that time to the theoretical study of the truths of nature. For what are places of prayer in the different cities but schools of wisdom . . . and every virtue, by which duties to God and men are perceived and correctly performed?" (*Mos.* 2.215–16). Philo's identification of places of prayer as being places of study as well is corroborated by the testimony of Josephus (*Against Apion* 2.17 §175), and is confirmed by the Theodotus inscription, which dates to the beginning of the first century C.E.[56] Josephus also praises the equal emphasis placed by Judaism on both the knowledge and practice of the Torah (*Against Apion* 2.16–17 §§172–73). A similar emphasis is found in rabbinic literature. Indeed, the rabbis even claimed that study is greater than practice, since it leads to action (*b. Qid.* 40b). Although Rabbi Yoḥanan considered it a duty and privilege for scholars to shoulder the burden of administration (*b. Shab.* 114a), there were others who regarded all occupation, with the exception of Torah study, as worthless (*Exod. Rab.* 6.5).[57] Now an analogous issue had exercised the Greco-Roman world in the form of the question about the superiority of the contemplative over the practical life, and that controversy is repeatedly echoed in Philo's writings. There is, however, a degree of ambiguity in his pronouncements on this topic, which reflects a similar ambivalence in his philosophic sources.

In a number of passages, Philo places the contemplative and practical lives on a par. At *LA* 1.57–58 he says that virtue is both theoretical and practical, since it involves philosophy, which includes logic, ethics, and physics, and — being the art of the whole of life — it also involves all kinds of actions. Theoretical virtue is indeed perfect in beauty, but its practice too is a prize to be striven for. Elsewhere he says that body and soul want to relieve each other, so that while the body is working, the soul enjoys a respite, but when the body takes its rest, the soul resumes its work; and thus the best forms of life, the theoretical and the practical, take their turn in replacing each other.[58] At *Decal.* 100, he bids man always follow God, who had devoted six days to *praxis* and the seventh to *theōria*, and not neglect this great archetype of the two best lives, the practical and the contemplative. Finally, Philo reproaches those who devote themselves either wholly to the service of God or wholly to companionship with their fellow human beings. "Both are incomplete in virtue; they alone have it entire who are highly esteemed in both spheres" (*Decal.* 108–10).

On the other hand, there are passages where Philo clearly gives priority to the contemplative life. "What life," he asks, "is better than a contemplative life, or more appropriate to a rational being?" (*Mig.* 47). At *QG* 4.47, after enumerating three ways of life, the contemplative, the active, and the pleasurable, he declares the contemplative to be great and excellent, the pleasurable slight and unbeautiful, and the active, which touches on both, small and not small, small by reason of being close to pleasure, great because of its nearness and kinship to contemplation. He often speaks in praise of solitude and leisure for the contemplation of nature (*Abr.* 22–23; *Prob.* 63) and asserts that the wise avoid gatherings of busybodies, such as lawcourts, council chambers, markets, and any assemblage of rash men (*Spec.* 2.44), and they will be prepared to abandon country, kin, and friends (*Praem.* 17–19). He describes the wise men as those who have dissolved their earthly element and have been transformed into disembodied minds in their desire to be in their totality well-pleasing to God (*Mut.* 33). In a moving auto-biographical outpouring, he reveals his own innate affinity with the life of the mind:

> There was a time when I devoted myself to philosophy and the contemplation of the universe and its contents, when I enjoyed the beauty, extreme loveliness and true felicity of its [all-encompassing] Mind, when I consorted constantly with divine principles and doctrines, wherein I rejoiced with a joy which knew no surfeit or satiety. (*Spec.* 3.1)

Sometimes he appears to reconcile his divided sentiments regarding the two types of life by relegating the active life to youth and the contemplative to old age (*Praem.* 51), suggesting that the one must precede the other (*Fug.* 36). Yet his ideal seems to be the sect of the Therapeutae, who are devoted to the contemplative life and regard as the true elders not those of silvery brow but those who from their earliest years have spent the prime of their youth and the flower of their maturity in the contemplative branch of philosophy (*Cont.* 67).

There is nothing at all surprising, however, in Philo's ambivalence with regard to the ideal life, since divergent views on this theme had already manifested themselves in the Greek philosophical tradition. Plato maintains a rather austere view in the *Phaedo* and *Theaetetus,* whereas in the *Republic,* although he ranks the philosopher's life above that of the love of victory and the love of gain (581C), he envisages a supreme political role for the philosopher, at least in the ideal state there conceived. Similarly, although Aristotle awards the palm to the contemplative life and concludes that a life guided by practical virtue is happy only in a secondary sense (*Ethica Nichomachea* 10.7), he stresses that virtue and happiness could only exhibit themselves in action (*Politica* 7.3), and when they are engaged in studying the moral activities he treats them as good in themselves.[59] Among Aristotle's disciples, Dicaearchus champions the active life and Theophrastus the contemplative (Cicero *De finibus* 5.57; Dicaearchus, frags. 29 and 31, Wehrli). Epicurus's wise man will not take part in politics except in an emergency (Diogenes Laertius 10.119). The Stoa, on the other hand, said that he will engage in public affairs unless something prevents him, and it advocated the *bios logikos,* combining *theōria* and *praxis,* since "a rational being is expressly produced for contemplation and for action" (Diogenes Laertius 7.130). "The wise man," say the Stoics, "will take part in politics, if nothing hinders him, and will marry and beget children. He will not live in solitude, for he is naturally made for society and action" (Diogenes Laertius 8.121, 123). The Stoic emphasis was thus apparently on *praxis,* but as M. T. Griffin has noted:

> The fact that none of the masters of the Old Stoa had followed their own precepts was, in Seneca's day, a commonplace, providing the occasion for ridicule or complex explanation, and Plutarch's account in *Stoic Self-Contradictions* (1033 BE) shows how, with a little malice, one could convict the founders of the Stoa of innumerable inconsistencies.[60]

In sum, though Philo recognized the importance of political activity, which required the participation of the wise man, in his heart of hearts he was captive to the ideal of pure contemplation, which allowed him only grudgingly to enter the communal domain.

Mysticism

The question of Philo's mysticism has been much debated, and although there is no clear evidence that Philo was a practicing mystic, there can be little doubt that a strong penchant for theoretical or intellectual mysticism colors much of his writing and forms an essential component of his religiosity. We have already discussed Philo's allegory of the soul's ascent to the intelligible realm up to the very edge of a dazzling vision that discloses the truly Existent without revealing its essence. There is much that is reminiscent here of the ascent of the soul in Plato's *Symposium*, which after transcending single instances of the beautiful, plunges into the wider sea of intellectual beauty, where it beholds on a sudden a wondrous vision of that which exists "itself by itself, eternal and singular," the ultimate source of all particular beauty. It transcends all knowledge and logos and may be grasped through itself alone (210–12). We are in the presence here of a First Principle analogous to the Form of the Good in *Republic* 6 (508–9), which is beyond even being and is the source of all knowledge and truth.[61]

E. R. Dodds has correctly noted that the ecstatic form of prophecy as defined by Philo is not a description of mystical union but a state of temporary possession.

> It is the supernatural spirit which descends into a human body, not the man who raises himself above the body. The earliest application of the word *ekstasis* to mystical experience is in Plotinus 6.9.11.22, where mystical union is described as "an *ekstasis*, a simplification, and surrender (*epidosis*, alternatively 'expansion') of the self, an aspiration towards contact which is at once a stillness and a mental effort of adaptation." (6.9.8.19)[62]

Philo, however, speaks also of another form of prophecy, which may be conveniently designated "hermeneutical" and is mediated not through ecstatic possession but through the divine voice. Whereas in the state of ecstatic possession the prophet's sovereign mind is entirely preempted by the divine Spirit so that he becomes a passive medium, hermeneutical prophecy does not render its recipient passive. It is clear from Philo's description of the giving of the Decalogue, which serves as the paradigm for prophecy through the divine voice, that, far from being preempted, the inspired mind in this case is extraordinarily quickened and sharpened (*Decal.* 35). Since the notion of ecstatic prophecy is employed by Philo only to explain the prophet's ability to predict the future, whereas the core of the Mosaic prophecy, the special laws, are delivered by him in his role of hermeneutical prophet, it is in this form of prophecy that we must seek to locate Philo's conception of mystical union. In his allegorical interpretation of the divine voice as the projection of a special "rational soul full of clearness and distinctness" making unmediated contact with the inspired mind that "makes the first advance and goes out to meet the conveyed meanings," it is not difficult to discern a reference to the activation of the intuitive intellect, by means of which one grasps the fundamental principles of universal being viewed as a unified whole. Philo was here following a Middle Platonic tradition that explained Socrates' famous *daimonion* or sign as the special sensitivity of his purified intellect to respond to the unuttered words of a daemon making voiceless contact with it (Plutarch *Moralia* 588E).[63] In Philo's hermeneutical prophecy, then, we may detect the notion of a union of the human mind with the Divine Mind or, in Dodds's terms, a psychic ascent rather than a supernatural descent.

An analysis of Philo's mystical passages reveals at once that, unlike Plotinus, who envisaged and actually experienced union with the ineffable One (4.8.1.1), Philo envisaged (though he may not actually have experienced) only a union with the Divine Mind, or that aspect of deity which is manifest as Logos. Like most mystics, he is convinced that humanity's goal and ultimate bliss lie in the knowledge or vision of God.[64] Indeed, the mere quest is sufficient of itself to give a foretaste of gladness (*Post.* 20).

> The limit of happiness is the presence of God, which completely fills the whole soul with His whole incorporeal and eternal light. And the limit of misery is His passing on the way . . . for the soul to be separated from the contemplation of the Existent One is the most complete of evils. (*QG* 4.4)

The soul has a natural longing and love for God and is drawn to Him by a surpassing beauty:

> When the mind is possessed by divine love, when it exerts itself to reach the innermost shrine, when it moves forward with all effort and zeal, under the impact of the divine inspiration it forgets everything else, forgets itself, and retains memory and attachment for Him alone whose attendant and servant it is. (*Som.* 2.232)

The first step leading to God is the recognition of one's own nothingness, which induces one to depart from oneself (*Her.* 69):

> For when above all he knew himself, then above all did Abraham despair of himself, in order that he might arrive at a precise knowledge of the truly Existent. And this is how it is: He who has profoundly comprehended himself, profoundly despairs of himself, having perceived in advance the absolute nothingness of created being. And the man who has despaired of himself knows the Existent. (*Som.* 1.60)

Having gone out of himself, the devotee is now asked to attach himself completely to God:

For in truth the mind that has been utterly purified, and that renounces all things belonging to creation, knows and recognizes but One alone, the Uncreated, to whom it has drawn nigh, and by whom it has been taken as a partner. For who is able to say "God Himself is alone to me," save one who clings to nothing that comes after Him? (*Plant.* 64)

This attainment to God involves the realization that it is God alone who ácts and as long as the mind "supposes itself to be the author of anything it is far away from making room for God" (*LA* 1.82). In the fragment from the lost fourth book of his *Legum Allegoriae,* Philo writes: "But when Moses affirms the first and better principle, namely, that God acts not as man, he ascribes the powers and causes of all things to God, leaving no work for a created being, but showing it to be inactive and passive." Those uninitiated, however, "in the great mysteries about the sovereignty and authority of the Uncreated and the exceeding nothingness of the created, do not as yet recognize this truth" (Harris, *Fragments:* 8).[65] Moreover, in abandoning body and sense perception, the mind is now absorbed in a form of intellectual prayer that is wordless and unencumbered by petition (*Fug.* 92).[66]

The mystic vision of God is a timeless experience that carries the soul to the uttermost bounds of the universe and enables it to gaze upon the divine Logos (*Conf.* 95–97). At *Ebr.* 152 (cf. *Det.* 89) we read:

What else was signified by the words, "I will pour out my soul before the Lord" but "I will consecrate it all to him, I will undo all the shackles that bound it securely, which the empty cares of mortal life had fastened upon it; I will carry it abroad, extend and diffuse it, so that it shall touch the bounds of the All, and hasten to that loveliest and most glorious of visions, the vision of the Uncreated."

The mystic state is further described as producing tranquillity and stability (*Gig.* 49; *Deus* 12), and it is sometimes indicated that it supervenes suddenly (*Sacr.* 78–79). It is also frequently described as a condition of sober intoxication, which is invariably depicted in a highly spirited and enthusiastic manner. The best known passage is *Op.* 70:

Again, when soaring upward the mind has spied the atmosphere and its changes, it is borne yet higher to the ether and the celestial revolution, and is carried around with the dances of the planets and fixed stars, in accordance with the laws of music, following the love of wisdom that guides it. When it has transcended all sensible substances, at that point it longs for the intelligible, and on beholding in that realm beauties beyond measure, the patterns and originals of the sensible things in the world below, it is possessed by a sober intoxication like those seized with Corybantic frenzy, and is inspired, filled by another sort of longing and a more fitting desire. Escorted by this to the uppermost vault of things intelligible, it seems to be on its way to the Great King himself; but while it keenly strives to see Him, pure and untempered rays of concentrated light stream forth like a flood, so that through its flashing bursts, the eye of the understanding spins with dizziness.[67]

Finally, like most mystics, Philo is keely aware of the inability of the human person to maintain a steady vision of the divine and the consequent ebb and flow that characterize that type of experience (*Som.* 2.233).

In an autobiographical vein, Philo sometimes describes his own personal experiences and speaks of an inner voice within his soul which is God-possessed and divines where it does not know (*Cher.* 27). At *Mig.* 34–35, he describes such an experience more spaciously:

> I feel no shame in describing my own experience, a thing I know from its having occurred numberless times. On occasion, after deciding to follow the standard procedure of writing on philosophical doctrines and knowing precisely the elements of my composition, I have found my understanding sterile and barren and have abandoned my project without result. . . . At other times I have come empty and have suddenly become full, the ideas descending like snow, so that under the impact of divine possession I had been filled with Corybantic frenzy and become ignorant of everything, place, people present, myself, what was said and what was written. For I acquired expression, ideas, an enjoyment of light, sharp-sighted vision, exceedingly distinct clarity of objects, such as might occur through the eyes as the result of the clearest display.

Our detailed examination of Philo's mystical passages thus indicates that they contain most of the characteristic earmarks of mystical experience. These may now be briefly summarized: Knowledge of God is supreme bliss, with the corollary that separation from God is the greatest of evils; the soul's intense yearning for the divine; recognition of one's nothingness and the need to go out of oneself; attachment to God; the realization that it is God alone who acts; a preference for contemplative prayer; a timeless union with the All; the serenity that results from the mystic experience; the suddenness with which the vision appears; the notion of sober intoxication; the ecstatic condition of the soul in the mystic state; and finally the ebb and flow of the mystical experience. We may thus conclude that Philo was certainly a "mystical theorist" (if not a practicing mystic)[68] to his very core and that his philosophical writings cannot be adequately understood if this signal fact is in any way obscured.[69]

Notes

1. The following abbreviations for the works of Philo are used in this chapter: *Abr.* = *On Abraham* (*De Abrahamo*); *Cher.* = *On the Cherubim* (*De Cherubim*); *Conf.* = *On the Confusion of Tongues* (*De Confusione Linguarum*); *Congr.* = *On the Preliminary Studies* (*De Congressu quaerendae Eruditionis gratia*); *Cont.* = *On the Contemplative Life* (*De Vita Contemplativa*); *Decal.* = *On the Decalogue* (*De Decalogo*); *Det.* = *The Worse Attacks the Better* (*Quod Deterius Potiori insidiari solet*); *Deus* = *On the Unchangeableness of God* (*Quod Deus immutabilis sit*); *Ebr.* = *On Drunkenness* (*De Ebrietate*); *Fug.* = *On Flight and Finding* (*De Fuga et Inventione*); *Gig.* = *On the Giants* (*De Gigantibus*); *Her.* = *Who Is the Heir* (*Quis Rerum Divinarum Heres*); *LA* = *Allegorical Interpretation* (*Legum Allegoriae*); *Mig.* = *On the Migration of Abraham* (*De Migratione Abrahami*); *Mos.* = *On the Life of Moses* (*De Vita Mosis*); *Mut.* = *On the Change of Names* (*De Mutatione Nominum*); *Op.* = *On the Creation* (*De Opificio Mundi*); *Plant.* = *On Noah's Work as a Planter* (*De Plantatione*); *Post.* = *On the Posterity and Exile of Cain* (*De Posteritate Caini*); *Praem.* = *On Rewards and Punishments* (*De Praemiis et Poenis*); *Prob.* = *Every Good Man is Free* (*Quod Omnis Probus Liber sit*); *Prov.* = *On Providence* (*De Providentia*); *QE* = *Questions and Answers on Exodus* (*Quaestiones et Solutiones in Exodum*); *QG* = *Questions and Answers on Genesis* (*Quaestiones et Solutiones in Genesin*); *Sacr.* = *On the Sacrifices of Abel and Cain* (*De Sacrificiis et Caini*); *Sobr.* = *On Sobriety* (*De Sobrietate*); *Som.* = *On Dreams* (*De Somniis*); *Spec.* = *On the Special Laws* (*De Specialibus Legibus*).

2. David Winston, *Philo of Alexandria,* 2–6. For a review and critique of the various approaches to Philo, including my own, see D. T. Runia, "Philo of Alexandria and the Timaeus of Plato," 5–22.

3. G. Scholem, *Über einige Grundbegriffe des Judentums* (Frankfurt am Main: Suhrkamp Verlag, 1970) 101.

4. See *QE* 2.124; *Conf.* 41; *Mig.* 103; *Conf.* 63, 146; *Deus* 31; *Her.* 205; *Fug.* 112; *Mos.* 2.134; *LA* 3.96; Eusebius *Praeparatio Evangelica* 7.131.

5. John Dillon, *The Middle Platonists,* 126–28, 346–49.

6. David Winston, "The Book of Wisdom's Theory of Cosmogony," *History of Religions* 11 (1971) 185–202, esp. 199 n. 41.

7. Dillon, *Platonists,* 45–46, 252.

8. For example, Ps 33:6; Sir 42:15; 43:26; cf. *Sib. Or.* 3:20. See H. A. Wolfson, *Philo,* 1:253–54.

9. See *Ancient Near Eastern Texts Relating to the Old Testament,* ed. J. B. Pritchard, 3rd ed. (Princeton, NJ: Princeton University Press, 1969) 428.

10. David Winston, *The Wisdom of Solomon* (Garden City, NY: Doubleday, 1979) 34–36.

11. For Philo's allegorical terminology, see J. Leopold, "Rhetoric and Allegory," in *Two Treatises of Philo of Alexandria,* ed. David Winston and John Dillon, 155–70.

12. Isaak Heinemann, *Philons griechische und jüdische Bildung,* 498–500.

13. Rudolf Pfeiffer, *History of Classical Scholarship* (Oxford: Clarendon Press, 1968) 237–40; Heraclite, *Allégories d'Homère,* ed. Felix Buffière (Paris: Société d'Édition 'Les Belles Lettres,' 1962) XXXVI.

14. Our account of Aristobulus represents a close summary of Nikolaus Walter, *Der Toraausleger Aristobulos* (Berlin: Akademie-Verlag, 1964) 124–71; see also Yehoshua Gutman, *The Beginnings of Jewish-Hellenistic Literature* [Hebrew] (Jerusalem: Mossad Bialik, 1958) 1:186–220; P. M. Fraser, *Ptolemaic Alexandria* (Oxford: Clarendon Press, 1972) 694–96.

15. Martin Hengel, *Judaism and Hellenism: Studies in their Encounter in Palestine during the Early Hellenistic Period,* trans. J. Bowden from 2nd rev. ed. (Philadelphia: Fortress, 1974) 1:164–69.

16. For a detailed comparison between Wisdom of Solomon and Philo, see Winston, *Wisdom,* 59–63.

17. W. O. E. Oesterly and G. H. Box, *The Religion and Worship of the Synagogue* (London: Sir Isaac Pitman & Sons, 1911) 169.

18. See G. Scholem, *Elements of the Kabbalah and its Symbolism* [Hebrew] (Jerusalem: Mossad Bialik, 1976) 260–62.

19. See E. E. Urbach, *The Sages: Their Concepts and Beliefs,* trans. I. Abrahams (Jerusalem: Magnes Press, 1975) 1:68, 74; J. Freudenthal, *Hellenistische Studien* (Breslau, 1875) 1:73; Heinrich Grätz in *Monatsschrift für Geschichte und Wissenschaft des Judentums* 30 (1881) 443; Wilhelm Bacher in *Jewish Quarterly Review* 3 (1891) 357–60. See also *m. Abot* 3:23; *Sifre Deut.* 48; *b. Nedarim* 62a.

20. On the other hand, there is a very close parallel between *Exod. Rab.* 5.9 (=Tanh. Shemot 70a) and Philo *Som.* 1.86. See Hans Bietenhard, "Logos Theologie im Rabbinat, in *Aufstieg und Niedergang der römischen Welt* 2.19.2, ed. W. Haase (Berlin and New York: de Gruyter, 1979) 580–617.

21. *Cher.* 27–28; *Sacr.* 59; *Her.* 166; *Abr.* 124–25; *QE* 2.68; *Fug.* 95; Winston, *Philo,* 23–24.

22. Eduard Zeller, *Die Philosophie der Griechen in ihren geschichtlichen Entwicklung* (Leipzig, 1923; reprint, Hildesheim: Olms, 1963) 3.2.407–9; Julius Guttmann, *Philosophies of Judaism: The History of Jewish Philosophy from Biblical Times to Franz Rosenzweig,* trans. D. W. Silverman (New York: Holt, Rinehart & Winston, 1964), pp. 25–26; Max Pohlenz, *Kleine Schriften* (Hildesheim: Olms, 1965) 1:335.

23. For a radically different interpretation, see Wolfson, *Philo,* 1:271–89.

24. É. Bréhier, *Les idées philosophiques et religieuses de Philon d'Alexandrie,* 74.

25. Plutarch *Moralia* 1051F, 1052B; Seneca *De Ira* 7.31.4; cf. 2.27.1.

26. *Op.* 16, 44, 77; *LA* 1.35; *Deus* 75; *Post.* 73; *Her.* 272; *Abr.* 204; *Mos.* 1.287, etc.

27. Winston and Dillon, *Two Treatises,* 311; cf. Pseudo-Aristeas 254.

28. For this Philonic deviation, see my forthcoming essay, *The Limits of Jewish Piety and Greek Philosophy in Philo's Thought,* chap. 3, "The Nature of God."

29. Cicero *Academicae quaestiones* 2.131; Plutarch *Moralia* 443C, 444B, 451C; Albinus *Didaskalikos* 30.5.6, Louis; Aulus Gellius *Noctes Atticae* 1.26.11; Maximus of Tyre *Oratio* 1.19b; 27.116b. Apuleius seems to be the only exponent of Middle Platonism who openly adopted the ideal of *apatheia* instead of *metriopatheia;* see S. R. C. Lilla, *Clement of Alexandria* (Oxford: Oxford University Press, 1971) 99–106.

30. See my forthcoming study, cited in n. 28.

31. *LA* 3.4; *Det.* 13, 95, 155; *Op.* 154; *QE* 2.34; *Congr.* 44; *Plant.* 32; *Post.* 1, 51; *Som.* 1.92–94.

32. David M. Hay, "Philo's References to Other Allegorists," *Studia Philonica* 6 (1979–80) 52, 58.

33. *Abr.* 201–4; *Fug.* 166–67; *Som.* 1.160; *Sobr.* 8; *Congr.* 36; *Det.* 46; *Mut.* 1; Cicero *Tusculanae disputationes* 3.82.

34. Cf. M. Aurelius 4.41: "Thou art a little soul bearing up a corpse, as Epictetus said" (not found in the latter's extant works).

35. Cf. Plato *Republic* 585B; *Timaeus* 86B; *Sophista* 228–29.

36. Cf. Plato *Phaedo* 81C; *Timaeus* 90A–D; Cicero *De deorum natura* 2.140.

37. *LA* 1.107–8; cf. Plato (*Gorgias* 493A; *Cratylus* 400B; Aristotle *Protrep.* fr. 10b, Ross.

38. See Felix Buffière, *Les Mythes d'Homère et la pensée grecque* (Paris' Études Augustiniennes, 1956) 365, 395; Jean Pépin, *Mythe et allégorie: Les origines grecques et les contestations judéo-chrétiennes* (Paris: Montaigne, 1958); 199–200; Pierre Boyancé, "Sur le discours d'Anchise," *Mélanges Dumézil, Latomus* 45 (1960) 60–76; idem, "*Études Philoniennes,*" *Revue des Études Grecques* 76 (1963) 74–77. For Philo's theory of metempsychosis, which apparently did not include animal reincarnation, on which subject he is silent, see Winston, *Wisdom,* 27–28.

39. *Abr.* 68–71, 119–32, 217–24; *Mig.* 176–95; *Som.* 1.41–60; *Gig.* 62–64; Samuel Sandmel, *Philo's Place in Judaism* (Cincinnati, OH: Hebrew Union College Press, 1956) 96–211.

40. *Ethica Nicomachea* 10.9.1179b20; *Politica* 8.13.1332a40; *Ethica Eudemia* 1.1.1214a16; cf. Diogenes Laertius 5.18; Winston, *Philo,* 374 n. 494.

41. *Congr.* 34–35; *Mut.* 256; *QG* 1.8; *Sacr.* 64, 78; *Deus* 92–93; *LA* 3.125; *Mig.* 167, and Colson's note ad loc. Cf., however, *Post.* 95, and Colson and Whittaker's note ad loc.

42. E. R. Dodds, *Pagan and Christian in an Age of Anxiety* (Cambridge: University Press, 1965) 10–11; A. J. Festugière, *La Révélation d'Hermès Trismégiste* (Paris: Lecoffre, 1949) 2:449–59.

43. Cf. *Agr.* 130; *Plant.* 164; *Spec.* 1.191, 203, 275, 283–84; 2.35.

44. Cf. Apollonius of Tyana *Epistulae* 27.

45. E. R. Dodds, *The Greeks and the Irrational* (Boston: Beacon, 1957) 222.

46. Cf. *Sib. Or.* 4.24–30; *Testament of Levi* 3.5–6; *Sir.* 35.1–5; *Corpus Hermeticum* 1.31–32; 13.19.

47. Cf. Pseudo-Plato *Epinomis* 983E; Cicero *De deorum natura* 3.26; *De re publica* 6.15; *De legibus* 2.26; Plutarch *Moralia* 477C; Pseudo-Heraclitus *Ep.* 4; Seneca *Epistulae* 90.28; *De beneficiis* 7.7.3.

48. Jean Pépin, *Idées grecques sur l'Homme et sur Dieu* (Paris: Société d'Éditions 'Les Belles Lettres,' 1971) 71–86; Winston and Dillon, *Two Treatises,* 252–53.

49. Diogenes Laertius 7.119; *SVF* 3.605; Cicero *Div.* 2.129.

50. Cf. *LA* 2.50; *Mos.* 2.288; Valentin Nikiprowetzky, "La Spiritualisation des sacrifices et le culte sacrificiel au Temple de Jerusalem chez Philon d'Alexandrie," *Semitica* 17 (1967) 97–116; Ronald Williamson, *Philo and the Epistle to the Hebrews,* Arbeiten zur Literatur und Geschichte des hellenistischen Judentums 4 (Leiden: Brill, 1970) 160–83; L. W. Thompson, "Hebrews 9 and Hellenistic Concepts of Sacrifice," *Journal of Biblical Literature* 98 (1979) 567–78; R. D. Hecht, "Patterns of Exegesis in Philo's Interpretation of Leviticus," *Studia Philonica* 6 (1979–80) 77–155.

51. Hos 11:1, 4; Deut 7:7–10; 10:12, 15; Jer 31:2; Isa 63:9; Mal 1:2; Moshe Greenberg, "On the Refinement of the Conception of Prayer in Hebrew Scriptures," *AJS Review* 1 (1976) 59–60.

52. Moshe Greenberg, "Of the Refinement of the Conception of Prayer in Hebrew Scripture," *AJS Review* 1 (1976) 71–72.

53. *Abr.* 6, 58–59; *Sobr.* 64; *Plant.* 49, 52; *Fug.* 164; *Mig.* 171; *Som.* 1.163; *Congr.* 7; *Cont.* 27, 89; C. W. Larson, "Prayer of Petition in Philo," *Journal of Biblical Literature* 65 (1946) 185–203.

54. Kurt von Fritz, "Greek Prayers," *Review of Religion* 10 (1945–46) 5–39.

55. R. T. Wallis, "Nous as Experience," in *The Significance of Neoplatonism,* ed. R. B. Harris (Norfolk, VA: International Society for Neoplatonic Studies, Old Dominion University, 1976) 121–53. Cf. Plotinus 4.3.30.5; 5.5.1.38–39.

56. Emil Schürer, *The History of the Jewish People in the Age of Jesus Christ,* rev. and ed. Geza Vermes, F. Millar, M. Black (Edinburgh: T. & T. Clark, 1979) 2:425.

57. Urbach, *The Sages,* 603–20.

58. *Spec.* 2.64; cf. *QG* 4.29; *Mos.* 1.48; 2.130; *QE* 2.31; *Decal.* 100–101; *Praem.* 11.

59. John M. Cooper, *Reason and Human Good in Aristotle* (Cambridge, MA: Harvard University Press, 1975) 144–80.

60. M. T. Griffin, *Seneca: A Philosopher in Politics* (Oxford: Clarendon Press, 1976) 340. The ambiguities in the Stoic position are fully exemplified in Seneca's writings; see Griffin, chap. 10, and my forthcoming study, cited in n. 28, chap. 2, "Prayer and Study," which is reproduced here in a considerably abbreviated form.

61. A. J. Festugière, *Contemplation et vie contemplative selon Platon,* 3rd ed. (Paris: Gabalda, 1967) part 1, chap. 4.

62. Dodds, *Pagan and Christian,* 71–72.

63. For a full discussion, see my forthcoming study, cited in n. 28, chap. 5, "Prophecy and Revelation."

64. *Decal.* 81; *Det.* 86; *Abr.* 58; *Praem.* 14.

65. For Philo's doctrine of free will, see Winston and Dillon, *Two Treatises,* 181–95.

66. For the contemplative mode of prayer in Hasidism, see Rivka Shatz-Uffenheimer, *Quietistic Elements in Hasidic Thought* [Hebrew] (Jerusalem: Magnes Press, 1968), 22–31, 95–110.

67. Cf. *Ebr.* 145; *Fug.* 166; *LA* 1.82; 3:82; *Prob.* 13; *Fug.* 32; *Mos.* 1.187; *Cont.* 89.

68. Dodds, *Pagan and Christian,* 70.

69. Winston, *Philo,* 33–35.

Bibliography

The older literature on Philo is fully recorded by E. R. Goodenough and Goodhart in Goodenough, *Politics.* An excellent annotated bibliography for the years 1937 to 1962 is provided by Feldman. Further bibliographies are provided in every issue of *Studia Philonica,* beginning in 1972; Earle Hilgert's bibliography is forthcoming in *Aufstieg und Niedergang der römischen Welt* (Berlin: de Gruyter, forthcoming). There is an excellent translation of Philo by F. H. Colson (and G. H. Whittaker for vols. 1–4) in the Loeb Classical Library (Cambridge, MA: Harvard University Press; London: Heinemann, 1929–1962), 10 vols., plus two supplementary volumes containing the *Questions and Answers on Genesis and Exodus* (1953), translated from the Armenian by Ralph Marcus. A brief anthology of Philo's writings which emphasizes his contemplative side is Lewy. A more comprehensive anthology of Philo's works is Winston, *Philo of Alexandria.* There are fully annotated editions of Philo's *In Flaccum, Legatio ad Gaium,* and *De Animalibus* by Herbert Box, E. M. Smallwood, and Abraham Terien, respectively. There is now also a full commentary (with an extensive introduction by several hands) on Philo's *The Giants* and *That God is Unchangeable* by Winston and Dillon.

The best general study of Philo is still Bréhier. An older but still useful account of Philo's Platonism is Billings, which is now supplemented and greatly advanced by the excellent dissertation of Runia. An excellent account of Philo's place within the Middle Platonic tradition is the chapter on Philo in Dillon. The large monographs by Völker and Wolfson are indispensable for their very rich presentations of data, though very one-sided in their interpretations. Two useful general introductions to Philo are Good-enough, *Introduction,* and Sandmel. A good summary chapter on Philo is that by Chadwick in *The Cambridge History of Later Greek and Early Medieval Philosophy.* A fundamental study on Philo's relationship to Palestinian Judaism and Greek culture is Heinemann. A very rich and important study of Philo's exegetical approach is Nikiprowetzky. Useful accounts of Philo's sexual imagery and theory of education may be found in Baer and in Mendelson. A highly stimulating but idiosyncratic account of

Philo's mysticism is Goodenough, *By Light, Light*. A detailed analysis of Philo's allegory of the soul is to be found in Marguerite Harl's extensive introduction to her edition of *Quis Rerum Divinarum Heres Sit* in *Les Oeuvres de Philon d'Alexandrie*. A brief analysis of Philo's mysticism may be found in Louth. For an account of Philo's ethical theory against its mystical framework, see my forthcoming essay in *Aufstieg und Niedergang der römischen Welt* 2.21 (Berlin: de Gruyter).

Baer, R. A. *Philo's Use of the Categories Male and Female*. Leiden: Brill, 1970.

Billings, Thomas H. *The Platonism of Philo Judaeus*. Chicago: University of Chicago Press, 1919.

Box, Herbert, ed. *Philonis Alexandrini, In Flaccum*. London and New York: Oxford University Press, 1939.

Bréhier, Émile. *Les idées philosophiques et religieuses de Philon d'Alexandrie*. Paris: Librairie Philosophique J. Vrin, 1950.

Dillon, John. *The Middle Platonists: 80 B.C. to A.D. 220*. Ithaca, NY Cornell University Press, 1977.

Feldman, Louis. *Studies in Judaica: Scholarship on Philo and Josephus (1937-62)*. New York: Yeshiva University, n.d.

Goodenough, E. R. *By Light, Light: The Mystic Gospel of Hellenistic Judaism*. New Haven, CT: Yale University Press, 1935.

———. *An Introduction to Philo Judaeus*. 2nd ed. Oxford: Barnes & Noble, 1962.

———. *The Politics of Philo Judaeus: Practice and Theory*. New Haven, CT: Yale University Press, 1938; reprint, Hildesheim: Olms, 1967.

Harl, Marguerite, ed. *Philo, Quis Rerum Divinarum Heres Sit*. Vol. 15 of Les Oeuvres de Philon d'Alexandrie, ed. R. Arnaldez, J. Pouilloux, C. Mondesert. Paris: Cerf, 1966.

Heinemann, Isaak. *Philons griechische und jüdische Bildung*. Breslau: Marcus, 1932; reprint, Hildesheim: Olms, 1962.

Lewy, Hans. *Philo: Selections*. Oxford, 1946. [Reprinted in *Three Jewish Philosophers*. Cleveland, New York, Philadelphia: East and West Library, 1961.]

Louth, Andrew. *The Origins of the Christian Mystical Tradition from Plato to Denys*. Oxford: Clarendon Press, 1981.

Mendelson, Alan. *Secular Education in Philo of Alexandria*. Cincinnati, OH: Hebrew Union College Press, 1982.

Nikiprowetzky, Valentin. *Le Commentaire de l'écriture chez Philon d'Alexandrie*. Leiden: Brill, 1977.

Runia, D. T. "Philo of Alexandria and the *Timaeus* of Plato." Diss., Alblasserdam, 1983.

Sandmel, Samuel. *Philo of Alexandria: An Introduction*. New York and Oxford: Oxford University Press, 1979.

Smallwood, E. M., ed. *Philonis Alexandrini, Legatio ad Gaium*. Leiden: Brill, 1961.

Terien, Abraham. *Philonis Alexandrini, De Animalibus*. Studies in Hellenistic Judaism, 1. Chico, CA: Scholars Press, 1981.

Völker, Walther. *Fortschritt und Vollendung bei Philo von Alexandrien*. Leipzig: Hinrichs, 1938.

Winston, David. *Philo of Alexandria, The Contemplative Life, The Giants, and Selections*. New York, Ramsey, NJ, and Toronto: Paulist Press, 1981.

———, and John Dillon. *Two Treatises of Philo of Alexandria: A Commentary on De Gigantibus and Quod Deus Sit Immutabilis*. Brown Judaic Studies 25. Chico, CA: Scholars Press, 1983.

Wolfson, H. A. *Philo: Foundations of Religious Philosophy in Judaism, Christianity and Islam*. Cambridge, MA: Harvard University Press, 1947.

9

Law and Spirit in Talmudic Religion

R O B E R T   G O L D E N B E R G

The Central Feature of Rabbinic Religion

CLASSICAL JUDAISM, drawing directly on its biblical antecedents, tends to emphasize act over intention, behavior over thought. Righteousness is chiefly a matter of proper behavior, not correct belief or appropriate intention. Divine punishment is always depicted in the historical books of Scripture as the result of wrong behavior;[1] the concept of heresy is unknown in the Hebrew Bible, and hypocrisy, although recognized in the Wisdom books as an undesirable trait, is never identified as the cause of national disaster.

The surviving materials indicate that the leaders of the various forms of postbiblical Judaism saw their chief tasks as formulating the correct rules for Jewish life and then inducing their followers (ideally the entire house of Israel) to obey them. This was clearly true of the sect at Qumran, despite the talk in their writings of the "spirits" of good and evil,[2] and it represents the starting point even of Philo of Alexandria, although he then proceeded to find deep spiritual meanings in those same rules.

Philo makes clear, however, that other movements in Jewish thinking, movements whose own writings have generally not survived, had begun to reverse this already ancient preference for law over spirit. In a famous passage, the great allegorizer inveighs against those even more radical than himself:

> 89. There are some who, regarding laws in their literal sense in the light of symbols of matters belonging to the intellect, are overpunctilious about the latter, while treating the former with easy-going neglect. Such men I for my part should blame for handling the matter in too easy and off-hand a manner: they ought to have given careful attention to both aims, to a more

full and exact investigation of what is not seen and in what is seen to be stewards without reproach.

90. As it is, as though they were living alone by themselves in a wilderness, or as though they had become disembodied souls, and knew neither city nor village nor household nor any company of human beings at all, overlooking all that the mass of men regard, they explore reality in all its naked absoluteness. . . .

93. Nay, we should look on all these outward observances as resembling the body, and their inner meanings as resembling the soul. It follows that, exactly as we have to take thought for the body, because it is the abode of the soul, so we must pay heed to the letter of the laws. If we keep and observe these, we shall gain a clearer conception of those things of which these are the symbols; and besides that we shall not incur the censure of the many and the charges they are sure to bring against us. (*On the Migration of Abraham* 89–90, 93).[3]

Philo takes issue here with the idea that the laws of Scripture can be disregarded once their spiritual purpose has been achieved. Although he concedes that the ultimate meaning of any passage in the Torah lies beyond its legal content, that the laws of the Torah are meant to convey meaningful instruction and not merely to regulate behavior, Philo insists nevertheless that these laws must be accepted and obeyed as laws. To do otherwise, he writes, is to act as though the soul has no need for the body and to disregard society's legitimate demand that its members conform to accepted public norms.[4] Philo's position, then, seems to be that indeed the significance of the various commandments in the Torah lies in what they teach—that is, what they contribute to the life of the spirit—and that the provisions of the laws are merely a necessary means of conveying this meaning, no more than instruments of a higher purpose, though necessary just the same.

The only surviving body of first-century Jewish writing that embodies the more radical view rejected by Philo is not usually considered in its Jewish context. The writings of the Christian apostle Paul, however, clearly reflect the same line of thought, even if certain nuances are different, and even if the central figure of Jesus Christ naturally was absent from the religious ideas of Philo's Alexandrian rivals. Paul concedes that the law is "holy, and the commandment . . . just and good" (Rom 7:12)[5] or at least that it had served a useful purpose as "our custodian until Christ came" (Gal 3:24), but now its purpose has indeed been achieved. Now the promised redeemer has come, that all "might receive the promise of the Spirit" through faith (Gal 3:14), and under these new circumstances "the written letter kills, while the Spirit gives life" (2 Cor 3:6). Paul's logic, then, is the same as that of the Alexandrian radicals: the law served a great and holy purpose in preparing its followers for an even greater salvation (or insight) that was to follow. That higher teaching is now directly available; to remain concerned with or loyal to the detailed, no-longer-necessary rules of the old Scriptures is benighted stubbornness. The new builders have rejected what once had been the cornerstone.

Following the triumph of the Christian religion, Paul's view of these matters became normative for Western civilization.[6] It is therefore important to keep in mind that rabbinic thinking on these subjects, whether in the not-yet-Christian Galilee or in non-Christian Babylonia, was formed independently of Paul's influence. For the authors of classical rabbinic literature, there is no fundamental conflict between Law (or the letter) and Spirit (or grace). In place of the elemental dichotomies of Pauline thought, ancient rabbis saw the kind of unity hinted at in Philo's image of body and soul. The meaning of divine revelation was not separable from its detailed contents; any such separation implied that the Torah was imperfect and might be superseded by a clearer and more direct statement of its "true" significance. The life of Torah could not for the rabbis be redeemed through grace, because the giving of the Torah had already been God's greatest grace. Rabbis could not speak of Torah *and* grace because they thought of Torah *as* grace.[7] In rabbinic thinking there was no need to emancipate the human spirit from the shackles of a stultifying legalism. The law nourishes the spirit; it does not kill but saves from death.[8]

Rabbinic Judaism takes for granted that true worship means obedience to sacred law, to the laws of the Torah as originally revealed to Moses on Mount Sinai and as later elaborated by Moses' rabbinic successors. At Mount Sinai Israel had entered into a covenant with the Creator of the Universe, and Israel's obligations under that covenant had been set forth as the commandments of the Torah. If "religion" is to be understood as loyalty to the divine covenant, any distinction between religion and obedience to the Torah was thus out of the question. As a corollary of this conception, the rabbis understood that study of the Torah was the highest possible religious activity. Through careful elaboration of the written and oral revelation transmitted through Moses, it was possible to discover more and more ways in which God's will might be fulfilled. To enlarge the range of the law was therefore not to add to its burdensome weight but rather to strengthen the link between the covenant community and its God.[9]

Extremely close attention to the details of the law, both as subject for study and as norm for behavior, became the central feature of rabbinic religion. In this respect the standard Christian description of Judaism as "legalism" is not inaccurate; it must only be kept in mind that rabbis cultivated this scholastic behaviorism in a spirit of joy and gratitude. They saw the Torah and its rules as an open door to the divine throne room and not at all as an obstacle blocking that same passage.

Kawwanah ("Consciousness")

To be sure, rabbinic literature reflects clear awareness of the dangers that a legalistic spirituality must face. A key term in the confrontation with such dangers is *kawwanah*—"consciousness" or "intention." The term appears in a number of contexts. In the case of prayer, the rabbinic tradition recognized that prayer without *kawwanah* is somehow flawed, and later codifiers ruled that statutory prayer recited without *kawwanah* must be repeated and that one who knows that *kawwanah* will be impossible for him can under some circumstances be relieved of the obligation to pray.[10] *Kawwanah* in this context must be understood to mean attention to the words or ability to direct them heavenward in a properly worshipful attitude. These are not the same, of course—one is intellectual and the other emotional in focus— and it is interesting that no clear definition of *kawwanah* is ever offered by these same codifiers. Prayer, however, is by its nature a special case. In connection with other sorts of ritual action, the rabbinic conception of *kawwanah* becomes more elusive.

As rabbis understood it, the Torah requires numerous ritual actions, each to be performed at stated occasions. Examples of such "commandments" (*mizwot*) would be the eating of unleavened bread (*mazzah*) on the first night of Passover[11] or the blowing of the ram's horn (*shofar*) on Rosh Hashanah, the fall new year celebration. Questions naturally arise: Does the requirement to perform such acts include any specified mental state? Does *any* performance of the act serve to fulfill the divine command, or is it necessary, since the act is "religious," that one have a particular attitude as well? Must one, for example, *intend* to fulfill the will of God? Must one at least be *aware* that the act does fulfill it? If no intention toward God is required, must one at least perform the act consciously, or willingly? Does the act fulfill the commandment even when performed absentmindedly, or unconsciously? What if the act is performed under compulsion?

These questions may well presuppose farfetched circumstances. The idea of eating unleavened bread "under compulsion" strains credulity. Yet the Talmud raises such hypothetical possibilities, and its purpose in doing so seems clear. The Mishnah indicates that earlier sages had indeed required some degree of self-consciousness (*kawwanah*) for proper performance of the commandments; the Mishnah denies that one who recites the *shema'* or hears the *shofar* without "directing the heart" has properly fulfilled the commandment in question.[12] By proposing such bizarre possibilities as that Persian magi might come and force feed *mazzah* to Jews on Passover[13] the Babylonian Amoraim reduced the requirement of *kawwanah* to the barest minimum that can be imagined. To recite *shema'* with *kawwanah* thus means to pay attention to the words, unlike one proofreading a scroll. To hear the ram's horn with *kawwanah* means not to mistake the sound for a donkey's bray.

Talmudic "legalism," then, retreated from the tendency of the Mishnah and restored the primacy of act over intention. Truly pious intention—the conscious desire while performing a certain act to fulfill thereby, without expectation of reward, the express command of God—is desirable, to be sure, but cannot be demanded, measured, or even reliably observed. Hortatory passages found scattered throughout rabbinic literature reveal that rabbis did harbor concern for their disciples' inner lives but that they were careful to separate their concern from the more central task of defining the religion's rules and requirements.[14] Rabbinic ethics reflect the recognition that religious life could not be entirely contained within "the four cubits of the law." The concept of *lifnim mi-shurat ha-din* ("within [or beyond] the line of the law") served to encourage people to disregard the limits of their legal obligation.[15] A similar quasi-legal phrase is "exempt in human law but liable in Divine law";[16] this phrase, usually applied to nonactionable negligence and the like, again recognizes that human actions can be of a sort that satisfies legal norms but are morally or religiously flawed. Perhaps most interesting in this connection is the use of the very term *mizwah* (commandment) to designate actions that people should feel obliged to carry out even when the law cannot compel them to do so; this use of the term can be found in contexts of both ritual and civil law.[17]

In short, Talmudic teachings on a wide variety of subjects suggest that ancient rabbis saw religion as primarily a matter of adhering to a set of divinely revealed (or sanctioned) rules, but that they recognized as well the need for approaching these rules in a certain frame of mind, lest they lose their proper religious effect. And this in turn suggests that rabbinic legalism shared the wider perception, already observed here in both Paul and Philo, that the law was designed to produce certain results. Obedience was not merely a formal principle. It sprang from recognition that the law was in itself beneficial and worthy of being obeyed. The dictum that the reward of one commandment is another commandment (*m. Abot* 4:2) was not the rabbis' only word on the subject. It was also understood that those who bent to the yoke of the law could be transformed into the sort of people they presumably wanted to become, the sort of people in any event that the Creator (and the rabbis) wanted them to be. This is the meaning of the famous teaching that "the commandments were given to purify man";[18] legalism is thus the disciplined pursuit of a desired goal and not the behavioral equivalent of "blind faith," or an accountant's strategy for getting into heaven.

Previous scholars have already investigated these themes (see the bibliographical remarks below), and little purpose would be served here by producing one more loose collection of rabbinic dicta on the subjects of the law and rabbis' joy in fulfilling it. As is well known, the haphazard, unsystematic arrangement of rabbinic literature is not well suited to the study of theological questions. Rabbis did not produce lengthy essays in which particular important religious questions were methodically investigated. Instead, the modern student of ancient Judaism finds in talmudic literature an immense variety of relatively brief discussions and an even larger number of unconnected sayings, most of them ostensibly concerned with some technical matter, many of them embedded in contexts that seem altogether irrelevant to the concerns of the particular saying. When one examines the standard surveys of rabbinic theology, one is struck by the observation that on any given page it is likely that no two citations will have been drawn from a common context. It thus becomes very difficult to imagine what the authors of the respective dicta were actually discussing on the day they spoke the quoted words.[19]

The Case of the Sabbath

In an effort to limit this difficulty, the rest of this chapter will focus on a single element in ancient Jewish religion—the Sabbath. The Sabbath was a central institution of ancient Jewish life, widely known and tenaciously maintained; indeed, "the observance of the Sabbath was one of the best known Jewish customs in the Roman world."[20] Jews everywhere abstained from their normal activities on this day and engaged instead in a variety of distinctive practices, both at home and in their synagogues. Jewish Sabbath observance thus enforced both the sense of unity that Jews felt with one another and also the sense of separation that they felt with respect to the surrounding world.

Now these observances—especially for rabbis and their followers—entailed familiarity with and acceptance of a large number of rules.[21] Many of these were proscriptive in character and gave rise to the widespread Roman conception that the Sabbath encouraged the Jews to lead lives of indolence and was itself a day of deprivation. This restrictive side of the Sabbath is the one most emphasized in the New Testament:[22] there we read of Jesus' being rebuked because his disciples violated various Sabbath taboos, or of Paul's rebuking his converts because they in turn wished to observe them or to impose them on others. At the same time, however, rabbinic sources follow in Philo's path by depicting the Sabbath as a day of profound enjoyment.[23] Picking up the hint of Isaiah 58:13, rabbis developed the conception that the Sabbath was essentially joyful and liberating; Rabbi Hanina b. Isaac described the day as offering a foretaste of the very joys of Paradise.[24]

This combination of strict legal regulation with a sense of liberation and ease is characteristic of the rabbinic approach to the law.[25] The Sabbath thus offers a key example of the rabbinic quest for a law-based spirituality, and it will be useful to examine in greater detail how this quest was pursued. In the pages that follow, certain features of rabbinic Sabbath law that shed light on rabbis' underlying religious conceptions will be examined. To understand the nature of the Sabbath and its role in rabbinic religion is to approach the very heart of rabbinic Judaism.

The Question of Muqzeh

Chapter 17 of *m. Shab.* deals with a prohibition against handling certain types of objects on the Sabbath. It offers a somewhat more abstract treatment of a theme that first arises at *m. Shab.* 3:6: "A new lamp may be handled [on the Sabbath], but not an old one. R. Simeon says, All lamps may be handled, except for a lamp [actually] burning on the Sabbath."[26] Neither in the isolated dispute found at 3:6 nor in the more general rules found in chapter 17 is the ground of such a prohibition laid out. The closest one finds is the explanation (at 17:1) that the door of a house (if detached) may not be handled on the Sabbath "because it is not in readiness" when the Sabbath begins. This conception presumably arises from the mythic significance of the Sabbath as celebrating the completion of creation. The world to be enjoyed on the Sabbath is the world that already existed when the Sabbath first began.

Post-Mishnaic rabbis evidently found this lack of explanation intolerable. Inventing a new technical term (*muqzeh,* "set aside"), the Amoraim proceeded to establish a whole set of types of forbidden activities. Some objects are *muqzeh* because their usual employment constitutes a forbidden activity; some because the objects themselves are repulsive and thus would reduce the pleasurable nature of the Sabbath, and so forth. The dispute in *m. Shab.* 3:6 was in this way transformed from a seemingly groundless disagreement over a seemingly random detail into a way of illustrating a basic conceptual disagreement. It could now be held that Rabbi Judah (identified in the parallel sources as the authority behind the initial, anonymous opinion in *m. Shab.*) accepted the principle of "*muqzeh* on account of repulsiveness" while Rabbi Simeon rejected it. Judah therefore forbade the handling of any lamp once it had become sooty through prior use, but Simeon forbade handling a lamp only if it was currently lit. Such a lamp is "*muqzeh* on account of a prohibition," that is, out of fear that the lamp may go out as it is being carried around[27] —and this category of proscription was accepted by everyone.

Examples of such transformation could be multiplied many times. True to its legalistic character, rabbinic law always maintained its focus on behavioral detail, forbidding this or permitting that. But as time went on, larger and larger groups of unconnected items came to be gathered together under the rubric of some general principle ("If an object is considered repulsive, handling that object is forbidden on the Sabbath"), and these principles in turn carried the discussion farther and farther away from the realm of behavior. To decide *why* Simeon permits and Judah forbids is of no necessary relevance to the task of deciding which opinion to adopt; to *make* such explanations into the basis for legal decisions had to be a separate, later development, and it never fully came about.[28]

If later rabbis had wanted to resolve ambiguity in the law or to settle disputes between earlier authorities by reference to general principles of the kind just mentioned, they could easily have done so, but in fact they did not. Such philosophical analyses of the basis of various teachers' opinions served the growing scholasticism of amoraic Torah study, but they did not directly affect the substance of the law. The Talmud recognizes that detailed halakhic rulings can reflect principles of law or theology, that they do conceivably spring from more abstract understandings of how the Sabbath ought to be celebrated, but it is interested in these more general principles only for their contribution to the theoretical elaboration of the law. Practical decisions are reached by other means.

The result is an odd situation in which no one is really interested in the role of "repulsiveness" in determining Sabbath law, although the whole discussion nevertheless presumes the basic importance of that concept. The Amoraim evince little interest in the idea and offer few examples of their own of how such a principle might lead to specific rulings. Yet they take for granted that the notion was basic to their predecessors' treatment of the same theme, and for that reason they seem to feel obliged to keep the category as part of their own discussions. The tannaitic documents, for their part, never use the word *muqzeh* at all, let alone provide an explanation of the conceptions underlying it. Further instances of this combination— detailed legal regulations that clearly reflect abstract legal (or philosophical) presuppositions but never stop to explain or even cite them—will presently appear. This is the foundation of the "growing scholasticism" of rabbinic legal thinking just mentioned. The term "scholasticism" is meant to suggest that rabbinic legal discourse was no longer interested in simple clarification or application or enforcement of the law. Instead, to be engaged in the study of the law had become a religious activity to be cultivated in its own right. Rabbis sought to mold the innumerable rules inherited from the past into a coherent system, with all laws attributed to a given master kept consistent with one another, with each master's set of rules wherever possible kept distinct from every other master's, and wherever possible with every detail traced back to some abstract principle that rationalized it and linked it to others.

Such scholasticism can now serve to illuminate the character of rabbinic spirituality. Rabbinic Judaism was a religion more congenial to certain religious goals and characteristics than to others. It valued alert, conscious intellectuality more than depth of feeling or experience; it cultivated clarity of expression more eagerly than inexpressible profundity. It was more interested in the relative compatibility of numerous statements than in the relative brilliance of any one of them. And for these reasons, it tended to direct attention to behavioral rules; for discussion of such rules, the favored characteristics of mind were the most naturally appropriate. The *via contemplativa* did not lead to the doorway of the talmudic academy.

Heating Water for the Bath

The following account appears at *b. Shab.* 40a:

> R. Simeon b. Pazzi quoted R. Joshua b. Levi in the name of Bar Qappara: In the beginning [people] would bathe [on the Sabbath] in water that had been heated on Sabbath Eve, [but] the attendants began to heat [water] on the Sabbath and say, "It was heated on Sabbath Eve." They[29] forbade [bathing in] hot water but permitted sweating [on account of the heat of the bathhouse or the water], but still [people] would bathe in hot water and say, "we were sweating." They forbade sweating, but permitted the hot [waters] of Tiberias [which were natural springs requiring no forbidden human labor; the term is used here generically], but still [people] would bathe in water heated by fire and say, "We bathed in the hot waters of Tiberias." They forbade them the hot waters of Tiberias but permitted [the use of] cold water. When they saw the situation could not be maintained [literally, the matter would not stand], they permitted them the hot waters of Tiberias, but sweating [i.e., from a source of artificial heat] remained in its place [i.e., forbidden].

The Jerusalem Talmud tells a related but different story (*y. Shab.* 3:36a):

> At first, [people] would block the furnace on Sabbath Eve and come in and bathe on the Sabbath. They were suspected of filling it with wood on

Sabbath Eve so it would keep burning on the Sabbath, so they[30] forbade them to bathe but permitted them to sweat. They were suspected of coming in to bathe and saying, "We were sweating," so they forbade them to bathe or to sweat. There were two bathing-places there, one of sweet water [heated by fire] and one of salt water [the "hot waters of Tiberias"—see above]; [the people] were suspected of uncovering [i.e., removing] the boards [covering the furnace] and bathing in the sweet water and saying, "We were bathing in the salt water," so they forbade them everything. Once [the people] had accepted the limitation, [the authorities] permitted more and more, until they permitted them water from a cave [heated by some natural means] and the hot waters of Tiberias, but they did not permit [people] to bring bathing-clothes. . . .

Now the anonymous "they" who issued all these rulings make no claim that one rule or another is the proper interpretation of the scriptural passages from which Sabbath rules are derived. Questions of meaning or of determining the actual intent of the divine lawgiver do not arise here at all. Instead, the religious goal here seems to be simply to get people to obey the law as the sages have determined it. If the sages think the people are taking advantage of loopholes in the law, they make it stricter. If the sages see they have gone so far that the people will no longer follow them, they retreat a bit. The point here is not that the law should conform to some predetermined model of Sabbath observance, but that it should work.[31]

The spirituality here is one of discipline and communal uniformity. The purpose of these various alterations in the law is to establish in principle that rabbis could determine the standards of religious behavior for the entire community, and then to arrange in practice for some such standard to gain acceptance. The divinity of the particular rules of the Torah, then, reflects the divinity of the system that is their ultimate sanction and sanctifies in turn the kind of life to which they give rise; the holiness does not depend on the specific contents of the laws themselves. The content of the law does not always matter; what does matter is that all agree on a certain content, so that the law can be obeyed.[32]

Studded Sandals

M. Shab. 6:2 forbids men to wear studded sandals (sandals with nails protruding from the soles) on the Sabbath. From the context, it seems clear that the prohibition represents a judgment that such footwear is not a common ornament or decoration, and so falls under the prohibition of bearing burdens on the Sabbath, or perhaps more specifically that studded sandals were considered too martial to be appropriate for the Sabbath.[33] Both Talmuds, however, explain this rule not as an inference in principle from some prior conception of how the Sabbath should be observed but rather as a reaction to a terrible particular event. The various stories told are not entirely clear or consistent with one another, but it is reported that a group of Jews hiding from soldiers during some persecution died on account of such sandals; either the sound of the soldiers' heavy tread, amplified by the nails in their footgear, had thrown the concealed Jews into a panic so that they trampled one another and were killed, or the Jews themselves had been wearing studded sandals, so that as they pressed to escape their pursuers they trampled one another and died.[34]

Now the notion that a certain enactment should have originated as commemoration of some event is known from elsewhere as well,[35] but especially interesting here are the explanations of why this particular ban is limited to the Sabbath. The Babylonian Talmud (*Shab.* 60a) simply states that the incident in question also occurred on the Sabbath, but the Jerusalem (*Shab.* 6:2–8a) observes that "a person does not usually own two pairs of sandals, one for the Sabbath and one for weekdays." In other words, the rule against wearing such sandals is formulated in terms of the Sabbath, but it is intended to drive them out of use altogether! S. Lieberman was the first to see the implication here that rabbinic authorities would use the ritual laws of the Sabbath in order to achieve social purposes to which those laws were in principle quite irrelevant.[36]

This rule remains within the spiritual world of "discipline and communal uniformity" mentioned above. The new element here, however, is that the religious impulse underlying that world might be consciously manipulated by the leaders of the community for reasons that lie outside the spiritual realm. Thus, it is not quite sufficient to state (as above) that "the content of the law [did] not always matter"; the content of the law very often did matter, but not always because of the spiritual purpose achieved through obeying it.

The Question of Minima

Chapters 8 and 9 of *m. Shab.* contain an extended development of the theme of *m. Shab.* 7:3:

> Whatever is fit to be stored and is of a sort that people do store, if [a person] carried it outside on the Sabbath he is liable for a sin-offering on that account. And whatever is not fit to be stored and is of a sort that people do not store, if [a person] carried it outside on the Sabbath he is not liable unless he had stored it.

The section ends with a related rule, given at 10:1:

One who stores away [a substance] for seed, or as a sample, or as a remedy, and [then] carried it outside on the Sabbath, is liable [for penalty] on [account of] any quantity whatever. But any [other] person is liable only [on account of] the [stipulated] measure. . . .

The point of these rules is as follows. The last of the thirty-nine basic categories of forbidden labor is "he who carries outside from one domain to another." In other words, one of the general rules of Sabbath law is that all objects are to remain for the entire Sabbath in that "domain" (specified location) where they were to be found when the Sabbath began. To transfer an object from one domain to another (e.g., to bring something into one's house, or out of it into a public thoroughfare) is to violate this law.[37] M. Shab. 7:3 limits this law with a proviso: trivial quantities of various substances do not count. If a given object is "of a sort that people do not store," that is, if no one would want it because no one could imagine a use for it, then one who inadvertently carries that object outside has incurred no penalty. To be sure, if by storing it the individual in question has indicated that the object does have value or significance (at least for him), then this proviso cannot be expected to apply.

M.. Shab. 10:1 further teaches that set amounts have been worked out for all sorts of substances, determinations of what the smallest significant amount of those substances is held to be. People who do "store" smaller amounts (e.g., for seed, or as a merchant's sample, or as medicine) are held responsible for their further handling of these materials, but ordinary people, people whose previous behavior has given no indication that they do value such minute quantities, are immune from penalty as long as they handle quantities smaller than these stipulated minima.

A few examples of how this works will suffice:

One who carries out wine—enough to mix the cup. Milk—for a swallow. Honey—to put on a scab. Oil—to anoint a small limb. Water—to rub off [or rub on, or dissolve] eye-ointment. All remaining liquids—a quarter [of a log]. (m. Shab. 8:1)

Leather—enough to make an amulet. Parchment—to write on it the small paragraph from phylacteries, namely, "Hear, O Israel."[38] Ink—to write two letters. Eye-paint—enough to paint one eye. (m. Shab. 8:5)

A sherd—enough to insert between one board and another; [this is] R. Judah['s opinion], but R. Meir says, Enough to scrape fire with it. R. Yose says, Enough to contain a quarter[-log of fluid. The last two then seek to prove their opinions through exegesis of Isaiah 30:14]. (m. Shab. 8:7)

Now all this seems to be "legalism" run wild. To make any sense at all of this material, one is obliged to remember the general character of the

Sabbath as defined by the notion of forbidden labor; one must recall that "carrying out" is one such activity; and one must remember the modifications of the idea of "carrying out" provided in *m. Shab.* 7:3 and 10:1. At that point, there arises at least the possibility that someone might find lists of this sort useful. Beyond that lies the "spirituality of discipline and communal uniformity" already discussed; this explains why people are not left to form their own ideas of how much milk, or bone, or eye shadow, or how many walnut shells, or how much urine matters and how much is trivial. For rabbis to set out lists of this kind, they had to believe that proper Sabbath observance is made possible only if the norms of behavior for any imaginable circumstance have been stated in advance with the greatest possible precision. It was not enough to believe that God's will was expressed through the law; instead, it was necessary to see that God's will *was* the law, precisely in its quality as law—fully worked out, highly detailed, leaving nothing to chance or to private interpretation. Rabbinic legalism is not the cultural expression of a theology from which it can be separated; it is the only possible way that theology could have formed the basis of the life of a community. "God's will" was like a pitch approaching home plate; just as the pitch is neither a ball nor a strike until the umpire gives a ruling, so too "God's will" had no content at all until the rabbis' teaching turned it into law.

But here too it is not sufficient to see the details of the law as chosen arbitrarily or at random simply to make the system work. The very idea that minimum usable quantities can be determined for every imaginable substance shows considerable abstract thinking had already taken place. Such minima presume that every substance has a culturally determined standard use; milk is simply swallowed, but wine is mixed in cups. Paper (8:2) is used for writing tax collectors' marks, but even used paper (8:2) can serve to wrap the mouth of a small perfume jar. Underlying all this is the additional premise, even more abstract in nature, that an act involving a quantity of any substance smaller than the designated minimum is not a purposive, productive act (intentional exceptions are recognized, as already noted) and therefore is not a real act at all. That is why such an act cannot be construed as forbidden Sabbath labor. Labor, to violate the laws of the Sabbath, must be consequential.[39] It must have an intended result and must achieve that result, after the model of the primordial labor of creation. Otherwise, it is trivial and of no concern.

It thus emerges that the most legalistic of discussions can turn out to embody or reflect significant premises, at the highest level of abstraction, concerning the nature of the world and of human action. Legalistic thinking conceals such premises; it tends not to discuss them in their own right.

But they are there, and they endow talmudic religion with a deeper reso-
nance than is usually noted. The implied metaphysics of rabbinic legalism
goes far beyond the question of the law itself.

The "Fathers of Labor"

M. Shab. 7:2 offers a list of forbidden activities that seems at first glance to
define the range of forbidden Sabbath labor:

> The main classes of work are forty save one: sowing, ploughing, reaping,
> binding sheaves, threshing, winnowing, cleansing crops, grinding, sifting,
> kneading, baking, shearing wool, washing or beating or dyeing it, spinning,
> weaving, making two loops, weaving two threads, separating two threads,
> tying [a knot], loosening [a knot], sewing two stitches, tearing in order to sew
> two stitches, hunting a gazelle, slaughtering or flaying or salting it or curing
> its skin, scraping it or cutting it up, writing two letters, erasing in order to
> write two letters, building, pulling down, putting out a fire, lighting a fire,
> striking with a hammer and taking out aught from one domain into another.
> These are the main classes of work: forty save one.[40]

If this list really is a basic definition, however, its placement in the middle
of a chapter and the placement of that chapter somewhere toward the
middle of the tractate seem very odd. What is more, this is hardly a
comprehensive list of forbidden labors; some of the most obvious entries for
such a list, such as buying and selling, are noticeably absent. This list too
is in fact an oblique reference, in the midst of a highly legalistic context,
to abstract philosophical conceptions.

In the hands of the Amoraim, this list of forbidden "fathers of labor" was
indeed turned into a lawyer's instrument. The Mishnah itself places 7:2 after
7:1; this paragraph contains the rule that one who performs many labors
of the same sort is liable for only one penalty, but one who performs labors
of many different sorts can be penalized on account of each one by itself.
In this connection, the list in 7:2 was taken to provide a basis for deciding
which labors are "of the same sort," namely, those which can be derived
from a single one of the thirty-nine basic categories, those which are all the
"descendants" of one "father."

In its origins, however, the list derived from a different purpose.[41] As
Yitzhak Gilat has observed, the Amoraim already saw that the elements of
this list fall into groups: the first eleven represent the "order of bread," that
is, of baking,[42] and so on. Gilat also correctly associates the list with the
story of Ben Zoma, who arose one morning and said: "How the first Adam
had to work before he tasted bread! He plowed, and sowed, and reaped, and
gathered, and threshed, and winnowed, and cleansed, and ground, and

sifted, and mixed [dough], and baked, and after that he ate, while I get up in the morning and find all this before me" (*t. Ber.* 7:5).[43] Here, in an *aggadic* setting, a very similar list serves to enumerate the stages of the preparation of bread. The thinking that preceded such a list, like the thinking that preceded the stipulations of minima considered above, represents an effort to understand the components of ordinary society and culture. Both projects reveal a thoughtful effort to uncover the assumptions and the mechanisms by which communities function. Whether the list appears in a folkloric setting, as in the story about Ben Zoma, or in the legal setting, as in *m. Shab.*, it teaches the same lesson about the minds of those who first compiled it.

Seen in this new context, *t. Shab.* 7:2 turns out to be an itemized description of the indispensable bases of organized human life: the preparation of bread (up to "baking"), of clothing (up to "sewing" and "tearing in order to sew"), of written matter (*not* of edible meat, despite the beginning of this series; the conclusion—writing and erasing—makes this clear), and of shelter and the organization of space (up to the end).[44]

Here too, then, behind the legalistic formulation of their thinking the rabbis of the Talmud had achieved highly abstract conceptions of the nature of human activity and its basic features. Rabbinic legalism was a cultural style as much as anything else, a style adopted no doubt because it conformed to the rabbis' most fundamental beliefs, but one that nevertheless left them the opportunity to speculate as far as they wished about those matters that "stand at the highest pinnacles of the world."

The Legalism of Rabbinic Religion

Rabbinic attention is always directed primarily at the regulation of behavioral detail, that is, at the *law*. This is why the traditional term "legalism," for all its occasional derogatory implications, may be used to describe the characteristic tone of rabbinic religion. The rabbis of the Talmud saw their task as one of determining the details of a vast system of religious law and then of encouraging (compelling, when they could) obedience to that law. The underlying assumption of rabbinic spirituality is that true obedience to God, true fulfillment of Israel's covenant obligations,[45] means acceptance of and submission to this law: determining as precisely as possible the proper rule for governing action in every conceivable situation and then acting according to that rule.

On the other hand, it must be reiterated that this attitude did not normally bring those religious consequences that critiques of legalism (usually Christian critiques) have alleged. Instead of self-righteous complacency, rabbis generally exhibit joyous gratitude for the giving of the law, sober self-examination with regard to their own fulfillment of its requirements and continual striving for self-improvement with regard to their future attitudes and deeds. All this was accompanied by full confidence in divine mercy and compassion; this last is the "spiritual" element in the more usual sense of the term that made the rest possible. It provided a link between a perfect law and its flawed practitioners.

Attention to detail, though necessary for a legalistic system of the kind here described, managed to avoid the blindness to larger questions that its critics have also claimed to see. On the contrary, rabbinic literature suggests that the ancient rabbis possessed a sharp sense of the larger consequences or broader implications of their rule. The discussion of the bathhouse and the hot waters of Tiberias makes clear that rules were determined with an eye to their probable reception and that the ability or willingness of people to live by a certain law were factors rabbis considered before promulgating it. The Jerusalem Talmud's remark about studded sandals also suggests that the details of rabbinic law were sometimes worked out on the basis of their expected consequences. In both these cases, the sources exhibit a clear sense that the human community to whom the divine demand for obedience was addressed possessed great freedom in determining precisely what law to obey. The spirituality of obedience required that there be a law, but the *contents* of the law might be determined by the obedient community itself, on grounds of its (or its leaders') own choosing.

Legal rules, even of the most detailed sort, also provided ancient rabbis with grounds for developing abstract philosophical conceptions, even if these were then formulated in a strikingly nonphilosophical way. Thus, the question of minimum culpable quantities of various substances contains some sort of conception—even if not explicit—of the nature of human action and the religious significance of human intention. The list of the "fathers" of forbidden labor similarly reflects a long history of contemplating the nature of human culture.

The rabbis themselves sought in the *aggadah* to express the wider religious implications of their legal enactments. The conception of "Sabbath joy" as a legal obligation[46] suggests the interplay between rule based religion and its own emotional or spiritual goals. The well-known remark that redemption would not arrive until all Israel properly observed the Sabbath (*b. Shab.* 118b) likewise suggests that rabbis saw obeying these rules as a way to redemption, not merely as a self-justifying discipline.[47]

Other details of the talmudic treatment of the Sabbath similarly hint at the spirituality, or intentionality, which underlay these rules. Two stories will suffice:

> Caesar [i.e., the Emperor] said to R. Joshua b. Hananiah, "Why does Sabbath food have such a [pleasant] aroma?" He said to him, "We have a certain spice—it is called Sabbath—that we put into it, and its aroma comes forth." He said to him, "Give us some of it." He said to him, "Whoever observes the Sabbath—[this spice] is effective for him; whoever does not observe the Sabbath—[this spice] does no good." (b. Shab. 119a)

This is really a story about the Sabbath and not about legalism at all, but certain relevant insights do emerge from it. One, of course, is the recognition that the Sabbath was associated with pleasure and physical enjoyment. The New Testament makes clear that by the first century Jewish Sabbath observance was condemned in certain quarters as joyless and burdensome;[48] a story like this provides a response to such accusations. It is to be noted that the heathen emperor is the one made to express this recognition. The idea is not put forward merely as a Jewish defense against other people's denigrating their way of life.

More specifically, the story revolves around cooking. This was an activity that the Sabbath particularly restricted. Foods could not be newly prepared on the Sabbath, and even reheating food already cooked was possible only within certain very restrictive limitations. Yet this very Sabbath food is portrayed as so aromatic that it brings itself to the Roman ruler's attention and arouses his envy. The rules of Sabbath observance appear here as instruments for achieving highly desirable spiritual and even bodily experiences, not at all as extrinsic to such goals or as obstacles to their attainment.

Finally, this next story reveals how the rules of Sabbath observance generated a rhythm of life that carried over into the rest of the week:

> Once a certain pious man went out to walk in his vineyard on the Sabbath, saw there a break [in the vineyard wall], and resolved to repair it. After the Sabbath he said to himself, "Since I resolved to repair it [on the Sabbath] I shall never repair it at all."
>
> What did the Holy One, blessed be He, do for him? He provided him a growth [lit., booth] of caper-bush that grew up into [the breach in the wall] and repaired it. From [that bush the man] drew his food and his livelihood for the rest of his days. (y. Shab. 15:3 15a–b; cf. b. Shab. 150b)

In its context, the point of this story is that unnecessary planning or speech is to be avoided on the Sabbath; in the sequel in the Jerusalem Talmud, Rabbi Hanina reports that the authorities barely excused greeting other people on the Sabbath. The story of the caper-bush tells of a world in which people control their thoughts on the Sabbath according to the same norms that guide their actions and receive a full reward of blessedness for doing so, not only in the spiritual realm but also in the workaday world that they seem to be rejecting. Behavioral rules have thus become a spiritual guide; rabbinic legalism serves to unite act and intention, not (as in Paul) to highlight their inherent conflict.

The Spirituality of Legalism

The rabbis of the Talmud were well aware of their own role in framing this religious style. They had no illusions that they were merely and passively carrying out a divine decree. There were, to be sure, aspects of Jewish law that they viewed in such a light,[49] but the Sabbath was a paradigm of something different: "The laws of the Sabbath . . . are like mountains suspended by a hair, little Scripture and many rules; they have nothing on which they can lean" (*t. 'Eruv.* 8:23; cf. *m. Ḥag.* 1:8, etc.). The rabbis who transmitted this remark and taught it to their disciples knew that the philosophy that underlay the laws of minimum quantity, or the list of "fathers of labor," was the framers' own; the effects produced by the ban on studded sandals or the social compromise reflected in the rules concerning hot baths were those toward which human authorities—these rabbis' own predecessors—had chosen to strive. This is a legalism, then, in which the law is a carefully honed artifact, worked out not merely with human consent, as Exodus 19–24 might be taken to imply, but with active human involvement. The divine law that rabbis expected all Jews to obey was as much their own legislation as the Creator's, and they knew this. In the passage just quoted, the rabbis openly acknowledged this to be the case, and presumably most other Jews, if they were at all educated, were aware of it as well.

The spirituality of legalism is therefore really dual; there are two kinds of legalism here, distinguished from each other by their respective practitioners' degree of learning. "The law" offers one kind of spiritual experience to those who help to shape it and another to the masses of the community whom it serves to shape in turn. These latter, like the "pious man" who left his wall unrepaired, strive to obey; the Torah comes into their world and gives it meaning. The former, however, enter the world of the Torah and bring their own meaning with them. The meaning of revelation, in the rabbis' view, is the meaning they themselves assign to it. Every time a rabbi offers new teaching, the amount of Torah in the world is increased, and the event of revelation is somehow replicated. In this sense too the rabbi might "enlarge Torah and make it mightier"; the rabbinic stance toward Torah was in certain respects as much like that of its Giver as it was like that of their fellow Jews.[50]

A full account of the spirituality of rabbinic legalism must therefore include the fact that rabbis were enabled by their conception of law to see themselves more fully "in the image of God" than anyone else. Not only their native endowment was godlike (this might be said of anyone), but their function was too. To live a life of Torah was not only to submit joyfully and lovingly to the "yoke" of a sacred covenant—this too might be said of anyone, or at least of all Israel—it was also to continue the shaping of that covenant, its application to unforeseen circumstances and its extension to new areas of human existence. There is a kind of grateful humility here, but a remarkable assertiveness as well. The innermost heart of rabbinic religion is the place where these two emotions finally merge into one.

Notes

1. See, for example, Leviticus 26, Deuteronomy 28; also 2 Kings 17, Nehemiah 9.

2. See most clearly the *Manual of Discipline* or *Community Rule* (1QS) 3:18.

3. Loeb Classical Library, vol. 4, pp. 183–85.

4. Philo recognizes here that the law-centered character of Jewish religion is linked to its strong communal emphasis. This matter will reappear below.

5. All citations of the New Testament are from the Revised Standard Version.

6. That is, it is now taken for granted that true religious meaning is meaning that addresses the inner spirit, that intention is of greater moral consequence than action, that the inner invisible aspect of human existence, rather than its exposed behavioral aspect, is the locus of its most profound significance.

7. See R. J. Z. Werblowsky, "Tora als Gnade," *Kairos* 15 (1973) 156–63.

8. This idea was an old one. See Psalm 119 and numerous other, shorter statements of the theme.

9. This was the rabbinic understanding of Isa 42:21—"to enlarge the Torah and make it mightier."

10. See, for example, Maimonides, *Code,* Laws of Prayer 4:15–17; 10:1.

11. This required ritual consumption of *mazzah* is to be distinguished from the more general prohibition against eating leavened bread during the whole week of Passover.

12. See *m. Ber.* 2:1; *m. Rosh Hash.* 3:7. It should be kept in mind that the *shema'* is technically a recitation, not a prayer; the earlier remarks about *kawwanah* in prayer should not automatically be taken to include the *shema'.*

13. See *b. Rosh Hash.* 28a.

14. See *Sifre Deut.* 33, on Deut 6:6; also *b. Ber.* 63b. It can be speculated that even this concern reflects a fear that without proper conscious alertness people eventually lose interest in the rules themselves.

15. At *b. B. Mez.* 83a, a litigant was *compelled* to disregard this limit, but this highly paradoxical result does not seem to have been very frequent.

16. See *b. B. Mez.* 82b, *b. B. Qam.* 29a, *b. Git.* 53a, etc.

17. In a ritual context (Sabbath pleasure): *b. Shab.* 25b; in a civil context (carrying out a dying person's wishes): *b. Ket.* 70a.

18. See *Gen. Rab.* 44:1 and elsewhere, different citations of this saying attribute it to various authorities.

19. This accepts for the moment the premise that the identified teacher did in fact speak the words in question. There are often reasons to doubt this premise, but the present context does not require that such reasons be considered. It should also be noted that the Talmud itself sometimes leaves the original contexts of rabbinic dicta open to some doubt.

20. Harry J. Leon, *The Jews of Ancient Rome* (Philadelphia: Jewish Publication Society, 1960) 3.

21. See Jacob Neusner, *History of the Jews in Babylonia* (Leiden: Brill, 1969) 4:178.

22. See Mark 2:23–26 and parallels; John 5:1–18; Rom 14:5–6; Gal 4:10–11; Col 2:16–17.

23. See *On the Special Laws* 2.56–64; *On the Life of Moses* 2.209–11; and elsewhere. See also R. Goldenberg, "The Jewish Sabbath in the Roman World," in *Aufstieg und Niedergang der Römischen Welt* 2.19.1, ed. W. Haase (Berlin and New York: de Gruyter, 1979) 414–47, esp. 427–29.

24. *Gen. Rab.* 17:5; 44:17. See also *b. Ber.* 57b.

25. Consider the well-known statement "Who is truly free? He who is occupied with the Law" (*Abot* 6:2, with reference to Exod 32:16).

26. See also the parallel sources at *t. Shab.* 3:13, *b. Shab.* 44a, *y. Shab.* 3:7 6b.

27. Extinguishing a flame is forbidden on the Sabbath.

28. A set of general rules indicating which authority to prefer in the event of a conflict can be found at *b. 'Eruv.* 46b, but even these rules are simply provided, not explained.

29. "They" presumably are representatives of rabbinic authority, but neither "their" identity nor the nature of "their" authority is clearly indicated.

30. See above. The story refers both to the masses and to the rabbinic authorities as "they"; the reader must keep things straight.

31. The two stories offer different explanations of how the final law was determined. According to the Babylonian Talmud, the sages simply discovered that people would accept their rulings only up to a certain point, a point past which "the situation could not be maintained." The Jerusalem Talmud, on the other hand, asserts that finally the sages' control was entirely accepted, at which point they reversed their course and began to ease the concrete provisions of their rulings.

32. I first heard the idea expressed here from my former teacher Professor David Weiss Halivni, but the context was different, and he in any event would not be responsible for the way I have applied it.

33. So G. Alon, *Studies in Jewish History* (in Hebrew; n.p., *Ha-Kibbutz ha-Me'uhad*, 1967) 1:108 n. 79, though his interpretation of the Mishnah should have recognized both these possibilities.

34. Probably in the time of Hadrian, but see the Soncino Press translation, *Shabbat*, p. 280 n. 6.

35. See Kossovsky's concordance to the Babylonian Talmud, vol. 30 (Jerusalem: Ministry of Education and Culture, Government of Israel, and Jewish Theological Seminary of America, 1973) p. 1183, s.v. *ma'aseh she-hayah*.

36. See S. Lieberman, *Hellenism in Jewish Palestine* (New York: Jewish Theological Seminary, 1962) 139–40.

37. This rule may in some sense be traced back to Jer 17:21–22.

38. That is, Deut 6:4–9.

39. See the *midrash* at *b. Hag.* 10b on the biblical phrase *melekhet mahshevet* (skillful labor). It is not clear whether this limitation on the concept of prohibited labor was grounded in abstract thinking or in exegesis.

40. Trans. H. Danby (Oxford: Oxford University Press, 1933) 106.

41. See Y. Gilat, "On the 39 Fathers of Sabbath Labor," *Tarbiz* 29 (1960) 222–28.

42. Rabbi Papa, *b. Shab.* 74b; see also *y. Shab.* 7:2 10c, "the order of a meal."

43. See also *b. Ber.* 58a, *y. Ber.* 9:2 13c.

44. It is a striking illumination of the rabbis' thinking that culture without writing, that is, without the Torah, apparently was quite unthinkable to them.

45. In rabbinic thinking, as in its biblical antecedent, "obedience to God" is always in the first instance the *community*'s obligation.

46. *B. Shab.* 118a; see also n. 17 above.

47. It should be noted that these two discussions—of Sabbath joy and of the Sabbath as redemptive—occur consecutively in the Talmud. The two contexts were linked; Sabbath joy in this world, as already noted, is a kind of foretaste of the utter bliss of the next. Also, the essentially lawyerlike quality of the rabbinic editors' minds is revealed in the way all nonlegal digressions get lumped together, so that the talmudic text can then return to its real task.

48. See above, n. 22.

49. See *Sifra, Qedoshim,* ch. 11:22.

50. See J. Neusner, *Talmudic Judaism in Sasanian Babylonia: Essays and Studies,* Studies in Judaism in Late Antiquity 14 (Leiden: Brill, 1976) 46–77.

Bibliography

Every generation produces its "standard" survey of ancient rabbinic theology. For the twentieth century, these have been (in chronological order) Schechter, Moore, Urbach. With respect to the particular question of the Law and its significance, see Schechter, 116–69; Moore, 235–80, 507–34; Urbach, 286–419 [Eng. trans.] See also Sanders, 33–59, 183–205.

Readers will also find useful the extracts in C. G. Montefiore and H. Loewe, 116–73.

Montefiore, C. G., and H. Loewe, *A Rabbinic Anthology.* Originally published in 1938; reprint, Cleveland: Meridian; Philadelphia: Jewish Publication Society, 1960.

Moore, George R., *Judaism.* Cambridge, MA: Harvard University Press, 1927.

Sanders, E. P., *Paul and Palestinian Judaism.* Philadelphia: Fortress, 1977.

Schechter, Solomon, *Aspects of Rabbinic Theology.* Originally published in 1909; reprint, New York: Schocken, 1961.

Urbach, E. E., *The Sages.* Jerusalem: Magnes, 1969 [Hebrew], 1975 [English].

The modern Hebrew term *halakhah* is frequently used to translate the concept "law." In ancient rabbinic Hebrew, however, this term rarely if ever had the abstract meaning thus imputed to it. Rabbis would study *halakhot,* that is, the legal substance of various rules, but it did not normally occur to them to seek the religious significance of "the law" as such. When they are described by modern writers as expressing gratitude, etc. for "the law" the term found in the source is *Torah.* The rabbinic conception of Torah *included* the element of law that has been discussed in this chapter but was not limited to it. A modern writer may say that the rabbinic religion is a religion of law, but ancient rabbis saw it as an indivisible revelation containing rules but much else besides. Readers of the modern literature should keep this in mind.

10

Ascetical Aspects
of Ancient Judaism

STEVEN D. FRAADE

In the world to come each person will have to give an accounting for everything which his eyes saw but he did not eat. *y. Qidd.*
4:12 (66d)

Whoever accepts the pleasures of this world is denied the pleasures of the world to come. And whoever does not accept the pleasures of this world is granted the pleasures of the world to come.
Avot de-Rabbi Nathan 28

Posing the Problem

"**A**SCETICISM**,**" AS THE TERM is most commonly employed in the study of religion, is a *modern* construct identified with a set of diverse phenomena, which are thought collectively to constitute a coherent way of viewing the world and acting in it.[1] How one defines "asceticism" is determined by one's choice of which of the constituent elements are essential to the encompassing construct and which are not. "Asceticism," thus, is used to differentiate those religious systems and their components that satisfy the definition by including its essential elements from those that do not. Unfortunately, there is no scholarly consensus concerning how "asceticism" (and its related terms) should be defined when employed in the study of religion, nor are the ways in which it is defined, whether explicitly or implicitly, consistently applied in the comparison of religions and religious traditions. This is due to a number of factors:

First, definitions of asceticism are often based on the salient characteristics of a particular, *familiar* model. For instance, someone familiar with the example of the Christian "desert fathers," who flourished in Egypt during the third and fourth centuries,[2] might consider as a definitive component of asceticism practices of self-inflicted bodily suffering that are not as characteristic of other pietistic systems generally labeled ascetic (e.g., ancient Syrian Christianity, Buddhism, and varieties of ancient Judaism to be discussed below). Thus, a particular form of asceticism becomes the model against which others are judged; if they differ too much from the model, they are said to be "diluted" forms of asceticism, or not properly ascetic at all. Obviously, scholars who begin with different models will end up with different definitions, including and excluding different religious systems under the rubric of asceticism. The arbitrariness of these choices should be apparent.[3]

Second, the word "asceticism" (and its relatives) has assumed in modern parlance negative connotations. By "asceticism" is often understood an extreme, *pathological* pattern of self-abnegation and flight from the world in the face of a less than hospitable social and historical environment.[4] In particular, such simplistic psychologizing is anachronistically introduced into the contexts of ancient cultures, which presupposed notions of psychic (that is, spiritual) well-being different from those of modern cultures. Such negative views of asceticism find their way into the arsenal of weapons employed in interreligious polemic and apologetic, even as practiced by scholars of religion. Given the prevalence of such negative views of asceticism, scholarly claims that a religious tradition, especially if that of the author, is free from or only slightly blemished by asceticism need to be examined critically.[5]

Third, many definitions and descriptions of asceticism are at fault not for deriving from too limited a model (the first point above) but for corresponding to no significant historical model at all, being rather *caricatures* of asceticism, whose features have been exaggerated under the influence of prevailing negative prejudices and polemical motivations (the second point above).[6]

Fourth, scholars frequently argue that the extent to which a particular religious practice (or complex of practices) is considered ascetic is determined by the purpose that motivates that practice. Unfortunately, motivations for particular religious practices are frequently difficult to discern. They are most often left unarticulated, and when articulated are either ambiguous, manifold, fluid, or inconsistent within a particular religious system. The criterion of motivation of purpose provides a window through which the subjective predispositions discussed in the previous points are bound to enter. For instance, some argue that to be *truly* ascetic, abstinence and self-imposed hardship require *complete* contempt for the body, its needs, emotions, and worldly surroundings as an "end in itself." Abstinence or self-imposed hardship that is not so total or permanent or is undertaken for the sake of moral or spiritual advancement, or in response to specific historical circumstances or in conformity with religious law, is determined not to be ascetic.[7] Not only do such narrow views of what constitutes asceticism omit from consideration varieties of religious life that could shed valuable light on the phenomenology of asceticism, but they are predicated on ascetic models that (as stated in the previous point) are caricatures, unrepresentative of even the more severe varieties of asceticism of any historical consequence.

An alternate course has been charted by those scholars of religion, usually of a sociological bent, who view asceticism as a broad phenomenon comprising several types. Such typologies recognize that asceticism can include religious systems with differing degrees of abstinence, of distrust of bodily needs and material "goods," of exclusivity and separatism vis-à-vis the world and its immediate social contexts, of individualism and communalism, and may be motivated by a variety of "ends." Thus, Max Weber developed a typology that distinguishes "innerworldly" from "otherworldly" asceticism, and J. M. Yinger distinguished the asceticism of the "church" from that of the "sect."[8] Although these typologies derive from models within the history of Christianity and therefore do not transfer smoothly to varieties of ancient Judaism,[9] they begin to move away from the preoccupation with defining a single ascetic archetype, against which religious systems or subsystems as wholes are judged to be *either ascetic or nonascetic.*[10] Rather, they view asceticism as representing a *side* of religion in general, being variously manifested in different religious systems, as determined in part by their different social and historical contexts. Asceticism, then, is descriptive of important *aspects* of a religious system but not of its *whole.*

This broader understanding of asceticism sees it as responding, in a variety of ways, to a *tension* inherent in all religious systems: humans (whether individually or collectively) aspire to advance ever closer to an ideal of spiritual fulfillment and perfection, while confronting a self and a world that continually set obstacles in that path, whatever its particular course. How can one proceed along that path with a whole, undivided, undistracted "heart" (all one's energies and intentions) while living among the distractions of the present world?[11] How can one relate to and commune with a transcendent, supernatural order, to submit wholeheartedly to the divine will, while living a worldly existence ruled by appetites and archons? These are the broad religious issues, with obvious social and psychological implications, which the ascetic aspects of a religious system address.[12]

This approach allows ascetic responses to the above mentioned tensions to assume a variety of social shapes and to be motivated by a variety of religious ends or ideals, which are roughly divisible into three categories: (1) fellowship or communion (whether ecstatic or rational) with the transcendent order (God in theistic religions); (2) disciplined, correct (moral/righteous) behavior; and (3) reparation of ruptures in the individual's or community's fellowship with the transcendent order caused by failures (conscious and intentional or not) to behave correctly.[13] In different religious systems these ideals may be variously combined and emphasized, and the ascetic methods for achieving them may vary in kind or in intensity.

Having recognized some of the pitfalls of too narrow a definition of asceticism, we should beware of a definition that is so broad as to make it indistinguishable from religion in general, which thereby renders it meaningless as a useful descriptive term in the comparative study of religions. Before attempting to chart a course between too narrow and too broad an understanding of asceticism, it is important to recognize that this is not a problem invented by modern scholarship, but a tension inherent in the term "asceticism" and its Greek root *askēsis*, as a brief history of the ancient usage of the latter will demonstrate.[14]

The Greek noun *askēsis* derives from the verb *askeō*, whose etymology is unknown, and which first appears in Homer meaning to "work" or "fashion" raw materials so as to manufacture a handiwork.[15] The verb and its derivatives soon come to mean exercise or training, both of soldiers for war and of athletes for games.[16] It then comes to refer to practice and exercise that leads to moral as well as physical excellence.[17] As athletic and military training require both the positive strengthening of one's physical faculties and the negative abstention from weakening habits, so too philosophical and spiritual training require both affirmation and renunciation. This dual sense of *askēsis* is particularly popularized by Stoics and Cynics and is increasingly applied to the exercise of religion: spiritual training requires a constant guard against the distracting and weakening influences of the passions.[18] Although several Greco-Roman philosophical schools shared this twofold ideal of *askēsis,* they differed sharply, even internally, regarding the recommended extent and manner of the renunciation that it required.

The understanding of *askēsis* as disciplined, willful religious practice is evidenced among Greek-speaking Jews in Greco-Roman times, especially the Alexandrian Jewish Bible exegete Philo.[19] It is from Philo, most likely, that this sense of *askēsis* is adopted by early Christian church fathers, who place increasing emphasis on its negative side of self-control (*egkrateia* and *sōphrosynē*).[20] Eventually, the word is more fully identified with the suppression of desire and becomes a technical term for the austerity of eremitical and monastic life and practices.[21]

Thus, from early in its history *askēsis* carried the broad sense of exercise and self-discipline, and soon acquired the concomitant meaning of self-control and self-denial with respect to physical and sensual impulses which were thought to hamper the attainment of moral and spiritual excellence. Although radical dualism is an important component in some ancient expressions of *askēsis* (Orphism, Platonism, and Pythagoreanism), it neither defines the term nor the point of view it denotes.[22] For the ancients, including Jews, *askēsis* was not simply the *negative* denial of world, body, sense, pleasure, and emotion, but the willful and arduous training and testing, often through abstention from what was generally permitted, of one's creaturely faculties in the *positive* pursuit of moral and spiritual perfection.

A definition of religious asceticism, therefore, should be specific enough to include its two main components: (1) the exercise of disciplined effort toward the goal of spiritual perfection (however understood), which requires (2) abstention (whether total or partial, permanent or temporary, individualistic or communalistic) from the satisfaction of otherwise permitted earthly, creaturely desires.[23] Within such a broad definition the ascetic aspects of different religious systems may be seen to exhibit different traits, which in being compared can shed light on the complex role of asceticism in religion in general. This role is complex in that asceticism is most often manifested not as a simple creed but as a tension between these two positive and negative components, both of which are in constant tension as well with the personal and social exigencies of worldly existence, and neither of which is ever fully realized in life, except perhaps in theory.

I turn now to the question of whether it is fruitful to look at ancient Judaism (and by extension, although not to be treated here, Judaism of later periods) in terms of its ascetic aspects. The question is not: Is ancient Judaism ascetic or nonascetic? but: How is asceticism, as defined above, manifested and responded to in the ancient varieties of Judaism, including that of the rabbis? Is the generally accepted and often repeated view that Judaism in its early stages eschewed asceticism root and branch to be perpetuated? The fact that I have already rejected the question that premises this view should by now tip the reader to my negative response. But how much can positively be said and what historical implications are then to be deduced are still to be explored.

I will introduce the application of these methodological observations to the study of ancient Judaism with a summary of the views of two eminent Israeli scholars of classical Judaism who provide two very different pictures.

Yitzhak Fritz Baer, in a Hebrew book titled *Israel Among the Nations,* put forward the radical thesis that Judaism of prerabbinic times, especially in the period between Alexander's conquest of Palestine in 331 B.C.E. and the Maccabean revolt in 167 B.C.E., was typified by an ascetic idealism that, although later diluted, left its permanent mark on rabbinic law and belief. Baer argues that the *ḥasidim rishonim* ("early pietists") of rabbinic literature were a circle of Jews who in the early Hellenistic period forged a religious ideology based on the social and spiritual ideals of Israelite prophecy *plus* the Greek ascetic ideals of Plato, the Cynics, the Stoics, and the Pythagoreans. That ideology required living one's life in relation to heavenly laws, constantly striving toward moral, spiritual, and intellectual advancement through various forms of self-discipline: the practice of purity, abstinence, renunciation of material goods, and even martyrdom. All this was to be in the context of an ideal society (fellowship) based on mutual trust and a natural economy. These ideals were expressed in a pietistic, ascetic legal code or "Torah" (proto-Mishnah).

According to Baer, the "early pietists" saw in the Maccabean uprising and the consequent restoration of Jewish sovereignty an opportunity to put their idealistic program into practice through the creation of a truly theocratic state. However, as ideals met the realities of obstacles to their implementation, the former were gradually compromised until finally, after the destruction of the Temple and the ascendancy of rabbinic Judaism, they were deferred to a future-worldly realization. However, remnants of the original "ascetic Torah" lie embedded in the corpora of rabbinic literature, especially the Mishnah and *baraytot* (mishnaic traditions outside the Mishnah), waiting to be culled and combined so as to reconstruct the original, uncompromised ascetic ideal. According to Baer, this ascetic ideal was held also by circles influenced by the "early pietists": Philo, the Essenes, the Pharisees, and, eventually, early Christian monastic groups. These Jewish pietists are a historical bridge between the asceticism of Hellenism (particularly Pythagoreanism) and early Christianity.[24]

Ephraim E. Urbach responded negatively to Baer's thesis, arguing that much of what Baer refers to as asceticism in ancient Judaism is far from it. According to Urbach, where truly ascetic movements and practices do appear in ancient Judaism they are narrow, short-lived, and syncretistic. What is most important, they need to be understood as responses to specific historical events: the destruction of the Temple in 70 C.E., the Hadrianic persecutions and failed Bar Kokhba revolt of 135, and the anti-Jewish decrees of amoraic times. They are, then, idiosyncratic intrusions into an otherwise nonascetic, even antiascetic, tradition.

Classical Judaism's greatness, says Urbach, was its rejection of what Baer calls the "ascetic Torah." Real asceticism, as exemplified in Philo, Hellenism, and throughout the church fathers, is based on the dualistic opposition of soul and body and is aimed at liberating the former from the latter, which is without value. This notion, says Urbach, is *absolutely* absent from rabbinic writings. Rabbinic forms of abstinence and acceptance of suffering are motivated, rather, by a fear of sin, a need to combat one's impulse to do evil, and a need for acts of atoning penitence, especially after the destruction of the Temple. They are not performed as acts of worship "for their own sakes." They are part of the *halakhah* (rabbinic law), which runs counter to asceticism. Most telling for Urbach is the fact that three distinguishing characteristics of Hellenistic and Christian asceticism are virtually absent from rabbinic Judaism: self-inflicted physical injury (except for fasting), celibacy, and the establishment of separate ascetic societies or orders.[25]

Here, then, are two strikingly different views of the place of asceticism in ancient Judaism. Although both contribute to our understanding, each is seriously flawed in its methodology. For my present purposes only the following points need be made:

Baer and Urbach implicitly presuppose very different definitions of asceticism. Baer understands it principally in its broader, positive sense of moral and spiritual self-discipline and exercise, whereas Urbach understands it in its narrower, negative sense of dualistic abnegation of the body.

Baer's attempt to extract the teachings of third-century B.C.E. pietists from third-century C.E. collections of rabbinic teachings and laws is methodologically dubious. It is not at all clear that the "early pietists" of rabbinic literature refer to a separate group in pre-Hasmonean (or even Hasmonean) times.[26] Baer's understanding of *askēsis* as spiritual and moral self discipline is at times so broad that virtually any aphorism recommending correct living can be included under it. In fact, several of the examples from rabbinic literature which he adduces for a prerabbinic "ascetic Torah" fail to convince for this reason.[27]

Urbach's implied definition of *askēsis,* on the other hand, is unrepresentative and somewhat of a caricature. It does not do justice to Philo, Hellenistic *askēsis,* or the church fathers from which it is said to derive. As I have argued, radically dualistic renunciation of the body is an important part of some varieties of asceticism, but is not definitive of them or of asceticism in general. Nor for that matter is abstinence, when motivated by the fear of sin, the desire to curb the impulse to do evil, or the need for atoning penitence, necessarily nonascetic. A careful examination of Urbach's many references to extensive rabbinic fasting and other forms of abstinence and to positive rabbinic views of suffering suggests that these are more than isolated responses to a few specific historical events. And even if, as is certainly the case, catastrophic events engender ascetic responses, these responses need to be viewed as sharpened expressions of tensions and tendencies already present, if perhaps dormant or held in check, but no less ascetic. Urbach's *own* evidence suggests a more complex and diverse attitude among the rabbis toward asceticism.

Despite these criticisms, both Baer and Urbach make valuable contributions to the discussion of asceticism in ancient Judaism. Baer is correct in suggesting that *askēsis* in ancient Judaism needs to be taken more seriously, not as something uniform or static but as an important and vital component in the development of Judaism in its varieties, as it was for other Greco-Roman religions with which ancient Judaism both shared and competed. The predominantly negative view of *askēsis*, which Jewish scholars hold in common with modern culture and which they appropriate for their own apologetic purposes, blinds them either to admitting its existence or to according to it anything but a negative role. Urbach is correct in suggesting some of the significant ways in which Jewish *askēsis* differed from that of other Greco-Roman religions and in showing, albeit unintentionally, that it was not so totally suppressed by the rabbis as Baer argues.

In combination, the views of these two scholars suggest the need for a new approach. Ancient Jewish "asceticism," as I have argued the term should be defined, cannot be interpreted simply as a reflex of specific historical events or foreign influences, both of which are important to consider, but as a perennial side of Judaism as it struggles with the tension between the realization of transcendent ideals and the confronting of this-worldly obstacles to that realization. There is no simple way to resolve that tension either for Judaism in general or for any of its ancient varieties. How much abstinence and hardship, both for individuals and for a society, should be advocated or tolerated in furthering those ideals and removing those obstacles? It is the *variety* and *complexity* of responses to that never-answered question that should be the proper subject for the study of the place of *askēsis* in Judaism.

A number of recent scholarly advances make the subject of this essay all the more pertinent today: knowledge of the Dead Sea Scrolls, a library of an Essene, separatist, pietistic community having ascetic characteristics; burgeoning interest in other Jewish literatures of Second Temple times, with their often pietistic, apocalyptic, and ascetic leanings; greater willingness to view even rabbinic Judaism as residing in a Hellenistic neighborhood; the growing recognition that rabbinic Judaism could include within its walls more mystical speculation (at least), magical praxis, and general diversity than was formerly admitted; renewed interest in the ascetic side of early Christianity, East and West, and the question of its Hellenistic and *Jewish* connections; and the growing sense that all of the above are interconnected and not simply isolated and heretical embarrassments.

Obviously, in the space remaining a systematic treatment of these issues is impossible.[28] Rather, I shall illustrate through exemplification the path that such a treatment should follow: first, a brief sketch of prerabbinic Jewish manifestations of the "ascetic tension," which will serve as a backdrop for the examination of a select number of rabbinic passages that exemplify that tension, both between rabbinic Judaism and its predecessors and within the ranks of the rabbis.

Askēsis in Prerabbinic Judaism

The Jewish literature that falls roughly between the last books of the canonical Hebrew Bible (200 B.C.E.) and the earliest rabbinic collections (200 C.E.) comes from a variety of social and religious contexts which scholars are only now beginning to reconstruct; it is not of one cloth. Still, in a survey as brief as this one must be, we may discern in this literature some general developments pertinent to our topic: first, an increasing preoccupation, among individuals and religious groups, with the dichotomy of this-wordly life and otherworldly demands and hopes; and, second, an increasing resort to ascetic practices as responses to that tension. The following is intended merely to exemplify and not to exhaust the evidence.

The Books of the Apocrypha and Pseudepigrapha[29]

This literature evidences a growing concern with living in accordance with the high moral and spiritual demands of the Torah and Prophets, with transcending mortality and living in communion with God's will and wisdom, and at the same time with the formidable obstacles of human sin and the forces of evil. Repeatedly, ascetic practices are depicted as means to living such lives, to obtaining such access, and to overcoming such obstacles.

These practices are employed for such purposes as: (a) preparing to receive a revelation or vision; (b) accompanying supplication to God, whether for revelation, wisdom, divine protection, or healing; (c) repenting for intentional and unintentional sins; (d) curbing the appetites and passions and guarding against sin.[30] The specific practices mentioned include the following, often in combination: (a) fasting; (b) other forms of voluntary dietary restriction (e.g., no wine or meat); (c) abstaining from washing or anointing; (d) sexual continence (temporary or permanent); (e) simple, coarse dress; and (f) flight to an uninhabited "wilderness."[31]

It would be naive to attempt to explain each of the above, but the following points, suggested by the same literature, are pertinent: (1) By doing without something that is otherwise permitted, a person demonstrates humility and self-sacrifice before God, appearing, as it were, cap in hand.[32] (2) In desiring access to God, one hopes to approach the realm of the sacred or holy (like the Temple) and therefore must prepare by separating from what renders impure (e.g., sex) and mortal (e.g., food).[33] (3) Even if one's self has been prepared, the surrounding human society may not be a fitting environment for attaining divine fellowship; a desert or a mountaintop is better suited, and the simplicity of primitivistic dress or diet is appropriate as well.[34] (4) Although Israelite dualism is, in general, not as radical as certain Greek forms which influenced it, it does presuppose a "spirit" that links humans with God and a "body" that links them with the earth and animals, and it favors the former over the latter. Access to God may be thought to require a strengthening of the former by weakening and guarding against the impulses of the latter. The greater the grip of those impulses, the greater the need for measures to break their hold.[35] (5) One of the frequently heard answers to the question of theodicy ("Why do the righteous suffer?") is that such suffering is a test of faith, testing the pious ones' acceptance of God's inscrutable will. It is only a small step to welcome such suffering and then another step to seek (even if unconsciously) it and the reward for its acceptance.[36] (6) Such ascetic practices could be resorted to temporarily, during times of particular need or danger, or permanently, in constant preparation for and expectation of otherworldly contact during life and finally at death.

We find frequent references, as in the prophets, to the sincerity and singleness of heart that distinguish the truly pious abstinent from the one who mistakenly believes that such practices by themselves "work."[37] Despite such concerns that ascetic practices not be for show, it was inevitable that they served as signs that a person or group of persons was committed wholeheartedly to a life of righteousness and piety, distinguished by simplicity, purity, temperance, and self-sacrifice. Such were the signs of having surrendered into God's hands, as it were, and not into those of worldly passions and powers. Such practices when adopted by a group served not only to mark a collective path to the sacred but also to mark off the group from the surrounding society and its perceived dangers.[38]

What relation such ascetic practices had to the official Temple cult, which similarly promised access to the sacred, atonement from sin, and respite from the dangers and impurities of the world and likewise required abstinence of those who entered, especially of its officiants, is not clear. It should not be assumed, however, that these practices reflect an alienation from the Temple, a lack of confidence in it, or a protest against it. It could just as easily be said that they were often thought to complement and supplement the Temple rites. If their proliferation is explained by the failure of the centralized cult to do its job, this may be because that job of reconciling heaven and earth, life and death, had grown too enormous and pressured for one centralized institution to perform.[39]

The following three examples are offered as a sampler:

2 Baruch 20:5–6:
Therefore, go away and sanctify yourself for seven days and do not eat bread and do not drink water and do not speak to anybody. And after this time come to this place and I shall reveal myself to you, and I shall speak to you true things, and I shall command you with regard to the course of times, for they will come and will not tarry.[40]

1 Enoch 108:8–9:
Those who love God have loved neither gold nor silver, nor all the good things which are in the world, but have given over their bodies to suffering—who from the time of their very being have not longed after earthly food, and who regarded themselves as a (mere) passing breath. And they have observed this matter, the Lord having put them through much testing; then he received their pure spirits so that they should bless his name.[41]

Testament of Joseph 3:4–5 (Joseph upon being lured by Potiphar's wife):
But I recalled my father's words, went weeping into my quarters, and prayed to the Lord. For those seven years I fasted, and yet seemed to the Egyptians like someone who was living luxuriously, for those who fast for the sake of God receive graciousness of countenance. If my master was absent, I drank no wine; for three-day periods I would take no food but give it to the poor and the ill.[42]

Philo Judaeus (20 B.C.E.–ca. 50 C.E.)[43]

Although the Alexandrian Jewish philosopher and Bible exegete Philo may or may not be representative of the attitudes of his hellenized Jewish contemporaries in Egypt, his writings are an excellent illustration of what I have called the "ascetic tension" in Judaism.

Philo inherits from Plato a radically dualistic conception of the universe. In this view, the material world of sense perception is an imperfect reflection of the intelligible order which emanates from God. The human soul finds its fulfillment through separation from the world of material desires, a world that lacks true reality, and through participation in the life of the spirit and divine intellect; the soul finally reunites the true self with its divine source and thereby achieves immortality.[44]

Like Cynics and Stoics, Philo views this process as a long, gradual, and arduous one. The ability of the body with its desires and of the material world with its allurements to entice and entrap the higher self is considerable. Life correctly lived is a constant combat against the principal enemies of pleasure, desire, and impulse, the principal weapons in this struggle being reason, temperance (*egkrateia*) and moral effort (*ponos*). This battle takes the form of repetitive preparatory exercises, or wrestling bouts, which gradually strengthen the soul and its virtues, force pleasure and the senses into submission, and convert passion (pathē) into emotional tranquillity (*apatheia* and *eupatheia*). Abstinence is an important element in this program of training. Through such a program the soul, like plaster (*Agr.* 37.160), gradually becomes settled and solid, in preparation for an eventual life devoted to contemplation of and ultimate mystical reunion with the universe's spiritual source. But this is not a struggle in which the human will can succeed unassisted. It needs the guidance of divinely originating wisdom in overcoming the passions. But even so, the soul needs a foretaste of the mystical outcome of the struggle, which it receives through divine grace, if it is to have the courage and energy to sustain the struggle. To what extent it is, in reality, possible fully to win the contest during one's lifetime is unclear, since Philo suggests that even the best are at times overcome by the false attractions of worldly goods and are unable to escape sin. Thus far, Philo's view of ascetic perfection is highly individualistic and world denying.

Philo, however, does not expound his philosophy primarily in the abstract, but in the context of commenting on the Bible (in Greek translation) and on Jewish life of his time. And here his denial of value to the body, its material needs and pleasures, and to social life is not as absolute and consistent as the above summary of his ideals would suggest. Whereas Moses and the Therapeutae represent the ideal of complete victory over the passions and lives totally committed to the contemplation of the divine truth and mystery,[45] Jacob and the Essenes represent the more realistic intermediary stage of the "man in progress," engaged in spiritual training in the context of an "active life."[46] Although Jacob is the embodiment of Philo's ideal of the life of training, wrestling, or *askēsis*, being called *ho askētēs* ("The Practicer"), he is not yet ready fully to engage pleasure in battle, fleeing the contest for a while until he is stronger.[47]

Such strength is only *gradually* achieved with the help of the command-ments of the Torah, which are often interpreted by Philo as exercises intended to strengthen the soul by repeatedly accustoming it to abstinence from and moderation of desires for food, drink, sex, etc.[48] Thus, although Philo's dualistic ideal leads him to idealize virginity as a precondition of communion with God and to claim that the wise person nourished by study has no need for even the most necessary food and drink, the reality of active life necessitates all of these, moderated, to be sure, through con-stant self-discipline and temporary abstinence.[49] Even the impulses may serve positive functions if harnessed by reason (*Mos.* 1.26).

Similarly, although Philo idealizes flight to the wilderness so as to engage in total contemplation, this should not be attempted until one has devel-oped the necessary self-discipline *within* the context of a socially and politically active life. Those who think that they can shortcut the process by prematurely fleeing society or by undertaking severe, sullen practices of self-abnegation before they are spiritually prepared display a false and vain *askēsis:*

> If then thou observest anyone not taking food or drink when he should, or refusing to use the bath and oil, or careless about his clothing or sleeping on the ground, and occupying wretched lodgings and then on the strength of all this fancying that he is practicing self-control (*egkrateia*), take pity on his mistake, and show him the true method of self-control; for all these practices of his are fruitless and wearisome labours, prostrating the soul and body by starving and in other ways maltreating them. (*Det.* 19–21)

> Truth would probably blame those who without examination abandon the transactions and business activity of civic life and profess to despise fame and pleasure. For they are pretending, and do not really despise these things; they are only putting forward their filthiness as a bait, on the pretext that they are lovers of propriety and self control and patient endurance. (*Fug.* 6.33–34)

> First enter practical business life, household-management and statesman-ship—master each domain—only then are you qualified for your migration to a different and more excellent way of life. For the practical comes before the contemplative life; it is a sort of prelude to a more advanced contest; and it is well to have fought it out first. (*Fug.* 36).

After citing the example of the Levites, who served in the Temple until the age of fifty (Num 4:3) before earning the prize of a contemplative life, Philo continues:

> And apart from this, it is a vital matter that those who venture to make the claims of God their aim and study should first have fully met those of men;

for it is sheer folly to suppose that you will reach the greater while you are incapable of mastering the lesser. Therefore first make yourselves familiar with virtue as exercised in our dealings with men to the end that you may be introduced to that also which has to do with our relation to God. (*Fug.* 38).[50]

Thus, Philo scorns the ascetic who thinks that *askēsis* consists simply in the practice of self-abnegation and flight from the world. Anyone who must *display* feats of self-denial does not practice true self-control, which is an inner struggle, a long, gradual process that must first be fought amidst society's temptations. I detect in this tension between a radically dualistic, contemplative ideal and a more moderate, socially engaged life of self-discipline a tension within Philo's own life. Although he desires (having tasted) the life of the Therapeutae, he feels obliged to shoulder political responsibilities on behalf of the Jewish community of Alexandria; he frustratingly defers the contemplative life to a "future" realization.[51] However, to reduce the ascetic tension in Philo's writings to being auto-biographically determined is a mistake since it is a tension that is very much evident in the Greek philosophical and Jewish biblical traditions on which he is dependent: believing in one's heroic spiritual potential, yet realizing the limitations of one's present self; yearning to obtain the rewards of a different "world," yet being consumed by the demands of this.[52]

The Essenes[53]

Ever since the discovery of the Dead Sea Scrolls in 1947 and increasingly as their contents have been published and interpreted, scholars have begun to acknowledge that the ascetic tendencies exhibited by certain Jewish writings of the Second Temple period are neither as theoretical nor as idiosyncratic as had once been thought. For now we have a picture, albeit fuzzy, of a Jewish group rooted in the Hebrew Bible and committed to the fulfillment of its precepts (of course, as they understood them), which incorporated many ascetic practices into its *communal* way of life.[54] Those practices included celibacy (at least for a major segment of the movement), a materially simple life free of private possessions, temperance in food and drink, avoidance of oil, simplicity of dress, reserve in speech, desert separatism (for those at Qumran), strict rules of ritual purity and of Sabbath observance—all part of a collective and individual discipline that made them in Philo's eyes "athletes of virtue" (*Prob.* 88).

The ascetic leanings of the Essenes—and here I will focus on the evidence of the Dead Sea Scrolls—need to be understood in relation to three inter-related aspects of their ideology: their dualistic view of the world, their eschatological view of their place in Israelite history, and their view of themselves as a Temple and priesthood in exile from Jerusalem.

Although the dualistic leanings of the Dead Sea Scrolls are not entirely consistent throughout, which suggests development over time or internal diversity, they may be summarized as follows: The natural world is God's creation and is to be celebrated, but it has come under the rule of demonic forces of evil, both spiritually and politically. Humans as flesh (*basar*) come under that rule, being lured from the righteous and pious observance of God's Torah. God comes to the aid of His elect (the Qumran sectarians) by bestowing His guiding spirit (*ruah*) upon them. This spirit cleanses them of sin, enables them to overcome successfully the forces and temptations of evil, leads them to true knowledge of God through the correct interpretation of His revealed truth (Scriptures). God also provides the community with teachers (particularly the Teacher of Righteousness) who are especially imbued with the divine spirit and who guide the community in its practice and study. The community is an outpost of the divine "spirit of truth" in the midst of a world ruled by the "spirit of falsehood."[55]

The Qumran group understood itself to be living in the last days of the present age, awaiting a final battle between itself ("the sons of light") and the forces of darkness, in which the latter would be destroyed and the world would be restored to the rule of God's spirit, messianically embodied. Thus, their disciplined way of life was intended to ensure their constant preparedness, individually and communally, for that seismic event, for which they would provide the ranks of pure, holy warriors.[56]

The Essene community seems to have originated, at least in its move to Qumran, in a split from the priesthood in Jerusalem. In their view, even the Temple had come under the rule of evil forces (the Wicked Priest), which negated its role as the atoning medium for Israel. The Qumran group was organized hierarchically, with priests filling the central functions of teachers, judges, and officiants in the ritual. The community as a whole viewed itself as containing the divine sanctuary, much like the wilderness camp of the Israelites during the journey from Egypt to Canaan. They believed their camp, like the holy sanctuary, to be a fitting dwelling place for the divine spirit, through the intermediacy of angels. Although it is doubtful that the Dead Sea sectarians conducted sacrificial rites, their *discipline* and *suffering* were viewed as having atoning power, both for themselves and for Israel. They were a spiritual Temple awaiting and preparing for the restoration of the true Temple in Jerusalem.[57]

These preoccupations give the ascetic practices of the Essenes a particular flavor different from the ascetic aspects of other varieties of ancient Judaism previously discussed, but not without similarities. These peculiarities, however, make the practices no less ascetic: abstinence is an important component in their disciplinary training leading to spiritual perfection. What is significant is the degree to which the ascetic aspects of Essene practice and ideology are communalistic in focus. They distinguish less the practicing (in Philo's sense) individual from his or her society than the unity of the sanctified community (*yaḥad*) from the outside world. They are concerned less with the fate of the individual soul than with the role and vindication of the community as a whole in the larger national and cosmic redemption. It is through participation in the discipline of the exclusive community that the individual member is "cleansed" by the divine spirit.

One of the aspects of the Essenes which most distinguishes them from other varieties of ancient Judaism—and this was noted long before the Dead Sea Scrolls were discovered—is their celibate nature, at least as reported by the ancient observers, Philo, Josephus, and Pliny.[58] These explain Essene celibacy as being motivated by a desire to avoid the lure of sexual desire represented (according to them) by women and marriage, a lure that threatens to compromise the Essenes' ascetic liberty, their wholehearted pursuit of piety and study, and the bonds of their community. Josephus, however, states that the Essenes are not categorically opposed to marriage in principle and that "another" order of Essenes, valuing the obligation to procreate, do marry and have children but adopt an ordered sexuality which guards against sexual self-indulgence.

However, one of the interesting ways in which the Dead Sea Scrolls do not fully agree with the reports of the ancient observers is that they seem to *assume* the existence of women and marriage within the order and do not speak of permanent celibacy, being instead careful to exclude women from aspects of the community's life in which they might threaten its ritual purity.[59]

Some scholars have suggested that this discrepancy between the Qumran scrolls and other ancient sources indicates diversity within the movement with regard to the practice of celibacy. Others suggest that the observers projected a Cynic-Stoic ideal of celibacy onto the movement. Most recently, some scholars have suggested that the rule of celibacy was only incumbent upon a man when he had reached the age of twenty-five, the age at which he would enter service in the holy "army" and be eligible for other offices within the community. Before this (from the age of twenty), he would have been free to marry and to fulfill the obligation of procreation, perhaps in a location other than the central camp at Qumran.[60]

While this thesis does not yet represent a scholarly consensus, it raises the possibility that the ascetic ideals of the Qumran group had to be adjusted to the *community's* ability to fulfill them (as well, perhaps, to the scriptural mandate to procreate). This could be done by assigning to a suborder the complete fulfillment of some of the group's ideals which all of its members were not yet ready to fulfill. In other words, the Essenes institutionalized an "elitist" *askēsis* within the community which did not threaten the community's ideal image of itself but served to fulfill that ideal on the community's behalf.

This same phenomenon of an "elitist *askēsis*" as a way of bridging the gap between the movement's ideal and its ability to fulfill it is reflected, I believe, in the following passage, which describes the Qumran "Council" (1QS 8:1–19):

> In the Council of the Community there shall be twelve men and three Priests, perfectly versed in all that is revealed of the Law, whose works shall be truth, righteousness, justice, lovingkindness, and humility. They shall preserve the faith in the Land with steadfastness and meekness and shall atone for sin by the practice of justice and by suffering the sorrows of affliction. They shall walk with all men according to the standard of truth and the rule of the time. . . . It shall be an Everlasting plantation, a House of Holiness for Israel, an Assembly of Supreme Holiness [Holy of Holies] for Aaron. They shall be witnesses to the truth at the Judgement, and shall be the elect of Goodwill who shall atone for the Land and pay the wicked their reward. . . . It shall be a Most Holy Dwelling for Aaron, with everlasting knowledge of the Covenant of justice, and shall offer up sweet fragrance. It shall be a House of Perfection and Truth in Israel that they may establish a Covenant according to the everlasting precepts. And they shall be an agreeable offering, atoning for the Land and determining the judgement of wickedness, and there shall be no more iniquity.[61]

The practice of a collective religious, ascetic discipline that provides room for and perhaps encourages a more rigorous discipline on the part of the collective's elites is also a focus of "ascetic tension" within rabbinic Judaism and early Christianity, the former of which we will now consider.

Ascetic Tensions in Rabbinic Judaism[62]

The relation of rabbinic Judaism, which formally begins with the destruction of the Temple in 70 C.E. and the gathering of Rabban Yohanan ben Zakkai and his students at Yavneh (Jamnia), to earlier varieties of Judaism is a complex matter that does not yield to simple formulas. The prerabbinic group with which the rabbinic movement has the greatest affinities is that of the Pharisees, whose name, Hebrew *perushim*, originally meant something like "separatists."[63] The exact character of this group—which is mentioned in the New Testament, by Josephus, and in early rabbinic writings, but which did not leave us any of its own writings—is a matter of scholarly controversy and is probably impossible to determine with certainty.[64] What seems clear is that the Pharisees dedicated their lives to the careful study and strict practice of Torah precepts received from earlier generations of pietists. They organized themselves separately but not in isolation from the larger Israelite society, which they sought to influence, whether directly or indirectly. The Pharisees are noted for having been scrupulous in the practice of ritual purity, especially at meals: they ate their common meals as though they were priests eating sanctified offerings, being especially careful to protect the table from impurity.[65] They are also reported to have been particularly careful concerning Sabbath observance and tithing and were known for their fasting, simple living, and close-knit communities. According to one later rabbinic tradition (*Avot de-Rabbi Nathan* 5), they expected their self-denial in this world to be rewarded in the future world.

The ideal of *perishut,* for which the Pharisees were named, is also a positive value in rabbinic literature, where we find *perushim* used to describe the holy vocation of Israel as a *people:*

> "You shall be holy, for I, the Lord your God, am holy" (Lev 19:1): You shall be separate/abstinent (*perushim*). (*Sifra Qedoshim* 1)[66]

> "You shall be to Me a Kingdom of Priests and a holy nation" (Exod 19:6). "Holy nation": The Israelites were fit to eat Holy Things before they made the Golden Calf. After they made the Calf this privilege was taken from them and given to the priests. . . . "Holy nation": Holy and sanctified, separated (*perushim*) from the nations of the world and from their abominations. (*Mek. Bahodesh* 2)[67]

Thus, the Israelites in ideally being a holy nation, a priestly people, are to aim to be priestlike, that is, consecrated to God. They are to be *perushim* in the double sense, first, of being separate and distinct from the other nations and, second, by virtue of abstaining from their indulgences.

In another context, *perishut* is a *stage* in the attaining of spiritual perfection:

> It is taught: "Be on your guard against anything evil" (Deut 23:10): A person should not have impure thoughts during the day, lest he encounter impurity at night. From here R. Phineas ben Jair says: Heedfulness leads to cleanliness, cleanliness leads to abstinence (*perishut*), abstinence leads to purity, purity leads to holiness, holiness leads to modesty, modesty leads to fear of sin, fear of sin leads to saintliness, saintliness leads to the Holy Spirit, the Holy Spirit leads to the revivification of the dead. . . . (*b. 'Avod. Zar.* 20b)[68]

Yet in still other contexts it is suggested that, although *perishut* remains an ideal, not all who aspire to it do so in the right way or with the correct motivation. In learning of Rabbi Akiba's martyrdom, during which he finally had the opportunity to love God with all his soul by dying for the Torah, we are told that there are seven types of *perushim*. The first six perform abstinences ostentatiously, overzealously, in order to gain merit, or mechanically. The seventh and highest level of abstinence is that of one who is abstinent out of love of God, like Abraham, who turned his impulse to do evil into an impulse to do good.[69]

Thus, we find a clear tension within rabbinic literature between the promoting of abstinence as an ideal to which all of Israel should, in fact are commanded to, aspire and the realization that many who undertake forms of *perishut* do so for vain, self-serving reasons.[70]

This tension is evident, in even more striking fashion, in another rabbinic tradition that employs the word *perushim*:

> Rabban Simeon ben Gamaliel (var.: Rabbi Ishmael) said: From the day when the Temple was destroyed, it would have been reasonable not to eat meat, and not to drink wine. But a court only decrees for the community things which they can bear. He said: Since they are ordering us not to study Torah, let us decree for Israel that they not marry. But then Israel will be desolate and the seed of Abraham will cease. Rather, they allowed Israel [these things], since it is better that they err unintentionally than intentionally. When the Temple was destroyed abstainers (*perushim*) multiplied in Israel, who did not eat meat, nor drink wine. R. Joshua confronted them saying: My sons, why do you not eat meat? They said to him: How can we eat meat when every day a Continual Burnt Offering was offered on the altar, and now it has ceased? He asked them: Why do you not drink wine? The answered him: How can we drink wine, which was poured on the altar, and now has ceased? He said to them: So too we should not eat figs and grapes, from which First Fruits were offered on the festival of 'Azeret [*Shavuot*], and we should not eat bread, from which were brought Two Loaves and the Show-bread, and we should not drink water, from which was poured the Water-offering on the Festival [*Sukkot*]. They were silent. He said to them: Not to mourn at all is impossible, for it has already been decreed, and to mourn too much is impossible. Rather, the sages have said: A person should plaster his house but leave a small area uncovered, as a memorial to Jerusalem.[71]

Once again *perushim* are identified with abstinence, now in response to the catastrophe of the destruction of the Temple. According to the view attributed to Rabban Simeon ben Gamaliel (or Rabbi Ishmael), their response is logical. They deny themselves pleasure out of a sense of mourning and probably penitence in the face of this tremendous event.[72] Their reported response is a common one, and many examples could be brought from rabbinic *halakhah* and *aggadah* in which similar reactions to catastrophe are mentioned approvingly: in the face of such divine judgment against the people how can one continue "business as usual"?[73] What bothers the rabbis is the fact that a *group* of Jews undertakes a theoretically proper course of abstinence which the *community as a whole* cannot bear. The rabbis prefer a milder and more symbolic form of self-denial which the whole community can successfully sustain and legally institutionalize (under rabbinic authority).

The relation of the *perushim* mentioned in this text to the Pharisees mentioned by Josephus and the New Testament is difficult to determine. Many scholars, beginning with the presupposition that rabbinic Judaism is antithetical to asceticism, assume that here (and elsewhere) *perushim* associated with ascetic practices cannot have anything to do with "our" Pharisees and must be "heretics." However, it is possible that the Pharisaic movement, which Josephus calls a philosophy and which modern scholars call a sect, was more diverse than is commonly presumed and was not wholly or immediately absorbed by the rabbinic movement. Some Pharisees moderated their asceticism in the process of trying to fill the vacuum of national leadership created by the destruction of the Temple.[74] Such rabbis knew that for their authority and program to be accepted they had to adapt their ideology to the needs and capabilities of the whole people, ideally expected to be a people of *perushim*. Other Pharisees may have persisted in a more elitist and voluntaristic asceticism, against which the rabbis had to turn, even while admitting the theoretical correctness of their ascetic ways. Thus, *perushim* and *perishut* remained rabbinic ideals. However, now they were no longer the ideals of a separatist group within Israel but of a separatist Israel, struggling to find new means to remain separate from the nations and consecrated to God, despite the loss of Temple and national sovereignty.

This tension was resolved neither easily nor quickly, but was internalized within the rabbinic movement. The rabbis differed regarding the extent to which a rabbinic elite should itself adopt an abstinent course of conduct more demanding than what could be expected of the people under its authority. Did the *halakhah* determine both the norms and *limits* of abstinence, or were individuals free to abstain from what was otherwise permitted, thereby separating themselves from the community for purposes of penitence, mourning, self-discipline, overcoming the impulse to do evil, or preparing for prayer, study, a vision, or death? This question, never answered within rabbinic Judaism, was inherited by medieval Jewish philosophers, mystics, and legal authorities.[75]

A few more examples will have to suffice for now, which illustrate some other aspects of the ascetic tension within rabbinic Judaism:

Said Simeon the Righteous [high priest, ca. 190 B.C.E.]: In all my life I ate the Guilt Offering of a Nazirite only once. It happened that a man came to me from the south, and I saw that he had beautiful eyes, a handsome face, and curly locks. I said to him: "My son, why did you want to destroy such lovely hair?" He said to me: "I was a shepherd in my village and I came to fill water from the river. When I looked at my reflection my impulse to do evil overcame me and sought to drive me from the world. I said to him: 'Evil one, you should not pride yourself in something which is not yours, in something which is destined to become dust and worms. Behold I vow to shave you off for the sake of heaven.'" I patted his head and kissed him, saying: "My son, may there be many like you who do God's will in Israel. In you is fulfilled what Scripture says: 'If anyone, man or woman, who distinctly utters a Nazirite vow, to set himself apart *for the Lord. . . .*' (Num 6:2)" (*t. Nazir* 4.7)[76]

There is ample evidence that the practice of Nazirite vows, biblically prescribed in Numbers 6, was widely undertaken in Second Temple times for various durations and for a variety of reasons: penitence, divine favor, self-discipline.[77] It was a way for an Israelite man or woman to achieve a high, priestly (even High Priestly) level of holiness through abstaining for a given period (according to the Mishnah, a minimum of thirty days) from wine, grape products, contact with the dead, even of one's immediate family, and cutting of one's hair. At the end of the vowed period, or should contact with the dead cancel the vow, the hair was shorn and offered with other sacrifices on the altar.[78]

Simeon the Righteous's general reluctance to accept the offerings of a Nazirite probably stems from a strong tendency in rabbinic literature, going back to the Mishnah, of viewing the Nazirite negatively. Apparently, many who enthusiastically vowed to undertake this obligation did so impulsively, for an inappropriate reason and without seriously considering whether they would be able to fulfill the vow.[79] This negative view is consonant with rabbinic concerns about vowing in general: it is better not to vow than to vow and not fulfill.[80] The rabbis go so far as to call the Nazirite a "sinner":

"And [the Priest] shall make expiation on his behalf [on account of contact with a corpse]" (Num 6:11): For he sinned against his soul (*nefesh*). R. Eleazar Hakappar says: Against which soul did he sin that he needs expiation? For he denied his soul wine. And we can argue *a fortiori:* If one who denies his soul wine needs expiation, how much more so one who denies himself everything. R. Ishmael says: Scripture [in speaking of expiation] refers only to the impure Nazirite, as it says: "And shall make expiation on his behalf for the guilt that he incurred through the corpse," for he became impure from contact with the dead. (*Sifre Num.* 30 and parallels)

Such radical exegesis, taking a biblically prescribed institution which declares the abstinent Nazirite to be "Holy to the Lord," in some ways equal to the *high priest,* and declaring him a sinner, can only be understood as a polemic. We probably have here a polemic either against the continued practice of Nazirite vows (unlikely in the absence of the Temple), or of individualized vows of abstinence in general, which the Nazirite comes to represent.[81] To be sure, Rabbi Ishmael rejects this exegesis, arguing that Scripture speaks only of the *defiled* Nazirite as a sinner.[82]

It is interest that despite such negative views of the Nazirite, other rabbis are said to refer to the Nazirite as "holy" and "saintly": "And if one who denies himself only one thing [wine] is called 'holy,' how much more so one who denies himself every thing" (*b. Ta'anit* 11a-b). It would seem impossible to reconcile this view with that of Rabbi Eleazar Hakappar. How can the Nazirite, and by extension other abstainers, be called both "sinner" and "holy"?

Taken as a whole, the tradition may be suggestive of a middle path, distinguishing, as does Simeon the Righteous, between those who undertake the Nazirite vow, and vows in general, rashly or for vain reasons and those who do so only after having considered their ability to complete the vow as a form of religious self-discipline: their goal is not to be noticed, not to gain merit, but to control or convert their impulse to do evil.[83] As one later rabbi explains, the Nazirite whom Simeon the Righteous praises vows with complete integrity: "his mouth and his heart are in full consonance" (*y. Ned.* 1.1, and parallels).

Finally, two texts which deal with sexual abstinence:

> It is taught: R. Eleazar says: Whoever does not engage in being fruitful and multiplying is like one who sheds blood, as it says: "Whoever sheds the blood of man, by man shall his blood be shed" (Gen 9:6), and immediately thereafter it says: "Be fruitful and multiply" (9:7) . . . [R. Simeon] ben Azzai says: It is as if he sheds blood and decreases the (divine) likeness, as it says "Be fruitful and multiply" (Gen 1:28) [after saying "in the image of God He created him" (1:27)]. They said to Ben Azzai: There are those who interpret well and perform well, those who perform well and do not interpret well, but you interpret well and do not perform well [he was celibate]. He said to them: What can I do? My soul clings in love to the Torah; let the world be sustained by others.[84] (*b. Yebam.* 636)

Although Ben Azzai's path of permanent continence is rejected by rabbinic law, which affirms the obligation of procreation for all, his reasoning, or that attributed to him, is reflective of an aspect of the ascetic tension within Judaism: If the central religious obligation is that of study of Torah (and attachment to God through it), then worldly preoccupations such as family are bound to be distracting, for reasons of time, energy, and purity.

It is interesting that elsewhere the ideal of complete, ascetic, continent availability to Torah is articulated in the *aggadah*. But halakhically such a "division of labor" as Ben Azzai proposes, which the Essenes seem to have adopted, is rejected in favor of an ordered sexuality which, although it affirms the ideal of sexual abstinence as a way to spiritual perfection, recommends moderate sexual activity, especially for the sage.[85] Sanctification was possible both through *temporary abstinence* and through *moderation* in what was permitted. The idea that one could sanctify oneself through engaging in permitted sexual intercourse with a correct religious intention is, to my knowledge, unique among the varieties of ancient Judaism.[86]

Thus, a tension is exhibited between the ideals of the study of Torah in purity and complete attachment, and of fulfilling one's duties as a father and husband, a tension that is differently resolved by different rabbis:

> Once R. Judah had a seminal emission while walking along the river shore. His students said to Him: Our teacher, instruct us in the laws of *derekh erez* ("proper manners"). He went down to the river and immersed himself and then taught them. They said to him: This is not what you have instructed us concerning the teaching of laws of *derekh erez* [that they do not require ritual purity]. He said to them: Even though I am lenient with others, I am strict with myself. . . . Our sages teach: Someone who has a seminal emission and has nine kabs of water poured on him [rather than fully immersing himself in forty se'ahs of water] is purified. Nahum of Gimzo whispered this to R. Akiba, R. Akiba whispered it to Ben Azzai, and Ben Azzai went and taught it to his students in the market. Two Palestinian Amoraim disagreed about this: . . . One said he [Ben Azzai] taught it, one said he whispered it. The first said he taught it so that neither Torah nor procreation would be neglected. The other said he whispered it so that the students of the sages would not hang around their wives like roosters. R. Jannai said: I have heard of some that are lenient [requiring only nine kabs] and of others who are strict [requiring forty se'ahs]. Whoever is strict with himself in this regard will have his days and years prolonged. (*b. Ber. 22a*)

Thus, although rules of sexual purity were liberalized for men—presumably so as not to discourage marital relations—others continued to impose upon themselves a stricter rule. The tension between sexuality and a sage's preoccupation with Torah study is unresolved.[87]

Many other aspects of the ascetic tension in rabbinic Judaism could be discussed: the degree to which voluntary abstinence is a fitting accompaniment to study and prayer, yet in excess lessens one's energy to serve the Master (*y. Dem. 7.4*); traditions of sages who undertake extensive fasts as penance for seemingly minor wrongdoings (*b. B. Mes. 85a*); fasting as a substitute for sacrifice (*b. Ber. 17a*); the practice of regular fasting twice a week;[88] the physical dangers of extreme abstinence to the individual and the burdens he places thereby on the community (b. Ta'anit 11b; 22b); the value of suffering as a form of atonement for one's sins, a sign of God's love, and a guarantee of reward in the world to come (b. Qid. 40b); piety beyond the law as a way of guarding against sin (b. B. Meṣ. 35a); abstinence as an aid in mystical experience (Hekhalot texts, e.g., Hekhalot Rabbati 30; cf. y. Kelim 9.3); ascetic tensions in the observance of the Sabbath (b. Shabb. 11a).[89]

For now, however, the presence of an ascetic tension within rabbinic Judaism has been well enough demonstrated. This tension never disappeared.[90] In many ways it is strikingly similar to such tensions in pre-rabbinic varieties of Judaism and within early Christianity (which could not be treated here). Yet in other ways the ascetic tensions within rabbinic Judaism are distinctively rabbinic.

Like the authors of the Apocrypha and Pseudepigrapha, the rabbis are acutely aware of the dichotomy between people's spiritual potential and the obstacles to the realization of that potential presented by their inner impulses and the lures of the world. Penitential abstinence is one way of dealing with that tension if not of resolving it. Like the literature of the Apocrypha and Pseudepigrapha, rabbinic writings know of some who desired more direct experience of heaven, either in life or at death, and employed ascetic means to that end. Maintaining a separation between heaven and earth while allowing each to influence the other is a common religious problem for which different ascetic responses were sought. Sanctification of oneself through abstinence is common to rabbinic and pre-rabbinic Judaisms (e.g., 2 Baruch 20:5, cited above). Sanctification through ordered and directed indulgence in pleasure (though not for pleasure's sake) is, as far as I can tell, a distinctive rabbinic contribution to the history of Judaism.

Late biblical and postbiblical Judaisms, by increasing the ethical, pietistic, and legal expectations placed on the individual, had to find ways of dealing with the psychic and social pressures thereby created. Ideals of perfection are one thing; dealing with an individual's and a religious society's continuing failure to realize them is another. One of the ways in which asceticism deals with this problem is by defining discrete areas of self-control in which the individual's (and society's) will can be exercised successfully in fulfillment of transcendent purposes.[91]

Like the writings of Philo, rabbinic traditions exhibit a tension between a radically ascetic (even dualistic) ideal and the need to fulfill that ideal within society. They too are critical of those who seek a quick, and overly individualistic, ascetic path to the realization of that ideal, if only because it was a path not open to them as community leaders. Unlike the writings of the Apocrypha and Pseudepigrapha and Philo, and like the Dead Sea Scrolls, rabbinic writings express concern for the spiritual perfection of the individual and the ascetic means to that end primarily within the context of a communal, institutionalized discipline. This creates tensions between the desires and abilities of (and perhaps needs for) pietistic circles which adopt levels of asceticism beyond that prescribed by custom and law ("elitist *askēsis*") and the dangers of separatism within Jewish society. This tension is particularly acute if those pietists wish to serve not only as religious models but as religious and communal leaders as well. The solution to this tension sought by a movement eventually dispersed over continents, living in the midst of other peoples, and wishing to bring all of Israel under its wings was to be much more complex than that "achieved" by a relatively small group, living in the desert, with control over who entered and left, and preparing for an imminent end of history. For the rabbis, it was a tension, as expressed in the *Mekilta* (*Baḥodesh* 2), between being both a "kingdom of *priests*" and a "holy *nation*": sanctified to God while living among yet apart from the nations and their ways.

These, then, are only some of the ascetic aspects of the history of ancient Judaism, with implications for the historical study of later varieties of Judaism. The tensions that I have described never disappeared. At times they produced movement that revitalized Jewish life and institutions, but at times that movement threatened to upset the difficult equilibrium of Jewish pietism and Jewish society. Future scholarship will have to delve deeper and more systematically into these ascetic aspects of Judaism, free, it is hoped, from the fog of interreligious polemic and apologetic.

Notes

1. This is not to deny that the term "asceticism" has ancient semantic roots, a subject to which I will return shortly. Much the same can be said for mysticism, apocalypticism, and gnosticism, with which asceticism often overlaps. Limitations of space have prevented me from providing a full scholarly apparatus in this and the notes that follow. This lack will be rectified in a monograph which I am preparing on the subject of this essay.

2. All dates are C.E. unless otherwise noted.

3. The alternative of defining "asceticism" so broadly as to be meaningless will be discussed below. I wish to stress that the fact that different scholars differently define and apply the term "asceticism" is not simply a problem of semantics, but of historical interpretation, as I will show below for the case of ancient Judaism.

4. Others have criticized this bias against asceticism: J. Evola, *The Doctrine of Awakening: A Study on the Buddhist Ascesis* (London: Luzac, 1951) 3–15; Oscar

Hardman, *The Ideals of Asceticism*, 3–4 (with examples); William James, *The Varieties of Religious Experience: A Study in Human Nature* (1902; reprint, New York: Modern Library, 1936) 291–304, 352–61; James A. Montgomery, "Ascetic Strains in Early Judaism," *Journal of Biblical Literature* 51 (1932) 183–87. Hardman (p. 14) cites Sir Bernard Shaw's definition of asceticism: "thinking you are moral when you are uncomfortable."

5. This tendency is evidenced among scholars who argue that Judaism in general and Judaism of the rabbis in particular is antithetical to asceticism. They often appear to be implicitly responding to Christian anti-Jewish polemics going back to the New Testament which portray Judaism as the "legalistic" enslavement to this-worldly rules of the flesh. The argument that Judaism is defined by the centrality of legal observance and therefore contains no asceticism is used, interestingly, both by those who make of this a virtue and by those who make of it a weakness. For example, see Emil G. Hirsch, "Asceticism," *Jewish Encyclopedia* (London and New York: Funk & Wagnalls, 1902–) 2:166–67; M. Lazarus, *The Ethics of Judaism*, trans. H. Szold, 2 vols. (Philadelphia: Jewish Publication Society, 1900–1901) 2:119–22; A. E. Suffrin, "Asceticism (Jewish)," in *Encyclopaedia of Religion and Ethics* (New York: Scribner, 1910) 2:97–99; H. Strathmann, "Askese," *Reallexikon für Antike und Christentum* (Stuttgart: Hiersemann, 1950) 1.1:750; idem, *Geschichte der frühchristlichen Askese* (Leipzig: A. Deichertsche Verlagsbuchhandlung Werner Scholl, 1914) 16–40 ("Der unasketlische Grundzug der palästinensisch-jüdischen Frömmigkeit"). The Jewish-Christian polemic with regard to asceticism is more complex than here indicated, and I hope to return to it in a projected monograph on the subject of this essay.

6. Examples will be provided below. For now, note how the *Oxford English Dictionary* (1:483) defines "ascetic" and "asceticism" in terms of "extreme" and "severe" abstinence and austerity, begging the question: At what point is abstinence "extreme," except as subjectively determined? Such definitions, however, *do* follow common popular usage, as exemplified by the earliest English use of "asceticism" cited by the *OED:* "Doomed to a life of celibacy by the asceticism which had corrupted the simplicity of Christianity" (Sir Thomas Browne, 1646).

7. Such are the arguments most often adduced in denying asceticism a place in the history of ancient Judaism. For examples, see the sources cited above, n. 5, and my discussion below of E. E. Urbach's position on the matter. For a classic statement of the antithesis between the motives of asceticism and the principles of classical Judaism, see George Foot Moore, *Judaism in the First Centuries of the Christian Era*, 3 vols. (Cambridge, MA: Harvard University Press, 1927–40), 2:263–65. For the same view in homiletical form, see Ahad Ha-'Am (Asher Ginzberg), "Flesh and Spirit," in *Selected Essays of Ahad Ha'am*, trans. and ed. Leon Simon (Philadelphia: Jewish Publication Society, 1962) 139–158. For a denial of motivation as a criterion in determining whether a pattern of abstinence and self-imposed hardship is a form of asceticism, see Bernhard Lohse, *Askese und Mönchtum in der Antike und in der alten Kirche* (Munich and Vienna: R. Oldenbourg, 1969) 12.

8. Max Weber, *The Sociology of Religion*, trans. E. Fischoff from the 4th rev. German ed., 1956 (Boston: Beacon, 1963) 164–81; J. Milton Yinger, *Religion, Society and the Individual: An Introduction to the Sociology of Religion* (New York: Macmillan, 1957) 417–20, 519–21. For another review of the literature on asceticism and Judaism, see Allan Lazaroff, "Bayha's Asceticism Against its Rabbinic and Islamic Background," *Journal of Jewish Studies* 21 (1970) 11–20.

9. Weber in fact denies asceticism any place in Judaism, since Judaism does not conform fully enough to his model of "innerworldly" asceticism derived from Puritanism,

with its religious vocation of socially transforming the present world. See Weber, *Ancient Judaism*, trans. Hans H. Gerth (New York: Free Press, 1952) 403–10; idem, *Sociology of Religion*, 246, 256–58.

10. Weber is inconsistent here; see preceding note.

11. The ideal of an "undivided heart" in service of God is discussed by Peter Brown (*Virginity and Society: Sexuality and its Renunciation in Late Antiquity*, forthcoming) as a central factor in the development of early Christianity's preoccupation with sexual continence.

12. For other exponents of this broad view of asceticism, see Oscar Hardman, *The Ideal of Asceticism;* James A. Montgomery, "Ascetic Strains in Early Judaism"; Bernhard Lohse, *Askese und Mönchtum*, 11–15; Ernst Troeltsch, *The Social Teaching of the Christian Churches*, trans. O. Wyon, 2 vols. (New York: Macmillan, 1931) 1:102, 239, 245; M. Olphe-Galliard, "Ascèse, Ascétisme: II. Development historique," in *Dictionnaire de spiritualité*, 1: 938–60; Joseph Bonsirven, *Le Judaisme Palestinien au Temps de Jésus Christ*, 2:280–91. This view of asceticism was long ago articulated by Emil Durkheim (*The Elementary Forms of Religious Life: A Study in Religious Sociology*, trans. J. W. Swain [New York: Macmillan, 1915] 309–17): "Asceticism is not a rare, exceptional and nearly abnormal fruit of the religious life, as some have supposed it to be; on the contrary, it is one of its essential elements." For most of the above, except where caricatures of Judaism still cloud the picture, a broader view of asceticism permits a more balanced assessment of its place in Judaism.

13. This division is from Oscar Hardman, *Ideal of Asceticism*.

14. For the following survey I have benefited from Bernhard Lohse, *Askese und Mönchtum*, 12–14; M. Olphe-Galliard, "Ascèse, Ascétisme: II. Development historique," 939–41; Joseph Ward Swain, *The Hellenic Origins of Christian Asceticism* (Diss., Columbia University; privately published, New York, 1916) 47; H. Strathmann, "Askese," in *Reallexikon für antike und Christentum* 1.1: 749–50; Hans Windisch, "*askeō*," in *Theological Dictionary of the New Testament* (Grand Rapids, MI: Eerdmans, 1964–) 1:494–96.

15. *Iliad* 3.388; 4.110; 10.438.

16. Thucydides 2.39, 5.67; Xenophon *Hipparchicus* 8.1.

17. For example, Hesiod *Opera et dies* 287ff.; Democritus *Frag.* 242; Herodotus 1.96, 7.209; Plato *Euthydemus* 283A, *Gorgias* 527E, *Respublica* 7.536B; Aristotle *Ethica Nicomachea* 9.9.7.

18. For example, Isocrates *Busiris* 26; Epictetus *Discourses* 3.12 and *Enchiridion* 47; Strabo *Geographus* 15.1.29, 61. For the analogy between physical and spiritual training, see Epictetus *Discourses* 3.12.16; Diogenes Laertius 6 (Diogenes) 70–71.

19. See 2 Macc 15:4 (*observance* of the Sabbath); 4 Macc 12:11 (*observers* of righteousness); 4 Macc 13:22 (*observance* of God's law). Similarly, Josephus speaks of Jewish knowledge and interpretation of the Law as *askēsis* (*Antiquities* 20.12.1 §§264–65). For the discipline of the Essenes and Therapeutae referred to as *askēsis*, see Josephus *War* 2.8.10 §§150–53; Philo *Hypothetica* (in Eusebius *Praep. Evang.* 8.11); Eusebius *Church History* 2.16–17. Philo's frequent use of *askēsis* and related words to describe religious "practice," will be discussed below. The argument that scrupulous Jewish observance of the commandments is incompatible with asceticism (see above, n. 5) finds no basis in ancient testimonies. Note, for instance, Col 2:16–23.

20. Clement of Alexandria *Paedagogus* 1.7, *Stromateis* 1.5; 4.22; Origen *Against Celsus* 7.48. It is interesting that *askēsis* appears only once in the New Testament, in Acts 24:16, in the general sense of exerting oneself religiously. The *idea* of self-discipline

(*egkrateia*) and renunciation of bodily needs as a requirement of spiritual contest is expressed by Paul in 1 Cor 9:25–27 and 1 Tim 4:7–8.

21. See G. W. H. Lampe, *A Patristic Greek Lexicon* (Oxford: Clarendon Press, 1961), p. 244, s.v. *askēsis*, 6.

22. See E. R. Dodds, *Pagan and Christian in an Age of Anxiety* (Cambridge: University Press, 1968) 27–42; Peter Brown, *The Making of Late Antiquity* (Cambridge, MA and London: Harvard University Press, 1978); Henry A. Fischel, *Rabbinic Literature and Greco-Roman Philosophy: A Study of Epicurea and Rhetorica in Early Midrashic Writings*, Studia Post-Biblica 21 (Leiden: Brill, 1973) 80 n. 100.

23. "Otherwise permitted" is intentionally vague, leaving open the possibility of its applying to both individuals in relation to their immediate societies and communities in relation to the broader society. Of the many definitions of asceticism that have been proposed, ranging from overly broad to overly narrow, that of Arthur Vööbus agrees most closely with the one I have proposed: "Asceticism, in religion, is the practice of the denial of physical or psychological desires in order to attain a spiritual ideal or goal" ("Asceticism," in *Encyclopaedia Britannica*, 15th ed., 2:135.

24. Yitzhak Fritz Baer, *Yisra'el ba-'Amim*, 20–57; Baer wrote also a series of articles in the Hebrew quarterly *Zion:* 17 (1952) 1–55, 173; 18 (1953) 91–108; 27 (1962) 117–55. Baer's thesis is developed by Zeev Falk, "From the Mishnah of the Pious Ones," [Hebrew] in *Benjamin De Vries Memorial Volume*, ed. E. Z. Melamed (Jerusalem: University of Tel Aviv, 1968–69) 62–69. Much the same view of the "early pietists," similarly extracted from later rabbinic texts but lacking Baer's emphasis on *askēsis*, is found in Adolph Büchler, *Types of Jewish-Palestinian Piety* (London: Oxford University Press, 1922).

25. Ephraim E. Urbach, "Ascesis and Suffering in Talmudic and Midrashic Sources," (Hebrew) in *Yitzhak F. Baer Jubilee Volume*, 48–68; summarized in Urbach, *The Sages: Their Concepts and Beliefs*, trans. I. Abrahams (Jerusalem: Magnes Press, 1975) 12, 443–48.

26. See S. Safrai, "The Teaching of the Pietists in Mishnaic Literature," *Journal of Jewish Studies* 16 (1965) 15–33; idem, "The Pharisees and the Hasidim," *Service International de Documentation Judeo-Chretienne* 10 (1977) 12–16.

27. For example, the statement attributed to Simeon the Just, "By three things is the world sustained: by the Law, by the [Temple-]service, and by deeds of loving-kindness" (*m. Abot* 1:2), is considered by Baer to be a cornerstone of the "ascetic Torah."

28. I shall discuss the first two points, and I shall duly treat the others in a monograph on the subject of this essay.

29. Although the ascetic practices recounted in these books are generally associated with biblical or legendary figures and are not presented as descriptions of or prescriptions for contemporary society, they presumably are projections from current practices and attitudes of the author's milieu. For a treatment of our topic in this literature, focusing on the *Testaments of the Twelve Patriarchs*, see Robert Eppell, *Le Piétisme Juif dans les Testaments des douze Patriarches* (Strasbourg: Imprimerie Alsacienne, 1930) 112–13, 147–57.

30. For (a) see Dan 9:3; 10:2–3, 12; *Apocalypse of Abraham* 9; 4 Ezra 5:13ff.; 5:20; 6:30, 35; *2 Baruch* 9:2; 20:5–6; *Martyrdom of Isaiah* 2:7–11; *1 Enoch* 83:2; 85:3. For (b) see Jud 4:9–13; 1 Macc 3:47–51; 2 Macc 13:10–12; Tob 12:8; *2 Baruch* 9:2. For (c) and (d) see 4 Macc 1:31–35; *Apocalypse of Elijah* 1:13–22; *Life of Adam and Eve* 5–6; *Testament of Joseph* 3:4–5; 4:8; *Testament of Judah* 15:4; *Testament of Reuben* 1:10; *Testament of Simeon* 3:4; *Testament of Moses* 9:1–7; *Letter of Aristeas* 15–55. The lines between these purposes

are not always distinct. Thus, it is sometimes unclear whether abstinence is intended to atone for a past sin or to guard against a future sin.

31. For (a) see most of the sources listed in the previous note. For (b) see Dan 10:2–3, 12; *Apocalypse of Abraham* 9; 4 Ezra 9:26; 12:51; *Martyrdom of Isaiah* 2:7–11; *Testament of Joseph* 3:4–5; *Testament of Judah* 15:4; *Testament of Reuben* 1:10; cf. Matt 3:4 (John the Baptist). For (c) see Dan 10:2–3; *Apocalypse of Abraham* 9. For (d) see Jud 8:4–8; Wisdom of Solomon 3:13; *Jubilees* 50:8; *Testament of Naphtali* 8:8; *Testament of Issachar* 2; 3:5; 7:2, 3; *Testament of Joseph* 3:4–5; 4:1–2; 9:2. On sex as a source of ritual impurity, see below, n. 33. A frequent theme is of sex for procreation alone and not for lust. See Tob 8:7 (cf. 6:17). For sexual morality setting Israel apart from other peoples, see below, n. 41. For (e) see *Martyrdom of Isaiah* 2:7–11; *Testament of Issachar* 4:2; cf. Matt 3:4 (John the Baptist); Josephus *Life* 2.11 (Bannus). For (f) see 1 Macc 2:29; *Martyrdom of Isaiah* 2:7–11; 4 Ezra 9:26; 12:51.

32. Many of the ascetic practices, especially those connected with penitence, are common to mourning customs. Both require visible signs of self-denial and humility. It is not always possible to determine when the motivation for an ascetic practice is mourning, when penitence, and when another form of petition before God, since they are often intertwined.

33. On sexual intercourse rendering one ritually impure, see Lev 15:18; 1 Sam 21:5–6. On priestly abstinence prior to officiating, see Lev 10:9. According to the Mishnah (*Yoma* 1:1), the high priest separated from his wife seven days before the Day of Atonement. Similarly, Exod 19:10, 15 relates that the Israelites prepared for the revelation at Sinai by being continent for three days, thereby "sanctifying" themselves. Moses is said to have fasted the whole time he was on the mountain (Exod 34:28; Deut 9:9, 18; cf. Elijah, 1 Kgs 19:8; Daniel, Dan 9:3; 10:2–3, 12). *Testament of Naphtali* 8:8 recommends a time for intercourse with one's wife and a time to abstain for prayer. For examples of abstinence in preparing for the receiving of a revelation or vision, see the examples in n. 30, above.

34. For examples, see above, n. 31. The obvious biblical antecedent is Israel's experience in the wilderness, romanticized by the prophets as a place of intimacy with God and of future redemption (Hos 2:14–17; Isa 32:16).

35. See above, n. 22. Note 4 Macc 1:1, 13, 31–35, where the dietary commandments of temperance assist in establishing inspired reason's rule over the passions and appetites. The goal of this type of ascetic dualism is not the destruction of the flesh but its harnessing by the spirit. The strongest dualism expressed in this literature is in Wisdom of Solomon 9:15, where a corruptible body weighs down the soul, preventing it from discerning wisdom, which comes through the spirit from God. This is still not Plato's image of the soul imprisoned in the body.

36. On the importance of accepting suffering as God's gracious chastening of the righteous and as a means of atonement, see *Psalms of Solomon* 3:3–9; 7:3–8; 8:29–40; 10; 13:5–9; 16:14–15; and *1 Enoch* 108:7–10, quoted below.

37. Ben Sira 34:25–26; *Testament of Asher* 2:8; *Testament of Judah* 13; cf. Isa 58; Jer 14:12; Zech 7:3–9.

38. On Israel's being distinguished from the other peoples by its sexual morality, see *Letter of Aristeas* 150–55; *Sibylline Oracles* 3:594–95.

39. Note the example of the institution of the *ma'amadot*, which according to the Mishnah (*Ta'anit* 4:2–3) existed in Second Temple times as an opportunity for the Israelites to fast in their towns for four days of the week during which the priestly course representing them offered sacrifices in the Temple. Undoubtedly, some groups favoring ascetic practice, such as the Qumran sectarians, were alienated from the

Temple priesthood, and their practices may be seen as an *alternative* to participation in the official cult. However, this need not have been true for asceticism in general.

40. Translation from *The Old Testament Pseudepigrapha*, ed. James H. Charlesworth (Garden City, NY: Doubleday, 1983) 1:627.

41. Ibid., 1:88.

42. Ibid., 1:820. On the shining faces of the abstinent, see 4 Ezra 7:125.

43. Treatments of Philo's ascetic side can be found in the standard works on his philosophy. Of particular value are: Thomas H. Billings, *The Platonism of Philo Judaeus* (Chicago: University of Chicago Press, 1919) 68–87; Henry Chadwick, "Philo and the Beginnings of Christian Thought," in *The Cambridge History of Later Greek and Early Medieval Philosophy*, ed. A. H. Armstrong (Cambridge: University Press, 1967) 137–57; John Dillon, *The Middle Platonists: 80 B.C. to A.D. 220* (Ithaca, NY: Cornell University Press, 1977) 139–83; Erwin R. Goodenough, *The Politics of Philo Judaeus: Practice and Theory* (New Haven, CT: Yale University Press, 1938) 28–29; 66–76; Marguerite Harl, "Adam et les deux Arbres du Paradis chez Philo d'Alexandrie," *Recherches de Science Religieuse* 50 (1962) 321–88; David Winston, "Was Philo a Mystic?" in *Studies in Jewish Mysticism*, 15–39, as well as Winston's essay in this volume, chapter 8. For an understanding of the Greek philosophical roots of Philo's asceticism, see Clifford Herschel Moore, "Greek and Roman Ascetic Tendencies," in *Harvard Essays on Classical Subjects*, 97–140; and the literature cited above, n. 14. The citations and translations from Philo's writings that follow are from the Loeb Classical Library edition. In addition to the abbreviations of works of Philo listed in the preceding chapter, n. 1, the following abbreviation is used in this discussion: *Agr.* = *On Agriculture* (*De Agricultura*).

44. For the Platonic notion of the soul imprisoned in the body, see *Her.* 68, 85, 273; *Mut.* 173; *Som.* 1.139, 181; *Deus* 111–15; *Ebr.* 101; *Abr.* 9. For the constant vigilance of the mind against the passions, see *LA* 2.27–30: when the one is awake the other sleeps.

45. Both have treatises devoted to them: *The Life of Moses* and *The Contemplative Life*. For a statement of Moses' subjugation and eradication of the passions through the practice (*askēsis*) of temperance, see *Mos.* 1.25–29.

46. The expression "man in progress" is a Stoic tag, applied by Philo to Jacob in contrast to Moses, the "perfect man," in *LA* 3.140. Philo contrasts the "active life" of the Essenes with the "contemplative life" of the Therapeutae in *Cont.* 1.

47. Whereas Moses rids himself of all pleasure, Jacob, the man of gradual improvement, does not reject pleasure in its entirety, rather "welcoming simple and unavoidable pleasure, while declining that which is excessive and over elaborate in the way of delicacies" (*LA* 3.140). On Jacob's initial flight from confronting pleasure, see *Fug.* 7.39, 43, 45. For a Greek parallel, see Epictetus *Discourses* 3.12.12. For Philo, Abraham, Isaac, and Jacob represent respectively the three Sophist components of moral education: acquired learning (*mathēsis*), nature (*physis*), and practice (*askēsis*).

48. See for example his interpretations of the laws of the Seventh Year (*Spec.* 2.104–9), of the Nazirite (*Spec.* 1.247–54), of Yom Kippur (*Spec.* 2.194–98), of firstfruits (*Spec.* 4.98–101), and of unleavened bread (*Spec.* 2.159–61). Whereas the "perfect man" denies pleasure of his own initiative, "the practicer" must be commanded what to do, thereby guided by divine reason.

49. For the ideal of virginity as a precondition of communion with God, see *Cher.* 50 and *Mos.* 2.68–70. See also his explanation of Essene continence (*Hypothetica* in Eusebius *Praep. Evang.* 8.11). The celibate Therapeutae, Philo says, chose wisdom alone as their life mates: *Cont.* 68. On Moses' abstinence from food and drink as a way of cleansing himself of pleasure in preparation for receiving revelation, see *LA* 3.141–42.

50. For other rejections of excessive abstinence or world flight, see *Mig.* 90–91; *Fug.*

4.25; 5.28–31; 6.33; *Spec.* 4.102. Note in these Philo's favoring of an Aristotelian "middle way": Do not reject wealth but use it charitably. Do not hesitate to attend a luxurious repast, but drink in moderation, etc. For remarkably similar rejections of excessive asceticism, see Seneca *Epistulae* 5.1–6.

51. For this tension within his own life see *Spec.* 3.1–6; *LA* 2.84–88.

52. This tension between the ideal of world renunciation and the role of the philosopher in politically transforming society is evident in Plato as well. Cynics and Stoics are similarly torn between the ideal of complete rejection of passion and an acceptance (if not valuing) of those "natural" impulses that require satisfaction. For a succinct statement of the Stoic attitude to passion and pleasure, see F. H. Sandbach, *The Stoics,* Ancient Culture and Society (New York: Norton; London: Chatto and Windus, 1975) 59–68.

53. I assume here that the Jewish sectarians at Qumran were at the center of the Essene movement described by Josephus, Philo, and Pliny. The Therapeutae, referred to above in my discussion of Philo (nn. 45, 46, 49), will not be dealt with here since Philo's idealization of them is our only source of information. For the abbreviations of the titles of the Qumran writings, see Joseph A. Fitzmyer, *The Dead Sea Scrolls: Major Publications and Tools for Study* (Sources for Biblical Study 8; Missoula, MT: Society of Biblical Literature and Scholars Press, 1975) 3–8.

54. As noted above, n. 19, the term *askēsis* was used by Greek-speaking Jews and Christians in referring to the Essenes' discipline.

55. See David Flusser, "The Dualism of 'Flesh and Spirit' in the Dead Sea Scrolls and the New Testament" (Hebrew), *Tarbiz* 27 (1957–58) 158–65. For good examples, see 1QS 3:13–4:1; 4:19–22; 1QH 11:10–14.

56. See Matthew Black, *The Scrolls and Christian Origins: Studies in the Jewish Background of the New Testament* (New York: Scribner, 1961) 16, 29–30; idem, "The Tradition of Hasidaean-Essene Asceticism: Its Origins and Influence," in *Aspects du Judéo-Christianisme,* 19–33. Black's reconstruction of a Nazirite background for the Essene holy warrior is highly speculative.

57. The Qumran camp is to be kept pure from defilement, since the holy angels dwell with the congregation: 1QSa 2:3–9. On the presence of angels amidst the congregation see 1QM 7:1–7; 1QH 11:10–14. On the sexual purity of the camp, see below, n. 59.

58. See Pliny *Nat. Hist.* 5.13.73; Josephus, *War* 2.8.2 §§ 119–21; 2.8.13 §§ 160–61; Philo *Hypothetica* (in Eusebius *Praep. Evang.* 8.11).

59. See above, n. 33. On the sanctity of the camp, see Deut 23:9–14; 2 Sam 11:7–13. For the Essene concern that the Temple in Jerusalem had been defiled by sexual contamination, see CD 5:6–7. Similarly, 1QSa 1:26 requires that when the whole assembly gathers for judgment, or for the Council of the Community, or for war, each member must prepare by being "sanctified" the previous three days. This is taken to refer to sexual abstinence, following the model of the revelation at Sinai (Exod 19:10–15). In 1QM 7:1–7 boys and women are forbidden from entering the camps during war, as are those with blemishes and men who have had night emissions. The recently published *Temple Scroll* (45–46) spells out similar measures for protecting the purity of the "Temple City."

60. According to Num 1:22 men enter the holy army at twenty. Yet 1QSa 1:8–11 states that the Qumran sectarians are enrolled in the community at twenty, at which age they are first permitted to marry since they can then distinguish between good and evil. At twenty-five, the age at which Levites begin their service, they enter the lowest rank of office within the community/army (see 1QM 7:1–7). For this thesis, see Abel Isaksson, *Marriage and Ministry in the New Temple* (Lund: Gleerup, 1965) 45–65. On

the relation of Qumran celibacy to ritual purity, see Antoine Guillaumont, "A propos du celibat des Esseniens," in *Hommages à André Dupont-Sommer* (Paris: Maisonneuve, 1971) 395–404; A. Marx, "Les racines du célibat essénien," *Revue de Qumran* 7 (1970) 323–42. On the question of Qumran celibacy, see now Lawrence H. Schiffman, *Sectarian Law in the Dead Sea Scrolls: Courts, Testimony and the Penal Code,* Brown Judaic Studies 33 (Chico: Scholars Press, 1983) 13, 64, 214–15. Scholars of Syrian Christianity have recently drawn attention to the parallels between Essene celibacy and that of the Syriac *Qyama;* see Antoine Guillaumont, "Monachisme et éthique judéochrétienne," in *Judéo-Christianisme,* 199–218; Robert Murray, "The Exhortation to Candidates for Ascetical Vows at Baptism in the Early Christian Church," *New Testament Studies* 21 (1974–75) 59–80.

61. Translated by Geza Vermes, *The Dead Sea Scrolls in English* (Harmondsworth: Penguin Books, 1962) 85.

62. Because of the volume and diversity of the rabbinic corpus and the present limitations of space, the following discussion must be selective and not systematic. My thesis, proposed in the introduction and to be illustrated now, is that there is no single rabbinic view of asceticism. Rather, asceticism has to be viewed as one important aspect of rabbinic Judaism, often in tension with others. Therefore, future study will have to focus on the degree to which these aspects and tensions are *differently* expressed in specific rabbinic corpora, in association with particular circles of sages, and in relation to specific areas of law and lore.

63. For the most recent discussion, see A. I. Baumgarten, "The Name of the Pharisees," *Journal of Biblical Literature* 102 (1983) 411–28. Baumgarten's argument that the name Pharisees meant "interpreters" is not to my mind convincing. It is based largely on Josephus's use of the Greek *akribeia,* often translated "exact," in describing the Pharisees as "exact interpreters of the law." However, *akribeia* when used in relation to law often has the sense of "strictness," as in Josephus *Antiquities* 20.2.4 §43, and in Acts 26:5, the latter referring to the Pharisees. In patristic Greek *akribēs* is used for the "scrupulousness" of ascetic life. See Lampe, *Patristic Greek Lexicon,* p. 64. It would seem that the name *perushim* was originally a positive term, used to describe the Pharisees, whether by themselves or by others, as being exacting and hence somewhat separatist in their study *and* observance of the Torah.

64. For two opposing views, see Jacob Neusner, *From Politics to Piety,* 2nd ed. (New York: Ktav, 1979); and Ellis Rivkin, *A Hidden Revolution: The Pharisees' Search for the Kingdom Within* (Nashville: Abingdon, 1978).

65. Jacob Neusner stresses the Pharisaic emphasis on purity. However, whether the Pharisees were defined by their preoccupation with purity or whether this was only one concern of theirs, part of a broader ethos, is difficult to know, given the paucity of unbiased witnesses. Purity was clearly a central element in the Essene ascetic discipline, as it was for Pythagorean asceticism.

66. Similarly, *Sifra Shemini* 12.4; *Sifra Qedoshim* 11.21; and *Lev. Rab.* 24.4: "Just as I [God] am Holy so too you be Holy. Just as I am *parush,* so too you be *perushim.*" The same sense can be found in *Sifra Qedoshim* 9.2, where the emphasis is on separation from the idolatrous nations and their ways. Similarly, *Sifre Deut.* 104; *y. Yebam.* 2.4 (3d); Rashi ad Lev 19:1. On sanctifying oneself by refraining from what is biblically permitted, usually taken to refer to sexual relations, see *b. Yebam.* 20a.

67. On Israel's having once been fit to eat holy things, see *Mek. Pisha* 1.

68. According to the Munich manuscript. The same tradition is found in *m. Sota* 9:15, with *perishut* in the printed editions but not in the chief manuscripts. Earlier in the

same mishnah we find: "When Rabban Gamaliel the Elder died, the honor of the Torah ceased, and purity and abstinence (*perishut*) died."

69. *y. Ber.* 9.7 (14b); *y. Soṭa* 5.7 (20c); *b. Soṭa* 22b. In *m. Soṭa* 3:4 *perishut* is positively referred to in the sense of sexual restraint, and then the "afflictions of the *perushim*" are mentioned negatively. The commentators take *perushim* here to refer to those people who adopt ascetic ways for this-worldly benefits. See Maimonides and the Meiri ad loc.

70. We saw much the same tension in Philo and noted a Stoic parallel (above, n. 50). The critique of excessive asceticism for one's own honor is a frequent theme of early Christian literature, in both the New Testament (sometimes directed against the Pharisees) and the writings of the church fathers (see Col 2:16–23; Matt 6; Luke 18:12; Origen, *Against Celsus* 5.49).

71. *T. Soṭa* 15.10–12; *b. Baba Batra* 60b.

72. E. Urbach argues that such abstinence was motivated by a desire to find alternatives to the Temple cult (see above, n. 25). The examples of the following note, and the text itself, suggest self-denial primarily as an expression of mourning or loss.

73. For instance, *t. Ta'anit* 3.11 forbids wine or meat during the meal preceding the fast day of the Ninth of Av (mourning the destruction of the Temple). Similarly, *b. Mo'ed Qat.* 23b stipulates abstention from meat and wine between death and burial. In *aggadah*, note *Mekilta of R. Simeon bar Yoḥai* ad Exod 18:27, in which the Rechabites are said to have been commanded to live abstinent lives in *anticipation* of the destruction of the Temple. *Gen. Rab.* 31.12 (and parallels) states that Noah and his family (and the animals) were forbidden sexual intercourse while in the ark and concludes in the name of R. Abin: "If you see poverty and famine come to the world, regard your wife as menstruous" (that is, abstain from sex). As *Tanḥuma Noaḥ* 17 (ed. Buber) has God say: "Can it be that while I angrily destroy the world you build?" The same text shows how Joseph abstained from procreation during the famine. Note, however, that according to one tradition, Noah continued his sexual abstinence after leaving the ark, which one rabbi views positively as a sign of holiness, and another views negatively.

74. The tension between an originally separatist, individualistic, and elitist *askēsis* and the desire of its adherents to exert influence and wield authority within a broader religious and social circle is well exemplified in the evolution of early Christian monastic asceticism. See especially Philip Rousseau, *Ascetics, Authority, and the Church in the Age of Jerome and Cassian.*

75. Note Maimonides's wavering position: *Moreh* 3.33, 48, 49; *Hilk. Talm. Tor.* 3.12; *Hilk. De'ot* 1.5; 3.1, 2; 6.1; *Mish. Tor. Ned.* 13.23–25; *Shemon. Peraq.* 4; *Mishnah Commentary, Avot* intro. 4; *Avot* 5:6; *Sanh.* 4:7. Similarly Judah Halevi, *Kuzari* 2.50; 3.1–7. Contrast Bahya Ibn Paquda, *Hovot ha-Levavot* 9. On Bahya's asceticism, see Allan Lazaroff, "Bahya's Asceticism," 11–38. On the penitential asceticism of the German pietists (*Hasidey Ashkenaz*), and its tensions, see Ivan G. Marcus, *Piety and Society: The Jewish Pietists of Medieval Germany.*

76. See also *Sifre Num.* 22; and later parallels, some of which are cited in the following notes.

77. See 1 Macc 3:47–51; Josephus *Antiquities* 19.6.1 § 294; *War* 2.15.1 §313; Acts 18:18; 21:23–24; *m. Nazir* 3:6; *y. Ber.* 7.2 (11b). A burial inscription that refers to members of a family as Nazirites has been uncovered; see N. Avigad, "The Burial-Vault of a Nazirite Family on Mount Scopus," *Israel Exploration Journal* 21 (1971) 185–200.

78. According to Josephus (*Antiquities* 4.4.4 §12), the Nazirite, at the completion of the vow, offers his or her dedicated hair in sacrifice, giving the shorn locks *to the priest.* On the priestly aspects of the Nazirite, see Jacob Milgrom, "Nazirite," *Encyclopaedia*

Judaica, 12:909–910. For the sanctity of the Nazirite compared to that of the high priest, see *m. Nazir* 7:1.

79. For negative views see *m. Ned.* 1:1; *t. Ned.* 1.1; *m. Nazir* 1:7; 2:3 (cf. *m. Ned.* 2:3); and sources cited in the following notes. For a positive view of the Nazirite, see *Sifre Zuṭa* 9.6: "Because he acts in an abstinent (*perishut*) and pure way he is called 'holy.' And furthermore, Scripture considers him equal to a prophet. . . ." For the connecting of the verb *nzr* ("dedicate") with *prsh* ("separate"), see *Sifra Zavim* 9:6; *Sifra Emor* 4.1; *Targum Onqelos* Lev 15:31.

80. *y. Ned.* 1.1 (36d). However, vows are also viewed positively: "Vows are a fence around abstinence (*perishut*)" (*m. Abot* 3:13). In other words, the successful fulfillment of vows strengthens one's ability to abstain (Maimonides). Both the Pharisees and the Essenes are said to have taken oaths quite seriously. See Josephus *Antiquities* 17.2.4 §42; *War* 2.8.6 §135; Matt 23:16–22.

81. Hence, the argument *a fortiori*. Similarly, in *b. Taʿanit* 11a Samuel extends the argument to *anyone* who undertakes a fast (*taʿanit*). In *b . B. Qam.* 91b our tradition is cited against one who rends his garments too much in mourning.

82. On this debate, whether all Nazirites are sinners or only impure ones (having rashly undertaken vows they could not keep), see *b. Ned.* 10a, tosafot, s.v. *kullan.*

83. On overcoming or converting one's impulse to do evil, see *Sifre Deut.* 33; *y. Soṭa* 5.7; *y. Sanh.* 2.3; *b. Qid.* 81b; *b. Yoma* 69b. Such examples notwithstanding, it may be said that the ascetic control of one's impulses does not occupy nearly as central a place in rabbinic asceticism as it does in Philo and Cynic and Stoic writers (or Maimonides). Penitential asceticism, however, is much more evident. See Moses Beer, "On Penances and Penitents in the Literature of *HaZaL*" *(Hebrew), Zion* 46 (1980–81) 159–81.

84. See also *t. Yebam.* 8.7; *Gen. Rab.* 34.14. On Moses' continence at Sinai (and before), see my discussion of Philo above, and *Sifre Num.* 99; *b. Yoma* 4b; *Avot de-Rabbi Nathan* 2, 9; *Gen. Rab.* 48.14; *Exod. Rab.* 19.3; 46.3; *b. Shab.* 87a; *Midr. Ps.* 146.4; *Zohar* 3.148a.

85. See *m. Ketub.* 5:6. The ideal of sexual continence is more often expressed in *aggadah,* whereas ordered sexuality is prescribed in the *halakhah.* Like the Essenes, who, according to Josephus, had celibate and marrying orders, the rabbis found a way to incorporate both types of sexual self-discipline. Yet the two remain in tension. Note *Midr. Ps.* 146.4, where the expression "he sets free the bound" (Ps 146:7) is interpreted in various ways to refer to the expectation of release from rules of abstinence in the world to come. According to one view God will then permit intercourse with a menstruant wife since the discipline of ordered sexuality will no longer be necessary, whereas according to another view intercourse will be altogether forbidden since the *shekhinah* (divine presence) will constantly dwell among humanity.

86. See *b. Yebam.* 20a: "Sanctify yourself in what is permitted to you." See *b. Shevu.* 18b; *b. Shab.* 53b.

87. Note Zipporah's bitterness at Moses' continence in *Sifre Num.* 99 and parallels. For abstinence and hardship in combination with Torah study, see *b. ʿEruv.* 54a; *b. Soṭa* 21b; *Avot de-Rabbi Nathan* 11; *m. Abot* 6:4, 5; *Sifre Deut.* 306. Cf. Eusebius's description of Origen's ascetic concentration on study in *Church History* 6.3.9–13.

88. On rabbinic fasting see S. Lowy, "The Motivation of Fasting in Talmudic Literature," *Journal of Jewish Studies* 9 (1958) 19–38. On the practice of regular fasting every Monday and Thursday see G. Alon in *Tarbiz* 4 (1932–33) 285–91.

89. A distinct tension can be discerned regarding the practice of fasting on the Sabbath. See Yitzhak D. Gilat, "On Fasting on the Sabbath" (Hebrew), *Tarbiz* 52 (1982) 1–16.

90. See above, n. 75.

91. For the important role of human will in the mishnaic law, see Jacob Neusner, *Judaism: The Evidence of the Mishnah (Chicago: University of Chicago Press, 1981)* 270–281. Human volition is especially central to Cynic and Stoic views of asceticism.

Bibliography

For general surveys of asceticism in various religious traditions the best place to begin is still the series of entries under "Asceticism" in *Encyclopedia of Religion and Ethics* (New York: Scribner, 1910) 2:63–111, even though the treatment of Jewish asceticism by A. E. Suffrin (pp. 97–99) is not satisfactory, since it, like most earlier treatments, tends to minimize (whether due to a positive or negative bias) the ascetic side of Judaism (see above, n. 5). For a survey whose presuppositions about asceticism (including its place in Judaism) are closer to my own, see M. Olphe-Galliard. For a more succinct survey, see Vööbus, "Asceticism," and for a still useful early attempt to develop a typology of asceticism, see Hardman.

Earlier efforts to rectify the prevailing view that asceticism is absent from or only aberrant within Judaism can be found in Montgomery; Bonsirven; Lazaroff; and Baer. For a more reserved approach to asceticism in ancient Judaism, see Urbach, "Ascesis." For ascetic aspects of Philo's philosophy and ethics, see Winston. On the asceticism of the Essenes and Dead Sea sectarians, see Black. Regarding the ascetic aspects of early rabbinic Judaism, no comprehensive treatment has yet been attempted. In addition to the differing perspectives of Baer and Urbach, further reading may include more detailed studies of specific areas in which ascetic tensions within Judaism are manifested, such as fasting: Lowy; Gilat. On ascetic tensions within medieval German Jewish pietism, see Marcus, and for asceticism in Bahya ibn Paquda, against the background of rabbinic Judaism and Islam, see Lazaroff.

Although a vast literature treats Western Christian asceticism, especially the phenomena of the Desert Fathers and subsequent monastic movements (a good place to start is Chitty), the social and phenomenological underpinnings of those phenomena and the comparative light they might shed on the ascetic aspects of ancient Judaism remain uncertain. See for now Rousseau; and Kretschmar. Recent study of Syrian Christian asceticism has pointed to even more suggestive analogues for the investigation of asceticism in ancient Judaism: see Vööbus, *History of Asceticism*, and Guillaumont. For the Greco-Roman background of ancient Jewish asceticism, an area in need of further investigation, a good place to begin would be Moore.

Baer, Yitzhak Fritz. *Yisra'el ba-'amim.* Jerusalem: Bialik Institute, 1955.

Black, Matthew. "The Tradition of Hasidaean-Essene Asceticism: Its Origins and Influence." In *Aspects du Judéo-Christianisme*, 19–33. Edited by M. Simon et al. Travaux du Centre d'Études Supérieures Specialisé d'Histoire des Religions de Strasbourg. Paris: Presses universitaires de France, 1965.

Bonsirven, Joseph. *Le Judaisme Palestinien au Temps de Jésus Christ*, 2:280-91. Paris: Beauchesne, 1935.

Chitty, D. J. *The Desert a City: An Introduction to the Study of Egyptian and Palestinian Monasticism under the Christian Empire.* Oxford: Blackwell, 1966.

Gilat, Yitzhak D. "On Fasting on the Sabbath" [Hebrew, with an English summary]. *Tarbiz* 52 (1982) 1-16.

Guillaumont, Antoine. "Monachisme et éthique judéo-chrétienne." In *Judéo-Christi-anisme: Recherches historiques et théologiques offertes en hommage au Cardinal Jean Danielou*, 199-218. Paris: Recherches de Science Religieuse, 1972.

Hardman, Oscar. *The Ideals of Asceticism: An Essay in the Comparative Study of Religion*. London: SPCK, 1924.

Kretschmar, Georg. "Ein Beitrag zur Frage nach dem Ursprung frühchristlicher Askese." *Zeitschrift für Theologie und Kirche* 64 (1961) 27-67.

Lazaroff, Allan, "Bahyā's Asceticism Against its Rabbinic and Islamic Background." *Journal of Jewish Studies* 21 (1970) 11-38.

Lowy, S. "The Motivation of Fasting in Talmudic Literature." *Journal of Jewish Studies* 9 (1958) 19-38.

Marcus, Ivan G. *Piety and Society: The Jewish Pietists of Medieval Germany*. Leiden: Brill, 1981.

Montgomery, James A. "Ascetic Strains in Early Judaism." *Journal of Biblical Literature* 51 (1932) 183-87.

Moore, Clifford Herschel. "Greek and Roman Ascetic Tendencies." In *Harvard Essays on Classical Subjects*, 97–140. Edited by H. W. Smyth. Boston: Houghton Mifflin, 1912.

Olphe-Gailliard, M. "Ascèse. Ascétisme: II. Development historique." In *Dictionnaire de spiritualité, ascétique, et mystique, doctrine et histoire*, 1:938–60. (Paris: Beauchesne, 1937).

Rousseau, Philip. *Ascetics, Authority, and the Church in the Age of Jerome and Cassian*. Oxford: Oxford University Press, 1978.

Urbach, Ephraim E. "Ascesis and Suffering in Talmudic and Midrashic Sources" [Hebrew]. In *Yitzhak F. Baer Jubilee Volume*, 48–68. Edited by S. W. Baron et al. Jerusalem: Historical Society of Israel, 1960. [Summarized in Urbach, *The Sages: Their Concepts and Beliefs*. Translated by I. Abrahams (Jerusalem: Magnes Press, 1975) 12, 443-48.

Vööbus, Arthur. "Asceticism." In *Encyclopaedia Britannica*, 2:135-37, 15th ed. (Chicago: Encyclopaedia Britannica, 1957).

———. *A History of Asceticism in the Syrian Orient*. 2 vols. Louvain: Corpus Christi-anorum Orientalium, 1958-60.

Winston, David. "Was Philo a Mystic?" In *Studies in Jewish Mysticism*, 15-39. Edited by Joseph Dan and Frank Talmage. New York: Ktav; Cambridge, MA: Association for Jewish Studies, 1982.

11

The Religious Experience of the *Merkavah*

Joseph Dan

Jewish Mystical Schools in Late Antiquity

THE APPEARANCE of Jewish mystical schools in late antiquity gave a new dimension to Jewish spirituality as expressed in the classical rabbinic works of the Talmud and Midrash. The mystical teachings of these schools are preserved in the Hekhalot and Merkavah literature, the accepted appellation of the earliest Jewish mystical writings, produced from the tannaitic (second century C.E.) to the late geonic period (tenth century). These works, written in Ereẓ Israel and in Babylonia, in Hebrew and Aramaic, describe in about twenty-five treatises the first mystical world view produced by Jewish culture.

When the main centers of Jewish culture moved to Europe in the tenth and eleventh centuries, there were Jewish scholars, poets, and philosophers who continued to describe the divine worlds in terms and symbols used by these ancient mystics, until, late in the twelfth century and the beginning of the thirteenth, the symbolism of the Hekhalot mystics was incorporated into the new systems of the emerging European schools of Jewish mysticism—the Kabbalah in southern France and northern Spain, and Ashkenazi Hasidism, the Jewish pietism of medieval Germany, especially in the Rhineland. Thus, for nearly a thousand years, Hekhalot and Merkavah mysticism was the dominant element in Jewish nonrationalistic spirituality. It flourished side by side with the great legal systems of Judaism, the Mishnah and the Talmuds of Ereẓ Israel and Babylonia, with the great schools of the Geonim, the heads of the legal academies in Babylonia, and the early Jewish philosophers and lawyers who shaped Jewish culture in medieval Europe.

In order to achieve such long-lasting impact on Jewish mystical thought, Hekhalot mysticism surely must have reflected deep-seated religious and spiritual needs of at least a select portion of the Jewish religious leadership. Indeed, as will be shown below, Hekhalot mysticism discovered in the Bible and in Jewish traditional religious sources a new dimension of inner experience, which enriched Jewish culture and religious practice. The following is a brief outline of the historical development, the major texts, and the mystical ideas found in the treatises of Hekhalot and Merkavah literature.

The celestial chariot (Hebrew: *merkavah*), described by the prophet Ezekiel in the first chapter of his book, seems to have been the subject of homiletical speculation long before the development of Jewish mysticism in the tannaitic period. Indeed, there is a suggestion that the book of Ezekiel itself includes passages that are interpretations of the first revelation of the divine chariot to the prophet. In tannaitic sources the speculation concerning and interpretation of various elements of the divine chariot is called *ma'aseh merkavah* and is regarded as an esoteric subject of homiletical interpretation (*midrash*). It is not surprising that the wonderful picture presented by Ezekiel, which described in vivid terms the hosts of angels, the celestial beasts, the wheels of the chariot, the clouds, the storm and the fire surrounding it, the divine glow (*nogah, hashmal*) observed emanating from it, and the many other elements of the divine revelation, intrigued Jewish commentators, who included the study of this chapter among other descriptions of divine visions and revelations as parts of the subject of *ma'aseh merkavah*.

Talmudic literature relates in some detail several homiletical discussions of the *merkavah,* but the esoteric nature of this subject is apparent in the fact that, although information is given concerning the specific circumstances of the sermon, little or nothing is revealed concerning the actual content of the midrash. It seems that Rabbi Yohanan ben Zakkai and his disciples, in the period immediately following the destruction of the Second Temple (70 C.E.), frequently dealt with speculation on Ezekiel's chariot, and the talmudic sources preserve detailed stories about the miracles that occurred on these occasions. Fire would descend from heaven and envelop the rabbis dealing with the divine chariot, and the trees and angels would somehow "participate" in the religious experience. These descriptions, however, are not essentially different from similar ones concerning homiletical commentaries on other subjects, and there is no reason whatsoever to conclude from them that the study of *ma'aseh merkavah* in these contexts is connected with mystical experience or mystical speculation. The *esoteric* character of this study is evident, and the sources include references to the severe results of improperly dealing with them; but there is no proof that mystical practice is involved here.

The same tannaitic sources also include elements of cosmological speculations connected with the homiletical interpretation of the first chapter of the book of Genesis, describing the creation. These speculations, also regarded as esoteric, are called in our sources *ma'aseh bereshit*, "the work of Genesis." The talmudic and midrashic sources usually present these speculations side by side with the homiletical references to Ezekiel's chariot, and it seems that they were combined into one system of esoteric speculation which included cosmology, cosmogony, and the celestial worlds into one secret whole, referred to in Ecclesiasticus's *nistarot*, which are above and below, in the past and in the future.

Some of the works of the Hekhalot and Merkavah literature belong to this exegetical-homiletical genre of *ma'aseh merkavah* and *ma'aseh bereshit*. The early descriptive-homiletical treatise known as *Re'uyot Yehezkel* (*The Visions of Ezekiel*) does not include any reference to active mystical experience; its main subject is the interpretation of Ezekiel's prophetic vision. According to this work, Ezekiel saw the divine chariot reflected in the waters of the river Kvar; he was looking at the reflected sky in the river when the skies opened and in them he saw the chariot, the angels, the holy beasts, the wheels, the rainbow; then the sky which was above this vision opened as well, and in it he saw a second chariot, throne, angels, etc., and so on until the seventh chariot in the seventh sky—all reflected in the river's waters. There is no doubt that the circle from which this work originated dealt with radical, innovative exegesis of *ma'aseh merkavah*, but no clear mystical element, in the proper sense, can be attributed to this activity.

A similar attitude can be found in one of the most important works of this literature—*Sefer ha-Razim* (*The Book of Mysteries*). This work, parts of which were known throughout the Middle Ages and modern times, was reconstructed with the assistance of newly identified genizah fragments by M. Margaliot. It contains seven chapters, each dedicated to a detailed description of the divine hosts in each of the seven firmaments in the manner of *ma'aseh merkavah* homiletics. The first chapter is dedicated to the lowest firmament, and each chapter ascends one step higher. *Sefer ha-Razim* is essentially a book of magical formulas; it lists the names of the divine powers and archangels and provides detailed magical recipes for how they can be made to fulfill the wishes of the user, wishes that include victory in war, protection from thieves, persuading a king to grant one's requests, and even love potions. The magical incantations included in this book contain many Greek terms and symbols, and even a prayer to Helios can be found, which reflects a Hellenistic Jewish syncretism.

These magical instructions are concentrated in the first chapter and the second, and their role diminishes as the author ascends from one heaven to another. In the seventh chapter, which describes the seventh and highest firmament, there is no magical element; it is a pure *ma'aseh merkavah* homiletical description. It seems therefore that *Sefer ha-Razim* represents one trend in the development of *ma'aseh merkavah* speculations: the employment of the esoteric knowledge of the divine chariot and its surroundings for magical purposes. No element of mysticism proper can be found in this work, and mysticism is absent from other magical treatises in Hekhalot literature as well, including *Harba de-Mosheh* (*The Sword of Moses*), a later collection of magical formulas, or the *Havdalah of Rabbi Akiba*, recently published by Gershom Scholem.

It seems, therefore, that we must conclude that the ancient tradition of speculation on and exegesis of Ezekiel's vision produced in the talmudic period several schools whose teachings are reflected in the literature that has reached us. One continued the homiletical interpretation of the biblical vision in an esoteric manner; another used the same material to assist in the development of magical formulas and practices; and one—the most important for our subject—produced a mystical system.

From Speculation to Experience

The appearance of Jewish mysticism in the talmudic period occurred, so it seems, *when active mystical ascent to the divine world replaced passive homiletical speculation in the midrashic manner concerning the chariot envisioned by Ezekiel.* This transition from interpretation to mystical activity marks the first stage in the development of Jewish mysticism, which continued for many centuries and eventually influenced the appearance of the major school of Jewish mysticism in medieval Christian Europe—the Kabbalah. The transition from the midrash of *ma'aseh merkavah* to the mysticism of the *yordey ha-merkavah* ("the descenders to the chariot") signifies a most meaningful and influential new departure in the history of Jewish spirituality.

The historical details concerning this radical change are not known to us, nor do we know the names of the early mystics who were responsible for this transition. There are, however, several sources that can be attributed to the tannaitic period which seem to indicate that this change occurred in or around the school of Rabbi Akiba ben Yosef, in the first third of the second century C.E. These indications include two new elements that were added to the traditional midrash of *ma'aseh merkavah:* the ascent to the divine world, and a new, radical understanding of the Song of Songs as a self-portrait of God.

The first indication of a new concept, that of possible ascent to the divine world and the viewing of its secrets, is found in the well-known parable of the four scholars who entered the *pardes* (literally, "the orchard"). This story, in its shortest and probably authentic version in the *tosefta,* relates that four scholars entered the *pardes:* Ben Zoma who "peeked" and died, Ben Azai who "peeked" and was hurt (usually understood to mean "went out of his mind"), Elisha ben Avuya, the famous heretic known as Aḥer, "the Other," who "cut off the shoots," usually understood as a reference to a grave sin or heresy, and Rabbi Akiba, who "entered in peace and came out in peace."

This obscure tale has been a celebrated subject of scholarship in the last century and a half, and its interpretations by scholars have differed radically. The two extreme positions in contemporary scholarship were expressed by G. Scholem and E. E. Urbach. Scholem suggested that this parable is a brief statement related to a much more detailed description of the mystical ascent of Rabbi Akiba to the celestial palaces, the *hekhalot,* as found in the mystical work *Hekhalot Zutarti, (The Lesser Book of Hekhalot).* According to him, this esoteric parable is a reflection of the developed practice of descent to the chariot as found in Hekhalot mysticism. Urbach insisted that this passage in the *tosefta* does not include any specific information concerning the content of the mystical experience and should be regarded as an opaque parable. Urbach did not accept the usual interpretation of the *pardes* as related to "paradise," a relation that led many scholars, including Scholem, to compare this passage to the traditions concerning Paul's ascension to paradise. According to him, the *pardes* is a part of the usual rabbinic format of parables about kings and their palaces and gardens.

Even if we accept only the minimalist conclusions of Urbach, the parable still indicates that Rabbi Akiba and his three contemporaries engaged in a mystical journey full of physical and religious dangers and that only Rabbi Akiba completed it successfully, spiritually and physically unhurt. Urbach is undoubtedly correct in stressing that the *tosefta* parable itself does not include any specific information concerning the nature of the experience and that it does not mention even one term that can connect it directly with the current homiletics concerning the first chapter of Ezekiel. It is quite clear, however, that the parable denotes a novel religious phenomenon, one closely connected with Rabbi Akiba and his generation. The story itself, as presented in the *tosefta* does not include any Hekhalot mystical terminology, and Scholem's suggestion cannot be regarded as proved. In other versions of the story in talmudic literature, especially that of the Babylonian Talmud, there are clear references to ideas and terms that are found in the Hekhalot books, but they may have been later additions to the original text.

The minimal conclusion, that a new, mystical experience did occur in the circle of Rabbi Akiba, is strengthened when we connect this parable with the other new group of ideas that emerged in that school, based on the new interpretation of the Song of Songs. In all versions of the *pardes* parable a biblical verse is quoted as explaining the fate of each of the four scholars. The verse applied to Rabbi Akiba is from the Song of Songs, "and the King brought me to his chambers." The "chambers" of the chariot and of heaven often appear in Hekhalot literature. But the connection between Rabbi Akiba and this book of the Bible does not end here. S. Lieberman has dedicated a penetrating study to this subject. It was Rabbi Akiba, in a mishnaic source, who claimed that the Song of Songs was the holiest book in the Bible—a strange conclusion indeed when the apparent content of the work is taken into consideration. Rabbi Akiba claimed in another source that the Song of Songs was "given" to Israel on Mount Sinai, together with the Pentateuch, using the same terminology that describes the "giving" of the Torah to the people of Israel. Therefore, the author of the book can hardly be King Solomon, the son of David, who lived many centuries after the giving of the Torah. Rather "Solomon" must refer to "the king who owns peace," God Himself, a literal interpretation of the name "Solomon" (*shelomoh*).

We do not have any indication of such an attitude toward the Song of Songs before Rabbi Akiba. It is possible to assume, therefore, that these two new phenomena are connected, namely, the ascent to the divine world and the new approach to the Song of Songs. In order to understand this connection we must turn to the concept of God as expressed in Hekhalot mysticism.

The most important text of Hekhalot mysticism, as far as the concept of God is concerned, is the treatise known as *Shi'ur Qomah* (*The Measurement of the Height* of the divine figure). This ancient treatise, which is attributed in our texts to Rabbi Akiba and Rabbi Ishmael ben Elisha, "The High Priest," is one of the most radical expressions in Hebrew literature of an anthropomorphic concept of God, and it caused great embarrassment to medieval Jewish thinkers who had to explain how it was possible that the authors of the Mishnah could have produced such a seemingly crude, anthropomorphic work. This brief treatise includes three lists: a list of the limbs of the divine figure—crown, forehead, beard, neck, eyes, hands, fingers, etc.; a list of the names of these limbs–in most cases incomprehensible, long sequences of Hebrew letters which are not combined into recognizable words; and a list of the measurements of these limbs, given in tens of millions of parasangs. It is quite evident that even though details of this divine figure are given only in the *Shi'ur Qomah,* other Hekhalot texts, when referring to God, relate to the same enormous figure that is described, named, and measured in this treatise.

Gershom Scholem has pointed out the fact that the anthropomorphism of the *Shi'ur Qomah* is based upon an understanding of the Song of Songs, especially those verses that describe in detail the male figure in the biblical work. Medieval mystics also seem to have known this connection between the Song of Solomon and the description of God in ancient Jewish mysticism. Scholem has suggested that this esoteric meaning of the Song of Songs was already known to Origen early in the third century and that when he spoke of the esoteric interpretation of this biblical work by the Jews of his time he meant the ideas incorporated in the *Shi'ur Qomah.* The evidence from talmudic and midrashic literature collected by S. Lieberman seems to support the possibility that the ideas of the *Shi'ur Qomah* originated in the tannaitic period, in the late second century C.E.

The appearance of the *Shi'ur Qomah* is not dependent on the earlier, traditional *ma'aseh merkavah* speculation. It is the result of a new understanding of the Song of Songs and of a mystical attempt to understand—and possibly to reach—the divine world by mystical means. The *Shi'ur Qomah* itself uses very little material that is based on the homiletical interpretation of Ezekiel's visions. Other Hekhalot mystical texts, especially *Hekhalot Rabbati* and *Hekhalot Zutarti* (The Greater and the Lesser Books of Hekhalot), combine the image of the *Shi'ur Qomah* figure sitting upon the celestial throne of glory in the seventh heavenly palace with the tradition of exegetical interpretation of the various elements of the *merkavah* descriptions.

The divine figure in the *Shi'ur Qomah* is called *Yozrenu* or *Yozer Bereshit,* that is, the Creator. The text of the *Shi'ur Qomah* itself does not denote clearly that the Creator is a separate figure from the supreme Godhead and that the anthropomorphic figure in the seventh palace is a demiurgic power standing beside God but not identical with Him. It is possible that such a view existed among the early Jewish mystics, but the school or schools of the writers of Hekhalot literature that has reached us objected to this view and suppressed it.

The relationship between the *Shi'ur Qomah* and the Song of Songs verses that describe the physical body of the Lover needs clarification. When the *Shi'ur Qomah* is read within the framework of medieval or modern concepts of God, the anthropomorphic descriptions seem to be crude and offensive. It is doubtful, however, that the author of this work had any such purpose or that this impression reflects the historical meaning of the ancient concept of God. The measurements of the various limbs of the Creator given in this treatise are given in units of *'alfey revavot*—thousands of tens of thousands of parasangs. The text itself gives the key to the meaning of these figures. Every parasang is three miles; every mile is two thousand *'amot* (feet); every *'amah* is three *zeratot* (fingers). This means that the basic unit of measurement is 180 billion "fingers." The author, however, states clearly: each "finger" is from one end of the world to the other end.

It is quite clear that the mystics who evolved this concept of the divine figure did not intend to describe it in measurements that could be understood by human beings; quite to the contrary, they presented a picture which, in its time and place, was completely beyond human comprehension. What for a medieval philosopher would seem to be a crude anthropomorphic picture was in fact an attempt to demonstrate the distance between human terms and divine terms, by using these huge, astronomical numbers. It is probable that the same attitude is found also in the *Shi'ur Qomah*'s list of names for the limbs of the Creator: the incomprehensible lists of letters denote the distance between these limbs and human understanding rather than bringing them closer to human terms, in language as in numbers.

It is possible to assume that the *Shi'ur Qomah* mystical speculation is a polemical answer to the simplistic interpretation of the Song of Songs as a divine self-portrait. The reader of the biblical book may learn from the text that God has a neck, hands, and feet, but the *Shi'ur Qomah* explains that His hands are not like human hands because of their astronomical size and incomprehensible names, and the same is true for all other limbs. In truly ironic fashion, this early mystical attempt to remove simplistic anthropomorphic notions of the Song of Songs, seen as given by God on Mount Sinai, was misread by later generations as the very epitome of crude anthropomorphism.

It is possible to conclude from this analysis that there were, in fact, three distinct phases in the emergence of ancient Jewish mysticism in the talmudic period. The first, representing a group of sources rather than a mystical endeavor, was the *ma'aseh merkavah* speculation in a homiletical manner. The second was the appearance of the new interpretation of the Song of Songs, coupled with the esoteric practice of the "entrance to the *pardes*," at the time of Rabbi Akiba. And the third, represented by the *Shi'ur Qomah* and other Hekhalot texts, combined the earlier material into a mystical system of the ascent to the divine palaces.

The Ascent in the Hekhalot Literature

Two detailed descriptions of a mystical ascent to the divine chariot have reached us—that of Rabbi Akiba, included in the work known as *Hekhalot Zutarti* (*The Lesser Book of Hekhalot*) and that of Rabbi Ishmael, presented in *Hekhalot Rabbati* (*The Greater Book of Hekhalot*), which is the most extensive and detailed extant book of Hekhalot literature. Other works contain many references to the practice of the ascension to the chariot, especially *Sefer Hekhalot,* known also as the Hebrew book of Enoch or *3 Enoch,* and the treatise published by G. Scholem under the title "*Ma'aseh Merkavah.*"

The two ascensions, those of Rabbi Akiba and Rabbi Ishmael, are described in a similar manner, and there is some material in key sections that is common to both. The problem of which of these two is the original version is a most complicated one. It seems to me that the balance of evidence will tend to show that the description of the ascension in *Hekhalot Zutarti* is the earlier one, because it does not contain as much legendary and mythical material as the *Hekhalot Rabbati* version contains.

Both treatises are based on a story: *Hekhalot Zutarti* retells the talmudic story of the four sages who entered the *pardes,* including most of the narrative material added in the later talmudic versions; *Hekhalot Rabbati* presents the story of the ten martyrs, the legend about the sufferings of ten sages who were executed by the Roman emperor, probably following the Bar Kokhba rebellion. In the detailed description of Rabbi Akiba's ascension, nothing can be found that conflicts with the accepted talmudic account, whereas *Hekhalot Rabbati* contains many elements that are unacceptable to the usual talmudic chronology and history. These elements include the list of the ten martyrs, who could not have died together and whose deaths are described in talmudic sources in a different manner. *Hekhalot Rabbati* includes the description of the Hekhalot mystics living and practicing in Jerusalem, around the Temple, but many of the sages mentioned were born after the destruction of the Temple. Rabbi Ishmael himself is introduced in this treatise as a "high priest the son of high priest," a completely legendary description. Furthermore, although we know from talmudic sources that Rabbi Akiba was connected with the various mystical practices and beliefs mentioned above, nothing in the traditional sources hints at Rabbi Ishmael's involvement in such matters, and the whole picture seems to be mythical. Rabbi Nehunia ben ha-Kanah, who is described in *Hekhalot Rabbati* as Rabbi Ishmael's teacher and the head of the circle of mystics, is not mentioned in talmudic sources in such a context at all. It seems, therefore, that *Hekhalot Zutarti* contains the earliest version that we have of a mystical ascent.

The term *hekhalot* itself cannot be found in the *ma'aseh merkavah* homiletical material, and it may be the innovation of the circle of mystics who developed the *Shi'ur Qomah* speculation and the new interpretation of the Song of Songs. Whereas earlier speculations emphasized the seven heavens that contain seven chariots, in *Hekhalot Zutarti* and later sources the seven celestial palaces are the basic structural element of the divine realm. The Hebrew term *hekhal* may refer either to the temple or to a king's palace, and it seems that in the Hekhalot books the emphasis is on the palace rather than the temple (following, probably, the Song of Songs metaphor). The main task of the mystic is to ascend from one palace to another, until he reaches the seventh and highest, where the divine figure, described in the *Shi'ur Qomah,* is seated on the throne of glory. Most of the material concerning this ascent in the *Hekhalot Zutarti* is concerned with the dangers that the mystic encounters on his way (based on the tragic fate of the three sages in the talmudic story of the *pardes*), and the ways in which these can be overcome.

The elements of "king" and "palace" are the dominant ones: each celestial palace has a gate, and a group of archangels guards every gate. In order to enter, the mystic must overcome increasing opposition of these guards, which becomes more powerful as the ascent continues. He must be familiar with the names of these guards, a knowledge that gives him magical powers over them. He must be equipped with special "seals," probably esoteric divine names, which constitute permissions to proceed, and he has to undergo several tests, which prove that his character as well as ancestry allow him to be included among the select few who see "The King in His Beauty." The text does not mince words when describing the cruel fate of those who fail the tests and prove themselves unworthy to proceed.

Rabbi Akiba's successful mystical ascension is concluded when he faces the divine figure, whose most esoteric names are nothing but the anthropomorphic verses in the Song of Songs 5:10–16, which serve as a basis for the *Shi'ur Qomah* description. He can then ask anything he wishes, and it seems that even in this highest stage of mystical achievement the magical element is not absent: God cannot refuse the request—even if it is of earthly needs—of the ascender who reaches the seventh palace. This journey, including the names of God, the names of the guards and their functions, and the description of the obstacles to be overcome, became the basic description of a mystical experience not only for the Hekhalot literature; its impact on later Jewish mysticism, up to and including the modern Hasidim of the eighteenth century, was enormous.

A central element of the mystical experience described in *Hekhalot Zutarti* and other sources is the hymns—those sung by the mystic himself on his journey and those which he hears the various classes of angels sing in the various palaces and around the throne of glory. Although *Hekhalot Zutarti* contains only a few such hymns, *Hekhalot Rabbati* presents many; and other Hekhalot works, especially the *Ma'aseh Merkavah* text, constitute anthologies of such early Hebrew mystical poetry. Some of these hymns are based on traditional Jewish prayers, and others were included in the prayer book by editors who took them from the vast anthology of Hekhalot literature.

Rabbi Ishmael's ascension to the chariot is described as an answer to an immediate necessity: the circle of mystics received the information that the Roman emperor was about to execute ten sages as a retribution for the sin of Jacob's ten sons when they sold their brother Joseph to slavery in Egypt. Rabbi Nehunia ben ha-Kanah did not know whether this decision was a whim of the emperor or a divine decree. If it were just a whim, the great magicians would have had no difficulty in annulling it, as, according to *Hekhalot Rabbati*, one of them had done on another occasion. Rabbi Nehunia, therefore, sent "the least of his disciples," Rabbi Ishmael, to the celestial palaces to investigate the background of the emperor's decision. *Hekhalot Rabbati* is an account of this mystical journey, but only a small part is dedicated to the actual immediate problem. Most of the book is a description of the palaces, of the ways in which the mystical ascent can be achieved, and of the hymns that Rabbi Ishmael heard during his ascent.

One passage in this work reveals more than others the actual concept of Hekhalot literature concerning mystical experience. When the information from Rome concerning the martydom of the ten sages first reached the circle of mystics, Rabbi Nehunia himself was "ascending to the chariot." He had to be called back immediately, so that the news could be told and a decision made. According to this description, Rabbi Nehunia's body was lying lifeless on earth, and his soul had to be called from the celestial realm to which it had departed and rejoined with the body.

This was done by Rabbi Nehunia's disciples in a complicated way. They made their teacher's body touch a piece of cloth to which the least suspicion —in fact, unjustified suspicion—of uncleanliness was attached. This suspicion was enough for Rabbi Nehunia to have to withdraw from the divine realm, but it was not enough to designate him as ritually unclean and thus make him the victim of the wrath of the angels. It is evident, therefore, that the Hekhalot mystics regarded their experiences as involving an actual departure of the soul from the body, the physical part remaining on earth while the spirit ascended to the divine chariot. Dreams or visions in the regular sense are not mentioned in this context; the experience is one of a complete departure of the mystic's spirit from its physical enclosure and its free roaming among the divine palaces.

The truth concerning the Roman emperor's decree, which is revealed to Rabbi Ishmael, is apocalyptic in nature. God did give permission to the archangel of Rome, Samael, to execute the ten martyrs because of the ancient sin of Joseph's brothers. However, Samael achieved this only by agreeing that in return Rome itself would be completely destroyed; all its people, beasts, and even precious metals would disintegrate, and the world would be freed of its yoke. The martyrdom, according to the concept of these mystics, was a welcome sacrifice for the achievement of a great mission—the destruction of the center of all evil and the freedom of Jews from Roman persecutions.

The Ascent and Transformation of Enoch

Sefer Hekhalot, or the Hebrew book of Enoch, is dedicated to the description of a different kind of mystical ascent. Its two opening chapters relate the ascension of Rabbi Ishmael to the palaces in a way similar to that described in *Hekhalot Rabbati,* but the manner of the presentation seems to denote that this practice was regarded as commonplace and usual—therefore told very briefly. The next thirteen chapters of this treatise describe the ancient ascension of Enoch, the son of Yared, the biblical hero who did not die, "for God had taken him" (Gen 5:24). Enoch, who was the hero of an ascent story in the literature of the Second Commonwealth period, has become in this work the archangel Metatron, the "Prince of the Countenance," a divine power second only to God himself.

According to this text, Enoch was chosen by God to serve as a witness for the sins of the human race which brought about the deluge. The divine power Anafiel was sent to earth to bring him up to the divine realm to reside there and prove that the harsh decision of God concerning the deluge was justified. But when he ascended, a process of transformation began during which Enoch became Metatron.

Twelve chapters of this treatise describe the process of the transformation of this human being into a supreme divine power. Enoch's flesh was turned into fire, his dimensions grew until they became *Shi'ur Qomah* dimensions, wings of fire grew around him, his body became full of eyes, a fiery garment was put around him, and he rode a chariot of fire driven by fiery horses.

But above all he received divine knowledge; he knew every secret above and below, including the secrets of the process of creation. He became the supreme leader of all the archangels, who bowed before him. According to this work, Elisha ben Avuya, the great heretic, ascended to the chariot and saw Enoch-Metatron sitting on a throne of glory surrounded by all the divine rulers of the nations. Mistakenly thinking Metatron to be a power equal to God Himself, the heretic declared: "There are two powers in heaven." In order to prevent the repetition of such a mistake God again sent Anafiel to Metatron to give him sixty lashes of fire in order to prove who is Master and who is His servant.

The body of the work, after these first fifteen chapters, is dedicated to the detailed description of the celestial realm as given to Rabbi Ishmael by Metatron. This is the most elaborate description of the seven Hekhalot, the archangels, the throne of glory, and the chariot in ancient Jewish mystical literature. There is a possibility that this part of the treatise is in fact an anthology of material gathered from many sources, some of them unknown to us, and presented by an unknown ancient editor as revelations transmitted by Rabbi Ishmael.

The figure of Metatron is central in ancient Jewish mysticism, even though he is not mentioned in some of the ancient texts, including *Hekhalot Rabbati* (where the chief angel is called Soria). The possibility that Metatron represents a demiurgic figure was obvious to many scholars who studied this mysterious figure, and there is an impressive body of evidence to support such a conclusion, not only in Hekhalot literature and midrashic material but also in non-Jewish gnostic sources. It seems quite possible that ancient Jewish mysticism did believe in a secondary divine power which assisted God in the process of creation. If so, it is easier to understand the background of this bizarre myth of the transformation of Enoch into Metatron. If Metatron was originally Enoch son of Yared, he can be a supreme divine power in the present but he certainly could not have had any function in the process of creation, which took place before he was born. This treatise, *Sefer Hekhalot* or the Hebrew book of Enoch, can be understood as an antidualistic polemical work that was intended to remove any possibility of belief in a second demiurgic power, just as our *Shi'ur Qomah* can be understood as an antianthropomorphic polemical work. It seems quite probable that the works of Hekhalot mysticism that have reached us are a second, conservative layer of mystical speculation, which hides a previous, more radical one, that believed in Metatron as a demiurge and in the literal understanding of Song of Songs verses as actual descriptions of the physical appearance of God.

Sefer Hekhalot also includes a list, the "Seventy names of Metatron," a document that can serve as an example for the process of the editing of this treatise. The list, which appears also in the great anthology of ancient Jewish mystical material compiled probably in the geonic period, *The Alphabet of Rabbi Akiba*, and later was published in a special treatise with an Ashkenazi-Hasidic commentary under the title *Sefer ha-Hesheq*, includes in its various recensions between ninety and ninety-four names; yet it is constantly described as the "seventy names of Metatron." It seems that an ancient list of divine names, which the Hekhalot mystics inherited from previous Jewish mystical traditions, was adopted into the *Sefer Hekhalot* framework as the list of the seventy names of Enoch-Metatron, without even an explanation of the difference in the number of elements in it.

Whereas the *Shi'ur Qomah* traditions represent the theological aspect of mystical ascension in those circles, *Sefer Hekhalot* denotes the existence of cosmogonical and cosmological speculations among the ancient Jewish mystics. In these speculations the figure of Metatron, probably under different names, was central, and the texts clearly denote the existence of a body of secrets concerning the process of creation. Some of the ancient mystical works that have reached us deal with these secrets in detail.

Sefer Yezirah: An Early Speculative Text

The most famous text of ancient Jewish mysticism—and probably the one least understood—is the *Sefer Yezirah* (*The Book of Creation*), which was written, as far as we can know today, about the fourth century. This work is enigmatic because it is very brief, and it contains a unique terminology, no parallel to which exists anywhere in midrashic or Hekhalot literature. *Sefer Yezirah* is a book that deals with cosmogony and cosmology, often with a scientific attitude, though some mystical elements can be discovered in it and some of its passages reveal a connection with Hekhalot mysticism.

The central idea of *Sefer Yezirah* is based on an old Jewish tradition. According to the first paragraph of this treatise, God created the world by using thirty-two "mystical paths of wisdom," which are the twenty-two letters of the Hebrew alphabet and the ten basic numbers, called in this work *sefirot*. The belief that the creation was the result of ten *ma'amarot* ("utterances") is based on a count of God's utterances in the first chapter of Genesis; this is found in the Mishnah itself. *Sefer Yezirah* continued in this direction, developing an original linguistic terminology to explain the process of creation by the hidden powers of the Hebrew language.

Creation, according to *Sefer Yezirah,* is the result of the action of God by thirty-two mystical "paths" (*netivot peli'ot*), which represent the twenty-two letters of the Hebrew alphabet, to which the author of *Sefer Yezirah* adds ten more principles, which are called *sefirot belimah*. This enigmatic term was adopted eight centuries later by the Kabbalists, who used it to denote the ten divine hypostases of the Godhead in their medieval gnostic concept of the pleroma. *Sefer Yezirah* itself, of course, does not know about any such concept, and the meaning of the term has to be decided according to the meager context offered by the ancient work itself.

It is quite certain that the *Sefer Yezirah* includes more than one meaning for the term *sefirot*. In the opening paragraph, which describes the mystical paths of creation, this term seems to denote nothing more than the ten first numbers. Later on in the first chapter the characteristics of these *sefirot* are described, and it seems that the author expresses by them his cosmological view, according to which there are five dimensions, or ten directions, of the infinite expansion of the cosmos in the divine plan. The ten *sefirot* are the six directions of space (up, down, north, south, east, west), the two directions of time (beginning, end), and a fifth dimension called here "good" and "evil." These ten directions are infinite, as expressed by the term *'omeq*, endless depth, which is added to each *sefirah*. According to this, it seems that the ten *sefirot* represent the expansion of the universe, and the twenty-two letters are the actual means by which specific beings were created. It is as if God, according to *Sefer Yezirah*, created the world using a typewriter—twenty-two letters and ten numbers.

Later in the book, however, the *sefirot* are discussed again, and this time only four are mentioned, even though their number is restated as ten ("ten and not eleven, ten and not nine"). The four *sefirot* represent the evolution of the elements from the divine realm. The first is the Spirit of the Living God (*ruah 'elohim hayyim*); the second, the appearance of air, or wind (*ruah*), from the divine being. The third is the evolution of the element of water from the air or wind, and the fourth, the appearance of fire from the water. Obviously the author did not recognize earth as a fourth element, and he explains it by the thesis that earth is a form of snow, which is derived from water, and thus is not an independent element. The text provides no answer to the question of the meaning of the other six *sefirot* in this system (the notion that the six directions of space should be added has no basis in the work itself though it is frequently mentioned by scholars). The central number has changed in this presentation from ten to three, and it is possible that these three elements represent the "central" *sefirot*, as the three letters *aleph*, *mem*, and *shin* (associated also with air, water, and fire) are the "mothers" (*'imot*) of the twenty-two letters of the alphabet.

Another aspect of the *sefirot* in this brief treatise is their mystical significance. In a short passage the author associates the ten *sefirot* with various elements of the description of the holy chariot in Ezekiel 1 and states that the ten *sefirot* have "an appearance like that of lightning," that is, they can be seen, at least in a mystical way. The *sefirot*, therefore, have a cosmological aspect as the dimensions of the universe, a cosmogonical aspect in the development of the elements, and a mystical one as part of the vision of Ezekiel's chariot.

It should be noted that the *Sefer Yezirah* does not discuss in any way the process of creation as described in the first chapter of Genesis. There is no reference to the creation of heaven or earth, of beasts or human beings. It seems that the purpose of this work is to explain what is missing in the biblical chapter: the creation of wind, water, and fire, unmentioned in Genesis; the vast space of the cosmos; and generally the situation prior to the ten utterances of God, by which the earth and all that is on it were brought forth. In this sense the treatise can be construed as explaining the meaning of the enigmatic biblical term *tohu wa-vohu*, ("null and void"), which in Genesis refers to what was before the process of creation started.

The theory of language presented by the *Sefer Yezirah* is very complicated, and it is deeply connected by the author to universal processes, to the meaning of time, and to human psychology and the nature of the soul. The ancient writer understood the Hebrew language to be derived from a set of roots, each of two letters (unlike the Arabic grammar which was adopted by Jewish linguists in the Middle Ages, according to which every word is derived from a root of three letters). Thus, a rather small number of roots (231 possible combinations of two of the twenty-two letters, called in the treatise "the gates of the wheel") is the source of all existence, and there exists at least a hint that the knowledge of these roots and their combinations can be used in order to repeat the divine process of creation. The power to create is inherent within the language and, when used in the proper way, can be employed for the purpose of creation. The Talmud tells the story of two fourth-century sages who created a calf using *hilkhot yezirah* ("the rules of creation"), and it is very difficult to decide whether there is here an ancient reference to our text. In the Middle Ages and modern times the *Sefer Yezirah* was supposedly used by mystics and magicians in order to create a homunculus, a *golem*.

Sefer Yezirah, together with some other works and sections of works dealing with cosmology and cosmogony (the most important other work is *Seder Rabba de-Bereshit*, which consists of detailed descriptions of the creation of heaven and earth, the realms of the chariot and the angels, and also of the celestial Garden of Eden and of hell), represents the ancient

Jewish mystics' deep interest in the search for the origins and laws of existence, expressions of the hidden powers of God which were revealed in creation. In almost all these texts and fragments it is very difficult to distinguish categorically between the "work of the chariot" and the "work of genesis." Common terminology, as well as similar attitudes, can be found, even though there are important differences. Ancient Jewish mysticism saw the mystical powers of God not only in the celestial realm of the *merkavah* but also in the cosmos itself, in its intrinsic structure and countless manifestations. Science and mysticism were not antagonistic or mutually exclusive for these mystics; they believed that exploration of the meaning of the universe could serve also to approach the secrets of the Godhead, which produced a comprehensive, though hardly systematic, mystical world view. Many elements of this world view remained alive for several centuries and were used by the medieval mystics, the founders of the Kabbalah and the Ashkenazi Hasidic movements in the second half of the twelfth century, to create their systems of mystical symbols, the basis of medieval Jewish mysticism.

The Magical Element in Early Jewish Mysticism

Cosmology and mysticism are not the only two elements combined in ancient Jewish mystical texts. Another major dimension of this literature is represented by the works of magic included in it. The interest in magic was indeed a central one for the Hekhalot mystics. In *Hekhalot Zutarti,* when Rabbi Akiba has successfully passed through the various gates, presented all the "seals"—thus overcoming the wrath of the guardian angels— and is at last in the presence of God Himself sitting on the throne of glory in the seventh *hekhal,* the author of the text gives Rabbi Akiba's words as a magical formula. In effect he states that anyone who reaches this stage can now ask for whatever he wishes, and his request must be answered by God. The redactor of this text did not feel a contradiction between the maximal achievement of mystical unity with God at the peak of the process of ascension and the presentation of a magical demand. Similarly, the redactor or editor of *Hekhalot Rabbati* saw no wrong in opening this work, which describes the mystical ascension of Rabbi Ishmael the High Priest, with two chapters describing the supernatural powers of the "descenders to the chariot," their ability to overcome their enemies and their mastery of the magic arts.

The magical literature included in Hekhalot literature is extensive and includes purely magical works like the *Harba de Mosheh* (*The Sword of Moses*), the *Havdalah of Rabbi Akiba,* mainly dedicated to charms and formulas against the evil powers that operate during the week after the Sabbath, and the *Hakarat Panim we-Sidrey Sirtutin,* dedicated to psycho-gnomical and chiromantical analysis of the character and fate of a person according to the lines of his forehead and hands.

Sometimes magic and mysticism are so closely connected that it is nearly impossible to separate them, as in the practice of the revelation of the Prince of the Torah, the divine power that teaches sacred learning without effort and makes the student unable to forget what he has learned. Hekhalot literature includes a series of formulas and holy names that enable the mystic to make the Prince of the Torah appear before him. In a late treatise appended to *Hekhalot Rabbati* in printed editions and in some manuscripts we find a story about the revelation of this power to the builders of the Second Temple in Jerusalem after the exile in Babylonia, where the revelation of this secret is described as a theophany greater than those which had occurred during the period of the First Temple. There is no doubt that the author of this treatise regarded the process of calling upon the Prince of the Torah as a mystical and not a magical one, even though the origin of the process might have been a magical mnemonic practice.

Ancient Jewish mysticism presents, therefore, a variegated and extensive mystical world view. Besides the purely mystical process of the ascension to the divine chariot, the authors of this literature regarded the secret of Genesis, the construction of the world, the Hebrew alphabet, the names of celestial powers and the holy names of God Himself, and earthly magical practices as one whole, one mystical attitude and way of life. Cosmogony and cosmology, anthropology and psychology, join magic on the one hand and *halakhah* and the study of the Torah on the other, to become building blocks of this new spiritual enthusiasm, which the awakening of Jewish mysticism in the talmudic era brought about.

The historical relationship between rabbinic Judaism and the circles of mystics has not yet been completely clarified: Were the mystics an integral part of rabbinic Judaism, or were they a section of what is often called "heterodox Judaism," separated from the "mainstream" of talmudic-midrashic schools? But from the cultural and spiritual point of view it cannot be doubted that this rich and colorful literature, which deals with so many aspects of mystical experience and mystical world view, contributed immensely to the Jewish culture of that period, adding to it a new mystical dimension and laying the foundation for a second mystical awakening within Judaism in the high Middle Ages.

Bibliography

A few Hekhalot and Merkavah texts were published in traditional editions, but their versions are usually unreliable. Most of the important texts can be found in the three great anthologies of this literature: Jellinek; Wertheimer; and Mussajoff. Since 1981, however, the scholarly world has been using another work as a source for Hekhalot texts: Schaefer. In this edition are printed side by side the seven most important manuscripts of Hekhalot literature, in a way that enables the reader easily to compare each section and each sentence in the various manuscripts. There is no doubt that this book is now the standard source for most of the texts of ancient Jewish mysticism.

Modern study of Hekhalot and Merkavah mysticism begins with the works of Gershom Scholem. The chapter on the subject in *Major Trends* (pp. 40–78) is the first comprehensive study of the phenomenon as a whole. Scholem's most important study of the subject is his book *Jewish Gnosticism*. In the last decade several new book-length studies of the field have been published. Among them the most comprehensive, which serves as an introduction to the subject and to the particular texts is Gruenwald. A detailed textual study of the earliest sources of Merkavah literature in the Talmud is Halperin. A similar study was prepared by I. Chernus. A detailed study of one text is Cohen, and a brief typology of this literature as a whole is presented in Dan. Another aspect is studied in Segal, and the relationship between gnosticism and Jewish traditions is the subject of Fallon.

Cohen, M. S. *The Shiur Komah.* Lanham, MD: University Press of America, 1983.
Dan, Joseph. *Three Types of Ancient Jewish Mysticism.* Cincinnati: Hebrew Union College, forthcoming.
Fallon, F. T. *The Enthronement of Sabbaoth.* Leiden: Brill, 1977.
Gruenwald, I. *Apocalyptic and Merkabah Literature.* Leiden: Brill, 1980.
Halperin, D. *The Merkabah in Rabbinic Literature.* New Haven, CT: American Oriental Society, 1980.
Jellinek. A. *Bet ha-Midrash.* 6 vols. Jerusalem: Wahrmann, 1967.
Mussajoff, S. *Merkavah Shelemah.* Jerusalem: 1922.
Schaefer, Peter. *Synopse zur Hekhalot Literatur.* Tübingen: Mohr, 1981.
Scholem, Gershom. *Jewish Gnosticism, Merkabah Mysticism, and Talmudic Tradition.* 2nd ed. New York: Jewish Theological Seminary, 1965.
———. *Major Trends in Jewish Mysticism.* 2nd ed. New York: Schocken Books, 1954.
Segal, A. F. *Two Powers in Heaven.* Leiden: Brill, 1977.
Wertheimer, S. A. *Battey Midrashot.* 2 vols. Mosad ha-Rav Kook, 1950–53.

Part Three

REFLECTIONS
The Medieval Age

I know You by a name, high and renowned.
I see You in Your acts but not by sight.
The secrets of Your knowledge have wearied sages.
Your supreme knowing is above our state.
I search You out, and, among my thoughts,
I find You, I see You, within my own heart.
You have breathed in me a soul, linked to Your throne,
Living in a body, low and contrite.
A man who is seen and cannot see, can he grasp
The glory of the unseen, seeing Great?

Isaac Ibn Gi'at

Heal me, my God, and I shall be healed.
Let not Your anger burn, to remove me from the earth.
My potion, my medicament, depends on You
For its weakness, or its strength, its failure or its worth.
You are the one that chooses. It is not I.
For You know what is good and what is ill.
Not on my own healing do I rely.
I look only towards Your power to heal.

Judah Halevi

The Secret of Sabbath:
She is Sabbath!
United in the secret of One
to draw down upon Her the secret of One.

The prayer for the entrance of Sabbath:
The holy Throne of Glory is united in the secret of One,
prepared for the High Holy King to rest upon Her.
When Sabbath enters She is alone,
separated from the Other Side,
all judgments removed from Her.
Basking in the oneness of holy light,
She is crowned over and over to face the Holy King.
All powers of wrath and masters of judgment flee from Her.
There is no power in all the worlds aside from Her.
Her face shines with a light from beyond;
She is crowned below by the holy people,
and all of them are crowned with new souls.
Then the beginning of prayer
to bless Her with joy and beaming faces. . .

Zohar 2:135a–b

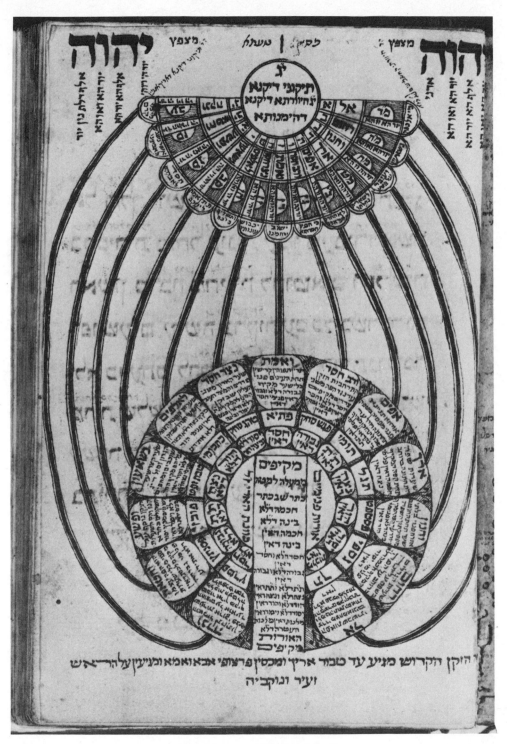

9. The thirteen *middot* ("attributes")
of God's Mercy, Mic. 4599, f. 345

10. Hispano-Mauresque Seder Plate

בעל הבית ובני ביתו יעשו אלו הכלים בליל פסח

11. "Reciting the Haggadah," Manuscript illumination,
Fourteenth century Spanish *Haggadah*

12. Page from a Spanish *Haggadah*,
Manuscript illumination, ca. 1300, #A, 13

12

Apples of Gold:
The Inner Meaning of
Sacred Texts in Medieval Judaism

FRANK TALMAGE

Allegory as a Characteristic Feature
of Medieval Jewish Literature

IN HIS ANTI-CHRISTIAN POLEMIC, the *Book of the Covenant,* Joseph Kimhi, the twelfth-century Narbonnese biblical exegete and grammarian, has his stereotypical Christian antagonist remark, "You understand most of the Torah literally while we understand it figuratively. Your entire reading of the Bible is erroneous for you resemble him who gnaws at the bone, while we suck at the marrow within. You are like the beast that eats the chaff, while we eat the wheat."[1] To have made such a statement, Joseph Kimhi's stereotypical Christian would have had to have read only stereotypical Jewish exegesis. He, like most Christian theologians, no doubt knew full well that Jews were anything but die-hard literalists.[2] What was meant by Jewish literalism was failure to accept the christological interpretation of the Hebrew Scriptures, and the term was used at times to vilify the Jewish reading of the Bible as "carnal" and at times to support periodic Christian efforts at interpreting *literaliter,* according to the literal or historical sense. Indeed, modern students of the history of exegesis emphasize this aspect of Hebrew biblical commentary. Some, like Beryl Smalley, might wish to show its importance for the development of the school of St. Victor;[3] others purport to emphasize its relevance for the contemporary exegete.[4] They are all correct, of course, but they tell only part of the story. Medieval Jewish biblical exegesis operated on many levels, according to the time, the place, and the predilection of the individual writer. The categories

313

most frequently discussed are those of *peshaṭ* and *derash,* the relationship of the so-called plain sense to the rabbinic hermeneutic. Our concern, though, is with a different set of polarities, that of *nigleh* (*zāhir*) and *nistar* (*bāṭin*), exoteric and esoteric, a dominant mode of exegesis in that part of the later medieval Jewish world more affected by Islamic culture than by Latin — Spain and Provence and, by extension, Italy. For lack of better terms — and indeed more precise terminology waits to be established — the categories of "allegory"[5] and "symbol" are frequently used, and we may use these categories as long as we are aware that what is spoken of here is not, as in so much of Christian exegesis, figural allegory, in which the type represents the antitype and in which the old prefigures the new. To be sure, such typological exegesis was not unknown to Judaism and was used far more extensively than is generally supposed. Indeed, the proverb "the actions of the fathers are an indication of those of the sons,"[6] in which the rabbis saw repetitiveness of the behavior of one generation of patriarchs after the other, was taken up by the thirteenth-century Geronese exegete Moses ben Naḥman (Naḥmanides), whereas his contemporary, Baḥya ben Asher, points out that the exodus from Egypt is a *figura* (*dimyon*) of the future redemption.[7] One of the most striking examples of Jewish typological exegesis is to be found in the commentary of Isaac ben Joseph Ha-Kohen (Spain, turn of the fifteenth century) on Ruth. There the book of Ruth is read as a prefiguration of the future history of Israel, and its characters are types (*mashal*) of those yet to come — Elimelech of the House of David, Naomi of the kingdom of Israel, Ruth of the faithful tribes of Judah and Benjamin, Orpah of the wayward ten tribes who followed Jeroboam, and so forth. In turn, Ha-Kohen's contemporary, Isaac Abravanel, from the evidence of the midrash, finds Adam to be a type of Israel, the true man, into whom God breathed His spirit, the Torah, and placed him in the Garden of Eden, the land of Israel.[8]

Yet by and large, without the need to demonstrate the concordance of two testaments, typology does not become the dominant mode. Rather the allegory that we shall be treating, more accurately termed reification allegory,[9] is the heir of the Greek allegorizers of Homer, Hesiod, Ovid,[10] and of Philo of Alexandria, an "imposed allegory"[11] in which the surface meaning[12] of a classical or canonical text, not truly intended by its author to be allegorical, is taken to envelop higher esoteric truth, the way the shell envelops the nut. This exoteric sense, the *nigleh,* may be useful as in Maimonides's *Guide for the Perplexed* (introduction; Pines, p. 12), or it may impede, as is suggested in the mystical classic the *Zohar.* But either way, the reader — the *discerning* reader — must probe beyond, must plummet beneath, must penetrate ever farther (*Guide* 1:26, 1:33, 2:48). Nor is it only

Scripture that is read allegorically, but even "parables of foxes," secular literature with an ostensibly diversionary intent, are, as in the Christian European tradition, to be read as a key to profounder, more arcane truths. In this way, even the fifteenth-century rhymed prose narrative of Don Vidal Benvenist, the *Romance of Epher and Dinah*,[13] an unabashedly scatological piece, is declared by its author to be not just a cheap piece of entertainment, not to contain, as Dante would have said, simply *diletto* but also *ammaestramento* (*Convivio* 1.2, 21.1), moral and psychological truths, couched in their present garb only to draw and hold the interest of prurient youth. And, in case we do not believe him (and we should indeed not be too hasty in dismissing his claim),[14] Benvenist, unlike the thirteenth-century Spanish savants, Judah al-Harizi and Isaac Ibn Sahula, who merely allude to the didactic nature of their rhymed prose narratives (*maqāmāt*), the *Tahkemoni* and the *Mashal ha-qadmoni*,[15]—actually undertakes to establish his claim in detail in his own allegorical interpretation of the tale. For so many in this Islamic-Jewish world of southern Europe, allegory was not merely a hermeneutic mode; it was a state of mind. It was not simply a way of looking at the world; it was a way of constructing the world. It was used in a variety of ways as abundant as the variety of its metaphors. For Maimonides, it was that of Prov 25:11:

> The Sage has said, *A word fitly spoken is like apples of gold in settings (maskiyyot) of silver.* Hear now an elucidation of the thought that he has set forth. The term *maskiyyot* denotes filigree traceries; I mean to say traceries in which there are apertures with very small eyelets, like the handiwork of silversmiths. They are so called because a glance penetrates through them; for in the (Aramaic) translation of the Bible the Hebrew *wa-yashqef*—meaning, he glanced—is translated *wa-istekhel*. The Sage accordingly said that a saying uttered with a view to two meanings is like an apple of gold overlaid with silver filigree-work having very small holes. . . . When looked at from a distance or with imperfect attention, it is deemed to be an apple of silver; but when a keen sighted observer looks at it with full attention, its interior becomes clear to him and he knows that it is of gold.[16] The parables of the prophets, peace be on them, are similar. Their external meaning contains wisdom that is useful for beliefs concerned with truth as it is. (*Guide*, introduction; Pines, pp. 11–12)

The quest for "truth as it is" is the quest then for the golden apple; as in *midrashim* cited by Maimonides (*Guide*, introduction; Pines, p. 11), it is the attempt to retrieve the coin at the bottom of the well by attaching cord to cord until one reaches bottom (*Song Rab.* 1:1) to make, as with the Muslim mystics' method of *istinbāt*,[17] the inner meaning surface; it is the search for the lost pearl found with the aid of a penny candle (*Song Rab.* 1:1); it is, as in the *Zohar*, the shelling of the nut with its numerous shells and layers

(*Zohar Ḥadash, Midrash Ruth* 39c), or the soul encased in its body encased in its garments, or the tree with its roots, bark, cortex, branches, leaves, flowers, and fruit alluding to seven layers of meaning (*Zohar* 3:202a).[18] But one of the most prevalent, and perhaps the most telling, images is that of the palace. This is the palace that entices but eludes, that beckons but only to those worthy of entrance.[19] At the end of the *Guide* (3:51; Pines, pp. 618–20), Maimonides expresses the search for "truth as it is" in terms of this palace metaphor. It is a long and arduous journey from the entrance to the center, but how great the reward when one reaches the inner court. Maimonides's palace metaphor gives rise to the epithet of the Kabbalists, "sons of the palace,"[20] adopted by them from that famous passage in the *Zohar*, which, employing that common motif of Iberian and early Jewish literature, the guarded woman,[21] places the Torah and the seductive and coquettish princess in the palace's inner court.

For the Torah resembles a beautiful and stately damsel, who is hidden in a secluded chamber of her palace and who has a secret lover, unknown to all others. For love of her he keeps passing the gate of her house, looking this way and that in search of her. She knows that her lover haunts the gate of her house. What does she do? She opens the door of her hidden chamber ever so little, and for a moment reveals her face to her lover, but hides it again forthwith. Were anyone with her lover, he would see nothing and perceive nothing. He alone sees it and he is drawn to her with his heart and soul and his whole being, and he knows that for love of him she disclosed herself to him for one moment, aflame with love for him. So is it with the word of the Torah, which reveals herself only to those who love her. The Torah knows that the mystic [*ḥakhim libba*, literally, "the wise of heart"] haunts the gate of her house. What does she do? From within her hidden palace she discloses her face and beckons to him and returns forthwith to her place and hides. Those who are there see nothing and know nothing, only he alone, and he is drawn to her with his heart and soul and his whole being. Thus the Torah reveals herself and hides, and goes out in love of her lover and arouses love in him. Come and see: this is the way of the Torah. At first, when she wishes to reveal herself to a man, she gives him a momentary sign. If he understands, well and good; if not, she sends to him and calls him a simpleton. To the messenger she sends to him the Torah says: tell the simpleton to come here that I may speak to him. As it is written (Prov 9:16): "Whoso is simple, let him turn in hither, she saith to him that wanteth understanding." When he comes to her, she begins from behind a curtain to speak words in keeping with his understanding, until very slowly insight comes to him, and this is called *derashah*. Then through a light veil she speaks allegorical words (*millin de-ḥidah*) and that is what is meant by *haggadah*. Only then, when he has become familiar with her, does she reveal herself to him face to face and speak to him of all her hidden secrets and all her hidden ways, which have been in her heart from the beginning. Such a man is then termed perfect, a "master," that is to say, a "bridegroom of the Torah" in the strictest sense, the master of the house, to whom she discloses all her secrets, concealing nothing. (*Zohar* 2:99a–b)

It is here that we must pause for a moment, for we in the Occident may not be fully able to appreciate what these particular structures really are. Generally, when we think of palaces, it is to those of Europe that we turn—Windsor, Hampton Court, Vienna, El Escorial, Leningrad, or, one should say, St. Petersburg—these awesome structures with their seemingly interminable corridors opening on to seemingly endless chambers and apartments and serving as cavernous display cases for royal treasures and objects of art intended to dazzle one so privileged as to be permitted to enter. Endless corridors, endless tunnels, endless doors—the palaces known to Kafka,[22] the palaces that express the sentiment of their builders and occupants: "I am might, I am power, I stand forever." Charles V of Spain attempted to build such a palace in Granada to which that odd little Moorish relic they call the Alhambra would serve as an annex to provide comic relief to the awesome dignity of his own. But that "arrogant intrusion," as Washington Irving called it, was not to be completed. Rather it was the Alhambra itself, that gracious ode in stucco and stone, that was to be the centerpiece not only of Granada but of our story. In marked contrast to the palace of Charles V, which speaks of self-glorification, the Alhambra proclaims a different message. In recurrent arabesques, "open designs without beginning, end, or repose, in pursuit of unattainable being, alternating between 'inner' and 'outer,'" as Américo Castro put it,[23] the Alhambra declares *wa-lā ghālib illa allāh* ("There is no Victorious One but God"),[24] and it is indeed toward heaven that the structure, with its star-shaped skylights and its stucco stalagmites, points. But it is the horizontal plane that concerns us here. Here one finds not tedious and monotonous corridors but dramatically arranged courts and chambers, so placed that one beckons to the other or, more properly, the others, for there is generally an option. A passage will lead now to the right, now to the left, now to a cul-de-sac, now to another passage where the whole march begins anew. It is a maze and a labyrinth—not one that discourages but one that entices, as the archways lead one to another, at first perhaps to disappointment, but finally, with persistence, to the princess or the golden apple.[25]

Thus, the architecture and the literature of Moorish Spain and its satellites go hand in hand.[26] In one of his *maqāmāt*,[27] or rhymed prose tales, Jacob ben Eleazar, a younger contemporary of Joseph Kimhi, recounts the love of the youth Sahar for his beloved princess Kimah, who is sequestered in just such a labyrinthine palace as we have described. In his desperation, Sahar wanders through the palace, which is described in terms made to order for a 1930s Hollywood musical stage set. Bevies of lovely maidens try to seduce him but to no avail. He struggles on through rooms walled in with glass flooded with water from behind so that he thinks he is in fact submerged and is drowning. Yet he perseveres. In each chamber, hangings with elegantly written love poems,[28] each more tantalizing than the previous, point the way until finally, when he finds himself at the point of desperation, he is led or leads himself to the object of his desire.

The palace, then, is the analogue in the Islamic-Jewish context of the labyrinthine forest or maze of the threshold episodes in Dante and Spenser, which provide the key to what approach one is to take to the text that follows.[29] Both the forest and the palace have their dangers, but it is the forward motion, the kinetic force against resistance, the overcoming of the conflict, the resolution of the quest, which are the searcher's salvation,[30] for, as the thirteenth-century Spaniard Baḥya ben Asher would point out, it is the exoteric which represents darkness while the esoteric is the gem which illumines.[31] Allegory, then, is not for the casual stroller in the gardens of the palace but for the one who dares to enter and is worthy of entering its portals. It is for the one who is willing to invest the hard labor and energy required, "the great effort at plowing and the need for being goaded. For the metaphor of plowing for the finding of the worthwhile esoteric sense and allegories (ḥidot) has long been widespread: If you had not plowed with my heifer, you had not found out my riddle (ḥidah) (Jud. 14:18). And this is because plowing is an activity which uncovers and lays bare the concealed thing sought after."[32]

> Allegory presupposes readers assiduous in interpreting (rather than simply following or responding to) a narrative. The greatest allegories are intransigent and elusive . . . because they are concerned with a highly complex kind of truth, a matter of relationships and process rather than statement. The elusiveness of truth is a measure of its value. . . .[33]

To read a text, then, was to seek the truth that eluded, in other words, to practice allegory. For the type of medieval mentality we are surveying, as for certain of today's literary critics, all reading was in some sense *allegoresis,* an allegorical reading.[34] Such a reader was literally inundated with allegory, expressed as it was in literature, in art, in architecture, and in homily at divine service, for which, as in Christianity,[35] greater or lesser preachers, such as Jacob Anatoli (Italy, thirteenth century), Isaac Arama (Spain, fifteenth century), and Abraham Saba (Portugal and Fez, turn of fifteenth century), prepared their sermons. It is to the types and uses of this all-pervasive *allegoresis* that we now direct our attention.

Fourfold Schemes of Interpretation

The polysemous nature of Scripture was long accepted in Judaism. Tradition spoke of "seventy faces (panim) of the Torah,"[36] the concept of 'faces' (*wujūh*) being found in Islamic exegesis as well.[37] On the Christian side, one of the loveliest images was that of John Scotus Erigena, who noted that "the sense of the divine utterances is manifold and infinite, just as in one single feather of the peacock one sees a marvelous and beautiful variety of innumerable colors" (*De Div. Nat.* 4:5, *PL* 122: 749). This acceptance of polysemy would make allegory possible for "the language of allegory makes relationships significant by extending the original identities of which they are composed with as many clusters of meanings as the traffic of the dominant idea will bear."[38] In Christianity, this polysemy had long been formalized into a system: the four senses of Scripture.[39] In Judaism, this crystallization took place in several texts that appeared in Spain in the latter half of the thirteenth century. We have already seen this description of a fourfold sense in the passage from the *Zohar* cited earlier in this paper, and Bahya ben Asher, the exegete and homilist, took a similar approach in his Torah commentary. There he lists "the way of *peshat*" or, for want of a better term, the plain sense; the "way of *midrash*" or the rabbinic hermeneutic; "the way of reason" or philosophical interpretation; and "the Lord's way" or "the way of truth," which is the kabbalistic interpretation (Introduction to Torah commentary). The system soon formally received the name of *pardes*, an acronym for *peshat*, *remez* (literally, "allusion" or philosophical allegory), *derashah*, and *sod* or the kabbalistic sense.[40] Whether there is a historical association between the Christian and Jewish quadruplex systems, an association already made by Pico della Mirandola,[41] has been a subject of some debate.[42] One point about it, however, should be made clear: the four senses of Christianity are not those of Judaism. The former received a variety of names, but most commonly they were termed literal, allegorical, moral or tropological, and anagogical. One of the best known and clearest formulations is that of Dante in his Epistle to Can Grande:

> For the better illustration of this method of exposition we may apply it to the following verses: "When Israel went out of Egypt, the house of Jacob from a people of strange language; Judah was his sanctuary, and Israel his dominion" (Ps 114:1–2). For if we consider the letter alone, the thing signified to us is the going out of the children of Israel from Egypt in the time of Moses; if the allegory, our redemption through Christ is signified; if the moral sense, the conversion of the soul from the sorrow and misery of sin

to a state of grace is signified; if the anagogical, the passing of the sanctified soul from the bondage of the corruption of this world to the liberty of everlasting glory is signified.[43]

If we examine these four senses, we find that the "letter" could indeed correspond to the Jewish *peshaṭ*. Yet the allegory meant here is typology, and although, as we have seen above, typology is not altogether alien to Jewish exegesis and although philosophical allegory is not entirely absent from medieval Christian exegesis,[44] Dante's allegory is not our *remez*. To be sure, moral exegesis of Scripture was part and parcel of Jewish interpretation, and, to take one example: Levi ben Gerson (Gersonides, Provence, fourteenth century) established a formal system of *to'aliyyot* (i.e., the Aristotelian *utilitas*) *middiyyot* (moral lessons)[45] in his biblical commentaries. Moral homilies go back, of course, to the midrash and rabbinic literature—one of the most remarkable being that cited in Maimonides's *Guide* (3:43), in which the verse "You shall have a paddle upon your weapon (*'azenekha*)" (Deut 23:14) is explained: "Do not read *'azenekha* but *'oznekha* your ear [the Hebrew consonantal spelling is the same in both words]. This teaches us that whenever a man hears a reprehensible thing, he should put his finger into his ear" (*b. Ket.* 15a). Yet although so much of rabbinic *derashah* is moral, it does deal with other categories, and moral interpretations can be found beyond the confines of rabbinic homily. The anagogical too is not unknown to Jewish exegesis. As an example, the *Zohar* interprets the "legalistic" passage "If a man sell his daughter to be a maidservant, she shall not go out as the manservants do" (Exod 21:7) in terms of redemption of the soul, that is, leaving this world not as a slave, laden within sin, but pure (*Zohar* 2:94b). The redemption of the soul after death is dealt with at length in an elegant fashion in Abraham Saba's *'Eshkol ha-kofer* on Esther (Drohobycz, 1903, pp. 46–58), where Mordecai (*marei dakhya*, "pure myrrh") is taken to refer to the pure body and Esther represents the hidden (*nisteret*) soul after death. The twelve months during which the soul is purified are indicated by the twelve months during which each maiden had to wait to be allowed into the presence of the King (God) after their purification. Yet though the redemption of the soul is certainly a central concern of the Kabbalah, it is not all of it, and the equation of anagogy and *sod* will not work. In terms of content then, *pardes* is not the fourfold Christian system.[46] The question of the development of the fourfold system needs further investigation. For the present, one might be inclined to go along with the coy, jocularly serious or earnestly humorous Abraham Ibn Ezra (twelfth century, Spain) who likened the four senses of Scripture to the four functions of the nose—to ventilate the brain, to drain it of mucus, to smell, and to improve one's appearance.[47]

Whatever the historical development be,[48] our principal concern is with the two categories of *remez* (philosophical *allegoresis*) and *sod* (kabbalistic interpretation), which we have chosen to treat together under the category of esoteric interpretation. Although such joint treatment has not been at all conventional, we hope that it will be justified in the course of this essay.

Motivations for Allegorization

Not all biblical texts lent themselves equally to esoteric interpretation. Some were obvious candidates: Proverbs, with its Hebrew title of *mishlei* ("parables") and its reference to the "words of the sages and their enigmas (*hidot*)," the most obscure kind of allegory[49]—according to such diverse philologists as the turn-of-the-seventh-century bishop Isidore of Seville (*Etym.* 1.37.26) and the thirteenth-century Narbonnese exegete David Kimhi (*Commentary* on Ezek 17:2; cf. Maimonides, *Guide*, introduction; Pines, p. 13)—and with its references to wayward and virtuous women and to wisdom's building her seven-pillared house, crying aloud at the street-corners, was a favorite with the philosophical allegorists. Recurrent in such commentaries is the notion that Proverbs is to be understood on two levels—one exoteric, that is, as a book of practical wisdom, and one esoteric, as intended only for the elite, for it is the elite, and only they, who not only will benefit from the inner meaning but also will not be harmed by its exposure to it. For the unprepared or incapable, examination of the inner sense will not be salutary but, moreover, will be harmful. That the truth must be kept from dolts was a common theme among practitioners of allegory and *allegorēsis* throughout the centuries. As George Chapman, a post-Elizabethan allegorist, would later put it, "Learning hath delighted . . . to hide her selfe from the base and profane Vulgare."[50] Maimonides made clear that the Torah speaks in the language of human beings (*b. Yeb.* 71a; *b. B. Mes̱.* 31b) in order to make it "possible for the young, the women, and all the people to begin with it and to learn it. Now it is not within their power to understand these matters as they truly are" (*Guide* 1:33; Pines, p. 71). Thus "it behooves to explain the matter to those whose souls grasp at human perfection and, by dint of expatiating a little on the point in question just as we have done, to put an end to the fantasies that come to them from the age of infancy" (*Guide* 1:36; p. 57).

Maimonides's spiritual disciple, Zerahiah ben Isaac ben Shealtiel Hen of thirteenth-century Barcelona, writing in Rome, expresses these sentiments more explicitly in the prologue to his commentary on Proverbs:

My intention in this work is to explain the Proverbs of Solomon after the fashion of science and inward speculation (*ha-ʿiyyun ha-penimi*) everywhere that understanding according to science or an esoteric explanation is called for. . . .

Now this book . . . has three functions. The first is to refer to matters which have an explicit benefit for the masses . . . and their behavior and interaction. The second . . . is to explain ethical matters of which their exoteric sense has an explicit benefit for the masses and their esoteric sense contains matters which are to be understood according to one's intellect and comprehension. The third, . . . which is the ultimate, is to allude to esoteric matters which are therapeutic for the sick soul and a benefit for the wise soul and its virtues in exalted divine matters. And because by their nature these matters are esoteric and concealed from the masses, and *because the natures of most people are not receptive to them and their intellects cannot cope with them,* King Solomon was forced to conceal them and assumed that whoever was disposed to understand that which he concealed would do so with a slight hint.[51]

According to Rabbi Zerahiah, then, Solomon's writing in allegory was protective, protective for the masses who simply could not cope with such subtle thoughts but protective as well for the esoteric teachings themselves lest they be misinterpreted by those unsuited for them. The *Zohar* goes so far as to explain the rebellion of the generation of the Tower of Babel by the suggestion that God revealed the secrets of esoteric wisdom to the world and they were immediately misinterpreted and misemployed. Not only Adam and Noah but also Abraham, Isaac, and Jacob failed to grasp them properly. It was only Moses who succeeded in understanding them (*Zohar* 1:75b–76a).

According to Samuel Ibn Tibbon's somewhat more sophisticated historicizing theory of protective camouflaging of the esoteric, there was a gradual reduction of the concealment of philosophical truths over the ages. Moses, writing the Torah for a people under the direct influence of a pagan and materialistic world, left certain philosophical truths well hidden lest they be perverted by the masses. In the course of time, David and Solomon (Psalms, Proverbs, Ecclesiastes, Song of Songs) could be more relaxed, even though contemporary pagan influences prevented them from revealing the truth openly:

Moses . . . had to conceal many beliefs and to present them as something other than they were. . . . Now whereas he did conceal them from the multitude and showed them to be different from what they were, he undoubtedly transmitted them orally to Joshua and to the seventy elders together with the rest of the oral Torah. He also alluded to many to let the wise know about them in their proper place, . . . until David and Solomon came and added hints to those secrets, once they saw the need to conceal them had lessened.[52]

Yet other motivations for allegorization are expressed in the context of commentaries on the Song of Songs. This book had been considered problematic since rabbinic times (*m. Yad.* 3:5) because of its blatantly erotic and sensuous surface meaning. The rabbis therefore warned: "He who recites a verse of the Song of Songs and treats it as a [secular] air . . . brings evil into the world, for the Torah puts on sackcloth, appears before God and complains: Your children have made of me a fiddle played by scoffers" (*b. Sanh.* 101a). Yet it was precisely because of its unlikely sacrality[53] that the Song of Songs was to play second fiddle to no other biblical book and was eagerly embraced by philosophers and Kabbalists alike in a rich variety of esoteric interpretations. Commentaries as diverse as that of Ezra of Gerona in the twelfth century and that pseudo-Joseph Kimhi bewail those who take the book as a love song.[54] Yet it was just that aspect which Ezra's contemporary, the rationalist North African Judah ben Joseph Ibn Aknin, saw as positive. Similar to the sentiments expressed in the context of Don Vidal Benvenist's *Epher and Dinah* is Ibn Aknin's idea that Solomon's writing in an appealing, belletristic style "was to make it attractive to the masses":[55]

> and when they became a little more learned they would reflect that it cannot be thought of the like of him that he intended the exoteric sense of the husk of the words . . . , and those that followed him . . . placed it in the biblical canon and esteemed it more than their own words . . . and urged people to study it for it contains exalted secrets and they would thus be prompted to investigate [them]. . . . *For this is the way of the Indians in the book they called* Kalila wa-Dimna [a cycle of fables that originated in India and was widely circulated in medieval Europe]. *They spoke in fables in the form of discussions between animals and birds and went as far as to decorate it with illustrations so that the masses would run and savor its wisdom and take pleasure in it until their intellect strengthens*[56] and would examine and find the insights and wisdom bound within.[57]

With a book like Song of Songs then, *allegorēsis* has a redemptive quality,[58] for it redeems it from embarrassment in the face of possible misinterpreters and scoffers. Indeed, there is an additional dimension here. A number of early Christian theologians had rejected the sacred character of Song of Songs, but, as part of the canon, it was taken as an allegory of the love of Christ for the church and was made part and parcel of the christological heritage.[59] Islam, however, had no such vested interest, and a Muslim, whose religion so prided itself on the sublimity and incomparability of the Qur'an, could well wonder at the inclusion of the Song of Songs in a collection of sacred writings. Indeed, Ibn Aknin relates a charming story in which he shows how *allegorēsis* saved the prestige of Judaism in the face of a rival religion.

> The physician Abu-l-Hasan ben Kamniel related . . . : I visited the Almora-vide King and found a Jewish physician with him . . . who was explaining the Song of Songs according to its exoteric sense as a love song. I rebuked that physician and condemned him before the king and said . . . : "This man is a stupid ignoramus and knows nothing of our Torah . . . [I then explained that the text was an allegory] and I convinced the king of this and explained its meaning and purpose to him . . . and disembarrassed him of the feeling of contempt which that blithering ignoramus of a physician had prompted in him. . . . . In this incident, God's name was sanctified.[60]

   If Song of Songs was considered to be problematic because of its erotic character, the narratives (as opposed to the laws) of the Torah were considered to be no less so for other reasons. Some of these narratives, like the story of the fall replete with talking serpent, were considered to be perhaps a bit taxing on one's credulity. There were Jewish Celsuses, too, who considered such things old wives' tales.[61] Some things might well have happened, as Scripture states,[62] but they are recounted primarily to provide the foundation for a more sophisticated superstructure. Other things, such as the tales of the patriarchs—like, as we shall see, many rabbinic *aggadot*[63] —were considered by some to be frankly rather trivial and less than worthy of a divine revelation. Rabbi Azriel of Gerona, on the evidence of *b. Hul.* 60b, reiterates that "there are passages in the Torah and Scriptures which would appear worthy of being burnt to those who do not know their real interpretation" (*Perush ha-'aggadot, p. 37).*[64] And so, as C. S. Lewis observed, esoteric interpretation, as "the most obvious way of turning primitive documents to meet the ethical or polemical demands of the moment,"[65] moved in. Surely one of the most daring expressions of this attitude is a passage found in the *Zohar* (3:152a), which merits citation here in full:

> Rabbi Simeon said: Alas for the man who regards the Torah as a book of mere tales and profane matters. If this were so, we might even today write a Torah dealing in such matters and still more excellent. In regard to earthly things, the kings and princes of the world possess more valuable materials. We could use them as a model for composing a Torah of this kind. But in reality the words of the Torah are higher words and higher mysteries. When even the angels come down into the world [to fulfill a mission], they don the garment of this world, and if they did not, they could not survive in this world and the world could not endure them. And if this is true even of the angels, how much truer it is of the Torah, with which He created them and all the worlds and through which they all subsist. When she descends into the world, how could the world endure it if she did not don earthly garments?

If anyone should suppose that the Torah herself is this garment and nothing else, let him give up the ghost. Such a man will have no share in the world to come. That is why David (Ps 119:18) said: "Open thou mine eyes, that I may behold wondrous things out of thy Torah," namely, that which is beneath the garment of the Torah. Come and behold: there are garments that everyone sees, and when fools see a man in a garment that seems beautiful to them, they do not look more closely. But more important than the garment is the body, and more important than the body is the soul. So likewise the Torah has a body, which consists of the commandments and ordinances of the Torah, which are called *gufei torah*, "bodies of the Torah." This body is cloaked in garments, which consist of wordly stories.[66] Fools see only the garment, which is the narrative part of the Torah; they know no more and fail to see what is under the garment. Those who know more see not only the garment but also the body that is under the garment. But the truly wise, the servants of the Supreme King, those who stood at the foot of Mount Sinai, look only upon the soul, which is the true foundation of the entire Torah, and one day indeed it will be given them to behold the innermost soul of the Torah.

Thus, the truly wise, that is, the mystic, will perceive not only the inner meaning but will one day, in this life or the next, attain an innermost ultimate understanding. It is then that he will realize that if he finds anything in the Torah that appears vacuous, it is only because of a deficiency within him,[67] that nothing is superfluous,[68] that the driest genealogical and geographical lists are redolent of supernal wisdom for "there is no difference between the [list of] captains of Esau and the Ten Commandments for it is all one entity and one structure" and that "Rabban Yohanan ben Zakkai would expound three hundred *halakhot* through the mystery of supernal wisdom on the verse 'And the name of his wife was Mehetabel the daughter of Matred the daughter of Me-zahav (Gen 36:39)'" (*Zohar Hadash* 12d).[69] Nor was it only the mystics who spoke so. Even the alleged archrationalist Levi ben Abraham ben Hayyim, the scapegoat of the Maimonidean controversy of 1304–1305, expressed essentially the same notion using precisely the same verses.[70]

Concerning other texts, of course, little apology was necessary. The first chapters of Genesis and of Ezekiel were believed to contain esoteric teachings from rabbinic times. The rabbis (*b. Hag.* 11b) and the medieval Kabbalists treated these texts, the *ma'aseh bereshit* ("work of creation") and the *ma'aseh merkavah* ("work of the chariot") as repositories of mystical lore, while the medieval rationalists, Maimonides foremost among them (e.g., *Guide*, introduction; Pines, p. 6), took them as referring to natural science and metaphysics respectively. Thus, Joseph Kimhi's son, David, a staunch Maimonidean but one who practiced restraint in the composition of allegorical commentaries, allowed himself free rein in his "secret" commentaries on these texts. In the Hexaemeron commentary, the Garden of Eden represents the active intellect and the tree of life the human intellect, while the tree of knowledge of good and evil symbolizes the material intellect. The virtuous human intellect strives toward the active intellect by pursuing the divine sciences, while the material intellect languishes because of its material lusts. In the same fashion, the roles of the cast of human characters are spelled out: Cain, the materialist agriculturalist, was devoid of intellectual attainments; Abel, who hungered after luxuries, was potentially more intelligent but allowed his intellect to go to waste; Seth, who was born of another woman (for Eve had returned to her source), ate from the tree of life, and was "good seed," shared the human intellect with Adam and was the true founder of humanity. The esoteric Ezekiel commentary, inspired by Maimonides, goes into elaborate detail concerning the creatures, the wheels, the four faces, the rider, and so forth in order to explain "this obscure vision . . . and incomprehensible utterance" (*Commentary* on Ezekiel, introduction).[71]

The Appropriateness of *Allegorēsis* in a Biblical Commentary

Exegetical gymnastics such as these raised the question of the place of *allegorēsis* in a biblical commentary. Joseph Kimhi, for example, interprets Prov 9:1, "Wisdom has built her house; she has hewn out her seven pillars," as referring to "the seven cognitive capacities by which man knows the Creator of the world and all that is in it. They are the five senses in man and two which are not physical—the reports of informants and the science of deductive reasoning. . . . ."[72] In other words, he reads a medieval epistemological theory into the scriptural text. Yet when his son, David—who, as we recall, did not shrink from writing allegorical commentaries on the first chapters of Genesis and Ezekiel and found the "exoteric sense of [the Garden of Eden story] very garbled (Commentary on Gen 3:1)—comments on that verse in his own commentary on Proverbs, he avoids any such "modernizing" tendency and instead of citing a philosophical interpretation "reverts" to a midrashic type of comment. If this strikes us as odd, it is odder still that it is not David's last word on the subject. In his relatively lengthy introduction to Psalm 119, he explains Prov 9:1 very much in the same fashion as had his father. In the same way, Rabbi David gives several rationalistic interpretations of Proverbs—which are not found at all in his commentary on Proverbs—in the introduction to his Genesis commentary. For example:

"My son, let them not depart from your eyes, keep sound wisdom (*tushiyyah*) and thought (*mezimmah*) (Prov 3:22)." . . . "Keep sound wisdom (*tushiyyah*)" refers to the exoteric [element] in the secrets of the Torah. The word *tushiyyah* is derived from the word *yesh* ["being"], which generally refers to the sensible, and that is the exoteric. And he said *mezimmah* which means "thought" with reference to the esoteric which is understood through ratiocination. He said that one should always guard the exoteric and the esoteric in the Torah in his heart.[73]

This anomaly may perhaps be clarified by looking at a similar anomaly. In explaining Jer 17:12, Rabbi David remarks:

"The throne of glory, on high from the beginning, the place of our sanctuary." The rabbis referred this to the Temple and said "Seven things were created before the world was created. One of them was the place of the Temple . . ." (Mid. Tehillim 90). They said too that the Temple faces the throne of glory (Gen. R. 49:7). The commentators have followed this approach. In the *Sefer Yeẓirah* [*Book of Creation*, an early cosmogonic work], it says: "the holy sanctuary is set in the middle" (*Sefer Yeẓirah* 4:3). I have dealt with this at length in my commentary on Psalms.

Indeed we find such an esoteric explanation in Kimhi's comment on Ps 132:2. The reason for this exegetical displacement is alluded to in the continuation of the preceding passage from the Jeremiah commentary: "[*The esoteric explanation*] *is good but it is not connected to the preceding or following verses.*" And again at Jer 9:23, he cites Maimonides's rationalistic explanation (*Guide* 3:54) with approval, finding it "fitting" but "not related to the context." *His* function on the other hand is clear: "I have clearly explained these two verses for you according to the subject of the chapter in relation to the context." Kimhi's purpose thus becomes evident. In the introduction to his commentary on Proverbs he notes:

When I considered the various biblical commentaries and I examined all that my wise predecessors expounded, . . . I found that everyone had his own opinion concerning the Book of Proverbs and this confused the mass of people. Some of the exegetes say that Solomon likened the Torah to a beautiful wise woman and idolatry to a wicked alien woman. Some explained that he likened matter to the harlot and the intellectual form to the good and wise woman. They all cite proofs to confirm their opinions.[74]

Kimhi believed—like Maimonides, like Jacob Anatoli,[75] like a host of others—that Solomon wrote this book with two intents, one esoteric and one exoteric, one philosophical and the other practical. In explicating "the lovely hind and graceful doe" of Prov 5:19, he hedges: "Rabbi Jonah [Ibn Janah] explained it allegorically as referring to wisdom. It is possible that

the author of the book wrote it with two intents in mind but it is probable
that he spoke about the woman." Yet at Prov 5:3 he openly admits: "There
is another meaning to this parable but we shall explain it only according
to its plain sense."[76]

To explain "according to its plain sense" was considered, then, to be at the
root of the scientific exegetical enterprise. Scripture can and should be
understood according to its esoteric sense: one should go beyond the silver
traceries to perceive the golden apple. But that is the task of the philosopher
and rationalist investigator. The primary responsibility of exegete as exegete is not to reveal what God or the inspired authors did not choose to
reveal openly but only to clarify the immediate message of their words.
When one takes a text out of its context, one may interpret it as one wishes;
in context, however, one must remain faithful to its apparent intent.

The Techniques of *Allegorēsis*

Esoteric interpretation was not arbitrary and whimsical. The techniques of
allegorēsis, whether the philosophical brand or the kabbalistic, were based
on textual manipulations made possible by certain attitudes toward
language—and in particular, the sacred language, that of Scripture.

> Allegorical narrative and allegoresis both respond to the linguistic context;
> in those periods when language is felt to be a numinous object in its own
> right, allegorical criticism and allegorical narrative will both appear, the one
> focusing on the manipulations the reader can make with a text and the other
> creating a text designed to manipulate the reader.[77]

And in the low Middle Ages, that great and golden age of allegory, such
a conception of the numinous quality of language was not lacking. The
often quoted kabbalistic tradition cited by Naḥmanides states:

> The entire Torah consists of the names of God and . . . the words we read
> can be divided in a very different way, so as to form [esoteric] names. . . . The
> statement in the *aggadah* to the effect that the Torah was originally written
> with black fire on white fire (*y. Sheq.* 6:1) obviously confirms our opinion
> that the writing was continuous, without division into words, which made
> it possible to read it either as a sequence of [esoteric] names or in the tradi-
> tional way as history and commandments. Thus the Torah as given to Moses
> was divided into words in such a way as to be read as divine commandments.
> But at the same time he received the oral tradition, according to which it was
> to be read as a sequence of names.

The question of the magical uses of this theory aside,[79] it laid the foundation for such manipulation of the text as follows. Mentioning Rashi's interpretation of the first three words of Genesis, *be-reshit bara Elohim*, as "at the

beginning of God's creation" (NJV: "When God began to create . . ."),
Nahmanides adds an interpretation according to the "way of truth," that is,
the Kabbalah, according to which the second *sefirah* (*ḥokhmah*) emanated
(*bara*) the third *sefirah* (*elohim*). Each *sefirah* in the kabbalistic systems of
exegesis is assigned one or more divine names as well as a plethora of
epithets and cognomens which make the biblical text a network of allusions
to what transpires in the world of the *sefirot*, to be deciphered by those who
know the code. But these allusions and this system of code words were
supplemented by a very fundamental technique in interpretation of this
sort—paronomasia, or plays on words.[80] This was, of course, hardly an
innovation in Jewish literature, for it was one of the pillars of rabbinic
hermeneutics and midrash. Yet it was turned to good use in the new
medieval kabbalistic midrash. For example, continuing the creation
account, the *Zohar* relates:

> "And Melchizedek the King of Salem (*shalem*) brought out bread and wine"
> (Gen 14:18). Rabbi Simeon began his discourse: "In Salem (*shalem*) also is set
> his tabernacle," etc. (Ps 76:3). Come and see: when the Holy One, blessed be
> He, desired to create the world, he drew a flame (the *sefirah gevurah*) from
> the scintilla of darkness (here apparently the *sefirah binah*) and blew one
> spark against the other: it dimmed and then glowed, and He drew from the
> depths (the *sefirah hokhmah*) one drop (the *sefirah hesed*) and joined them
> together and through them created the world. The flame (*gevurah*) rose and
> ensconced itself on the left and the drop (*hesed*) rose and ensconced itself on
> the right, they being intermeshed and entangled, ascending and descending
> [in disharmony]. A current of wholeness (*shalim*, i.e., the *sefirah tif'eret*)
> went forth and immediately both sides became one. [*Tif'eret*] resided bet-
> ween them [*hesed* and *gevurah*] and they were bound with each other. Then
> was there peace (*shelam*) above and peace below and the ladder [the *sefirot*]
> was firm. . . . Then "Melchizedek was the King of Salem," the King of Salem,
> to be sure, the king who governs in wholeness (*bi-shelemu*). (*Zohar* 1:86b–87a)

Thus, a temporary disarray in the creation of the "sefirotic" world is
resolved with the creation of *tif'eret*, so that the Holy One, blessed be He,
is the King of Salem (*shalem*) who brings peace (*shelam*) and wholeness
(*shelemu*) to the world.

But it was not only the Kabbalah that employed paronomasia; philosophical allegory made extensive use of it as well. Thus, in explaining the
meaning of the book of Job, Maimonides plays on the name of Job's homeland, Uz, pointing out that among other things it is the imperative of the
verb ʿuz: "It is as if [Scripture] said to you: 'Meditate and reflect on this
parable, grasp its meaning, and see what the true opinion is'" (*Guide* 3:22).
Thus, the exhortation to scrutinize the book of Job for its true message is
alluded to in an apparently incidental reference to a place name.

The use of paronomasia was limited only by the philological (or pseudo-philological) ingenuity of the writer. To one post-Maimonidean, the sons of Leah symbolized the senses, since one of the sons of Dan is called Hushim (Hebrew: *ḥushim*, "senses"). In this way, Reuben is sight (*re'ut*), Simeon (*Shim'on*) hearing (*shema'*), and so forth,[81] an approach not all that different from that of the early Christians who saw Simon of Cyrene as representing the five senses because he came from the Lybian Pentapolis![82] Joseph Ibn Kaspi (Provence, turn of the fourteenth century), who was generally, although not absolutely, disinclined from allegory,[83] interpreted the cherubim (*keruvim*) as the separate intellects who are "mounted (*rekhuvim*) on stones of fire."[84] Isaac Arama, the fifteenth-century Spanish homilist, takes Abraham's saddling his ass (*wa-yaḥavosh 'et ḥamoro*, Gen 22:3) to refer to the subduing of his material component (*kevishat he-ḥeleq ha-ḥomri*),[85] and Isaac ben Yedaiah, in his commentary on the *aggadot*, even interprets Zion (*ẓiyyon*) as "the intellectual signification (*ha-ẓiyyun*) . . . that is in man."[86]

A second important technique was the use of stock metaphors. As we have seen, harking back to ancient allegorical traditions, male and female were standard representations of matter and form;[87] water, which according to rabbinic tradition represented Torah, now could refer to philosophical wisdom;[88] "evil waters" (Ps 124:5), by association with Christian baptism, alluded to apostasy[89] or, as in the flood story, the waters of sin, against which one is protected by an ark of good deeds with three levels representing mathematics, physics, metaphysics,[90] and so forth. Although this was seldom developed into a full-fledged formalized system, as it was in the *aggadic allegorēsis* of Isaac ben Yedaiah, its traces were clearly marked.

Yet it was not only the words and letters of the sacred text which were vehicles of esoteric interpretation; it was the numbers as well. As M.-D. Chenu has observed: "Numbers were like the thoughts of God, and in decoding their meaning one discovered the secret of a world whose harmony derived from 'measure and number and weight' (Wisd. 11:21)."[91] Numerical manipulations in the form of *gemaṭria* and other techniques were integral elements of early rabbinic exegesis as well, but the Middle Ages developed numerical interpretation in elaborate schemes designed to reveal the mysteries of the universe. The interpretation of the four rivers of Eden, which had its origin in the allegorization of the Eden story by Solomon Ibn Gabirol quoted by Abraham Ibn Ezra, was oft repeated.[92] But this is trivial compared with David Kimhi's almost encyclopedic listing of the meaning of the number four in Ezekiel 1 in his esoteric commentary on that chapter.

[It refers to] ... the four elements from which the lower world was formed and the world of the four species: mineral, vegetable, animal, and rational. The great luminaries which direct the lower worlds move in fours, for the sun moves in its course through the four seasons of the year and the moon in four phases in a month. The day is divided into four periods against the four elements. Similarly the animal and vegetable kingdoms are in fours. . . . . In a like fashion, the government of the microcosm is related to the number four for the governors of the human body are four: the nutritive, the sensitive, the imaginative, and the appetitive. The nutritive is divided into four faculties: the ingestive, the retentive, the digestive, and the eliminative, with the four qualities: heat, cold, dryness and humidity. Item, the four humors through which the body is maintained: blood, white gall, red gall, and black gall. Item, the four prime problems: existence, what, how, and why . . . and four is the first perfect square. Again $1+2+3+4$ is equal to ten. . . .[93]

But if this listing presumed to be exhaustive—as it is unquestionably exhausting—other numerical symbolical references taxed one's energy by taxing one's wit, for some ingenuity had to be used in deciphering them. Thus, the *Zohar* tells us that on the Sabbath, "the Torah is crowned in perfect crowns, on this day the [sound of] joy and delectation is heard in 250 worlds" (*Zohar* 2:88b). It is hardly obvious that the number 250 refers to the 248 limbs[94] of the *shekhinah*, the *sefirah malkhut*, who is embracing in dance the two *sefirot*, *hesed* and *gevurah*—thus 250.

The examples adduced here are perhaps extreme and indeed are deliberately chosen in order to put into relief the kind of approach taken. This does not mean, though, that esoteric interpretation, especially philosophical *allegorēsis*, did not have its rules. One of the earliest pronouncements on the limits of "nonliteral" interpretation was that of the tenth-century Iraqi scholar, Saadya Gaon, whose statement has become a classic:

We, the congregation of Israelites, accept in its literal sense and its universally recognized meaning whatever is recorded in the books of God that have been transmitted to us. The only exceptions to this rule are those instances in which the generally recognized and usual rendering would lead to one of the four [following] results: either (a) the contradiction of the observation of the senses . . . ; or (b) the contravention of reason . . . ; or (c) a conflict with some other Scriptural utterance; or finally, (d) a conflict with what has been transmitted by rabbinic tradition. . . . Now the method of interpretation to be adopted in these exceptional cases is to look for a rending of the expressions [that are in doubt], which would be permissible in the usages of the Hebrew language and would make it possible for the contradictions to be reconciled.[95]

This statement is of course intended to a great extent to deal with the problem of anthropomorphisms and anthropopathisms, that is, individual metaphors, rather than the extended metaphor which is allegory as well as certain very specific problems, although allegory is by no means excluded. Yet it was the spirit of this statement that kept a check on what was to be allegorized not only by him but by Abraham Ibn Ezra.[96] It was really not until the generations of Maimonides and the post-Maimonideans that esoteric interpretation among the philosophers was used not only for limited, apologetic purposes but also, as we have seen, as a natural mode of exegesis. Yet even then *allegorēsis* had, officially at least, its limitations. And if, in Goethe's felicitous phrase, "it is in his restraint that the master reveals himself," Maimonides once again proved himself the master. Although Maimonides clearly approved of *allegorēsis,* he used it only to a very limited extent in the *Guide*—and where he did do so he indicated that there was a certain artistry in esoteric exegesis. When a passage is selected for *allegorēsis,* not every word has to be exploited. As Spenser warned in the preface to the *Faerie Queene:* "Many adventures are intermeddled rather as Accidents than intendments."[97] Thus, in the introduction to the *Guide,* Maimonides advises that there are two kinds of prophetic parables.

> In some of these parables each word has a meaning, while in others the parable as a whole indicates the whole of the intended meaning. In such a parable very many words are to be found, not every one of which adds something to the intended meaning. They serve rather to embellish the parable and to render it more coherent or to conceal further the intended meaning, hence the speech proceeds in such a way as to accord with everything required by the parable's external meaning. Understand this well. (Pines, p. 12)

As an example of the first kind, Maimonides cites Gen 28:12–13, the account of Jacob's ladder; as an example of the second, Prov 7:6–21, the story of the harlot. Explaining that the passage is an allegory in which the harlot represents matter, the cause of all bodily pleasures, against the pursuit of which one is warned, Maimonides insists that certain phrases are completely tangential to the narrative.

> What can be submitted for the words, *"Sacrifices of peace-offerings were due from me, this day have I paid my vows"* (7:14). What subject is indicated by the words, *"I have decked my couch with coverlets?"* (7:16) And what subject is added to the general propositions by the words, *"For my husband is not at home?"* (7:19)

He warns then:

> [When the reader] find[s] in some chapter of this Treatise I have explained the meaning of a parable and have drawn your attention to the general proposition signified by it, you should not inquire into all the details occurring in the parable, nor should you wish to find significations corresponding to

them. For doing so would lead you into one of two ways: either into turning aside from the parable's intended subject, or into assuming an obligation to interpret things not susceptible of interpretation and that have not been ingested with a view to interpretation. (*Guide,* introduction; Pines, p. 14)

These, of course, are the words of a master, of one who knew how to practice restraint, of one who knew how not to outdo himself. And indeed, on these verses, where the master gave guidance, the disciples followed, although elsewhere they might be less discreet and judicious. In this way, Zerahiah Ḥen in his rather lengthy commentary on Proverbs was faithful to the master and refrained from explicating three verses in Proverbs 7 which Maimonides considered decorative, although he was prolix on the others; whereas Immanuel of Rome singled these verses out as coming only to flesh out the chapter.[98]

Samuel Ibn Tibbon saw another reason for this sort of literary "padding." Connecting it with the Maimonidean style of esoteric writing, in which the truth is hidden in a web of repetition and contradiction in order to conceal it from the masses, he states:

This is the way of concealment used by Ecclesiastes in his book in order to make his rhetoric more difficult, by the use of equivocity, by both dropping and adding necessary connections [between themes] and this makes it possible for someone to interpret in a way counter to the intended interpretation . . . but the man of understanding will understand. . . . It should not occur to you that [Ecclesiastes] is needlessly repetitious. . . . Any time he repeats himself or appears to contradict himself he does it intentionally, and the intelligent reader will understand what he wanted to innovate by this repetition, and which of the two contradictory teachings is the truth which the author wishes to communicate.[99]

Again then, deliberate obfuscation helps draw the ways of the labyrinthine maze from which the adept must seek to extricate himself.

Allegorical Interpretation of Rabbinic Literature

The problems encountered by medieval Judaism in reading the Bible were to be no less severe when it came to interpreting rabbinic midrash, especially the *aggadah* or nonlegal material. It was once again not just a question of individual anthropomorphic or anthropopathic phrases but of entire passages—passages that were the products of an essentially oriental literature, couched in the language and painted in the colors of the oriental imagination, which were now to be read by those who professed—with the rise of Islam, the absorption of Greek culture, and the translation of Judaism to Western Europe—an occidental religion. In his *Kuzari,* the twelfth-century Andalusian thinker, Judah Halevi, raises this problem in the imaginary dialogue between a Jewish sage and the king of the Khazar nation, who had just converted to Judaism and was receiving instruction in his new religion. The sage admits that there may indeed be many a thing in rabbinic literature "which is considered less attractive today," but "was held proper in those days." Taking the opening, the king indeed notes that "the application of such verses once for legal deductions, another time for homiletic purposes, does not tally with their real meaning. Their *aggadot* and tales are often against reason." The sage advises that rather than consider the rabbis deficient in the art of dialectic, one must take the apparently difficult *aggadot* either "as basis and introduction for explanations and injunctions" in the case of the anthropomorphic and anthropopathic *aggadot* or the "tales of visions and spirits, a matter which is not strange in such pious men." Others are clearly esoteric "parables employed to express mysterious teachings which were not to be made public. For they are of no use to the masses and were handed over to a few select persons for research and investigation, if a proper person suitable—one in an age, *or in several*—could be found. Other sayings appear senseless on the face of them, but that they have their meaning, becomes apparent after but a little reflection" (emphasis added).

The *aggadot*, then, are not to be taken lightly, for, like certain biblical passages, they are reserved for a limited elite. As an example, Halevi cites a passage from *b. Pes.* 54b and *b. Ned.* 39b:

> "Seven things were created prior to the world: Paradise, the Torah, the just, Israel, the throne of glory, Jerusalem, and the Messiah, the son of David." This is similar to the saying of some philosophers: "The primary thought includes the final deed." It was the object of divine wisdom in the creation of the world to create the Torah, which was the essence of wisdom, and whose bearers are the just, among whom stands the throne of glory and the truly righteous, who are the most select, viz. Israel, and the proper place for them was Jerusalem, and only the best of men, viz. the Messiah, son of David, could be associated with them, and they all entered Paradise. Figuratively speaking, one must assume that they were created prior to the world. (*Kuzari* 3:67–73).[100]

Thus, the difficult passages are to be taken as allegories and metaphors. Maimonides formalizes this principle by categorizing in several places three approaches to *aggadah*, two erroneous and one correct. Two classes take the words of the *aggadah* literally: one accepts them at face value and imagines that the sages "have said these things in order to explain the meaning of the text in question," and the other "holds the [*midrashim*] in slight esteem and holds them up to ridicule, since it is clear and manifest that this is not the meaning of the biblical text in question." The fundamentalist "first class strives and fights with a view to proving, as they deem, the correctness of the *midrashim* and to defending them and think that this is the true meaning of the [biblical] text and that the *midrashim* have the same status as the traditional legal decisions." But both classes are gravely in error, for literalism can lead only to blind fundamentalism, on the one hand, or mocking rejection on the other. What both groups must realize is that the *aggadot* "have the character of poetical conceits whose meaning is not obscure for someone endowed with understanding. At that time this method was generally known and used by everybody, just as the poets use poetical expressions." To illustrate this, Maimonides cites the *aggadah* from *b. Ket.* 15a (quoted above) which plays on Deut 23:14, according to which the command to have a paddle (*yated*) on one's weapon ('*azenekha*) is interpreted as a moral homily according to which one should plug one's ear ('*oznekha*) on hearing something reprehensible. Maimonides rails:

> Would that I knew whether, in the opinion of these ignoramuses, this tannaite believed this to be the interpretation of the text, that such was the purpose of this commandment. . . . I do not think that anyone of sound intellect will be of this opinion. But this is a most witty poetical conceit by means of which he instills a noble moral quality . . . and he props it up through a reference to a [biblical] text, as is done in poetical compositions.[101]

Although the example brought by Maimonides is not allegorical, the principle is established. As Judah Halevi put it, the biblical text is a fulcrum on which the true meaning of the parable turns. Although he himself would not, as a rule, allegorize the *aggadah,* he most certainly opened the door for others to do so.[102] His rather limited expositions would be developed by a wide variety of writers into interpretations such as the following explication of an apparently fanciful passage from *b. Baba Batra* 75a by Shem Tov ben Isaac Shaprut:

> Rabbah stated in the name of . . . R. Johanan: The Holy One, blessed be He, will in time to come make a tabernacle for the righteous from the skin of Leviathan; for it is said "Can you fill tabernacles with his skin" (Job 40:31). If a man is worthy, a tabernacle is made for him. If a man is [sufficiently] worthy, a covering is made for him; if he is not worthy [even of this], a necklace is made for him; if he is not worthy [even of this] an amulet is made for him. . . .
> Know that the skin ('*or*) alludes to light ('*or*) and emanation which the soul acquires as they said in the *haggadah:* "And the Lord God made . . . garments of skin ('*or*) (Gen 3:21), i.e. , garments of light ('*or*)" (*Gen. Rab.* 20:12). The sage clarified for us the purpose of the resurrection of the dead. He said that it is [to enable] man to acquire the perfection which he had not acquired previously because of all extraneous matters which prevent apprehension,

and at the time of the resurrection there will be no tempter (*satan*) or evil affliction and one will be able to apprehend that which he is lacking. He also advised that one should not think that at that time all will be equal for there will be differentiation according to [the degree of] apprehension for there are those who apprehend a great deal and those who apprehend a bit. . . . *Now reader, see how all these* haggadot *explain great secrets and awesome matters hidden from the eyes of the sages. Praised be God who revealed their intention to us so we could understand their inner meaning.*[103]

Although there would be not a few who, like Ibn Shaprut, would attempt to penetrate the true meaning of the rabbinic dicta, Maimonides, like Judah Halevi, was less than optimistic about the possibility. Whereas the latter saw only "one in an age or in several," Maimonides says that the third class of people, those who truly understand, are so few that they can be considered a class only in the sense that the sun is considered a species.[104] And in principle they were correct, for opposition to *allegorēsis* of the *aggadot* was rife especially during the time of the thirteenth-century Maimonidean controversy. Those who favored esoteric interpretation of the *aggadah* constantly harked back to earlier authorities to establish the legitimacy of their approach—David Kimhi to the Geonim[105] and Yedaiah Ha-Penini of Beziers who argued:

It is not today that we started to allegorize the *haggadot* . . . and understand them in a manner other than their exoteric sense. I will say that we are not only permitted to do so but that we are commanded by the master of blessed memory [Maimonides] to be concerned for the honor of our sainted sages and to clarify and explain them in a fashion which will be compatible with the truth without the roots of the faith being affected.[106]

Such justificatory statements have, to a great extent, led some to see in the philosophical *allegorēsis* of the midrash an apologetic tendency, a sense of embarrassment in confronting the fanciful and at times "irrational" *aggadah*. Such *aggadot* had been, it is true, under attack by forces outside of rabbinic Judaism to show the alleged absurdity of rabbinic traditions and teachings.[107] Karaism, Islam, and Christianity all contributed their share to attacking the midrashic heritage.[108] It is true too that such *aggadot* were problematic for those biblical exegetes who were interested in following the plain sense of Scripture.[109] But this did not necessarily mean that the "rationalists," more than any other Jews, were embarrassed by the *aggadah*. Rather, the huge exegetical enterprise undertaken by them shows a conviction (note the enthusiastic conclusion of Ibn Shaprut's remarks cited above!) that rabbinic tradition contains the teachings of Greek philosophy. It was the task of the exegete of *aggadah* to decipher these teachings, which the rabbis masked in fanciful guise very much for the same reasons that the biblical writers ostensibly masked their esoteric teachings in disguise—to hide the truth from dolts,[110] to make their teachings more appealing to the masses, and so forth. In this way, the motivation of the philosophizers would be similar to that of the Kabbalists in their quest to extract kabbalistic teachings from rabbinic midrash and thereby demonstrate the antiquity of the Kabbalah. Thus, Rabbi Azriel of Gerona in the thirteenth century would write a commentary on the *aggadot* in which many passages would be explained according to the sefirotic system. The anthropomorphic passage about God's wearing phylacteries is explained in terms of the ten *sefirot:* the four compartments of the head phylactery represent the first four *sefirot,* the fifth *sefirah,* "strength," is represented by the "left hand of God," on which the hand phylactery is placed on the basis of the proof text Isa 26:8. That the word *yadekhah* ("your hand") in "It will be as a sign on your hand" (Exod 13:16) is spelled with a superfluous *heh,* the fifth letter of the Hebrew alphabet shows, too, that the phylactery placed on the left hand is the fifth *sefirah.* The lower five *sefirot* are represented by the knot of the phylacteries, which, according to tradition, was revealed to Moses when he was shown God's back (Exod 33:24).[111]

Esoteric Interpretation of the Commandments: Allegory versus Symbol

The search for the esoteric sense of *aggadah* had, as do all matters *aggadic*—its halakhic parallel, the quest for the inner meaning of the *mizwot,* of the commandments of the Torah according to their traditional rabbinic interpretations. The imperative of seeking out this meaning is given a striking rationale by Jacob Anatoli. He harks back to the Christian argument, familiar to us from the statement from Joseph Kimhi's *Book of the Covenant* with which we began this paper, that "we eat the husks while they eat the fruit" and argues that this is indeed the case. The problem is that "their fruit is the fruit of falsehood, while the fruit of truth, as bequeathed by Moses, is not cultivated because of Jewish negligence and superficiality in reading the Scriptures."[112]

The entire question of this esoteric interpretation of the commandments has far-reaching consequences not only in terms of the history of exegesis but in terms of Jewish religious history as well. It is here also that some have seen a strong line of demarcation between the approach of the philosophers and that of the Kabbalists. According to this dichotomy, the *allegorēsis* of the philosophers had the potential for leading to the abandonment of the actual observance of the commandment itself. In other words, there was a potential (and at times allegedly actual) antinomianism, since, according to this conception, if one understood the philosophical rationale of a commandment there was no longer any need to perform it in deed. In contrast, kabbalistic exegesis of the commandments is held to be symbolic, the symbol—in this case, the commandment—retaining its own integrity.

> The thing which becomes a symbol retains its original form and its original context. It does not become, so to speak, an empty shell, into which another content is poured; in itself, through its own existence, it makes another reality transparent which cannot appear in any other form. If allegory can be defined as the representation of an expressible something by another expressible something, the mystical symbol is an expressible representation of something which lies beyond the sphere of expression and communication.[113]

Before examining the validity of this point of view, let us review the treatment of a particular *mizwah*, namely, that of dwelling in a booth or *sukkah* during the Feast of Tabernacles (Lev 23:42–43), in the philosophical tradition and the *Zohar*.

In dealing with the former, our primary concern is not with the issue of *ta'amei ha-mizwot*, the enterprise of explaining the reasons for which the commandments were actually given, but with actual allegorization of the commandment. The *ta'am* or reason is fairly straightforward. Whether Maimonides, Gersonides, or others, all agree that the reason for the commandment is that one dwell in the *sukkah* in order to be reminded of the days of poverty in the desert, so that he may be grateful to God for his present prosperity, or to be reminded of the miracles performed in the desert.[114] Allegorization, on the other hand, follows the pattern we have been observing. Bahya ben Asher, who combined philosophy with Kabbalah, explains the minimal seven handspans required for the width of the *sukkah*[115] as representing the seven liberal arts, the ten for the height the ten commandments, and the seventy square handspans of each side the seventy "faces" of the Torah.[116] According to Gersonides, the covering (*sikkukh*) of the *sukkah*, made of some material that is naturally grown from the earth, has the function of teaching that, as one becomes aged and the veil (*masakh*) of matter is removed from the intellect and becomes fragile like the covering of the *sukkah*, one must not think one can abandon the study of the natural sciences and engage only in metaphysics but must still engage in the former since they lead to the latter, and ultimately to the awe of God.[117] Hasdai Crescas again interprets the covering of the *sukkah* allegorically:

> As the body is the vehicle for the soul which is the form of man and shelters him, the covering is the essence of the *sukkah* and shelters him. Thus the Torah commanded that it be made of material which grows from the ground

to indicate submission and that it not be subject to defilement in order to alert us concerning the purity of our souls.[118]

Moving now from these rationalistic allegorizations of elements of the *sukkah*, let us review one kabbalistic, specifically Zoharic, interpretation.[119]

Among the interpretations of the *Zohar* of the Feast of Tabernacles is that of the invitation into the *sukkah* of "guests," *'ushpizin*, a word related to one found in rabbinic literature meaning "inn"[120] but given the connotation of "guest" by the author, probably under the influence of the Castilian *huésped*. This apparently extraneous bit of philology is useful in that it dates to the Middle Ages the custom of *'ushpizin*, a custom widely practiced until today even by Jews totally unaware of its Zoharic origins. According to this custom, seven heavenly guests, Abraham, Isaac, Jacob, Moses, Aaron, Joseph, and David, are invited into the *sukkah* on each of the seven days of the holiday. These heavenly guests are the seven heavenly days, that is, the seven lower *sefirot*, and by the fulfillment of the precept, the unity of the seven *sefirot* is brought about.

> R. Abba said: It is written: "In booths shall you dwell, seven days" (Lev 23:42). The *Zohar* reads the verse as if the seven supernal days, the seven *sefirot*, are being addressed. And afterwards: "they shall dwell in booths" (Lev 23:42). . . . The first is for the guests (*'ushpizin*), the second for those of this world. The first for the guests as when R. Himnuna the Elder entered the *sukkah*, he rejoiced and stood at the entrance of the *sukkah* from within and said: "Let us invite the guests, let us set the table." He stood and blessed and said: "'You shall dwell in booths seven days' (Lev 23:42). Be seated, O supernal guests, be seated! Be seated, O guests of faith, be seated!" He raised his hands and rejoiced and said: "Happy is our portion, happy the portion of Israel as it is written 'for the portion of the Lord is His people'"(Num 32:9), and he would sit down. The second [verse, Lev 23:42], refers to those of this world, for he who has a portion in his people and in the holy land sits in the shadow of faith to receive the guests and rejoice in this world and the next. (*Zohar* 3:103b–104a).

It is at this point that the *Zohar* adds its own dimension to its understanding of the performance of the commandments. Their purpose, the unification of the upper world, the world of the *sefirot*, is not accomplished unless there is a corresponding fulfillment below in this world. Therefore, the invitation of the heavenly guests will be to no avail for they will not grace the *sukkah*, unless *earthly* guests, the poor (and, for Bahya ben Asher, the scholars,[121] for who can be poorer than they?), are invited as well.

> Nonetheless, one must give pleasure to the poor. For what reason? Because the portion of the guests (*'ushpizin*) which he invited belongs to the poor. And he who sits in the shadow of the faith, and does not give them their

portion has them all get up and leave saying: "Do not eat the bread of him that has an evil eye" (Prov 23:6), for it develops that the table he set was intended for him and not for the Holy One, blessed be He. Concerning him, it is said: "I will spread dung upon your faces" (Mal 2:3), "the dung of your sacrifices" (Mal 2:3), and not *My* sacrifices. Woe to him when the guests of faith get up and leave his table. (*Zohar* 3.104a).

In this way, the esoteric level of the commandment has no validity unless the exoteric level—the literal observance of the commandment—is fulfilled. Further, the purpose of the commandment according to the philosophers, the recollection of the Israelites' poverty in the desert, is translated here into action, recollection through concern for the poor. And he who shows no such concern for the poor, the representatives of the patriarchs who symbolize the *sefirot*, is cursed in the roundest and most colorful terms.

> Rabbi Abba said: Abraham would always stand at the crossroads to invite guests and set the table for them. Now, when they invite him and all the righteous ones and King David and do not give them their portion, Abraham gets up from the table and says: "Depart, I pray you, from the tents of these wicked men" (Num 16:26) and they all leave with him. Isaac says: "The belly of the wicked shall want" (Prov 13:25). Jacob says: "The morsel you have eaten you shall vomit up" (Prov 23:8). The rest of the righteous say: "For all tables are full of filthy vomit and no place is clean" (Isa 28:8). King David [representative of the *sefirah malkhut*, which serves as the agent for punishing the wicked] says [this verse] and exerts retribution.... (*Zohar* 3:104a)

But he who fulfills the commandment in sincerity, even if his means only allow him to do so in the humblest capacity, is greatly blessed.

> Rabbi Eleazar said: The Torah has not laid a burden on man greater than he can bear, as it is written: "every man shall give as he is able" (Deut 16:17). Let not one say: first, I shall eat to satiety and quench my thirst and shall give to the poor what remains; but the first portion is for the guests. And if he gives pleasure to the guests and satisfies them, the Holy One, blessed be He, rejoices with him and Abraham invokes the verse: "Then shall you delight in the Lord" (Isa 58:14) while Isaac invokes the verse: "No weapon that is formed against you shall prosper" (Isa 54:17). (*Zohar* 3:104a)

What does an example such as this teach us of the effect of esoteric exegesis on halakhic practice? Despite the presence of ostensibly antinomian passages in Zoharic literature, the *Tiqquney Zohar* and *Ra'ya Meheimna* and in kabbalistic literature in general,[122] the prevalent trend is a confirmation of the actual observance of the *mizwah* since only that which has a correspondence in the lower world can have reality in the upper world. The question that needs examination, then, is the widespread view that philosophical *allegorēsis* led to abandonment of the observance of *halakhah*. There are two bases for this view, one historical and one literary critical. The former stems largely from the criticism heard during the Maimonidean controversy of the thirteenth century in which, among other things, the allegorists, in their attempt to imitate Maimonides, "made dark light and light dark" and "went out against Eden, the Garden of God, for which all Israel longs; it was a beautiful sight to behold . . . after them it was a desolation."[123] According to these critics the very foundations of the faith were shaken by the allegorization of the creation story, since the observance of the Sabbath rests on the principle of creation.[124] They tell too of actual ritual indifference, laxity in prayer, and so forth.[125]

The latter, literary-critical view, which sees in philosophical *allegorēsis* a catalyst for the abandonment of halakhic observance, is the distinction between allegory, in which the literal sense is nulled or annulled, and symbol, in which that which is symbolized participates in the symbol—in this case, the *mizwah*—and therefore the precept itself cannot be annulled.

The difficulty with the first critique of philosophical *allegorēsis*, stemming primarily from the acrimonious feuding of the Maimonidean controversy, is that we have virtually no evidence that these charges had any validity. As is true with so many heresy hunts throughout history, our literary records present the point of view of the accusers rather than that of the accused. The latter, the so-called philosophizers or rationalists, continually protest their orthodoxy, and indeed the sources give us scant reason to doubt them. The one example continuously branded as an archheretic, Levi ben Ḥayyim, was in reality hardly immoderate in his views and was lauded by his familiars for his piety. If negligence in religious observance did exist, it seems to have been due more to general indifference rather than to sophisticated intellectual considerations.[126]

The second critique, the literary-critical, with its distinction between allegory and symbol, has its origins in Goethe and since his time has undergone numerous modifications and metamorphoses.[127] To a certain extent, this literary-critical crux seems to mirror or at least parallel the distinction made in modern times between allegory and typology in Christian biblical exegesis. The former, with its roots in Philo and Origen is seen as discarding the literal or historical sense; the latter, with its purpose of establishing the link between one historical reality and another, is seen as preserving it.[128] Typology is, then, "a legitimate extension of the literal sense, while word allegory is something entirely alien: the former is in truth exegesis, the latter is not."[129] This approach has led to a general embarrassment on the part of modern Christian exegetes with allegory, that is, moral allegory, which is a "rationalistic phenomenon" over against typology, which is "concerned with tying into facts, not spiritual truths."[130]

To transfer the problematics of modern Christian biblical exegesis and certain outmoded theories of literary criticism to concerns of medieval Jewish theology is, to say the least, fraught with difficulties.[131] For one thing, patristic and medieval Christian exegesis repeated, by and large, its insistence that the spiritual senses, tropology and so forth, that which the moderns call allegory, in no way annuls but indeed validates the literal or historical: "Spiritual understanding is founded on the literal and pre-supposes it."[132] It is true, of course, that Christian recognition of the literal sense did not necessarily imply literal fulfillment. Whereas even the proph-ecies concerning Jerusalem, which had been traditionally spiritualized in Christian tradition, were taken literally when historical circumstances made it desirable, that is, with the establishment of the Crusader king-dom,[133] the fulfillment of the ritual commandments was not, for they were considered a category unto themselves.[134] In no way, however, should we commit the fallacy of drawing an analogy between Jewish spiritualization and allegorization of the commandments and that of Christianity against its background of conceptions of a new dispensation and freedom from the "law."[135]

And so we find Jacob Anatoli, the object of so much criticism in the Maimonidean controversy, stressing in the very context of his sermon for Tabernacles that "true opinions need deeds in order to reinforce them."[136] Yet the fifteenth-century Spanish Jewish philosopher, Joseph Albo, address-ing himself to Christian spiritualization of the commandments, notes in his *Book of Roots* that the Torah is called "testimony" (Exod 25:21, Ps 132:12) to signify that the words of the Torah are to be taken at their face value, like the testimony of witnesses in a court case, and that we must not give them figurative interpretations (*we-lo na'aseh lahem zurot*) or read into them conditions or time limitations that are not explicitly stated. He insists that "no man has the power to abolish the literal meaning of the commandments by interpretation." At the same time, however, many passages in the Torah "bear allusion to more noble and celestial things. Thus, the account of the tabernacle refers to real things, and at the same time bears allusion to sublime and celestial things. . . ." In sum, "there are in the Torah expressions which allude to other nobler and more sublime things, and yet are also true in their literal meaning. *This is especially true of the commandments.* They do allude to noble and sublime things, but at the same time there is an important purpose in themselves and in their performance."[137]

Thus are the words of a "philosopher," writing, it is true, ostensibly against the background of an anti-Christian polemic but essentially reiterating the traditional Jewish view that multiple interpretation of Scripture leaves each level of interpretation intact. And this is indeed in complete harmony with what reading or practicing allegory is all about. As C. S. Lewis has warned, one must be wary of the danger of "attend[ing] to the signification in the abstract and . . . throw[ing] aside the allegorical imagery as something which has done its work."[138] For the one cannot dispense with the other, in that "allegory calls attention to the 'other'—in a word to God, or to some sort of possible 'sacredness'; by interfolded correspondences between word and word, one woven web of sense (one text) calls attention to the plexed (or 'folded') artistry of another text."[139] Allegory is not then a throwing away but, as W. Y. Tindall notes—if we transfer his use of the term "symbol" to ours of "allegory"—a "throwing . . . together."[140]

Thus, the dichotomy between rationalistic *allegorēsis* and kabbalistic interpretation would have to be tempered, first of all, on literary-critical grounds.[141] Moreover, certain Kabbalists themselves were prepared to make use of philosophical allegory itself as a legitimate mode of interpretation even though it was not the kabbalistic truth. Bahya ben Asher in his *Kad ha-Qemah* discusses the very *mizwah*, *sukkah*, with which we began.

> Therefore one must fulfill the precept of *sukkah* concretely (*be-murgash*) and consider its ideational (*be-muskal*) character, [for . . . it is the latter which is] its ultimate purpose . . . for the physical (*gashmit*) level is not like the ideational (*sikhlit*) level. Now it is known that our forefathers experienced both at the Red Sea: . . . the physical crossing . . . when they physically perceived that remarkable miracle and the metaphysical perception as our rabbis said: "A maidservant at the Red Sea saw what Ezekiel ben Buzi did not" (*Mekhilta*, *Shirah* 3). Thus it is the essence of the fulfillment of a *mizwah* that one contemplates its essence which is its metaphysical and esoteric element. But one is fulfilled only through both, for even though one knows the esoteric level (*nistar*) of a precept, one is not exempted from fulfilling it on the exoteric level (*nigleh*). Of this it is written: "The hidden things (*ha-nistarot*) are the Lord our God's and the revealed things (*ha-niglot*) are for us and our sons" (Deut 29:28), . . . i.e., we are under the obligation to fulfill them exoterically for with a knowledge of the esoteric we cannot possibly be exempted from the exoteric.[142]

What does exist here is a hierarchy in the levels of meaning, whether in the Kabbalists' four senses, in the simpler formulation of the eleventh-century Spanish philosopher Bahya Ibn Paquda that "the rational and practical commandments . . . are only a means by which to ascend to the intellectual perception which is the ultimate purpose intended in the creation of the human species in this world,"[143] or in that of his later namesake, Bahya ben Asher, falling back on Maimonides's parable: "For the superiority of the esoteric over the exoteric is as the superiority of gold over silver."[144] But hierarchy does not mean abrogation. The more precious the apple of gold, the more must it be guarded by its silver encasement.

Afterword

As a postscript, one may inquire about what remains of this treasure of gold and silver which medieval Judaism bequeathed to posterity. Is it, like so many Hebrew manuscripts of the period, to be placed on the block at Sotheby's and be ultimately viewed as a museum piece or hidden in a dark climate-controlled vault to be taken out occasionally at the request of some odd antiquarian or doctoral student researching a dissertation? Or indeed has it had and does it have a more vital function to fulfill? We have noted previously the embarrassment of modern Christian biblical scholars and theologians at certain types of allegorical exegesis, not only among Protestants, who might be expected to be freer in dispensing with the patristic or medieval legacy,[145] but among Catholics as well. As for Judaism, one would be hard pressed to find very many modern Jews who would accept medieval philosophical *allegorēsis* at face value although kabbalistic interpretation in various modifications and among diverse sectors of the contemporary Jewish world still retains meaning. Yet this is not the real point at issue.

One of the most difficult concepts to convey to the student embarking on a study of a religious tradition or a particular form of that tradition is that it is not the intention or desire of the instructor to indoctrinate or catechize the student but rather to have the latter appreciate it on its own terms and, if possible, to empathize with its adherents, to penetrate *their* minds—even as an outsider looking in; to see with *their* eyes—even through the glass darkly. If one were to study medieval Jewish esoteric exegesis in this light, one would appreciate that perhaps its most significant legacy for modern Judaism has not been any particular doctrinal interpretation or form of interpretation but the very principle of freedom of interpretation itself, that the Scriptures, biblical or postbiblical, bear more than one meaning, that a modernist approach to a text need not rule out a commitment to belief in tradition. Thus, one retains one's foundation without fundamentalism, one's faith in the Creator without creationism.

This was put on a sardonic level by Walter Kaufmann in his "Dialogue Between Satan and an Atheist." Complaining that arguing with Jews about Scripture never got him anywhere, Satan laments: "They knew the texts as well as I did, made connections from verse to verse across a hundred pages much more nimbly than I did, and were never, absolutely never, fazed by anything I said. . . . Usually they produced some rabbi who, more than a thousand years ago, had made my point and been given some classical answer.[146]

When asked why he could not show that their interpretations were untenable, Satan replies that that was not the point at issue:

> For they considered the whole thing a game, and they played it according to special rules; by their rules, their arguments were tenable. *They never claimed that Moses had meant all the things they put into his mouth.* Of course not. But according to the rules of the game it could be argued that an interpretation of the words of Moses was correct in spite of that—even several conflicting ones.[147]

Through the art of interpretation—the game, if you will—Moses' hard, chiseled tablets become pliable, malleable, flexible—no more to be shattered but to retain their wholeness and integrity.

Thus, when the late Chief Rabbi of Palestine, Abraham Isaac ha-Kohen Kook, was asked concerning the legitimacy of the findings of modern biblical scholarship for the pious Jew, he replied, relying on some of the texts we have cited above, that although one need not blindly accept them, neither must one blindly reject them: "For the purpose of the Torah is not to tell us simple facts and stories. Its essence is that which lies within (*tokh*), the inner elucidation of the material."[148] If anything, he continues, should modern biblical scholarship challenge traditional understanding of the Torah, all the better! For it will spur on the pious Jew to probe more deeply and search out the Torah's profounder intents.[149] Yes, a game it may all be, but it is one that has allowed Judaism to be continued to be played out in earnest.

Notes

This paper was written in connection with a larger project supported by the Social Sciences and Humanities Research Council of Canada. My thanks to Rivka Hurwitz and Barry Walfish for their keen interest and bibliographical references and to Moshe Idel for numerous suggestions and his generosity in allowing me to think through with him many of the formulations found here.

1. Joseph Kimhi, *Book of the Covenant,* trans. Frank Talmage (Toronto: Pontifical Institute of Medieval Studies, 1972) 46–47.

2. H. A. Wolfson, *The Philosophy of the Church Fathers,* 2 vols., 3rd rev. ed. (Cambridge, MA: Harvard University Press, 1970) 1:74–75. Cf. G. R. Evans, *The Language and Logic of the Bible: The Early Middle Ages* (Cambridge: University Press, 1984) 155, but contrast pp. 14–15.

3. Beryl Smalley, *The Study of the Bible in the Middle Ages,* passim.

4. See the *Enziqlopedyah Miqra'it*, s.v. "TeNaKh, parshanut"; reprinted as *Parshanut ha-Miqra ha-Yehudit*, ed. Moshe Greenberg (Jerusalem: Mosad Bialik, 1983).

5. Our use of the term allegory in this essay in general does not include the meta-phorical interpretation of individual anthropomorphisms and anthropopathisms. See Isaak Heinemann, "Scientific Allegorization During the Jewish Middle Ages," in *Studies in Jewish Thought*, 247–48.

6. Based on *Tanhuma, Lekh Lekha* 9.

7. See Amos Funkenstein, "Nahmanides' Symbolical Reading of History," in *Studies in Jewish Mysticism*, ed. Joseph Dan and Frank Talmage (Cambridge, MA: Association for Jewish Studies, 1982) 129–50; expanded Hebrew version: "Parshanuto ha-Tipologit shel ha-RaMBaN," *Zion* 45 (1979–80) 35–49; Bahya ben Asher, *Kad ha-Qemah*; Ner hanukkah, Sukkah, in *Kitvey Rabbenu Bahya* (Jerusalem: Mosad Ha-Rav Kook, 1969) 269, 276; Abraham Saba, *Şeror ha-Mor*, 5 vols. in 1 (Warsaw, 1878/80), 4:23b, 5:5b, 32a–b.

8. Isaac ben Joseph Ha-Kohen, *Perush Megillat Rut Megalleh Sod ha-Ge'ulah* (Sabio-netta, 1551); Isaac Abravanel, *Commentary* on Gen 3:22 (Warsaw, 1861/62) p. 22a based on *Gen. Rab.* 19:9.

9. That is, making a thing (*res*) of an abstract notion. See *Dictionary of the Middle Ages*, s.v. "Allegory."

10. See *Encyclopedia of Religion and Ethics*, s.v. "Allegory, Allegorical Interpretation"; Ernst Curtius, *European Literature and the Latin Middle Ages*, trans. W. R. Trask, Bollingen Series 36 (New York: Pantheon Books, 1953) 203–7; Jean Pepin, *Mythe et allégorie: Les origines grecques et les contestations judéo-chrétiennes* (Paris: Editions Montaigne, 1958); Edwin Honig, *Dark Conceit: The Making of Allegory* (London: Faber & Fabar, 1959) 28–31; R. P. C. Hanson, *Allegory and Event* (London: SCM, 1959) 56–62.

11. See Rosemond Tuve, *Allegorical Imagery: Some Medieval Books and Their Posterity* (Princeton, NJ: Princeton University Press, 1966) 219–333: John MacQueen, *Allegory* (London: Methuen, 1970) 15, 46–49.

12. Hillel of Verona in the thirteenth century actually refers to the "superficial" sense of texts following the Christian terminology "iuxta superficiem littere"; see *Tagmuley ha-Nefesh*, ed. Joseph Sermoneta (Jerusalem: Israel Academy of Sciences and Humani-ties, 1981) 146 (*mi shetah peshatei ha-miqra . . .*), 179 (*divrey aggadot . . . nir'im be-shitham ha-hison maskimim 'im peshatei qesat miqra'ot*, 193 (*be-shitham ha-hison*).

13. Vidal Benvenist, *'Efer we-Dinah* (Constantinople, 1516).

14. On the didactic function of medieval belles lettres, see Edward A. Bloom, "The Allegorical Principle," *ELH* 18 (1951) 164–74; Maria Rosa Lida de Malkiel, *Two Spanish Masterpieces: The Book of Good Love and the Celestina* (Urbana: University of Illinois Press, 1961) 24–33; cf. D. W. Foster, *Christian Allegory in Early Hispanic Poetry* (Lexington: University Press of Kentucky, 1970) 93, 100–1 n. 32; Gay Clifford, *The Transformations of Allegory* (London and Boston: Routledge & Kegan Paul, 1974) 37–39. Robert Hollander, *Allegory in Dante's Commedia* (Princeton: Princeton Univer-sity Press, 1969) 54. For a more skeptical view, see Stephen Gilman, *The Spain of Fernando de Rojas* (Princeton: Princeton University Press, 1972) 361–62.

15. Judah al-Harizi, *Tahkemoni*, ed. Y. Toporowski (Tel-Aviv: Mahbarot le-Sifrut, 1952) 13–14; Isaac Ibn Sahula, *Mashal ha-Qadmoni* (Brescia, 1491; photoreprint, Jeru-salem: Kedem, 1976–77) introduction (p. 1): "See the parable and allegory . . . and inner allusion and wisdom within it."

16. On the similar conception of the "pierced technique" in Carolingian art and

exegesis, see Smalley, *Study of the Bible,* 2: ". . . we are invited to look not at the text but through it."

17. Paul Nwiya, *Exégèse coranique et langage mystique* (Beirut: Dar-el-Machreq éditeurs, 1970) 34.

18. Cf. Saba, *Şeror ha-Mor,* 1:28a. These images are, of course, universal and common to the Latin, romance, and English traditions. See D. W. Robertson, Jr., "Some Medieval Literary Terminology with Special Reference to Chrétien de Troyes," *Studies in Philology* 48 (1951) 669–92, and esp. the glossary on p. 692. One of the loveliest expressions is the utterance of Dame Nature in Alain de Lille's *De planctu naturae:* "Do you not know that in the shallow surface of literature the poetic lyre sounds a false note, but within speaks to those hearers of a loftier understanding, in that the chaff of outer falsity cast aside, the reader finds within the sweeter kernel of truth" (*PL* 210:451; English: Alain de Lille, *The Complaint of Nature,* trans. Douglas Moffat, Yale Studies in English 36 [New York: Henry Holt, 1908] 40). This motif is ultimately charmingly satirized by Jonathan Swift in *A Tale of a Tub,* where Wisdom, among other things, is declared to be ". . . a Nut, which unless you chuse with Judgment may cost you a Tooth, and pay you with nothing but a worm" (ed. A. G. Guithkeich and D. Nicholl Smith[Oxford: Oxford University Press, 1920] 66).

19. Cf. Origen *Selecta in Psalmos,* Ps. 1, *PG* (*Patrologiae cursus completus. Series graeca,* ed. J. P. Migne [Paris: J. P. Migne, 1857–66]) 12, col. 1080, cited in Hanson, *Allegory and Event,* 180.

20. The theme of the mystical descent into the palace is carried through in Nahmanides's poem "Me-rosh mi-qadmey 'olamim," printed in Jefim Schirmann, *Ha-Shirah ha-'Ivrit bi-Sefarad u-vi-Provans,* 2 vols. in 4, 2nd ed. (Jerusalem: Mossad Bialik, 1960) 2:322–25. On the development of the theme from the *Zohar* to Moses Hayyim Luzzatto's *Migdal 'oz,* see Fischel Lachover, *'Al Gevul ha-Yashan we-he-Ḥadash* (Jerusalem: Bialik Institute, 1951) 40–51.

21. *Tanhuma, Piqqudey,* 96: "Testimony means Torah. This is likened to a king who had a daughter and built her a palace. He set her within seven chambers and declared: 'If any one reaches my daughter, it is as if he reaches me'"; Américo Castro, *The Structure of Spanish History* (Princeton, NJ: Princeton University Press, 1954) 445–46.

22. Kafka's castle was actually a complex of small buildings, but the effect of sameness and interminability is that described here for they were "innumerable" and the village itself that led to the castle "seemed to have no end; again and again the same little houses . . ." (*The Castle,* trans. Willa and Edwin Muir [London: Penguin, 1970] 16, 17).

23. Castro, *Structure,* 432.

24. On the significance of this iconographic inscription, see Oleg Grabar, *The Alhambra* (Cambridge, MA: Harvard University Press, 1978) 135.

25. On the complexities and drama of the structure of the Alhambra, see Grabar, *Alhambra,* 56–58, 64, 114, 199–200.

26. On allegory in the visual arts and the visual element in allegory, see Clifford, *Transformations,* 71–93; and on the relation between thought and architecture in the Latin Middle Ages, see Erwin Panofsky, *Gothic Architecture and Scholasticism* (Cleveland, OH: World, 1957); O. G. Von Simson, "The Gothic Cathedral: Design and Meaning," in *Change in Medieval Society: Europe North of the Alps, 1050–1500,* ed. Sylvia L. Thrupp (New York: Meredith, 1964) 168–87; Emile Mâle, *The Gothic Image: Religious Art in France of the Thirteenth Century,* trans. Dora Hussey (New York: Harper & Brothers, 1958; reprint of *Religious Art in France: A Study in Medieval Iconography and Its Sources of Inspiration* [London: Dent & Sons, 1913]); Henri de Lubac, *Exégèse médiévale: Les quatre sens de l'écriture,* 2 parts in 4 vols. (Paris: Aubier, 1959–63)

2:2:4–60. For a striking example of modern architectural imagery in literary definition, see W. Y. Tindall, *The Literary Symbol* (New York: Columbia University Press, 1955) 229.

27. Jacob ben Eleazar, " 'Ahavat Sahar we-Khimarh," in Jefim Schirmann, ed., "Sippurey ha-Ahavah shel Ya'aqov ben 'El'azar," *Yedi'ot ha-Makhon le-Ḥeqer ha-Shirah ha-'Ivrit* 5 (1939) 247–66.

28. Cf. Grabar, *Alhambra*, 100–101.

29. See A. C. Hamilton, *The Structure of Allegory in the Faerie Queene* (Oxford: Oxford University Press, 1961) 34–35.

30. See Clifford, *Transformations*, 14–35.

31. Baḥya ben Asher, *Kad ha-Qemaḥ*, Sukkah, in *Kitvey Rabbenu Baḥya*, ed. Chavel, p. 274.

32. Jacob Anatoli, *Malmad ha-Talmidim* (Lyck: Mekize Nirdamim, 1866) introduction, p. [6].

33. Clifford, *Transformations*, 53.

34. Northrop Frye, *Anatomy of Criticism: Four Essays* (Princeton: Princeton University Press, 1957) 89; Maureen Quilligan, *The Language of Allegory: Defining the Genre* (Ithaca, NY and London: Cornell University Press, 1979) 15–16.

35. See Harry Caplan, "The Four Senses of Scriptural Interpretation and the Mediaeval Theory of Preaching," *Speculum* 4 (1925) 282–91; Angus Fletcher, *Allegory: The Theory of a Symbolic Mode* (Ithaca, NY: Cornell University Press, 1964) 5.

36. Wilhelm Bacher, "L'Exégèse biblique dans le Zohar," *Revue des études juives* 22 (1891) 35; Gershom G. Scholem, "The Meaning of the Torah in Jewish Mysticism," in *On the Kabbalah and its Symbolism*, 62–63.

37. Ignaz Goldziher, *Die Richtungen der Islamischen Koranauslegung* (Leiden: Brill, 1920) 84–85, 115–16; cf. Nwiya, *Exégèse coranique*, 109–56 and passim. The concept, as presented by Nwiya, is somewhat more complex than in Judaism. On the seeming inexhaustibility of meanings of a biblical text, see the analysis of Guiseppe (Joseph) Sermoneta, "Prophecy in the Writings of R. Yehuda Romano," in Isadore Twersky, ed., *Studies in Medieval Jewish History and Literature–II* (Cambridge, MA and London: Harvard University Press, 1984) 337–51.

38. Edwin Honig, *Dark Conceit*, 114.

39. See de Lubac, *Exégèse médiévale*.

40. Scholem, "Meaning of the Torah," 56–59.

41. Ibid., 62 n. 1.

42. Wilhelm Bacher ("Das Merkwort PRDS in der jüdischen Bibelexegese," *Zeitschrift für die alttestamentliche Wissenschaft* 13 [1893] 294–305) and Gershom Scholem ("Meaning of the Torah," 61–62) were inclined to see such a connection, but Peretz Sandler ("Li-Ve'ayat PaRDeS we-ha-Shitah ha-Merubba'at," in *Sefer Auerbach* [Jerusalem: Ha-Hevrah le-Ḥeqer ha-Miqra, 1954/55] 222–35) tended to reject it.

43. *Letters of Dante*, trans. Paget Toynbee, 2nd ed. (Oxford: Clarendon Press, 1966) 198; cf. *Convivio* 2.1.3–6. See also MacQueen, *Allegory*, 54–58.

44. Robert Hollander, *Allegory in Dante's* Commedia (Princeton, NJ: Princeton University Press, 1969) 252; de Lubac, *Exégèse médiévale*, 2:2:37–39, 168.

45. Compare the schema of Abraham Maimonides, *Ma'amar 'al odot Derashot HaZaL*, printed in Jacob Ibn Habib, *'Eyn Ya'aqov*, photoreprint ed., 5 vols. (Jerusalem: 'Am 'Olam, 1960–61) 1:16 (*ha-derekh ha-rishon, ha-derekh ha-sheni*).

46. Joseph Sermoneta has seen a correspondence between the fourfold system and Hillel of Verona's classification of rabbinic *aggadah* into six categories (*Tagmuley ha-Nefesh* 2:2, p. 181n.). Although there may be some formal correspondence, this is not

the issue. Hillel is not dealing with multiple approaches to the interpretation of a single text but to the classification of different texts.

47. David Rosin, "Reime und Gedichte des Abraham Ibn Ezra," pt. 2, *Jahresbericht des jüdisch-theologischen Seminars* (Breslau, 1887), p. 60. It is of interest to note here that Angus Fletcher has pointed out that the fourfold scheme of exegesis is a semantic translation of the Aristotelian four causes. The tropological or moral sense would correspond to the efficient cause. (*Allegory*, 313 n. 12).

48. On this point, an examination of Islamic exegesis may be fruitful: see Nwiya, *Exégèse coranique*, 210–11. In general, much could be learned from one competent in both Islamic and Jewish biblical exegesis.

49. The twelfth-century northern French exegete Joseph Bekhor Shor, living in a different intellectual climate, railed against "the nations of the world who say that what Moses said is *allegoria*, that is, riddle and parable (*ḥidah u-mashal*)" (*Commentary* on Num 12:8).

50. Cited in Quilligan, *Language of Allegory*, 27; cf. the passage from Sir John Harrington's preface to his translation of Orlando Furioso cited in Edward A. Bloom, "The Allegorical Principle," *ELH* 18 (1951) 177; P. J. Korshin, *Typologies in England 1650–1750* (Princeton, NJ: Princeton University Press, 1982) 159–60. Such statements are reminiscent of the classic statement of Cassiodorus following Augustine, *In Ps.*, Preface, 15 (Corpus Christianorum scriptorum Latinorum 97; Louvain: Corpus Christianorum scriptorum Latinorum) 19.50–54.

51. Zerahiah ben Isaac ben Shealtiel Hen, *'Imrey Da'at*, ed. Josef Schwarz (Vienna, 1871).

52. Samuel Ibn Tibbon, *Ma'amar Yiqqawu ha-Mayim* (Pressburg, 1837) 174; cited in Aviezer Ravitzky, "Samuel Ibn Tibbon and the Esoteric Character of the *Guide of the Perplexed*," *AJS Review* 6 (1981) 113 and see pp. 111–13. See also Ibn Tibbon's introduction to his commentary on Ecclesiastes cited in Sermoneta, "Prophecy in . . . Yehuda Romano," 340–41, n. 5.

53. See Quilligan, *Language of Allegory*, 30–31.

54. Commentary of Ezra, printed in *Kitvey Rabbenu Mosheh ben Nahman*, ed. C. B. Chavel, 2 vols. (Jerusalem: Mosad Ha-Rav Kook, 1963/64) 480; French translation: *Le commentaire d'Ezra de Gérone sur le cantique des cantiques*, trans. Georges Vajda, 44; Pseudo-Joseph Kimhi is cited in Siegmund Salfeld, *Das Hohelied Salomo's bei den jüdischen Erklärern des Mittelalters* (Berlin, 1879) 53n.

55. See Hanson, *Allegory and Event*, 238. See also Augustine *On the Trinity* 11.2: "The Holy Scriptures, as is fitting for little ones, did not shun any kind of verbal expression through which our understanding might be nourished and rise step by step to divine and sublime things"; and the formulation of the eighth-century Muslim mystique Muqātil Ibn Sulaymān: "God described that which is in His realm (*'indahu*) [i.e., Paradise] by means of that which is in [man's] realm (*'indahum*) in order to direct their hearts to Him"; see Nwiya, *Exégèse coranique*, 101.

56. This is the rationale expressed by the seventh-century Arab compiler of *Kalila wa-Dimnah*, Abdullah Ibn al-Muqaffa'; see Castro, *Structure*, 427–28.

57. Joseph ben Judah Ibn Aknin, *Hitgallut ha-Sodot we-Hofa'at ha-Me'orot*, ed. A. S. Halkin (Jerusalem: Mekize Nirdamim, 1964) 2–5; idem, "Ibn 'Aknin's Commentary on the Song of Songs," *Alexander Marx Jubilee Volume* 407.

58. See Quilligan, *Language of Allegory*, 79–85. Compare the attitude of Isaiah b. Yedaiah toward the *aggadah* as "pandering" to the masses (Marc Saperstein, *Decoding the Rabbis: A Thirteenth-Century Commentary on the Aggadah*, 27) and the similar views

of Joseph Ibn Kaspi (Basil Herring, *Joseph Ibn Kaspi's* Gevia' Kesef: *A Study in Medieval Jewish Philosophic Bible Commentary* [New York: Ktav, 1982] 58-59).

59. See Halkin, "Ibn 'Aknin's Commentary," 390–91; Johan Chydenius, "The Typological Problem in Dante," in *Commentationes Humanarum Litterarum*, Societas Scientiarum Fennica 25 (Helsinki: Finska vetenskaps-societen, 1961) 121–26.

60. Ibn Aknin, *Hitgallut*, 490–91; Halkin, "Ibn Aknin's Commentary," 391–92.

61. Origen *Against Celsus* 4.38–39; see also Anatoli's condemnation of those who read the prophets superficially as if they were old wives' tales (*ke-derekh sippur havlei ha-zeqenot*) (*Malmad*, introduction, p. [10]).

62. See Heinemann, "Scientific Allegorization," 258-59.

63. Maimonides, *Ma'amar*, 15; Saperstein, *Decoding the Rabbis*, 22, 45–46.

64. On this passage, see Moshe Idel, "Tefisat ha-Torah be-Sifrut ha-Hekhalot we-Gilguleha ba-Qabbalah," *Meḥqerei Yerushalayim be-Maḥshevet Yisra'el* 1 (1981) 51.

65. C. S. Lewis, *Allegory of Love* (London: Oxford University Press, 1936) 62; see also Smalley, *Study of the Bible*, 2; de Lubac, *Exégèse médiévale*, 1:44.

66. On the vestment image in John Scotus Erigena, see de Lubac, *Exégèse médiévale*, 1:121–25.

67. Pseudo-Naḥmanides, *Ma'amar 'al penimiyyut ha-Torah*, ed. C. B. Chavel, *Kitvey Rabbenu Mosheh ben Naḥman*, 2:468. On the possible authorship of this text see Ephraim Gottlieb, "Berurim be-Khitvey R. Yosef Giqatila," in *Meḥqarim be-Sifrut ha-Qabbalah*, ed. Joseph Hacker (Tel Aviv: University of Tel Aviv Press, 1976) 128–31; see also Abba Mari ben Joseph, *Minḥat Qena'ot* (Pressburg, 1838) 5.

68. Pseudo-Naḥmanides, *Ma'amar*, 2:468; Isaiah Tishbi, ed., *Perush ha-Aggadot le-Rabbi 'Azri'el* (Jerusalem: Mekize Nirdamim, 1945) 38.

69. Azriel, *Perush ha-'Aggadot*, 37–38; see also Saba, *Ṣeror ha-Mor*, 1:49b.

70. A. S. Halkin, "Why Was Levi ben Hayyim Hounded," *Proceedings of the American Academy of Jewish Research* 34 (1966) 71.

71. Frank Talmage, *David Kimhi: The Man and the Commentaries* (Cambridge, MA and London: Harvard University Press, 1975) 121–22.

72. Joseph Kimhi, *Sefer ha-Galui*, ed. H. J. Mathews (Berlin: Mekize Nirdamim, 1887) 1; idem, Commentary to Prov 9:1, *Sefer Ḥuqqah*, ed. Ber Dubrowo (Breslau, 1865–66) 12a; see also Jonah Ibn Janah, *Sefer ha-Riqmah*, ed. Michael Wilensky, 2nd ed., 2 vols. (Jerusalem: Ha-'Aqademyah la-Lashon ha-'Ivrit, 1963–64) 380.

73. Introduction to Genesis, ed. Avraham Golan, *Petiḥah le-Ferush ha-Torah* (Jerusalem: privately published, 1982) 3.

74. MS Vat. Ebr. 89, fol. 2r.

75. Anatoli, *Malmad*, introduction, p. [6].

76. MS Vat. Ebr. 89, fols. 19v, 17v.

77. Quilligan, *Language of Allegory*, 281.

78. Moses ben Naḥman, *Perush ha-Torah le-Rabbenu Moshe ben Naḥman*, ed. C. B. Chavel, 2 vols. (Jerusalem: Mosad Ha-Rav Kook, 1958/59) 1:6; English from Scholem, "Meaning of the Torah," 38. On this theory in general, see Scholem, "The Meaning of the Torah," 37–38.

79. Scholem, "The Meaning of the Torah."

80. On punning and wordplay in allegorical narrative, see Quilligan, *Language of Allegory*, 33–51. A scholar of English has insightfully noted the suitability of Hebrew for this sort of interpretation. "The study of Hebrew . . . and the existence of English Bibles with alternatives in the margin, may have had influence on the capacity of English for ambiguity; Donne, Herbert, Jonson, and Crashaw were Hebrew scholars, and the flowering of poetry at the end of the sixteenth century corresponded with the

first thorough permeation of the English language by the translated texts. This is of interest because Hebrew, having very unreliable tenses, extraordinary idioms, and a strong taste for puns, possesses all the poetical advantages of a thorough primitive disorder" (William Empson, *Seven Types of Ambiguity* [New York: Meridian Books, 1955] 219).

81. David Kaufmann, "Hoshen mishpaṭ" (Letter of Simeon b. Joseph to Menaḥem b. Simeon) in *Jubelschrift zum neunzigsten Geburtstag des Dr. L. Zunz* (Breslau, 1886), Hebrew section, pp. 158–59.

82. Herring, *Gevia' Kesef,* 37–40.

83. Hanson, *Allegory and Event,* 133.

84. Joseph Ibn Kaspi, *Menorat Kesef* in *'Asarah Keley Kesef,* ed. Isaac last (Pressburg, 1902) 109; and in general see Herring, *Gevia' Kesef,* 52–54.

85. Isaac Arama, *'Aqedat Yizḥaq* (Pressburg, 1849) 1:143a; see Saperstein, *Decoding the Rabbis,* 113; Kaufmann, "Hoshen mishpaṭ," Hebrew section, p. 160.

86. Saperstein, *Decoding the Rabbis,* 75.

87. Ibid., 27, 60, 233–34 n. 50.

88. *B. Ta'anit* 6a; Rashi on Isa 55:1; Maimonides, *Guide* 1:30, Pines, p. 64; Kimhi on Isa 55:1 synthesizes the traditions, saying "Torah *and* science," as does jacob Anatoli, *Malmad, ha-Talmidim* 57a–58a. See also Saperstein, *Decoding the Rabbis,* 73–75.

89. *Kitvey Pulmos shel Profiat Duran,* ed. Frank Talmage (Jerusalem: Dinur Center, 1981) introduction, p. 12; Anatoli, *Malmad,* 12a.

90. See Saperstein, *Decoding the Rabbis,* 47–78.

91. M.-D. Chenu, "The Symbolist Mentality," in *Nature, Man, and Society in the Twelfth Century* (Chicago and London: University of Chicago Press, 1968) 106; see also de Lubac, *Exégèse médiévale,* 2:2:7–40; Evans, *Language and Logic,* 59–66.

92. See Saperstein, *Decoding the Rabbis,* 57.

93. From Talmage, *David Kimhi,* 122.

94. According to rabbinic reckoning (*m. 'Oholot* 1:8), the body has 248 limbs.

95. Saadya ben Joseph Gaon, *The Book of Beliefs and Opinions,* trans. Samuel Rosenblatt (New Haven, CT: Yale University Press, 1948) 2:17, p. 415.

96. Heinemann, "Scientific Allegorization," 252–55.

97. See also Alain de Lille: "All other elements, which some say are to be taken differently should be referred not to prophecy, but to visual picturing" (*De sex alis cherubim,* PL 210; 171).

98. Zerahiah ben Shealtiel Hen, *'Imrey Da'at,* 42; Immanuel of Rome, *Perush Sefer Mishlei* (Naples, 1687; reprint, Jerusalem: National and University Library, 1981) 39.

99. Samuel Ibn Tibbon, *Commentary on Ecclesiastes,* quoted in Ravitzky, "Samuel Ibn Tibbon," 111.

100. Trans. Hartwig Hirschfeld (1905; reprint, New York: Schocken Books, 1964) 192-96.

101. *Guide* 3:45; Pines, p. 573; cf. *Guide,* introduction; Pines, 9–10; Commentary on the Mishnah, introduction, ed. Joseph Kafih, 6 vols. (Jerusalem: Mosad Ha-Rav Kook, 1963/64– 1968/69) 1:20–21; Simon Rawidowicz, "On Interpretation," *Proceedings of the American Academy of Jewish Research* 26 (1957) 102–5.

102. More elaborate schematizations of the *aggadah* are provided by Maimonides's son Abraham in his *Ma'amar* and in Hillel of Verona's *Tagmuley ha-Nefesh,* 179–91; see above, n. 45.

103. Shem Tov ben Isaac Shaprut, *Pardes Rimmonim* (Zhitomir, 1866) 22–23; cf. Isadore Twersky, "R. Yeda'yah ha-Penini u-Ferusho la-'Aggadah," in *Studies in Jewish Religious and Intellectual History Presented to A. Altmann,* ed. Siegfried Stein and

Raphael Loewe (University, AL: University of Alabama Press, 1979), Hebrew section, p. 71.

104. Moses Maimonides, introduction to *Pereq Ḥeleq*, ed. Kafih, 2:202; English translation: *A Maimonides Reader*, ed. Isadore Twersky (New York: Behrman House, 1972) 408-9.

105. Talmage, *David Kimhi*, 122-23.

106. Yedaiah Ha-Penini Bedersi, *Ketav Hitnaṣṣelut*, printed in *She'elot u-Teshuvot ha-RaSHBA* (Benei Berak, 1957/58) 158 n. 418; see also D. J. Silver, *Maimonidean Criticism and the Maimonidean Controversy, 1180-1240* (Leiden: Brill, 1965) 119, 125, 192; and Twersky, "R. Yeda'yah ha-Penini," 63-82.

107. See Gershom G. Scholem, *Major Trends in Jewish Mysticism* (New York: Schocken Books, 1946) 30-32.

108. See Chen Merhavia, *Ha-Talmud bi-Re'i ha-Naẓrut* (Jerusalem: Bialik Institute, 1970); Talmage, *David Kimhi*, 77-83; Saperstein, *Decoding the Rabbis*, 1-20; Twersky, "R. Yeda'yah ha-Penini," 65, 71-72.

109. See, e.g., Talmage, *David Kimhi*, 72-83, 125-34.

110. See Saperstein, *Decoding the Rabbis*,, 25.

111. Azriel, *Perush ha-Aggadot*, 4-5; the passage is paraphrased more fully in Saperstein, *Decoding the Rabbis*, 16-17.

112. Anatoli, *Malmad*, introduction, p. [9].

113. Scholem, *Major Trends*, 27; Isaiah Tishbi, *Mishnat ha-Zohar*, 2 vols. (Jerusalem: Bialik Institute, 1957) 2:364-65; Isaiah Tishbi, *Netivei 'emunah u-minut* (Tel Aviv: Massada, 1964) 11-22, esp. 20; see also Hanson, *Allegory and Event*, 63; and the full treatment by Daniel Matt in his essay in this volume, chapter 14.

114. Maimonides, *Guide* 3:43, Pines, p. 572; Gersonides, Commentary on the Torah, ad loc. Cf. Joseph Ibn Kaspi, *Guide to Knowledge*, in *Hebrew Ethical Wills*, ed. Israel Abrahams; 1 vol. in 2 (Philadelphia: Jewish Publication Society, 1926) 135.

115. Cf. Maimonides, M.T., Hil. Sukkah 4:1.

116. Baḥya ben Asher, *Kad ha-Qemaḥ*, Sukkah, ed. Chavel, p. 279.

117. Gersonides, Commentary, *'emor*, third *to'elet*.

118. Crescas, *'Or 'adonai* 2.6.2 (Vienna, 1859) p. 59a.

119. For an example, though, of *kabbalistic* allegory of this *mizwah*, using philosophical style but kabbalistic content, see Jacob ben Sheshet, *Meshiv Devarim Nekhoḥim*, ed. Georges Vajda (Jerusalem: Israel Academy of Sciences and Humanities, 1968) 177-78.

120. For example, *b. Meg.* 26a, *b. Giṭ.* 44b.

121. Baḥya ben Asher, *Kad ha-Qemaḥ*, 276-77.

122. Scholem, "Meaning of the Torah," 83-86.

123. Joseph ben Todros Abulafia in *Ginzey nistarot*, ed. Jacob Kobak; 3 (1872) 150-51; cited from Silver, *Maimonidean Criticism*, 181.

124. Judah Alfakhar, in *Qovez teshuvot ha-RaMBaM we-'iggerotaw*, ed. A. L. Lichtenberg (Leipzig: L. Schnauss, 1859) 16; cited from Silver, *Maimonidean Criticism*, 176.

125. *Ginzei nistarot*, 3:165; see also Silver, *Maimonidean Criticism*, 145, 157, 188, 189, 192; Saperstein, *Decoding the Rabbis*, 138-39 and notes. Compare the attitude of the twelfth-century Muslim philosopher Averroes (Ibn Rushd), as discussed by Herring (*Gevi'a Kesef*, 40, with appropriate bibliography).

126. See Heinemann, "Scientific Allegorization," 260-61; Y. F. Baer, *A History of the Jews in Christian Spain*, trans. Louis Schoffman, 2 vols. (Philadelphia: Jewish Publication Society, 1971) 1:289-305: Halkin, "Why Was Levi b. Ḥayyim Hounded," 65-76; idem, "Yedaiah Bedershi's Apology," in *Jewish Medieval and Renaissance Studies*, ed. Alexander Altmann (Cambridge, MA: Harvard University Press, 1967) 165-84;

Charles Touati, "La Controverse de 1303–1306 autour des études philosophiques et scientifiques," *Revue des études juives* 127 (1968) 21–37.

127. See the succinct formulation of Saperstein (*Decoding the Rabbis*, 219–20 n. 62). For echoes of the Goethian view of symbol, see Johan Huizinga, *Waning of the Middle Ages* (Garden City, NY: Doubleday, 1959) 205; Auerbach, "Figura," 56–57; C. R. Post, *Mediaeval Spanish Allegory* (Cambridge, MA: Harvard University Press, 1915) 4–5; Fletcher, *Allegory*, 13–14. Hollander goes so far as to call the spirit of allegory gnostic (*Allegory in Dante's* Commedia, 5, 11).

128. Wolfson, *Philosophy of the Church Fathers*, 31, 34.

129. Jean Daniélou, *From Shadows to Reality: Studies in the Biblical Typology of the Fathers* (London: Burns & Oates, 1960) ; *Sacramentum Futuri: Etudes sur les origines de la typologie biblique* (Paris: Beauchesne, 1950) 64–65.

130. Gerhard von Rad, "Typological Interpretation of the Old Testament," trans. John Bright, in *Essays In Old Testament Hermeneutics*, ed. Claus Westermann (Richmond, VA: M. E. Bratcher, 1963) 21. On embarrassment over allegory in general, see G. W. H. Lampe and K. J. Woolcombe, *Essays on Typology* (London: SCM, 1951); Chydenius, "Typological Problem in Dante," 23; de Lubac, *Exégèse médiévale*, 2:2:128–30; Hanson, *Allegory and Event*, 89. Erich Auerbach's celebrated essay takes fairly much the same strand, substituting the concept of "figura" for typology ("Figura," in *Scenes from the Drama of European Literature*, 11–76; esp. 30, 54–55).

131. For the dichotomy allegory–symbol, one could substitute the bipolar system of Roman Jakobson, F. de Saussure, and C. Lévi-Strauss of metaphor (corresponding to philosophical allegory) and metonymy (corresponding to kabbalistic interpretation). The former is based on similarity and analogy, and the latter connotes contiguity and participation. See Roman Jakobson and Morris Halle, *Fundamentals of Language* (The Hague: Mouton, 1952) 26–82; Hayden White, *Metahistory* (Baltimore, MD: Johns Hopkins University Press, 1973) 31–38; Gerhart B. Ladner, "Medieval and Modern Understanding of Symbolism: A Comparison," *Speculum* 54 (1979) 229. However, although this system is superficially attractive, it would seem to do little to relieve the problems created by the allegory–symbol polarity. For reservations on the Scholem-Tishbi dichotomy from a contemporary literary critical point of view, see Uri Shoham, *Ha-mashma'ut ha-'Aheret* (Tel Aviv: Tel Aviv University, 1982) 61–64.

132. Thomas Aquinas, *Summa Theologiae* 1.1.9; see also Augustine, *Literal Commentary on Genesis* 8.1 (CSEL 28:1, 229; PL 34:273); de Lubac, *Exégèse médiévale*, 1:44; Chenu, "The Symbolist Mentality," 110–11, 132–33; Auerbach, "Figura," 36, 39.

133. See Johan Chydenius, "The Typological Problem in Dante," 51–91; Joshua Prawer, "Jerusalem in the Christian and Jewish Perspectives of the Early Middle Ages," *Gli Ebrei nell'alto medioevo, Settimane di studio del Centro Italiano di studi sull'alto medioevo, 1978* 26 (1980) 2 parts, 2:743.

134. Idem, "The Theory of Medieval Symbolism," *EHL* 27.2 (1970) 24, 34–35. Nonetheless, in Christianity as well theory does not become totally divorced from deed. See Evans, *Language and Logic*, 56: "When the Bible uses allegory, it tells us of something which has been done, not simply so that we may know of it, but in a way that refers beyond itself, so that we may understand that something else has been done or is to be done. The emphasis here is consistently upon what those 'things done' or 'things to be done' signify, that is, upon the meaningfulness of the things themselves, not the words."

135. On multiple interpretation as opposed to reinterpretation, see pp. 254–55, 59.

136. Anatoli, *Malmad*, 187a.

137. Joseph Albo, *Sefer ha-'Iqqarim*, ed. Isaac Husik, 5 vols. (Philadelphia: Jewish

Publication Society, 1930) 3:21, 192–95. Compare the especially strong statement of Hillel of Verona on taking the rabbinic interpretation of the commandments figuratively: "One must not understand them figuratively (*be-derekh mashal*) in order to free oneself from the straightforward sense of the explicit commandment, nor say that such-and such a commandment means such-and-such and it is enough for me to understand that meaning alone. There is no need for me to fulfill it literally. Any one who says this is not part of the Jewish people nor of the followers of Moses our Master and it is forbidden to speak to him. May God remove him from us!" (*Hegyon ha-Nefesh*, 182–83); see also the emphatic disquisition of Immanuel of Rome, *Perush Sefer Mishlei*, 159–61.

138. Lewis, *Allegory of Love*, 125.

139. Quilligan, *Allegory*, 152.

140. Tindall, *The Literary Symbol*, 116; see also Nwiya, *Exégèse coranique*, 67–68: "The allegorical is not the abstraction of the letter nor its negation nor its truth; it is only the way by which the imagination breaks the narrow circle of the letter—that of the law—to gain access to a world which is no longer ruled by the intangible categories of permitted and forbidden."

141. Maintaining the polarity of allegory–symbol, R. Goetschel has attempted to demonstrate that, for all their differences, the interpretations of Jacob's encounter with the angel in Judah Ibn Aknin (via Baḥya ben Asher) and the *Zohar* stem from a single "*epistēmē*"; see R. Geotschel, "Interpretation rationaliste et interpretation mystique du combat de Jacob avec l'ange dans l'exégèse juive du moyen âge," *Lectures bibliques* (Brussels, 1980) 41–54, esp. 48-49.

142. Baḥya ven Asher, *Kad ha-Qemaḥ*, Sukkah, ed. Chavel, p. 280.

143. Baḥya Ibn Paquda, *Ḥovot ha-Levavot*, ed. Moses Hyamson, 5 vols. (New York, 1925–27) 3:2, p. 192.

144. Baḥya ben Asher, *Kad ha-Qemaḥ*, ed. Chavel, p. 274, based on Maimonides, *Guide*, introduction, trans. Pines, p. 12; cf. Anatoli, *Malmad*, introduction, p. 4.

145. Ibid., 163–64. See Hanson, *Allegory and Event*, 126–27.

146. Walter Kaufmann, *Critique of Religion and Philosophy* (Garden City, NY: Doubleday, Anchor Books, 1961) 256.

147. Ibid. (emphasis added).

148. Abraham Isaac ha-Kohen Kook, *Iggerot*, 3 vols. (Jerusalem: Mosad Ha-Rav Kook, 1961–65) Letter 134, 1:163. Compare the attitude of Philo and Origen toward the positive value of biblical inconsistencies and difficulties along with Hanson's charming comparison to one of G. K. Chesterton's "Father Brown" stories, in which the latter deliberately sets a number of small objects out of place on his route through London as a trail for another (Hanson, *Allegory and Event*, 264).

149. Hanson, *Allegory and Event*, 126–27.

Bibliography

Medieval Jewish biblical exegesis has received surprisingly little attention from scholars since the early days of the *Wissenschaft des Judentums* in nineteenth-century Germany. Those surveys that do exist have been done primarily by biblicists, whose concerns do not necessarily coincide with those of medievalists or historians of religion, and the type of interpretation discussed here is generally not treated.

An older, schematic treatment of the subject is Ginzburg (the term "allegory" is used here to refer to any non-"plain sense" type of interpretation). Far more probing and highly recommended is Heinemann, a somewhat stilted if still readable translation of the German original. Rawidowicz is an essay on exegesis as an accommodation to changing historical circumstances written as a vehicle for the author's own ideology of Jewish history. The most eloquent and accessible essay on kabbalistic exegesis in English is Scholem.

Indispensable for an understanding of the nature of so much medieval exegesis, Christian or Jewish, is Smalley. Auerbach is an illuminating and rich study of the development of the concept of figural interpretation in Christian exegesis. Chenu is a rich essay on allegorical interpretation against the background of medieval intellectual history.

Virtually no original texts relevant to this study have been translated into English, apart from, of course, a classic model of an approach to allegorical exegesis, Moses Maimonides's *Guide of the Perplexed*. Halkin will give the student a good sense of Ibn Aknin's approach. Vajda is a complete annotated French translation of Ezra of Gerona's kabbalistic commentary on the Song of Songs. A good introduction to philosophical allegoresis of rabbinic midrash is Saperstein.

Auerbach, Erich. "Figura." In *Scenes from the Drama of European Literature: Six Essays*, 11–76. New York: Meridian, 1959.

Chenu, M.-D. "The Symbolist Mentality." In *Nature, Man, and Society in the Twelfth Century*, 99–145. Translated by Jerome Taylor and Lester K. Little. Chicago and London: University of Chicago Press, 1968.

Ginzberg, Louis. "The Allegorical Interpretation of Scripture." In *On Jewish Lore and Law*, 125–58. Philadelphia: Jewish Publication Society, 1958.

Halkin, Abraham. "*Ibn 'Aknin's Commentary on the Song of Songs*." In *Alexander Marx Jubilee Volume*, 389–424. New York: Jewish Theological Seminary, 1950.

Heinemann, Isaak. "Scientific Allegorization During the Jewish Middle Ages." In *Studies in Jewish Thought*, 247–69. Edited by Alfred Jospe. Detroit, MI: Wayne State University Press, 1981. [German original: "Die wissenschaftliche Allegoristik des jüdischen Mittelalters," *Hebrew Union College Annual* 23 (1950–51) 611–43.]

Maimonides, Moses. *Guide for the Perplexed*. Trans. by Schlomo Pines. Chicago: University of Chicago Press, 1963.

Rawidowicz, Simon. "On Interpretation." *Proceedings of the American Academy of Jewish Research* 26 (1957) 83–126.

Saperstein, Marc. *Decoding the Rabbis: A Thirteenth Century Commentary on the Aggadot*. Cambridge, MA, and London: Harvard University Press, 1980.

Scholem, Gershom. "The Meaning of the Torah in Jewish Mysticism." In *On the Kabbalah and Its Symbolism*, 32-86. Translated by Ralph Manheim. New York: Schocken Books, 1965.

Smalley, Beryl. *The Study of the Bible in the Middle Ages*. Oxford: Blackwell, 1952. Reprint, Notre Dame, IN: University of Notre Dame Press, 1964.

Vajda, Georges, trans. *Le commentaire d'Ezra de Gérone sur le cantique des cantiques*. Paris: Aubier Montaigne, 1969.

13

The Devotional Ideals of Ashkenazic Pietism

IVAN G. MARCUS

EW DEVOTIONAL IDEALS were a central feature of the first religious revival movement of European Judaism, the German-Jewish pietists who have been known since the fourteenth century as *ḥasidey ashkenaz* (see the text translated below, p. 360). Their views about the theory and practice of Jewish worship must be placed within the context of their novel religious program. To appreciate the former, we must consider briefly the latter.

The novel pietistic movement emerged in the late-twelfth-century Rhenish communities of Mainz, Worms, and Speyer, and in the Bavarian community of Regensburg. Piety and pietism are not the same. The former refers to all forms of legitimate expression within a religious culture. Pietism in Judaism, usually called "hasidism," refers to particular types of elite religious expression, which are sometimes grounded in special claims about the divine will and at other times, in claims about religious fellowship as well.

Among the known authors of the medieval German hasidic movement, three figures in the Qalonimos family stand out: Rabbi Samuel ben Qalonimos the Elder (fl. mid-twelfth century), to whom is attributed a short work called *Sefer ha-Yir'ah* (*Book of the Fear of God*); his younger son, Rabbi Judah the Pietist (d. 1217), the author of the pietistic code called *Sefer Ḥasidim* (*Book of the Pietists*); and his cousin and main student, Rabbi Eleazar ben Judah of Worms (d. ca. 1230), the editor and author of books of pietism, esoteric theology, religious law, and biblical commentary; synagogue poet; and participant in communal synods.[1]

Among the types of sources written by the pietists, one is of special interest to the student of religious spirituality. Even to give it a conventional label is to risk prejudging what it can tell us. These sources are not what is commonly called "documentary," such as communal ordinances, economic or social records, traces of one-time events. Nor are they compilations of religious law or answers to questions of appeal asked of legists (*responsa*). They are not philosophical treatises, in the sense of responding to the Hellenic tradition; nor mystical speculations on the nature of the Godhead; nor scholastic Talmud commentaries which make distinctions in order to avoid the appearance of contradictions. Reference books call these writings "ethical" or "moralistic," in the specific sense of being practical handbooks in which world views appropriated from legal, philosophical, or mystical theories are applied to everyday life.[2] In short, they are viewed as practical religious guidebooks, not as independent theoretical and practical religious manuals.

These discursive, prescriptive treatises, arranged as collections of fragmentary comments, chart the nature of reality and the Jew's place in it as much as do legal, philosophical, and mystical writings in Judaism. They develop a world view and ethos that are pietistic, instead of legal, philosophical, or mystical. Moreover, these sources consist of a deeply layered texture which permits innovation to be disguised as tradition. They often are couched in a mosaic of biblical quotations, rabbinic paraphrase from the Talmuds, and midrashic literature of late antiquity and the Middle Ages, and include a significant body of moralistic tales or *exempla* that may have served originally as handbooks for sermons. To be sure, the author speaks in his own voice even when he puts forward quotations from classical Judaism, for it is he who has done the selecting or paraphrasing. These pietistic sources illustrate in a particularly graphic manner how a traditional religious culture develops by what Michael Hill refers to as "revolution by tradition."[3]

Far from being simply practical handbooks, *Sefer ha-Yir'ah, Sefer Hasidim,* and Eleazar's pietistic writings portray a new theoretical religious ideal of personal salvation in Judaism, and in so doing they also define a new model of the ideal Jew, the pietist or German-Jewish *hasid*. In its central teaching, pietism requires of the pietist Jew complete obedience to an infinite demand generated by the will of God, now conceptualized as hidden as well as partially revealed. As a result of their multilayered view about God's will and revelation, the pietist authors instruct the *hasid* not only to observe all of the religious obligations required of ordinary Jews but also to strive to discover limitless new obligations hidden in Scripture and not explicitly revealed at Sinai in either the oral or written traditions. In addition, all aspects of the pietist's life are to be lived in total dedication to serving God, comparable to the burnt offering that was totally consumed on the Temple altar, to Abraham's willingness to sacrifice Isaac, and to Job's loyalty under divine trial.

Indeed, according to the new ideal, all of life is a preparation for the afterlife, and this-worldly experience is a divine trial. God constantly tests the *hasid* by tempting him with erotic or ego pleasures, which he must resist despite the suffering experienced as a result. His energy is rather to be directed properly, not at self but at selflessly serving the deity out of an all-consuming love:

> Pay attention to how some people risk their very lives for the sake of personal honor. For example, knights go into the thick of battle and even sacrifice themselves to enhance their own reputation and to avoid being humiliated. Moreover, consider how many stratagems respectable women adopt in order to avoid being discovered after they become pregnant as the result of an affair. Not to speak of thieves! If these people work so hard for only momentary benefits, how much the more should (a pietist) be resourceful for the sake of his Creator. (*SHP*, 985)[4]

A central preoccupation of the pietists is with the scales of salvation. For them, there is a measurable relationship between the sinful pleasure experienced in this world and the punishment it earns in the next:

> For according to what one enjoys in this world, one loses (reward) in the world to come. But one who suffers constantly in this world, as from a wicked wife whom he cannot divorce, or from constant poverty or from government harassment . . . that kind of pain is equivalent to Hell itself, so long as one accepts it in this world out of the love (of God). (*SHP*, 277)

Although Judah the Pietist's *Sefer Ḥasidim* and Eleazar of Worms's pietistic writings share this view about a personal eschatology, they differed about the social implications of pietism. Thus, *Sefer Ḥasidim* illuminates the ideal religious life not of individual pietists alone but also of an ideal community that follows the pietist way of total service to God. Led by charismatic leaders called "sages" (*hakhamim*), pietists in *Sefer Ḥasidim* are described as struggling to live among a nonpietist Jewish majority and Christians, both of whom pose a threat to the pietists' way of life. To minimize outside influence on them, the authors generally advise pietists to avoid contact with the others unless they, the pietists, can do so from a position of relative strength.

In Eleazar of Worms's writings, on the other hand, there are no references to groups of pietists, no socioreligious agenda, no leadership by sages. His emphasis is completely personalist and is directed at promoting the salvation of the individual pietist, who is no longer clearly differentiated from a Jew who is pious.

Individual Capacity and Praying

Although the German pietists always projected an impossibly demanding religious goal for the *hasid*, they were paradoxically also aware of the importance of allowing for individual intellectual and religious differences, and they adjusted their requirements in accordance with them. Thus, pietists are to debate with nonpietists about religious matters if they can win but not if they are not talented enough to defeat the nonpietist. Similarly, a child's ability is to be taken into account when a pietist father determines his son's curriculum. He should study Talmud only if he is capable of so doing; otherwise, biblical studies are all he need do. Again, when it comes to giving atoning penances to sinning pietists and others, a remarkable new figure of Judah the Pietist's socioreligious formulation of pietism, the sage-penancer, is to give the repentent sinner a penance he is likely to do and not one that is too difficult for him.

One feature of German Hasidism that indicates especially well how the high demands of pietism were adjusted to the individual capacities of the God-fearing is their devotional ideal. Here, as in the Qalonimide authors' pietistic writings as a whole, almost impossible demands were modified in accordance with the capacities of different people. Not everyone is a religious virtuoso, and for this reason the devotional ideal is in actuality a range of demands from extremes of intellectual and spiritual rigor to the minimal one of praying with correct motivation alone.

The Qalonimides' remarks about prayer vary from elaborate esoteric commentaries designed for the special initiates like themselves, to instructions for more limited pietists on how to pray with "concentrated attention"[5] (*kawwanah*), to the parable of an illiterate and inarticulate Jewish cattle herder who cannot recall even the minimum required Jewish prayers but chooses to pray spontaneously anyway.

At one end of the devotional spectrum is a body of esoteric commentary on the standard prayers. Although others had written commentaries on liturgical poems (*piyyutim*), composed over the centuries and differing from place to place, the German pietists were the first to write commentaries on the ancient required prayers shared by all Jews. In the course of writing down one version of his prayer commentary, Eleazar of Worms introduces a chain of tradition in which he claims that the commentary itself derives from the sages who instituted the ancient prayers.[6]

Although the pietists claimed that these traditions were ancient and therefore authoritative, the traditions were written down only in the late twelfth century in the Rhineland because of special circumstances. As the pietists tell us themselves, other Jews were not reciting the same texts of the prayers as were the German pietists, and they viewed this "deviation" as religiously harmful. The pietists' esoteric traditions on the prayers were based on word and number associations whose effectiveness depended on the exact wording of the prayers being recited. To deviate from the texts would have cosmic implications and would nullify the mystical correspondences which the pietists claimed obtained between word frequencies in the prayers, the Bible, and numerical patterns in nature. As Judah the Pietist and his disciple Eleazar of Worms indicated more than once:

> You inhabitants of France and the Islands of the Sea (England) who err utterly and completely, for you invent lies and add several words in your prayers of which the early sages who formulated the prayers never dreamed. . . . Every benediction which they formulated is measured exactly in its number of words and letters, for if it were not so, our prayer would be like the song of the uncircumcised non-Jews. Therefore, give heed and repent, and do not go on doing this evil thing, adding and omitting letters and words from the prayers." (Jerusalem MS 8° 3296, frag. 7a)[7]

Elsewhere the pietists indicate that the risk incurred from liturgical deviance is significant. Because some French Jews have tampered with the liturgy, "they cause exile to themselves and their children until the end of all generations" (Jerusalem MS 8° 3296, frag. 2). Evidently it was this danger that prompted them to write down their esoteric prayer traditions. Once written down, the commentary lore was no longer esoteric. To what extent did knowledge of the numerical associations become part and parcel of Jewish worship among the pietists? Put another way, How do the pietistic writings portray Jewish worship?

The Range of Prayer Techniques

Although there is no evidence that the German pietists meditated on numerological word associations during their worship,[9] some evidence suggests that a few virtuosi did more than strive to concentrate on the words of the prayers themselves. It is significant that the first explicit reference to the German pietists describes them as being involved with the intellectual activity of deriving esoteric associations from the prayers. In his code of Jewish law, *Arba'ah Turim* (*Oraḥ Hayyim,* section 113), R. Jacob b. Asher (d. 1340) refers to the pietists as follows:

> My brother, R. Yehiel, may his memory be blessed, reports: The German pietists interpret (biblical) cross-references (see *b. B. Qam.* 82a). They would measure and count the numerical value of the number of words in the prayers and benedictions and (figure out accordingly) with reference to what (special meanings) they were so formulated.

To be sure, this brief reference does not claim that any pietists dwelt on the esoteric prayer associations while at prayer, but there is a hint that something related did take place, at least in the case of the sage. In *Sefer Hasidim* Judah the Pietist relates an exemplum about a town that had a larger and a smaller synagogue which a visiting sage would attend alternately. At one point, he stopped going to the larger synagogue, and this aroused the curiosity of people:

> He said to them, "In the large synagogue people rush through the (preliminary) benedictions and the Psalms. They interrupt (and prevent) the prayers (from being recited) at the correct time (of the morning). This does not happen in the small synagogue. (There,) they say the benedictions and prayers of praise deliberately (*be-meshekh*) and I derive benefit (for the sake of) the Holy One, blessed be He. For when I draw out (the prayers,) I can count on my fingers how many A's (*'alafin*), how many B's (*betin*), and how many of each and every (other) letter (there are) in a particular song of praise. After I return home, I think of a reason why there are just so many (of each letter in the various prayers). (*SHP*, 1575)

The indication in this story that the protagonist is a "sage" and not an ordinary pietist may mean that such originality was the province of a few adepts within the pietist movement and was not the practice of most. Still, the exemplum does suggest that the activity of generating new prayer associations was not merely theoretical but was considered an ongoing process that took place in connection with the drawn out recitation of prayers. Rabbi Jacob ben Asher, we recall, emphasized not the German pietists' meditating on prayer commentaries but their counting the words of the prayers, as in the exemplum. These sources suggest that the pietists did not meditate on the words of the esoteric prayer associations, but some did more than concentrate on the prayers: they also counted the frequencies of the letters found in the words of the prayers.

To be sure, for the pietist who was not a sage, the devotional ideal focused not on the numbers of the letters or words but on the meaning of the words themselves. Without concentrated attention on them, prayer would not be effective (*SHP*, 446). Judah the Pietist likens praying to a house built on the foundation of concentrated attention: remove the latter and the former collapses (*SHP*, 441). He required *kawwanah* at all times, not just at specified times, in order to fulfill the religious obligation of reciting the fixed prayers (see *m. Ber.* 5:1; *t. Ber.* 3:6; 2:2; *Sifre Deut.* 41; *b. Ta'anit* 2a; cf. *b. Rosh Hash.* 28a and *b. Pes.* 114b).

The pietists had to learn many skills in order to pray properly. Anticipating the eighteenth-century Polish Hasidic movement, the pietists called for prayer with melodies as much as possible. As Eleazar of Worms put it

in his poetical introduction to *Hilkhot Ḥasidut* (*Laws of Pietism*), "A benediction deserves a pleasant melody / the glory of song is in much rejoicing /
a supplicating voice (requires) drawing out (the prayers) with concentrated
attention" (*ḥemshekh be-khiwun*).

To pray with concentrated attention, the pietists were supposed to pray
slowly, in a drawn out fashion (*be-meshekh*), and they were not left to their
own devices as to how to increase their concentration and avoid distractions. In addition to criticizing rapid, mechanical praying (*SHP*, 11, 418,
421, 450, 479, 1577, etc.), the pietist authors insist that discipline is needed
to keep distracting thoughts (*hirhurim*) at bay. Even thoughts about Torah
study during prayer are to be avoided, though they are better than ones
related to the banalities of everyday existence (*SHP*, 445, 1581, 1602; cf. 38).
To concentrate properly when one is sad, wine may help to lift one's spirits
(*SHP*, 61). At all times, one needs silence all around (*SHP*, 456), not people
who talk (*SHP*, 1602) or who are emotionally unstable (*SHP*, 458). Those
who go in and out of the synagogue must be ignored (*SHP*, 1582): the pietist
should shut his eyes so as not to see them and "break his concentration"
(*SHP*, 1582). Another technique for avoiding visual distractions is for the
pietist to wear his prayer shawl over his eyes so that it blocks his view on
all sides (*SHP*, 1584; cf. 1 Kgs 19:13). In the evening, when the prayer shawl
is not ordinarily worn, he should look toward the floor. A sudden urge to
laugh is to be checked with specific remedies: he should shut his eyes tight,
pull in his stomach, and grind his teeth together (*SHP*, 1584).

A balance had to be struck between ways of avoiding distractions and
inadvertently calling attention to himself in a way that might make others
laugh at him and disturb him even more (*SHP*, 1587). To be sure, scorn
would earn the pietist who suffered it a reward in the next world (*SHP*,
1589, etc.), but it was even more desirable to avoid losing one's concentration. If a pietist found himself unavoidably sitting next to a nonpietist—a
practice to be avoided since the latter's evil thoughts would chase away the
divine presence (*shekhinah*) (*SHP*, 403)—the pietist should close his eyes at
various times, such as when reciting the daily penitential prayers (*taḥanun*)
(*SHP*, 1586). But since he is likely to be able to sustain this kind of concentration only for short prayers, he should generally pray looking down, and
his mind should be directed toward heaven (*SHP*, 1583; cf. *b. Yeb.* 105b).
The exception is that when he recites the special morning and evening
benedictions that refer to the celestial regularity of the day and night, he
is to look up toward the heavens (*SHP*, 1582).

The matter of correct theological direction of the pietist's concentration,
even if different from his physical orientation, is taken up in many different

contexts in pietist writings. In *Sefer Ḥasidim,* Judah the Pietist poses the issue in connection with his version of the talmudic comment: "When a man prays, the *shekhinah* is before him, as it is said, 'I have set the Lord always before me'" (Ps 16:8) (*b. Sanh.* 22a):

> Even though it is written "the Lord . . . *before* me," he should direct his concentration only upwards towards Heaven. Since he does not know where the Temple is located, when he prays he should meditate with his mind as though the divine Glory (*ha-kavod*) were within four cubits in front of him, and (God's) Highness (*rumo*) is way up in Heaven.
>
> When a dwarf speaks to a man (of ordinary height), does he not look (up) at the face of the "giant," and not (look straight) at his trunk?[10] Similarly, although the Creator is everywhere, (Scripture) said (one who prays) should do (it) in the direction of (His) greatness (?), as it is said, "Pour out thy heart like water before the *face* of the Lord" (Lam 2:19). Because human beings are down here (in relation to God on high,) they must elevate their soul and mind. For this reason, the mind of one who prays should be (directed) upwards (*SHP,* 1585).

The question of the direction toward which the pietist should pray has become a theological one: On which aspect of the deity should the one who prays concentrate? It is not possible to review here in any detail the various aspects of the deity in the esoteric theology of the German pietists, but it is necessary to stress one point. In *Sefer Ḥasidim,* Eleazar of Worms's works (e.g., "Introduction" to *Hilkhot Ḥasidut,* p. 3: "direct your mind at your Creator"), and in those prayer texts on God's unity and meditations that Joseph Dan has called "exoteric,"[11] the authors insist that prayer should be directed at the highest conception of God, called here "His Highness" and elsewhere, "the Creator" (*ha-bore'*). In one of the pietists' esoteric theological texts,[12] a different solution is proposed. As Dan has suggested, it seems that Judah the Pietist distinguished between the elite and the ordinary pietist. The former were to meditate on the emanated Glory (*ha-kavod*), which some viewed as being attached (*daveq*) to the unknowable Creator; the latter are to concentrate on God on high, the Creator.[13]

The elaborately detailed demand that the pietist pray with concentrated attention on the words he utters could not apply to would-be pietists who lacked the capacity to remember the words themselves. Samuel the Pietist takes it for granted that women lack this capacity and that some men do as well. Adjustments had to be made in such a person's devotional ideal:

> And if someone comes to you who does not understand Hebrew but is a God-fearer or a woman, tell them to learn the order of the service in a language that they understand. Prayer consists of the mind understanding

(what is said). If a person's mind does not comprehend what comes out of his mouth, in what way does he derive any benefit? (*Sefer ha-Yir'ah; SHP*, 11)

For the would-be pietist who is totally incapable of remembering the prayers at all, sincere motivation is sufficient, but only for such a person. Samuel the Pietist's parable of the cattle herder adopts an international tale about the sincere but inept pray-er and fits it into the German pietistic devotional ideal by placing it inside a qualifying framework.[14] Correctly understood, this tale represents the other extreme in the devotional ideal from that of the sage mentioned earlier. The author does not propose as an ideal of German pietism that unconventional, naïve prayer uttered with sincerity is more important than prescribed Jewish worship. Rather, the point is that it is better than nothing at all when a God-fearer is severely limited intellectually:[15]

> A man should perform every religious commandment that he can, and what he cannot perform, he should think of performing.
>
> This lesson can be likened to this story: Once there was a man who was a cattle herder and he did not know how to pray properly. Every day he said, "Master of the universe, You know full well that even though I normally charge everyone else a fee, if You had animals and gave them to me to guard, I would guard them for free—because I love You." And he was a Jew.[16]
>
> One time a scholar was out walking and found the cattle herder praying in this way. He said, "Fool! Do not pray that way."
>
> The herder replied, "How then, should I pray?"
>
> The scholar immediately taught him the required blessings, the *Shema'* reading, and the *Tefillah* prayer[17] so that the herder would no longer pray as he had before.
>
> After the scholar had left, the herder forgot everything that he had been taught. He did not say the prayers that the scholar had taught him.
>
> But he also was afraid to say the prayer he formerly said because the righteous[18] scholar had forbidden him.
>
> In a dream at night, the scholar saw himself being told, "If you do not go and tell the cattle herder to pray as he did before you met him, beware the misfortune that awaits you. You have robbed Me of a man who deserves the world to come."
>
> The scholar immediately went to the cattle herder and asked, "What prayers are you saying?"
>
> He replied, "None at all. I forgot the prayers you taught me, and you told me not to say, 'If He had animals. . . .'"
>
> The sage responded, "I dreamed such and such. Say what you used to say."
>
> This is the case of a man who had no Torah and no good deeds. Yet he merely thought of performing good deeds and God counted it as a great thing. For "the Merciful wants the heart."[19] That is why a man should think good thoughts toward the Holy One, blessed be He. (*Sefer ha-Yir'ah; SHP*, 4–6)

Notes

1. The pietistic works are now being translated by the present writer.

2. Joseph Dan, "Ethical Literature," *Encyclopaedia Judaica* (1971) 6:926–32.

3. Michael Hill, *The Religious Order* (London: Heinemann, 1973) 85–103.

4. Translations from *Sefer Hasidim,* cited as *SHP* followed by paragraph number, are from Hebrew manuscript Parma, Biblioteca Palatina 3280 (Catalogue De Rossi, 1133), published with many errors by Jehuda Wistinetzki and Jacob Freimann (Frankfurt am Main: Wahrmann, 1924)

5. The phrase is borrowed from Mircea Eliade, *No Souvenirs* (New York: Harper & Row, 1977) 230.

6. E. E. Urbach, ed., *'Arugat ha-Bosem,* 4 vols. (Jerusalem: Meqize Nirdamim, 1939–63) 4:73–111; Joseph Dan, "The Emergence of Mystical Prayer" in *Studies in Jewish Mysticism,* 87.

7. Translated by Joseph Dan ("The Emergence of Mystical Prayer," 89).

8. Translated by Joseph Dan ("The Emergence of Mystical Prayer," 89).

9. See Dan, "The Emergence of Mystical Prayer," 91–92.

10. This text explicates the emphasis of thinking upward during prayer found in a passage in Oxford MS Opp. 540 (Catalogue Neubauer, 1567), fol. 9b published by Joseph Dan (*'iyyunim be-Sifrut shel Hasidei Ashkenaz* [Ramat Gan: Masada, 1975] 169) and discussed in his *Torat ha-Sod shel Hasidut Ashkenaz* (Jerusalem: Mosad Bialik, 1968) 136. The allusion in the passage to *Seder Eliyahu Rabbah,* chap. 9 (ed. M. Friedmann, p. 46), does not mention prayer directed *upward,* which is the key to that passage and is central to the exemplum of the dwarf in *SHP,* 1585.

11. See Joseph Dan, "*'Sifrut ha-Yihud'* shel Hasidei Ashkenaz," *Qiryat Sefer* 41 (1966) 533–44 and his English "Introduction" to *Shir ha-Yihud: The Hymn of Divine Unity* (Jerusalem: Magnes, 1981) vii–ix.

12. See n. 7.

13. Dan, *Torat ha-Sod,* 129–43, 164–68.

14. Joseph Dan, *Ha-Sippur ha-'ivri bi-yemey ha-Beynayim* (Jerusalem: Keter, 1974) 179–80.

15. This tale appeared in my "Narrative Fantasies from *Sefer Hasidim*" in *Fiction* (Rabbinic Fantasy), ed. Mark Mirsky and David Stern, 7, 1–2 (1983) 140–41 and is reprinted here with permission.

16. This gloss is one sign that the author knew that the original tale was not about a Jewish protagonist.

17. These prayers are the core of the daily evening and morning liturgy.

18. The use of the term *zaddiq* (a righteous man) in connection with the scholar is ambiguous. On the one hand, a learned person who teaches a Jew how to pray is righteous. On the other hand, in our story, the scholar may appear righteous to the cattle herder, but the reader knows that he is acting incorrectly.

19. Rashi on *b. Sanh.* 106b.

Bibliography

The most extensive treatment of pietism is Marcus. Soloveitchik dwells on important elements of the pietistic ideal. The theological writings of the pietists are treated briefly in the third chapter of Scholem and at greater length in Dan, *The Esoteric Theology.* The most important English study of the pietists' prayer ideal is Dan, "The Emergence."

Dan, Joseph. "The Emergence of Mystical Prayer." In *Studies in Jewish Mysticism*, 85–120. Edited by Joseph Dan and Frank Talmage. New York: Ktav, 1982.

———. *The Esoteric Theology of German Hasidism* [Hebrew]. Jerusalem. Bialik Institute, 1968. [A summary appeared in Dan, "Hasidei Ashkenaz," in *Encyclopaedia Judaica*, 7:1377-79.

Marcus, Ivan G. *Piety and Society: The Jewish Pietists of Medieval Germany.* Leiden: Brill, 1981.

Scholem, Gershom. *Major Trends in Jewish Mysticism*, 3rd ed. New York: Schocken, 1954.

Soloveitchik, Haym. "Three Themes in the Sefer Hasidim." *AJS Review* 1 (1976) 311–57.

14

The Mystic and the *Mizwot*

Daniel C. Matt

THE MYSTIC WHO DECIDES, or feels compelled, to remain in society is bound to develop a particular understanding of that society's moral and legal demands. The mystic's own constant demand, to experience directly the reality of God, must be aligned with the dictates of tradition and law. Whether or not complete alignment is possible, the social mystic will make the attempt, and the social mystic is likely to try to convince others that the attempt is worthwhile and vital, that the alignment of legal and mystical realms is not an imposition or an overlap of one realm on the other, that the two are, in fact, one. Abiding in the presence of God, the social mystic abides by the law.

In Kabbalah, the mystical branch of Judaism, there is ample evidence of the spiritualization of law. Expounding *ta'amey ha-mizwot* (mystical "reasons for the commandments") constitutes an entire genre of kabbalistic literature. The systematic search for reasons for the commandments was initially undertaken by Jewish philosophers, who applied rational standards to the laws of the Torah. The Jewish mystics followed the lead of the philosophers, at times accepting their formulations, more often disputing with them and offering mystical reasons. Both the philosophers and the mystics were dissatisfied with a naïve, unreflective observance of *mizwot*. For both types of thinkers it was no longer sufficient to follow God's word simply because He had commanded it. There was a need to understand the motivation behind the *mizwah* ("commandment"), the rationale or mystical secret inherent in the divine law.

The Bible and Rabbinic Literature

The formulation of reasons for individual *mizwot* is not a medieval invention. The Torah itself justifies certain commands: work is forbidden on the

Sabbath "for in six days YHWH made heaven and earth, the sea, and all that is in them, and He rested on the seventh day" (Exod 20:11). The motive clauses of the Torah distinguish it from most other ancient legal corpora. These explanatory, ethical, religious, and historical comments appeal to the human conscience and provide pedagogical motivation for observing the law. Israel is enjoined: "Do not take a bribe, for a bribe blinds the wise and perverts the words of the righteous" (Exod 23:8). The following verse reads: "Do not oppress a stranger; you know the soul of a stranger, for you were strangers in the land of Egypt." Leviticus is more demanding: "The stranger who resides with you shall be as a native among you; you shall love him as yourself, for you were strangers in the land of Egypt" (Lev 19:34). A child's question on Passover, "What is this service to you?" (Exod 12:26), that is, "Why do you do this?," is to be answered by explaining the historical background of the exodus. The social benefit of certain mizwot is emphasized. A false witness is to be punished "as he schemed to do to his fellow. Thus you will sweep out evil from your midst; others will hear and be afraid, and such evil things will not again be done in your midst" (Deut 19:19–20). The laws have been commanded "for our lasting good, to keep us alive, as we are today" (Deut 6:24). Israel is famous for its just divine legislation: "This is your wisdom and understanding in the eyes of the nations, who shall hear all these statutes and say, 'Surely, this great nation is a wise and understanding people'" (Deut 4:6).

In rabbinic literature there is an awareness that not all biblical legislation is respected by the nations. Sifra (on Lev 18:4) distinguishes between mishpatim ("judgments") and huqqim ("decrees"). Mishpatim include prohibitions against robbery, incest, murder, idolatry, and cursing God's name. Even if these had not been recorded in the Torah, they would still be valid. Huqqim, on the other hand, are divine decrees that do not seem so reasonable. These include the prohibition against wearing garments made of both wool and flax, the purification ritual of the leper, the red heifer, and the scapegoat designated for Azazel on Yom Kippur. Both the nations of the world and the evil inclination within attempt to refute the huqqim, but Israel is instructed: "I, YHWH, have thus decreed; you are not allowed to object."

The heteronomous quality of the divine command is cherished by the rabbis. "Greater is one who is commanded and acts than one who is not commanded and acts" (b. Qid. 31a). An individual who determines on his own the right way to act is inferior to one who submits to the yoke of the mizwot, which is to be accepted along with the yoke of the kingdom of heaven (m. Ber. 2:2). By obeying the mizwot, Israel affirms that God redeemed them from the slavery of Egypt and transformed them into servants of the divine will. "I brought you up from the land of Egypt on condition that you accept upon yourselves the yoke of the *mizwot*. Whoever acknowledges this yoke acknowledges the Exodus. Whoever denies this yoke denies the Exodus" (*Sifra* on Lev 11:45). "I redeemed you so that I would decree and you would fulfill" (*Sifre Num.* 115).

It is not that the *mizwot* are without purpose. On the contrary, "the *mizwot* were given solely to refine humanity" (*Gen. Rab.* 44:1). The announcement of specific reasons, however, might undermine observance. "Why were the reasons for [the *mizwot* of] Torah not revealed? Because the reasons for two passages were revealed and the great one of the world stumbled on them" (*b. Sanh.* 21b). The reference is to King Solomon's transgression of Deut 17:16–17, where an Israelite king is forbidden to amass wives, in order that his heart not go astray, and forbidden to amass horses, in order that he not rely on Egypt. The overt mention of the reason apparently tempts one to indulge in the transgression and avoid the predicted consequence.

The reasons for the *mizwot* are "matters concealed by the Ancient of Days"; they will be revealed only in the world to come (*b. Pes.* 119a; *Pesiqta de Rab Kahana* 4:7; Rashi on Song 1:2). Until then it is dangerous to attempt to fathom each commandment, because one thereby measures the *mizwah* by reason, by the reasoning power of the human subject of the commanding King. Loyal subjects should obey and not question, probe, or rationalize. Yet the King is also a Father who lovingly instructs His children for the sake of intimate delight:

> Israel is beloved! The Bible surrounds them with *mizwot*: *tefillin* ["phylacteries"] on the head and arm, a *mezuzah* [slip of parchment] on the door, *zizit* [a "fringe"] on their clothes. . . . This may be compared to a king of flesh-and-blood who said to his wife, "Adorn yourself with all your jewelry so that you will be desirable to me." So the Blessed Holy One said to Israel, "My children, distinguish yourselves with *mizwot* so that you will be desirable to Me." (*Sifre on Deut.* 36)

In Hellenistic literature the *mizwot* are presented as rational legislation designed to produce a virtuous people (see *Letter of Aristeas* 142–47). Philo of Alexandria made the first attempt at a systematic exposition of the reasons for the *mizwot*. He maintained that the Mosaic law implants all virtues and that every *mizwah* has a rational purpose, though he employed the allegorical method to explain the sacrifices and festivals. The *mizwot* are not to be taken literally whenever this would compel one "to admit anything base or unworthy of their dignity" (*The Worse Attacks the Better* 5:13). Yet Philo criticizes those who concentrate on the symbolic message and treat the literal meaning "with light-hearted neglect." One ought to give "careful attention to both aims, to an accurate investigation of the invisible and also to an irreproachable observance of the visible."

> Why, we shall be ignoring the sanctity of the Temple and a thousand other things, if we are going to pay heed to nothing except what is shown us by the inner meaning of things. . . . If we keep and observe these [laws], we shall gain a clearer conception of those things of which these are symbols; and besides that, we shall not incur the censure of the many and the charges they are sure to bring against us. (*On the Migration of Abraham* 16:89–93)

Medieval Jewish Philosophy

Saadiah Gaon (882–942) divided the *miẓwot* into *sikhliyyot*, "rational," and *shim'iyyot*, those "heard" through revelation alone. Revelation merely re-iterates the rational commands, whereas it initiates the cultic and ceremonial laws of the Bible and makes them imperative. These latter are not irrational or without usefulness; the festivals, for example, enable one to engage in spiritual activity and human fellowship (*Emunot we-De'ot* 3:5).

Judah Halevi (ca. 1075–1141) viewed the *miẓwot* as a way to attain "the connection with the divine influence" (*Kuzari* 3:23). According to him, the heretic Elisha ben Avuya (second century) made the mistake of discarding the means once he had glimpsed the end. He reasoned that "these actions are but instruments that lead up to spiritual heights. Having attained the heights, I have no need for the actions prescribed in the Torah" (*Kuzari* 3:65). It is best not to analyze the *miẓwot* but simply to accept them "with all one's heart. . . . However, one who descends from this highest grade to scrutiny does well to seek a reason for these commandments that are based on wisdom, instead of casting misconstructions and doubts that lead to corruption" (*Kuzari* 2:26).

Moses Maimonides (1135–1204) made the most ambitious, comprehensive attempt to rationalize the *miẓwot*. He rejected Saadiah's distinction between rational and revelational *miẓwot*. "Every commandment and prohibition . . . is consequent upon wisdom and aims at some end" (*Moreh Nevukhim* [*Guide of the Perplexed*] 3:26). It is a human duty to understand the meaning of the *miẓwot*. If "you perform a commandment merely with your limbs, as if you were digging a hole in the ground or hewing wood in the forest, without reflecting either upon the meaning of that action, or upon Him from whom the commandment proceeds, or upon the end of the action, you should not think that you have achieved the end" (*Guide* 3:51). If no reason can be discovered, "the lack is in your comprehension."

As for himself, Maimonides states that there are "only very few command-ments . . . whose cause has not yet become clear to me" (*Guide* 3:26).

The Torah hid most of the reasons for the *mizwot*, because they are too profound to be understood by the masses and also because people would be tempted to dispense with the actual *mizwah* and content themselves with fulfilling its intention. "Thus the integrity of religion would be destroyed" (*Sefer ha-Mizwot*, end). Knowing the purpose or inner meaning must not become a substitute for normative performance; observance must not be reduced to a function of reason. "Whoever interprets the *mizwot* in a way that conflicts with their literal sense is a liar, evil, and a heretic" (*Mishneh Torah* [*MT*], *Melakhim* 11:3 [uncensored version]).

Maimonides's search for the reasons for the *mizwot* was motivated by his conviction that natural reason accords with divine authority. He was also stimulated by Christian and Moslem claims that the law of Moses had been abrogated. "Others declare that the *mizwot* had an esoteric meaning and were not intended to be taken literally; that the Messiah has already come and revealed their occult significance" (*MT, Melakhim* 11:4 [uncensored ver-sion]). In contrast to Justin Martyr, who, in his *Dialogue with Trypho*, stated that the Mosaic law was a punishment for Jewish recalcitrance, Maimonides writes: "The ordinances of the Law were meant to bring upon the world not vengeance, but mercy, loving-kindness, and peace" (*MT, Shabbat* 2:3). Torah is no oppressive burden; it guides the human being to focus solely on God, "training you to occupy yourself with His commandments, and not with that which is other than He" (*Guide* 3:51). "The essence of the true divine religion lies in the deeper meaning of its positive and negative precepts, every one of which will aid the human being in his striving after perfection" (*Iggeret Teman*).

The *mizwot* aim at perfection of the body and perfection of the soul. The former, which consists of practical and moral virtues, is a prerequisite for the latter, which consists of correct opinions and beliefs. The *mizwot* are intended to fashion a just society in which the individual will be able to devote himself to intellectual perfection, "to become fully rational." "To this ultimate perfection there belong neither actions nor moral qualities. It consists solely of opinions toward which speculation has led and that inves-tigation has rendered compulsory" (*Guide* 3:27). Yet Maimonides is aware that true opinions "do not last unless they are accompanied by actions that strengthen them . . . and perpetuate them among the multitude" (*Guide* 2:31).

The Torah is especially concerned with one false opinion: idolatry. "The entire purpose of . . . our law and the pivot around which it turns consists in the effacement of [idolatry]" (*Guide* 3:29). Maimonides explains many of

the *huqqim* as measures intended to combat idolatry; for example, the prohibition against boiling a kid in its mother's milk is a rejection of pagan
custom (*Guide* 3:48). He thus accepts historical causation as a factor in
revelation and a means of rationalization. He immersed himself in the study
of the idolatrous Sabians in order to understand the background of the
Torah's cultic legislation. "From these books it became clear to me what the
reason is for all those commandments that everyone comes to think of as
having no reason at all other than the decree of Scripture" (*Letter on
Astrology*).

In a radical move, Maimonides contends that the sacrificial cult was a concession by God to the idolatrous habits of the Israelites, who were steeped
in paganism. It was a gracious divine ruse by which God transferred the
institution of sacrifice from idols to Himself, thus effacing idolatry. If
sacrifices had been forbidden outright, Israel would have insisted on continuing to offer them to false gods because the human being, "according to
his nature, is incapable of abandoning suddenly all to which he is accustomed" (*Guide* 3:32; cf. Lev 17:7; *Lev. Rab.* 22:8). Thus, sacrifices in general
have a purpose. Their details, however (which animals and how many), are
not subject to rationalization: "They were given merely for the sake of
commanding something. . . . All those who occupy themselves with finding
causes for any of these particulars are stricken with a prolonged madness,
in the course of which they do not put an end to an incongruity but rather
increase the number of incongruities" (*Guide* 3:26).

Maimonides provides utilitarian explanations for a number of *miẓwot*.
The incense burned in the Temple improved the smell caused by the sacrifices (*Guide* 3:45). The pig is forbidden because it is filthy; in fact, all foods
forbidden by the Torah are nutritionally unwholesome (*Guide* 3:48). The
calf whose neck is broken when a local murder cannot be solved (Deut 21)
is not a means of ritual atonement but a means of identifying the murderer.
The various ritual actions cause people to investigate, to search for relevant
information; thereby the killer may become known (*Guide* 3:40). The
utilitarian treatment of *miẓwot* is characteristic of Maimonides's *Guide of
the Perplexed*, in which historical causation and social rationales are prominent. In his legal code, the *Mishneh Torah*, there is little trace of historical
motivation. Here the *miẓwot* are an edifying force and a way to express
intimacy with the divine. "When one loves God properly, he will immediately fulfill all the *miẓwot* out of love" (*MT, Teshuvah* 10:2).

The Response of Kabbalah

The medieval Jewish philosophers employed the scientific idealism of
Greece to explain and strengthen the religious idealism of the *miẓwot*. They

defended the commandments against the attacks of philosophic antinomianism and Christian polemics. They countered Jewish apathy with fervent, spiritual rationalism, claiming that without meaningful reasons, the value of *miẓwot* is diminished and God's glory lessened. There were philosophers, such as Judah Halevi and Ḥasdai Crescas, who rejected the criteria of general culture, but most tried to explain the *miẓwot* scientifically, to define Judaism in terms operative outside of Judaism, and to demonstrate that Torah accords with nature. In doing so, they highlighted autonomous conscience rather than the heteronomous divine command, which was not recognized in Greek philosophy. There was no intention of opposing tradition. An apologetic tone characterized the philosophic discussion of *ta'amey ha-miẓwot,* and indeed assent to tradition was part of the epistemology of medieval religious philosophy.

There were Jewish thinkers and codifiers who opposed the rationalization of the *miẓwot.* Jacob ben Asher, discussing the prohibition against shaving the beard, writes: "We do not need to search for a reason for the *miẓwot* because they are decrees of the King, incumbent upon us even if we do not know the reason."[1] Joseph Albo praises those who do not pretend to be wiser than God but walk innocently in His Torah (*'Iqqarim* 3:27).

The Kabbalists were not so innocent. They studied Maimonides's *Guide* and understood the need for an ideology of *miẓwot* but were not satisfied with a rationalistic one. Isaac of Akko (Acre) writes: "Even though the words of the *Guide of the Perplexed* purify the mind . . . , his *ta'amey ha-miẓwot* are flimsy and totally inadequate."[2] Todros ben Joseph ha-Levi Abulafia charges Maimonides with "fabricating reasons for the *miẓwot*" (*Oẓar ha-Kavod, Shab.* 28b). Todros's father claimed that Maimonides eventually regretted the "blemished reasons" he had provided and sought to retract those parts of the *Guide.*[3] This wishful thinking conveys the traditionalists' profound disappointment with the consequences of the philosophers' program in Spain. The Geronese poet Meshullam ben Solomon Da Piera complains that "weak minds found in him [Maimonides] a stumbling block, though he only innovated to awaken the sleepers." He notes too that the rebellious draw on the *Guide.*[4] Maimonides was not the direct cause of the violation of the commandments, but, as Judah Alfakhar charged, the *Guide* "serves as a pretext for the wayward and defiant."[5] Religious laxity and rationalism are linked by Joseph ben Todros Abulafia, who divides the promoters of the *Guide* into two groups. The first is one of "hypocrites who make a sham of the Torah and freely indulge in secret transgression. . . . They assume the mantle of righteousness but it clothes them not." The second group is composed of "rich pleasure-seekers who remove the age-old boundaries . . . , who thrust the poor off the road and abandon the paths of righteousness, neglecting the Torah out of wealth."[6] Here Spanish

Maimunists are seen as either hypocritical intellectuals or hedonistic aristo-crats. However, the *Guide* influenced wider circles. Joseph complains that since it was translated from Arabic into Hebrew, "every one of the rabble considers himself a philosopher. . . . They profane the sacred and absolve themselves of the duties of prayer and *tefillin*."[7]

The rationalistic approach to *mizwot* served as a convenient justification for certain Jews. Jacob ben Sheshet, a strong kabbalistic opponent of the "heretical" tendencies of philosophy, writes in his *Sha'ar ha-Shamayim:*

> We have heard that there are those in Israel who have broken through the fence and the barrier, and invented things in their minds, thus casting truth down to the ground. . . . They spread an evil report and speak falsely about God, saying that the *mizwot* were intended merely to protect the health of the body or to protect one's money and property or to protect the well-being of the state, not for punishment and reward. They provide Jacob with in-numerable strange gods! May the mouths of the liars be shut! [Ps 63:12]. They have thought up thoughts in order to find reasons to engage in all sorts of abominations. They have strayed after Greek wisdom.[8]

These heretics claim that, since the purpose of prayer "is solely to purify the mind," there is no point in using words; meditation on the divine is preferable. "How can we say 'Answer us,' 'Rise and save us' to one who has no body nor physical attributes? What good is it to say to Him, 'Blessed are You'?"[9] The rarefied conception of God conflicts with traditional forms. Jacob remarks: "It is vain and evil to absolve oneself of obligatory prayer while cleaving through the intellect to [divine] thought."[10] Isaac of Akko dreams that he sees a "curse against the rebels who believe only in the Infinite [nature of God] . . . and neither pray nor bless, for they say, 'What need does He have for our prayers? What benefit can He derive from our blessings?'" Isaac castigates "the foolish philosophers . . . , ignorant of the ten *sefirot* [stages of divine manifestation], the Name of the Blessed Holy One. Their faith is deficient and wrong, for they disdain prayer and bless-ings and are frivolous toward the *mizwot*."[11]

There were sincere and insincere rationalists, but the Kabbalists attacked anyone whose views threatened traditional observance. Jewish aristocrats and courtiers, who assimilated into the upper levels of Christian society, were eager to explain away and discard cumbersome ritual. Joseph ben Shalom Ashkenazi attacks them:

> They look upon the *mizwot* as mere customs or hygienic measures, theoriz-ing that the health of the body is therapeutic to the soul. The *mizwot* become a subject for philosophic speculation, and philosophy itself a rationalization of their indulgence in sensual pleasure. . . . Hence they are ever in pursuit of iniquity; they are quick to shed blood and eager to fornicate and ready to

violate all the precepts of Torah. . . . As if this were not bad énough, they attribute their troublesome error to the great rabbi Maimonides. God forbid that he inclined toward any of these matters![12]

The religious nihilism, personal ambition, and political ruthlessness of certain courtiers are portrayed vividly in the poetry of Todros ben Yehudah ha-Levi Abulafia, who was himself involved with the royal court. He lashes out at "so-called Jews who cherish Christian faith, who walk in darkness, from Moses' Law estranged, who transgress the sages' precepts, too blind to esteem the Hebrew faith. They think that spending the night studying Talmud is a lonely pursuit. To know the Hebrew alphabet is sufficient." They "transgress every positive commandment and enact the negative ones."[13]

Moses de León in his *Sefer ha-Rimmon* reacts bitterly against assimilated Jews who embraced a rationalistic ideology to justify their neglect of tradition:

> They engaged in the study of these books [of philosophy] and their minds were so attracted that they abandoned the words of Torah and the *mizwot* and discarded them. . . . When they are alone with one another, they ridicule and mock [the words of the rabbis] and delight in the words of the Greeks and their assistants [the medieval philosophers]. They kiss their words! Furthermore, I have seen them on the Fesitval of Sukkot standing in their places in the synagogue, watching the servants of God circling with palm branches around the Torah scroll in the ark, laughing at them and mocking them, saying that they are fools without any knowledge. Meanwhile, they have no palm branch and no citron. They claim, "Has not the Torah said to take these in order to 'rejoice in the presence of YHWH your God for seven days' [Lev 23:40]? Do you think these species will make us happy? Silver and gold ornaments and fine clothes make us happier!" And they say. "Do you think we have to bless God? Does He need this? Foolishness!" Eventually there are no *tefillin* on their heads. When asked why, they respond, "*Tefillin* are only intended to be 'a reminder between your eyes' [Exod 13:9]. Since they are intended as a reminder, it is better to mention the Creator with our mouths several times a day. That is a better and more fitting reminder!" They take those books and see those words and say, "This is the Torah of truth!"[14]

Not only lazy scoffers but sincere religious seekers were captivated by the philosophic approach. An anonymous student of Abraham Abulafia who studied the *Guide of the Perplexed* under a Jewish philosopher writes:

> God is my witness! If I had not previously acquired strength of faith by what little I had learned of the Torah and the Talmud, my observance of many of the *mizwot* would have been ruined, although the fire of pure intention was ablaze in my heart. What this teacher communicated to me in the way

of philosophy did not suffice, until God had me meet a godly man, a kabbalist, who taught me the general outlines of the way of Kabbalah.[15]

Without a strong traditional basis, philosophy is likely to be detrimental
to religious practice. "One who has been raised on books of logic and
philosophy and has not occupied himself beforehand with our holy Torah,
both the Written and the Oral, will disdain the *mizwot* and prayer."[16]

The philosophers had sought to defend and justify tradition by the application of reason. Skepticism had to be confronted directly. Saadiah Gaon
introduced his *Emunot we-De'ot* with words of desperation: "I have seen
people drowning in the sea of doubt; the waters of error have already
covered them. There is no diver who can raise them from the depths, no
swimmer who can grasp their hand and pull them out." Jacob ben Sheshet
points out that Maimonides sought to base Torah on nature and the *mizwot*
on reason because of "heretics and non-believers who say, 'What is the
reason for such-and-such a *mizwah*? The intellect does not tolerate it; it is
only an allegory!'" (*Meshiv Devarim Nekhohim*, p. 145). In the introduction
to his translation of Maimonides's *Shemonah Peraqim*, Samuel Ibn Tibbon
argues that one should not merely affirm religious teachings on faith;
through wisdom one should know their truth. It is better to demonstrate
the existence of God by logical proof than to simply accept it on the basis
of *qabbalah*, "tradition." The Kabbalists, known in the *Zohar* as *beney mehei-
manuta* ("sons of faith"), felt called upon to champion the primacy of faith.
Perhaps they feared consequences such as those predicted by Heinrich
Heine: "From the moment a religion solicits the aid of philosophy, its ruin
is inevitable."[17]

The philosophers had succeeded in demonstrating that most of the *mizwot* were reasonable. The Kabbalists felt that they had thereby subordinated the divine command to human reason. No one was more aware of
the philosophic agenda than the mystics. Isaac of Akko writes in his *Me'irat
'Eynayim:* "Some of our people show off their wisdom of nature and say
that we should force ourselves to take everything in the Torah and base it
upon nature by any means of interpretation, however far-fetched. We must
not say that it is beyond nature" (p. 157). Nahmanides criticizes Maimonides
for "reducing miracles and increasing nature" (*Kitvey Ramban* 1:154). He
charges that Aristotle failed to comprehend the supernatural:

> We must muzzle the mouths of those who show off their wisdom of nature,
> who follow after the Greek who denied everything except what he could
> perceive by the senses and stirred his mind to think, he and his wicked
> students, that anything he could not comprehend by logical reasoning was
> not true. (*Commentary* on Lev 16:8)

Early Kabbalah

Mystical reasons for the *miẓwot* became a central feature of Kabbalah. Meir ben Solomon Abi Sahula (early fourteenth century) in his commentary on *Sefer Yeẓirah* mentions two fields of kabbalistic study: the doctrine of the ten *sefirot* and the elucidation of *taʿamey ha-miẓwot*.[18] The two are closely related.

Already in *Sefer ha-Bahir*, the earliest text of Kabbalah, edited toward the end of the twelfth century in Provence, the esoteric meaning of the *miẓwot* is related to the *sefirot*, the ten stages of divine manifestation.[19] Only a few *miẓwot* (*tefillin*, *ẓiẓit*, *lulav* [palm branch], *terumah* [offering]) are discussed, but the point is made that the fulfillment of a *miẓwah* signifies the activity of a *sefirah* or the combined activity of several *sefirot*. Furthermore, such fulfillment contributes to the maintenance and operation of the *sefirot*.

> There is one pillar extending from the earth to the sky. *Ẓaddiq* [Righteous One] is its name, named after the righteous. If there are righteous humans in the world, it is strengthened; if not, it is weakened. It supports the entire world, as it is written: "*Ẓaddiq* is the foundation of the world" [Prov 10:25]. If it is weak, the world cannot continue to exist. Thus if there is even only one righteous human, he supports the world.[20]

The ninth *sefirah*, *Ẓaddiq* or *Yesod* ("foundation"), is said to include all the *miẓwot* (*Bahir* §184). By stating that its potency is affected by human action, the *Bahir* adumbrates the kabbalistic theme of *ẓorekh gavoha*, the "need on high," the radical insight that the divine realm is dependent on human effort.

The tenth *sefirah*, *Malkhut*, serves as the focus of much of the *taʿamey ha-miẓwot* in the *Bahir*. Since *Malkhut* ("kingdom") receives the flow of emanation from *Ẓaddiq*, She too includes all the *miẓwot*. "The first light . . . was very great and no creature was able to gaze upon it. The Blessed Holy One took one-thousandth of its splendor and fashioned a precious stone, beautifully set, and included in her all the *miẓwot*" (*Bahir* §190). She is "the bride, adorned and crowned with all the *miẓwot*" (*Bahir* §196).

Isaac the Blind (ca. 1160–1235), the son of Abraham ben David of Posquières, transmitted various *taʿamey ha-miẓwot* and apparently composed an entire book on the subject, which was quoted by Kabbalists of the thirteenth and fourteenth centuries and subsequently disappeared.[21] In his commentary on *Sefer Yeẓirah* (1:6) Isaac cites Ps 119:96: "I have seen an end to every purpose, but Your *miẓwah* is very broad." He remarks: "Although Your *miẓwah* seems finite at first, it expands to infinity. While all perishable things are finite, the human being can never fully comprehend Your *mizwah.*" The concrete, determinate act appears limited but leads the mystic toward *Eyn Sof,* the "infinite" and unknowable nature of the divine.

In the kabbalistic center of Gerona, traditions received from Isaac the Blind were spread to wider circles, against the wishes of Isaac himself,[22] while new teachings were also developed. Detailed mystical explanations were provided for various *miẓwot,* mostly *ḥuqqim:* mixed species, sabbatical and jubilee years, circumcision, incest, *lulav* and *etrog* ("citron"), *ẓiẓit,* and sacrifices.

Ezra ben Solomon of Gerona (d. 1238 or 1245) was the first to provide kabbalistic explanations as part of an extended list of *miẓwot,* which he included in his commentary on the Song of Songs, attributed to Nahmanides.[23] Ezra follows Maimonides's enumeration of the command-ments, making certain changes and adding new reasons. He intended to provide reasons only for those *miẓwot* that were not explained in the Torah (*Kitvey Ramban* 2:496). Actually he offers kabbalistic reasons for only a small number of *miẓwot,* several of which are already explained in the biblical text. The general purpose of the *miẓwot* is that the evil inclination be subjugated to the good inclination, that the body be drawn after the power of the soul (*Kitvey Ramban* 2:497). "The *miẓwot* are the body of purity and holiness. One who engages in them purifies and sanctifies himself" (*Kitvey Ramban* 2:548). It is forbidden to take vengeance or bear a grudge (Lev 19:18) not merely because these are antisocial (as Maimonides had taught) but because one who does so "fails to walk in the ways of the Blessed Holy One" (*Kitvey Ramban* 2:547). The *miẓwot* are a means of imitating and contacting the divine. "The *miẓwot* are the *middot,*" the various divine "qualities" (*Kitvey Ramban* 2:538). These *middot,* the seven lower *sefirot,* are called "the edifice of the *miẓwot*")*Kitvey Ramban* 2:538).

> The performance of a *mizwah* is the light of life [of a *sefirah*]. One who acts below maintains its power. . . . He walks in the ways of light, does not depart from it, basks within it. When the soul is detached from the body, that light draws the soul . . . , for that quality draws her. . . . The splendor of the soul ascends and stands in a high and intimate place, within the glory of the Blessed Holy One. (*Kitvey Ramban* 2:528)

Azriel ben Menaḥem of Gerona (early thirteenth century), Ezra's younger contemporary, does not discuss the *miẓwot* in detail. In his *Commentary on the Aggadot* (pp. 38–39) he writes: "Even though there are light and weighty *miẓwot,* all the *miẓwot* are divine glory." He concludes: "All the *miẓwot* have one end, and their end is infinite. Whoever is engaged in *miẓwot* must be in awe of the *mizwah,* as if he were crowned and adorned with its glory."

In the Geronese circle, creative kabbalistic exegesis was openly encouraged by Jacob ben Sheshet (mid-thirteenth century). He writes in his *Ha-Emunah we-ha-Bittahon* (also attributed to Nahmanides): "It is a *mizwah* for every wise person to innovate in Torah according to his capacity" (*Kitvey Ramban* 2:364). After one mystical innovation he comments: "Do not think that this is far-fetched. If I had not invented it in my mind, I would say that it was transmitted to Moses at Sinai" (*Kitvey Ramban* 2:370). In another book, he defends and qualifies his method:

I know that there are those among the pious and the wise of Israel who will indict me for having written reasons for two or three *mizwot* of the Torah, thus opening the possibility of providing reasons for many *mizwot* according to the path of wisdom. Behold I bring a proof that any wise person may provide a reason for any *mizwah* whose reason has not been explained in the Torah. The benefit will be great and his reward too, for he makes the *mizwah* beautiful in the eyes of the nations, and they will say, "Surely, this great nation is a wise and understanding people" [Deut 4:6].[24] For they contend against us, "What is the reason for this *mizwah* and that one? They are nothing but allegories!" When we provide them with reasons that they cannot deny, they will say, "Come, let us ascend to the house of YHWH, to the house of the God of Jacob. He will instruct us in His ways; we will walk in His paths" [Isa 2:3]. . . . So let no pious or wise person find it difficult to provide a reason for those *mizwot* whose reason is not stated explicitly in the Torah, as long as he does not claim that such a reason is the essence of the transmission of that *mizwah*. Rather, let him say that if such-and-such a *mizwah* had not been given, it should have been given for such-and-such a reason. (*Meshiv Devarim Nekhohim*, 83)

Jacob is eager to convince the skeptics that the *mizwot* are worth taking literally; they should not be allegorized away. Previously we saw that he ascribes a similar motivation to Maimonides. To accomplish his task, Jacob is willing to provide reasons, not necessarily the original reasons, but ones that adequately justify the *mizwot*.

Moses Nahmanides (1194–1270), the most famous rabbinic figure of Gerona, helped the young kabbalistic movement gain acceptance. This he accomplished despite his own hesitancy to spread the secrets. His involvement in mystical study, coupled with his halakhic authority, paved the way for future Kabbalists and helped convince Jewry that mystical teachings were compatible with rabbinic Judaism, that, in fact, Kabbalah conveyed the true meaning of Torah. His *Commentary on the Torah*, written in the land of Israel toward the end of his life, is a blend of exoteric and esoteric exegesis. The latter appears only in occasional hints introduced by the phrase "according to the way of truth." Nahmanides gives notice in his introduction that these hints cannot be understood through one's own intellectual effort but only by a perceptive student who learns directly from a wise Kabbalist. He rarely invents kabbalistic teachings or mystical reasons for the *mizwot*. In discussing the command against incest, he writes: "We have no tradition concerning this, but according to reasoning, there is in this matter one of the secrets of Creation connected with the soul" (*Commentary* Lev 18:6).[25] Usually he transmits what he has learned from Geronese colleagues and teachers. His creative exegesis was mostly confined to *peshat* (the "literal" meaning), polemics, and *halakhah* (e.g., *Hiddushey ha-Ramban*).

Nahmanides agrees with Maimonides that the *mizwot* have reasons. "Every one has a reason and a benefit and serves to improve the human being." The benefits of the *mizwot* are "preventing physical harm or wrong beliefs or unseemly character traits, or recalling the miracles and wonders of the Creator, and knowing God." "Our lack of knowledge of the reasons for [the commandments of] Torah derives solely from the blindness of our intellect" (*Commentary* on Deut 22:6).

The *mishpatim* are intended to "bring about good life" (*Commentary* on Deut 6:24); they are "desired by everyone, needed by everyone. Without them, civilized life is impossible" (*Commentary* on Lev 26:15). The *huqqim* are "*mizwot* whose reasons have not been revealed to the masses. Fools reject them and say, 'Why does God desire that I not wear this garment woven of fine linen and blue wool? How do we benefit by burning a cow and sprinkling the ashes on ourselves?'" (*Commentary* on Lev 26:15). It is precisely these apparently irrational *huqqim* that are "God's secrets in the Torah. In thinking about them, people do not derive pleasure as they do from the *mishpatim*, but all of them have a proper reason and perfect benefit. . . . One who combines two species alters and denies the act of Creation, as if he thinks that the Blessed Holy One has not completed His world perfectly, and he wants to help in the creation of the world by adding creatures to it" (*Commentary* on Lev 19:19).[26]

God's decrees are heteronomous but not irrational. They are publicized because of their beneficial intent, but their reasons are revealed only to those who are close to the King. "The *huqqim* are decrees of the King. Now a decree is that which arises in the mind of the king, who is wise in the management of his kingdom. He knows the need and benefit of the command he ordains, but he does not reveal it to the people, only to his wise advisers" (*Commentary* on Lev 18:6).

In discussing the sacrifices, Nahmanides attacks Maimonides's historical explanations.[27] The claim that the sacrifices were a concession to Israel's idolatrous nature is not mentioned by Nahmanides. He assails Maimonides's view that since the Egyptians and Chaldeans worshiped cattle and sheep, Israel was commanded to sacrifice these to God in order to demon-strate the falsehood of such beliefs (*Guide* 3:46). "God forbid that [the sacrifices] have no purpose and intention other than eliminating idolatrous opinions from the minds of fools" (*Commentary* on Lev 1:9). The fact that Abel, son of Adam and Eve, offered sacrifices is significant for Naḥmanides because at that point in human history there was no idol worship. "This should muzzle the mouths of those who speak foolishness concerning the reason for the sacrifices" (*Commentary* on Gen 4:4).[28] A better explanation is that the sacrifice takes the place of the sinner. "One's own blood should be spilled and one's body burned, were it not for the loving-kindness of the Creator, who accepts this offering as a substitute and ransom, its blood in place of his blood, life for life" (*Commentary* on Lev 1:9).[29]

A mystical reason for sacrifices is suggested by Naḥmanides in his dis-cussion of Adam's role in the Garden of Eden. Adam was placed there "to till it and tend it" (Gen 2:15), which the Midrash (*Gen. Rab.* 16:8) inter-preted as referring to sacrifices. Naḥmanides comments: "By means of the sacrifices blessing emanates to the higher powers, and from them to the plants of the Garden of Eden" (*Commentary* on Gen 2:8). The sacrifice provides emanation to the *sefirot.* This notion is rooted in the *Bahir* (§109), which suggests a derivation of the Hebrew word for sacrifice, *qorban:* "Why is it called *qorban?* Because it draws near [*meqarev*] the holy powers." The *qorban* is a sacrament unifying the *sefirot* and ensuring the flow of emana-tion from the Infinite source. An anonymous contemporary of Naḥman-ides describes the *qorban* as a symbol of the union of the human soul with the *sefirot:* "The meaning of the *qorban* is to raise the low [human] desire in order to draw it near and unite it with the desire of the higher powers, which are His names [the *sefirot*], and then to draw the higher desire and the lower desire to one desire [the highest *sefirah,* called Desire]" (Tishby, *Mishnat ha-Zohar,* 2:197–98).

We have referred to Maimonides's utilitarian explanation of the calf whose neck is broken when a local murder cannot be solved. Naḥmanides quotes this reason in his comment on Deut 21:4: "People will speak about it a great deal; perhaps the matter will be revealed." Such an explanation is inadequate for Naḥmanides because although "according to this reason, the stratagem is useful, the act is not desirable in and of itself." He concludes that the reason for killing the calf is similar to the reason for the scapegoat on Yom Kippur and the ritual of the red heifer. This is spelled out by Naḥmanides's successors and commentators. Isaac of Akko writes that Naḥmanides's point is to convey "the secret without a stratagem" (*Me'irat 'Eynayim,* p. 233). Baḥya ben Asher in his commentary on Deut 21:1 states: "The calf was offered to the attribute of judgment so that it . . . not rule over us." Menaḥem Recanati says similarly, "The reason for this *miẓwah* has been hinted to me . . . : so that the attribute of judgment affect it [the calf] and not the world" (*Ṭaʿamey ha-Miẓwot,* p. 73d).

In enumerating the 613 *miẓwot,* Naḥmanides frequently differs with Maimonides. One of their differences involves the issue of prayer. Maimonides lists prayer as the fifth positive command. Naḥmanides objects: "Certainly the matter of prayer is not an obligation at all but derives from the Creator's quality of grace toward us, that He hears and responds whenever we call out to Him" (*Sefer ha-Miẓwot,* p. 156). The mystic experiences prayer not as the fulfillment of an obligation but as a gift, an intimate moment with God. The *miẓwot,* as well, are not mere obligations. They resonate with one's essential nature. "The human being is vanity and air, nothing at all, but reverence is the essence of his creation. His eyes and head and all his limbs are as nothing; the *miẓwot* are his body and limbs and soul" (*Kitvey Ramban* 1:203).

The Zohar

The theme of *ṭaʿamey ha-miẓwot,* which played a significant role in the teachings of the Geronese Kabbalists, was enhanced as Kabbalah developed in Castile. It became a basic genre of kabbalistic literature, alongside biblical exegesis and explanations of the ten *sefirot.*

Joseph Gikatilla (1248–ca. 1325) in his *Ginnat Egoz* complains of heresy in Spain, of those who deny Torah and prophecy, men of reason who feel that they can dispense with ritual observance. He produced two types of compositions on the *miẓwot.* His *Kelaley ha-Miẓwot* is a talmudic encyclopedia clarifying halakhic concepts. This deals neither with *sefirot* nor letter mysticism but occasionally discusses spiritual aspects of observance. Gikatilla also wrote mystical explanations of about a dozen individual *miẓwot.*[30]

Gikatilla opposes the attempt to enumerate the 613 commandments. One who undertakes this acts as if the Torah "were in his eyes like one of the chronicles produced for one of the wise men of the nations. . . . There is no greater renunciation or nullification of *miẓwot* than [the act of] one who decides and decrees that the *miẓwot* he counted are the ones given to Moses at Sinai and not others."[31]

Gikatilla seeks to discover the nature of the phenomenon of *miẓwah,* not merely the details. "Whoever engages in the details of the *miẓwot* and has not merited to attain the explanation of their principles is like one who has a pearl and does not know its powers and qualities" (*Kelaley ha-Miẓwot*). Every *miẓwah* has unique powers and effects. The reward of a *miẓwah* is the remedy that derives from its power. Conversely, punishment is simply the removal of a *mizwah*'s protection. This notion is repeated in Gikatilla's *Sha'arey Zedeq:* "Whoever fails to observe one of the *mizwot* is denied the good that derives from its observance, as one who does not sow his field fails to reap, or as one who does not wear clothes finds his body chilled" (p. 12b). This naturalistic, mechanistic explanation of the function of the *mizwot* is supplemented in Gikatilla's *Sha'arey Orah,* where he emphasizes the mystical aspect: "Come and see the power of the righteous, who adhere to Torah and *mizwot* and are empowered to unite all the *sefirot*" (p. 38).

The righteous unite the *sefirot* but are careful not to unite that which must be kept separate. They "establish all inner things in their place within and outer things without. Nothing leaves its boundary" (*Sha'arey Zedeq,* p. 12b). Gikatilla understands the word *hoq* ("decree") in the sense of "a prescribed limit, a boundary" that divides the outside forces from divinity (*Sha'arey Zedeq,* pp. 13b–14a). In explaining the *hoq* of *sha'atnez* (the forbidden combination of wool and linen), Gikatilla reveals the intense conservatism of Kabbalah: "All created things are good, nothing is evil, if they remain in the place and retain the characteristics assigned them by God." *Sha'atnez* violates the principle of defined boundaries. "Whoever joins the things that are separate, such as one man's wife with another man, destroys the world. For this reason *sha'atnez* [is forbidden]."[32] Certain of the *huqqim* may not be "tolerated by the intellect" (*Kelaley ha-Mizwot*), but "we should fulfill them and not analyze them critically by asking, 'Why were they given to us?' We should guard the boundary of the border [*hoq gevul*] of reflecting on and thinking about them. We should not cross that border" (*Sha'arey Orah,* p. 53).

The *Zohar,* the masterpiece of Spanish Kabbalah composed in Aramaic by Gikatilla's colleague, Moses de León, adopts a different strategy. It loves to question, to challenge, to cross borders, and then to return home with renewed devotion and transformed understanding. "It is not a sin when one examines Torah precisely and asks questions to illuminate its words" (*Zohar* 3:192a). The *Zohar* confronts problematic *mizwot* directly with its questions and provides its own answers.

> What is the reason for sacrificing an animal? It would be better for a person to break his spirit and engage in repentance. Why should he slaughter an animal, burn it in fire on the altar? But it is a mystery.... The mystery of the sacrifices includes many mysteries, which can be revealed only to the truly righteous, from whom the mystery of their Master is not concealed. (*Zohar* 3:240b)

The *Zohar* reveals various aspects of the mystery. In several passages (e.g., 3:5a) it follows the teaching of the *Bahir* that the *qorban* is intended to unite the *sefirot* "until all turn into one, complete oneness . . . so that compassion fill all the worlds . . . and everything be sweetened." The *qorban* is intended especially to join the feminine and masculine aspects of divinity, *Shekhinah* ("presence," another name for *Malkhut*) and *Tif'eret* ("beauty"). As the burnt offering ascends, *Shekhinah* "ascends and joins with the Holy King [*Tif'eret*] in complete union" (3:107b). Similarly, on Yom Kippur, when the high priest offers a sin offering to atone for the people, he is, in effect, uniting the King and Queen. It is because of the intimacy of this moment that the Torah instructs: "No one [else] shall be present in the Tent of Meeting" (Lev 16:17; *Zohar* 3:66b). The union is initiated by sacrifice. "The smoke ascends and an arousal of love is bound and aroused above. One stands facing the other. The fire is kindled and shines by means of the arousal below" (1:247b–248a). The divine union produces an abundance of light and atonement of sin (1:206b). Thus, the efficacy of sacrifice is maintained by the *Zohar*, and Maimonides's historical relativization is countered by an emphasis on the cosmic significance of the act. Israel is included in the ecstasy, for as the fire of *Shekhinah* consumes the offering, the people achieve mystical communion with Her and, miraculously, are not destroyed. "You who cleave to YHWH your God are alive every one of you today" (Deut 4:4; *Zohar* 1:51b).

A different spiritualization appears in another passage: "The essence of the *qorban* . . . is to offer before the Blessed Holy One the desire of one's heart, spirit, and soul. This is more precious to Him than anything!" (3:9b). Elsewhere the *Zohar* maintains that the flesh of the sacrifice is offered to the demonic, the Other Side, while the intention of the heart is directed toward God. "The desire ascends to one place and the flesh to one place" (1:65a). The scapegoat loaded with Israel's sins and designated for Azazel on Yom Kippur (Lev 16:7–22) is understood as a bribe offered to the demonic accuser to silence him. The basis for this interpretation is found in the late Midrash *Pirqey de-Rabbi Eli'ezer* (chap. 46): "They gave him [Satan] a bribe on Yom Kippur so that he would not interfere with Israel's sacrifice." The *Zohar* adds that by means of this device the accuser is transformed into an advocate of Israel.[33]

The *Zohar* questions the details of biblical ritual and law in order to provide mystical answers. Concerning the wave offering, the *yanuqa*, the *Wunderkind* of the *Zohar*, asks: "What difference does it make whether he waves it or lowers it?" (3:188b). The *etrog*, one of the four species taken on *Sukkot*, the Feast of Booths, is called "the fruit of a lovely tree" (Lev 23:40). The *Zohar* asks: "Now, is the *etrog* from a lovely tree? There are so many thorns all around it! Yet you say it is the fruit of a lovely tree? But the mystery of the word . . ." (3:24a). The mystery is that the tree is the cosmic tree of the *sefirot,* beautiful indeed. Its fruit is *Shekhinah,* the yield of emanation.

Maimonides had claimed that the details of certain *mizwot* need not be explained and "were given merely for the sake of commanding something." Nothing could be further from the *Zohar*'s truth. "Rabbi Shim'on said, 'If human beings knew the words of Torah, they would know that every single word and letter contains precious, supernal mysteries.' . . . Piles upon piles of mysteries of wisdom depend on each one. . . . Every word contains many mysteries, reasons, roots, and branches."[34] Problematic words and verses require the gaze of contemplation. "Every weak or fragile word in the Torah—when you contemplate and know it, you will find it as strong as a hammer that shatters rocks" (3:6b; cf. Jer 23:29). "There are many verses in the Torah that seem as if they should not have been written. Yet we see that they are all supernal mysteries" (2:217b).[35] "This verse—one who sees it but does not contemplate it is like one who does not taste a dish" (2:217b). The mystical reason (*ta'am*) for a particular word or verse or *mizwah* is its unique taste (*ta'am*), which is accessible only to one who contemplates and engages the text. The *Zohar* attacks the radical rationalists who read the Torah critically and question its divine origin and thus undermine its authority: "Woe to those sinners of the world who neither know nor perceive the words of Torah. . . . Those close-minded fools . . . —not only do they fail to know; they even say that those words are defective and useless" (1:163a).

The *Zohar* seeks deeper layers of Torah in order to reinforce the foundations of faith. "New and ancient words of Torah are revealed . . . to draw Israel close to their Father above" (1:243a). "We must not destroy the faith of all; we must maintain it!" (1:136a [*Midrash ha-Ne'elam*]). The success of the *Zohar*'s program is attested by Pinhas of Koretz, an eighteenth-century Hasidic rabbi, who declared, "The *Zohar* has kept me Jewish."[36]

Kabbalistic creativity is essential to this venture. Thus it is a *mizwah* "to study Torah, to engage in it, and to expand it every day" (1:12b). God rejoices in new words of Torah: "The moment a new word of Torah comes forth from the mouth of a human being, that word ascends and presents herself before the Blessed Holy One. He lifts up the word and kisses her" (1:4b). The Kabbalists are not simply inventing secrets; they are discovering them, gathering them from the rich field of the divine presence. Moses Cordovero explains why the *Zohar* calls the Kabbalists "reapers of the field": "The reapers of the field are the Comrades, masters of this wisdom, because *Malkhut* [*Shekhinah*] is called the Apple field; She grows sprouts of secrets and new flowerings of Torah. Those who constantly create new interpretations of Torah are harvesting Her" (*Or ha-Hammah* on *Zohar* 3:106a).

Moses de León attributed the *Zohar* to the circle of the mishnaic teacher Shim'on bar Yohai, whose ancient authority sanctioned publication of the secrets (3:79a):

> The generation in which Rabbi Shim'on is present is completely worthy and devoted, completely sin-fearing. *Shekhinah* dwells among them. This is not so in other generations. So words are expressed openly and not concealed. In other generations this is not so: secret words from above cannot be revealed, and those who know are afraid.

Moses felt an urgent need to reveal the secret meaning of Torah and *mizwot* because laxity in observance was prevalent, because of the inroads of rationalism and heresy, as well as to more mundane factors: laziness and ignorance. The moralistic literature of the times lists a number of neglected *mizwot: tefillin, mezuzah, sukkah,* the ritual washing of hands, circumcision, and sexual morality. The *Zohar* emphasizes the importance of all of these by providing them with kabbalistic reasons.

Though it rarely discusses mystical experience, the *Zohar* is eager to highlight the mystical significance of *mizwot.* Living according to Torah is the surest way to encounter God. "When a human being observes the commands of Torah, *Shekhinah* walks with him constantly and never departs from him" (1:230a). The author speaks with the passion of a mystical moralist. If one invites the poor into his *sukkah,* seven biblical heroes abide there with him. If one arrives early at the synagogue, *Shekhinah* joins Herself to him. Every day lived in accordance with Torah is woven into the soul's garment of splendor.[37]

Maimonides had claimed that the ultimate perfection consists only of true opinions, not actions (*Guide* 3:27). The *Zohar* counters: "The action below is always essential in order to arouse above. Come and see: One who says that the action is not always essential, or pronouncing words or producing sounds, may his spirit deflate!" (*Zohar* 3:105a).[38] The interdependence of human and divine action is emphasized continually: "As they manifest an action below, so it is aroused above" (3:119a). "Once a human being arouses an arousal, an arousal above is aroused" (1:77b; cf. 3:31b, 38b). This is why the shewbread had always to be present on the table of acacia wood in the tabernacle, for "blessing does not appear at an empty place" (2:153b; cf. Nahmanides's *Commentary* on Exod 25:24). Human behavior influences the *sefirot.* If one is kind and loving, the *sefirah* of *Hesed* ("loving-kindness") is aroused (3:92a–b). The correspondence between *mizwot* and *sefirot* is vital: "All the commands of Torah are united with the body of the King, some with the head, some with the torso, some with the hands, some with the feet. No command is apart from the body. So one who transgresses any command is like one who sins against the body of the King" (2:85b)[39] Each *miẓwah* represents a divine limb, quality, or attribute. The entire body of the *sefirot*. the body of the King, is the body of primordial Adam; so "the commands of Torah are all in the mystery of Adam" (2:162b). The *miẓwot* are the means of attaining the knowledge of God's being and one's own deep structure.

> All the commands are limbs through which the mystery of faith is perceived. One who does not contemplate and gaze at the mysteries of the commands of Torah does not know how the limbs are mysteriously arrayed. The limbs of the body are all arrayed according to the mystery of the commands. Even though there are great and exalted limbs, all of them—small and great—if one is removed, even the smallest, that person is blemished. All the more so, one who detracts even one command from the commands of Torah causes a blemish where there should be none. (2:165b)

In the Talmud (*b. Mak.* 23b) Rabbi Simlai had suggested the correspondence between the 248 human limbs and the 248 positive commandments, and between the 365 days of the year and the 365 prohibitions. Each limb was intended to fulfill a *miẓwah,* each day to sanctify the human being by restricting him to the realm of the permissible. The *Zohar* expands this conception by daring to describe the limbs of the divine. The *miẓwot* reflect the basic divine and human structure. Through enacting the *miẓwot,* the human microcosm links up with his divine archetype, in whose image he has been created.

The *miẓwot* both reflect and influence the *sefirot.* They are an opportunity to regain the wholeness that was lost when Adam disobeyed the first "thou shalt not." By eating of the fruit of the tree of knowledge, he split the feminine and masculine halves of divinity, *Shekhinah* and *Tif'eret.*[40] He asserted his conscious independence from God's will. The *miẓwot* are an invitation to realign the human and divine wills, a mystical means to restore the harmony between the Blessed Holy One and His *Shekhinah.* The human being thus comes to the aid of God. He can raise *Shekhinah* from the dust of exile (1:191b) and actualize divine being. Of one who performs the *miẓwot,* God says, "'It is as if he has made Me.'... Since they [the Blessed Holy One and His *Shekhinah*] are aroused above you to join together..., you have indeed made them" (3:113a).[41]

The purpose of the *miẓwot* is to promote the *ziwwuga qaddisha* ("the holy union"). The Sabbath is an especially appropriate occasion. The Sabbath Queen, *Shekhinah,* is welcomed and crowned by Israel and ushered into the presence of the King, the Blessed Holy One. The Sabbath is God's wedding celebration (3:105a). Mystics imitate this divine union on Sabbath eve (1:112a [*Midrash ha-Ne'elam*]).

The power of human action also has negative potential. The prophet Isaiah had written: "Your iniquities have been a barrier between you and your God. Your sins have hidden His face from you; He does not hear" (59:2). The *Zohar* states that "sins of the world cause the Blessed Holy One to ascend above, above" (2:58b). Moreover, sinners "cause a defect above" and interfere with the flow of emanation (3:297a–b). They "separate the Queen from the King, and the King from the Queen. Thus He is not called One, for He is only called One when they are in one union. Woe to those sinners who cause separation above!" (3:16b). Adam's cosmic mistake is thereby repeated. The *Zohar* interprets Isa 50:1: "For your crimes, your mother was sent away," as referring to *Shekhinah*, who is "banished along with you" (3:115a). The effects of sin correspond precisely to the act. "One who joins himself to another man's wife causes a defect in the [divine] union, for the union of *Keneset Yisra'el* [*Shekhinah*] is with the Blessed Holy One alone" (3:44b).

The demonic is empowered by human sin. "What draws down that [impure] spirit? You must admit, the act that reveals the Other Side [the demonic]" (3:86b). "If sinners did not draw the impure spirit down to the world, it would not be present" (2:269a). "The Other Side is present only because of the actions of the world, so that he can become defiled through them" (2:180b). In this scenario, ethical and mythological strands are interwoven. Slander or gossip stimulates the tortuous serpent, who "raises its rough skin . . . and is aroused from head to tail. . . . Its whole body is aroused . . . to act as an informer on high" (2:265a).

Every word has its effect above. The Kabbalist is an ethical mystic, constantly aware of the need to act righteously. *Miẓwot* fuel the light of the soul (3:187a). They reinforce the connection between the human part and the divine whole. "Israel should be adorned with Torah and *miẓwot*, so that they will always cleave to the Blessed Holy One" (*Zohar Ḥadash, Rut*, 84d [*Midrash ha-Ne'elam*]).

One approaches the divine by imitation. "He has commanded them to walk in His ways, literally, to resemble Him in everything" (*Zohar* 1:10a). The ritual washing of the hands must be performed perfectly because the ten fingers symbolize the ten *sefirot*, or in the words of the *Zohar*, "the hands of a human being inhabit the height of the world" (3:186a).[42] The action below succeeds in arousing a holy action above only if it mirrors the divine model (3:38b). As the *sefirot* provide the flow of emanation one to the other, so humans must provide for the poor. This is the most effective way to regain the stature of Adam (1:13b). Wearing *tefillin* is another way "to complete oneself in the image above, as it is written [Gen 1:27]: 'God created Adam in His image'" (1:13b). The Talmud (*b. Ber.* 6a) had described

God as wearing *tefillin*. The *Zohar* teaches that "one who is arrayed in them is in the image of God" (1:14a) and makes himself a chariot for the divine presence (1:129b [*Midrash ha-Ne'elam*]). Wearing this crown, he is king on earth, as God is King above (3:269b). He is expected to imitate the divine lover:

> One who puts on *tefillin,* when he puts on the *tefillah* of the hand, must extend his left hand toward *Keneset Yisra'el* [*Shekhinah*] and bind the knot with his right hand, so as to embrace Her, in order to fulfill the verse: "His left hand is under my head; with his right he embraces me" [Song 2:6]. Thus one should present himself as above and crown himself in all. Then he is a totally perfect human being, complete in supernal holiness. God calls out to him, "Israel, in whom I will be glorified" [Isa 49:3]. (*Zohar* 3:55a)

The first *mizwah* in the Torah, "Be fruitful and multiply" (Gen 1:28), presents another opportunity to imitate the *sefirot*. In both human and divine realms, male and female are incomplete unless they are joined. "Any image not embracing male and female is not sublime and true" (1:55b). According to the Midrash (*Gen. Rab.* 8:1), Adam was originally an androgynous being. The *sefirot,* which constitute the body of primordial Adam, are also androgynous. From the union of *Tif'eret* (the Blessed Holy One) and *Malkhut* (*Shekhinah*) all souls are born; these souls too, in their original nature, are androgynous (1:85b). Only because of Adam's sin has this androgynous nature been lost (3:43b). As male or female, humans are only "half a body" (3:7b), but by joining together and engendering new life, each couple regains wholeness and manifests the oneness of God (3:7a, 81a–b). The Talmud (*b. Yebam.* 63b) had taught that "Whoever does not engage in engendering new life . . . , it is as if he lessens the image" in which Adam and Eve were created. Ezra of Gerona identifies this image with *Tif'eret* and *Malkhut* (*Kitvey Ramban* 2:523–24). The *Zohar* urges one "to extend the image of the supernal King through the world," "to extend the [cosmic] tree" (1:186b; 2:109a) by fulfilling this *mizwah*. Joseph of Hamadan wrote, soon after the composition of the *Zohar,* that one who is fruitful "maintains the image of the chain" of *sefirot*.[43]

In the Wake of the Zohar

Gershom Scholem estimated that the *Zohar* was completed by 1286. In 1287 Moses de León wrote *Sefer ha-Rimmon* (*The Book of the Pomegranate*) in Guadalajara. This is an extensive discussion of over one hundred *mizwot* "that are always necessary."[44] The title alludes to a rabbinic saying: "Even the empty ones of Israel are filled with *mizwot* as a pomegranate [is filled with seeds]" (*b. Ber.* 57a).[45] *Sefer ha-Rimmon* is, in effect, a kabbalistic manual that demonstrates how everyday halakhic observance can flower into mystical practice.

Though he never cites the *Zohar* by name, Moses de León draws on it and occasionally refers to it obliquely: "They have said in the Midrash," "I have seen in the Yerushalmi," "I have seen this matter in a deep place." His own creative exegesis is evident throughout, as he discovers and expounds the sefirotic symbolism of each *mizwah*. The role of received kabbalistic tradition is reduced.[46]

We have seen (see above n. 14) how *Sefer ha-Rimmon* condemns those who refused to observe the rituals of Sukkot. In another passage we find a description of the mystical significance of the act: "By human action below, a power above is aroused. . . . Nothing in the lower world is for naught. . . . When this [palm branch along with the other species] is held below, the power appointed over it is aroused." By holding the four species together (see Lev 23:40) and waving them in all directions, one activates and demonstrates the union of the *sefirot*. The performance of the *mizwah* initiates the human worshiper into the mysterious extent of God's oneness: "God is one, God's secret is one, all the worlds below and above are secretly one. . . . Meditate on this matter, and you will find that His true existence is linked with and concatenates throughout all the worlds" (*Sefer ha-Rimmon*, fols. 46b–47a).

The *mizwot* are a mystical technique available to the masses, a legislated "secret by which the upper and lower realms are maintained" (fol. 101b). "The secret of fulfilling the *mizwot* is the mending of all the worlds and drawing down the emanation of the desire and will from above" (fol. 106b). *Sefer ha-Rimmon* was intended to bridge the gap between the Kabbalists, the "remnant called by God,"[47] and the common people. Ironically, it failed to achieve popularity and was never published, whereas the esoteric *Zohar* was read even by those who could not understand its lyrical Aramaic. Yet *Sefer ha-Rimmon* is remarkable for its attempt to spread a spiritualized understanding of *mizwot* and to inculcate mystical observance. The book closes with a verse cited over thirty times in the *Zohar,* a motto of the Kabbalists (Isa 60:21): "Your people, all of them righteous, will inherit the land forever; a sprout of My planting, the work of My hands, making Me glorious!"

Toward the end of the thirteenth or the beginning of the fourteenth century, the *Ra'aya Meheimna* (*The Faithful Shepherd*) was composed. This work of *ta'amey ha-mizwot* was modeled on the *Zohar;* it was a successful enough imitation that it came to be printed as part of the *Zohar.* The work criticizes the rich leaders of the community for their neglect of *mizwot,* their indulgence in sensual pleasure, and their oppression of the Kabbalists and the poor. "They are neglectful of Torah and neglect those who engage in it."[48]

Like the Franciscan Spirituals, the author of the *Ra'aya Meheimna* predicts the appearance of a spiritual doctrine that will supersede the ruling materialistic one. The *Ra'aya Meheimna* contrasts the tree of life, which represents a pure, spiritual understanding of Torah, with the tree of knowledge of good and evil, the talmudic halakhah that contains excessive prohibitions and restrictions. The first tablets given to Moses at Sinai conveyed the teachings of the tree of life, but when these tablets were broken, the tree of knowledge of good and evil became dominant, and the Torah took on a more limited, material form. The Mishnah, the code that is the core of the Talmud, is "the grave of Moses" (*Zohar* 1:27b [*Tiqquney Zohar*]). Through mystical meditation, Kabbalists regain the essence of the tree of life; their understanding of Torah accords with the original revelation.[49]

The anonymous author is not antinomian; the *mizwot* are essential. Through them the concealed God is known (3:230a [*Ra'aya Meheimna*]). "Happy is one who [by engaging in each *mizwah*] causes God to dwell in each of his limbs." The Kabbalist strives to be "complete in his limbs, so that they all be perfect in the image of the Blessed Holy One. If one limb is deficient, he is not in the image" and must undergo the ordeal of transmigration to obtain another chance at perfection (*Tiqquney Zohar* 70, p. 132a).

The goal is to imitate and affect the divine. Moses is praised by Elijah because "in every commandment your effort was to unite the Blessed Holy One and His *Shekhinah*" (*Zohar* 2:119a [*Ra'aya Meheimna*]). Mystical understanding and enactment of the *mizwot* serve to "light up the Queen, to strip Her of the dark clothes of literalness and adorn Her with garments of shining colors of the mysteries of Torah" (*Zohar* 3:215b [*Ra'aya Meheimna*]).[50] In messianic time the tree of life will triumph over the tree of knowledge of good and evil. Until then the Kabbalist must keep the spark alive. The author of the *Ra'aya Meheimna* encourages mystical observance of the *mizwot* but questions the authority of rabbinic Judaism.

Around the time of the composition of the *Ra'aya Meheimna*, an extensive work on the commandments, entitled simply *Sefer Ta'amey ha-Mizwot*, was written by Joseph of Hamadan.[51] This Kabbalist, who perhaps came to Spain from Persia, explains over two hundred *mizwot*. He sometimes presents Maimonides's explanations as the *peshat* (the literal sense), but he lists numerous kabbalistic reasons, one after the other. He justifies his new revelations with this claim: "Who am I, who is my family, that I should recount the secrets of Torah? But this is my comfort in my affliction [Ps 119:50]: Not I am the revealer, but rather God."[52]

The human role is to effect divine union. By fulfilling any *miẓwah,* one marries the divine bride and groom; by transgressing a *miẓwah,* "it is as if he delivers a writ of divorce" (*Sefer Ṭa'amey ha-Miẓwot,* negative commandment 2, fol. 132a). Two of Joseph's formulations enshrine the human–divine interaction. Every *miẓwah* "applies above" (*shekhiaḥ kelappey ma'lah*), that is, God not only commands but performs the *miẓwot.* That is why the Torah says, "Keep My *miẓwot*" (Lev 26:3), "literally, 'My *miẓwot,*' which I perform!"[53] The divine performance is an interplay between the *sefirot,* which correspond to various *miẓwot.* This dimension of enactment is the archetype of human activity. "The entire Torah applies above. Once it was given to Moses at Sinai, it took on physical form."[54] The corresponding human enactment is an imitation of divinity; one thereby "maintains the form [of *sefirot*] and is an actual image of God" (positive commandment 84, p. 389). The correlation between *miẓwot* and divine limbs, outlined by the *Zohar,* is taken to extremes in *Sefer Ṭa'amey ha-Miẓwot;* the eating of *mazzah* on Passover, for example, stimulates the first joint of the right thumb of the divine body.[55] By performing the *miẓwot,* one strengthens both his own and the divine limbs. Joseph refers to this process as "limb strengthening limb" (*ever maḥaziq ever*), "which means that when one's limbs are complete, and one maintains all the limbs of the Torah, namely, the 613 *miẓwot,* one thereby maintains all the limbs of the chariot [the *sefirot*] and strengthens them."[56] On the other hand, "Whoever detracts a *miẓwah,* has eaten a limb of the living [divine] being" (negative commandment 58, fol. 206a).

Menahem Recanati (late thirteenth to early fourteenth centuries) wrote a book of *ta'amey ha-miẓwot* that covers some one hundred commandments. He encourages the reader to "raise . . . a *miẓwah* to a higher matter wherever you can in the Torah . . . , even if you have not received [this mystical innovation] from a wise kabbalist or seen it in one of the books of the wise." But he cautions, "Do not claim that the matter is not according to its literal meaning. One must believe that it is precisely according to its literal meaning and alludes to a higher matter."[57]

Recanati was affected by the revelations of the *Zohar.* He drew on it openly and frequently. "I found in the *Wondrous Book of Zohar* awesome things concerning this *miẓwah.* . . . He was encouraged to reveal his own discoveries by the example of the *Zohar:* "I could not write explicitly what I had intended concerning this great secret, for there are things that a person cannot express in speech, much less write down. But what I found in the *Wondrous Book of Zohar* emboldened me. . . ."[58]

The *miẓwot* are embroidered into the *sefirot* (Recanati, *Commentary on the Torah*, p. 23b). Thus, God and the *mizwot* are inseparable. "Torah is not outside of God; God is not something outside of Torah. So the sages of Kabbalah have said that God is Torah."[59] The reason for a *mizwah* is its divine analogue. "This is the principle: One is permitted only that which alludes above, nothing that causes a defect" (*Sefer Ta'amey ha-Mizwot*, p. 81b). Genuine fulfillment of the *mizwot* enriches the flow of emanation (p. 3a) while enabling one to receive and reflect more (p. 74d).

> A light surrounded by thin glass shines more brightly than a light surrounded by thick glass. . . . So it is with a human soul. Although souls are equal, a difference arises because of the material in which they are planted. . . . It is only right that the body . . . not be nourished on that which dulls the mind and veils the intellect. It is well-known that the soul functions better if she is nourished on pure, fine food than on impure, coarse food. This is the meaning of the prohibition of foods, according to what appears to me and according to what I have seen in the books of the wise, may their memory be a blessing.

✳ ✳ ✳

We have surveyed most of the kabbalistic compositions on *ta'amey ha-mizwot* from the late twelfth to the early fourteenth centuries. One of the distinguishing features of the mystical approach is its insistence on the divine need for the human act. Although there are occasional references to such a need in rabbinic literature (see n. 20), the usual view is reflected in the following midrashic teaching: "What does the Blessed Holy One care whether you slaughter an animal and eat it, or stab it and eat it? Do you cause Him any benefit or harm? What does He care whether you eat pure food or carcasses? . . . Behold, the *mizwot* were given only to refine [*le-zaref*] human beings" (*Tanhuma Shemini* 8).[60] The *mizwot* are purposeful, but their purpose is to benefit humanity, not divinity. The Kabbalists reverse this teaching by understanding the key word *le-zaref* according to its other meaning, "to join"; thus "the *mizwot* were given only to join human beings" to God. "They are the thread that binds those who fulfill them with God . . . like a thread joining two pieces of cloth." The infinite nature of God, *Eyn Sof*, is unaffected by human activity, but the *sefirot*, the dynamic aspects of His being, are vitally affected.[61] The heretical rationalists had challenged, "What need does He have for our prayers?" (above, n. 11). Meir Ibn Gabbai (sixteenth century) discounts any need except the divine. Prayer for personal needs "contaminates the sanctuary." Even one's spiritual needs should not be the focus, only God's unity (*'Avodat ha-Qodesh*, 2:6). By engaging in *mizwot,* Israel channels and radiates the divine light. "If Israel were not in the world to draw forth emanation by . . . fulfilling the *mizwot,* who would draw it forth? How could God possibly emanate without someone to draw it forth?" (Isaac of Akko, *Me'irat Eynayim,* p. 126).

Each *mizwah* has cosmic impact. "The upper world needs the arousal of the lower world" (*Zohar* 1:82b). Nahmanides and subsequent Kabbalists refer to this profound relationship by the phrase *zorekh gavoha,* "a need on high."[62] As explained by Ibn Gabbai, "When She dwells below, She dwells above [with *Tif'eret*], and She does not dwell above unless She dwells below. So the presence of *Shekhinah* below is a need on high" (*'Avodat ha Qodesh,* 2:2).

Israel helps to satisfy this need by their holy action, which welcomes the divine into the world. They thereby "open the upper source and draw down the emanation of blessing and light" to *Shekhinah* and the lower realms. The world is sustained by this influx engendered by human deeds, "even though they are not intending it for themselves" (*'Avodat ha-Qodesh,* 2:16). This perspective contrasts sharply with the philosophical approach. "The *mizwot* are not intended to teach beneficial opinions, as Maimonides taught, but rather to maintain the existence of the world. . . . What brought Maimonides to rationalize the secrets of Torah was his lack of knowledge of the true *qabbalah* . . . and his pursuit of foreign sciences" (Ibn Gabbai, *Tola'at Ya'aqov,* p. 5b).

The philosophers had tried to explain the *mizwot* in human terms, as a guide to physical, intellectual, and spiritual well-being. The *mizwot* are a means to an end; some of them, for example, sacrifices, were adapted to the national state of mind. Such historical relativism is repugnant to the Kabbalists. To them, each *mizwah* is a holy entity, independent of time-bound reality, eternally charged with divine energy. *Mizwot* are elements of the divine structure and the human microcosm. Their social effect is a mere reflection of their cosmic effect. They perfect not only the human being but all of existence. The hidden meaning of each *mizwah* is its function in, and correlation with, the hidden life of God. Performance has the theurgic value of maintaining the harmony of the *sefirot;* it is literally divine service. The symbolic potential of the *mizwah* can be realized only through enactment. Knowledge of the processes is a prerequisite, but the deed itself is essential. This kind of spiritualization poses no threat to traditional observance; it only renders it more vital.

The philosophers placed theory above ritual practice. "Indifference toward the specific form of Jewish law and tradition . . . could be considered the hallmark of the philosopher, who, living as he does a theoretical life, is not concerned with the outward forms of legal and cultic observance or with popular religious beliefs."[63] Maimonides set out to counter this indifference and to demonstrate correct beliefs and the reasonableness of Torah and *mizwot;* beliefs are strengthened by actions. Yet, in his parable of the ruler in the palace near the end of the *Guide of the Perplexed* (3:51), he states that the multitude of adherents of the Law "never see the ruler's habitation." Since they fail to engage in philosophical speculation, they are characterized as "ignoramuses who observe the commandments."

Maimonides thought it foolish to search for reasons for every detail of the *mizwot.* For the Kabbalists, "there is no part of a *mizwah* that is not intended for the purpose of the felicity of the soul and the unification of God" (*'Avodat ha-Qodesh,* 2:3). Biblical law, rabbinic formulation, and later customs are all presented as symbols of metaphysical realities. The hala-khically valid differences between developmental stages of religious praxis are blurred, while the commitment to punctiliousness is reinforced.[64]

Though Kabbalah objected to viewing the *mizwot* as a didactic means of spreading correct theological opinions, its own *ta'amey ha-mizwot* are themselves an attempt to inculcate a mythical consciousness in which Torah is "restored to her ancientry."[65] This bold attempt is all the more startling since much of its raw material is law, an essentially rational system conceived in a decisive break with myth. Kabbalah constructs its mythical realm out of the elements of this law. The commands of the ruler of the world become sacraments and mystery rites that simultaneously reflect and influence the pulsating life of the universe. The code of law becomes a secret code. Judaism is transformed into a mystery religion; symbolic and magical aspects of the *mizwot* are alternately emphasized. The mystic integrates himself into the pattern of the cosmos and stimulates the flow of emana-tion. His ritual act represents the divine and calls it forth. Whereas the philosophers had sought to rationalize the *mizwot* in earthly terms, the Kabbalists expand the dimensions. The human actor is now a protagonist in the cosmic drama. The *mizwot* are "literally the essence of life" (Gikatilla, *Ginnat Egoz,* p. 28a), his life and God's. They are not reducible to autono-mous reason; nor are they simply imposed heteronomously. As extensions of the divine qualities, they permeate the universe and constitute its fabric. The human who lives by them is attuned to the rhythm of being. He is imitating God, who, according to Joseph of Hamadan, enacts all the *mizwot.*

Of course, it is not enough to perform the *mizwot* as commandments "learned by rote" (Isa 29:13). One must know the sefirotic correspondence of the act, "where the *mizwah* touches, what is its goal, to what it alludes" (*Sefer ha-Peli'ah,* p. 4b). "If one does not know the secret of a *mizwah,* one cannot fulfill it properly" (*Galya Raza,* p. 65). Knowledge of *ta'amey ha-mizwot* engenders *kawwanah,* "intention, direction," awareness of the profound nature of each act. The rabbis of the Talmud had argued over whether or not *mizwot* require *kawwanah* (*b. Rosh Hash.* 28b); the Kabbalists demand it. *Kawwanah* "must precede a *mizwah*" (*Tiqquney Zohar,* Introduction, p. 6a). "One who performs a *mizwah* without *kawwanah* or contemplation has acted imperfectly" (*Kitvey Ramban,* 1:150).

Prayer was the first ritual affected by Kabbalah. Independent of outward action, it was easily transformed into a comprehensive exercise in inward meditation, in which the full force of spirituality could be expressed. The *kawwanot* of prayer, pertaining to individual words, focus the mystic's consciousness on particular *sefirot.* Guided by these *kawwanot,* the Kabbalist journeys from self to divine and, finally attaining the rung of mystical nothingness, he offers up his ego. Prayer, historically and spiritually, assumes the role of sacrifice.[66]

It would seem that other *mizwot* do not lend themselves to meditation or contemplative immersion. Yet Kabbalah offered instruction on how to concentrate thought upon the significance of each action as it is performed. While fulfilling the *mizwot,* the mystic sees himself taking "a contemplative walk in the spiritual world. At every stage of his activity, *kawwanah* indicates to him the place where he stands in the ascent of the soul."[67] The *sefirot* provide the framework for the ascent and are realigned by it. As the Kabbalist climbs and probes, he repairs the fractured unity of God through his directed action. "We have the power . . . to strengthen the *sefirot* in their natural state of pure thought, according to the abundance of action" (Recanati, *Commentary on the Torah,* p. 51c).

This metaphysical commitment to action distinguishes Kabbalah from philosophy. It is not sufficient to believe in an infinite God. The Kabbalists criticized the philosophers, "whose wisdom is based solely on negation."[68] By negating those aspects of divinity that infringed on a pure spiritual theology, the philosophers diluted traditional, dynamic faith. "Those who deny the proper attributes of God speak out until faith has been drained."[69] Kabbalah learned a great deal from philosophy and based its own mystical theosophy on some of the insights of Neoplatonism and Aristotelianism. The infinite reality of God, *Eyn Sof,* is inaccessible to thought and has no attributes. But the Kabbalists claim to surpass the philosophers. "Their heads reach the place where our feet stand."[70] Theological understanding and speculation are incomplete without deeds. Through ritual, God's inner life (the *sefirot*) is explored and known, imitated and affected. These *sefirot* are the manifestations of *Eyn Sof,* the divine attributes. Here God thinks, feels, and responds. The *sefirot* link *Eyn Sof* with the world; *mizwot* are the mystical tool that enable one to contact the otherwise unknowable God.

In an age when tradition was threatened, Kabbalah offered a conservative spiritualization. Judaism is reinterpreted as a system of mystical symbolism, in which mythical imagery and legal formulations coexist and reinforce one another. Law is the dynamic essence of God. By accepting the "precious yoke" of *mizwot*,[71] the Kabbalist takes on cosmic responsibility and a discipline that promises intimate experience of the divine. Kabbalah succeeded in renewing the significance of Torah and *mizwot*. It encouraged reformist tendencies in Spain and stimulated a religious awakening after the Spanish exile. To the politically powerless Jew, it offered an opportunity to rule metaphysical reality through activating the symbolic machinery of the *sefirot*. From 1500 to 1800 Kabbalah was Jewish theology, mysticism was normal. *Mizwot* were enacted "for the sake of the unification of the Blessed Holy One and His *Shekhinah*."[72]

Kabbalah created a mystical ideology of law that highlighted the connection between Israel and the *mizwot*. These *mizwot* are Israel's distinguishing feature (*Sifre Deut.* 43). "If, God forbid, they were not distinguished by them, they would be like the nations of the world" (*Ma'arekhet ha-Elohut*, p. 207a). The *mizwot* are a token of God's love. "Out of love for them, He drew them close to Him and gave them the Torah" (*Zohar* 2:47a). Israel's faithfulness is proven by their observance. "Idolatrous humanity seduces and oppresses them, but they stand firm in their religious practices" (1:237b). Removed from her source, the soul is sustained by Torah. "The soul finds comfort after being separated from her mother, *Shekhinah*. She finds comfort in Torah."[73] The *mizwot* provide comfort and are also a guide to *devequt*, "communion." "One must prepare in order to be able to bind his thought to God. This [preparation] is the fulfillment of the *mizwot* with all one's strength."[74]

By formulating mystical reasons for the *mizwot*, Kabbalah asserts their potency but also betrays its own sophistication. It is not content with accepting traditional commands at face value. There is an urge to "look at what is under the garment" of Torah (*Zohar* 3:152a). Nonmystical traditionalists saw the divine origin of the *mizwot* as sufficient reason to obey. To offer any other reasons, to correlate divine command with human reason, was seen as an affront to the arbitrary will of God, as a weakening of the religious value of the *mizwot*. One should submit to the yoke and not question. "There is no reason for the Law other than the will of the Creator" (*Guide* 3:48). Maimonides had rejected this opinion, and the Kabbalists, who began as his students, could not return to a naïve faith. Yet rationalistic *ta'amey ha-mizwot* did not quench their mystical fervor, and they had evidence that such reasoning undermined halakhic observance. Despite their commitment to the law, the Kabbalists had also been influenced by Bahya Ibn Paquda's *Duties of the Heart* and by *Sefer Hasidim*, which attacked cut-and-dried legalism. Moses de León criticizes those who are satisfied with knowing the letter of the law: "Having attained this, which is one level, why does he not ascend from wisdom to wisdom, from level to level?"[75] The Kabbalists took the radical step of claiming that God commands because He needs. The human servant becomes God's partner.

Kabbalistic *taʿamey ha-mizwot* extend the limits of religious experience. The experiential emphasis invites a pun on the two meanings of *taʿam:* "reason" and "taste." At God's table, one finds "many tasty dishes, various *taʿamey Torah,* sweeter than all foods and delicacies of the world." "We will be able to prepare tasty reasons [*matʿamim*] for His *huqqim,* such as He loves." "The *mizwot* have hidden *teʿamim.* Those who taste them taste in this world the goodness hidden away for the righteous in the hereafter."[76] The Psalmist had sung (34:9): "Taste and see how good God is." The Kabbalists encourage one to taste each *mizwah,* to discover its unique divine essence. The delight is shared by God, for the fulfillment of a *mizwah* is a divine aphrodisiac promoting union above.

The kabbalistic art of providing *taʿamey ha-mizwot* develops gradually. In Gerona mystical reasons are transmitted mostly for *huqqim* and other *mizwot* that lack an explicit reason. Though Jacob ben Sheshet encouraged creativity, Nahmanides recommended hearing "the reason for the *mizwot* in a proper manner through *qabbalah,*" that is, received from a master as an esoteric tradition (*Kitvey Ramban,* 1:190). Still he wrote that "every one of God's *mizwot* has many reasons; each has many benefits for the body and the soul" (*Commentary* on Exod 20:23). The *Zohar* introduced abundant use of symbolic interpretation. Even if a clear reason for a *mizwah* had been stated in the Torah, the *Zohar* did not hesitate to offer a deeper, higher reason. Though Todros Abulafia criticized Maimonides for "fabricating reasons for the commandments," Kabbalists in the thirteenth and fourteenth centuries reveled in creating "new-ancient words" that provided the *mizwot* with mystical flavor. Rich flavors were offered in de León's *Book of the Pomegranate* and Joseph of Hamadan's *Sefer Taʿamey ha-Mizwot.* Here *aggadah* and *halakhah* are interwoven; legend, fantasy, and spirituality blend with law and *mizwah.*

Tradition has been defined as "doctrine not written by its first author."[77] If certain of the Kabbalists broke this law by creating new traditions of *taʿamey ha-mizwot,* their purpose was to reinforce traditional structures, check backsliding, counter the consequences of rationalism, and celebrate mystical awareness. Their kabbalistic reasons for the commandments conveyed esoteric doctrines. The doctrine of reincarnation, for example, was spread by the Kabbalists under the guise of the biblical *mizwah* of levirate marriage. The brother of a childless deceased husband marries the widow to enable the dead man's soul to reincarnate in a son born to the new couple. Thus, the deceased may merit children in his second *gilgul* ("rolling" into a new body, reincarnation), "and his name will not be obliterated from Israel."[78] The *mizwot* do not merely serve as handy proof texts. They constitute a framework for daily mystical experience. Despite its esotericism, Kabbalah could be transmitted through the *mizwot.*

This is not to deny the antinomian potential of certain kabbalistic formulations. "When Adam put on the skin of the serpent, his nature became material, so necessitating a Torah that gave material commandments."[79] Mystics naturally looked forward to the messianic age, when they could recover Adam's original, ethereal form and understand the mysteries of Torah. According to another text, there is one letter missing in our alphabet. Only because of this do we read positive and negative *mizwot* in the Torah. In the next cosmic cycle of time, the letter will be restored and the Torah will appear differently.[80] When mysticism joined forces with messianism, the potential antinomianism surfaced. Followers of Shabbetai Zevi envisioned a new understanding of Torah, in which "the *mizwot* are totally spiritual, even 'You shall not plow with an ox and an ass together' [Deut 22:10]." Shabbetai himself is credited with the infamous blessing: "Blessed are You, YHWH our God, King of the universe, who permits the forbidden."[81]

The Kabbalists we have surveyed could not have answered "Amen" to such a blessing. The secret behind the *mizwah* enriched and did not replace the act. There was a tendency to expand rather than dissolve the concept of *mizwah.* The Hasidic master Dov Baer, the Maggid of Mezhirech, developing earlier themes, says: "One who fulfills 'Know Him in all your ways' [Prov 3:6] has infinite *mizwot.*"[82]

Mystical exegesis served a social function by reducing the potential conflict between traditional authority and the authority claimed by the mystic. The Kabbalists identified their own experience with tradition. Often, as we have seen, their *ta'amey ha-mizwot* stray far from the *peshat,* the literal sense, in order to highlight the mystical dimension of a *mizwah.* Sometimes they insist on the literal understanding of a *mizwah,* even if earlier commentators have substituted other meanings. The command to cleave to God (Deut 10:20; 11:22; 13:5; 30:20) had been questioned in the Talmud (*b. Ket.* 111b; cf. *b. Sot.* 14a): "Is it possible for a human being to cleave to *Shekhinah?* Is it not written: 'YHWH your God is a consuming fire' [Deut 4:24]?" Rather, one should aid scholars and imitate divine qualities; then it is as if one cleaves to *Shekhinah.* Maimonides describes the state of communion near the end of his *Guide* (3:51); yet in his enumeration of the *mizwot,* he adopts the more modest interpretation of the Talmud.[83] Kabbalists gave special attention to *devequt*, "cleaving" to God. Isaac the Blind is reported to have said: "The essence of the service of the enlightened and of those who contemplate His name is 'Cleave to Him' [Deut 13:5]."[84] Nahmanides (on Deut 11:22) speaks of those who attain this state and become "a dwelling place for *Shekhinah*." The *mizwah* of *devequt* was so basic to Kabbalah that its literalness had to be preserved. Joseph Gikatilla (*Sha'arey Orah*. p. 166) cites a rabbinic principle (*b. Shab.* 63a): "A biblical verse cannot lose its literal meaning." He concludes: "'Cleave to Him,' cleave undoubtedly. As to what the rabbis have said: 'Is it possible for a human being to cleave to *Shekhinah*?,' it certainly is!"

Notes

1. Jacob ben Asher, *Tur, Yoreh De'ah*, 181; cf. Rashi on Lev 19:19; Ibn Ezra on Lev 19:27; 21:5; idem, *Yesod Mora'*, chap. 8; Maimonides, *Sefer ha-Mizwot*, ed. H. Chavel (JerusalemL Mosad ha-Rav Kook, 1981), negative commandment 44, p. 275; idem, *Mishneh Torah. 'Avodah Zarah* 12:7.

2. Isaac of Akko, *Me'irat 'Eynayim*. ed. Amos Goldreich (Ph.D. diss., Hebrew University, 1981) 157; cf. Bahya ben Asher on Exod 30:1; *Ma'arekhet ha-Elohut* (Jerusalem: Meqor Hayyim, 1963), *Minhat Yehudah*, p. 35a.

3. See the letter of Joseph ben Todros published by S. Halberstamm in *Jeschurun* 8 (1872) 36; cf. Gershom Scholem in *Tarbiz* 6 (1935) 341.

4. *Yedi'ot ha-Makhon le-Heqer ha-Shirah ha-'Ivrit bi-Yrushalayim* 4 (1938) 34, 56.

5. Yitzhak Baer, *A History of the Jews in Christian Spain*, 1:107-8.

6. *Jeschurun* 8 (1872) 44; cf. Bernard Septimus, *Hispano-Jewish Culture in Transition* (Cambridge, MA: Harvard Univesity Press, 1982) 94.

7. *Jeschurun* 8 (1872) 37.

8. *Ozar Nehnad* 3 (1860) 163.

9. Ibid., 164.

10. Ibid., 165.

11. *Ozar Hayyim;* see *Me'irat 'Eynayim*. ed. Goldreich, 411, 414; cf. *Tiqquney Zohar* 70, p. 131b; G. Scholem, *On the Kabbalah and Its Symbolism*, 90.

12. *Qiryat Sefer* 4 (1928) 297–98.

13. Baer, *History*, 1:239, 241; idem in *Zion* 2 (1937) 19–55.

14. *Sefer ha-Rimmon*, British Museum MS 759, fol. 107a-b; I have corrected the text according to Cambridge MS Add. 1516, fol. 107b. Cf. G. Scholem, *Major Trends in Jewish Mysticism* (New York: Schocken Books, 1961) 397–98 n. 154. On *tefillin*, see Ibn Ezra and Rashbam on Exod 13:9.

15. *Qiryat Sefer* 1 (1924) 133–34; Scholem, *Major Trends*, 148–49.

16. Quoted by Isaac of Akko in the name of Nahmanides; see *Me'irat 'Eynayim*, ed. Goldreich, 414; Moshe Idel *AJS Review* 5 (1980) 19.

17. Heinrich Heine, *Religion and Philosophy in Germany*, chap. 2.

18. Scholem, *Reshit ha-Qabbalah* (Jerusalem: Schocken, 1948) 17; cf. Ezra of Gerona, *Kitvey Ramban*, ed. H. Chavel (Jerusalem: Mosad ha-Rav Kook, 1964) 2:479; Nahmanides, *Kitvey Ramban*, 1:190; Eleazar of Worms in *Sefer Razi'el* (Amsterdam, 1701) 7b.

Joseph Jabez in his *Commentary on Avot* (3:12) defines Kabbalah as "the knowledge of *ta'amey ha-mizwot*."

19. On the *sefirot*, see Scholem, *Major Trends*, 207–39; *On the Kabbalah*, 88–116, and my *Zohar: The Book of Enlightenment*, 33–38.

20. *Sefer ha-Bahir* §102; cf. *b. Hag.* 12b; *Pesiqta de Rab Kahana* 25:1; *Lam. Rab.* 1:33.

21. Scholem, *Reshit ha-Qabbalah*, 113.

22. Scholem, *Sefer Bialik*, ed. J. Fichman (Tel Aviv: Omanut, 1934) 141–55.

23. *Kitvey Ramban* 2:496–97, 521–48; cf. Jacob Katz *Zion* 44 (1979) 159–67.

24. Cf. Ibn Ezra, *Yesod Mora'*, chap. 8; Maimonides, *Guide* 3:31.

25. See *Qiryat Sefer* 6 (1930) 417–18.

26. Cf. Ezra of Gerona, *Kitvey Ramban*, 2:544.

27. But see *Commentary* on Lev 2:11, where he admits that Maimonides's explanation of one sacrificial detail may be correct.

28. Cf. Todros Abulafia, *Ozar ha-Kavod*, on *Shab.* 28b; Isaiah Tishby, *Mishnat ha-Zohar*, 2:196.

29. Cf. *Lev. Rab.* 3:5; Ibn Ezra on Lev 1:4; idem, *Yesod Mora'*, chap. 8; *Kitvey Ramban* 1:164.

30. On *Kelaley ha-Mizwot*, see Efraim Gottlieb, *Mehqarim be-Sifrut ha-Qabbalah* (Tel Aviv: Tel Aviv University, 1976) 121–28; on the *sodot*, see Alexander Altmann in *Qiryat Sefer* 40 (1965) 269–76.

31. Gottlieb, *Mehqarim*, 121–22. Nahmanides says that he is suspect of anyone who claims to know exactly which *mizwot* constitute the 613 (end of *hassagot* to Maimonides's *Sefer ha-Mizwot*, 408); cf. Isadore Twersky, *Introduction to the Code of Maimonides*, 249 n. 25.

32. See *Qiryat Sefer* 40 (1965) 272; see also above, n. 26.

33. *Zohar* 1:174b; 3:102a, 203a; cf. Tishby, *Mishnat ha-Zohar*, 2:206–20.

34. *Zohar* 2:55b; 3:79b, 265a., cf. Scholem, *On the Kabbalah*, 62–63.

35. Cf. Azriel, *Perush ha-Aggadot*, ed. Tishby (Jerusalem: Mekize Nirdamim, 1945) 37: "To one who does not understand their meaning, certain portions and verses of the Torah seem fit to be burned. But to one who has come to know their interpretation, they appear as essential components of Torah."

36. See Scholem, *Major Trends*, 156–57.

37. *Zohar* 1:224a–b; 2:131a–b; 3:103b–104a. I have translated and discussed these passages in *Zohar: The Book of Enlightenment.*

38. See above, "The Response of Kabbalah."

39. Yehuda Liebes (*Peraqim be-Millon Sefer ha-Zohar* [Jerusalem: Hebrew University, 1982] 226) compares *gufa de-malka* ("body of the King") with *corpus domini.*

40. See *Zohar* 1:53b and my discussion in *Zohar*, 54, 214–16.

41. Cf. 3:110b; *Lev. Rab.* 35:7; Tishby, *Mishnat ha-Zohar*, 2:435; M. Idel in *Mehqerey Yerushalayim* 1 (1981) 64, n. 145.

42. Cf. *Sefer Yezirah* 1:3; *Bahir*, §124; Azriel, *Perush ha-Aggadot*, 27–28; Nahmanides on Exod 30:19.

43. Joseph of Hamadan, *Sefer Ta'amey ha-Mizwot*, ed. M. Meier (Ph.D. diss., Brandeis University, 1974) 439; see also my edition of David ben Yehudah he-Hasid's *Book of Mirrors* (Chico, CA: Scholars Press, 1982) Introduction, p. 34 n. 238.

44. British Museum MS 759, fol. 4a. Here, for lack of space, I discuss only briefly several books of *ta'amey ha-mizwot* from the immediately post-Zoharic period.

45. See also *Song Rab.* 4:3; cf. *Zohar* 2:100a; *Zohar Hadash, Rut* 83d (*Midrash ha-Ne'elam*); *Sefer ha-Rimmon*, fols. 3b, 67b.

46. M. Idel, "We Have No Kabbalistic Tradition on This," in *Rabbi Moses Nahmanides*, ed. I. Twersky (Cambridge, MA: Harvard University Press, 1983) 71.

47. Joel 3:5; *Sefer ha-Rimmon*, fol. 95b; cf. *b. Sanh.* 92a; Twersky, *Introduction to the Code of Maimonides*, 64 n. 109.

48. *Zohar* 1:25b. This section (1:22a–29a) belongs to *Tiqquney Zohar*, written by the author of *Ra'aya Meheimna;* see Scholem, *Major Trends*, 188.

49. See Baer, *History*, 1:270–77; idem in *Zion* 5 (1940) 1–44; Scholem, *On the Kabbalah*, 66–71; Tishby, *Mishnat ha-Zohar*, 2:37598.

50. Cf. Bahir. §196; *Tarbiz* 5 (1934) 322; *Zohar* 1:8a, 23a–b (*Tiqquney Zohar*); *Zohar Hadash, Shir ha-Shirim* 64a; Isaac of Akko, *Me'irat 'Eynayim*, 61–62, 414–15.

51. See Altmann in *Qiryat Sefer* 40 (1965) 256–76, 405–12; and Meier's edition of the positive commandments (above, n. 43). For the negative commandments, I have consulted Jerusalem MS 8° 597.

52. Joseph of Hamadan, *Ta'amey ha-Mizwot*, negative commandments, Introduction, fol. 129a. Cf. David ibn Abi Zimra's reaction to one of Joseph's formulations (*Mezudat David* [Zolkiew: S. Stiller, 1862] p. 15c): "He made this up and we should not listen to him." Nevertheless, Ibn Zimra made abundant use of the book.

53. *Ta'amey ha-Mizwot*, positive commandment 8, p. 44; cf. *The Book of Mirrors*, 260; *y. Rosh. Hash.* 1:3, 57b; *Lev. Rab.* 35:3. Many Kabbalists elaborate the tradition (*b. Ber.* 6a) that God wears *tefillin*.

54. See *Qiryat Sefer* 40 (1965) 407.

55. *Ta'amey ha-Mizwot*, positive commandment 54, p. 224; see the table prepared by Meier in his introduction.

56. The expression derives from Ibn Ezra, *Yesod Mora'*, chap. 5; see Yehuda Avida in *Sinai* 14 (Vol. 29) (1957) 401–2; Altmann in *Qiryat Sefer* 40 (1965) 275; and *Zohar* 1:170b. See also Gikatilla, *Sha'arei Orah* (Warsaw: Orgelbrand, 1883) 4: "If one succeeds in purifying a limb, that limb becomes like a throne for the sublime, inner entity called by that name"; Recanati, *Commentary on the Torah* (Lemberg: Cohn and Budweiser, 1881) 47c–d, 51b–c; Joseph of Hamadan, *Ta'amey ha-Mizwot*, 427–29; and the *hadīth qudsī* (Annemarie Schimmel, *Mystical Dimensions of Islam* [Chapel Hill: University of North Carolina, 1975] 43): "When I love a servant, I, the Lord, am his ear, so that he hears by Me; I am his eye, so that he sees by Me; I am his tongue, so that he speaks by Me; and I am his hand, so that he takes by Me."

57. Recanati, *Sefer Ta'amey ha-Mizwot* (London: S. Lieberman, 1962), Introduction, pp. 2a, 13a; compare the similar statements by Philo and Jacob ben Sheshet (cited above, sections 2 and 5); and Bahya ben Asher on Deut 29:28.

58. *Ta'amey ha-Mizwot*, pp. 68d, 77d; cf. 66d, 75d; *Zohar* 2:237a.

59. *Ta'amey ha-Mizwot*, Introduction, pp. 2a–b, 13a; cf. Scholem, *On the Kabbalah*, 43–44; Idel in *Mehqerey Yerushalayim* 1 (1981) 63–64, 68.

60. See also *Gen. Rab.* 44:1; Ibn Ezra, *Yesod Mora'*, chap. 7; Maimonides, *Guide* 3:26; Nahmanides on Deut 22:6; Gikatilla, *Ginnat Egoz* (Hanau: Eliezer Mehoqeq, 1615) p. 28a; Rashba, in *Eyn Ya'aqov* on *Sukkah* 28a; and Job 7:20; 22:2–3; and 35:6–7: "If you sin, what do you do to Him? . . . If you are righteous, what do you give Him?"

61. Meir ibn Gabbai, *'Avodat ha-Qodesh* (Warsaw: Lewin-Epstein, 1890) 2:3, 16; cf. Shem Tov ben Shem Tov, *Sefer ha-'Emunot* (Jerusalem, 1969) 10:2; *Tiqquney Zohar*, 70, p. 131b; and Hayyim of Volozhin, *Nefesh ha-Hayyim* (Vilna, 1837) 2:4: "From the aspect of His essence, leaving aside His connection with the worlds, there is no place at all for Torah and *mizwot*. . . . All human activity, whether good or evil, has no effect at all on His essence."

62. Naḥmanides on Exod 29:46; cf. Shem Tov ibn Gaon, *Keter Shem Tov* in *Ma'or va-Shemesh*, ed. Y. Coriat (Leghorn, 1839) 396; and Baḥya ben Asher, ad loc.; *b. Sanh.* 74a; *Midr. Ps.* 31:9.

63. Shlomo Pines, in the introduction to his translation of Maimonides's *Guide of the Perplexed* (Chicago: University of Chicago Press, 1963) 116–17 n. 96.

64. See Katz in *Tarbiẓ* 50 (1981) 405–22.

65. *Zohar* 2:147a; cf. my *Zohar*, 131, 256.

66. See G. Scholem, "The Concept of *Kavvanah* in Early Kabbalah," in *Studies in Jewish Thought*, ed. Alfred Jospe (Detroit: Wayne State University Press, 1981) 162–80; Tishby, *Mishnat ha-Zohar*, 2:197–98, 254.

67. G. Scholem, *Ha-Qabbalah be-Gerona* (Jerusalem: Akademon, 1964) 348–49.

68. Isaac of Akko; see Scholem, *Ha-Qabbalah be-Gerona*, p. 113.

69. Meshullam Da Piera; see *Yedi'ot ha-Makhon* 4 (1938) 113.

70. Moses of Burgos, cited by Isaac of Akko; see *Me'irat 'Eynayim*, pp. 56, 62, 416; Scholem in *Tarbiẓ* 5 (1934) 318; idem, *Major Trends*, 24; 354 n. 22; idem, *Ha-Qabbalah be-Gerona*, 111–13.

71. *Sefer ha-Rimmon*, Bodleian MS 1607, fol. 101a.

72. See Scholem, *Major Trends*, 275–76; 413 n. 97; cf. *Zohar* 2:119a (*Ra'aya Meheimna*), cited above in section 7.

73. Joseph of Hamadan, *Ta'amey ha-Miẓwot*; see Altmann in *Tif'eret Yisra'el*, ed. H. Zimmels (London: Soncino Press, 1967), Hebrew volume, p. 63.

74. Isaac of Akko, *Me'irat 'Eynayim*, p. 218; cf. Ibn Ezra on Deut 31:16; David Kimhi on Ps 19:9.

75. Moses de León, *Or Zaru'a*; see *Qoveẓ al Yad* 9 (1980) 249.

76. *Zohar* 3:271b (*Ra'aya Meheimna*); *Galya Raza*, ed. Rachel Elior (Jerusalem: Hebrew University, 1981) 65 (cf. Gen 27:9); *Ma'arekhet ha-Elohut*, Introduction to *Minhat Yehudah*, p. 1a (cf. *b. Ḥag.* 12a; *Zohar* 2:148b–149a). For similar puns see *Sefer ha-Rimmon*, fol. 45a; Ralbag on Leviticus, end of *Parashat Ẓaw*; Eliyah Ḥalfan, cited by Meir Benayahu in *Da'at* 5 (1980) 88; Mordecai Jaffe, *Levush ha-Tekhelet* (Venice, 1620) 3d.

77. Robert Bellarmine, the Italian cardinal and theologian, (1542–1621), cited by Donald R. Kelley, *Foundations of Modern Historical Scholarship* (New York: Columbia University Press, 1970) 153.

78. Deut 25:6; cf. Ezra, *Kitvey Ramban*, 2:537; Naḥmanides on Gen 38:8; *Qiryat Sefer* 6 (1930) 417–18; *Zohar* 3:215b (*Ra'aya Meheimna*); Scholem, *On the Kabbalah*, 345; idem, *Pirqey Yesod be-Havanat ha-Qabbalah u-Semaleha* (Jerusalem: Bialik Institute, 1976) 308–57; Gottlieb, *Meḥqarim*, 370–96; Katz in *Da'at* 4 (1980) 67–70; *Tarbiẓ* 51 (1982) 59–106; Benayahu in *Da'at* 5 (1980) 82–84.

79. Abraham Azulai, *Hesed le-Avraham*, drawing on Moses Cordovero; see Scholem, *On the Kabbalah*, 71–72.

80. See Scholem, *On the Kabbalah*, 81.

81. See Scholem, *Meḥqarim u-Meqorot le-Toledot ha-Shabbta'ut ve-Gilguleha* (Jerusalem: Bialik Institute, 1982) 96; idem, *Major Trends*, 319, 421 n. 70.

82. Dov Baer, *Or Torah* (Jerusalem, 1968) 147a; cf. *Lev. Rab.* 22:2; Baḥya ibn Paquda, *Ḥovot ha-Levavot*, Introduction; Ibn Ezra, *Yesod Mora'*, chap. 2; Baḥya ben Asher, *Commentary on the Torah*, Introduction.

83. *Sefer ha-Miẓwot*, positive commandment 6, pp. 155–57; cf. Naḥmanides's animadversion, pp. 160–63.

84. Ezra, *Commentary on Song of Songs, Kitvey Ramban* 2:522; cf. Azriel, *Perush*

ha-Aggadot, 16; Hayyim Honeh in *Sinai* 6 (Vol. 11) (1942) 86–99; Scholem, *The Messianic Idea in Judaism* (New York: Schocken Books, 1971) 203–27; Tishby, *Mishnat ha-Zohar*, 2:280–306; Chayim Henoch, *Ha-Ramban ke-Hoqer we-khi-Mequbbal* (Jerusalem: Harry Fischel Institute, 1978) 243–61.

Bibliography

A survey of *ṭa'amey ha-miẓwot* ("reasons for the commandments") is provided by Alexander Altman and Gershom Scholem in *Encyclopaedia Judaica* (5:783–92); this covers rabbinic, Hellenistic, medieval, philosophic, kabbalistic, and modern thought. Hebrew readers can consult Heinemann. Rabbinic *ṭa'amey ha-miẓwot* are discussed in Urbach (1:365–99, 2:845–57). On Maimonides, see Twersky (pp. 373–447). Further investigation of the Kabbalah may begin with Scholem's works, particularly the essay on Torah. The *Zohar* was rendered into English by Harry Sperling and Maurice Simon. I have translated a selection of passages from the *Zohar* and provided commentary in *Zohar*. Readers will benefit from Tishby, which should appear soon in English. In the second volume Tishby traces the development of *ṭa'amey ha-miẓwot* in early Kabbalah (pp. 429–42) and then provides annotated translations of *Zohar* passages on the *miẓwot*. See also Faierstein. Other titles can be found in the notes to the present essay. For the historical setting, see the first volume of Baer.

Baer, Yitzhak. *History of the Jews in Christian Spain*. Philadelphia: Jewish Publication Society, 1966.

Faierstein, Morris. "'God's Need for the Commandments' in Medieval Kabbalah." *Conservative Judaism* 36 (1982) 45–59.

Heinemann, Isaak. *Ṭa'amey ha-Miẓwot be-Sifrut Yisra'el*. Jerusalem: Jewish Agency, 1966.

Matt, Daniel C. *Zohar: The Book of Enlightenment*. Ramsey, NJ: Paulist Press, 1984.

Scholem, Gershom. *Major Trends in Jewish Mysticism*. 3rd ed. New York: Schocken Books, 1954.

———. *On the Kabbalah and Its Symbolism*. Jerusalem: Keter, 1974.

Tishby, Isaiah. *Mishnat ha-Zohar*. Jerusalem: Bialik Institute, 1961.

Twersky, Isadore. *Introduction to the Code of Maimonides*. New Haven, CT: Yale University Press, 1980.

Urbach, Ephraim. *The Sages: Their Concepts and Beliefs*. Trans. by I. Abrahams. Jerusalem: Magnes Press, 1975.

15

Hitbodedut as Concentration in Ecstatic Kabbalah

MOSHE IDEL

Individual and Community in Jewish Spirituality

R ABBINIC JUDAISM, more than as the religion of a people, took shape as the religion of Jewish communities.[1] From the time that the Temple cult ceased, those commandments applying to Israel as a nation ceased to have validity or contemporary force; the most significant religious-social framework that remained—and was even strengthened—following the destruction of the Temple was the community, whose focus was the synagogue. The common divine worship—prayer—was transformed into the center of religious life; it required the assembling of ten men as an essential precondition for the performance of many of its most important components. Halakhic thought made the gathering of the community a more and more essential part of the religious cult and rejected, directly or indirectly, tendencies toward individualistic separatism. Prayer, Torah study, circumcision, and marriage all became understood as events which the individual performs within society and in which he must participate. Solitude as a religious value or as a means of attaining religious ends was preserved as a part of sacred history: the solitude of Moses on Mount Sinai, that of Elijah in the desert, and that of the high priest in the Holy of Holies became ideals that were part of the heritage of the past. The individual was no longer able to achieve perfection by separation from the company of other men: he was now required to join them in order to achieve religious wholeness.

This tendency, the literary expressions of which appear in the Talmud and the Midrash, was inherited by the Kabbalah. The very fact that several of its leading thinkers—the RABaD (Rabbi Abraham ben David of Posquières, ca. 1125–1198), the RaMBaN (Rabbi Moses ben Naḥman, 1194–1270), and the RaShBA (Rabbi Solomon ben Abraham Adret, ca. 1235–ca. 1310)—were themselves halakhic authorities and simultaneously communal leaders is sufficient proof of the need for continuity. The Kabbalists accepted the framework of the *mizwot* as self-evident and fought for its strengthening and protection against challenges, both internal and external. The strikingly small number of original prayers composed by the Kabbalists, the exegetical nature of kabbalistic literature from its earliest inception, and, above all, the nonexistence of separate kabbalistic groups or societies who separated themselves from the organized framework of the people as a whole are all indirect evidence of a conscious and deliberate tendency to avoid turning the Kabbalah into a focus of controversy and division among the members of the community. We thus find here an interesting phenomenon, different from analogous processes in Christianity and Islam, regarding the organization of groups with mystical tendencies.

In the latter two religions, mysticism is associated with the formation of brotherhoods or monastic orders, and most of the mystical literature, whether Christian or Moslem, is written within their framework. It follows from this that the full realization of the life of the spirit is connected, in both religions, with the choice of a way of life markedly different from that of most of their coreligionists. This way of life is sometimes characterized by separation from the life of the "lay" society; at other times the monk or devotee may continue to be active within society but will observe special norms and practices. These organizational forms are based upon the voluntary acceptance of limitations and obligations over and above those normally accepted as religious norms on the part of their members, on the assumption that these rules of behavior constitute a framework that makes the development of the life of the spirit possible. Generally speaking, the establishment of organizations of this type is associated with the quest by these or other individuals for personal religious or spiritual attainments. The "mobile" and nomadic character of both Christian and Muslim religious orders also stems from this.

At the time of its inception as a historical phenomenon, the Kabbalah did not know of any special organizational system; there were no specific practices or customs designed especially for the Kabbalists. The spiritual life was generally strengthened by intensifying the spiritual effort invested in the fulfillment of the *mizwot,* which as such were obligatory upon the entire people, or by deepening the understanding of the reasons underlying the *mizwot.* At times, nonhalakhic means of attaining communion with God were set, but these were designed so as not to conflict even indirectly with the fulfillment of the *mizwot.* Moreover, the carrying out of these practices was, in any event, extremely limited in time and was not intended to replace the halakhic framework. Nor did they demand for themselves authority comparable to that of the halakhah. In practice, Kabbalah may be defined as a sort of *regula* of the Jewish religion: because of the broad scope of the halakhic system, the fulfillment of the 613 commandments could be seen as a religious challenge which, despite its being normative, allowed for departure from the norm when the *mizwot* were performed with kabbalistic intentions. If the *regula* in Christianity was intended to add religious demands, expressed in both internal and external behavioral changes, the Kabbalah, generally speaking, was concerned with inner change and, at least in the beginning, did not tend to add or detract from the halakhic norm. The external difference in behavior between the Kabbalist, the philosopher, and the halakhist was far smaller than that between a monk and a lay Christian. It suffices to contrast the abstention from marriage as a decisive factor in the formation of monasticism or the special dress of both the monks and the Sufis with the total absence of anything of this kind among the Kabbalists. Put differently, the transformation of an ordinary Jew into a Kabbalist did not involve any discontinuity in his outward behavior, as opposed to what generally happened to one who joined a Sufi brotherhood or a monastic order.

Against the background of what we have said above, the appearance of the first discussions of the religious value of seclusion (*hitbodedut*) in medieval Jewish texts must be seen as indication of external influence. This is clearly the case in the discussions of the subject in the book *Hovot ha-Levavot* (*Duties of the Heart*) by Rabbi Bahya Ibn Paquda (second half of the eleventh century), in which the Sufi influence is clear; this phenomenon reappears in the circle of Pietists (*Hasidim*) associated with Rabbi Abraham Maimonides (1186–1237).

I wish to discuss here the specific meaning of the term *hitbodedut* within a particular kabbalistic school, namely, that of prophetic Kabbalah founded by Rabbi Abraham Abulafia (1240–ca. 1291), and the influence of that school upon the Kabbalah of Safed. I will analyze here the texts in which the term *hitbodedut* has the specific meaning of "concentrated thought," as part of a clearly defined mystical technique. This meaning may have been influenced by the Sufi understanding of inner contemplation or spiritual meditation or by the Sufi terms *tagrid* or *tafrid,* whose meaning approximates that of *hitbodedut* in some texts of prophetic Kabbalah.

This meaning does not appear in any of the major Hebrew dictionaires. Nor have students of Jewish philosophy or of Kabbalah discussed this meaning of the term, but there is no doubt that this understanding will contribute to a more exact interpretation of several important philosophic texts that until now have been differently understood.[2]

The Sufi Background

The connection between pronouncing the name of God and *hitbodedut,* in the sense of seclusion in a special place, is already present in Sufism. The similarity of Rabbi Abraham Abulafia's approach to this subject to the Sufi system is well known, and one need not assume that this is mere chance. It is possible that he learned of this approach from his teacher, Rabbi Baruch Togarmi, who was apparently of Eastern background, to judge by the name. Sufism may also have influenced Abulafia directly, even though there is no evidence from his writings that he had any contact with Muslim mystics. The precise way in which certain Sufi elements entered Abulafia's thought must remain an open question; however, it is appropriate to discuss here, in relation to *hitbodedut,* a description of the Sufi practice of *dhikr,* which was likely to have been known to Jewish authors from the mid-thirteenth century on: I refer to a passage in Rabbi Abraham Ibn Hasdai's Hebrew translation of a work by the Persian Muslim theologian, jurist, and mystic Abu Hamid Al-Ghazali (1058–1111), known as *Mozney Ẓedeq.* The Sufi "path" is portrayed in the Hebrew version as follows:

I decided to follow this path, and I took counsel with an old teacher of the Sufi worship as to how I ought to behave regarding continual reading of the books of religion. And he answered me thus: Know that the path towards this matter is to cut off and cease completely all of those things by which one is attached to this world, until your heart will not think at all of wife, or children, or money or home or wisdom or rulership. But bring yourself to a place such that their presence or absence becomes a matter of indifference. Then seclude yourself in a corner and make do with the divine service of the commandments as ordered, and sit with a heart empty of all thoughts and worry, and let all your thoughts be only of the supreme God. And accustom your tongue to say the name of the living God, let it not cease to call upon the Lord continually, as in the saying of the prophet, "let them not depart from your mouth" (Isa 59:1). And all this in order to understand God and to apprehend Him, until you reach the stage that, were you to allow your tongue to move by itself, it would run quickly to say this, because of its habit to do this thing. And afterwards accustom yourself to another thing, that is, to meditate in your heart and soul, in your thoughts alone, without any movement of your tongue. And then become accustomed to another thing, that there remain in your heart only the meaning of the words, not the letters of the words or the form of speech, but only the subject itself, abstract, firmly fixed in your heart, as something obligatory and constant. The choice is in your hand only up to this limit. After that there is no choice; you can but constantly remove the sickness of destructive lusts—but after that your own [free] will ceases, and yours is only to hope for that which may appear, of the opening of the gates of mercy, what is seen of Him to those who cleave to the exalted Name, which is a small part of what was seen by the prophets . . . but the level of those who cling to God cannot be told, nor their exalted qualities, and their imagination, and their [moral] virtues. These are the ways of the Sufis.[3]

The final goal of the Sufi path, as described in this Hebrew text, is to cling to God. The essence of this clinging is discussed immediately before the passage quoted above:

And to always hope and wait for God to open for him the gates of mercy, as these things were revealed to those who cling to Him and to the prophets, and their souls acquired that perfection of which man is capable — not through learning, but by separation from this world and *hitbodedut* and casting off all desires, and making his goal to receive God with all his heart and all his soul. And whoever shall be with God, God will be with him. (*Mozney Zedeq*, pp. 48–49)

According to the Hebrew version of Al-Ghazali, the Sufis had a fixed path by which they attained communion with God, which involved several clearly delimited stages: (1) separation from the world; (2) indifference or equanimity; (3) solitude (*hitbodedut*); (4) repetition of God's name; (5) communion with God. Despite the general similarity between certain of the various stations on the way toward *devequt* (clinging to God) in Al-Ghazali and parallel steps in Abulafia, the difference between the approaches of these two mystics is clear. First, equanimity is mentioned neither in any of Abulafia's own writings nor in the book *Sha'arey Zedeq*, which belongs to his circle. Second, in Al-Ghazali *hitbodedut* refers to physical solitude in a secluded room, whereas in Abulafia it is sometimes understood in this way but at other times, where it is a precondition for pronouncing the names of God, it is understood in the sense of concentration of one's mental activity. Third, the recitations in Al-Ghazali differ from those in Abulafia: Al-Ghazali proposes pronouncing the name with one's tongue, in one's heart, and fixing its meaning in one's thought; Abulafia proposes reading the name and combining its letters in writing, verbally, and in one's thought. From this, it follows that we cannot base his system upon that of Al-Ghazali, at least not directly and not in full.

Hitbodedut in the Writings of Abraham Abulafia

Most of the discussions of *hitbodedut* that were written prior to Abulafia saw it as an activity engaged in by Moses, the prophets, and the pious men of ancient times. The approach of both Jewish philosophers and Kabbalists was based on the assumption that prophecy was a phenomenon of the past. For this reason, their discussions of this subject must be seen primarily as literary activity—exegesis of the Bible or of talmudic sayings—rather than as rules for actual practice.

This situation was radically changed in the writings of Rabbi Abraham Abulafia. As one who saw himself as a prophet and messiah, he believed that his particular form of Kabbalah paved the way for mystical experience for all who would follow his path. For this reason, the tone of his writing is clearly practical; his writings, from which we shall quote below, are intended as guides to "prophecy" for his contemporaries, and the autobiographical hints therein leave no doubt that he himself followed these techniques and enjoyed their fruits. These two facts are clear signs of the actualization of the discussion concerning *hitbodedut*, whose effects are also felt among later Kabbalists, under the direct or indirect influence of Abulafia's writings.

In the commentary on his work *Sefer ha-'Edut*, written on the occasion of his abortive attempt in 1280 to meet with Pope Nicholas III, Abulafia writes:

> The Pope commanded all the guards of his house, when he was in Soriano . . . that should Raziel [thus Abulafia designates himself] come to speak with him in the name of the Jews, that they take him immediately, and that he not see him at all, but that he be taken outside of the city and burnt. . . . And this matter was made known to Raziel, but he paid no attention to the words of those who said this, but he practiced *hitbodedut* and saw visions and wrote them down, and thus came about this book.

The close connection between *hitbodedut* and revelation is better explained if we assume that Abulafia concentrated in order to receive an illumination which would guide him in this critical situation, when he was also pressed for time. From what we know, Abulafia arrived at the palace in Soriano right at the time he wrote these things, so that it is difficult to imagine that he found a house or room in which to seclude himself, as he advises in his other writings. It is clear that this is not a casual suggestion, nor a historical description of the prophets, but a firsthand account of the use of *hitbodedut* in order to attain revelation. *Hitbodedut* in the sense of concentration appears to have been part of a way of life, and not only a sporadic activity performed in times of trouble or danger. In an epistle known as *The Seven Paths of the Torah* (*Sheva' Netivot ha-Torah*), Abulafia enumerates a long list of works which he learned, but which did not bring him to "prophecy":

> But none of this brought me to apprehension of the Active Intellect, to the point that I could take pride in prophecy, that I could fulfill the verse, "For in this shall the proud man take pride . . ." [Jer 9:23] until I received this

apprehension in actuality, and I placed my soul in my hands according to the way of the Kabbalists, in knowing the Name alone. Yet nevertheless there were strong obstacles against me because of my sins, and they held me back from the path of *hitbodedut,* until the Holy Spirit left me, as is the case today.[4]

Abulafia here states explicitly that it was only the actual practical use of the technique of combination of letters of the divine name which brought about these revelations. This technique is referred to as "the way of the Kabbalists," and it constitutes the particular kabbalistic method advocated by him. The expression "the way of *hitbodedut,*" may also allude to this, for which reason it makes sense to assume here that *hitbodedut* refers not to isolation from society but to the use of a kabbalistic technique of combining letters, for which mental concentration is indispensable. An alternative interpretation of this incident, that Abulafia was unsuccessful in isolating himself from society, seems to me to be incorrect: we know that he attempted to disseminate his teachings in public and that he was persecuted by his opponents, who certainly would not have objected were the prophet-messiah to abandon his public activity and withdraw to some isolated place to engage in his own private, peculiar form of Kabbalah. It seems to me that Abulafia's comments concerning "obstacles" are to be interpreted as referring to disturbances, whether internal or external, to his own powers of concentration.

Support for this understanding of Abulafia's comments may be found elsewhere in his epistle *Sheva' Netivot ha-Torah.* In the description of the seven ways to interpret the Torah, he mentions, at the end of the fifth path:

This path is the beginning of the wisdom of letter-combination in general, and is only fitting to those who fear God and take heed of His name [Mal 3:16]. And the sixth path . . . is suitable to those who practice concentration (*hitbodedut*), who wish to approach God, in a closeness such that His activity—may He be blessed—will be known in them to themselves.

It also seems to me that one may discern here the connection between the "practitioners of *hitbodedut*" and the "science of letter-combination." In this passage, as well, he speaks of closeness to God, but it is still only a stage preceding the seventh path, that appropriate to "prophets," through which there comes about the "apprehension of the essence of the Ineffable Name." It follows from this that the "path of *hitbodedut*" is an earlier stage in the process intended for the attainment of prophecy. It must be stressed that, despite the "objective" description of the practitioners of concentration, this is not only a theoretical discussion; the seven ways of reading or of interpreting the Torah do not refer to the distant past, but constitute a living option for the members of Abulafia's own generation, he having been the one to restore these older ways of reading. Abulafia saw himself as a prophet both to himself and to others—that is, as one who had undergone the final two stages along the path outlined in his epistle. For this reason, it seems that his words must be seen as an autobiographical testimony, from which point of view this text should be combined with the two previous quotations, whose autobiographical character is quite evident.

A close relationship between letter-combination and *hitbodedut* appears in the book *Ḥayyey ha-ʿOlam ha-Baʾ*:

> He must also be very expert in the secrets of the Torah and its wisdom, so that he may know what will occur to him in the circles [the concentric circles on which the letters to be combined are written] of the combination, and he will arouse himself to think of the image of the Divine prophetic Intellect. And when he begins to practice letter-combination in his *hitbodedut,* he will feel fear and trembling, and the hairs of his head will stand up and his limbs will tremble. (MS Oxford 1582, fols. 116-12a)

Here, *hitbodedut* designates the special concentration required by the Kabbalist in order to combine letters. This intense concentration involves physical side effects that would be difficult to explain were they caused only by withdrawal from society.

In conclusion, we should emphasize the innovation involved in Abulafia's understanding of *hitbodedut* as concentration. According to extant kabbalistic sources, he seems to have been the first Kabbalist to connect *hitbodedut* with a practical, detailed system to give the concept *hitbodedut* real content: essentially, the combination of letters and the vocalization associated with them. Later we shall see that the presence of an association between *hitbodedut* and letter-combination or the recitation of divine names is likely to be a conclusive sign of the direct or indirect influence of Abulafia's kabbalistic system.

Most of the texts to be discussed below were written in the Middle East, or by authors of Eastern origin. This striking fact is doubtless connected, first of all, with the relationship between Abulafia's system and Sufism, a relationship acknowledged by the Kabbalists themselves. Second, as Abulafia's Kabbalah was subject to intense attack by the RaShBA, its influence within Spain itself was limited, which created an imbalance between the spread of prophetic Kabbalah in the East and its curtailment in the West. On the other hand, there is considerable discussion of *hitbodedut* among Jewish philosophers in Provence and Spain during the thirteenth to fifteenth centuries, albeit lacking in Abulafia's practical tone, in which classical prophecy is interpreted as a phenomenon attained through the help of *hitbodedut,* whether this is understood as concentration or as withdrawal from society. These discussions are likewise associated with Arabic philosophical texts, such as *Sefer Hanhagat ha-Mitboded* by Ibn Bajjah, or *Sefer Hay Ben Yoqtan* by Ibn Tufail, and they later influenced the development of Kabbalah during the sixteenth century. On the other hand, the Spanish Jewish thinkers contemporary with the Kabbalists were influenced neither by Abulafia's doctrine of *hitbodedut* or that of his disciples nor by the Jewish-Sufic approaches of the school of Abraham Maimonides (1186–1237).

In the Abulafian Tradition

Among those works closest to Abulafia's system, one must include the book *Sha'arey Zedeq;* this work, composed in Palestine in 1290 or 1295, clearly reflects knowledge of the Sufi approach. For our purposes, the anonymous author's comments concerning the influence of letter-combination and *hitbodedut* are of particular significance: "And I, through the power of combination and of *hitbodedut,* there happened to me what happened with the light that I saw going with me, as I have mentioned in the book *Sha'arey Zedeq.*"[5]

The experience of the "light," which occurs as a result of letter-combination and *hitbodedut,* forms an interesting parallel to the Holy Spirit mentioned in the above quotations. Moreover, the author of *Sha'arey Zedeq* also experiences "speech" as a result of the combination of the letters of the Holy Name. This provides additional evidence of the practical use of *hitbodedut* in the sense of concentration. It seems to me that the term recurs in this sense in two additional passages in *Sha'arey Zedeq.* One of these passages speaks of the progress of the philosopher beyond natural wisdom to divine wisdom and of the possibility that on some rare occasions the following might occur:

> He should greatly refine and draw downward the thought, and seek to concentrate on it, that no man should contaminate his thought . . . and he will see that he has great power in all the wisdoms, for such is its nature, and he will say that a given matter was revealed to him as if a prophecy, and he will not know the cause (MS Jerusalem 8°148, fol. 59b)

Hitbodedut is described here as a departure from the ordinary course of thought among the philosophers, which results in a revelation whose source no one can identify. In order to exemplify this path, the author relates a story pertaining to the Muslim philosopher Avicenna (980–1037):

> I found in the words of one of the great philosophers of his generation, namely, ibn Sina, in which he said that he would concentrate while composing his great works, and when a certain subject or matter would be difficult

for him, he would contemplate its intermediate proposition and draw his thought to it. And if the matter was still difficult, he would continue to think about it and drink a cup of strong wine, so as to fall asleep . . . and the difficulty in that subject would be solved for him. (MS Jerusalem 8°148, fol. 60a–b)

It seems to me that the preceding story does not refer to the withdrawal of that Arab philosopher from other people for two reasons: first, that *hitbodedut* and "drawing down of thought" are mentioned together in the first quotation from *Sha'arey Ẓedeq,* which we quoted above; since *hitbodedut* is there connected with thought, it makes sense to assume that elsewhere too this anonymous Kabbalist would use this term in a similar or identical sense. Second, in another story parallel to the one quoted above, preserved in the writings of Rabbi Isaac of Acre, who was apparently a contemporary of the author of *Sha'arey Ẓedeq,* solitude is not mentioned at all.

The Evidence of Isaac of Acre

Traces of Abulafia's understanding of *hitbodedut,* together with other additions whose source is apparently in the Pietistic-Sufi environment within which he grew up, are found in the works of Rabbi Isaac ben Samuel of Acre (late thirteenth to mid-fourteenth century). In the book *Me'irat 'Eynayim,* he writes:

He who merits the secret of communion [with the divine] will merit the secret of equanimity (*hishtawut*), and if he receives this secret, then he will also know the secret of *hitbodedut,* and once he has known the secret of *hitbodedut,* he will receive the Holy Spirit, and from that prophecy, until he shall prophesy and tell future things.[6]

Separation from or equanimity toward worldly things, which is called *hishtawut* ("equanimity"), makes possible *hitbodedut,* which here clearly refers to concentration. According to Rabbi Isaac, a condition of *ataraxia* ("absence of passion," a term used in the Cynic and Stoic tradition), is necessary for concentration, which leads, as in the case of Abulafia, to the Holy Spirit, and even to prophecy. One should note here the introduction into the context of kabbalistic thought of equanimity as a precondition of *hitbodedut*—an idea found neither in the writings of Abulafia nor in *Sha'arey Ẓedeq.* Its appearance in Rabbi Isaac of Acre is another important addition based on Sufi influence. Further on in the same passage, the author quotes another Kabbalist who has not yet been identified by scholars, referred to by the acronym ABNeR:

R. Abner said to me that a man who was a lover of wisdom came to one of the practitioners of concentration, and asked to be received as one of them. They replied: "My son, may you be blessed from heaven, for your intention is a good one. But please inform me, have you achieved equanimity (*hishtawut*) or not." He said to him: "Master, explain your words." He said to him: "My son, if there are two people, one who honors you and one of whom despises you, are they the same in your eyes or not?" He replied: "By the life of my soul, master, I derive pleasure and satisfaction from the one who honors me, and pain from the one who despises me, but I do not take vengeance or bear a grudge." He said to him: "My son, go in peace, for so long as you have not achieved equanimity, so that your soul feels the contempt done to you, you are not yet ready to link your thoughts on High, that you may come and concentrate. But go, and subdue your heart still more in truth, until you shall be equanimous, and then you may concentrate." And the cause of his equanimity is the attachment of his thoughts to God, for cleaving and attachment of the thought to God cause man to feel neither the honor nor the contempt that people show him.

We have here two traditions concerning the interrelationship among cleaving and equanimity and concentration. Rabbi Isaac's opinion, which places attachment to God in one's thought before equanimity, appears in the first quotation, as well as at the end of the second passage, beginning with the words "and the cause"; this conclusion constitutes, in my opinion, Rabbi Isaac's statement of his own view, which differs from that of "R. ABNeR," who claims that equanimity is the condition for attaining *devequt*, and that concentration (*hitbodedut*) is only possible thereafter. All this indicates that Rabbi Isaac had before him two traditions concerning this matter: one which he advocated and which was close to that of Abulafia, and the other that of the unknown Kabbalist "R. ABNeR." The appearance of the discussion concerning the connection between equanimity and concentration in "R. ABNeR" indicates that Rabbi Isaac was in contact with Kabbalists who were influenced by Sufism. Since "R. ABNeR" is already quoted by Rabbi Isaac at the beginning of his book *Me'irat 'Eynayim*, it makes sense to assume that Rabbi Isaac was familiar with Sufi concepts even before he began writing this book, which is today considered his earliest work.

In his book *Oẓar Ḥayyim*, Rabbi Isaac again discusses the question of *hitbodedut*:

I say that if a man does that which his soul [wishes] in the proper ways of *hitbodedut*, and his soul is immersed in this light, to look at it—then he will die like Ben Azzai who "looked and died." And it is not proper to do this, for "precious in the eyes of the Lord is the death of His righteous ones" (Ps 116:15), for whoever attempts to break through and to go beyond the

Partition will be stricken, and a serpent shall bite him. (MS Moscow-Ginzburg 775, fol. 138a; MS Oxford 1911, fol. 149b)

The expression "the ways of *hitbodedut*" is deserving of particular attention, recalling as it does the phrase we found above in Abulafia, *derekh ha-hitbodedut* (the path of *hitbodedut*). We noted there the close connection between concentration and letter-combination. Despite the fact that the letter-combinations are not mentioned in the passage from *Ozar Hayyim*, it seems to me possible that "the paths of *hitbodedut*" are in fact associated with them. Elsewhere in the same work, the author writes:

And by letter-combinations, unifications, and reversals, he shall call up the tree of the knowledge of good and evil, righteous knowledge and lying imagination, angels of mercy and angels of destruction, witnesses of innocence and of guilt, prosecutors and defenders, and he will be in danger of the same death as ben Azzai (MS Sassoon 919, fol. 215)

It is difficult to avoid noticing the parallel between the danger of death connected with Ben Azzai in the two passages cited and "the ways of *hitbodedut*" and "letter-combinations and unifications" as possible sources of danger. It follows from this that, as in Abulafia, *hitbodedut* in *Ozar Hayyim* is connected with the concentration needed to combine letters. Confirmation of this understanding of *hitbodedut* is found in another discussion in the book mentioned:

He who has been granted by God the spirit to concentrate and to engage in wisdom and in combination of letters and all its prerequisites, to separate himself from the objects of sensation and from physical pleasures, all of which are transient, and to pursue the Intellect and speak of it and of spiritual pleasures, which are eternal life (MS Moscow-Ginzburg 775, fol. 170a)

Here *hitbodedut*, that is, the ability to concentrate, is a gift from God, with the help of which one may progress in a process whose final end is clinging to spirituality. This process is connected with the Intellective Soul overpowering the appetitive:

And live a life of suffering in your house of meditation lest your appetitive soul overpower your intellective soul, for by this you will merit to bring into your intellective soul the divine plentitude, and in the Torah, that is to say, in the wisdom of combination and its prerequisites. (MS Moscow-Ginzburg 775, fol. 170b)

The purpose of meditation and letter-combination is to bring the spiritual abundance into the intellective soul or the Intellect; we learn this also from another source: "The wise man, who comes to isolate himself and to concentrate and to bring down into his soul the divine spirit, through

miraculous and awesome deeds . . . that itself is the divine spirit to attain
the intelligibles" (MS Sassoon 919, fol. 215).

Comparison of this passage with others quoted from *Ozar Hayyim* will
aid us in establishing the meaning here of the verb *hitboded*. In all other
passages, Rabbi Isaac used this verb, or a noun derived from it, to refer to
spiritual activity, for which reason the verbs *poresh* and *hitboded* should be
seen as referring to two distinct activities: separation from society or from
the objects of sensation, and intellectual concentration. This distinction
applies also to this pair of verbs in other passages from Rabbi Isaac: "It is
right in my eyes that those hermits (*perushim*) who practice concentration,
who have removed from their souls the sensuous things, of which the holy
spiritual poet R. Eliezer the Babylonian said . . ." (MS Moscow-Ginzburg
775, fol. 136a). Again: "This is the secret of the modest, hermitlike practitioners of concentration who flee from the sensual things and cling to the
intelligibles" (MS Moscow-Ginzburg 775, fol. 238b). The meaning of abandonment of the sensuous and clinging to the intelligibles, together with a
quite detailed description of the process, appears in an extremely important
passage attributed to Rabbi Isaac of Acre, quoted in the book *Reshit
Hokhmah* by Rabbi Elijah de Vidas:

> Thus we learn from one incident, recorded by R. Isaac of Acre, of blessed
> memory, who said that one day the princess came out of the bathhouse, and
> one of the idle people saw her and sighed a deep sigh and said: "Who would
> give me my wish, that I could do with her as I like!" And the princess
> answered and said: "That shall come to pass in the graveyard, but not here."
> When he heard these words he rejoiced, for he thought that she meant for
> him to go to the graveyard to wait for her there, and that she would come
> and he would do with her as he wished. But she did not mean this, but
> wished to say that only there (i.e., in death) great and small, young and old,
> despised and honored—all are equal, but not here, so that it is not possible
> that one of the masses should approach a princess. So that man rose and went
> to the graveyard and sat there, and devoted all his thoughts to her, and always
> thought of her form. And because of his great longing for her, he removed
> his thoughts from everything sensual, but put them continually on the form
> of that woman and her beauty. Day and night he sat there in the graveyard,
> there he ate and drank, and there he slept, for he said to himself, "If she does
> not come today, she will come tomorrow." This he did for many days, and
> because of his separation from the objects of sensation, and the exclusive
> attachment of his thought to one object and his concentration and his total
> longing, his soul was separated from the sensual things and attached itself
> only to the intelligibles, until it was separated from all sensual things, in-
> cluding that woman herself, and he communed with God. And after a short
> time he cast off all sensual things and he desired only the Divine Intellect,
> and he became a perfect servant and holy man of God, until his prayer was
> heard and his blessing was beneficial to all passers-by, so that all the

merchants and horsemen and foot-soldiers who passed by came to him to receive his blessing, until his fame spread far about. . . . Thus far is the quotation as far as it concerns us. And he went on at length concerning the high spiritual level of this ascetic, and R. Isaac of Acre wrote there in his account of the deeds of the ascetics, that he who does not desire a woman is like a donkey, or even less than one, the point being that from the objects of sensation one may apprehend the worship of God. (*Reshit Ḥokhmah, Ahavah* 4)

This story contains several of the concepts discussed above: communion in thought—"the attachment of the thought of his mind"—here precedes *hitbodedut,* that is, concentration, just as the secret of *devequt* precedes that of concentration in the *Me'irat 'Eynayim.* Moreover, the graveyard alludes, as we can see from the story itself, to a situation of equality of opposites, and from this point of view there is an interesting parallel to the secret of equanimity mentioned in *Me'irat 'Eynayim.* From a study of the story, one may assume that equanimity precedes communion and that the latter in turn precedes *hitbodedut,* so that we have here the order of the stages as presented by "R. ABNeR." For a deeper understanding of the significance of this parable, let us turn to another passage from the *Me'irat 'Eynayim:*

From the wise man R. Nathan, may he live long, I heard . . . that when man leaves the vain things of this world, and constantly attaches his thought and his soul above, his soul is called by the name of that supernal level which it attained, and to which it attached itself. How is this so? If the soul of the practitioner of *hitbodedut* was able to apprehend and to commune with the Passive Intellect, it is called "the Passive Intellect," as if it itself were the Passive Intellect; likewise, when it ascends further and apprehends the Acquired Intellect, it becomes the Acquired Intellect; and if it merited to apprehend to the level of the Active Intellect, it itself is the Active Intellect; but if it succeeds in clinging to the Divine Intellect, then happy is its lot, for it has returned to its foundation and its source, and it is literally called the Divine Intellect, and that man shall be called a man of God, that is, a divine man, creating worlds. (p. 222f.)

Here, as in the story of the princess, we read of a spiritual ascent, through which one becomes "a man of God." Both cases speak of *hitbodedut* and *devequt,* although in the latter case it is difficult to determine the exact relationship between the two concepts. Likewise, the supernatural qualities of the man of God are mentioned in both passages: here he is "a creator of worlds"; in the parable of the princess "his prayer is heard and his blessing is efficacious"; at the end of the first quotation from *Me'irat 'Eynayim* it speaks about prophecy which enables the prediction of the future.

Examination of all of the sources relating to *hitbodedut* that we have quoted from the writings of R. Isaac of Acre indicates that its purpose was to remove the thought process from objects of sensation and to lift it up to the intelligibles or even to the highest levels of the world of Intellect. The final goal of this process of ascent is to commune with God Himself, as is clear from the parable of the princess. This is even true in the quotation from Rabbi Nathan, in which *devequt* to the Divine Intellect is mentioned.

One might well ask whether one can identify the exact nature of the princess in this story. She is portrayed there exclusively as an earthly substance, but this level of understanding seems insufficient. The conclusion, quoted from *Reshit Hokhmah* in the name of Rabbi Isaac, states that "from the sensual one must understand the nature of divine service," in the context of "lust for a woman." Concentration on this desire causes the meditator to leave the world of the senses, that is, the physical form of the princess, and to cling to intelligibles, and afterward to God Himself. In *Me'irat 'Eynayim* the author writes: "It is not like your thoughts in the objects of sensation, but it speaks of the intelligibilia, which are commanded by the *'atarah*. The letter *'ayin* is the initial of the word *'atarah* [crown], which corresponds to the *sefirah* of *malkhut*, which is the *Shekhinah*." It follows from this that Rabbi Isaac identifies the intelligibilia with the *Shekhinah*. Furthermore, immediately following the passage quoted above he adds: "See the parable of the princess, etc., as explained in *Keter Shem Tov* [by Shem Tov Ibn Gaon]: 'the Torah [spoke here of] the unification of *'atarah*.'" The identification of the crown as the princess—referring to the *sefirah* of *malkhut*, which is in turn identified with the intellect—suggests a withdrawal from the objects of sensation, a distancing from the physical form of the princess, while attachment to the Intellect is seen as cleaving to the supernal, ideal princess—the *Shekhinah*—and then to God Himself. This clinging may be what is referred to as "divine service" by Rabbi Isaac, and the practitioner of concentration who clings to God may be the "perfect servant." One may also go a step further and interpret the expression "man of God" (*ish ha-elohim*) in the parable of the princess in an erotic sense: the mediator is transformed into the likes of Moses, the husband (*ish*) of the *Shekhinah*, symbolized here by the word "God" (*ha-elohim*). This is a common idea in Kabbalah, and such a possible interpretation should not be rejected out of hand. In the context of this discussion, we should mention the spiritual pleasures which, according to Rabbi Isaac, accompany attachment to the Intelligibles.

As we stated above, there is a similarity between the parable of the princess and Diotima's statement in Plato's *Symposium;* however, in her speech Diotima does not at all mention solitude, either in the sense of seclusion from society or in that of mental concentration. But these two forms

420   HITBODEDUT AS CONCENTRATION

of solitude are mentioned by the Muslim philosopher Averroes (1126–1198) in connection with Socrates' understanding of God:

> And he who among them belongs to the unique individuals, like Socrates, who choose isolation and separation from other people and retreat into their souls always, until those of great heart believed that through this dedication and forced contemplation of the above-mentioned forms, one shall arrive at the first form that can be apprehended. . . . (MS Berlin 216 [Or. Qu. 681], p. 325)

Here, as in the parable of the princess, it is possible to go from the intelligibles, or the forms, to the apprehension of God Himself, by means of solitude and mental concentration. Is the attribution of the practice of solitude to Socrates connected with the fact that he was the one to quote Diotima's comment in Plato's dialogue? In any event, Averroes's comment seems to reflect an older tradition concerning Socrates as a recluse, which was also cited by Rabbi Judah Halevi (ca. 1075–1141).

We saw above that *hitbodedut* was part of a technique of concentration and attachment of the human soul to God. However, according to Rabbi Isaac of Acre, *hitbodedut* is able in addition to serve as a means of drawing the divine pleroma down into the human soul:

> When man separates himself from the objects of sensation and concentrates and removes all the powers of his intellective soul from them, *but gives them a powerful elevation in order to perceive Divinity,* his thoughts shall draw down the abundance from above and it shall come to reside in his soul. And that which is written, "Once in each month" is to hint to the practitioner of *hitbodedut* that his withdrawal from all objects of sensation must not be absolute, but rather "half to God and half to yourselves," which is also the secret of the half-shekel, "the rich man should not add, nor the poor man subtract, from the half-a-shekel" (Exod 30:15), whose esoteric meaning is "half of one's soul," for *shekel* alludes to the soul.[7]

This evaluation of *hitbodedut* is already referred to in Abraham Ibn Ezra's commentary on Exod 3:14 (long version) and in Abulafia, but Rabbi Isaac of Acre seems to emphasize this approach more clearly and fostered its inclusion in later Kabbalah.

Shem Tov Ibn Gaon and His *Badday ha-Aron*

The approach of Rabbi Shem Tov ben Abraham Ibn Gaon (late thirteenth to fourteenth century) should be understood within the context of Abulafia and of Rabbi Isaac of Acre. His book *Baddey ha-Aron,* which was written at least partially in Safed, contains an interesting discussion of *hitbodedut:*

He should concentrate his mind until he hates this world and desires the world to come. And he should not be surprised that they [the Sages] said that one who is engaged in the secrets of the Chariot need not stand before a great man or an elder. . . . And he will see that there is no end to his intellect, and he shall delve deeply into the secrets of the Chariot and the structures of Creation, to the place where the mouth is unable to speak and the ear is unable to hear. Then he will see visions of God, as one who dreams and whose eyes are shut, as it is written, "I am asleep but my heart is awake, the voice of my beloved knocks . . ." (Song 5:2). And when he opens his eyes, and even more so if another person speaks to him, he will choose death over life, for it will seem to him that he has died, for he has forgotten what he saw. Then he will look into his mind as one looks at a book in which are written these great wonders. (MS Paris 840, fol. 45a)

By the power of his mental concentration, the Kabbalist turns to his inner self and discovers there amazing things, written as in a book; this situation of introspection is an extremely sensitive one, which may easily be disturbed by any outside stimulus. Note the use here of the expression "visions of God," which is indicative of a revelation that may be associated with the previous mention of the secrets of creation or the secrets of the chariot. According to Rabbi Shem Tov, this inner revelation is transformed into a source of the writing of this book:

When he has no friend with whom to practice concentration as he would wish, let him "sit by himself and be silent, for He has come upon him" (Lam 3:28). And he shall begin to write what he sees in his mind, as one who copies from a book that is written before him, black fire on white fire, in the true form of a sphere, like the sun, for the light has come upon him at that hour, and all the seas would not suffice for ink, nor all the rushes of the swamps for quills, as in the parable of the Sages, until the heavens be revealed to him as a book. (MS Paris 840, fols. 45b-46a)

Here, unlike in the first quotation, the Holy Spirit seems to move within the one meditating, and he must seek a companion with whom to practice concentration. It is also possible that these represent a series of different levels of events; the first passage speaks of one's attempts to reach the stage of mystical experience, from which it follows that *hitbodedut* also here means concentration; the second passage describes the experience itself, during which the meditator requires human company; this stage is described in some detail further on in Rabbi Shem Tov's description:

And they [i.e., the Kabbalists, "those who receive the truth in each generation"] did not have others with whom to practice concentration properly, for the spirit of their bellies disturbed them, and they secretly opened their mouths in wisdom, and they conversed with [their quills] of reed and marsh. (MS Paris 840, fols. 45b-46a)

We find here a unique understanding of the function of *hitbodedut:* companionship makes it possible for the meditator to relieve himself of the burden of his mystical experience; without him, the Kabbalist would have to write down his words and "speak with the reed," something which may later bring about disaster: "and it is possible that it will afterwards come into the hands of unworthy people, and strangers will husband Him, which is not as the law." Rabbi Shem Tov goes so far as to say that even the meditator himself is likely to become confused in his later understanding of the things revealed to him during the mystical experience.

> [These contents] . . . do not help a man nor does he understand them, unless he received a tradition by word of mouth. Even those who themselves write it may at times not understand it well at that time, and when the revelation [i.e., the appearance of the Holy Spirit] passes, he will look at them and not understand them, and even when they are explained, he will be unable to conceptualize them. (MS Paris 840, fols. 45b–46a)

The passages quoted above appear between two discussions concerning letter-combination; the first discussion opens with this sentence:

> And he shall arouse through his wisdom the thought, which is dormant in the sea of darkness, and say in his heart: "As I knew the form of the letters and they were inscribed on my heart, one next to its companion, I will examine each letter, in its combinations and its vocalizations, and its combination arising from the combination of letters, to levels without end, of levels of the letters, even though these also are without end." (MS Paris 840, fol. 44a)

This indicates that the mental concentration (i.e., *hitbodedut*) mentioned in the first passage from the book *Baddey ha-Aron* begins with an arousal connected with letter combination; this approach approximates the prophetic Kabbalah of Abulafia and his school. After the discussions of *hitbodedut,* Rabbi Shem Tov again mentions the combination of letters, and adds the advice that one deal only with the combinations of vocalization marks. At the conclusion, he says:

> But if he will understand the things which I have written concerning the thirty-two paths and the letters, one above the other, at once visible and invisible, and imagine them in his mind after receiving them verbally, and the light appears above him, or from fire, "for it is a spirit in man" [Job 32:8] that he shall know the hidden letters. (MS Paris 840, fol. 47a).

It is clear that Rabbi Shem Tov advises here a system of letter- and vocalization-combination in order to attain the experience of appearance of the light and of speech—"it is a spirit in man." This experience is very similar to the descriptions connected with *hitbodedut,* as quoted above. But these do not seem to be merely suggestions; the Kabbalist·writes further: "I also saw hidden and sealed mysteries, worthy of concealment, but the spirit pointed them out, and I could not go by without a hint to those who pay heed to the language of the dotted letters" (MS Paris 840, fol. 47b).

It makes sense to assume that this is a description of an experience of Rabbi Shem Tov himself, who, as is known, dealt with the textual tradition of the Bible and, as a result of this particular involvement, almost certainly arrived at an experience of light and spirit that obligated him to write down some of the things which are in *Baddey ha-Aron*. This teaches us that the Kabbalah with which he was involved was not only a matter of theory, or confined to the distant past, but a current practice in fourteenth-century Safed. The fact that the book *Baddey ha-Aron* was written in the Galilee, where Rabbi Isaac of Acre was also educated and where the anonymous author of *Sha'arey Zedeq* also almost certainly stayed, teaches us that Rabbi Shem Tov might have continued an ecstatic kabbalistic tradition that already existed in the land of Israel. In any event, in his first kabbalistic work, *Keter Shem Tov,* there are no traces of the ecstatic Kabbalah, such as we find in his later work.

To conclude our discussion of the work *Baddey ha-Aron,* let us return to the opening of the first passage we cited from this book and quote it in its fuller context:

> And do not be astounded by what the Sages said (*b. Sukk.* 28a) concerning Jonathan ben Uziel, namely, that when he was engged in the study of the Torah any bird which flew overhead was immediately consumed by fire. And he should concentrate in his mind . . . and he should not be surprised that they [the Sages] said that one who is engaged in the secrets of the Chariot need not stand up either before an elder or a great man. And he should understand the words of R. Akiba to Ben Zoma, "From whence and to where" [*b. Hag.* 15a] and their answers to one another, in which the second word was written without the *yod.* (MS Paris 840, fol. 45a)

Involvement in Torah and involvement in the secrets of the chariot are understood here as stages advancing mental contemplation. The meaning of involvement in Torah is explained above as profound involvement in the combinations of letters and vowels. The nature of the involvement in the secrets of the chariot according to Rabbi Shem Tov is not clear. We already saw above, in the writings of Rabbi Isaac of Acre, that the practice of *hitbodedut* is compared to the path of Ben Azzai and Rabbi Akiba when they entered into *pardes.* It is possible—and this requires proof—that involvement in the secrets of the chariot refers also to the science of combining letters; support for this interpretation may be found in the approach of Rabbi Abraham Abulafia, who sees in the secret of the chariot the combination of holy names. If this is so, *hitbodedut* depends upon involvement in the secrets of the chariot.

Sulam ha-'Aliyah of R. Judah Albotini

We read in another work that represents a loyal continuation of the path of prophetic Kabbalah, *Sulam ha-'Aliyah,* by R. Judah Albotini (d. 1519):

> By this he shall ascend to the level of equanimity, as that sage [cf. *Hagigah* 1:2] said to his student who asked him: "Will you teach us the secret of the Chariot?" He answered: "Have you achieved equanimity?" And the student did not understand what he was saying to him, until he explained the matter to him, namely, that all attributes are equal to him. And this was what he said to him, "If a man insulted you, and took away that which was yours, would you be angry and strict with him over this? And if he did the opposite, namely, to honor you and to give you many gifts, would you rejoice over this and feel it? And would you be feel in your soul that you were affected by these two opposites?" Then his master said to him, "If so, then you have not yet acquired the quality of equanimity, that is, that it should be equal to you whether it be honor or its opposite. And since such is the case, how can you ascend to the level of *hitbodedut,* which comes after you have achieved equanimity?[8]

The parallels between this story and that told by Rabbi Isaac of Acre in the name of "R. ABNeR" in his book *Me'irat 'Eynayim* are clear; nevertheless, one may not necessarily assume that this book is the direct source of Rabbi Judah's words here for several reasons: first, in Albotini equanimity (*hishtawut*) immediately precedes *hitbodedut,* as it does in Rabbi Isaac's view, whereas in "R. ABNeR" *hitdabbequt* (communion with the divine) comes between them. Second, despite the similarity in subject matter, this is not an exact quotation from the version in *Me'irat 'Eynayim.* Elsewhere in this book there are direct quotations from the writings of Abulafia and from the book *Sha'arey Zedeq,* but all of them are identified with appropriate references. Third, the attitude toward the activity of Ben Azzai differs in "R. ABNeR" and in Albotini: only the latter emphasizes this personality's high level. Fourth, *Sulam ha'Aliyah* quotes the talmudic saying concerning the teaching of the secret of the chariot, which is absent from *Me'irat 'Eynayim.* The addition of the expression "secrets of the chariot" (*ma'aseh merkavah*) in the specific context of this story indicates that this subject was seen as related to *hitbodedut.* According to Rabbi Judah, or his unknown source, Rabbi Eleazar ben Arakh was referring to *hitbodedut* when he used the phrase "secret of the chariot." However, in place of the preconditions mentioned in the Talmud, which emphasize wisdom—that is, "a wise man, who understands by himself"—*Sulam ha-'Aliyah* stresses the trait of *hishtawut*. This change, which is not accidental, relates to the tendency of the Sufis to diminish or even to negate completely the value of intellectual wisdom and learning. It is worthwhile to compare this approach to *hishtawut* with that of Rabbi Joseph Caro:

> He should have concern for nothing in the world, except for those things which pertain to the service of God, but all the things of this world should be equal in his eyes, everything and its opposite. For this is the secret of the wise man, who was asked by one who wished to practice union: "Have you achieved equanimity?" For the truth is that one for whom the good things of this world and its ills are not equal cannot practice union in a complete manner. (*Maggid Mesharim*, be-shalah)

According to R. Werblowsky this is a quotation from Ibn Paquda's *Hovot ha-Levavot*.[9] However, this passage seems even closer to Albotini: first, because both Caro and Albotini speak of a "sage" who answers the question, whereas Bahya refers to a *hasid* (pious man). Second, the use of the term *shaweh* (equanimous) is common to the two Kabbalists but is absent from Bahya. Third, the expression "from honor and from its opposite" is close to Caro's "a thing and its opposite." Despite this, we may not assume that Caro was influenced by the version in *Sulam ha-'Aliyah*, since he completely ignores the importance of *hitbodedut*. Moreover, as one can learn from their continuation, Caro's words were written outside of Palestine, and it seems unlikely that Albotini's work came there and was used without being cited by name. The similarity in the details between the two sources is indicative of a common source that was different from the version in *Hovot ha-Levavot*.

Let us now return to the book *Sulam ha-'Aliyah*. Rabbi Judah Albotini was apparently the first to state in an unambiguous way that *hitbodedut* differs from solitude:

> For the welfare of the body, that is, solitude brings about purity of the potencies and cleanness of qualities. Equanimity brings one to concentration of the soul, and concentration brings about the Holy Spirit, which brings one to prophecy, which is the highest level. If so, one of the necessary prerequisites for your path in concentration is that you first have the quality of equanimity, that you not become excited by anything.[10]

We find here another case in which a talmudic saying is incorporated in the discussion of *hitbodedut;* this use gives the two spiritual levels—*hishtawut* and *hitbodedut*—a privileged place within the sequence of stages bringing about the Holy Spirit in the talmudic tradition, and it indicates that these Sufi concepts were understood as matching—or even explaining and interpreting—the ancient Jewish tradition. However, this harmonistic claim has a harsh ring, from the standpoint of the talmudic tradition. Although *hishtawut* is claimed to fit a certain statement in the Talmud, at the same time it opposes certain central Jewish attitudes. The previous quotation continues:

> On the contrary, he must have joyfulness of soul and be happy with his lot, and think in his heart that he alone is one and rules over this entire, low world, and that there is no person, near or far, who will concern himself over him, nor anyone who can do him any evil or damage or harm or trouble, nor any good, for all the good of this world and its wealth is in his hands, and he needs nothing. Of this, the Sages said: "Prophecy does not dwell save upon one who is wise, courageous and wealthy" (*b. Shab.* 92a). And "Who is wealthy? He who rejoices in his lot (*m. Abot* 5:1)."

"Joy in one's lot" is here given a far-reaching interpretation from a Jewish point of view: it is taken to mean a feeling of total independence and separation from one's human environment. This matches Rabbi Shem Tov Ibn Gaon's approach to the contemplative's relationship to the members of his family, but it is certainly a far-reaching step compared with what is stated in the book *Baddey ha-Aron*. For Rabbi Judah, separation from the world constitutes a psychological state preceding ecstasy, for which reason—one may assume—it is more fixed and continues for a longer period than the separation caused at the time of *devequt* itself, according to Rabbi Shem Tov. The state of *hitbodedut* is attained by letter-combinations, just as it was by the Kabbalists of the school of Abulafia:

> . . . who was expert in the wisdom of *zeruf* and that of *dillug*. . . . Afterwards, let him perform this means of *hitbodedut,* in combination with the verse that he wishes to use from the Torah, and he should repeat this many times, or for a month, more or less, as he wishes, until he sees that he is perfect in that path, and so he shall further persist in this *hitbodedut*. . . ."[11]

The various systems of letter-combination are understood here as means of *hitbodedut,* or among its paths. We have here a system of intellectual exercises whose purpose, according to Albotini, is to prepare the soul to receive the Holy Spirit.

R. David Ibn Abi Zimra

One should note the influence of the interrelationship among *hitbodedut,* Holy Names, and the attainment of the Holy Spirit upon the approach of Rabbi David ben Solomon Ibn Abi Zimra (RaDBaZ, 1479–1573). This Kabbalist, who was acquainted with the system of Abulafia, writes in his book *Magen Dawid:* "I have already seen one who wrote that, through the concentration on the Holy Names in holiness and in purity, one may reach the stage of the Holy Spirit, even in our times, and this is a matter with which the enlightened man will not be in doubt about the matter of the Holy Names" (fol. 49b).

The author goes on to develop this idea more fully elsewhere; but, as opposed to what is said in this passage, which sees the acquisition of the Holy Spirit as possible in the present, the RaDBaZ explains the phenomenon of the Urim and Thummim as reached by means of *hitbodedut:*

> The matter of the Urim and Thummim . . . is that one of the Holy Names, known to the priest, was contained in the folds of the breastplate, and the priest would direct his attention and thought and intentions towards that Name and concentrate upon it, and be adorned with the Holy Spirit by that same name, and it would be pictured in his mind. (*Magen Dawid,* 18d–19a)

According to him, this phenomenon resembles prophecy: "For at times the prophet would direct his thoughts and contemplate, and with a slight arousal would understand the intentions of God, even in a mysterious metaphor or parable. And at times he would not be ready, and he would concentrate and see the vision and the parable" (*Magen Dawid,* fols. 18d–19a). The prophet was required to concentrate and to meditate in order to decipher for himself the contents of his vision: "For were the intention of your thoughts towards prophecy in great concentration, you would know by yourself and would not need to ask the meaning of the parable."

Hitbodedut in the Writings of R. Moses Cordovero

As we have seen, several motifs relating to *hitbodedut,* which originated in the circle of Rabbi Abraham Abulafia, reappeared at the beginning of the sixteenth century in the writings of two Kabbalists who were among the exiles from Spain and Portugal: Rabbi Judah Albotini and Rabbi David Ibn Zimra, both of whom lived and were active in Jerusalem. One must ask whether it is merely coincidence that interest in *hitbodedut* reemerged in sixteenth-century Palestine, after it was associated with Kabbalists active in the late thirteenth and the early fourteenth century who had a certain relationship to the land of Israel. This question becomes more serious in the light of the fact that the Spanish Kabbalists of the fourteenth and fifteenth centuries almost completely ignored the teaching of Rabbi Abraham Abulafia, and even during the generation of the Expulsion he was still regarded as the "black sheep" of Kabbalah in the eyes of many Spanish Kabbalists. The renewed interest of Palestinean Kabbalists of Spanish origin in the

Kabbalah of Abulafia and its offshoots points toward their encounter with the Eastern kabbalistic heritage, which combined prophetic Kabbalah with Jewish-Sufi pietism. The presumption that such a kabbalistic tradition, whose traces were lost for a period of slightly less than two hundred years, did exist may also explain the interest of the Safed Kabbalists during the latter half of the sixteenth century in Abulafia and Rabbi Isaac of Acre's doctrine of *hitbodedut*. I would conjecture that we are speaking here not only of the preservation and study of Abulafia's writings but also of a living kabbalistic tradition—which may explain the origins of Albotini's *Sulam ha-'Aliyah* and the centrality of *hitbodedut* and letter-combination among the Kabbalists of Safed from the middle of the sixteenth century on. In contrast, Spanish Kabbalah on the eve of the Expulsion, such as the circle of the author of *Sefer ha-Meshiv*, was much involved with techniques of revelation, including incantations for dream questions and formulas for automatic writing—concerns that were continued in the Kabbalah of Safed. However, as opposed to Abulafia, they did not emphasize the relationship between *hitbodedut* and letter-combination. In the writings of Rabbi Moshe Cordovero, we hear for the first time of an integration of Abulafia's doctrines within an overall summary of Spanish Kabbalah—namely, in his book *Pardes Rimmonim*. As opposed to the comprehensive work of Rabbi Meir Ibn Gabbai, which is based almost entirely on Spanish Kabbalah, Cordovero includes themes and quotations from the writings of Abraham Abulafia, giving them a standing unknown among the Spanish exilic Kabbalists active outside the land of Israel. This incorporation is quite clear in the discussion of *hitbodedut*, and its implications for the development of Kabbalah will be treated later in our discussion. There is no doubt that the Safed Kabbalists had copies of several of the most important writings of Abulafia and his disciples. Thus, for example, we read in Rabbi Moshe Cordovero's commentary on the *Zohar* passage known as "the *Sabba* (grandfather) of *Mishpatim*":

> And as '*ADaM* (man—i.e., the letters '*DM*) follows alphabetical order, [its letters symbolizing] world [i.e., location], year [i.e., time], soul [i.e., personhood], until he attaches himself to the secret of *neshamah, ruah, nefesh* [i.e., the three levels of soul], that is *NRN*, the secret of '*ShN*, in the secret of the letters which are transmuted in his mouth, and the secret of the vocalization signs, and the secret of the *hitbodedut* brought down to man by them, as is written in the book *Sha'arey Zedeq* by Rabbi Abraham Abulafia author of *Sefer Hayyey ha-'Olam ha-Ba*. (MS Cincinnati 586, fol. 45b)

This passage indicates that Cordovero had before him two of the principal works of prophetic Kabbalah; from them he learned, among other things, the secret of *hitbodedut*, which, as we have seen above, is connected with the combinations of letters and of vowels. Through *hitbodedut,* the soul becomes attached to the supernal hypostases known as *neshamah, ruah, nefesh.* We have here a Neoplatonic formulation of the understanding of *devequt,* influenced not a little by the approach of the author of *Sha'arey Zedeq.* A closer examination of the meaning of the word *hitbodedut* in this text would be worthwhile. It is clear that the stage portrayed here is one reached by the practitioner of concentration after the process of *zeruf* and not before it, which differs from the texts discussed until now. Here, *hitbodedut* is transformed into the final stage before *devequt.* One should compare Cordovero's unique use of this term with that of his disciple, Rabbi Ḥayyim Vital, who writes in the book *Sha'arey Qedushah,* apparently in the name of his teacher:

"The sons of prophets, who had before them drum and pipe, etc." [1 Sam 10:5] for by the sweetness of the sound of the music *hitbodedut* rests upon them, by the pleasantness of the sound, and they cast off their souls. And then the musician ceases his playing, but the prophetic disciples remain in the same supernal state of *devequt,* and they prophesy. (MS British Library 749, fol. 15b)

In this quotation from Vital, as in Cordovero, *hitbodedut* occurs as a result of the use of a certain technique, and in the wake of this concentration the soul attains the state of *devequt.* This intermediate situation may signify a kind of abnegation of the senses or isolation of the soul from objects of sensation, which enables it to attach itself to a higher level.

In *Pardes Rimmonim* (v. 2, fol. 97a), Cordovero paraphrases a very important passge from Rabbi Abraham Abulafia's book *Or ha-Sekhel,* defining *hitbodedut* as retirement to an isolated room and letter-combination. However, beyond these quotations one finds here an interesting discussion based upon the doctrines of Abulafia's school:

Several of the early ones explained that by the combination and transmutation of the seventy-two-letter holy name or the other names, after great *hitbodedut,* the righteous man, who is worthy and enlightened in such matters, will have a portion of the Divine Voice (*bat qol*) revealed to him, in the sense of, "The spirit of God spoke in me, and His word was on my lips" (2 Sam 23:2). For he combines together the potencies and unites them and arouses desire in them, each to its brother, as the *membrum virile* of man and his companion [i.e., the female], until there is poured upon him a spirit of abundance—on the condition that he be engaged in this thing, as a vessel prepared to and worthy of receiving the spirit, for if such is not the case, it will become cruel to be turned into "a degenerate wild vine" (cf. Jer 2:21). (*Pardes Rimmonim,* v. 2, fol. 69b)

Thus, *hitbodedut* in the sense of concentration advances the process of letter-combination, whose purpose is the attainment of the holy spirit, in the spirit of Abulafia's Kabbalah. The conclusion of this quotation favors the approach of Rabbi Isaac of Acre, in which combination enables the soul to receive the abundance or the spirituality. This expression is interpreted elsewhere as well in connection with *hitbodedut:* "The prophets, of blessed memory, used to acquire, by means of those letters, through great concentration and by virtue of their pure soul, that spirit embodied in the letters" (*Pardes Rimmonim,* v. 2, fol. 69b). The letters combined by the Kabbalist are transformed here into a sort of talisman, which absorbs the supernal abundance. After the spirituality is absorbed by means of the letters, it becomes attached within the soul, which is prepared for this by concentration. *Hitbodedut* is described as a process by which the soul is transferred from the world of matter to the world of spirit, on the one hand, or as a technique of spiritual elevation, through contemplation of sensory data and its stripping away, in order to understand the spiritual element within it. The mystical aspect of *hitbodedut* is clearly expressed in another book by Cordovero, namely, *Shi'ur Qomah:*

> The sons of the prophets, when they used to prepare themselves for prophecy, brought themselves [to a state of] happiness as in the verse, "Take me a musician, and when the musician plays . . ." (2 Kgs 3:15). And they would concentrate in accordance with their ability to do so, in attaining the wondrous levels and casting off the material, and strengthening the mind within the body, until they abandoned matter and did not perceive it at all, but their mind was entirely in the supernal orders and subjects. And they concentrate, and cast off the physical, and go away—and this matter is man's preparation on his own part.[12]

According to Cordovero, the "sons of the prophets," that is, the ancient Jewish mystics, had special methods of concentration: "according to their knowledge of concentration," which showed them how to cast off materiality and to prepare the dematerialized mind to apprehend the structure of the *sefirot:* "the sublime levels," "those supernal levels." We learn about the necessary transition between the physical and the spiritual from *Sefer Or Yaqar:*

> If one wishes to take pleasure in the understanding of his Creator, let him concentrate according to the accepted premises which he has learned, and let him look at a particular physical form, so that he may learn from it that which is alluded to in the spiritual worlds, and he will see the detailed organs of it, and the varied matters, and its lights. And from there he will come to understand the innermost secrets of the spirituality of that form, and he shall attain *devequt.* Such was the way of Adam in the garden of Eden. Now, if the cherubim were physical-spiritual beings, he may gaze at them and come

to contemplate and to apprehend from what is pictured here, in terms of the visual, that which makes sense to the mind—[proceeding] from the physical to the spiritual. (v. 10, p. 7)

The Kabbalist is able to acquire "knowledge of his Creator" through contemplation of the form of his own physical organs, by means of *hitbodedut.* This statement reminds us of Rabbi Isaac of Acre's story of the princess, which was quoted in the work of Cordovero's pupil, Rabbi Elijah de Vidas. Furthermore, according to Rabbi Isaac, "from the sensory you shall understand the intelligibilia, for from your flesh shall you know God [after Job 19:26]." We have here a kabbalistic variant of the saying "Know yourself and know your God," according to which concentration plays a central role in the transition between one's self—that is, one's body—and the Divine. *Hitbodedut* is a means of uncovering the supernal source of material being; the cessation of *hitbodedut* is likely to bring about a distorted understanding of phenomenon. Thus, we hear of Moses that:

Because he turned his heart away from prophetic concentration, in fleeing from the Creator's mission, turning his head in thinking that it was Amram, his father, who was calling him at that moment. For had he concentrated at that time, he would have understood how that voice was descending from the [cosmic] world of Creation to that of Formation, and from that of Formation into that of Action. . . . And the same happened to Samuel, at the beginning of his prophecy, that he did not concentrate, to understand the way of the voice, even though he was worthy of prophecy. So he thought that that voice was a human voice, that is, that of Eli, until he finally said, "Speak, for your servant hears" (1 Sam 3:10)—that is, that he concentrated and apprehended the stages of prophecy, and understood the descent of the divine voice.[13]

Here, *hitbodedut* is understood as a combination of concentration and meditation at one and the same time; it is the means enabling the human intellect to restore the essence of things to their supernal source, by apprehension of their essence. This is the way by which one turns to the upper world:

There are two aspects of *hokhmah:* the supernal aspect is turned towards the divine crown (*keter*), which aspect does not face downwards. . . . The second, lower aspect turns downwards. . . . Likewise man has two aspects: the first is that of his concentration upon his Creator, to add and acquire wisdom, and the second that by which he teaches others. (*Tomer Devorah,* 3).

It seems important to me to dwell upon a certain change in the use of the term *hitbodedut* in Cordovero's thought: concentrated thought enables one to uncover the hidden essence of the object of contemplation, through which one comes to understand the supernal source and the way in which the spiritual emanates down into the material world. According to Cordovero, the human intellect must cast off its physicality only in order to penetrate, by means of its concentration, beyond the physicality of other things, to uncover their spiritual nature and to arrive in the final analysis at God Himself. According to another text, Cordovero seems to state that there are certain subjects whose apprehension cannot be guaranteed even by *hitbodedut:*

> For the Torah is the secret of the upper Being which has come into existence below, and is not separated from the *sefirot,* but it nevertheless is present for those who exist below, while connected to the spiritual existence of the *sefirot.* When man concentrates in order to understand this mystery, he shall be astonished and be silent to his mind and not find it, for the Torah is not a separate being below. (*Or Yaqar, Tiqqunim,* MS Modena fol. 196b)

We find here an interesting approach, reminiscent of Rabbi Isaac of Acre's opinion that the mystic is unable to penetrate the secrets of the Torah.

Safed and the Dissemination of *Hitbodedut*

The penetration of the concept of *hitbodedut,* in the sense of intellectual concentration, into the writings of Rabbi Moshe Cordovero, sometimes combined with a technique of letter-combination, bore important implications beyond the absorption of prophetic Kabbalah within the framework of theurgic Spanish Kabbalah. This fact facilitated the dissemination of a number of elements associated with the technique of letter-combination in Kabbalah generally; but no less important was the enhanced importance of *hitbodedut* in texts written by Cordovero's disciples. I refer particularly to the major works of kabbalistic *mussar* written during the last third of the sixteenth century. As we have already seen above, Rabbi Elijah de Vidas used Rabbi Isaac of Acre's parable of the princess in his book *Reshit Hokhmah.* Elsewhere in his book, parables mentioning *hitbodedut* in the sense of seclusion from society also reappear. But it seems to me that de Vidas knew more of *hitbodedut* from his teacher than what survived in his writings. In *Sha'arey Qedushah,* Rabbi Hayyim Vital tells us:

> R. Elijah de Vidas, the author of the book *Reshit Hokhmah,* of blessed memory, told me in the name of his teacher, R. Moshe Cordovero, of blessed memory, the master of *Pardes* [esoteric-kabbalistic teaching], that whoever wishes to know whatever he wishes should accustom himself to holiness . . . and after he recites the *Shema'* on his bed he should concentrate in his mind somewhat. . . . (MS British Library 749, fol. 15b)

This indicates that traditions concerning the importance of *hitbodedut* were transmitted orally, and it is likely that Cordovero himself also had traditions that he did not put down in writing. This assumption makes sense also on the basis of examination of the extensive material concerning *hitbodedut* in the unpublished portion of Vital's *Sha'arey Qedushah*. This section is filled with quotations from the writings of Abulafia and Rabbi Isaac of Acre, as well as from unidentified material dealing with *hitbodedut*.

The third work from Cordovero's circle, Rabbi Eleazar Azikri's (sometimes mispronounced Azkari, 1533–1600) *Sefer Haredim*, in which Rabbi Isaac of Acre is also mentioned, discusses the practical implication of *hitbodedut* at some length. For our purposes, it is worthwhile to examine two passages in which, in my opinion, there is noticeable Sufi influence. The first appears in Azikri's mystical journal:

> It is written, "I have always placed God before me" (Ps 16:8). It is written in the book *Hovot ha-Levavot*, that it is inconceivable that a master and a slave, one being contemptible in the eyes of the other, or those who honor and those who despise him, should be equal in his eyes, as the *hasid* said to the man who wished to [mentally] concentrate, "You cannot do so unless you practice humility and, [receiving] insults, until you achieve equanimity.". . . And there are three conditions in this verse, *shiwiti* ("I placed"—literally, "I made equal"), that is, that I make everything equal before me, my praisers and my condemners, for I am a worm. (MS Jewish Theological Seminary, New York 809, fol. 210b)

It seems to me, despite the explicit mention of *Hovot ha-Levavot*, that one ought not to see in this work the direct source of Azikri for the following reasons. First, Bahya does not mention *hitbodedut* in connection with *hishtawut*. Second, Bahya does not mention here any interpretation of the verse from Psalms. Third, the language of the two passages differs in many details. Thus, one may assume that Azikri had in front of him an additional source, possibly one of the writings of Rabbi Isaac of Acre written under Sufi influence. Elsewhere Azikri quotes Rabbi Isaac ben Solomon Luria (ha-ARI, 1534–1572) as stating that *hitbodedut* "is helpful to the soul seven times more than study, and according to a man's strength and ability he should concentrate and meditate one day a week . . ." (*Haredim*, p. 256). This exaggerated valuation of *hitbodedut*, stated by Luria when he first started his own path as a contemplative, reflects the Sufi understanding of the supremacy of *hitbodedut* above study.

It should be noted that, despite the fact that in these texts the term *hitbodedut* does not appear in conjunction with the discussion of letter-combination or the uttering of divine names, one must assume that these constitute a technique used by Azikri when he practiced *hitbodedut*. In his mystical journal, he writes: "And at every moment he unites His names with joy and trembling, and he flees from society as much as is possible, and is completely silent, in a brilliant flame, alone, fearful and trembling, and the light which is above your head, make always into your teacher, and acquire a companion."[14] An interesting parallel to this appears in *Sefer Haredim,* which was, as is known, a very popular and widely known book: "But be enlightened in your mind, in the enlightenment of these matters (i.e., the *sefirot*) and imagine the letters of the names, that this is left to you, but to imagine more than the letters is tantamount [to arriving] at a corporeal conception. And visualizing the letters in the mind . . ." (p. 43). We find here a technique that is not identical to that of letter-combination, but a *dimayon*—that is, visualization—of the letters of the Divine Name, and this already appears in Abulafia and in Rabbi Isaac of Acre, and one may assume that the influence of these Kabbalists in these matters is also reflected in Azikri.

The incorporation of the concept of *hitbodedut* in the ethical writings of Cordovero's disciples constitutes the final stage in the process of penetration of *hitbodedut* into Jewish culture as a practical teaching. Abulafia's writings constituted the beginning of the process of absorption of the Sufi outlook within Kabbalah; however, his books were intended only for special individuals, and even though his writings were circulated in manuscript form their influence was largely confined to kabbalistic circles. The incorporation of the concept of *hitbodedut* into Cordovero's writings was an important step toward its dissemination among a far wider public, both because of the influence of the book *Pardes Rimmonim* and because of the incorporation of *hitbodedut* as a religious value in the Safed *mussar* works. However, although Cordovero still maintained the connection between *hitbodedut* and letter-combination, his disciples removed the instructions pertaining to the combination of letters. The fourth section of Vital's *Sha'arey Qedushah,* containing detailed instructions for letter-combination, was never printed. Azikri doubtless knew of the use of Divine Names in connection with revelation and made use of it, but he speaks little of this matter, whereas the connection between *hitbodedut* and letter-combination is entirely absent from de Vidas. It is certain that the relatively popular character of these *mussar* works was the reason for the concealing of this part of Abulafia's Kabbalah, but its other element—*hitbodedut*—continued, together with Rabbi Bahya ibn Paquda's views on the subject, to constitute a source of inspiration for the guidance of Jewish mystics. The influence of the views sketched above may be traced through the writings of the Hasidic mystics and possibly even in the writings of Rabbi Moses Hayim Luzzato.

In conclusion, we should discuss the place of the texts quoted above within the general framework of Jewish mysticism. The drawing of a new and detailed path was not a purely theoretical matter; one may assume that most of the Kabbalists quoted above underwent mystical experiences after taking the steps described above: mental concentration and letter-combination or the pronouncing of Divine Names. It should be mentioned that approaches which could be described as *unio mystica* appear in the writings of Rabbi Abraham Abulafia, Rabbi Isaac of Acre, Rabbi Judah Albotini, and de Vidas, or, as in the case of Azikri, coupled with ecstatic states. Therefore, the preceding discussion can serve as a kind of introduction to the more detailed analysis of one of the central subjects in the study of Jewish mysticism: the penetration of *unio mystica* into kabbalistic thought and practice.

Appendix: *Hitbodedut* and the Shutting of Eyes

One of the practical techniques advocated by the Kabbalists in order to attain a state of concentration—that is, *hitbodedut*—was the shutting of one's eyes. This technique is well known to us from Sufism and in connection with achieving *kawwanah* (direction, concentration) in prayer and for purposes of contemplating colors which become revealed in one's consciousness among the Kabbalists.

An anonymous Kabbalist saw "the essence of *hitbodedut*" in the act of closing one's eyes:

> And what is the essence of *hitbodedut*? By closing the eyes for a long time, and in accordance with the length of time, so shall be the greatness of the apprehension. Therefore, let his eyes always be shut until he attains apprehension of the Divine, and together with shutting his eyes negate every thought and every sound that he hears. (MS Paris, Alliance, 167 VI.B)

The connection between shutting one's eyes and *hitbodedut* here is in the shutting off of the person from the senses. This enhances concentration and facilitates the possibility of apprehension: the meditator enjoys Divine providence in accordance with the degree or level of comprehension. This connection between apprehension and providence indicates a possible influence of Maimonides's approach (*Guide* 3:51) to the relationship between them. At the beginning of the sixteenth century, Rabbi Judah Albotini wrote in his book *Sulam ha-'Aliyah:*

> That those who practice concentration, when they concentrate upon some subject or some profound interpretation, close their eyes, and nearly obliterate their own powers, in order to remove their hidden mind from potential into actualization, and to make that interpretation firm and to hew it out and impress it upon their souls.[15]

Here, as in the anonymous quotation, the shutting of the eyes is associated with those who practice concentration, on the one hand, and the capability of apprehension, on the other. Elsewhere Albotini adds the following sentence to the material copied from Rabbi Abraham Abulafia's *Ḥayyey ha-ʿOlam ha-Ba:* "Then, in that situation, he shall strongly shut his eyes and close them tightly, and all his body shall shake, with trembling and fear, and his knees. . . ."[16]

The practice of preceding the concentration necessary for apprehension by closing one's eyes found its way into one of the most famous works of Rabbi Ḥayyim Vital, namely, *Shaʿarey Qedushah.* According to the author, the fourth and final stage of the process of purification, whose ultimate purpose is the attainment of prophecy, includes seclusion in a special house:

> And he should shut his eyes, and remove his thoughts from all matters of this world, as though his soul had departed from him, like a dead person who feels nothing. . . . And he should imagine that his soul has departed and ascended, and he should envision the upper worlds, as though he stands in them. And if he performed some unification—he should think about it, to bring down by this, light and abundance into all the worlds, and he should intend to receive also his portion at the end. And he should concentrate in his thought, as though the spirit had rested upon him, until he awakens somewhat. . . . And after a few days he should return to meditate in the same manner, until he merits that the spirit rest upon him. (3:8)[17]

We find here a bold step, compared with its predecessors: the purpose of closing one's eyes in *hitbodedut* is now to merit the Holy Spirit, and no longer merely the realization of the intellect. Vital again suggests this practice for the purpose of *yiḥud* along the lines of Lurianic Kabbalah: "At the beginning you must shut and seal your eyes and concentrate for one hour, and then concentrate upon this—namely, the name MeTeTRoN—and divide it into three portions, each portion consisting of two letters, thus, *MeT TeR 'ON.*"[18] Again, in a magical formula in the possession of Rabbi Ḥayyim Vital, or written in his hand, we read: "To ask [a question] while awake: Enwrap yourself in *tallit* and *tefillin* and shut your eyes in concentration and recite: blessed memory" (. . . from a manuscript of our master, R. Ḥayyim Vital, quoted in *Sefer Meqor ha-Shemot* of M. Zaccuto, MS Laniado fol. 682).

One may clearly argue on the basis of these quotations that the suggestion of closing one's eyes to enable one to concentrate was adopted for various and peculiar reasons, which characterize systems of thoughts remote from one another. It is possible, by its means, to augment the intellect, to receive the Holy Spirit, or to ask waking questions or to perform mystical unifications.

In contrast to the understanding of *hitbodedut* as concentration and the shutting of the eyes as an earlier stage, which repeats itself in Rabbi Ḥayyim Vital, one finds also the opposite outlook in this Kabbalist. He advises:

> Meditate in a secluded house as above, and wrap yourself in a *tallit*, and sit and close your eyes and remove yourself from the material world, as if your soul had left your body, and ascended into the heavens. And after this casting off, read one *mishnah*, whichever one you wish, many times, time after time, and intend that your soul commune with the soul of the *tanna* mentioned in that *mishnah*. (MS British Library 749, fol. 162)

In another formula, which appears immediately thereafter, Vital advises:

> Meditate in a secluded house, and close your eyes, and if you wrap yourself in a *tallit* and wear *tefillin* this shall be better, and after you turn your thoughts completely and purify them, then do combinations in your thoughts, using any word that you wish in all its combinations. For we are not strict as to which word you combine, but in whichever one you wish, for example: 'RZ, 'ZR, R'Z, RZ', Z'R, ZR'. . . .

These descriptions of *hitbodedut* fit in many details the technique suggested by Rabbi Abraham Abulafia: that is, concentration in a secluded place, the wearing of *tallit* and *tefillin*, shutting one's eyes, and letter-combination. However, there is no doubt that to these details were added later approaches, including the attachment of the soul of the meditator to the soul of the *tanna* connected with the *mishnah* which is recited, or the ascent to the heavens. Despite this, we can state that Vital's descriptions give evidence of a continuation, with some changes, of the prophetic Kabbalah of the school of Abulafia. As this statement also holds true of other suggestions, which precede shutting one's eyes to concentrate, one may conclude that, with regard to *hitbodedut*, Rabbi Ḥayyim Vital was influenced by the various different versions of prophetic Kabbalah. His discussions of this subject, together with the material we have described above found in Rabbi Moshe Cordovero, indicate an impressive penetration of prophetic Kabbalah into theurgic Spanish Kabbalah, which had come to Safed without having been previously markedly influenced by Abulafia's teachings.

Notes

1. Full documentation and extended discussion of themes discussed in this article will be found in the author's forthcoming monograph on *hitbodedut* (in Hebrew). Space did not permit the full annotation of this article.

2. I shall deal here neither with this problem nor with the new understanding of kabbalistic texts written in Gerona or of other kabbalistic works unconnected with ecstatic Kabbalah. This subject will be discussed separately in a monograph now in preparation, which will include a detailed discussion of *hitbodedut* in the sense of isolation or removal from society.

3. Ed. J. Goldenthal (Leipzig, 1839) 49–51.

4. A. Jellinek, *Philosophie und Kabbala* (Leipzig, 1854) 1:21.

5. *Sefer Shoshan Sodot* (Korzek, 1784) fol. 60b.

6. *Me'irat 'Eynayim*, ed. A. Goldreich (diss., Hebrew University, 1981) 2:218.

7. *Revue des études juives* 115 n.s. 15 (1956) 66.

8. G. Scholem, *Kitvey Yad ba-Kabbalah* (Jerusalem, 1930) 226.

9. R. J. Z. Werblowsky, *Joseph Karo: Lawyer and Mystic* (London: Oxford University Press, 1962) 161.

10. G. Scholem, *Kitvey Yad ba-Kabbalah*, 226.

11. Ibid., 228–29.

12. Warsaw, 1885, 30d.

13. In R. Margaliot, *Mal'akhey 'Elyon*, Appendix, p. 21.

14. See *Mehqerey Yerushalayim be-Mahashevet Yisra'el* 1:3 (1982) 88.

15. See *Qiryat Sefer* 22 (1945) 163.

16. See Scholem, *Kitvey Yad ba-Kabbalah*, 227.

17. Beney Beraq, 1973, 115.

18. *Sha'ar Ruah ha-Qodesh* (Jerusalem, 1912) 7, 52.

Bibliography

Various matters with which this essay deals have also been touched upon in other writings of this author, mostly in Hebrew. In English, see Idel, "Unio Mystica." On the connection of music with matters discussed here, see Idel, "Music." This author's book on Abraham Abulafia and his teachings is due to appear in the series Judaism: Mysticism, Hermeneutics, and Religion, published by the State University of New York (SUNY Press). For an English summary of Abulafia's teachings see Scholem (pp. 119ff.). An important survey of the problem of mystical union in the Safed center of Kabbalah is Pachter.

Idel, Moshe. "Music and Prophetic Kabbalah." *Yuval* 4 (1982) 150ff.

———. "Unio Mystica in Abraham Abulafia." In *Studies in Medieval Jewish History and Literature*, vol. 3. Edited by I. Twersky. Cambridge, MA: Harvard University Press, 1986.

Pachter, Mordechai. "The Concept of Devekut in the Homiletical Ethical Writings of Sixteenth Century Safed." In *Studies in Medieval Jewish History and Literature*, vol. 2. Edited by I. Twersky. Cambridge, MA: Harvard University Press, 1984.

Scholem, Gershom. *Major Trends in Jewish Mysticism*. 3rd ed. New York: Schocken Books, 1954.

Contributors

ARTHUR GREEN, editor of this volume, is Dean of the Reconstructionist Rabbinical College, Associate Professor of Religious Studies at the University of Pennsylvania, and author of *Tormented Master: A Life of Rabbi Nahman of Bratslav* (1981).

JOSEPH DAN is Gershom Scholem Professor of Jewish Mysticism at the Hebrew University and Librarian of the Jewish National and University Library in Jerusalem. He is author of *Jewish Mysticism and Jewish Ethics* (1985).

MICHAEL FISHBANE is Samuel Lane Associate Professor of Jewish Religious History and Social Ethics at Brandeis University. He is author of *Biblical Interpretation in Ancient Israel* (1985).

STEVEN D. FRAADE is Associate Professor of Religious Studies at Yale University. He is author of *Enosh and His Generation: Pre-Israelite Hero and History in Postbiblical Interpretation* (1984).

ROBERT GOLDENBERG is Associate Professor of Judaic Studies and Director of Religious Studies, State University of New York, at Stony Brook. He is author of *The Sabbath-Law of Rabbi Meir* (1978).

MARTHA HIMMELFARB is Associate Professor and Robert Remsen Laidlaw '04 Preceptor in the Department of Religion at Princeton University. She is author of *Tours of Hell: An Apocalyptic Form in Jewish Christian Literature* (1983).

MOSHE IDEL is Senior Lecturer in Kabbalah, Hebrew University. He is author of *Mystical Experience in the Writings of Abraham Abulafia* (forthcoming).

JAMES L. KUGEL is Starr Professor of Hebrew Literature at Harvard University. He is author of *The Idea of Biblical Poetry* (1981).

JON D. LEVENSON is Associate Professor of Hebrew Bible in the Divinity School of the University of Chicago. He is author of *Sinai and Zion: An Entry into the Jewish Bible* (1985).

IVAN G. MARCUS is Associate Professor of Jewish History at The Jewish Theological Seminary of America. He is author of *Piety and Society: The Jewish Pietists of Medieval Germany* (1981).

DANIEL C. MATT is Associate Professor of Judaic Studies at Graduate Theological Union, Berkeley, California. He is author of *Zohar: The Book of Enlightenment* (1984).

439

JACOB NEUSNER is University Professor and Ungerleider Distinguished Scholar of Judaic Studies and Co-Director, Program in Judaic Studies, Brown University. He is author of numerous works on the History of Judaism in the Talmudic Period, including a five-volume *History of the Jews in Babylonia* (1965–70) as well as a translation of *The Talmud of the Land of Israel* (1982–).

JOEL ROSENBERG is Associate Professor of Hebrew Literature and Judaic Studies at Tufts University. His book *King and Kin: Political Allegory in the Bible* will be published this year.

S. DAVID SPERLING is Professor of Bible, Hebrew Union College–Jewish Institute of Religion in New York. He is co-author of *Handbook of Ancient Hebrew Letters* (1982).

FRANK TALMAGE is Professor in the Department of Near Eastern Studies at the University of Toronto. He is author of numerous books in the history of medieval Judaism and Jewish-Christian relations.

DAVID WINSTON is professor of Hellenistic and Jewish Studies at the Graduate Theological Union in Berkeley, California. He is editor of two treatises of Philo of Alexandria (with John Dillon; 1983) as well as many other studies on Philo and Judaism in the Hellenistic era.

Photographic Credits

The editor and publisher wish to thank the custodians of the works of art for supplying photographs and granting permission to use them.

1. The British Library

2. The Shrine of the Book, D. Samuel and Jeane H. Goltesman Center for Biblical Manuscripts, The Israel Museum, Jerusalem

3. Israel Exploration Society, Jerusalem

4. Yale University Art Gallery

5. The Jewish Theological Seminary of America, New York

6. Schloessinger Collection, The Israel Museum, Jerusalem

7. The Institute of Archaeology, The Hebrew University of Jerusalem

8. The Institute of Archaeology, The Hebrew University of Jerusalem

9. The Jewish Theological Seminary of America

10. The Israel Museum, Jerusalem

11. The British Library

12. The British Library

Indexes

Subjects

afterlife doctrines, 7, 145–46, 154, 160–61

angels, 6, 79, 80, 145, 146; as apocalyptic messengers, 184; divine council of, 150, 152; in Enoch's vision, 155, 159; priestly function of, 152; Qumran community and, 162, 267; wives of, 146, 148–49

apocalypse, 146–48, 161, 183–86. *See also* eschatology

archaeology, 8, 51, 90, 91

ascent, heavenly, 145–46, 148–54, 160–62, 291–93, 297–300; of Akiba, 292–94, 297, 298, 305; of Ishmael and Nehunia, 297, 299–301, 305

asceticism, 186, 253–56, 261–63, 266–69; bodily denial and, 254–55, 257, 259, 264–66, 270–71; celibacy and, 266, 268; diet and, 259, 260, 262, 265, 270–71; etymology of, 253, 256–57; Hellenistic views of, 256–61; Nazarites and, 273–74; Philo and, 256, 259, 263–66; rabbinic views of, 257–61; 270–73; tension and, 255–56, 261, 263, 266, 271, 276

Ashera worship, 16, 20, 29

atonement, 74–77, 147, 183, 188

Baal, 16, 20, 27, 156–57

Babylonian exile, 6, 13, 33, 114, 130; eschatology and, 146, 156; heavenly temple and, 151

biblical tradition, 82–84, 91–93; archaeology and, 8, 90, 91; Canaan and, 8–12, 90; canonization of, 45, 82–85; compilation of, 5; Creator as leader in, 105–6; criticism of, 7–8, 13, 89, 91; cyclical motifs of, 96, 101–4; Davidic and Mosaic covenant in, 100–1; demythologizing processes in, 157; event sequence and, 88–90, 94, 96; Hellenistic allegory and, 204–5, 211, 213; Hellenistic exegesis and, 88, 92, 199–200,

204; as a history of Israel, 106–7; intermarriage and, 9, 12; kings, poetry and, 97–98; literary aspects of, 90–93, 96–100; lore within, 105–6; Masoretic interpretation of, 83, 85, 135; monolatry and, 23–24, 27–28; monotheism and, 6, 13, 16–21; oral history and, 88–90, 92; poetic aspects of, 90, 94–99; prose and, 94–98; royal influences on, 94; Septuagint and, 83, 135; Ugarit and, 8–10, 90. *See also* Pentateuch; Psalms; Torah

Canaanite culture, 8–12, 90, 119, 150, 152

canonization, 45, 82–85, 136, 147, 176

Christian tradition, 83, 92, 147, 153, 174; of asceticism, 254, 256–59, 261; and Jewish exegesis, 313–14, 320, 323–24, 341–44; Judaic origin of, 187, 189–90; the law and, 233–34, 237–38, 371; monasticism and, 406; and Sabbath observance, 237–38, 248

cleanliness, 6, 7, 36, 54, 152; food and, 191–93; ritual forms of, 191, 192, 195, 216, 270

commandments, divine, 75, 86, 235, 367–70; Gikatilla on, 282–83, 400; Recanati on, 392–93; *Zohar* on, 383–93. *See also* Decalogue; law; Torah

contemplation, 64, 205, 220–23, 240, 266; Abulafia on, 407, 409–13, 422, 427–29; 434; Albotini on, 424–27, 435; alphabetic mysticism and, 411, 413, 416, 422–23; Azikri on, 433–35; Caro on, 425; Cordovero on, 428–32; essence, supernal source and, 431; Ibn Zimri on, 426–27; Isaac of Acre on, 414–20, 424, 430–33; *Sha'arey Zedeq* on, 413–14; Shem Tov on, 420–24; shutting of eyes and, 435–37; Sufi path of, 408–9, 413; Vital on, 429, 432, 436, 437

covenant, 10, 14, 16, 39, 50; with Gibeonites,

442

Names

Colophon

Jewish Spirituality: From the Bible through the Middle Ages,
Volume 13 of World Spirituality: An Encyclopedic History of the
Religious Quest, was designed by Maurya P. Horgan and Paul J. Kobelski.
The type is 11-point Garamond Antiqua and was set by
The Scriptorium, Denver, Colorado.